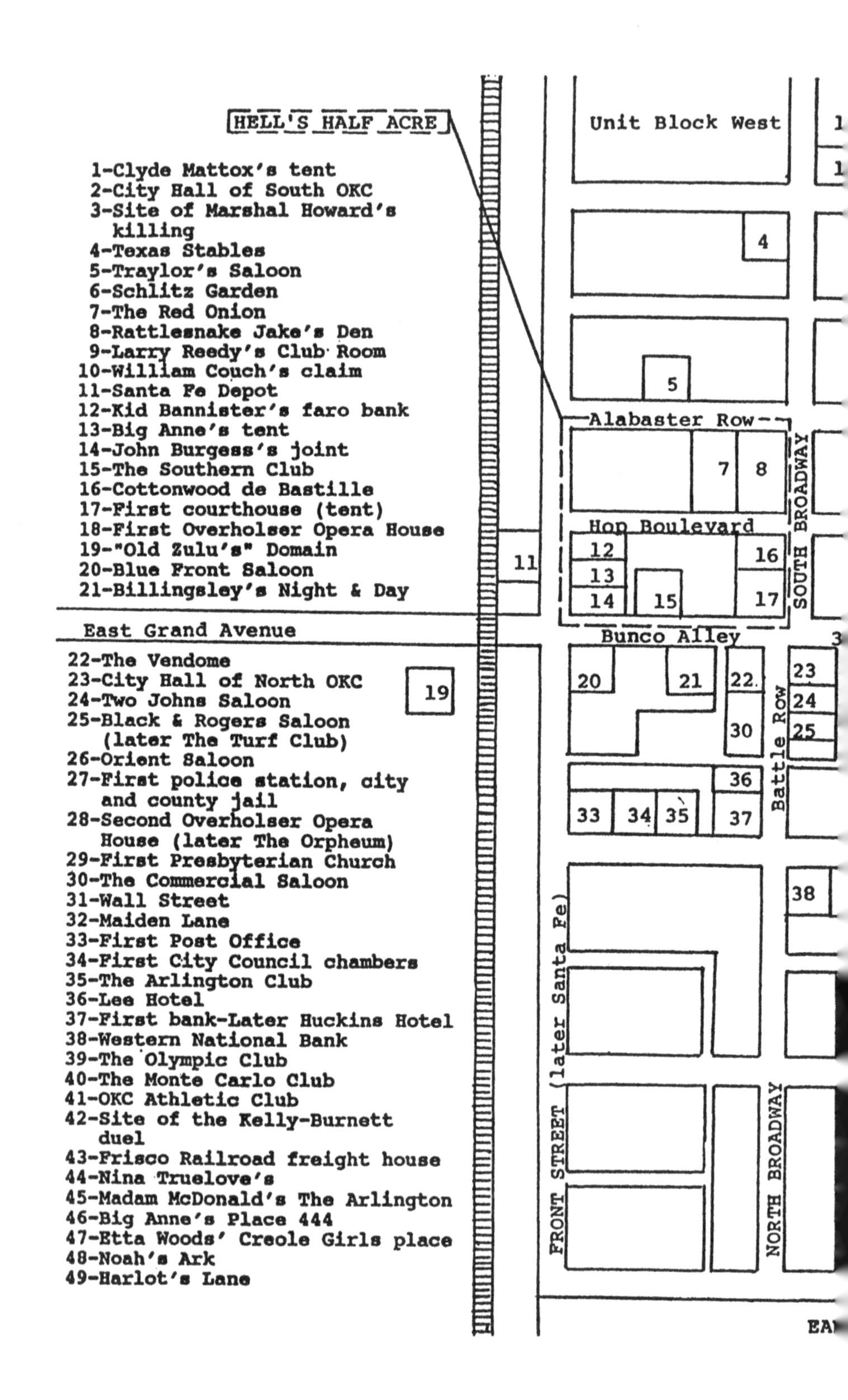
HELL'S HALF ACRE
1-Clyde Mattox's tent
2-City Hall of South OKC
3-Site of Marshal Howard's killing
4-Texas Stables
5-Traylor's Saloon
6-Schlitz Garden
7-The Red Onion
8-Rattlesnake Jake's Den
9-Larry Reedy's Club Room
10-William Couch's claim
11-Santa Fe Depot
12-Kid Bannister's faro bank
13-Big Anne's tent
14-John Burgess's joint
15-The Southern Club
16-Cottonwood de Bastille
17-First courthouse (tent)
18-First Overholser Opera House
19-"Old Zulu's" Domain
20-Blue Front Saloon
21-Billingsley's Night & Day
East Grand Avenue
22-The Vendome
23-City Hall of North OKC
24-Two Johns Saloon
25-Black & Rogers Saloon (later The Turf Club)
26-Orient Saloon
27-First police station, city and county jail
28-Second Overholser Opera House (later The Orpheum)
29-First Presbyterian Church
30-The Commercial Saloon
31-Wall Street
32-Maiden Lane
33-First Post Office
34-First City Council chambers
35-The Arlington Club
36-Lee Hotel
37-First bank-Later Huckins Hotel
38-Western National Bank
39-The Olympic Club
40-The Monte Carlo Club
41-OKC Athletic Club
42-Site of the Kelly-Burnett duel
43-Frisco Railroad freight house
44-Nina Truelove's
45-Madam McDonald's The Arlington
46-Big Anne's Place 444
47-Etta Woods' Creole Girls place
48-Noah's Ark
49-Harlot's Lane
Unit Block West
Alabaster Row
Hop Boulevard
Bunco Alley
Battle Row
SOUTH BROADWAY
NORTH BROADWAY
FRONT STREET (later Santa Fe)

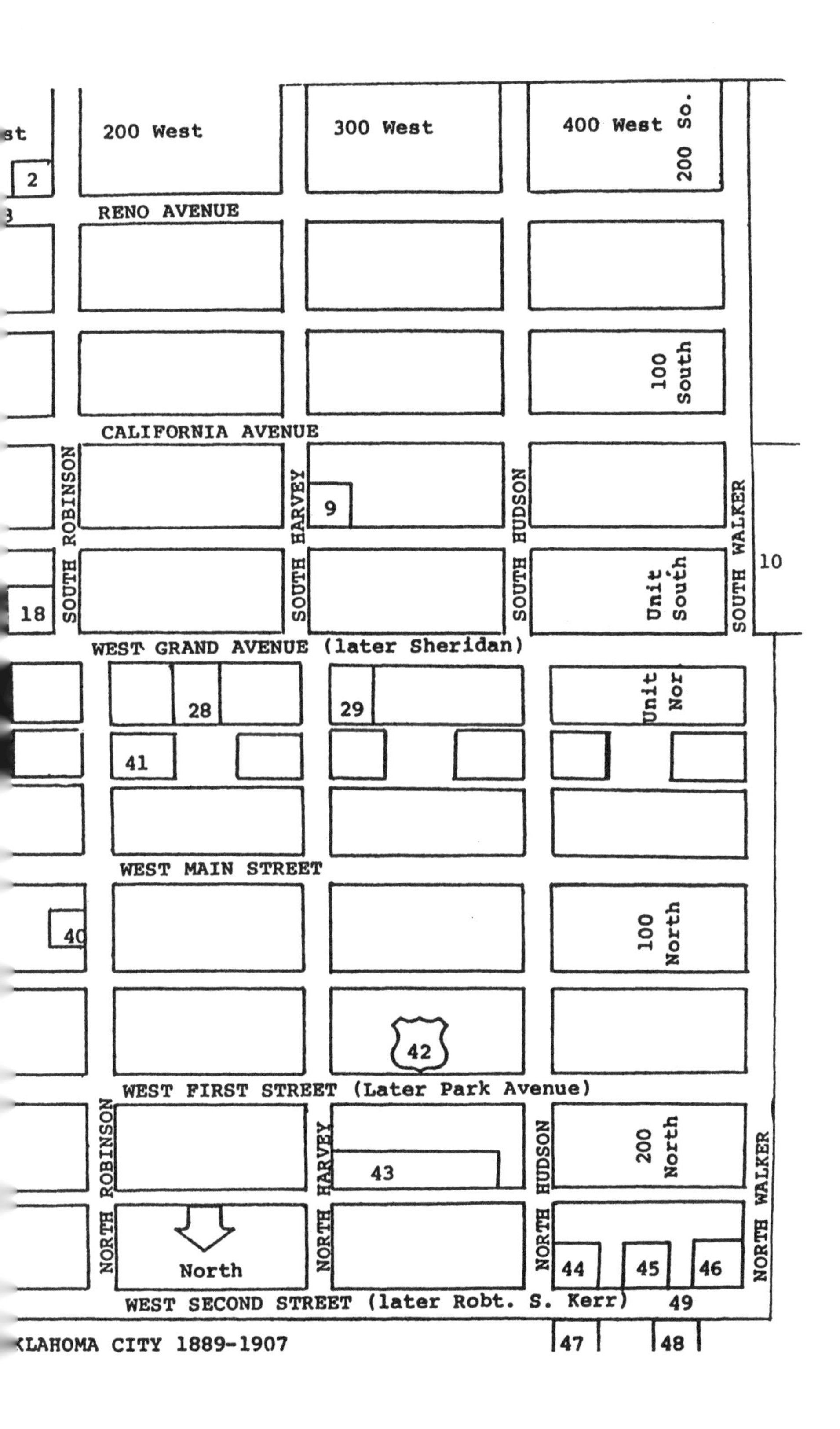

st
200 West
300 West
400 West
200 So.
2
RENO AVENUE
100 South
CALIFORNIA AVENUE
SOUTH ROBINSON
SOUTH HARVEY
9
SOUTH HUDSON
SOUTH WALKER
10
Unit South
18
WEST GRAND AVENUE (later Sheridan)
28
29
Unit Nor
41
WEST MAIN STREET
40
100 North
42
WEST FIRST STREET (Later Park Avenue)
NORTH ROBINSON
NORTH HARVEY
43
NORTH HUDSON
200 North
NORTH WALKER
North
44
45
46
WEST SECOND STREET (later Robt. S. Kerr)
49
KLAHOMA CITY 1889-1907
47
48

# OKLAHOMA JUSTICE

## THE OKLAHOMA CITY POLICE

*A Century of Gunfighters, Gangsters and Terrorists*

BY
RON OWENS

*Turner Publishing Company*
*Publisher's of America's History*

*Publishing Consultant: Keith R. Steele*

*Oklahoma Justice*
*Author: Ron Owens, Oklahoma City Police Department*



*Library of Congress Catalog Card No. 95-62081*
*ISBN:* 978-1-681-62348-1

*Limited Edition. Additional copies may be purchased from Turner Publishing Company.*

# ACKNOWLEDGEMENTS

When I began collecting the information that became this manuscript, it was intended as a brief, general account of the highlights of the history of the OCPD's first century; just a little old fashioned detective work. I had no idea, as it expanded, just how much assistance I would need from others and, in a sense, how much of a collaborative effort it would become. I would like to express my appreciation to some of them here.

To Captain C.E. "Ed" Hill of the OCPD, for goading me into this in the first place, and providing inspiration by jump-starting my interest and inquisitiveness during those periods when I got sick of it. Ed is also responsible for the herculean effort of collecting and preserving the OCPD's historical photographs, only a small fraction of which are represented in this work.

To the members of the OCPD, officers and civilian, past and present, who lived much of this history and made the rest of it, provided insights and personal information regarding much of it, and allowed me to share it with them for most of my adult life. Your chosen profession makes it obligatory that most of you will never be fully appreciated for the special people you are...but I know.

To The Oklahoma City Police Association for their support of the centennial commemorative yearbook that was the beginning of this history.

To the entire staffs of the Newspaper Archives and Library of the Oklahoma Historical Society, the Downtown and Ralph Ellison branches of the Oklahoma County Metropolitan Library System, and the File Room of The Daily Oklahoman newspaper, virtually all of whom I sought guidance and information from at one time or another.

To Dr. Bob Blackburn and Chester Cohen of the Oklahoma Historical Society for guidance and access to Dr. Blackburn's outstanding doctoral dissertation on Oklahoma law enforcement history.

To the following for access to historical files and materials; Nathan Barber of the OCPD Retired Police Officers Association; retired OCPD officers Richard Mullins and Russell Rigsby; Sam Watson of the Oklahoma Sheriff and Peace Officers Association; Ed Martin and Mike Shannon of the Oklahoma Publishing Company; Brad Robinson of Oklahoma Christian College; and Jim Roberts of the Oklahoma Department of Public Safety.

To Turner Publishing Company, for recording this information for posterity and giving the next guy a place to start. Especially to Keith Steele, for the patience, expertise and guidance shown to a fledgling author.

Without doubt, I have overlooked some people or failed to mention them specifically by name. To them, my apologies, my thanks and my acknowledgement of my indebtedness for their assistance, guidance, encouragement and inspiration.

# TABLE OF CONTENTS

# DEDICATION

TO
John Harden McBride 1862-1915
Spear Cushman Crossley 1867-1922
Austin Arthur Crossley 1884-1936
John Luther McBride 1898-1981

IT IS NOT THE CRITIC WHO COUNTS

Not the man who points out where the strong man stumbled or where the doer of deeds could have done better. The credit belongs to the man who is actually in the arena; Whose face is marred by dust and sweat and blood; Who strives valiantly; Who errs and comes short again and again; Who knows the great enthusiasms, the great devotions and spends himself in a worthy cause; Who at least knows in the end the triumph of high achievement; And who, at the worst, if he fails, at least fails while doing greatly, so that his place shall never be with those cold and timid souls who know neither victory nor defeat.

- Theodore Roosevelt -

Soldiers are policemen who act in unison;
Policemen are soldiers who act alone.

-Herbert Spencer
Social Statics (1851)-

A policeman is a composition of what all men are, a mingling of saint and sinner, dust and deity....Less than one half of one per cent of policemen misfit the uniform. He, of all men, is at once the most wanted and the most unwanted. He must be such a diplomat that he can settle differences between individuals so that each will think he won. But, if a policeman is pleasant, he's a flirt; if he's not, he's a grouch. He must be able to start breathing, stop bleeding, tie splints, and above all, be sure the victim goes home without a limp or expect to be sued. He must know every gun, draw on the run and hit where it doesn't hurt. He must be able to whip two men twice his size and half his age without damaging his uniform and without being "brutal". If you hit him, he's a coward; if he hits you, he's a bully. He must know where all the sin is and not partake. The policeman must chase bum leads to a dead end, stake out 10 nights to tag one witness who saw it happen—but refused to remember. The policeman must be a minister, a social worker, a diplomat, a tough guy and a gentleman. And, of course, he'll have to be a genius; for he'll have to feed and clothe a family on a policeman's salary.

-Tobias Wells-

# A PERSONAL PROLOGUE

Garnettville was founded on May 22, 1892, in the Unassigned Lands of Oklahoma Territory, in what was to become the far northeastern part of Oklahoma County. It was named for Eugene M. Garnett, the town's first postmaster. The name was changed to Luther on July 26, 1898, and was named after Luther Jones, the infant son of a prominent Oklahoma City businessman, Charles G. "Gristmill" Jones. Gristmill Jones built the first mill in central Oklahoma Territory in 1889 and became a prominent developer of real estate and railroads. He served terms as the Mayor of Oklahoma City from 1896-97 and 1901-03. He was also the originator and first President of the Oklahoma State Fair in 1907.

My uncle told me that he had been told by his mother, Mary Emma Crossley McBride, that when he was born in Luther on November 22, 1898, the doctor who delivered him told her that he was the first white male child born in Luther. Three black male children had been born before him and all of them had the name Luther incorporated in their names and she should follow suit. Thus he was christened John Luther McBride.

His own participation in law enforcement was limited to having been "drafted" periodically as a Reserve Deputy Sheriff under Oklahoma County Sheriff Ben Dancy in the early 1920s. This was during a period when Oklahoma City was having serious racial unrest with the Ku Klux Klan. He indicated that some incidents involving the lynchings of blacks in the southwest Oklahoma City stockyards area known as Packing Town were what caused the temporary necessity for the increase in the Sheriff's manpower. My uncle went on to become a civilian foreman at Tinker Air Force Base and retire after 25 years service. I gathered that his few forays into the field of law enforcement were somewhat expected of him because of his family connections to law enforcement. That was where he got most of the stories he entertained his young nephew with; his father and uncles.

Although I didn't realize it at the time, the skeleton for this book began taking shape while listening to stories at the knee of my uncle. The older brother of my divorced mother, he provided a father figure for a young boy and an example for a young man of what a man should be. A leathery, ruggedly outdoors type of man, he was also a paradoxical man with tough roots.

His father, my maternal grandfather, John Harden McBride, was born in Missouri in November of 1862. When he died 53 years later, he was the City Marshal of Beaver City, Oklahoma. The lingering stomach cancer that eventually killed him forced his only son to end his formal education not much beyond the elementary school level to help support the family. Despite his lack of formal education, John Luther McBride became a voracious reader, self educated in many areas and rose to a supervisory position in his chosen profession. A man's man who made his living in physical, outdoor work among other men, his speech was habitually coarse, blunt and liberally sprinkled with profanity. The rough exterior, however, concealed a kind heart, a gentle nature and inflexible personal integrity rooted in the best of the previous century's values when men did business on a handshake and your word of honor was more binding than any legal document. A better, kinder, more honest or honorable man never lived. He also instilled in me an interest in history and law enforcement that I didn't appreciate until I was much older. Thankfully, he lived long enough for me to tell him these things. He also lived long enough to tell me something about some of the men he learned his lessons from.

Spear Cushman Crossley was born on July 28, 1867, in Rockport, Missouri, into a family representative of the troubled border state's conflicting loyalties in the recently ended conflict. His father and an uncle had fought with the 93rd Illinois Infantry under Grant at Vicksburg, and with Sherman at Missionary Ridge and on the march on Atlanta. Another uncle rode with Confederate General Joe Shelby's cavalry. He had five brothers and a sister. The sister was to become my maternal grandmother, Mary Emma Crossley McBride. His family eventually relocated to Luther in far northeast Oklahoma County. He was in the hardware business before he became an Oklahoma County Deputy Sheriff, a position he held for over 20 years. He had a reputation for honesty, truthfulness, frankness, and considerate and humane treatment of his prisoners. Usually going about his duties with a lit cigar clenched in the left side of his mouth, he also had a reputation for not drawing his gun unless he intended to use it.

On June 3, 1922, he was hunting a man named Jack Moore who had robbed several people in the downtown Oklahoma City area. Moore was known to be armed with a pistol and considered himself tough enough that he wouldn't have to run from the law. Deputy Crossley went in a bar on Northwest Tenth Street in Oklahoma City looking for Moore without knowing that Moore had been warned he was coming. When Crossley entered the bar, Moore was behind him, pointed his pistol at him and said "Stick 'em up". The Luther Register of June 3, 1922, reported that Moore was shot in the stomach and thigh by Deputy Crossley but would recover to stand trial. He would, in fact, outlive the man who arrested him.

Another element of Spear Crossley's reputation was the fact that, unlike many officers of the day, he preferred to use violence only as a last resort. He had been known to talk armed fugitives into surrendering to him without a fight a number of times during his career. He was particularly effective with black fugitives because it became known that he would protect them from being beaten or lynched.

On Thursday, June 15, 1922, Deputy Crossley located such a fugitive driving a stolen car about a mile southeast of the old Oklahoma State Fairgrounds at Reno and Eastern Avenues in Oklahoma City. This area was later the site of Douglass High School. The black man was wanted for stealing a Packard automobile and had the car with him when he was discovered.

Deputy Crossley arrested the man and took him to jail without incident. Accompanied by other deputies, he then returned to the scene of the arrest to recover the stolen car. The rope that they tried to tow the car with broke after a short distance and they left to get another. Unknown to them, several Oklahoma City Police officers had driven by the location and noted the location of the stolen car. When the OCPD officers came back by, they saw that the car had been moved from its original location. Believing the thieves would return for the car, they decided to stake it out.

When the county officers returned and began to try to recover the car again, the city officers approached them. In the rural darkness, each group mistook the other for the car thieves. Each group later said the other group started firing first. After a few shots were exchanged, they began identifying themselves as law enforcement officers and calling for each other to surrender. Only then, too late, did they become aware of the error. Spear Crossley had been shot in the left eye by someone evidently using the glowing ember of his cigar as an aiming point. He died on the way to the hospital. John Luther McBride was notified in Luther of his uncle's death and drove to Oklahoma City that night to bring the body back to Luther for burial.

In the aftermath, a Coroner's jury determined that the fatal shot had been fired by Oklahoma City plainclothesman W.H. Flynn. Much was made in the local press about the fact that the city officers had been outside of their jurisdiction. At that time, that area was outside of the Oklahoma City limits and was in Oklahoma County's jurisdiction. Sheriff Ben Dancy lambasted the city police for not notifying his office when their officers were coming into the county for law enforcement purposes. Charges against Officer Flynn were contemplated but never filed. My uncle told me that the officer who shot "Uncle Spear" was so overcome with grief and guilt that he became an alcoholic, quit the police force and ended his days in a mental asylum. I don't know whether that is true or not. I do know that Officer W.H. Flynn is not pictured in the 1923 OCPD Annual.

Spear Cushman Crossley was eulogized as one of the most effective, fearless officers in Oklahoma law enforcement history. He had spent over 20 years in law enforcement, participated in over 250 raids, and been credited with solving a number of major cases. He was buried in Luther Cemetery with over 800 people in attendance, said to be the largest funeral in Luther to that time. Years later, his name, misspelled "S.C.Croosley", was carved into a block of Oklahoma granite in front of the Oklahoma Department of Public Safety headquarters three miles north of the location where he was slain.

Austin Arthur Crossley was born on August 26, 1884, in Thompsonville, Kansas. "Aus" came late to law enforcement, by default. On June 26, 1922, 11 days after Spear Crossley was killed in the line of duty, Aus was appointed as an Oklahoma County Deputy Sheriff to replace his slain brother. On February 20, 1931, he was hired as a Scout Car officer (Patrolman) by the Oklahoma City Police Department. His prior law enforcement experience apparently standing him in good stead, he was promoted to Raiding Squad Detective in May of 1931. He still held this rank when he collapsed in Police Headquarters and died on January 7, 1936, from a cerebral hemorrhage. He is buried at Luther, Oklahoma, within a few yards of his brother. At the time of his death a third brother, Orrin Wilkerson "Ole" Crossley, was a reserve officer on the Oklahoma City Police Department.

I later learned that the law enforcement profession has a strong tendency to be a "family" business. It frequently follows bloodlines much like the clergy and practitioners of medicine, law, and crime. In the appendices of this book is a current list of the more than 1300 employees of the Oklahoma City Police Department. The reader will note that, even beyond the plethora of common surnames, many of the names are the same. Just by a cursory examination of that list, I can easily recognize over 200 OCPD employees who have husbands, wives, fathers, mothers, sons, daughters, brothers, sisters or other blood relatives working in the same organization. That is over 15 percent of the total. If you included relatives of OCPD retirees, the number would be even higher. Many second, third and even fourth generation employees are on that list. If you included ex-wives, ex-husbands and current or former in-laws, the number would rise even more dramatically.

It was also this tendency, no doubt, that initially fostered the idea of law enforcement officers as a "brotherhood". This tendency plus the shared experiences of combat (physical, mortal or both) and the emotional trauma of getting to know more about people than is good for any human being, not unlike soldiers in wartime situations, makes cops extremely clannish.

Some of them take offense to being called cops. Most, I believe, do not. I never did. I grew up calling them cops and never meant it offensively. When I later became aware of the other appellations applied to them as a group (John Law, The Man, fuzz, Blue Dads, pigs, etc.), it became even less offensive. When I learned a few of the stories behind the name, it made even more sense. Two of the more believable stories are rooted in two of the earliest formal police forces, those of London and New York City.

In the early nineteenth century, Sir Robert Peel's police began patrolling the environs of London, England. They took their popular names as "Bobbies" from his first name. One legend has it that when they were signing their reports, they began abbreviating their official title, "Constable On Patrol", as "C.O.P.". Anyone familiar with a police officer's penchant for taking shortcuts on handwritten reports can readily believe this story.

The other most believable story deals with the New York City Police early in the same century. Not long after their creation as a formal law enforcement agency, it became necessary to differentiate between the ranks. The first and most obvious sign of this rank was the badge itself, and the relative value of the metal from which it was made. The Chief's badge was gold, those of lower ranking commanders were silver and those of the basic patrolmen were brass. Then as now, in armies and police departments, the quickest way to achieve action on a complaint was to approach the first line supervisor, the lowest ranking person authorized to give orders to a significant number of people. On the NYPD, this person was the Sergeant and his badge was made of copper. Therefore, when a citizen had a problem that required police intervention, the common expression on the street became "See the Copper", meaning take it to the Sergeant.

As most of them have experienced, I am sure, civilians have often asked me for a glimpse inside this closed, mysterious society. My answer has always been it isn't closed or mysterious. Many police officers have civilian friends. They just have to gain some understanding and acceptance of the suspicion, cynicism and realism created by working in a world they rarely if ever glimpse. Cops are just people. Besides coming in all sizes, shapes and colors, they come with all the normal human flaws and virtues. There are smart ones and dumb ones, competent and incompetent, honest and crooked, gentle and brutal, the whole spectrum of humanity. But the crooked, sadistic and idiots are a very small minority in the whole. They probably make up a smaller percentage of the whole than the percentage of doctors who abuse drugs, psychiatrists who have sex with their patients or clergymen who molest children. I have caused some controversy for making that statement publicly in the past. I'll probably cause some more for making it even more publicly here and now......but I still believe it.

If the previous paragraph sounds like a paraphrasing of the quotation by Tobias Wells included on the dedicatory page of this work, it probably is. Nevertheless, I believe most police officers, past and present, would probably agree with it. Though admittedly blatantly self-serving, it does illustrate the eternal "damned if you do, damned if you don't" nature of the police profession. Many examples of that paradox are illustrated herein.

Although no one but them seems to realize it, law enforcement officers are a minority too. Of the 260 million people in this country, only about half a million do this job, slightly less than one-fifth of one percent. A standard that was applied to police departments for many years was to try to achieve a ratio of one police officer for every 1,000 citizens. Most large cities now try to achieve two officers per 1,000 and, in some of the largest metropolitan areas, four or five officers per 1,000 is not uncommon. Of that representative 1,000 citizens, most will be honest, decent people. A small portion will be people who consider crime a full time occupation. Another portion will turn to crime when an opportunity presents itself. But most of those 1,000 will need the services of a police officer at some time whether it is because of a traffic accident, a lost child, a domestic argument or being victimized by the criminals. Herein lies the rationale for the "thin blue line" mentality of the police that tells them that Custer had pretty good odds after all.

If new law enforcement officers expect a lot of appreciation from the citizens for doing their jobs, they soon accept the reality that most people will never feel much kindness or affection toward people who have and exercise legal authority over them. If you visit Oklahoma City, you will find historical museums that pay homage to cowboys, softball, native American Indians, photography, aviation and space, firefighters and the 45th Infantry Division, to name a few. You will find none dedicated to law enforcement officers. Several attempts to establish one have been tried but all have been aborted by public apathy. A similar memorial planned for the United States Marshals Service has not come to fruition. Therefore, police officers' clannishness is somewhat forced upon them. Most of their recognition and appreciation will come from their peers. Many adopt the attitude that "If I'd wanted to be popular, I'd have joined the Fire Department". This book is for them also.

Now the disclaimers. First, my credentials. I am a middle-aged (if I live to my 90s) police officer. I have been a member of the Oklahoma City Police Department since December 1, 1969. I am a native of Oklahoma City and have lived there all of my life with the exception of a few years in my very early childhood. I have a college degree but it is not in history, english, literature or journalism. I am neither a journalist nor a historian. Most of my writing has been confined to police reports.

Next, my biases. Most of these will be very obvious to the reader. Through the vagaries of the system, I have managed to achieve the rank of Captain. Although I am now in the ranks of what are considered to be "police administrators", I was a very slow bloomer. The first 18 years of my career were spent in the ranks of Patrolman and Detective in what are considered areas of police operations; i.e. preventing crimes, investigating crimes and putting people in jail for committing them, which I feel is supposed to be the bottom line for a police department's existence. Therefore, it is with those jobs and the people who do them that my heart and sympathies lie.

Another set of biases comes with my personality, temperament and life experiences. To quote Dirty Harry Callahan, "a good man has to know his limitations". Political savoir-faire, tact and diplomacy are not among my strong points. I am something of a cynic in that I consider the current wave of "political correctness" ludicrous and, against all common sense, something of an idealist in that I have little patience with the principle of enforcing or applying the laws differently to different people because of their race, sex, color, creed, religion, sexual orientation, title, office, the size of their bank balance or any other factors. That kind of idealism is destined for a lot of frustration in our society, where money, power and political influence makes virtually everything negotiable. It also leads to the kind of cynicism it takes to make a statement like that.

Now a final word about mistakes. Being extremely human, I've made more than my share in my life. Joining the Oklahoma City Police Department on December 1, 1969, was not one of them. The portion of this history that occurred before that date was obtained entirely through research. I was present for the portion that occurred after that date, sometimes as a direct witness or participant.

Returning to the subject of mistakes, the odds are very high that some of them are in this book. If so, they are my errors and mine alone. If they are errors in judgement, interpretation or analysis, where they are attempted, I have no one to blame but myself and neither do you. If errors of fact, I won't whine about the difficulty of research except to say it was undoubtedly one of the toughest investigations in which I was ever involved.

Ron Owens    Oklahoma City, Oklahoma    July 1, 1994

# PREFACE

The subtitle of this book is somewhat misleading. It was intended to be, as it says, a history of the Oklahoma City Police Department's first century. Technically, that first century ended on August 9, 1990. This history goes several years beyond that point in an effort to be as current as possible.

Bearing in mind that I have no prior claim to the title of historian or author, it was not intended to be comprehensive or all-encompassing and by no means definitive—just a more thorough treatment of the subject than has been done before. That and to correct some misinformation uncovered in the initial research I had begun when I was assisting in the preparation of a centennial Oklahoma City Police Department yearbook in 1990. Entire books, television programs and motion pictures have been produced about some of the incidents just barely touched upon in this work. Some of them are referred to in the bibliography. Many other such works could be written about some of the other incidents in this work but have not been yet.

In the process of the writing, it became apparent to me that it was impossible to write the history of a police department without including some of the history of the City that is its' raison d'etre. I found it equally impossible to ignore the parallel political history of the City. The control of police departments by elected and appointed civil officials is a principle as sacrosanct in this country as civilian control of the military.

Another policeman-turned-author once said that most cities get the kind of police department they deserve. Just as an army is representative of the country it protects, so is a police department a mirror image of its' community. They are each made up primarily of their local sons, and now, daughters. Just as an army cannot win a war without the support of the people, as in Vietnam, a police department can only enforce those laws supported by the majority of the citizenry. Vocal minorities and influential majorities can and do pull them back and forth, then as now. If the majority of the citizens will brook no vice or crime or corruption, the police department will be allowed to eradicate them. If the citizenry tolerates it or even demands it, it will survive or even flourish.

The constants in this seesawing process are the lower level functionaries, the lower ranking officers of the police department and the lower level bureaucrats of civic government. The fluctuations are most visible in the upper reaches of these organizations; the administration of the police department and the higher levels of elected and appointed municipal officials. These are the people usually most visibly affected by the process I call "The Doctrine of Changing Fortunes".

This doctrine functioned most radically during the first half of this city's history. A man could quite literally be the Chief of Police one day and a patrolman walking a beat or directing traffic the next day. One officer advanced from Traffic Officer to Assistant Chief to Chief, then back to Patrolman and back up to Captain in nine years. Rank and position vacillated at the whim of a Mayor, a City Councilman, a City Manager or sometimes even a gambler or a bootlegger. In the very early days, it could even affect the lowly patrolman. More than a few officers were on and off the Department several times depending upon whether the powers that be were Democrats or Republicans. Many examples of all of these vagaries are contained herein. Things are much more civilized today. Those who risk those fates today have usually spent 20 years or more rising through the ranks and are eligible for pensions on a moment's notice. So now those of exalted status that offendeth or fall from grace just retire and go away.

The history of the Oklahoma City Police Department has been, understandably, just as chaotic as that of the City it serves. In attempting to measure that chaos, as good a barometer as any is probably an examination of the persons occupying the top position in that agency, the Chiefs of Police.

In its first century of existence, 46 men have served 49 separate terms as Chief of the Oklahoma City Police Department. They have been both elected and appointed. One was killed in the line of duty while serving in that office and two others were killed while serving in other law enforcement positions. Several others survived being shot while performing their duties.

Their terms of office range from eight days to 11 1/2 years but average less than two years per term. On one occasion, there were five Chiefs in the same year. On seven occasions, there were three Chiefs in the same year. Ten men served 12 separate terms during the turbulent decade of the 1920s. One Chief served three separate terms and two others served two separate terms. Two served for eight days at the same time, petulantly isolated in opposite ends of the police station. One senior commander retired after a squabble with one Chief, only to return from retirement within a few months to replace him as the new Chief. The office has been occupied by legendary gunfighters and career law enforcement officers who have served in almost every other imaginable municipal, county, state and federal law enforcement capacity. It has also been occupied by businessmen far out of their depth, politicians, sycophants, figureheads, martinets, political puppets, hacks, strident moralists, hypocrites, ambitious political aspirants....and one murderer.

Fairlawn Cemetery is situated in near northwest Oklahoma City. It covers the one-quarter square mile between Western and Shartel from Northwest 26th to Northwest 30th. Its' original location was considered to be " two and one-half miles northwest of town". It was the first formal cemetery founded in Oklahoma City after the Land Run of 1889 and it looks like it.

Looking at it from as much as half a mile away, it just looks old. The closer you get, the older it looks. This is not a modern cemetery with all the gravestones flat so the riding lawnmowers can groom the grounds effortlessly. The trees grow haphazardly where God intended and not where the landscapers put them. It isn't flat either. There are hills and low spots. The rains of a hundred springs and autumns have left standing water and allowed some of the gravestones to sink or tilt lopsided under their weight.

Its' age is also accentuated by the wrought iron and cyclone fencing buttressed up against the modern-made-to-look-old stone facade of the First Presbyterian Church bordering it on the south. Its' 200-foot spire towers over a myriad of Greco-Roman crypts, large and small gravestones, ornately carved and uniquely shaped in marble and granite. Many of them are hard to read now due to weathering or, unfortunately, vandalism. Some of the dates, although literally carved in stone, don't match the dates in newspapers or official accounts.

Visitors don't have to be students of architecture to appreciate the workmanship in the ornate granite and marble sculptures. City residents don't have to be students of history to appreciate the historical significance of the names carved into some of the more elaborate headstones....Overholser, Skirvin, Kirkpatrick, Colcord, Lee, Couch, Trosper.

As you might expect after more than a century, it is almost full now. Over two dozen OCPD officers are interred there. Eight were killed in the line of duty and 16 served as Chief. It has a large number of interesting, historical headstones and grave markers. Large and small, ornate and simple, overstated and understated, they are an interesting microcosm of a City's history;

BENJAMIN FRANKLIN CRAVATT<br>1908-1954<br>Detective - Oklahoma City

J.M. JONES<br>July 7, 1864 June 30, 1895

WILLIAM BRAZIER HENDREY<br>Jan. 19, 1863<br>June 1, 1938

TIMOTHY J. TELLEGEN<br>Texas<br>Pvt 6 Regt USMC 2 Division<br>World War I<br>July 23, 1896 May 21, 1960

DAD<br>M.C. BINION<br>1866-1941

LUTHER BISHOP<br>1885-1926

JACK LOVE
June 9, 1857 June 5, 1918
The world is better for this man having lived.

WILLIAM EDWARD SNELSON
December 30, 1870 May 4, 1951

OSCAR GRANT LEE
1863-1934

JOHN HUBATKA
May 9, 1866 August 16, 1932
Pioneer Officer

I.D. "IKE" ASHBURN
June 25, 1877 July 23, 1928

CHARLES C. POST
1871-1948

J.N. FIGHTMASTER
1858-1934

JESSE H. SOSBEE
1885-1922

MORRIS R. REAGAN
October 10, 1859 February 25, 1910

United Confederate Veterans
Dedicated June 3, 1923
These were men
whom power could not corrupt
whom death could not terrify
whom defeat could not dishonor

CARL S. GLITSCH
1875-1929

CHARLES A. BECKER
1878-1949

CAPTAIN WILLIAM L. COUCH
11/20/50 4/21/90

C.F. COLCORD
1859-1934

GEORGE W. JACKSON
5/14/48 4/12/98

REESE F. GALYON SR.
1893-1966

JOHN JOHNSTON WATT
1889-1939

REESE F. GALYON JR.
6/8/17 12/22/51

G.W.R.CHINN
March 19, 1843 March 2, 1910

SHIRLEY E. DYER
2/22/67 1/2/19

T.A. COUCH
3/12/05 Aged 48 years

COLUMBUS H. DEFORD
1845-1922

WILLIAM J. MCCLURE
July 12, 1842 June 19, 1895

And many, many more. This book is about Oklahoma City, its primary law enforcers and their agency. It is about the controls they have exerted, tried to exert or failed to exert over each other for the last century. It is also about the birth and growth of a town, a city and a state. It's also about Fairlawn and how it became a cemetery...and how it became full.

...he who is not forgotten is not dead.
—Samuel Butler
Note-Books (1912)—

# On My Watch—In Remembrance

Officer Michael John Ratikan
1943-1971
Lieutenant Darrell D. Pierce
1933-1972
Officer Joe McArthur
1945-1972
Master Patrolman
Kenneth W. Schoonover
1944-1972
Lieutenant Jim C. Pierce
1926-1973
Officer James Dewey
Chamblin
1943-1974
Lake Ranger
William L. Stewart Jr.
1948-1974
Sergeant Terry Glenn Lawson
1938-1977
Detective Larry Yandell
1936-1977
Officer Frank Winburn Chambers
1931-1978
Officer John Gerald Sanderson
1948-1978
Chief Elvin Wayne Lawson
1921-1979
Officer Garland Lee Garrison
1928-1979
Officer Norman V. Wilkerson
1931-1980
Officer John Arthur George
1954-1981
Detective Lowell D. Huckabee
1923-1981
Officer Benjamin R. Mize Jr.
1945-1981
Sergeant
Ernest Jesse Johnson III
1942-1982

Jailer Daisy Crabtree
1923-1982
Detective Charles M. Hinderliter
1921-1982
Lieutenant Bill Stubbs
1938-1982
Officer James Douglas Largent
1957-1983
Officer George Ryan Taylor
1951-1983
Lieutenant William Marcum
1911-1984
Detective Gary Lee Ward
1940-1985
Officer Edward John Yanish
1947-1985
Officer Danny Mercer
1947-1985
Officer Roscoe Scobey
1926-1985
Master Patrolman
Richard O. Riggs
1953-1986
Sergeant Leslie A. McCaleb
1940-1986
Sergeant William D. Lord
1943-1986
Specialist Wesley Gene Fansler
1930-1986
Captain John J. Byrd
1915-1987
Detective Morris Ned
1936-1987
George Beasley
1902-1987
Police Service Technician
L. Ann Einhorn
1948-1987
Detective Tony Allison Jr.
1949-1988

Officer Mark Weldon
1963-1989
Assistant Chief
Gerald Emmett
1927-1989
Sergeant Gary C. Scott
1935-1989
Detective Burke Lemay
1927-1990
Detective Robert Shahan
1942-1990
Officer Wayne E. Hamilton
1922-1990
Officer Delmar Warren Tooman
1962-1990
Sergeant Roy "Pat" Patterson
1912-1991
Captain Jim Perdue
1923-1993
Major Bill L. Peterman
1926-1993
Dispatcher Syrena Standlee
1954-1993
Detective Denver G. Kirby Sr.
1932-1993
Lieutenant Ellis Lee Bond Jr.
1937-1993
Detective Herbert C.
Hedgecock Jr.
1945-1994
Officer Danny Clark
1938-1994
Major Bruce M.W. Shaw
1931-1994
Lieutenant John Lewis LeMaster
1934-1994
Chief Hilton Geer
1918-1994

Life, misfortunes, isolation, abandonment, poverty,
are battlefields which have their heroes; obscure
heroes, sometimes greater than the illustrious heroes.
—Victor Hugo
Les Miserables (1862)—

# INTRODUCTION
# TWO DAYS IN OKLAHOMA CITY

One day in Oklahoma City, three prisoners escaped from the Oklahoma County Jail. All three were armed, desperate men, charged with murder. One had killed a Canadian County Deputy Sheriff, the others a Pottawatomie County Deputy Sheriff.

While one made his getaway in one direction, the other two ran out into the street, forcing a passing vehicle to swerve and stop. While unsuccessfully trying to get their commandeered vehicle moving, they saw three Oklahoma City Police officers running toward them with drawn weapons. Opening fire on the officers, a brief but fierce gunbattle erupted.

Struck in the head, one of the killers fell dead in the intersection. The other man ran down the street, wounded and dodging bullets in his wake. Behind him, one of the citizens lay wounded and one of the officers was lying in the street with a bullet through his chest. The policeman bled to death in minutes.

Another day in Oklahoma City, a silent holdup alarm was triggered. Another three Oklahoma City Police officers arrived on the scene with drawn weapons. As two of them covered the sides and back of the fast food restaurant, the third officer tried the entrance door. Finding it locked, he went in the exit door.

With no one in sight, the officer cautiously moved through the deserted dining area. As he approached the double kitchen doors, one of them burst open. A man stepped out, firing two shots into the officer at point blank range. Faster than you can snap your fingers twice, the officer went down, wounded in the head and chest.

Hearing the shots, one of the other officers ran to the back of the building. Taking cover at the corner, he saw a man run out of the back door with a gun. As the officer yelled at him to stop, the man turned toward him with the gun as he started getting into a car. The officer fired six shots. The car window disintegrated as the man fell over in the seat.

Two days in Oklahoma City. Two unusual days, thank God, but unfortunately not that unusual. Perhaps what was most unusual about those two days is the fact that there were more than 95 years between them.

The first incident occurred on June 30, 1895, at the intersection of Broadway and Grand (now Sheridan), one-half block from the Oklahoma County Jail at Maiden Lane and Wall Street. The unmoving getaway vehicle was a buggy with a balked horse. Outlaw Jim Casey died in the storm of gunfire from Chief Jones, Officers J. Stafford, G.W. Jackson and several assisting citizens. Superseding the "I don't want to get involved" attitudes of the future, keeping the peace was everybody's business in those days. Just ask the Dalton Brothers.

Bob Christian, wounded but not seriously, and his brother Bill escaped. Later traced to Arizona, then Mexico, they were never brought to justice for their crimes.

Chief of Police Milton Jones became the first Oklahoma City Police officer to die in the line of duty that day. The sixth man to hold the office in less than five years, he was one week short of his thirty-first birthday.

The second incident occurred on September 29, 1990, at a Long John Silvers restaurant in the 1200 block of South Meridian. Officer Delmar Warren Tooman became the twenty-eighth OCPD officer to lose his life in the performance of his duties. Officer Barry Lanzner's shots disabled Carl Elizabeth Whelan but he survived. While awaiting his trial for First Degree Murder, Whelan committed suicide in the Oklahoma County Jail several months later.

On May 3, 1991, Officer Tooman would be honored at the Oklahoma City Police Department's Tenth Annual Awards Banquet at the Myriad Convention Center. He would be posthumously awarded the Police Cross for his supreme sacrifice. Officer Lanzner would be awarded the Medal for Meritorious Service. The main entrance of the Myriad Convention

Center is less than 50 yards from the intersection where Chief Milton Jones was shot down 95 years before.

On Northeast 36th Street in Oklahoma City, on the south edge of Lincoln Park, is the 45th Infantry Division Museum. It is a memorial to their heroes of two wars that lasted six and one-half years. Directly south of it across 36th Street is the Oklahoma Department of Public Safety Headquarters. It contains the administrative offices of the Oklahoma Highway Patrol (OHP) and the Oklahoma State Bureau of Investigation (OSBI). The grounds also contain a Union Soldiers Cemetery, memorializing some of the fallen in our Civil War, still our country's most costly conflict in terms of lives lost.

In front of the DPS Headquarters is a memorial to the heroes of a war that never stops. Formally dedicated in May of 1969, a plaza around a central flagpost is ringed with dark gray and pink marble blocks. They resemble tombstones in more ways than one. On the blocks are chiseled the names of all the law enforcement officers who have died in the line of duty in Oklahoma or Indian Territories and the State of Oklahoma. As of July 1, 1994, the 537 names cover six of those blocks and the list is not complete. Twenty-eight of them belong to Oklahoma City Police officers. Many others died in or around Oklahoma City.

Appropriately, the oldest name on the memorial blocks is Chin-Chi-Kee, a Chickasaw Indian Lighthorseman (territorial policeman) killed on January 10, 1852. Hundreds of other names have been added to that distinguished roll since Chin-Chi-Kee, several of them since that of Delmar Warren Tooman. Tragically, they will not be the last.

If you thought the "Wild West" was all in Abilene, Dodge City, Wichita and Tombstone, consider this;

In the quarter of a century between 1872 and 1896, 103 Deputy United States Marshals were killed in the line of duty in Oklahoma and Indian Territories. Most were from "Hanging Judge" Isaac Parker's court of the Western District of Arkansas, a force that never numbered more than 200 at any one time. In the three decades between 1878 and 1907, when Oklahoma became the 46th State, at least 50 other law enforcement officers lost their lives in this "No Man's Land" including Sheriffs, Deputy Sheriffs, Chiefs of Police, city police officers, possemen, Indian Territorial Police and one Sheriff from Arkansas.

One of those martyred Deputy Marshals was Frank Dalton. He was killed on November 27, 1887, southeast of Sallisaw in what is now LeFlore County while trying to arrest a group of bootleggers. It is ironic that his three outlaw brothers gained fame breaking the laws that Frank died trying to enforce. Ranging from their home in Kingfisher County on the northwest border of Oklahoma County, the Daltons, their cousins the Youngers and friends Frank and Jesse James crisscrossed the Territory at will. So did the Doolins, Belle Starr, John Wesley Hardin, the Earps, the Mastersons and "every other hell raiser" that traveled between Kansas, Texas, Missouri, New Mexico or Arizona.

Almost every other major city in America was established and prospering when Oklahoma City was wild, open prairie. It is doubtful if any other state or city has packed as much significant history into such a short period of time.

# OKLAHOMA JUSTICE

## THE OKLAHOMA CITY POLICE

*A Century of Gunfighters, Gangsters and Terrorists*

BY
RON OWENS

# I — THE WILD WEST OKLAHOMA TERRITORY 1889 — 1899

One of the treaties the United States government signed with the Five Civilized Tribes of Oklahoma and Indian Territories stated that this land would be theirs for "as long as grass shall grow and waters run". For them, the grass stopped growing and the waters stopped running on April 22, 1889.

High noon on Monday, April 22, 1889, was signaled from the Red River to the Kansas line by bugles, train whistles, shouts, cannon fire and gunshots. The First Great Land Run had begun, the first of five land runs that would open Oklahoma and Indian Territories to legal, government-sanctioned white settlement over the next dozen years. The governmental sanctions had come during the first week of March. Outgoing President Grover Cleveland had signed a bill opening the nearly two million acres of the Unassigned Lands in the center of the territory on the last day before he was replaced by President-elect Benjamin Harrison.

When Harrison decided on the deadline of noon on April 22 for the opening, what more American way to settle it than a race? Every April 22nd to follow would be known as 89'ers Day throughout Oklahoma. Facetiously dubbed "the Harrison Horse Race", later authors would compare it as a subject of national attention to the first moon landing eight decades later. The echoes of the bugles and whistles would gradually fade. The sound of gunshots would remain.

*Indian Police at Oklahoma City - 1889.*

*A "Harrison Horse Race." Although this photo is of the Land Run that opened the Cherokee Outlet in September 1893, the opening of April 22, 1889, must have looked very similar.*

No one knows how many people entered the Central Oklahoma area that day. Estimates range from 20,000 to 100,000. They came on foot, horses, mules, oxen, buggies, sulkies, wagons, trains and bicycles. More than a few came "sooner" than they should. One witness compared the Land Run to a cattle stampede which was more than just an analogy. More than a few people were run over in the headlong rush and at least one man was trampled to death after being unhorsed. The dust raised by the churning feet, hooves and wheels was visible for miles on that clear day. Horses collapsed, wagons crashed together and overturned as kids were bounced out of them, the mayhem must have been spectacular.

The stage was set in preparation for a boom town like none other. Boom towns were not a unique phenomenon in the American West. Kansas railroads and cattle drives, the gold of California, Colorado and South Dakota's Black Hills, Nevada and Arizona's silver created their Abilene, Tombstone, Virginia City and Leadville. The prospect of free land in Indian Territory would create something truly unique.

Since the Civil War ended in 1865, Oklahoma and Indian Territories had become a melting pot of Americans like the coastal cities had become melting pots of international immigrants. Indians banished and shuffled from one home to another, disenfranchised negroes fleeing the Deep South plantation life, unreconstructed Confederate veterans looking for a place where Union authority and oversight was minimal, all these and more drifted in. In what would later become a state "noted for its eccentricities", the entire southeast portion of the state was to acquire the nickname of "Little Dixie". One of those "eccentricities" would be the impeachment of Governors, which Oklahoma has accomplished twice as many times as any other State.

For those readers preparing to gloat over their superiority in this area, I would refer you to the realities of politics in our American democracy. This statistic doesn't necessarily indicate that Oklahoma's governors are corrupt or incompetent twice as often as those of other states. Perhaps we just catch them and do something about it twice as often.

Thieves, killers, moonshiners, gunrunners, rustlers, farmers, ranchers, "Boomers" invading and squatting from neighboring states and territories all flocked to the wild, open land. For nearly a decade and a half, the only semblance of law in this raw, primitive 70,000 square miles was Judge Isaac Parker's Deputy U.S. Marshals operating out of the Western District of Arkansas in Fort Smith. Three days before the Run, Parker had just finished hanging the fifty-third and fifty-fourth miscreants to swing from his gallows. Save the occasional brush with hostile Indians, a peripatetic Deputy U.S. Marshal or solitary Army patrols, it was a land without restraints.

Some historians believe the Run came about as a punishment to the Indian tribes who had sided with the Confederacy during the Civil War. In 1861, the Confederacy entered into mutual defense treaties with nine Indian nations and tribes in what is now Oklahoma, then known as Indian Territory. The dispossessed red men didn't have any lost love for the soldiers in blue coats who had herded them and their families down the Trail of Tears to their relocated lands in Oklahoma three decades earlier. It is problematical whether they understood that some of those same men were now wearing gray coats. Nevertheless, many of the Indians were themselves slaveholders and, thus identifying with the Southern cause, at least 3,000 Indian warriors from these tribes fought for the Confederate Army, making a considerably larger contribution than is indicated by their numbers. They fought mostly in the Trans-Mississippi Department, that area of the Confederacy and the Border States west of the Mississippi River. Although not very adaptable to conventional military discipline, they were ruthless, courageous fighters. Though most of their service was in the Trans-Mississippi Department, near their homelands, it was not exclusively so. War whoops mixed with rebel yells in places like Fredericksburg and Appomattox also. Their battle flags were a variation of the Confederate Stars and Bars with a circle of 11 white stars representing the seceded southern states surrounding five red stars representing the Five Civilized Tribes.

The Indian Territory was definitely not a major theater of the war. However, being bordered on three sides by two of the largest states in the Confederacy (Texas and Arkansas) and on the fourth by the two most combative Border States (Missouri and Kansas), the Territory wasn't all that far removed from the war. There were at least 89 military actions in Indian Territory during the conflict. By comparison with the theater east of the Mississippi, no major battles were fought there nor were major casualties sustained there compared to the Antietams and Gettysburgs. Nevertheless, battles at Honey Springs, Fort Gibson, Chustenalah, Tulsey Town (Tulsa), Big Cabin, Cabin Creek and Spring Creek were ruthlessly fought. As an example of the dichotomies of this war, at Honey Springs, Oklahoma Indians fought on both the Union and Confederate sides. After years and sometimes decades of intertribal wars, Oklahoma's Indians were men accustomed to fighting but not particularly inclined to taking prisoners, thus the resulting casualty figures were proportionately higher than those of many more famous eastern battles. Their practice of scalping the fallen Yankees (against the orders of their commanders) also outraged the northern press, public and military, who were not very understanding of the social or religious significance it had for them.

They also didn't endear themselves to the Union by holding out for months after Lee surrendered at Appomattox. On May 26, 1865, the Army of the Trans-Mississippi became the last major Confederate army to surrender, almost seven weeks after Lee's capitulation. On June 23, Brigadier General Stand Watie surrendered his battalion of Cherokees, Creeks, Seminoles and Osages at Doaksville, near Fort Towson in southeastern Indian Territory. He was the last Confederate general officer to yield and his battalion was the last rebel force surrendered of any significant size. The last Confederate civil authorities to yield to the Union, on July 14, were Governor Winchester Colbert and the Council of the Chickasaw Nation. Writing of our Civil War in the next century, Winston Churchill called it "the noblest and least avoidable of all the great mass conflicts of which till then there was record." It was a war of strong passions and long memories. When the statue of Armed Freedom was placed atop the dome of the U.S. Capitol in 1863, it was not architectural happenstance that she spent the next 130 years facing south until removed for refurbishing in 1993.

Union Army records indicate that Indian Territory furnished 3,530 Indian troops to the Union during the war. Of those, 1,018 were killed in battle, over one-fourth. While the Confederate records are much less complete, Oklahoma's Indians on both sides sustained a larger percentage of losses than any of the states in that war. A post-war census showed that over a third of the entire Cherokee Nation had been obliterated. The strong passions and long memories of the conflict still endure in Oklahoma as much as they do throughout the Old South. That fact is inescapable if you visit the Confederate Room on the second floor of the Oklahoma Historical Society across the street from the State Capitol in Oklahoma City. The room is dominated by a huge Confederate battle flag, 8 feet high and 15 feet wide, covering most of one entire wall. Also framed in a place of honor on the wall is a smaller flag, only about five feet square—ragged, bleached-out, actually in pieces, some of them missing but carefully reconstructed within its frame. It was the red-fringed battle flag of Brigadier General Joseph O. Shelby's Missouri Cavalry Brigade.

At the end of the war, a militantly unreconstructed Shelby refused to surrender and headed for Mexico with some 200 of his veteran troopers rather than live under Union rule. By the time he reached the Mexican border, the force had grown almost to the size of a brigade and was accompanied by three other Confederate generals as well as the Confederate Governors of Louisiana and Texas. As he crossed the Rio Grande River at Eagle Pass, Texas, on the symbolic date of July 4, 1865, he ordered the battle flag weighted down with rocks and thrown into the river so it would never be captured. This was done but it was retrieved by a member of his 4th Missouri Cavalry and, years later, donated to the Oklahoma Historical Society. A brass plate on the frame proudly proclaims "THIS BATTLE FLAG OF GENERAL JOSEPH O. SHELBY WAS NEVER SURRENDERED". A plaque on the wall tells of the restoration of the room by the local chapters of the Sons of Confederate Veterans and the United Daughters of the Confederacy. It is dated 1976. Shelby would return to Missouri after two years but would remain the obstinate rebel for the remainder of his life. In 1893, he was appointed by President Cleveland as the United States Marshal for the Western District of Missouri, holding jurisdiction over much of the ground he contested with the Union during those years.

So, perhaps the Land Run was a punishment for the Indians of the Confederacy. Some historians believe the Run was part of an inevitable westward expansion. Some believe it was a governmental capitulation to the "Boomers" and their incessant invasions of this Territory over the previous decade. Probably all of these are partially true.

Four prospective townsites were already established at Guthrie, Kingfisher, along the South Canadian River south of Norman and at Oklahoma Station (eventually Oklahoma City). Law enforcement was to be provided initially by the Provost Marshal of the U.S. Army with the assistance of a small contingent of Judge Isaac Parker's Deputy U.S. Marshals headquartered in Guthrie. Captain Daniel F. Stiles made his headquarters just east of the Santa Fe railroad tracks in what is now the historic Bricktown area. Stiles had two companies of infantry and cavalry elements of the 10th and 5th Regiments at his disposal to accomplish this task.

On the morning of April 22, Oklahoma Station consisted of no more than a half dozen shacks; a depot building for the Atchison, Topeka & Santa Fe railroad, the railroad agent's shack, a Post Office of rough logs, a boarding house, section house, the Army Quartermaster agent's house and a stockade for the stagecoach line were all that marked a bleak outpost of civilization on the prairie. But the entrepreneurs who were eventually immortalized in the nickname of the "Sooner State" were already occupying the Santa Fe station.

These were the agents and surveyors of the Seminole Land and Improvement Company of Topeka, Kansas. They were led by William L. Couch, honorarily called "Captain", not because of any former military status but as the successor to the late Captain David Payne as leader of the Boomer movement that had repeatedly invaded the Territory for the last decade. A 39-year-old North Carolinian, Couch was to make the appellation "Seminole" synonymous with "Sooner".

Within minutes after the noon deadline, these men began platting and surveying west from the railroad tracks. The Seminole Company felt that the Run should start from the railroad tracks, not from the borders of the District. Years later, courts would rule against these

*Oklahoma City on April 26, 1889, four days old.*

*One of the thousands who made it without busting.*

organized Sooners but at noon on April 22, they were there in force. The outline of what was to become Main Street was already visible before the first legal settlers arrived from the south boundary shortly after 1 P.M.

These men, organized as the Oklahoma Colony Company or the Oklahoma Town Company, had named their company after the town of Colony, Kansas, where it had been formed. They had camped the night before on the banks of the South Canadian River, 15 miles to the south, and elected officers. They were led by Dr. Delos Walker who had been a Prohibition Party candidate for the governorship of Kansas before participating in the Land Run. Walker would later become the first president of the City School Board, one of the founders of the Anti-Saloon League at the turn of the century and have a street named for him like many of the others involved in the initial bedlam that was to become Oklahoma City.

There was a general impression among the Boomers making the Run that Oklahoma Station was to be the primary city in the newly

*OKC sprawls westward from the Santa Fe tracks in early May, 1889.*

opened lands, probably due to its central location and the presence of the railroad. The 320 acres surrounding the station would be divided into town lots and the first man to "settle" by driving a wooden stake into a plot was a landowner. By nightfall, at least 10,000 people would jam into the area. Tents blanketed the landscape, building frames were going up and some permanent wooden structures were erected by the next morning.

The Oklahoma Colony Company got off to a bad start. Their surveyor started laying out lots east of the railroad tracks only to discover that this area had been reserved for the military. Undismayed, they moved west across the tracks and began surveying southwards from Grand Avenue, heading straight south from the Seminole Company surveying northwards from Main Street. Well, not exactly straight.

Within a few days, the two surveys met at Clarke Street. This was the first street south of Main Street. It was later to be named Grand Avenue and, later still, Sheridan. Where the two surveys met, they naturally did not match. The Seminole survey had used the railroad tracks as a north-south line when they did not actually run true north. Stakes, claims and lots were everywhere including in the middle of areas platted as streets and alleys. Chaos reigned supreme.

In Guthrie, a similar situation was handled in a unique manner. After the official survey was completed, what was to become Oklahoma Avenue was staked off and everyone with claims between the stakes was given warning to move their belongings forthwith. Dozens of the grumbling dispossessed began arming themselves and lining up in the intended roadway to defend their claims. A short time later, four teams of mules with huge logs chained behind them were lined up at one end of the intended street. In front of them rode two men in their mid-30's, each armed with a rifle, two pistols and the determined look of men who knew how to use them.

The appearances were not deceiving. The two riders were William M. Tilghman and James P. Masterson. Both men's reputations preceded them and neither were exaggerated. Bill Tilghman's reputation as a buffalo hunter, indian fighter, army scout and peace officer stretched back to his teens. Like Tilghman, Jim Masterson had cut his teeth as a lawman in Dodge City during its heyday and his oldest brother, Ed, had been killed while serving as an Assistant City Marshal in Dodge. Many future histories would agree that, during his time, Jim was more respected as a lawman and more experienced as a gunfighter than his more famous older brother, Bat Masterson. Some would say that Bat's reputation eventually eclipsing that of his younger brother was due to a combination of superior literary skill, showmanship, self-promotion and Hollywood's latching on to the more colorful character.

The pair were unlikely to be deterred by the odds, either. Both were barely three months removed from their participation in the County Seat War between Cimarron and Ingalls, Kansas. Tilghman, Masterson and less than a dozen other lawmen had engaged in a day-long gunbattle with over 200 townsmen. Tilghman was still nursing a leg wound from that fracas when he and Masterson were deputized by Guthrie's Mayor C.P. Dyer to clear the soon-to-be Oklahoma Avenue. The mules were urged forward and the procession proceeded to clear the street all the way to the Santa Fe station, the logs flattening tents, luggage and everything else in their path. Although there were undoubtedly many unhappy claimants, none resisted.

Back at Oklahoma Station, town meetings, buckboard orators and committee appointments followed until a compromise was reached on that first Friday. The surveys were legitimized in spite of the fact that they were not in line with each other, in some places by 20 or 30 yards. The conflicting plots were united by two methods.

First, the infamous "jogs" in the streets north and south of Grand Avenue were made and, eventually, literally set in concrete.

One author aptly termed these jogs as "the scars of a bloodless conflict". For decades, people travelling north or south on Robinson, Harvey, Hudson and Walker Streets would find themselves confronted with a solid front of buildings as they approached Grand (or later Sheridan) Avenue. To continue down the same street, they would have to make a complete right turn and then a sharp left turn. These offset streets were a part of the City's history for the first century until Urban Renewal began correcting them in 1975. The last remaining one, at Sheridan and Walker, was corrected in 1990.

The second method used was to divide the ground between the alleys behind Main Street and Grand Avenue into lots facing east and west with a vacant court in the center of each block. These central courts were to be owned by the City. The alleyway extending north from Grand Avenue between Broadway and Robinson was named Wall Street and the alleyway running east and west between Broadway and Robinson was named Maiden Lane. The County Jail and later the City Jail were to be located at this mid-block intersection.

Such was the enmity between the competitors, these two areas started out as separate cities. They even named their streets differently in the beginning. North of Grand the east-west arteries were named "streets" and south of it they were somewhat more pretentious "avenues". The area north of Grand became known as the "Town of Oklahoma", North Oklahoma or simply Oklahoma. The suffix "City" became a common form of reference but wasn't officially recognized by the U.S. Post Office until July 1, 1923.

The north-south streets that bisected both towns were named, going west from the Santa Fe tracks, Front Street (later Santa Fe), Broadway, Robinson, Harvey, Hudson and Walker.

The town north of Grand Avenue extended for eight blocks with the streets named, successively, Main Street, and 1st through 7th Streets (later designated Northwest 1st through 7th). In the years to come, Northwest 1st Street would be renamed Park Avenue, 2nd Street would be named Robert S. Kerr and 3rd Street would become Dean A. McGee.

The area south of Grand Avenue became the town of South Oklahoma. Their avenues south of Grand Avenue became, successively, California, Reno, Washington, Noble, Chickasaw, Pottawatomie, Frisco, Choctaw and Canal Avenues. From Washington Avenue to Canal Avenue was later to become Southwest 1st through 7th. Both towns together initially consisted of 85 square blocks, less than two-thirds of a square mile. They held their own separate elections, had their own mayors, marshals and city officials. This chaos was to remain for over a year with the two groups forming ad hoc political parties.

The group representing North Oklahoma became known as the Seminoles after the land company they initially represented. The group representing South Oklahoma was originally given the derisive nickname "Kickers" because of their vocal disputes with the self-serving policies and decisions of the Seminole group. Since Indian names and words attached themselves so easily to all things in Oklahoma (itself an Indian word, derived from the Choctaw words for "red people"), the south group came to be known as the Kickapoos. These groups would be in contention for some time to come.

One of the Territorial Deputy U.S. Marshals was later quoted as saying that they operated on the principle that "There's no Sunday west of St. Louis and no God west of Fort Smith". In the first weeks, Captain Stiles did what he could to prevent the area from adding to its "hell ain't a foot from here" reputation but he had his hands full. Many of the initial settlers were of a type that Charles Colcord kindly referred to as "the adventurous class".

Deputy U.S. Marshal J.C. Varnum rode into town and said he was looking for man named Nolan who had killed a wealthy half-breed Chickasaw named Martin Colbert in a land dispute. Fourteen miles west of town, Varnum said he found another man lying dead on a claim with his killer calmly sitting on a log nearby. He said he was on the land first. Three miles west of Guthrie, another man tried staking out a previously staked claim. The first-comer put three rounds into him with a Winchester rifle.

It wasn't any calmer at Oklahoma Station. Two hundred and fifty armed men tried to jump a claim north of the city defended by ten men. Five hundred armed men raided a claim on the west side and began staking out lots. Detachments of troops arrived at both locations in time to prevent a full scale war. Two Boomers arguing over a lot attracted the attention of some soldiers. Charlie Quinly, one of the contestants, told them not to interfere. One of the troopers ignored the warning and Quinly immediately shot him.

An enterprising Chicago gambler named George Cole installed himself next to the town's only water well near Main and Broadway, demanding a nickel a cup for water. When a thirsty group began planning a hanging, soldiers ran Cole out of town.

Front Street (now Santa Fe) was the focal point of the earliest activity. By mid-afternoon of the first day, a sharply dressed gambler from Texas calling himself "Kid" Bannister set up a tent west of the Santa Fe Depot. A sign on the tent proudly proclaimed it to be the first "bank" in the Territory. And it was....a faro bank. The Kid was a local entrepreneur for the next 14 years until he was shot to death by the bartender of the Turf Club at 13 N. Broadway.

The first attempt at a real bank to prove successful, which was simultaneously a lumber dealership, was set up in a covered wagon within an hour of the beginning of the Run, west of what would later become the intersection of Main and Broadway. T.M. Richardson traded lumber for practically anything negotiable including the proverbial wooden nickels. He later established a more stable bank that would evolve into the First National Bank. This first incontestably legitimate bank was dubbed the Citizens Bank when it opened on May 30 on the southeast corner of Main and Broadway.

Next to the Kid's "bank" was John Burgess from Kansas with a buckboard full of booze. He played a game of catch-me-if-you-can with U.S. Marshals from that location for two years until he opened the most notorious of all the early saloons, the Two Johns, on the northwest corner of Grand and Broadway next to City Hall.

On the southwest corner of Grand and Front Street was the tent of "Big Anne" Wynn, who was to build a red light empire that would last for 20 years. One of 18 children, 26 years old and 200 pounds of aggressive womanhood, Anne was a shrewd, intelligent political manipulator and a veteran of plying her trade in the Colorado mining camps. She later moved her establishment to Northwest 2nd (now Robert S. Kerr) and Walker, became a power in City politics, amassed a $75,000 fortune and was never convicted of a crime.

In fact, the entire square block bounded by Broadway, Front, Grand and California became known as "Hell's Half Acre". The unit block of Grand Avenue between Broadway and Front Street was called "Bunco Alley" because of its profusion of gamblers and con-men. It was also the original red-light district before the City's center of prostitution was relocated to Northwest 2nd Street some years later.

The unit block of California between Front Street and Broadway became "Alabaster Row". This was akin to nicknaming a fat man "Slim". This south boundary of Hell's Half Acre was the segregated black complement to Bunco Alley and Battle Row combined. It was described as "a motley jumble of negro dives in plaster-board shacks and the rendezvous of notorious negro toughs".

The unit block of North Broadway from Grand to Main Street became "Battle Row". Four saloons occupied the east side of the block and the northeast corner of Grand and Broadway was occupied by The Vendome, the poshest whorehouse in town. Presided over by madam Ethel Clopton, it featured carpeting imported from Belgium and other classy appointments with prices to match.

The combative street name, however, stemmed from the half dozen buildings on the west side of the block; City Hall and five saloons with gambling parlors including the Black & Rogers and The Two Johns. This was the area newcomers would seek out if they were looking for action and entertainment of the traditional rougher variety. One author described a typical night on Battle Row thusly;

> "All along Battle Row, denizens of the saloons and gambling dens lived up to the traditional reputation of the wild west, with everybody aspiring to be a 'bad man'. Often a hundred horses tethered on either side of the street pawed and snorted to the whistling of bullets, the cracking of heads, and the blatant carousing of a weltering, fighting mass of cowboys, liquor-soaked tramps, tin-horn gamblers and excited city men, as all came tumbling out of a dozen saloons, shouting and smashing beer bottles over each other's heads and engaging in a hilarious free-for-all celebration".

The alley dividing Hell's Half Acre between Broadway and Front Street became known as "Hop Boulevard". This area became the home of The Southern Club, The Red Onion, Rattlesnake Jake's Den and the City's first jail, the "Cottonwood de Bastille".

One of the other early observers recorded his observations with crystal clarity;

> "History has never recorded an opening of Government land whereon there was assembled such a rash and motley colony of gamblers, cutthroats, refugees, demi mondaines, bootleggers and high-hat and low-pressure crooks...The spectacular array included the Kansas Jayhawker, the Missouri Puke, the Texas Ranger,

the Illinois sucker, et al. There were nesters, horsethieves, vagabonds, brand blotters, broncho busters, sheepherders, cowpunchers, spoofers, bull whackers, range riders, minute jacks, wildcatters, fourflushers...confidence men...tenderfeet, land whales, butterfly chasers, blue-sky promoters, sourdoughs...fellows with nicked reputations, geezers who had just been liberated from the hulks and had ugly corners of their lives to live down...There was Piute Charley, Cold Deck Mike, Alibi Pete, Alkali Ike, Comanche Hank, False Alarm Andy, Poker Jim, Rattlesnake Jack, Six-Shooter Bill and Cactus Sam. There were marksmen who were quick on the draw, who could throw a half dollar in the air and clip it with a bullet from their revolvers three times out of five....."

Despite the fact that there was little law and virtually no order in this newly populated city, most property disputes were not settled by bloodshed. Most of these pioneers were in fact reasonable and fair-minded men. More than one lot's ownership was decided by the flip of a coin, with the loser moving on to another location. Some just required a strong statement of principles to dissuade them. One somewhat faint-hearted claim jumper tried to negotiate a settler out of half of his 160-acre claim, offering to split it with him until the original claimant told him "he would take the whole 160 or six feet", i.e. enough for a grave. The barterer decided to move on. But, as with the present day, a small percentage of the populace raised more than enough hell to keep the newspapers full and these always made the more interesting stories. Whatever editorial space was left unoccupied by the troublemakers, the rampant and unrestrained politics of the budding metropolis provided more than enough to fill it up.

The early provisional governments tried to make some order out of all this. By April 27, South Oklahoma had elected a slate of City officials including George W. Patrick as Mayor and N.C. Helburn as City Marshal. On May 1, North Oklahoma followed suit, electing William L. Couch as Mayor, James B. Koonce as City Marshal and Joe Blackburn as City Clerk and Recorder.

Writing his autobiography more than four decades later, Charles F. Colcord would note that Kentuckians were about "as clannish as the Irish". Blackburn, often acting as Mayor in Couch's absence, appointed fellow Kentuckian Colcord as a policeman in the new boom town. Colcord would receive no formal salary for his duties but would be paid a portion of the fines levied against offenders. Colcord was a 29-year-old frontier veteran from an old Kentucky family of slaveholders and Confederate cavalrymen. After participating in the Land Run, Colcord had settled in a shack on Lot One of Block One, the first lot platted at what would later become Reno and Santa Fe on the Santa Fe right-of-way. He had traded a wagon and team of horses for it with George W. Patrick, the first Mayor of South Oklahoma and another Kentuckian. After purchasing food and candles, Colcord began his life as an Oklahoma entrepreneur with $10.45 in his pockets.

*One of the earliest Oklahoma City Police badges.*

On May 4, the first City Ordinance was passed, prohibiting claim jumping and providing for a $100 fine. Since the city had no jail, if serious offenders had no money to pay their fines, they had to work them out on a chain gang providing "civic improvements" to the city streets.

The small, informal police forces survived on these and other fines. Even then, the collection of the revenue was difficult. Drunks, the most prevalent offenders, were arbitrarily fined from $1 to $5, if they had it. If not, they were released anyway after they sobered up enough. It was not uncommon for individual officers to make 15 or 20 arrests daily. Police Court was initially held in any tent or shack that was available. The first Police Court was held in a tent on California Avenue and later moved north to Grand.

With the Army and the Federal Marshals restricted to enforcing Federal mandates, the daily business of keeping the peace, or trying, fell to the City Marshals and their deputies. These men were necessarily drawn from the populace and prior experience or noble motives were not prerequisites for the positions. The only apparent qualification was a willingness to confront the challenges of the office. Thus there was a high attrition rate among these men. Some appointments were measured in days. Sometimes the only way to tell who the lawmen were was who was running toward the sound of gunfire instead of away from it or ignoring it entirely.

Might made right. During that first summer, the citizens of Oklahoma Station were often left to solve their own disputes in their own ways. Often, those solutions relied upon the inventions of Samuel Colt.

Against the odds, the boom town made it almost two months before the first law enforcement officer was killed. Almost, but not quite. On June 13, 1889, a 19-year-old hellion named Clyde Mattox and Bill Hart were fired from the South Oklahoma police force. John S. Howard and Dan F. McKay were appointed in their places. The next day, Hart, Mattox and an associate called "Keech-Eye" were doing some serious drinking. Keech-Eye was a cross-eyed (hence his nickname) gambler who ran a dance hall on Washington Avenue (later Southwest 1st Street). Having an associate like this may provide some insight as to why the two men were dismissed from the police force.

The three disgruntled trouble-makers decided to parade some prostitutes down Reno and, when the girls were arrested, they would use this as an excuse to shoot up the town. Why they felt they needed an excuse is not clear. At any rate, when the "parade" commenced, the women were duly arrested by Marshals Howard and McKay. Mayor Fagan ordered them held without bond. McKay also arrested Bill Hart but not without resistance. Hart tried to shoot McKay but the Marshal, helped by a citizen, disarmed him and wrestled him into custody. Keech-Eye went to Mattox's tent at 110 West Reno and told him of Hart's arrest. Mattox grabbed his Winchester and headed for the Mayor's office. At 4 P.M. on June 14, a drunken, enraged Mattox began firing his rifle in front of the Mayor's office on Reno Avenue. Deputy Marshal Howard came to the door and Mattox fired at him. Howard and McKay both returned fire. McKay was struck once and Howard was struck twice but hit Mattox once before he fell. Mattox was grazed across the abdomen and ran off when he ran out of bullets. When it was discovered that Howard was mortally wounded, Mattox was pursued to the Texas Stables a block away on South Broadway, being shot once more along the way for good measure.

There he was finally subdued and arrested by, among others, Charles Colcord, Jim Koonce and Deputy U.S. Marshal George Thornton. Marshal McKay returned to duty the next day. Mattox was shot through the right lung and the bullet lodged in his back near the surface. Howard's father, a Doctor from Sanger, Texas, arrived on the train the next day to take his son's body back for burial.

Mattox survived his wounds and, through the vagaries of the criminal justice system of the day, was acquitted of Howard's murder. Not to worry, Mr. Mattox was easily his own worst enemy.

On December 12 of that same year, Mattox killed a negro named John Mullins in a dispute. Tried and sentenced to hang for that crime, he managed to win a new trial. While out on bond, Mattox was suspected of killing two of the witnesses to the Mullins murder.

The first witness, a negro, was at first believed to have been murdered by Mattox but suspicion eventually devolved upon one of Mattox's gambling associates, a "Doctor" East. East was tried and acquitted, deservedly so as it developed. Some years afterwards, Bill Hart was shot in a gambling dispute in Shawnee and a friend of his told of Hart confessing the negro's murder to him the day after it was committed. Mattox also went on a hunting trip to Seminole County with a white man who had witnessed the murder. That witness never returned from the hunting trip. In spite of these difficulties, at Mattox's retrial he was again convicted and sentenced to hang. The sentence was commuted to life imprisonment by President Cleveland and Mattox served eight years before he was pardoned in 1898. Pardoned but unreformed, we shall hear from Clyde Mattox again later.

The town was rampant with free enterprise, legitimate and otherwise. By the first of June, Main Street lots were selling for anywhere from $100 up to ten times that. During the early part of the summer, Charles Colcord sold his lot and shack on Lot One of Block One for $750. He used this money to purchase two adjoining lots at Fourth and North Broadway, immediately north of the future location of the Daily Oklahoman Building. He built a two-room house on these lots, brought his family in from Kansas and lived there for the next four years.

By mid-June, there were 570 businesses and 1,603 homes in the burgeoning boom town. The town governments continued having their growing pains. The first mayor of South Oklahoma, G.W. Patrick, resigned in less than a month amid charges of corruption. The treasurer, John Cochran, failed to post his bond and simply disappeared. The next mayor, T.J. Fagan, resigned when he heard of a movement to impeach him. The first marshal, N.C. Helburn, quickly decided the position was not for him. The relative stability of the marshal's position is evident from the chaos involving Clyde Mattox, Bill Hart, John Howard and Dan McKay. The town north of Grand wasn't exactly running smoothly either.

During the early summer of 1889, an armed drunk kept pestering a group of men and bragging "My name is Rip Rowser Bill and I've come to Oklahoma City to start a graveyard", his hand hovering menacingly near his pistol. For several days, Bill continued to repeatedly intrude in their affairs, continuing to make the same dire proclamation about "starting a graveyard in Oklahoma City".

During this period, the men formed an organization that they dubbed "Knights of the Cottonwood". Finally, after Bill shot several holes in a tent they were occupying, the men lost patience and decided that the man's manners better suited him for residence in Texas.

The committee members tied him up and, with some local officers, they hauled him down to the Santa Fe depot to wait for the midnight train to Texas. When they learned that the train was going to be three hours late, the officers left, deciding that the intervening time could be better spent elsewhere. When the officers left, several committee members and Bill were sitting beneath a big cottonwood tree.

When the officers returned at the appointed time to load him on the train, they found Bill swinging from a limb of the cottonwood. Locating and questioning the committee members, they contended that they had left Bill secured to a limb of the cottonwood tree and had limited his wanderings by means of a rope around his neck.

A rapidly assembled jury agreed with the men's contention that the rope had shrunk during the night's dampness, raising Bill off the ground and causing his death. The next morning, Bill was buried on the banks of the North Canadian River just south of the Military Reserve section now known as the Bricktown area. Thus he fulfilled his prophecy about "starting a graveyard in Oklahoma City". But not before he was fined $3.30, the amount found in his pockets, for carrying a concealed weapon.

If the town had a jail, perhaps old Bill wouldn't have ended up twisting slowly in the wind. The council passed an "occupation tax" to be imposed on every citizen, excluding preachers, according to their "worth and dignity". Presumably the tangible values assigned to these intangible qualities were arbitrarily assigned by the infinite wisdom of the city fathers. With the first $300 raised, the first jail was built on the southwest corner of Broadway and Grand. It was soon facetiously dubbed the "Cottonwood de Bastille" because of the native trees used for its construction. After a few months, it would be replaced with a more secure structure made of 2- by 8-inch lumber. A single cell, 14 feet by 16 feet, with a capacity of up to 17 prisoners and one-inch iron rods over the windows, was constructed at the mid-block intersection of Maiden Lane and Wall Street. The 2- by 8-inch boards were laid vertically for the floor and flat for the walls, making both 8 inches thick. The material was donated by local merchants and the labor by volunteers. This would become the later location for both the city and county jails.

*The Cottonwood Bastille-first city jail.*

All went well for a while. Police Judge "Posey" Violet handed out fines with great alacrity. Then a hitch developed. Several of the town lawyers refused to pay the occupation tax and were unceremoniously thrown in jail along with a variety of lot-jumpers, gamblers and the like. The lawyers sent one of their colleagues to Muskogee, 125 miles away, to plead their case before the Federal Court there. In freeing the recalcitrant lawyers and restraining Judge Violet from enforcing the occupation tax, Judge J.G. Foster said " The fact is, the whole affair of city government in Oklahoma is without warrant of positive law but is merely sanctioned by the needs of the people". Essentially, the Judge was paraphrasing the Guthrie resident who said "Law? For thirteen months, there was no law but what we made ourselves".

This must have been a setback for Mayor Couch, City Marshal James B. Koonce and the Mayor's brother, Thomas Abraham "Abe" Couch. They not only were without law but they had no authority to enact future law. Undaunted, the Seminole administration continued to pass ordinances that the judge and police enforced with fervor.

That first summer, Charles Colcord had received a Federal Deputy's commission from U.S. Marshal Richard Walker of Kansas to bolster the authority of his local police appointment.

Five months after the Run, the Seminoles and Kickapoos were still going at it hammer and tongs. During the City's first week, the Seminole-dominated City Council adopted a document known as the "Articles of Confederation". They then began referring to this document as the City Charter, indicating that it applied to both North and South Oklahoma City. The Kickapoos immediately began raising hell for their own charter. The dispute raged all that summer. In this experiment in democracy, nothing seemed to get accomplished without much wailing, railing and gnashing of teeth.

Sometimes the disputes even went beyond this, as reported in a local newspaper of September 20, 1889.According to the media report, an argument arose in the previous evening's City Council meeting about the adoption of another City Charter. Councilman John E. "Jack" Love, a Kickapoo, called for an election, it was voted down and the Seminole Mayor William Couch summarily adjourned the meeting. Councilman Love then made a few disparaging remarks about the local law enforcement officer's abilities.

Following the meeting, words were exchanged between the Couch brothers and Councilman Love. Although J.B. Koonce was the official City Marshal, apparently Abe Couch held some unofficial law enforcement status in his brother's administration. Nevertheless, the Couches definitely stepped out of their class when they decided to confront Jack Love.

John E. "Jack" Love was a 32-year-old Texan who entered Oklahoma with the Land Run. He was elected as a City Councilman a few months after the Run when attrition allowed the Kickapoos to secure a couple of seats for their sympathizers on the heavily weighted Seminole Council. Later to become a Deputy U.S. Marshal, one of the most prominent men in Woodward County including its first Sheriff and the first Chairman of the State Corporation Commission, Jack Love was not an inconsiderable man to be trifled with. Described as "six feet four inches in height and weighing two hundred and seventy-five pounds with no surplus flesh", one wonders what the Couches must have been thinking.

The upshot of it was Abe put his hand on his gun and called Love a liar. Love, singularly unimpressed and definitely unintimidated, immediately "hit straight out and knocked Abe about ten feet, clear into the street and into a mudhole". Mayor Couch then picked up a chair and went after Love. The melee moved outside, eventually involving the Mayor, his brother Abe, two Councilmen, the Recorder and City Marshal. It finally ended when Councilman Love had Abe on the ground "begging for mercy", and someone pistol-whipped Love from behind. Some credence is given to Abe Couch's unofficial status at the time by the paper's report that Abe messed up "his nice new uniform wallowing in the mud".

It wasn't the first time that Abe Couch's temper had gotten the better of him and it wasn't to be the last. In fact, it would be some years yet before it would be appreciated just how far out of control Abe's temper could get.

The Times lashed out at the Seminoles for refusing to have an election on the charter issue. The banner headlines were characteristic of the caustic, cynical humor of early Oklahoma political reporting;

DOG IN THE MANGER
CAN'T EAT THE HAY AND WON'T LET THE HORSE
THE MAYOR AND THREE COUNCILMEN AFRAID OF
A POPULAR VOTE

Two days after the City Council brawl, the Kickapoos tried to hold an election on their charter anyway. They had been warned. Captain Stiles had already stated he would equate any such effort as an effrontery equivalent to the rebellion of the Confederacy in 1861.

On the morning of September 21, some citizens approached the polling place in a keno room on Battle Row. Two of Stiles' troopers stationed at the door tried to bar their way and were rapidly overpowered. A full company of soldiers immediately filled Battle Row and cleared the street with fixed bayonets. "The Battle of the Charters" was over.

Much can be said about the prevailing condition of law and order by the fact that on November 11, 1889, Mayor Couch resigned and moved to his claim on the west side of town to protect it from lot-jumpers. His claim was on the southwest corner of Main and Walker, the later site of the first County Courthouse and, much later, the Montgomery Wards building and a Holiday Inn hotel.

Sidney Clarke became acting Mayor and called an election for November 27, 1889. The Kickapoos nominated Dr. Andrew Jackson Beale and the Seminoles Henry Overholser, who was to become an active civic leader for years to come. In a future City Directory, Overholser was to unabashedly list his occupation as "capitalist".

One endorsement Overholser could probably have done without came from S.H. Scott, a black lawyer and former Kickapoo sympathizer. While campaigning for Overholser before a group of his own race, Scott said "Heah me, my fellow votahs. Mr. Oberholser hab a white face but he hab a heart as black as yours or mine."

The election rapidly turned into the three-ring circus that was to typify Oklahoma politics. The bubbling cauldron that was Hell's Half Acre competed with the Salvation Army's drums for people's attention. Political partisans soliciting votes for their candidates stood shoulder to shoulder with gamblers ready to wager on the coming election. It was alleged that people in town only a week were being registered to vote. On election day itself, an act of prophetic symbolism occurred when a Kickapoo councilman was stabbed by a disgruntled Seminole sympathizer.

Dr. Beale won by 14 votes. A fellow Kentuckian, the new 53-year-old Mayor renewed Charles Colcord's appointment as policeman. The new Mayor never really gained control of the unwieldy young city. An epidemic of lot jumping immediately broke out. Beale issued a proclamation against it that was summarily ignored. The Kickapoo Mayor and Seminole Council were immediately at loggerheads.The Mayor decided to ignore the original plat agreed upon during the first week. The Council voted him down. He then tried to repeal ordinances requiring a certificate of title and recognizing the titles as lawful. Again, he was voted down. On December 18, Beale called for an election to be held on December 30 to fill the seats of two Seminole councilmen whose seats he had declared vacant because they had moved from their wards. With that straw, the camel's back broke.

The day before the intended election, December 29, U.S. Marshal R.A. Walker entered town from Kansas accompanied by U.S. Marshal Thomas Needles of Muskogee, who had just come from Washington D.C. They forbade the election and announced that the entire city was under the control of Deputy U.S. Marshals. Two days later, the U.S. Attorney General ordered the Marshals to maintain the status quo until Congress could organize the Territory and provide for municipal government. All ordinances were invalidated and all municipal officers discharged. Thus ended a rather remarkable experiment in self-government.

City Marshal Koonce, Abe Couch and the other hastily recruited officers may not have been the most shining examples of law enforcement but they were around when things got out of hand. Now the City had no protection other than two newly imported Deputy U.S. Marshals and they apparently were not overzealous. Liquor, gambling, prostitution and lot-jumping ran rampant. After three months of this anarchy, a temperance meeting was held at the First Methodist Church on March 24, 1890. The Deputies were roundly criticized and a committee conferred with Marshal Walker of Kansas. He removed the two lackadaisical Deputies and assured the citizens that help was on the way.

The help arrived in the form of two new Deputy U.S. Marshals. Ransom Payne was a cousin of former Boomer David Payne and a distant relative of Davy Crockett of Alamo fame. He chose Charles Colcord as his assistant. Obviously different men than their predecessors, they got everyone's attention rapidly. The Oklahoma Gazette reported "There is a new Deputy Marshal in town and he is raising hell!".

And raise hell they did indeed. Within ten days, Payne and Colcord locked up 30 saloon men and called in a company of troops to guard two train car loads of liquor they had confiscated. At long last, the law had arrived in Oklahoma City. Ironically, it came too late for one of the city's founding fathers.

The city's first provisional Mayor, William L. Couch had resigned five months before to establish and protect his claim at Main and Walker. Couch had been involved in a dispute over his claim with J.C. Adams almost from the day of the Run. On April 14, 1890, Couch got in a gunfight with Adams on and over this claim.

Fatally wounded, Couch died a week later and was buried in Fairlawn Cemetery on April 22, 1890, one year to the day after he helped found the city.

When Charles Colcord published his autobiography several decades later, he said that there were "lots of killings" in those days but people generally didn't pay much attention to them because they were usually "rough men killing rough men". Colcord's statement was borne out by the first census conducted in the territory in 1890. One territorial newspaper reported 110 violent deaths in the territory that year, one for every 2,350 citizens and more than four times the national average. By 1895, the number of deaths by frontier violence rose to over 250. Doubtlessly the publicity surrounding this statistic discouraged a good deal of immigration and probably encouraged some emigration from a better but more faint-hearted class of citizenry.

Couch's death generated more interest than any other in the city's first year. Adams was arrested by Deputy Marshal Colcord and taken to Wichita, Kansas, for trial. In another irony,

47 years later, the Oklahoma City Police Department would move into their newly constructed headquarters building. The streets bordering it on the north and south were, and still are, named Couch Drive and Colcord Drive.

Interestingly enough, after the initial excitement wore thin, the population of Oklahoma City decreased as many drifters, gamblers and general hangers-on moved on to greener pastures. Although most of the ones who stayed were a stable population trying to organize their community and establish their government, there were more than enough of these others types still around to keep things interesting.

Also within that first year, a local chapter of the Women's Christian Temperance Union was formed in the city. They would evolve into a conservative force in city politics to be reckoned with, stridently proclaiming for years that Oklahoma City was a "modern Sodom and Gomorrah" and the "Prince of Darkness's stronghold in Oklahoma". Unfortunately, the citizenry wouldn't do much to prove them wrong.

On May 2, 1890, President Benjamin Harrison signed the Organic Act establishing Oklahoma Territory. It created six counties (Logan, Oklahoma, Cleveland, Canadian, Kingfisher and Payne) with county seats at, respectively, Guthrie, Oklahoma City, Norman, El Reno, Kingfisher and Stillwater. At the first meeting of the legislature, Guthrie was named as the territorial capital, starting a not-always-friendly competition between the residents of Guthrie and Oklahoma City that would not be settled until statehood 17 years later. George W. Steele of Indiana was appointed as Territorial Governor. He appointed officers for the counties including County Commissioners and Sheriffs. The appointed Sheriff for Oklahoma County was a 45-year-old Tennessee native, Captain Columbus H. Deford, who, like many others of the day, continued to be known by the rank he held during the Civil War. On July 15, 1890, the County Commissioners ordered that the separate towns of [North] Oklahoma [City] and South Oklahoma [City] be incorporated together as a single entity with an official population of 5,086.

D.W. Gibbs was appointed to act as Mayor with the title Chairman of the Board of Trustees until a formal election could be held.Oklahoma City lost little time in establishing a provisional government and, almost immediately, a police agency. A week later, the fledgling city was divided into four wards. An imaginary line was drawn down the middle of Robinson and the middle of the first alley south of Main Street, bisecting the city into four quadrants numbered in a counterclockwise manner. The northeast quadrant became Ward One, the northwest one was Ward Two, the southwest Ward Three and the southeast sector was Ward Four. The available records of those first turbulent years are neither complete, accurate or unbiased. However, enough has been preserved to give a reasonably accurate picture of the growth of the city and its' police.

The new city's first legal election was set for August 9, 1890. The new legal anointment, however, did not change the settlers' character. Dr. I.W. Folsom, a second cousin of President Grover Cleveland's wife and the Democrat's first candidate for Mayor, was removed from the ticket after he appeared on Battle Row on the night of his nomination, got roaring drunk and rode down Main Street screaming his joy at being the City's "first legal Mayor".

He was replaced on the ticket by W.J. Gault, a local lumber dealer.On August 9, Gault was elected Mayor defeating the Republican candidate Henry Overholser. An aldermanic system of government was chosen. A mayor and eight aldermen (or City Councilmen) would be elected, two from each of the four wards into which the city was divided. Gault promptly created the Oklahoma City Police Department. During the first City Council meeting on August 12, he appointed Deputy U.S. Marshal Charles Colcord as the first Chief of Police at a salary of $60 a month. Colcord would retain his federal commission while serving as Chief. On August 21, four policemen were hired, one from each of the city's four wards; William R. McGill from Ward One, F.M. "Bud" Reynolds from Ward Two, John Hubatka from Ward Three and Abner J. Day from Ward Four. They were each to be paid $40 a month.

Hubatka was a huge 24-year-old Bohemian immigrant. A picture of the first Oklahoma City Police Department shows Chief Colcord seated with his four officers standing behind him. Reynolds would have needed to stand on a footstool to see over Hubatka's shoulder. The next biggest man in the group appears a good three inches shorter and 50 pounds lighter than the

*The first Oklahoma City Police Department - August 1890. Seated, Chief Charles F. Colcord. Standing left to right, F. M. 'Bud' Reynolds, William R. McGill, John Hubatka and Abner J. Day.*

Bohemian giant. He was destined to serve for the next four decades and become a legend in Oklahoma City law enforcement.

The photo shows the men wearing identical double breasted uniform coats with double rows of brass buttons. Colcord is wearing a five-pointed star and the others have solid heart-shaped shields. A collection of ammunition belts, holsters and Colts lie on the floor at their feet.

At their first meeting, the City Council leased a two-story brick building at 13 N. Broadway for $25 a month. The basement became the City Jail, the second floor housed Police Headquarters,Police Court and city offices while the ground floor housed the notorious Black and Rogers Saloon. This historic site is now occupied by the Sheraton Century Hotel.

It is not difficult to justify the Black and Rogers Saloon's reputation as "notorious". This saloon was a favorite meeting place of the Wolf Gang from Lexington. In the early part of Gault's second administration in 1891, a tough Texas gambler named George Shields, known as "Satan Shields", learned that some of the gang were in town to wreak vengeance against one of his friends. Shields went to Pettee's Hardware Store on Main Street, bought an ax handle and went around the corner to the Black and Rogers to confront six of the gang.

In less time than it takes to tell it, all six were unconscious on the floor. When they came to, all six were hauled before Police Judge Ben Miller, who fined them $100 each....for attempting suicide.

In the Fall of 1890, the Buffalo Bill Wild West Show came to town, setting up in a grove of trees in the North Canadian River basin. Although in this time and place it must have seemed somewhat anticlimactic, it still drew 16,000 spectators.

Also that Fall, Mayor Gault had asked Charles Colcord if he had considered running for Sheriff in the upcoming county elections. Colcord replied that he could not afford to finance a campaign. Gault, a good Democrat, encouraged him by loaning him $300 to finance his campaign.

The first county elections were held on February 3, 1891. As was already becoming the norm for Oklahoma politics, the headlines were screaming for reform, urging the replacement of the territorial Republican appointees. Chief of Police Colcord, with his sterling reputation and the endorsement of the Women's Christian Temperance Union, became the first elected Sheriff of Oklahoma County, replacing territorial appointee C.H. Deford. Colcord had been running against Deford and the independent candidate, Deputy U.S. Marshal George K. Thornton. Although Colcord beat Deford by only 175 votes out of almost 3,000 cast, he carried the entire Democratic ticket with him. Colcord resigned from the Chief's job to accept his new post at the City Council meeting on February 9 and soon hired his first deputies, Undersheriff Hugh Meyers (later killed in the line of duty near Purcell), J. Milton Jones, Webb Jones and Sam Bartell. Colcord would still retain his federal commission as a Deputy U.S. Marshal throughout his two-year term as Sheriff as he had while Chief of Police.

One of Colcord's first acts as Sheriff was to build a new county jail at Maiden Lane and Wall Street. After razing the old wooden structure, he imported steel cells from Cincinnati, Ohio, and built the new jail around them. During his term as Sheriff, Colcord also took over the operation of the federal jail in Guthrie. This jail had been built soon after the Land Run by a group of private investors who then contracted with the Federal Government to house their prisoners. Colcord bought the jail and operated it for five years with Deputy Webb Jones in charge.

Constantly evolving as a successful capitalist, Colcord was paid a dollar a day per prisoner, usually in county script that sold for 40 cents on the dollar but holding it until he could redeem it for its full value..

As soon as the election returns were counted, speculation was rife about the identity of the new Chief of Police or City Marshal, the terms often being used interchangeably. The local papers seemed to think that the favorite was W.H. Bean of South Oklahoma City. Mayor Gault proved them wrong when, during the same Council meeting in which Chief Colcord resigned, he nominated Thomas J. Word, who was immediately and unanimously confirmed by the Council. Word was known as a "fearless, conscientious, high-minded gentleman". In what was to become something of a tradition associated with the changing of Chiefs, even at this early stage, there were personnel changes. Officer Wiley Harris resigned and Taylor Hopkins was appointed to fill the vacancy. A local paper printed a diatribe against the magnanimity of the City Council for raising the Chief's salary to $65 a month and $50 monthly to each of half a dozen officers. To help offset this largesse, it was during Word's tenure in office that the $25 fine for carrying concealed weapons was adopted. But you could still carry all you wanted unconcealed and they continued to be frequently used.

THE EVENING GAZETTE
August 4, 1891

Hank Cunningham was arrested for riding his horse on the sidewalk and fighting last night. His trial will occur Friday morning at 10 O'Clock.

Word spent a relatively undistinguished 14 months in the Chief's job. A report to the City Council noted that during January of 1892, police had made 63 arrests and assessed $384 in fines. Although there continued to be the assorted burglaries, robberies, murders and more minor offenses, Word's principal attribute seems to have been his ability to keep out of the public eye. One of the rare mentions of his name in the local press during his tenure occurred ten days after Hank Cunningham's arrest noted in the above article. The Oklahoma Times-Journal of August 14th noted that during the previous day's City Council meeting "...Bills were allowed for street work and material. One, however, of 90 cents for ammo purchased by Marshal Word to kill dogs was defeated on the grounds that Policemen were hired for that purpose and should furnish their own guns and ammunition...".

The year 1892 marked the appearance of the first telephones in the city and a new Chief of Police. The April 18th City Council meeting dealt with impending changes in the police force. It was agreed that the Mayor would appoint the Chief and the Councilmen would appoint the individual policemen from their Wards. The appointments were Abner J. Day from Ward 1, Lee Tomlin from Ward 2, John E. Dolezal from Ward 3 and Tom Lewis from Ward 4. When circumstances required more manpower, the Mayor could appoint "special police" to be paid at a rate of $1.25 per day. J.E. Bell was appointed as a "policeman at large". Officers were to be on duty continuously from 7 A.M. until 10 P.M. You figure out the hourly pay rate.

There were 19 applications for the Chief's job on file including George W.R. Chinn, private detective Bill Ansley and Johnny Lewis of The Turf Club. But there were rumors that incoming Mayor Mitscher had already decided on a man who hadn't even filed an official application. In a little early-day investigative reporting, one newspaper noted that Oscar G. Lee had resigned his position as County Clerk of County B (later Pottawatomie County) and had moved his residence from Tecumseh to Oklahoma City. The rumors were true. There was a Council vote between Lee, Johnny Lewis and J.A. Bales that eliminated Bales. A tied vote between Lee and Lewis was broken by Mayor Mitscher casting the deciding vote for Lee. Lee was officially appointed on April 25 and posted his $6,000 bond the next week. William R. McGill, one of the four original officers, resigned the same day.

*Chief Oscar G. Lee-1892.*

The same Council meeting centered on wrangling about the size of the police force. A proposal was made to increase the size of the force to eight officers, two to be appointed from each of the four Wards. This was met by criticism, speculating on why the Gault administration had been able to get by with four officers but the new administration wanted twice that many. Evidently a cheaper compromise was reached since the members of Bill Ansley's Detective and Patrol Agency were "...given the power of policemen without compensation by the City". Official expansion of the force would wait another couple of years. Perhaps this was the birth of another old Oklahoma City tradition; trying to get something for nothing without much questioning of the quality of the something you're getting for nothing.

Although later a successful hotel developer, most notably of the plush Lee-Huckins Hotel, Lee took his duties seriously and evidently was up to the job. When two local hoodlums named Bud and Ping Fagg went on trial, Lee was ordered to clear the courtroom because it wouldn't hold all of the spectators.

One man, Bill McMichael, refused to leave, telling Lee to "go to hell". Lee disarmed him and McMichael landed at the bottom of the courthouse steps. Lee gave him back his gun, fully loaded, and told him not to come back or "I'll have to use force".

On October 5, 1892, the Dalton gang was decimated while trying to rob two banks simultaneously in Coffeyville, Kansas. A force of local lawmen and citizens killed Bob and Grat Dalton, Bill Powers and Dick Broadwell while seriously wounding and capturing Emmett Dalton. Bill Doolin would have been with them except for a lame horse that kept him from accompanying them to their date with destiny. The debacle illustrated some of the paradoxes and similarities of the sometimes confusing, thin line between lawmen and outlaws in the Old West. Not many of them maintained the sterling reputation of a Tilghman or a Colcord. Many operated, depending upon personalities and circumstances, on both sides of the law and many of them were personally acquainted from shared experiences. Their common bond seemed to be an expertise with firearms, and the physical courage and boldness of spirit to use them in imposing their will on other men, for better or worse, depending upon their motives. Bob and Grat Dalton had been Deputy U.S. Marshals some years before. Their brother Frank had been killed in the line of duty as a deputy. Dick Broadwell had been one of Charles Colcord's closest friends and Colcord later said that he had no idea that Broadwell had "gone wrong" until he saw his name on the list of the Coffeyville dead.

In January of 1893, Charles Colcord's term as Sheriff of Oklahoma County expired. Instead of running for another term, Colcord decided to pursue an appointment as United States Marshal for Oklahoma Territory from the newly installed Cleveland administration. Heck Thomas was also in the running but they were both beaten out by Evett Dumas Nix. Appointed on July 1, 1893, Nix offered the position of his Chief Deputy to Colcord but he declined. Colcord requested instead to be named the Deputy in charge of the Fourth District in Perry and Pawnee. Two and one-half months later, this area, the Cherokee Strip, was opened by another land run. Colcord made the run on a horse he had trained for two months for the ordeal. His anticipation paid off when he became the first person to file on a claim in Perry. He would remain there for the next six years, investing in livestock and land, and enforcing the law in a new boom town. Among his deputies were Bill Tilghman and Frank Canton.

Frank Canton was another example of the tenuous line between lawmen and outlaws. Twice elected Sheriff of Johnson County, Wyoming, and a veteran of the Johnson County Cattle War, Canton later became a renowned Deputy U.S. Marshal for Judge Isaac Parker and E. D. Nix in Oklahoma. He was one of Charles Colcord's deputies in the Fourth District and was walking with Colcord in Pawnee on November 6, 1896, when William "Bee" Dunn confronted him over a grudge, reaching for his gun. Canton killed Dunn with a single shot in the forehead. After his rowdy Oklahoma days, Canton went on to become a Deputy U.S. Marshal in Alaska during the gold rush days and, in the next century, returned to Oklahoma to join the National Guard. As a Brigadier General, he became the first Adjutant General of the state.

While Canton was working for him in Pawnee, Charles Colcord noticed that Canton seemed to be very fond of a Texan he used frequently as a posseman named George Horner. Colcord assumed it was because there was a resemblance between the two men. When Horner died, it provoked a uncharacteristically emotional response from Canton. Years later the explanation came out. Frank Canton was really Joseph Horner, George's brother. Joseph Horner was wanted in Texas for a gunfight in Texas in 1874 where three black U.S. cavalry troopers had been shot, one of them fatally. Joseph Horner disappeared from Texas and Frank Canton surfaced in Johnson County, Wyoming.

In this last bastion of the Wild West, stories of shootings, stabbings and killings of one type or another were almost daily fare in the territorial newspapers. Charles Colcord's statement about the almost blase' attitude of the citizenry toward these reports because they usually involved "rough men killing rough men" is indicative of the public attitude. Generally there was little sense of mourning for the victims or moral outrage. The primary criticisms were the bad public image the violence fostered in the press which would discourage immigration which would hurt business. After four and one-half years of white settlement, the biggest event in the territory to bring about a change in that attitude occurred in 1893. It also spelled the beginning of the end for the territory's worst gang of outlaws.

Ingalls, a small town ten miles east of Stillwater in Payne County, was a well-known hideout of the Dalton/Doolin gang. In late August of 1893, half a dozen of the fugitives were reliably reported to be in Ingalls including Bill Dalton, Bill Doolin, George "Bitter Creek" Newcomb, "Red" Buck Waightman, "Dynamite Dick" Clifton, "Tulsa" Jack Blake and Roy "Arkansas Tom" Daugherty.

On September 1, 1893, two covered wagons entered Ingalls, one from Stillwater and one from Guthrie. Concealed inside them was the ominous number of 13 Deputy U.S. Marshals; Thomas J. Hueston, his brother Ham Hueston, Lafayette Shadley, Dick Speed, H.A. "Hi" Thompson, Henry Keller, George Cox, M.A. Iauson, John Hixson, Jim Masterson, Doc Roberts, Ike Steel and Steve Burke. Bill Tilghman would have been leading one of the groups but he was recovering from a broken ankle.

Seeing Bitter Creek Newcomb leading his horse down the street, Marshal Dick Speed opened the battle prematurely by wounding Newcomb in the leg with his Winchester—prematurely because the other wagonload of Marshals hadn't taken cover yet. Seconds later, Arkansas Tom opened fire from a second-story window of the nearby hotel, killing Speed immediately. This caused a general melee of gunfire on both sides. The rest of the gang, firing from the saloon, distracted the officers attention from Arkansas Tom's strategic position above them. The next to fall was Marshal Tom Hueston, shot by Daugherty twice in the left side and bowels while trying to shield himself behind a pile of lumber. Then Lafe Shadley went down, shot three times while trying to climb through a fence by either Arkansas Tom, Bill Dalton or both.

Daugherty was trapped when the remaining officers surrounded the hotel and the rest of the gang escaped. Daugherty later surrendered to a preacher when the marshals were preparing to dynamite the hotel to the ground with him in it. Tom Hueston died from his wounds the next day and Lafe Shadley died the next day. Three Deputy Marshals were dead and only one of the gang in custody. Finally, the public, not to mention the Marshals, had it. Over the next three years, the Dalton/Doolin gang was hunted down to a man. Arkansas Tom Daugherty was one of the few to live to stand trial. He was sentenced to 50 years in prison.

After ten months in office, Oscar Lee went on to pursue his business interests and was replaced by Willis Ivers. If Colcord and Lee had been peaks in the office's integrity, Ivers provided the first valley. Ivers lasted less than six months before resigning and being charged with embezzling city funds.

In October of 1893, Edward F. "Frank" Cochran began the first of two separate terms as Chief of Police, part of a lifetime in law enforcement.The first month of Cochran's administration saw City Hall and the Police Department move into a new building. At that time, the city offices were scattered all over town, housed in whatever space was available. Since the Land Run, the Hill brothers had run a meat market on the northwest corner of Broadway and Grand. Earlier in the year, they had sold their two-story frame building to gambling and liquor interests. It rapidly became the biggest "joint" in town with the Buckhorn Saloon operating on the ground floor and the gaming house above.

It was common knowledge that the Hill brothers had been Sooners and the city quickly moved to invalidate their right to sell the two-story building on the lot. When the new owners refused to listen to such arguments, Mayor O.A. Mitscher (father of Admiral Marc Mitscher of World War II fame) ordered Chief Cochran to raid the premises and seize the building and equipment. Big John Hubatka led the raid, sweeping the building clean of occupants and ripping out the card tables and bar. By nightfall, the offices of the Oklahoma City government and Police Department were fully established in their new headquarters. It was reported that the next morning, more than a few embarrassed customers were turned away when, coming in to put their foot up on the rail and order their morning toddy, they were perplexed to find themselves in Police Headquarters instead of their favorite watering hole. The city offices were to remain there for nine years. Until Statehood arrived in 1907, liquor was legal and liquor licenses, at $250 a year, contributed greatly to the health of the city's coffers. Doubtlessly, it also contributed to the city's eternal wrangling over vice.

1893 was a particularly busy year for the Black and Rogers Saloon, occupying the ground floor of the building that previously housed the city offices. This year's activities alone would

*The new City Hall-1893.*

have engraved its name permanently in the legends of Battle Row. Sheriff John M. Fightmaster, the second elected Oklahoma County Sheriff, killed a miscreant known as "Scarface Joe" there one night. Dr. I.W. Folsom had an altercation there during the same year. The fallen-from-grace mayoral candidate evidently had a problem with the bottle. One night while in his cups, the good Doctor tried to use a Bowie knife on bartender Phil Rogers with no surgical cure in mind. He was dissuaded by a pistol-whipping delivered by Charles Colcord. Ada Curnutt, the only woman to act as a Deputy U.S. Marshal, arrested 19 men there one night for perjury in land contests. The 20-year-old daughter of a Methodist clergyman, Ms. Curnutt was actually the District Court Clerk in Norman. She was active again just before Christmas of 1893. The U.S. Marshal sent a wire to Norman that two wanted men named Reagan and Dolezal were in Oklahoma City and wired warrants for their arrest. There were no male deputies around so Ms. Curnutt boarded the train, armed with the warrants. Locating the two men in a saloon, possibly the very same Black and Rogers, she had a man go in and call them outside for her. The newspaper described them as "typical outlaws...bearded, armed and drunk". When they came out, Ms. Curnutt read them the warrants and placed them under arrest. When it appeared they wouldn't take her seriously, she offered to deputize every man within earshot as her posse to effect the arrests. Since the scene had naturally drawn a number of spectators, the lady seemed perfectly willing to make good on her threat and there seemed to be plenty of help available should she decide to call upon it, the two men succumbed to the inevitability of the situation and put their hands out to be cuffed. Following their safe delivery to the lockup, Ms. Curnutt was presumably free to return to her favorite leisure activity of hand-painting china.

The building the city vacated at 13 N. Broadway was soon to become the home of another infamous saloon, the Turf Exchange Saloon and Gambling House, also known as The Turf Club. The new owner, Tom Cook, was referred to as "a legitimate, gentlemanly gambler". In those days, that description could easily be applied to anyone who didn't cheat at cards and shot only those who did.

Even so, that didn't prevent his joint from acquiring a well-deserved reputation. Evidently a superstitious man, Mr. Cook changed the building number to 12 + 1 North Broadway. It was soon to have an unpropitious start into city folklore.

On February 13, 1894, former Chief Willis Ivers was tried and acquitted of embezzlement of city funds while in office. The next month, the Turf Saloon was to have, if not its first, one of its more sensational killings.

Hank Cunningham was a former Deputy Sheriff. One reason he was a "former" was an incident when he was bringing an Indian in to jail from the eastern side of Oklahoma County on October 10, 1890.

On the way, they stopped at a saloon and both got drunk. While drunk, they got in a shooting chase with two other men. An old man driving a wagon down the road was hit and killed by a stray bullet. Cunningham and the Indian were tried for the murder separately. Cunningham said the Indian did it and he was acquitted. The Indian said Cunningham did it and he was also acquitted. Such was the state of sophistication of the law in Oklahoma Territory at the time.

Cunningham had been staying on a claim east of the city and had been convicted of perjury in a court contest over the claim. A wealthy cattleman, W.J. "Bill" McClure, had put up Cunningham's bond but withdrew it upon his conviction. On Saturday, March 24, 1894, a drunken Cunningham began following McClure around, incessantly voicing his displeasure over the removal of the bond.

McClure kept trying to avoid Cunningham but the two finally came to blows in the Turf Saloon at 4 A.M. the next morning, coincidentally an Easter Sunday.

The bartender threw Cunningham out but he returned in minutes brandishing a leveled Winchester. McClure, without stopping to ask Cunningham his intentions, immediately invoked the unwritten Code of the West ("Do unto others before they do it unto you"). He took cover behind the bar and promptly emptied his .45 into the former lawman. Hit five times, Cunningham died on the floor. A coroner's jury and a local judge both agreed with McClure's interpretation of the unwritten Code and he was held blameless.

Six weeks later, Frank Cochran resigned to return to his former occupation of Deputy U.S. Marshal. Another former federal deputy, J. Milton Jones became Chief at a salary of $65 a month. He had from five to eight officers under him including J.H. Boles, C.T. Dunn, J.H. Reed, Lee Tomlin, George W. Jackson, J. Stafford and the ubiquitous John Hubatka. They were paid $50 monthly. Probably some of them were in attendance in late 1894 when the city had its first football game. Played at the intersection of Northwest 7th and Robinson, the "Terrors" beat the "Boomers" 24-0.

### OKLAHOMA DAILY TIMES-JOURNAL
January 7, 1895

#### NOTICE

Parties who have friends buried on the Military Quarter, Block 40, are requested to move them at once while the weather is still cold. By order of the Committee on Reservations, C.E. Dunn, Chairman.

### OKLAHOMA DAILY TIMES-JOURNAL
March 13, 1895

#### HE PAYS THE PENALTY
#### FIRST LEGAL HANGING IN OKLAHOMA

At 12:00 today, the murderer John Milligan was hanged until he was dead, dead, dead and the majesty of the law was maintained.

Probably the highlight of Chief Jones tenure was the first legal hanging in Oklahoma. The concerned subject was "a black man, 21 years old, five feet eight inches tall, weighing 187 pounds, wearing a size 10 shoe and size 17 collar". His name was variously reported as John Milligan or John Mulligan, with Milligan being the most frequently chosen spelling. Milligan had been raised as an adopted son by an old black couple, Gabe and Hannah Clark. With their

*A hanging in Oklahoma City.*

six-year-old granddaughter, they had all moved from their home in Tennessee to the Deep Fork township in northeast Oklahoma County the year after the Land Run.

Having attained his age of majority, John could now be expected to help support the family but it was not to be. John was a slacker, refusing to work and not earning his keep. Becoming fed up, his elderly benefactors gave him an ultimatum; begin pulling his own weight or get out.

On the night of November 6, 1893, John Milligan made his decision. After the Clarks went to sleep, Milligan attacked them in their slumber with an axe and straight razor. Although Hannah was killed outright, Gabe would survive for a few days before succumbing to his horrible wounds. Milligan then attacked the last witness, the little girl. Stealing $90 from the couple, Milligan made his escape.

Luck was not on his side. The crime was discovered rapidly and the little girl lived to identify him. Milligan was arrested in St. Louis and returned by Sheriff John Fightmaster for trial. Tried and sentenced to death, he escaped from the Oklahoma County jail on November 27, 1894, by squeezing his heavily muscled body through a fifteen-inch diameter ventilation pipe. His jailer that night was future OCPD Chief Ralph Cochran. Milligan eluded lawmen for two days before being arrested, ironically enough, the day before Thanksgiving by Ed and Will Fightmaster, brothers of the Sheriff, on their farm six miles south of Oklahoma City.

The adventure was still not over. Milligan escaped again, this time maintaining his freedom for only twelve hours before being recaptured near Choctaw. In January of 1895, he was granted a sixty-day stay of execution by the territorial governor but that stay expired in the second week of March. Milligan's execution was scheduled for noon on March 13.

A gallows was constructed behind the Hartwell Jewelry Company at 127 West Main Street. Its efficiency was tested with a bag filled with 200 pounds of sand. Contrary to the image of a public hanging, a stockade fence was built around the gallows in an attempt to limit the view of spectators. Human ingenuity and morbid curiosity being what they are, this did nothing to block the view from the roofs of the multiple story buildings in the area.

Official witnesses were to be limited to a "jury" of a dozen men, five friends of the condemned man, a physician to pronounce death, a representative of the County Attorney's office and the necessary lawmen.

March 13, 1895, would later be considered as a perfect day for an execution; gray, overcast, humid, and drizzling rain. Five minutes before noon, John Milligan mounted the thirteen steps to the gallows and listened to a recitation of the indictment of his crimes. Three minutes after noon, the trap was sprung. John Hubatka, a participant, gave the details to a reporter years later; "He was an immense fellow...In those days, we didn't have the electric chair. We had a lot of lynchings but this was the only legal hanging. So we had to borrow a special rope from Ft. Smith, Ark. Have you ever seen one of them? They're about an inch thick and they've got a slip knot as big as that— (cupping his hands to make a shape about the size of a small cabbage). That knot was the special feature. When the door was sprung the knot broke the fellow's neck so that he died immediately....Of course, some witnesses were permitted and the newspapermen were there but it wasn't much of a crowd. Captain DeFord, the sheriff; his son Jim; F.B. Owens and I had to take care of the hanging. That gallows was never used again."

Eighty-two years later, in 1977, Oklahoma would become the first State to adopt lethal injection as the method of execution. It would also be one of the last to stop using hanging. Like some of its badmen, old western traditions die slow and hard in Oklahoma.

The night of May 11, 1895, was an atypical Saturday night even for Oklahoma City. A series of events were due to happen that would graphically illustrate the prevailing character of the young city and its residents. It all started when Carrie Gribbin began beating her Salvation Army bass drum at the intersection of Bunco Alley and Broadway.

While Carrie collected coins from the righteous and prayed for the rest, a policeman pursued an untagged dog into Hop Boulevard. The officer, desensitized by having already killed 20 untagged dogs at the dog pound that afternoon, caught up with the dog as he was frantically scratching on the door of the Red Onion where his owner was drinking. Doing his duty with a single shot, the officer headed back toward Bunco Alley.

Alerted by the sound of the shot reverberating through the alley, the dog's owner came out of the Red Onion and found his dog dead in the alley. Drawing a knife and screaming with rage, he set off in pursuit of the officer, terrified citizens parting in his path. Shouts for the police brought four officers who disarmed the raging Irishman and dragged him to jail.

Moving away from this chaos, Carrie started east on Bunco Alley, still blissfully beating her drum. Just then, a buggy pulled by two horses being whipped by Mrs. John Young, the wife of the owner of the Silver Dollar Saloon, careened off of Santa Fe and raced west down Bunco Alley like the flames of hell were licking at their hindquarters. When they met Carrie and her thundering drum, the horses reared in terror, jerked the reins from their driver and veered to the side of the street. Mrs. Young was thrown out of the buggy, became caught in one of the wheels and was dragged down the street. Tipping over, the buggy crashed into a lightpost at the street's intersection with Wall Street, dumping the driver in front of the Orient Saloon while the frenzied horses continued west on Grand, dragging pieces of wreckage behind them. Mrs. Young's injuries were not serious.

While officers were cleaning up this mess, a cacophony of screams sent them running the half-block to the City Jail. The drunk Irishman whose dog had been assassinated had set the jail on fire. The officers running into the rear of the Battle Row saloons for water to fight the fire broke up a cockfight behind the Two Johns Saloon. In the resulting melee, a gambler beat a drunk to death with brass knuckles. When the jail fire was out, the officers rescued the gambler from a rapidly forming lynch mob, throwing him in the still smoldering jail.

The following Monday night, a group of citizens appeared before the City Council to protest. The object of their ire was not the dead dog, the drunken knife-wielding Irishman, the immolation of the City Jail, the riotous cockfight or the ensuing murder and near lynching. The focus of protest was the buggy accident which was directly attributable, according to the newspaper, to the "Salvation Army raising its usual din in front of the First National Bank". In a display of the citizen's priorities, they raised absolute hell about Carrie and her drum-beating, one citizen offering to "smash that damn drum into smithereens". This resulted in the immediate adoption of Ordinance Number 164 prohibiting such disturbances upon the city's streets.

When Carrie started beating her drum the next night, she was immediately arrested. Fined $5 in court, she refused to pay and was jailed. She was released on a writ obtained by her attorney,

*Chief J. Milton Jones-1895.*

Judge J.L. "Lot Jumping Jim" Brown, who appealed it to the Territorial Supreme Court.

Chief Jones was evidently an able, efficient and highly regarded officer. He served 13 months in office and appeared to be on his way to being the longest tenured Chief to date when tragedy struck.

During the Spring of 1895, Bob and Bill Christian were arrested for gunning down Pottawatomie County Deputy Sheriff Will Turner near Violet Springs on April 27. Tried and convicted, the pair were then transferred to the Oklahoma County Jail. A two-story wooden structure with steel cages on the ground floor at the intersection of Maiden Lane and Wall Street, it was then considered to be the most secure facility in the Territory.

James Casey and his brother, Vic, had killed Canadian County Deputy Sheriff Sam Farris in Yukon on May 21, 1894. Vic Casey later died from the wounds he suffered in the gunbattle and Jim Casey was sent to the Oklahoma County Jail to await trial. J.H. Garver was the jailer at Oklahoma County. When he placed the Christians in the same cell as Jim Casey, the three killers began planning their escape. After receiving guns and tools smuggled into the jail by Bob Christian's girlfriend, Jesse Findlay, the prisoners hid them in a stovepipe at the rear of their cell.

On Sunday afternoons, Garver traditionally allowed his prisoners to walk freely around the corridor outside their cells. On June 30, 1895, while Garver was not looking, the three men removed the guns from their hiding places. Overpowering Garver, they made their escape. Fleeing into an alley behind the jail, Bill Christian mounted Chief Jones' horse which was tied up nearby and headed southwest out of town. Bob Christian and Jim Casey ran out into Grand Avenue. They continued east towards Broadway, waving down a passing buggy and attempting to commandeer it for their escape. The furor had attracted the attention of Chief Jones and Officers Jackson and Stafford. As the three approached the scene, a gunfight ensued with several interested citizens joining in on the officers' side. It was later determined that Jim Casey shot Chief Jones and he was shot by the officers. When it was over, both Casey and Jones lay dead in the street.

The following Monday, thousands of Oklahomans paid their respects at the Chief's funeral. The Oklahoma Times-Journal eulogized him by saying "His modesty, manliness and fine sense of honor endeared him to all his intimate acquaintances and gained him the respect of the entire community." Jones was interred in Fairlawn Cemetery. An investigation showed the jailbreak to be the result of a conspiracy of seven people. The Christian's father and Tullis Welch were arrested but never tried. Jessie Findlay served 14 months in the County Jail. John Fessenden and Louis Miller were killed resisting arrest. John Reeves was sentenced to life imprisonment but was paroled after serving 11 years. Strangely, one of the oldest Deputy U.S. Marshals in the Territory, W.H. "Bill" Carr, was charged with supplying Bob Christian's gun to be smuggled in to him. Carr had been one of the Marshals that arrested Bob Christian and took the same gun away from him. Giving credence to those charges, Carr disappeared before his trial. Although he was later rumored to be living in Southeastern Oklahoma and serving in Cuba during the Spanish-American War, he was never brought to justice.

J.H. Garver, the errant jailer, was fired and charged with gross negligence. It was later proven that he had received a telegram from the Pottawatomie County Sheriff warning him about the planned jailbreak the day before it occurred but he ignored it. Tried and convicted, he was later sentenced to ten years but was pardoned after serving two years.

Lawmen had several running gun battles with the Christians and what was left of their gang all over southeastern Oklahoma for the next two months. Fessenden and Miller were killed in the process but the Christians got away and formed another gang in Arizona. Bill Christian's luck finally ran out in April of 1897 when he was killed near Clifton, Arizona. His brother Bob was arrested in Mexico six months later. Within two weeks, before extradition proceedings could be accomplished, Bob Christian escaped and was never heard from again.

The year of 1895 was rapidly becoming the swan song of the Doolin gang. On May 2, George "Bitter Creek" Newcomb and Charlie Pierce had been killed on the Dunn Ranch east of Ingalls in Payne County. On September 6, William F. "Little Bill" Raidler was located 25 miles northeast of Pawhuska in the Osage Hills by Bill Tilghman and Heck Thomas. When confronted by the officers, Little Bill decided to make a fight of it and was promptly filled with buckshot by Tilghman. Tougher than his diminutive size would indicate, Raidler survived his wounds and was sent to the Ohio State Penitentiary. There he would become acquainted with Al Jennings and an inmate serving three years for embezzlement, William Sidney Porter. Porter would later become famous for writing short stories under the pseudonym of O. Henry.

When Woodward County was created by the opening of the Cherokee Outlet in September of 1893, the choice of the first sheriff was left to the Territorial Governor. The man chosen by Governor Renfrow was Jack Love, former Oklahoma City Councilman and humbler of Abe Couch. By late 1895, Love had discharged his duties as Woodward County's first Sheriff and had entered private enterprise. One of his closest friends in Woodward was Temple Houston, local attorney and son of Texas legend Sam Houston.

Also residents of Woodward at the time were the Jennings family. Three of the four sons, Al, Ed and John, were local attorneys, sons of a county judge. Al Jennings, a red-headed bantam rooster barely five feet tall, was a former prosecuting attorney in Canadian County before the family migrated from El Reno. In early October of 1895, these two groups were to come together explosively.

On October 8, Houston was prosecuting a case involving the theft of beer from a railroad car with Ed and John Jennings acting as defense attorneys. During the trial, Houston and Ed Jennings became involved in a heated argument in court, insults were exchanged and guns were drawn but the situation was defused by bystanders before violence erupted. Later that night, Temple Houston and Jack Love were having a drink in the Cabinet Saloon in Woodward when Ed and John Jennings entered. The dispute began afresh and, absent cooler heads, a gun battle erupted. Ed Jennings was felled by a gunshot to the head, immediately and fatally. John Jennings, hit in the arm and chest, ran 200 feet down the street before collapsing from his wounds. Houston and Love were both unscathed "although several bullets passed through their clothes and hats". Both immediately turned themselves in and were released on bond.

In the resulting trial, Houston and Love were acquitted on the grounds of self defense. Al Jennings stormed from the courtroom, swearing vengeance. Al and his brother Frank hung around the area for several months but never "found" either Love or Houston although neither did anything to conceal himself. Perhaps, as one author suggested, they were mindful of both men's proven credentials with a gun and responded to the logic that "there was no use filling up the graveyards with Jenningses". Love's and Houston's participation in this saga now ended. Houston died prematurely in 1905. Love became the first chairman of the State Corporation Commission and remained in that position until his death in 1918.

During the summer of 1897, Al Jennings and his brother Frank started the "Jennings Gang" and entered into the outlaw life. Made up of several of the most inept losers imaginable, it derived what little "professionalism" it could claim from former Doolin associates Little Dick West and Dynamite Dick Clifton. The gang was to have an outlaw career of less than six months that one author called "one of the shortest and funniest on record".

By July of 1897, Deputy Marshals were hunting for them for the robbery of a post office in Foyil in far northeastern Oklahoma. On August 16, 1897, the gang stopped and boarded the Santa Fe train south of Edmond. Two attempts to blow open the safe with dynamite were unsuccessful and the gang rode away empty handed. The next day they encountered Deputy

U.S. Marshal Sam Bartell who was unaware of the Edmond train fiasco. They had a meal with Bartell and rode on. Two weeks later, they tried their luck on an MK&T train south of Muskogee. The gang piled surplus railroad ties on the track and set them afire to stop the train. The engineer, no novice, simply poured on the steam and drove through them without stopping.

The next three months saw a series of petty robberies (including one in which Al was identified when his mask slipped off) netting anywhere from a few hundred dollars to a feast on stolen whiskey and bananas, followed by chases and gun battles with pursuing Marshals. Predictably, the gang's only success in these encounters was escaping after absorbing some of the lawmen's bullets. On December 6, 1897, Marshals captured most of the gang, including Al and Frank, while they were sleeping in a wagon trying to get to Arkansas. Appropriately, not a shot was fired.

Tried in May of 1898, Al Jennings was given five years in Leavenworth for attempting (unsuccessfully, naturally) to kill a Deputy U.S. Marshal. Tried again in February of 1899 for robbing the U.S. Mail, Al was given a life sentence. He was not through, however, with his part in the history of Oklahoma or Oklahoma City.

### THE DAILY OKLAHOMAN
November 2, 1895

#### A PARSON ROLLED

Parson Leach of McCurtain, I.T. is the latest victim of the negro wenches of Oklahoma City who prey upon all persons who cross their path and bid defiance to the local police.

Parson Leach lost $7.50 and some of his innocence that night. Twenty black prostitutes went to jail but he couldn't identify the guilty ones. He still made it to the Presbyterian synod in Pauls Valley thanks to the trainfare provided by an anonymous Oklahoma City policeman. Parson Leach had been victimized by the minions of another one of Oklahoma City's unique characters. The organizer, leader and enforcer of a group of enterprising black prostitutes, she was known by the nickname "Old Zulu". Described as "a gigantic, six-foot frowsy headed Fury with a voice like a fog-horn and a countenance that would stop a clock", she was Big Anne Wynn's connection in the negro sections and the acknowledged "Queen of Avenue A" (East Grand Avenue). Usually carrying a pistol hidden down the front of her dress, when under the influence of spirits or drugs, "she was a whole regiment of hatpins, nails, teeth, feet and umbrellas, [and] policemen had to go in squads to arrest her".

Although probably arrested for every misdemeanor on the books, Old Zulu also provided public services such as encouraging the black populace to exercise their right to vote. She accomplished this by roaming the streets and alleys of East Grand and Alabaster Row on election day, armed with a club and loudly proclaiming "All yo' niggahs git tuh the polls an' don't be messin' 'round 'bout it nethah".

One day after terrorizing two blocks of East Grand, she was wrestled into Police Court by four officers to face Judge Highley. His sentence of $50 and six months in jail sent her into a tirade of tears and pleas of illness. The Judge then offered to drop the sentence and pay her way to Texas if she'd leave town. This brought on another deluge of tears and pleas to go home to Virginia but not Texas. When the Judge was adamant, Old Zulu said she'd rather go to jail than Texas...and she did.

### OKLAHOMA DAILY TIMES-JOURNAL
January 15, 1895

#### POLICE COURT

Judge Beatty was presiding when during the trial a well known offender, Stormy Jim, arrived in charge of a policeman, shuffled up to his honors desk and in a familiar tone asked the Judge "Did you want to see me?". "You are charged with Drunkenness and Disturbing the Peace by fighting. Are you guilty or not?", questioned the Judge. "Guilty", answered Stormy...The Judge fined him $9.00 to which he answered he did not give a .... for that, so his honor, after reprimanding the police for bringing an intoxicated prisoner to court, gave him five days more for insolent language.

*Chief J.H. Boles.*

On December 5, Bill Doolin was arrested by Bill Tilghman at a bath house in Eureka Springs, Arkansas. When the two got off the train in Guthrie, some 3000 people turned out to see the inheritor of the Dalton legacy. Since he had made the arrest alone and without firing a shot, Tilghman's reputation as the territory's premier lawman skyrocketed.

One of Jones' officers, J.H.Boles, was chosen to replace him but was apparently not a worthy successor. He lasted less than five months before having charges of misconduct preferred against him. Boles was charged in early December with having arrested a young couple while he was drunk on duty. The City Council refused to suspend the Chief while the charges were investigated and drew heavy fire in the press for that refusal. At the Council meeting on December 16, affidavits from the arrested couple and witnesses to the arrest were presented. They and a number of other witnesses attested that Chief Boles was drunk on the night of the false arrest. This testimony was from witnesses who were "without exception citizens of excellent standing". In his defense, Chief Boles presented 17 affidavits to prove his sobriety on that night. Most of them, evidently, were from pimps and prostitutes. The Council voted 6 to 1 for Boles' dismissal.

Officer George W. Jackson, a veteran of the gunfight with the Christians and Jim Casey, was appointed acting Chief of Police to date from December 15 but was not officially confirmed by the City Council until December 30, 1895.

The year 1896 began with the Republicans regaining City Hall with the election of Charles Graham "Gristmill" Jones as Mayor. On January 16, newspaper headlines trumpeted the capture of Bill Doolin in Arkansas and Marshal Bill Tilghman's reputation went up another notch. Typically, clamoring for reforms and vice sweeps began, targeting the saloons, gambling houses and brothels. The most notorious of the day appeared to be The Red Onion, operating on Alabaster Row on the north side of California Avenue between Broadway and Robinson.

OKLAHOMA DAILY TIMES-JOURNAL
January 21, 1896

We knew that Arkansas City would get in on the Doolin capture in some way. It is now reported that Doolin was captured through information given out by his sister-in-law. As the story goes Tilghman and Bill Ansley went into partnership on the deal. Ansley formerly lived here and worked the Santa Fe. Doolin's wife had a sister in Oklahoma City and Ansley was to court her and marry her if necessary to catch Doolin. He did so and after the marriage, Ansley got wind of the whereabouts of them, threw his wife over and put Tilghman on. It is now said that Ansley has skipped and Mrs. Ansley is hunting for him with a gun.

*Chief T.A. 'Abe' Couch"*

George W. Jackson didn't last long in the top job and was replaced on May 1, 1896, by T.A. "Abe" Couch, the late Mayor's brother who had suffered so cruelly at the hands of Councilman Jack Love a few years before. Finally, Abe had official sanction for his law enforcement role. But his luck wasn't to hold for long.

On July 5, there was a mass jail break at the federal jail in Guthrie. Among the escapees was Bill Doolin. The elite of the territory's lawmen immediately began fanning out in every direction looking for Doolin. Heck Thomas found him on August 24 near Lawson, on the Pawnee/Payne County line east of Stillwater. This time Bill Tilghman wasn't around to give Doolin a break. Thomas put at least 20 holes through him with a massive eight-gauge shotgun.

As 1897 began, the Supreme Court overturned City Ordinance 164, declaring it unconstitutional to forbid Carrie Gribbin to beat her Salvation Army drum. The author of the ordinance, Councilman Goodrich, was furious. Described by former City Manager Albert McRill as an "intense Republican", it has been suggested that Goodrich may have had an overblown sense of his own self importance because he was personally acquainted with President McKinley.

Goodrich was currently at odds with newspaper editor and fellow councilman Frank McMaster, who was just as fervently a Democrat as Goodrich was a Republican. This opposition set the stage for a City Council meeting that would knock Carrie's drum right off the docket. McMaster upset the applecart by accusing two councilmen (both Republicans) of stealing $20,000 from the city treasury.

Goodrich began assailing McMaster, refusing to use his name and referring to him as "that thing". The word "guttersnipe" was mentioned. I will now refer to McRill's recounting of the ensuing scene since I doubt if it could be improved upon;"Thereupon Alderman Lindsay, another staunch Democrat, called Alderman Goodrich a 'damned liar'. McMaster shouted at Lindsay to 'hit Goodrich'. Chairs began flying around the council-chamber. City Clerk George Spencer, a meek neutral, crawled under a table and 'spent a second in silent supplication'.

Chief of Police Abe Couch, who had seen chairs flying through the air when 'Jack' Love, the Kickapoo alderman, went on a rampage, did not interfere, nor did Mayor Jones who, as speaker of the Oklahoma legislature, had become accustomed to flying chairs, paperweights and spittoons.Goodrich shouted 'lemmeatim' and McMaster shrieked 'turn me loose'. Finally, McMaster aimed a Fitzsimmons' left at Goodrich, but it fell short..."

Although Abe Couch had decided to sit this one out, other officers restored order.

The Carrie Gribbin discussion postponed until the next Council meeting, the Daily Oklahoman set the stage by saying "A high old time is promised and those who are not financially able to attend the Corbett-Fitzsimmons' [world heavyweight championship] fight in Nevada should come early".

By the next meeting, however, Goodrich and McMaster were of a like mind on the Carrie Gribbins decision. Goodrich complained that it "gives them the right to beat their drums and howl and raise hell generally" while McMaster groused that the Salvation Army would keep at

*Officer Ike Ashburn with citizens-late 1890s."*

it until "it Kansasizes the whole town".

Nevertheless, the decision stood and Carrie could beat her drum to her heart's content, for all the good it did, no matter how many buggies got wrecked.

Late in 1896, the Territorial Legislature passed a law making the Chief of Police's post an elected one with a two-year term. Sworn in on April 1, 1897, the first elected Chief was Edward F. "Frank" Cochran, serving his second term in the office. Cochran was given a force of eight men and three bloodhounds with which to maintain order. Four of them who listed their occupation as policemen in the City Directory of that year were Joe Burnett, W.B. Hendrey, J. Stafford and M.J. McFarland. The highlights of his term were particularly bloody, two of them occurring during a single week in 1897.

The first incident occurred at Traylor's Saloon on Alabaster Row at 16 West California. Nineteen-year-old Patrolman Ike Ashburn and two other officers got in a "free-for-all shootout" with a house full of drunks, leaving six dead.

Several days later, there was another bloodbath at The Bucket of Blood in the 800 block of East 1st Street. A berserk Mexican with a Bowie knife killed eight patrons brandishing razors before being killed by an unnamed police officer.

Shortly thereafter, Kid Bannister shot a man in the Southern Club and chased everyone off of Bunco Alley. The Kid was brought to justice for this by being fined $10 and court costs.

On January 15, 1898, Clyde Mattox was released from prison with a pardon from President Grover Cleveland. It had taken three trials to get him convicted and his mother had expended an estate valued at $20,000 in her herculean legal battles on her son's behalf.

Clyde was either a slow learner or just plain mean because he was not through being a source of grief to his mother or Oklahoma.

Within a few years of the city's opening, the primary red light district had migrated from its original stronghold on Bunco Alley to line both sides of the 400 block of West 2nd Street.

*The Public Market area on California Street in the late 1890s.*

Gaining the nickname "Harlot's Lane", the area rivalled New Orleans' Basin Street, in one author's opinion, as a marketplace for sins of the flesh.

Going west from Hudson on 2nd Street, the first house of joy encountered would be that of Etta Woods and her Creole girls. Next was the house of Nina Truelove. Next was the Red Star of Madam Brentlinger, whose nom de guerre was Jean La Monte. She was another veteran of the mining camps of Leadville, Colorado, who had come to the city with Big Anne Wynn. Across the street was Madam McDonald's The Arlington, touted as the "most exclusive" house on the Lane.

Across the street from The Arlington was Noah's Ark, operated by "Big Liz" and "Dude" Walker. The far west end of the Lane was dominated by Big Anne Wynn's two-story Place 444, presided over by madam Effie Fisher, combining whiskey, dancing and sex all under one rollicking roof. Various smaller brothels were interspersed among these more notorious joints.

On April 7, 1898, the saga of the Dalton/Doolin/Jennings triumvirate came to an end. Richard "Little Dick" West was found on Turkey Creek in Kingfisher County by a posse led by Bill Tilghman and Heck Thomas. After riding with the Daltons and Bill Doolin, West had left the Jennings gang in disgust at their rank amateurism. West had been the hardest of the lot to track down and corner because of his aversion to sleeping in buildings. His habit of always sleeping outside had always given him sufficient warning of the approach of posses in the past to allow him to escape. but not this time. Surrounded and deciding to make a fight of it like a real outlaw, West went down in a blaze of gunfire and an era ended.

In early April of 1898, George W. Jackson became the second and last Chief of Police to die in the line of duty. Jackson had been serving as the "Night" or Assistant Chief since May of 1897. During the early morning hours of Sunday, January 16, 1898, two men were involved in an all night drinking bout from the previous Saturday evening. They were Oklahoma County Deputy Sheriff Bishop Armstrong and Fred Jones. Jones was the night bartender at the Compton Saloon and a brother of slain Chief Milton Jones. About 6 A.M. the two men went to Ethel Smith's "sporting house" on West 2nd Street. They soon went to another brothel across the street and began roaming between the two houses raising various kinds of hell. During one of the visits, Armstrong fired his gun. No one was hit but a black banjo player went for the law before someone was.George Jackson responded. As he was trying to enter the house, Armstrong met him in the doorway. The two men went down fighting until Jones approached and pulled Jackson off of Armstrong. Jones was holding a gun and Jackson told him to give it up. Jones then fired once, shattering Jackson's right hip. Jones began running down the street and Jackson began firing at him. One of the bullets hit Armstrong.

Jones turned himself in an hour later with his lawyer and was released on $2,000 bond. Over the next three months, Armstrong recuperated but Jackson's condition worsened. The paper noted that Jackson had been in ill health before the shooting and was "feeling his age" of 49 years. Jackson died on the afternoon of April 12.

Fred Jones was rearrested two days later in Tecumseh and returned to Oklahoma City the next day, the day of Jackson's funeral. The funeral procession to Fairlawn Cemetery on April 15 was "the largest the city had seen since that of Milton Jones three years previously".

February of 1899 was to be the coldest February in Oklahoma City's history. The temperature reached a bone-chilling 4 degrees, then went to 12 below zero and finally to 17 below zero, the coldest temperature ever recorded for any date. Things were frosty in City Hall too. Frank Cochran had served about 20 months before resigning on February 7, 1899, due to a stated "lack of harmony of several months standing" with city government. Cochran returned to his former position as a Deputy U.S. Marshal.

Chief G.W.R. Chinn.

George W.R. Chinn was appointed to serve the remaining two months of Cochran's term of office, resigning his seat on the City Council to accept the appointment. Chinn was the owner of the Oklahoma Transfer and Storage Company, a former sheriff in Missouri and former Deputy U.S. Marshal. Less than a week later, M.J. McFarland resigned as Assistant Chief. It is unknown whether this was the result of disharmony with the new Chief or political allegiance to the old one. William B. Hendrey, an officer under Cochran, was appointed Assistant Chief in his stead.

Democrat Hendrey ran against former County Sheriff Columbus H. DeFord in the spring elections. Chinn did not run. Hendrey won the election on April 5 and Chinn handed over his badge on April 11 after thanking the Council for "the opportunity to serve". Chinn returned to his transfer and storage business and Hendrey increased the force to 12 men.

*1900 OCPD with Chief William Hendrey at far right.*

# II — STATEHOOD, POLITICS AND PROHIBITION 1900-1909

The impending close of one century and the birth of a new one did little to tame the town or the Territory. It was still a dangerous place especially for con-men and gamblers. Bob Darnell, known as "Big Mitt", his brother Emmet, the "Butterfly Kid" and Jack Pecora all died in gunfights, just to name a few of the more notable ones. Charlie Harris, a gambler and gunfighter who had survived the Colorado mining towns, was gunned down on California Avenue. The Police Court was averaging $1,000 a month in fines.

Boom towns had been alternately springing up and withering all over the western United States for over half a century. Whether their impetus was gold, silver, oil, cattle, railroad or land run, they all had one thing in common; their populations were highly transient and their numbers fluctuated widely. That fact accounted for the overnight population of Oklahoma Station, estimated to be between 10,000 and 12,000 by Captain Daniel Stiles, dwindling to an official count of 5,086 slightly more than a year later when the city was incorporated. From that point, it slowly and steadily began building back up.

In spite of the fact that the population had nearly doubled in the first decade, growth and progress were slow. Much too slow for a town with pretensions of eventually becoming the

*Downtown Oklahoma City-early 1900s.*

*First County Courthouse-built on William Couch's old claim at Main and Walker.*

primary city and capital of a new state. By the time of the 1900 Census, the population was shown to be 9,990. This was 10 less than the minimum necessary to permit the city to issue bonds to finance public buildings. A number of persons swore that, although residents, they had not been counted. Elmer E. Brown, the publisher of the Oklahoma Daily Times-Journal, was designated to go to Washington D.C. and try to get the additional names included on the official rolls.

The Director of the Census, knowing of the contention between the two largest cities for dominance, was reportedly highly amused by the fact that Oklahoma City and Guthrie claimed exactly the same population figures. Nevertheless, he yielded to the newspaperman's explanations and included the names on the rolls. Within a couple of weeks, Mr. Brown was back home with a certificate showing Oklahoma City with an official population of 10,037. The population boom of the first decades of the 20th Century is directly related to that Census. Without the inclusion of those names, the bonds to finance the sewers, waterworks, public buildings and other facilities of a modern city could not have been issued. Slowly but surely, the city was growing up.

A building boom began with the new century. In March, Charles Colcord sold all his land, race horses, trotting horses and thoroughbred shorthorn cattle in Perry and returned to Oklahoma City with over $50,000, more than half of it in cash. He immediately bought two lots on the southeast corner of First and Broadway, where the Liberty National Bank now stands. He also assisted another former OCPD Chief with the first $5,000 in financing a new hotel.

On October 8, Buffalo Bill brought his show back to town, staying at ex-Chief Oscar Lee's new Lee Hotel on the southeast corner of Main and Broadway. The plushest hotel in the city, this four-story palace cost $100,000, boasted 150 rooms and the first electric elevators in town. These latter conveniences were not universally appreciated because, due to the state of the power supply in town at that time, whenever the elevators were used, the lights dimmed all over town. Another early guest was Teddy Roosevelt.

When the Spanish-American War started in 1898, the country had not had a major conflict in over three decades. Civil War veterans were all at or beyond middle age. Then as now, war was primarily a young man's job. Therefore, the largest pool of manpower that was experienced in shooting at people and getting shot at was in the western states and territories. That is exactly where Colonel Teddy Roosevelt's 1st U.S. Volunteer Cavalry, his beloved "Rough Riders", were recruited from, a large percentage of them from Oklahoma and Indian Territories. He called them " a splendid set of men, these Southwesterners—tall and sinewy, with resolute, weather-beaten faces, and eyes that looked a man straight in the face without flinching". When it came to providing combat experience, the hapless Cubans had nothing on Comanches, the Daltons and similar foes. Of the Oklahoma contingent, 23 had been killed and 105 wounded in that "little" war.

Now Roosevelt was the Governor of New York. In nine months, he would become the Vice President of the United States and, six months later, our youngest President following the assassination of President McKinley. On July 2, 1900, these events were totally unforeseen when Roosevelt held a reunion for his Rough Riders in the North Canadian River basin on the south edge of Oklahoma City. That night, he hosted a ball for them at 214 West Main, the unfinished Street and Reed Furniture Store. With everything bedecked in red, white and blue, Americanism was the main course.

Another familiar name resurfaced in the first year of the new century. Clyde Mattox, who had killed the first law enforcement officer in Oklahoma City 11 years earlier, became news again. Originally sentenced to hang, Mattox's sentence was commuted to life imprisonment by President Grover Cleveland. President McKinley pardoned him in 1897 because he was supposedly dying from tuberculosis.

Not only did the uncooperative Mattox refuse to die, on April 3, 1899, he stabbed a man to death in Ponca City. He was arrested for that crime by the Deputy U.S. Marshal in Perry at the time, Charles Colcord. Colcord had also helped arrest Mattox for Marshal Howard's murder in the summer of 1889. At the time of the arrest in Perry, Colcord allowed Mattox's mother, Mrs. S.W. Hatch, to talk him into going to their tent to let Mattox change clothes. The tent was separated into two rooms by a sheet hanging from the top. When Mattox sat down on a bed near the curtained-off room, he and his mother began acting nervously. Colcord, acting upon his instincts, drew his gun and led them both out to meet the Sheriff. Colcord later came

*1902 OCPD-The four men seated in the front row, left to right, are former Chief J.H. Boles, John Hubatka (with dog between his legs), Chief Ralph Cochran and his brother, former Chief E.F. 'Frank' Cochran.*

to feel that his actions were governed by impulsive paranoia until, some time later, he was told by Bill Tilghman what had almost occurred that night. Tilghman had been told the true story by Mrs. Hatch. One of Mattox's associates named Three-Finger Jack had been hiding behind the curtain that night and he had put a gun under the pillow on the bed where Clyde was sitting. The horses were saddled and waiting behind the tent, ready for their escape after they had killed the officer. Mrs. Hatch said that Clyde would have gone free that night and Colcord would have died except "Clyde lost his nerve". Sentenced to 12 years this time, Mattox was paroled by Governor Haskell on March 12, 1908. The Governor revoked the parole two years later because of yet another shooting. Mattox was pardoned again in July of 1911 and, this time, really died not long after his release.

Meanwhile, another future challenge for law enforcement appeared. Honking horns began echoing off downtown buildings as the first motorized cars began making their appearance on city streets, accompanied by the bleats and slashing hooves of terrified horses and the curses of their riders.

In January of 1901, former Chief Frank Cochran suffered grievous wounds in a gunfight with bank robbers in Bristow. Cochran was the Deputy U.S. Marshal stationed there at the time and was living across the street from the bank. He and his wife were awakened one night when the bank's safe was dynamited by at least three robbers. Telling his wife to get on the floor, Cochran armed himself and went to the window. He immediately attracted shotgun fire from the lookout man. Cochran was immediately felled by buckshot wounds in both shoulders, the right groin and the left leg. In spite of his wounds, Cochran ran across the street to the bank and fired at two men as they went out the back door of the bank.

Deputy U.S. Marshal Bill Tilghman captured two of the robbers two days later in Stroud. Frank Cochran would eventually lose his left leg as a result of his wounds and, although he never fully recovered from them, would never fully yield to them either.

Ralph W. Cochran, Frank's brother, was elected Chief in April of 1901 and increased the force to 18 men to police over 10,000 citizens. Frank Cochran returned to serve as a Desk Sergeant under his brother.

One of the seemingly eternal and continuing problems that law enforcement seems to burden itself with is jurisdictional disputes between agencies. These always cause many more problems than they solve and usually assist the criminals in their illegal pursuits. It is probably rooted in the political nature of their control systems and the ever-vigilant public scrutiny under which they are held. It is almost axiomatic for some police administrators to feel that the best way to curry political and public favor is to be better, faster, more thorough and efficient than surrounding jurisdictions. Realizing that it is impossible in this profession to be above criticism, they sometimes avoid a "be the best that you can be" attitude and just strive to be better than the guy next door. This dissipates heat by diverting criticism. It usually doesn't sit well with the agency the criticism is diverted toward. More than a few veteran law enforcement officers over the years have shaken their heads in exasperation and made comments to the effect that "crime is organized, why can't we get organized?". This isn't a new problem.

In the summer of 1901, a rift occurred between city and county law enforcement that was to continue, off and on, for several decades. It seemed to have its roots in partisan politics. The entire Democratic ticket was elected in the county elections in the fall of 1900. The municipal elections in the spring of 1901 saw the Republicans take over city government, headed by Mayor Charles G. "Gristmill" Jones. Thus there were political factions with opposing philosophies controlling law enforcement agencies with overlapping jurisdictions, responsible to the same citizens, with their every action (or lack of action) trumpeted daily by competing newspapers with the same opposing political philosophies.

Citizen complaints caused the City Council to consider shutting down the town's slot machines unless they produced more revenue from fines. The local police judge contended that fines had never been higher. While the Mayor, City Council and police judge were deliberating the fine points of this, the County Attorney ordered the Sheriff to shut down the slots and step up enforcement efforts on the saloons. The implication to the citizens was that while the city administration talked, the county acted. The Daily Oklahoman sardonically accused the County Attorney of having "a spasm of virtue". The County Attorney defended his "spasm" by alleging that the Chief of Police had "confessed himself powerless to control the turbulent element of the City". It was a response to public, press and political pressures that would wax and wane for years to come.

The politics of the time were chaotic but progress still persevered. On February 2, 1903, the first street car in the Territory was placed in operation by the Oklahoma Railway Company, run by John Shartel and Anton Classen. Delmar Gardens, a 140-acre entertainment complex, opened at Exchange and Western where the Public Market now stands. Lon Chaney, the "Man of 1,000 Faces", and Buster Keaton performed in plays there. Heavyweight champion John L. Sullivan held boxing exhibitions, Apache Chief Geronimo and Comanche Quanah Parker sold autographs there for dimes. Dan Patch, the famous pacing horse, and Barney Oldfield raced there.

Charles Colcord began building a new home at 421 N.W. 13, just north of the downtown area and on the southern edge of the Heritage Hills area, the elite residential edition of its day. An 11-bedroom Georgian-Colonial mansion with marble fireplaces, a solarium, billiard room and a ballroom, it was a far cry from the wooden shack Colcord had traded a wagon and horses for on Lot One of Block One 14 years earlier.

*Chief Orris H. Emrick-1903.*

One of the most cowardly murders in the city's history occurred on February 13, 1903. George Burton was known as a gambler, killer and, when he was drinking, a general troublemaker second only to Kid Bannister. He was allegedly a fugitive from Deadwood, South Dakota, for killing another gambler over a poker game. In the early afternoon of that date, Burton was drinking in the Two Johns Saloon when a man named Ray Love came in for a drink. As the railroad worker sidled up to the bar, he accidentally stepped on one of Burton's feet. Burton evidently had a bad case of corns and erupted with a stream of profanity at Love. Love tried to apologize to no avail and the two started swinging at each other. One of the larger patrons stepped in as peacemaker, grabbing Burton and shoving the smaller Love away. Love left immediately, going north on Broadway.

Burton was trying to get out of the larger man's grasp, swearing that he didn't have a gun, and the man let him go. Burton ran out of the

Two Johns and caught up with Love within 25 yards. Drawing a gun from his pocket, Burton hit Love in the back of the head, knocking him to the ground, and then shot him in the back as he lay there. Burton was arrested and tried for murder. He was convicted and sentenced to ten years imprisonment.

On April 7, 1903, Orris H. Emrick was elected Chief of Police on the Democratic ticket, defeating Republican John Hubatka. Sworn in six days later, Emrick was hailed as a highly respected businessman who had come to the city from Wichita, Kansas, in the Run of '89. Born in Warren County, Illinois, in 1854, Emrick had successfully operated the Emrick Transfer Company for the past 12 years and it was noted that this was his first experience in holding public office or, apparently, in law enforcement. A newspaper photo of the Chief showed a handsome man with short, dark hair going gray and a full mustache. He was wearing a uniform coat with his badge on his upper left breast. The badge was a five- pointed star surrounded by a wreath and hanging from a semicircular arc by two small chains.

The 1903 City Directory lauded the city as a metropolis of 30,000 population but admitted in the fine print that the "actual count" was 24,347. A reorganization of the police force increased the force to 22 men. Seven worked during the day, 13 worked nights and two served as detectives. They were listed in the paper as:

| | | |
|---|---|---|
| Orris H. Emrick, Chief | A.A. Lucas | W.L. Lett |
| H.E. Bunker | L.D. Fowler | Abe Couch, Detective |
| James Felts | Parker, Day Sergeant | Ike Armstrong |
| J.T. Brown, Assistant Chief | Walter McCoy | Frank Eenish |
| Joe Burnett | R.J. Colt | John Ballard |
| T.C. Parker | Fred W. Hagen, Detective | Charles Larrey |
| C.H. Coucher, Captain | H.C. Robertson | W.O. Parker |
| | | T.C. Warden |

A shooting of small consequence but one which provides insights into Oklahoma City politics of the time occurred about 6:30 P.M. on June 25, 1903. Political fixer Larry Reedy was currently serving as the Secretary of the local Horseshoer's Union. A man named Charles Swinghammer had quit the union because it restricted the number of hours he could work. An article soon appeared in a union paper branding Swinghammer "a scab" and urging others not to do business with him. Swinghammer blamed Reedy for writing the article. They crossed paths behind the Johnson-Larimore Hardware Store at 100 West Grand on that evening.

Reedy, accompanied by his brother, was immediately decked by Swinghammer. When the brother stepped forward, Swinghammer decked him as well. Larry Reedy then drew his .44 and fired twice. One bullet broke Swinghammer's right arm, the second bullet broke his left arm, exited and entered his jaw, breaking it in two places. Swinghammer was hauled to get medical treatment and Reedy landed in jail.....but not for long. Larry Reedy, after all, was not your average blacksmith.

A stocky, 200-pound former prizefighter, Reedy arrived in Oklahoma City just after the turn of the century. Fresh from an apprenticeship in Chicago's Loop District where he marked as many ballots as needed to insure the victory of the highest-bidding alderman candidate, he found fertile ground in Oklahoma City politics.

He quickly established himself in the largest precinct in the city, Precinct A of Ward Four in the southern part of town. Making the rounds of saloons, buying a few drinks and starting political conversations, it wasn't too difficult to figure out who was currently "in", politically speaking, who was currently "out" and who wanted to get back in. The local Democrats were anxious to get Republican Mayor Gristmill Jones back into private life so they purchased Mr. Reedy's favor.

His favor included the services of a group of bar-flies he organized into a gang that acquired the nickname "The Dirty Dozen". A slightly tamer precursor of Hitler's brownshirts, they intimidated and brawled their way through the ward until it acquired the nickname "The

*Mounted OCPD officers in front of the first County Courthouse.*

*Officer Ike Ashburn on a less stately mount.*

Bloody Fourth".

A true Democrat, Reedy was not partisan when it came to money and his services went to the highest bidder regardless of political philosophy or affiliation. Minor office-seekers were expected to start the bidding at $250, major city and county offices started at $500 and state offices or special circumstances like bond issues could go as high as $1,000.

Reedy was appointed as an "election inspector" in his adopted precinct. That was like having the cat guard the bird cage. Although there weren't more than 500 legal voters in the entire precinct, it soon became known that Reedy's precinct could deliver as many votes as necessary when the right price was paid. One might have expected someone who was able to ingratiate himself as thoroughly into city and county politics for more than a decade to rise above his Chicago tenderloin origins. Unfortunately this wasn't the case with Larry Reedy. The natural political belligerency that went with his chosen profession often led to fights and occasionally to the drawing of weapons. He was arrested innumerable times for carrying weapons, assaults and minor thefts of items as diverse as chickens, soap and phonograph records.

Although Reedy was not invulnerable to the law, he was fairly well protected from the brunt of it. This was primarily as a result of a close relationship with Police Judge J.T. Highley. The Judge was fervently pro-Labor and a co-publisher of The Labor Signal newspaper. Reedy's position as Secretary of the local Horseshoer's Union gave them a common bond to build on, on the surface. In their respective positions as elected official and political fixer, it can only be surmised what other bonds may have formed.

Officer Roe Burnett, Joe's brother, once brought Reedy before Judge Highley on a vagrancy charge. Highley released him in short order, then told Burnett to leave Reedy alone because "if it wasn't for Larry Reedy, not a damned one of us would have a job".

At any rate, Reedy rarely paid fines or served jail time for his transgressions. He occasionally prevented his arrest by producing a Deputy Sheriff's badge. When he was actually arrested, he was allowed to appeal the case until it died a natural death from neglect. The legal maxim that "justice delayed is justice denied" might have been invented with Larry Reedy in mind. Such was to be the case in Reedy vs. Swinghammer. It may also be worth noting that the paper that published the article calling Swinghammer "a scab" was the Labor Signal, published by Judge Highley.

Reedy was indicted on July 11, 1903, for shooting with intent to kill. The fact that his bond was immediately posted is not as significant as who posted it; Seymour Heyman, President of the Chamber of Commerce, John Threadgill, prominent builder of the hotel on the northeast corner of 2nd and North Broadway that bore his name and a City Councilman. The hapless Mr. Swinghammer was up against some heavy hitters in his quest for justice.

On the evening of July 4, 1903, Joseph "Kid" Bannister was out celebrating his independence with a friend, J.T. Phillips. One hopes the Kid enjoyed his evening because it was to be his last. The two were drinking at The Southern Club when the Kid decided to go to the Turf Exchange Club on Battle Row. Phillips tried to dissuade him by reminding him that Tom Cook, owner of the Turf Club, "had no use for [Bannister]". There had been hard feelings between the men for the last six months, when Cook's brother-in-law had been arrested for pistol-whipping Bannister. Undeterred, Bannister insisted.

When they arrived at the Turf Club about 10 P.M., Bannister went inside followed by Phillips. As the Kid proceeded inside, the Turf's "house policeman" (bouncer) stopped Phillips and was searching him for weapons. While the man was disarming him, they heard shots coming from inside the club. Tom Cook strode by a few seconds later, telling Phillips "I don't have anything against you but I told that goddam sonofabitch not to come to my house again". Proceeding inside, Phillips found Bannister dead on the floor, a .38 slug in his chest.

Officers Ike Ashburn and W.L. Letts arrived at the Turf Club only to discover that Cook had already walked the half block to the police station and surrendered himself. The officers found a .38 pistol under Bannister's body when they rolled him over. Albert McRill says the other patrons broke into a spontaneous cheer when it was announced that Bannister was dead. The next day's paper apparently concurred in the judgement by carrying the story under the headline "A Bad Man Shot Dead". A coroner's jury made it unanimous by finding the shooting justifiable and Tom Cook was released. Kid Bannister was interred in Fairlawn Cemetery, presumably with few in attendance to regret his demise.

DAILY OKLAHOMAN
July 7, 1903

CHANGES IN POLICE

Several members of the police force received letters yesterday evening from Mayor Van Winkle requesting them to tender their resignations to take effect Wednesday, July 8. The men whose resignations were requested are Officers Fowler, McCarthy, Baber, Emmett and Lewis. They are all republicans. No reason was assigned for the requested resignations.

An epochal gunfight occurred on January 13, 1904, that closed a chapter in western history and sent a message that law and order was in Oklahoma City to stay. Edward O. Kelly was on parole from Colorado for killing Bob Ford, the man who had killed Jesse James. Kelly had murdered Ford in Ford's dance hall in Creede, Colorado, on June 8, 1892. The jury took the charge all the more seriously because Kelly had committed the cowardly killing under color of authority while serving as a Deputy Town Marshal. The motive was shown to be a serious grudge between the two men stemming from either a stolen diamond ring, a stolen diamond scarf-pin or a woman. Convicted of second degree murder and sentenced to life imprisonment, Kelly spent the next ten years in prison before being paroled on October 3, 1902. A red-headed six-footer, Kelly, 46, was described as "resembling [former World Heavyweight boxing Champion] Bob Fitzsimmons". As it turned out, the two might have provided a good match except that Ed Kelly wasn't known for fighting fair.

When he arrived in Oklahoma City a month earlier, Kelly had been arrested by Officer Joe Burnett. Newspaper accounts noted that Kelly had been "mightily offended" and had nursed a grudge against Burnett ever since. This night Kelly was in a surly mood, having already been in jail once courtesy of Officer H.E. Bunker. When he got out of jail, Kelly armed himself with his customary two guns and began bragging that he was "gunning for a policeman". About 9 P.M., Kelly and Burnett's paths crossed on the south side of the 300 block of West 1st Street (later Park Avenue), now directly south of the Oklahoma County Courthouse.

Fully intent on living up to his boast, Kelly drew his gun, Burnett grabbed his gunhand and struck him with his nightstick. Then ensued an epic struggle that lasted 15 minutes, travelled 75 feet all the way around the corner and saw over a dozen shots fired. Anyone who has ever been in a fight can appreciate how long 15 minutes can be under such conditions. Both men emptied their guns while continuing to struggle, with Kelly cursing, biting and promising murder while Burnett called to bystanders to help him. No one wanted to get involved until a baggageman from the Frisco Depot, A.G. Paul, happened by. Wading into the melee to assist, Paul grabbed Kelly's gunhand. Burnett got his second gun with his newly-freed hand and shot

Kelly in the head. When it was over, Officer Burnett had flesh wounds in his left arm and left hip, part of one ear bitten off and two bullet holes in his overcoat which was on fire from the muzzle blast of Kelly's guns. Burnett survived to become an Assistant Chief on the force he served so well.

Ed Kelly's body remained in the morgue for the next two weeks, waiting for some relative or loved one to claim it. Indicative of the man's lifestyle, no one did. Finally, on January 28, the body was buried in an unmarked grave in Fairlawn Cemetery in a $12.50 casket provided at county expense.

In 1903, Henry Overholser had constructed the Overholser Opera House at 217 West Grand. The four story building cost $100,000 and had a capacity of 2,500 people to enjoy its ornately carved boxes, leather opera chairs, plush carpets and draperies. It boasted of having over 700 electric lights and the largest stage west of the Mississippi. From the stage floor to the roof was an awe-inspiring 72 feet. Later to become the Orpheum and still later the Warner Theater, it was the pride and joy of Oklahoma City social life.

*Officer Joe Burnett, pictured here as OCPD's Assistant Chief about 1910.*

In the alley behind the Opera House, in the location of what would later become the Harber and Cooper Theaters, was a three story building. This was the Oklahoma Athletic Club, where Jess Willard began his rise to the Heavyweight Championship of the world. The gymnasium, however, covered only the first floor of the building. Under separate management from the rest of the building, it served as what law enforcement officers call "a front". The two upper floors were the territory of Jake Barnes and a bastion of the "Big Four" syndicate that had controlled all the big time gambling in the city since the turn of the century.

At that time, the Big Four consisted of Jake Barnes, Clint Stout, Cecil Proctor and William "Bet You A Thousand" Monnahan. Between them, they owned and controlled all of the biggest, most lucrative gambling joints in the City including the Southern Club at 28 West Grand, The Olympic Club at 105 1/2 West Main, the Oklahoma Athletic Club and the Monte Carlo at 114 1/2 North Robinson. Their control extended beyond that, into city politics and politicians and thereby into law enforcement. Like organized crime figures of the future, they usually preferred to pull their strings behind the scenes and only rarely came out into the light. But the fall elections of 1904 had them worried. So the Big Four flexed their muscles.

A local attorney, R.M. Campbell, was the Democratic nominee for County Attorney. Running on a strong law enforcement platform, Mr. Campbell made some forthright but injudicious statements at a political rally in Edmond. Responding to a question from a member of the Women's Christian Temperance Union, he indicated he would prosecute the Big Four to the fullest extent of the law if elected.

The next morning, he found the Big Four waiting for him in his law office. When questioned as to his statements and whether he really meant them, he said he had. They then informed him in no uncertain terms that he would not be the next County Attorney. This was not portrayed as a threat, not as a hope, not as a wish on their part, just a flat statement of fact. Mr. Campbell was defeated by 81 votes.

On the evening of December 9, 1904, a local gambler named A.E. "Hoxie" Wachter gained a unique status among his peers by becoming the only known City resident to get shot by a man without arms. Actually John H. Payne did have arms, just very small ones. The victim of congenital birth defects, Payne's left arm was about five inches long and his right one was only a couple of inches longer. Having drifted into town a few days before, Payne began advertising himself as "The Armless Wonder" and giving shooting exhibitions in the joints around Hell's Half Acre. He carried his pistol in a pocket on the left side of his vest, cocked it with his chin and, according to witnesses, "fired it with the full dexterity and ease" of a man with normal appendages.

Hoxie had borrowed $20 from Payne the previous night. It was not intended to be a long term loan and Payne expected to be repaid promptly. When they ran into each other about 7:30 on the evening of the 9th in the Turf Exchange Saloon, Payne asked Hoxie if he had his $20. When he said he didn't, Payne asked how much he did have. Hoxie said he had a nickel and Payne said " Well, you know what's coming". Hoxie did indeed and bolted for the door. Payne fired three shots at the retreating gambler, hitting him twice, in the left leg and right thigh.

Officers Ike Ashburn and Roe Burnett heard the shots and ran to the fallen gambler. Payne was taken into custody by Captain Joe Burnett and Officer Lucas. Payne plead his case by explaining that he "didn't want to kill Wachter but merely desired to break his legs".

The beginning of the year 1905 saw no better example of the doctrine of changing fortunes than former Chief T.A. "Abe" Couch. Still serving as a detective on the OCPD, Couch had experienced more than his share of hard knocks already. Abe had suffered a public beating and humiliation at the hands of City Councilman Jack Love in the first few months after the city's opening. His brother William, the first provisional Mayor, had been killed in a gunfight over a claim before the City was a year old. Abe had served an honorable but undistinguished eleven months as Chief of the force in 1895-96. In June of 1899, Abe's wife had committed suicide by drinking carbolic acid. Almost six years later, at the age of 48, Abe was again, or still, a troubled man.

Since the previous summer, Abe had been romantically involved with Della Patterson, a divorcee also known as Della Johnson. He had been seeing her every night but was recently getting some competition from a young man named Clifford Shannon. He had evidently discussed his jealousy with Mrs. Patterson and he had been assured that she did not intend to see Shannon anymore.

Shortly after midnight on Saturday, February 25, 1905, Abe Couch was approaching Mrs. Patterson's rooming house at 116 West California when he saw a man leaving the building he thought he recognized as Clifford Shannon. Unsure, Couch followed the man several blocks to his home and then approached him, asking him if he was Shannon. In fact, it was Shannon but he took advantage of Couch's uncertainty by lying to him and giving him his roommate's name. Shannon later stated that Couch had his hand on his gun while he was questioning Shannon's identity and he felt that if he had identified himself correctly, Couch would have killed him on the spot.

Deterred but not mollified, Couch returned to Mrs. Patterson's rooms on West California. Upon entering her rooms, they became embroiled in a loud argument about her recent visitor. Mrs. Patterson admitted to Couch that it had been Shannon he had seen leaving. The loud recriminations attracted the attention of others roomers and Mrs. Patterson's 12-year-old son. In a jealous rage, Couch drew his pearl handled .45 and shot Della Patterson fatally in the face and the chest. When another roomer, Mrs. Maud Watts, tried to intervene, Couch shot her twice in the chest, killing her also. He then placed the gun to his temple and committed suicide.

Chief Emrick and Officer Sam Bartell were the first officers on the scene, finding Couch face down on the floor wearing a gray overcoat over his police uniform. Two days later, Abe Couch was laid to rest next to his brother in Fairlawn Cemetery. His pallbearers were Officers Slayton, Burnett, Humbarger, Ashburn, McCoy and Colt.

After almost two years, shifty Larry Reedy's trial for shooting Charles Swinghammer with intent to kill was scheduled for April 11, 1905. Larry couldn't seem to fit it into his schedule so the case was continued for a week. Still too busy to show up, Reedy was arrested in Dallas the next week and posted another bond at once. Swinghammer's pursuit of justice lengthened.

In the Spring elections of 1905, "Big John" Hubatka was elected Chief on the Republican

*The OCPD on July 14, 1905-Chief John Hubatka centered in the middle row.*

ticket, this time to last for two years. Orris H. Emrick went back to running Emrick Baggage Transfer and Storage, a business that survives in Oklahoma City to this day. The Police Department increased to 23 regular officers and five reserves, apparently all very much needed. Upon recalling these times in later days, T.D. Turner, the President of the Chamber of Commerce during this period remembered that "there were 90 saloons in the business section" and they accounted for "the killing of 1 to 3 men every 24 hours". Turner said that this rate of violence continued until city officials were able to curtail it somewhat by requiring the saloons to close on Sundays.

On a somewhat less harmful note, Old Zulu was still up to her old tricks. Sheriff George Garrison arrested her this year for rolling a man for $42. This time she was sentenced to 15 months in the Federal Penitentiary at Leavenworth, Kansas.

Finally, after almost three years, Larry Reedy went to trial for the Swinghammer shooting on May 24, 1906, but it hadn't been easy. The December after his last continuance, the County Attorney declared the charges to be "faulty" and dismissed them. Swinghammer raged at the injustice. Four months later the charges were refiled and the trial finally occurred.

Convicted of a lesser charge of shooting with intent to do bodily harm, Reedy was sentenced to a year and a day in Leavenworth Federal Penitentiary. But he couldn't fit that into his schedule either. With impending Statehood, the Constitutional Convention and municipal elections, Larry was going to be much too busy (and valuable) to be wasting his time making little rocks out of big rocks in Kansas.

Reedy's first chore was a little matter of rigging delegates to the Constitutional Convention. The 59th Congress passed the Oklahoma Statehood Bill on June 14, 1906, calling for delegates to be elected to a constitutional convention the following November. One of the Republican candidates was Judge James L. Brown, a fiery Kickapoo prohibitionist ever since he came in with the Run. Known as "Lot Jumping Jim" because of his initial delight in forcibly removing Sooners from their illegal claims, Brown was anathema to the saloon interests. They enlisted Reedy's aid and he "done 'em proud".

On election day, Reedy's Dirty Dozen were spreading plentiful money and booze, rousting voters out of the saloons and into the polls. Meanwhile, Reedy was improvising ballots from paper tablets when he ran out of official ballots. When the polls closed, he was locked in a hotel room on South Broadway with more tablets and the precinct ballot box. A "bucket brigade" of his minions relayed the latest tally from the County Courthouse, showing Judge Brown leading slightly. Finally, Reedy presented his precinct's ballot box. It contained more than a hundred votes more than were needed to defeat "Lot Jumping Jim". The newspapers screamed "Fraud" but to no avail. Reedy had earned his money again.

If his benefactors thought Reedy would throw himself into his work and allow his personal image to cool off, they were wrong. On July 17, 1906, Reedy was back in the County Jail, at least for a little while. He had been involved in a knife fight at his residence at 220 West Reno with Bailey Haines, a young soldier recently returned from the Philippines. A young lady was rumored to have been the impetus for the duel. Haines suffered cuts on his forehead, left hip and on his left shoulder down to the collarbone. Although he was hospitalized, Haines survived his wounds.

The spirit of forgiveness was alive and well during Oklahoma's last year as a territory. On February 2, 1907, Al Jennings was granted a full pardon by President Theodore Roosevelt. His life sentence had been commuted to five years by President McKinley in 1900 and he was released from prison in the summer of 1902. Having settled near Lawton, when he received his full pardon, Jennings moved to Oklahoma City and started a law office in the State National Bank Building. A staunch Democrat, he began keeping his eye on Oklahoma politics.

After months of typical Oklahoma politics, the Constitutional Convention finally completed their work. The oldest delegate was 68-year-old Clement V. Rogers. A quarter-blood Cherokee, a former Captain in the First Regiment of Confederate General Stand Watie's Cherokee Mounted Volunteers and the father of Will Rogers, one can detect the old man's influence on his famous cowboy/humorist son in his remark that "it would be a Godsend to this convention if there wasn't so damned many lawyers here". But lawyers there were and their influence was manifest. The State Constitution was a behemoth. Ten times longer than the U.S. Constitution, at 95 pages and 45,000 words it was the longest in the nation and took 18 hours to read. A statewide prohibition clause was included in the Constitution against the advice of many opponents, among them Charles Colcord. The opponents of prohibition claimed that it would substitute "3000 bootleggers for 30 saloons". Actually there were 70 saloons in Oklahoma City at the time but their claim was nevertheless prophetic.

On the first day of 1907, Chief Hubatka submitted a report to the City Clerk detailing the activities of the nearly 21 months of his administration. The OCPD now consisted of 25 men including four Detectives. The Chief stated that during that time, 7,112 arrests had been made and slightly over $28,000 collected by the Police Department had been turned over to the Police Judge.

Feeding the Prohibitionist's fires, the number of arrests for intoxication were highest (1,962) followed by prostitution arrests (1,173). The arrests were all enumerated within 75 types of offenses, all the way down to discharging bombs (2), females dressed in men's apparel (2), hay stacking in the City limits (1) and running automobiles without lights (also 1). The value of stolen goods was placed at almost $10,500 while the amount recovered was a little over $8,700. Case dispositions included 3,227 who paid their fines, 799 dismissed, 289 found not guilty and 236 ordered to leave town. The newspaper commented that the results were "at a minimum for a city of near 40,000".

Vice was the central issue of the 1907 City elections. It was a particularly nasty campaign, even by Oklahoma standards. For months before the election, the Daily Oklahoman carried on a campaign against the incumbent Chief John Hubatka. He was seen as the central figure of the Republican ticket which was portrayed as being tolerant of vice and intent upon letting the town run wide open in that respect. The Democrats were going all out against Hubatka's Republicans and events gave the Oklahoman more than enough grist for their mill.

Daily articles updated a police brutality complaint from a man from Kansas City. He alleged that officers had dragged him to jail with a broken leg, beaten him and refused him medical treatment. All of this was supposedly known of and ignored by Chief Hubatka. Bars were being allowed to run on Sundays with uniformed officers ignoring the drinking patrons. In at least one case, Chief Hubatka was alleged to have patronized one of the bars himself on a Sunday and been seen picking up a few beers to go.

On March 30, just days before the election, a confrontation in the Moss Bar at 7 North Broadway made the headlines. Officer Charles Armstrong, evidently a staunch Republican and supporter of Hubatka, confronted Ike Ashburn in the saloon. Ashburn was described as a "former officer and a current Democrat". The doctrine of changing fortunes, no doubt. During the confrontation, Armstrong tried to strike Ashburn with his nightstick but Ashburn took it away from him. Armstrong then drew his gun and tried to shoot Ashburn. As they struggled over the weapon, it fired and struck one of the bar's customers. The customer survived but it still fueled the Oklahoman's front pages for days. Then the Republicans made an accusation that the Democratic mayoral candidate Henry Scales had been in the bar at the time.

Hubatka also had a libel suit for $25,000 pending against the newspaper during this period. In some very convenient timing, he was called to testify in a hearing on this lawsuit just days before the election. Naturally, the entire transcript of his testimony ended up on the front page. To make matters worse, if possible, Hubatka testified horribly if he was quoted correctly. He alleged that he had never seen any gambling going on in Oklahoma City and had no knowledge of bars being open on Sundays. This was the coup de grace.

Although it was probably unnecessary to kick the quivering Republican corpse, on election night Larry Reedy was hard at work on his ballot box in his club room behind Sears Roebuck's store at Grand and Harvey. When Reedy's precinct returns were late coming in, as usual, Chief Hubatka went looking for him. Locating him at his club room, there was a shouting match through the closed door but Hubatka decided not to force his way in and confiscate the tardy ballot box. That decision cost him his job.

When Reedy's ballot box was presented and the votes tallied, it became a banner year for the Democrats. A new Mayor, Henry Scales, and a new Chief of Police, Charles Post, were swept into office on a reform ticket. As icing on the cake, Hubatka refused to turn in his badge when he was ousted from office. Four officers immediately resigned from the Department, refusing to work for the new Chief.

The paper noted that all officers were appointed by the Mayor except the Chief, who was elected. Patrolmen were now paid $55 a month for the first six months and then got a raise to $65. The Assistant Chief and one Captain, Joe Burnett, were paid $100 monthly. The population was over 32,000 now.

Henry Ford was just beginning to produce his Model T Fords. They sold for $850 with a four-cylinder, 20 horsepower engine that could drive them as fast as 40 miles per hour and came in "any color you choose as long as it's black". In less than a decade, assembly line techniques would produce them in half the time and drop the price to $360.

On April 4, the OCPD got a new patrol wagon. It was to be used for both patrol and ambulance functions and was kept at the J.H. Marshall Undertakers Parlor at 222 North Broadway when not in use. It was not destined for too much idle time right away.

Exercising his mandate, Chief Post waded into battle waving the reform banner, naming a "Flying Squadron" of officers under Assistant

*Chief Charles Post-1907.*

*OCPD-1907-left to right,Top Row-Roe Burnett, Jim Dillingham, Mike Conners, Will Light, Paul Lonnett, Will McIver and Rolley Organ.Row 2-Will Lett, Joe Soule, George Page, George Strouble, John McCarty, Bill Slayton, John Sadier and Wallace Parker.Row 3-M. Carol, Sgt. Webb, Chief Charles Post, Assistant Chief Tod Warden, Sgt. John Reeh and Jim Bowles.Bottom Row-W.T. Robertson, unknown and Shirley Dyer.*

Chief C.T. "Tod" Warden to clean out the bars and gambling houses. Warden's first raid, at the Olympic Club at 105 1/2 West Main proved to be a flop. Lookouts alerted the gamblers who hurriedly took all the gambling equipment up to the roof by way of a hidden passage and then escaped down the back stairs, leaving a sole janitor to greet the charging officers.

Former City Manager Albert McRill relates the tale of one of these lookout systems. A deputy sheriff who always served his warrants in a horse and buggy rig pulled by a pinto pony was on the gamblers payroll for $100 a month. A lookout was placed so he could watch the rig tied up next to the County Jail. If the Deputy was serving warrants that were not intended for his benefactors, he would drive north to Main Street when leaving the County Jail. If he had warrants naming his vice bosses, he'd turn south towards Grand. This would trigger a series of phone calls from the lookout and frenzied activity cleaning up the joints before the Deputy's arrival. When the Deputy arrived at the clubs, no gambling equipment would be visible and the gamblers would be gone. He would return the warrants unserved, being able to truthfully say he had observed no gambling equipment and the wanted men had not been present. The gamblers then just had to stay out of sight until they could arrange for their bond or to have the charges dismissed altogether. Nevertheless, the raiding continued and met with moderate success.

Cooperating with the new police attitude toward vice was Police Judge J.T. Highley. Charges in his court ranged from vagrancy ($30 fine or 30 minutes to get out of town) to open flirting by women on the street ($5 fine). One officer found that even the stern judge was

capable of some lightheartedness when he dismissed charges of "spooning in broad daylight" against two couples. Highley ruled that hugging in public between members of the opposite sexes was permissible, a tame forerunner of the rulings of the 1970s that allowed totally nude dancers.

The populace, like the times, were a paradox. Stabilized as always by the central core of small businessmen wanting to make a living and decent people just wanting to get by, the politics of the day were pushed back and forth between two opposing, equally vociferous groups. On the one hand were the bible-belters with their morally rigid codes demanding extinction of vice. On the other was that section of the populace who, while often not publicly condoning it, privately demanded their inalienable right to take a drink, place a bet and occasionally associate with ladies more "interesting" than their wives and sweethearts.

What the public wants, it usually gets. Within a year, the Flying Squadron had succumbed in part to the citizenry's demand for vice. Raids became less frequent, causing a local newspaper to note that Oklahoma City suffered from "a putrid social condition".

Perhaps no one person was more publicly representative of that condition than Big Anne Wynn. She would have been a noxious enough odor in the nostrils of the populace if she had kept to her place on Harlot's Lane, plying her trade. But there was more to Anne than that.

Clever, willful, opportunistic and manipulative, she had an innate sense of the interaction and interdependence between business, politics and vice. Sex, bribery, extortion and the quid-pro-quo were her tools and she used them masterfully. Hardly the public image of the garishly-dressed, heavily-painted, gum-popping floozy, she merged well in classier business and social circles. Composed, mannerly and fashionably dressed in tasteful style, she gained great influence spreading her plentiful cash among business, labor and politics.

Less than a month after the paper's pontificating upon the City's stench, something happened to lend it credence. At 2:00 A.M. on the morning of August 27, 1907, "Big Anne" Wynn's two-story "resort" at 312 East Grand Avenue burned to the ground in a spectacular conflagration. One man and three prostitutes died in the blaze and circumstances indicated arson.

Anne had been having increasing legal problems of late. She had moved her base of operations to the house on East Grand after she had been permanently enjoined against operating on West Second Street. Her legal problems were about to be compounded.

Although Anne had not been there during the fire (she was dining at The Southern Club), a coroner's jury was convinced that arson and murder had been committed. In spite of the fact that there was no obvious evidence against her initially, the coroner's jury indicted her and her black porter, "Judge" Peters, for arson and murder. Arrested for the first time in her 18 years in Oklahoma City, she entered a plea of not guilty and was held on an $18,500 bond. This time, no prominent citizens showed up to post her bond.

Some evidence finally did turn up but it was seven months later and even then it was inconsistent. Fannie Ritchey, one of Anne's former courtesans, alleged that Anne had conspired with one of her customers to rob and murder another of the resort's patrons. The body had been dumped in the North Canadian River bed, Anne had gone to The Southern Club to establish an alibi and "Judge" Peters had set the fire to destroy the scene of the crime.

Big Anne went to trial on May 19, 1908, but Fannie Ritchey's story didn't convince the jury and the charges were dismissed. In the Spring of 1909, Big Anne sold her holdings and moved to Los Angeles, her $75,000 fortune expended in her fight to cheat the gallows. She died in California a few years later.

On September 17, 1907, there was a general election on the proposed State Constitution and a Prohibition ordinance. The Prohibition clause was enthusiastically promoted by the influential religious community, the Women's Christian Temperance Union, the Anti-Saloon

League and soon-to-be-Governor Charles Haskell. The voters approved the State Constitution by a margin of greater than 2 to 1. President Teddy Roosevelt proclaimed that Statehood Day would be November 16, 1907. Oklahoma City voters voted overwhelmingly against the prohibition clause but the rural vote passed it, albeit by only slightly more than 18,000 votes out of nearly a quarter of a million cast. Thus Oklahoma entered the Union as the 46th State and one of only 5 dry states.

Prohibition formally went into effect at 10:16 A.M. on November 16, 1907, but the Governor told the County Sheriff to let the saloons stay open all day. That night, 560 saloons closed all across the new State of Oklahoma, 70 of them in Oklahoma City. The last saloon in Oklahoma City closed its doors at 11:50 P.M. after a local brewery poured 27,000 barrels of beer and an unknown amount of mash into the gutters. Souvenir postcards were issued showing men dipping beer out of the streets with buckets, their hats or any container available. Most of the town's women stayed home that night. Men, taking advantage of the cheap prices, hauled the booze away in everything imaginable, not the least of which was their bellies. One observer remarked that it seemed as though "Hades had taken a recess and was using Main and Broadway for a playground". Brawls were common that evening, climaxing when Fred Norris shot and killed Robert Johnson, a bartender at Ed Donley's saloon on 1st Street after an argument over a jug of booze.

Booze dumping parties continued to be a popular form of public entertainment. Another one during the first year of Prohibition saw 1,000 gallons of contraband beer dumped into the North Canadian River. The party lasted for four hours with 300 in attendance. Hundreds of drunken fish provided a fisherman's bonanza downstream at Spencer. One besotted catfish caught allegedly weighed 90 pounds. Even allowing for pre-Guinness hyperbole, this had to be a near-record size fish. Future Mayor Whit Grant made an environmentalist plea, saying that since they couldn't stop drunkenness, "let's try to confine it to the men and let the fishes at least die sober".

As a Statehood present, Larry Reedy got a full pardon on the Charles Swinghammer shooting conviction from Governor Charles Haskell. Among the benefactors who requested his pardon were the former president of the Chamber of Commerce (Heyman), John Threadgill, Oklahoma County Sheriff George Garrison, Oklahoma Secretary of State William Cross, President of the State Federation of Labor Luther Langston and State Commissioner of Charities and Corrections Kate Barnard. So much for justice, delayed, denied, defunct.

The night before Statehood also produced another interesting spectacle. The old Blue Front Saloon had been converted into a church and a revival was being conducted for the City's black population. Who should wander in off the street and find "enlightenment" but Old Zulu. She and 50 others were baptized the next morning in the North Canadian River. Predictably, it wouldn't last much longer than the shock of the cold water.

Not long thereafter, she was arrested in front of Noah's Ark on Harlot's Lane in a frenzied state of intoxication. The citizens were treated to a travelling sideshow when the Police Department's "hurry-up horse", Old Blue, pulled the new police wagon down the street, rocking from side to side while Old Zulu and four officers tussled inside. Arriving at the jail, she was thrown into the jail's only cell for women with five other ladies. She immediately whipped one of them, destroyed the stove, and went after the rest with the stovepipe. After her cellmates were mercifully released, Old Zulu was still bouncing off the walls, loudly braying that "it tuk nine of dem bulls to put me heah".

In May of 1908, state officers led by Attorney General Charles West and his Enforcement Attorney, Fred S. Caldwell, raided the two most blatant offenders of prohibition in Oklahoma City, if not the whole state, the Two Johns and the Southern Club. The absence of city and county officers was notable. The raiders sacked up three wagonloads of beer, gambling paraphernalia and proprietor John Burgess. From his cell in the county jail, a drunken Burgess roundly pronounced prohibition "a damned failure; she can never be enforced". Attorney General West was doing his duty enforcing the law and bootlegger Burgess was expressing his opinion on its practical applications. With all due respect to the differences in the two men's characters and motives, they were both right.

The City elections in March of 1909 were predictably stormy. Mayor Scales' primary opponent was E.O. Whitwell, a local Presbyterian minister and member of the Anti-Saloon League. Chief Post's political image had suffered from Big Anne's recent acquittal but this had little effect on the Mayor since the voters usually chose to blame the Chief of Police for vice enforcement or the lack thereof. Naturally, Whitwell had the support of the religious community in his contention that the town was "a lawless city" and needed cleaning up. A visiting evangelist from Tulsa commented that "Since my visit to Oklahoma City, I am confirmed in my belief that hell was made too little from the start".

The night before the primary election, Reverend Whitwell got a lesson in politics. Mayor Scales invited the ingenuous pastor to speak at one of his rallies north of the Lee Hotel. Five thousand people showed up. The good pastor should have known better. During the campaign, he had called the Mayor a drunkard and here he was going to the Mayor's rally in front of the Mayor's supporters.

In his introductory remarks, Scales naturally referred to the Reverend's charges and admitted that he enjoyed a drink now and then. He then treated the cheering throngs to a hilarious discourse on the joys of a properly prepared mint julep. He even admitted that he occasionally drank too much and became intoxicated. Then, roughly paraphrasing Winston Churchill, he stated "my condition on such occasions is only temporary and I get over it. But being a damn fool, like my opponent, is permanent. He can never get over it". Reverend Whitwell left the platform without taking his opportunity to speak to the jeering crowd.

The elections returned Mayor Scales to office and Chief John Hubatka defeated Charles Post, probably with no small thanks to Larry Reedy's Ward Four ballot box, paving the way for a return to vice activity at full force. Although Hubatka was rarely criticized for a lack of ability as a police administrator or investigator, he was frequently blasted in the media for his allegedly soft position on vice.

There were expectations of conflict between the Democratic Mayor, the Democratic majority on the City Council and the Republican Police Chief but the reality was to exceed all expectations. It started in earnest less than three weeks after the election.

Scales decided that the principle of "divide and conquer" had worked so well on the Romans, it might be equally effective on a police department. He was right. On May 17, Scales let go with both barrels of his bureaucratic scattergun by having the Council pass a new two-part ordinance. The first part created the position of Assistant Chief of Police to be appointed by the Mayor. The actual title was Night Chief of Police, his authority was equal to that of the Chief and he was to report directly to the Mayor. The second barrel of the ordinance created the Secret Service Department. This was to be a plainclothes detective force responsible only to the Mayor. They were equal in authority to the police force but not actually part of it and the Chief had absolutely no authority over them. The Secret Service was to be headed by a Chief who was also equal in authority to the Police Chief but answerable only to the Mayor.

Although the Council passed the ordinance, they didn't attach an emergency clause to it so it wouldn't take effect for 30 days. Hubatka spent that time railing against it, publicly questioning why the citizens bothered to elect a Chief of Police if the Mayor was going to be allowed total and absolute control of City law enforcement.

In the meantime, the Mayor, Council and Police Judge introduced the Chief to an old political weapon known as "the bureaucratic runaround". The stage was set for yet another battle between City Hall and law enforcement, where politics rather than effective crime fighting was to be the deciding factor.

Judge Highley did his part by dismissing charges against most of the vice figures arrested by Hubatka's officers. The Chief still had to present all of the Police Department's expenditures to the Council for their approval for payment. Most of the bills Hubatka presented for payment were "referred" to a claims committee and payments were held up for weeks. Cartoons appeared in the papers almost daily lampooning the infighting between the officials. One showed Chief Hubatka hanging precariously onto a branch in the top of a tree with the seat of his pants ripped out, yelling across a fence at two of his Councilmen supporters (a distinct minority) something to the effect of "What'll we try next?". A bulldog at the base of the tree with the Chief's pants seat clenched in his slavering jaws was labelled "The Council".

If the Police Court was turning gamblers and bootleggers loose in droves, they were cracking down on the violators of traffic regulations. They were trying to gain early control over an increasingly motorized society. Toward the end of May, two motorists were assessed fines of $10 each for speeding. One of them was Charles F. Colcord.

On June 10, 1909, George Burton was out of jail and raising hell again. Convicted of murdering Ray Love in 1903 and sentenced to ten years, Burton had completed a little over half that sentence when he had been paroled the previous December. Before he went to jail the first time, one of the many places he had made himself unwelcome was the Sasaric Saloon and gambling house at 12 1/2 S. Robinson, owned by Robert D. Kerr. It is unknown if Kerr was any relation to the more famous Kerrs of Oklahoma but it is known that he had no use for George Burton. That evening Burton was back at the Sasaric making himself just as unwelcome as ever. Drinking, cursing and threatening everyone generally, Burton was told to leave by Kerr. When Burton turned his wrath on the owner, Kerr slapped him. Burton left, threatening vengeance.

Half an hour later, a witness heard Burton say "Hell, just for some excitement, I'm going over and shoot Kerr". This he immediately proceeded to attempt. As Burton walked in the saloon, someone yelled a warning to Kerr, who was in the restroom. Kerr ran out with drawn gun and emptied it at Burton, hitting him five times.

Burton's funeral cortege consisted of 1 woman and 17 gamblers who came to bury a man who, in the words of the preacher, "has been hurried into the presence of God to give an account for the deeds done in the body". Nine months later, Kerr was acquitted of murder charges in Burton's death.

George Burton's earthly concerns were over but not so for Chief Hubatka. That same month he sought an injunction against the Mayor to prevent him from making appointments to his Assistant Chief and Secret Service positions. The injunction was not granted and on June 23, the Secret Service Department became a reality. Frank L. Staton was appointed Chief, Charles Clark was day Sergeant, Bert Mills was night Sergeant and the first Secret Service operatives were future Chief Webb Jones, W.W. Slaton, Will Graham, Rowland "Roe" Burnett (Joe's brother) and Ed Davis. Five days later, the Mayor appointed Joe Burnett as Assistant or Night Chief of Police.

Hubatka refused to acknowledge Burnett's authority or the validity of his appointment. He insisted that Burnett had no authority over his officers. Whereupon the Mayor had a letter delivered to Hubatka notifying him in no uncertain terms that Joe Burnett was the Night Chief of Police, assigned to duty between the hours of 6 P.M. and 6 A.M. During his duty hours, Burnett's authority was equal to that of Hubatka and he was answerable only to the Mayor. It was also noted that during Burnett's duty hours, the Chief's Office was his office. Hubatka's duty hours were to be from 6 A.M. to 6 P.M.

An editorial campaign by one of the local papers had begun to embarrass the City officials and, on July 28, Hubatka filed a lawsuit against Mayor Scales, the City Attorney and each member of the City Council and Secret Service Department. He charged the politicians with accepting graft from gambling interests and said the Secret Service officers had been appointed illegally. His lawsuit contended that he had been elected by the citizens to be Chief of Police 24 hours a day, not just between 6 A.M. and 6 P.M.

During this wrangling over authority and control over the police, the thieves and liquor merchants had a heyday. Twenty houses were burglarized in three days including the Mayor's. In August, 300 bootlegging joints were in successful operation and the gamblers were running more brazenly than ever. The population of the City had doubled to over 64,000 in the three years since Statehood and it was running wildly wide open.

On September 17, Mayor Scales, backed by a 7-2 Council vote, suspended Chief Hubatka for corruption in office and dereliction of duty, alleging that he had evidence of payoffs from bootleggers and gamblers. When the notice of suspension was delivered to him, Hubatka nonchalantly stuck it in his pocket, saying he'd "keep it to remember the Mayor by". The Chief then made it clear that he did not intend to honor the notice of suspension, he would wait for a court order before honoring it and refused to turn in his gold badge. The Mayor said he would present his evidence to the grand jury.

The grand jury handed down indictments on October 14. The evidence of payoffs from

*Looking west on Main Street of Oklahoma City in 1910.*

bootleggers and gamblers turned out to be against County officers. The Sheriff and two deputies were suspended and indicted for taking bribes. Chief Hubatka was indicted for forgery and embezzlement, having allegedly kept $20 of a prisoner's bond money. The Chief's secretary, G.W. "Sammy" Sampson, was indicted for altering records. Both men remained free after posting $2,000 bonds.

# III — VICE WAR AND WORLD WAR 1910-1919

*Officer Morris Reagan.*

As the new decade began, the Police Department got a slight break from public controversy as the latest grand jury began attacking the credibility of the Mayor's Secret Service Department. On January 22, they returned an indictment against Chief of the Secret Service Frank L. Staton for grand larceny. The incident had occurred the previous March when Staton was serving as a plainclothesman on the City force. The indictment alleged that while checking pawn shops for a $250 diamond ring as a result of a police complaint, Staton had found the ring. Instead of returning it to the owner, he had allegedly redeemed it for $115, less than half its value, and kept it. Staton scoffed at the indictment, claiming he could and would prove that the ring he was wearing was the same one he had been wearing when he first came to the City from Tennessee two years earlier. Evidently he did just that because nothing came of the indictment. The earlier indictments against Chief Hubatka were also quashed.

The Department lost another officer in the line of duty in 1910. Officer Morris R. Reagan was walking a beat in the 1000 block of North Broadway about 1:00 A.M. on February 25 when witnesses reported hearing a gunshot and seeing a black man running south on Broadway. Reagan, who had only been an officer for about three months, was found lying on the sidewalk shot once in the head, his gun still holstered. A horse-drawn buggyload of responding officers led by Assistant Chief Joe Burnett apprehended William Martin still running south on Broadway at N.W. 4th Street.

Officer Reagan's obituary noted that the 50-year-old officer had been the nephew of John R. Reagan, Postmaster General of the Confederacy under Jefferson Davis, a former U.S. Senator and President of the Historical Society of Texas. A few days later, Morris Reagan was buried in Fairlawn Cemetery during a drizzling rain. Attended by a cortege of relatives including his 80-year-old father, his 13-month-old son, and his brother Thomas who was a former OCPD officer, now a member of the Fire Department, Reagan was laid to rest next to his brother Tim who had died 17 years earlier. The family suffered a simultaneous tragedy when notified that on the same night Officer Reagan had been slain, one of his cousins, a Captain Fowler, had been killed while serving with the U.S. Army in Nicaragua.

THE DAILY OKLAHOMAN
February 27, 1910

POLICE COURT NOTES

D.H.Ward, charged by Chief of Police John Hubatka with reckless driving, was dismissed. Hubatka testified that he saw Ward's automobile collide with a market wagon in front of the court house.

"Little Bit", a negress, charged with loitering, told the court that she thought that a jail sentence would be a "little bit too strong". She was dismissed.

Otto Lorenz, facing a charge of keeping a boarding house which, according to the testimony of police officers, was not strictly up to the moral ethics of the city, told the court that he owned the establishment only two days, and that when he discovered its reputation immediately gave it away. He was dismissed.

James Duckwood, Robert Thorn, R.J. Brown and I.P. Limes, boys between the ages of 17 and 18, pleaded not guilty to a charge of vagrancy. They were dismissed on condition that they leave town.

A Mexican vagrant, unable to speak English, was fined $10 and costs on general principles.

Six days after Reagan's death, former Chief George W.R. Chinn was buried in Fairlawn just a few yards from Reagan's final resting place. Survived by his wife and three daughters, Chinn had succumbed to a long battle with diabetes at his home at 420 W. Frisco (later S.W. 5th) just 17 days short of his 67th birthday. Chinn had come to Oklahoma City from Missouri in the original Land Run. He had opened the first transfer and baggage business in the city and the first telephone in the city had been installed in his office. Having fought for the Confederate States Army during the Civil War, his funeral cortege included representation from the United Confederate Veterans as well as the OCPD.

Not quite two months after Officer Reagan's death, William Martin's preliminary hearing was held, the accused being represented by the law firm of Embry and Black. Newspaper accounts stated that the defendant was "disquieted" by the prosecuting attorney staring malevolently at him. The prosecutor was William R. Reagan, the slain officer's father and an eminent attorney in territorial days, trying his last case. Now 80 years old and hard of hearing, Reagan had to have some of the testimony repeated to him by assistants. Unashamedly biased, Reagan told reporters "In the old days, this man would never have stood trial". Although he didn't spell it out, there was little doubt about what he meant.

If his hearing was failing, Reagan's legal acumen was intact. The old man knew how to make a case. Officer James Rippey identified Martin as the man he had seen Officer Reagan stop and search several months earlier. Martin evidently took great umbrage with this action and told the officer that if he messed with him again, he'd kill him. Officer Veasey and the slain officer's brother Thomas, a fireman, both testified that Reagan had told them about a negro named Martin who was supposedly looking for him and threatening his life. Dr. J.W. Riley identified Martin as the man he had seen shortly before the shooting occurred a short distance away from the scene. Martin was indicted for the slaying.

While the Reagan/Martin preliminary hearing was in progress, another move was afoot to improve working conditions for officers. Every uniformed officer on the force signed a petition to be presented to the City Council requesting they be allowed to start working 8-hour days instead of the traditional 12 hours. They stated that it was unfair that all other city employees had adopted the 8-hour day but Police were still required to work 12 hours a day. Mayor Scales voiced his agreement with the petition, saying that between working their shifts and going to court, most officers actually put in 16-hour days. The Council approved and the OCPD went to 8-hour shifts.

After two and one-half years of statehood, it was finally time to decide where the state capital would be located. The two heavyweights in contention, Oklahoma City and Guthrie, and a smattering of minor contenders had been wrangling over this since the Organic Act was signed into law in 1890. The Act had established Guthrie as the temporary territorial capital and, almost immediately, the political machinations began. Petitions and counter petitions were circulated, conventions came and went. Finally, Governor Charles Haskell set an election for June 11, 1910. The citizens would decide between Oklahoma City, Guthrie and Shawnee. Then the campaigning began in earnest. Charles Colcord headed the Oklahoma City organization. Former City Manager Albert McRill says the Oklahoma City organization enlisted the talents of Larry Reedy when faced with the political realities of the stakes involved. Be that as it may, Colcord and his followers evidently did their jobs well. When the 135,944 votes were counted, Oklahoma City had garnered over 70 percent of them, more than triple those cast for Guthrie.

Governor Haskell received the news while attending a banquet in Tulsa on the night of June 11. Having missed the last train for Oklahoma City that night, he hurriedly arranged for a special train after midnight. Arriving at the Huckins Hotel on old Battle Row about 6:00 A.M., the Governor took a piece of the hotel's stationery, wrote a statement proclaiming Oklahoma City as the State capital and adjourned to the hotel coffee shop for breakfast. Although the official move was not scheduled to be accomplished until 1913, the Governor later said he decided to do it at once because he was tired of the Oklahoma State Capital newspaper's editor calling him a liar over this issue in every morning's edition.

Before leaving Tulsa, Haskell had instructed his private secretary, W.B. Anthony, to retrieve the State Seal from Guthrie and meet him at the Huckins. Anthony proceeded to the Secretary of State's office in a borrowed Cadillac and picked it up. Recriminations circulated for years about thieves in the night crawling in windows and smuggling the seal out in a bag of laundry but evidently it had merely been handed over to him wrapped in plain brown paper.

On Independence Day of 1910, Jack Johnson, the son of a former slave, became the first black World Heavyweight Boxing Champion by defeating Jim Jeffries in Reno, Nevada. Violence erupted in more than a dozen cities from New York to New Orleans. Both blacks and whites attacked members of the other race. Initial reports of gangs of whites ambushing and beating negroes in the near northeast area of the City were investigated and proved to be false.

Less than a week later, the Sunday newspaper carried a message for the citizenry just in case they were contemplating any similar unruliness. Pictured from border to border across the top of the page were the OCPD's 30-man night shift and the 16-man day shift. The accompanying article noted that the Department's 56 officers were led by Chief Hubatka, night Chief (Assistant Chief) Joe Burnett, Captains Clayton and Conners, Day Sergeant M. Murray and Night Sergeant A. Bradford. The officers were being drilled by Inspector S.R. Alexander, an 18-year veteran of the Chattanooga, Tennessee, Police. Inspector Alexander said the officers were being trained to deal with mass disturbances like riots and strikes because "the officers had no practice in working as a body". They were also engaging in target practice every Tuesday at the City Waterworks.

Oddly enough, it was during this time of dissension that the first police annual or yearbook was published. The 1910 Fire & Police Souvenir Book had 26 pages with a very ornate cover emblazoned with the badges of the Police and Fire Departments. The Police badge pictured is an eight-pointed star with "Oklahoma City Police" inscribed around an inner circle and a raised five-pointed star in the center.

Written and published by Louis A. Reed, the book pictured a 49-man force. It noted that no such history had ever been printed before and that the profits from the book went to the Fire and Police pension funds. The short biographies of Mayor Henry M. Scales and Chief John Hubatka made no mention of the animosity between them.

Following those biographies are photos of 36 uniformed officers and 12 plainclothesmen. Joe Burnett is Assistant Chief, Frank L. Staton is Chief of the Secret Service (the Detective force) and Shirley Dyer is Night Chief of the Secret Service. Shown among the 8 Secret Service men are Roe Burnett (Joe's brother), John Cassidy and future Chief F. Webb Jones. The photos of the 32 uniformed patrolmen are not identified by name but recognizable among them are Ike Ashburn as well as future Chiefs Jerry Smith and Rolley Organ. A separate page is dedicated to Officer Reagan under the bold headline "Officer Killed On Duty". The book also included pictures of 3 City Physicians, 2 Police reporters and a group shot of the 31-man Fire Department.

It was also during this year that the Bureau of Identification was formed. The forerunner of the Bureau of Records, it was administratively located under the Secret Service Department (Detective Bureau). Records, such as they were, were 3-by-5-inch pieces of cardboard containing a small frontal photograph of the offender's face. The front and back contained lines where the offender's name, aliases and offense were handwritten. Also included on the card were the offender's bertillon measurements; height, length of outer arms, length of trunk, cheek bone width, length and width of head, length of right ear and left foot, middle finger, little finger and forearm. B.I. Record Number 1 was of a man arrested for burglary and was dated August 23, 1910. For the first six arrests, it was an all male province. Then, on August 26, a diminutive 16-year-old girl named Ester Benson, alias Ester Roby alias Shorty Brown, was arrested by Officers Gordon and Jones in the river bottom west of Wheeler Park on South Western for "Masquerading in Male Attire". At 5-foot-2 1/2 inches tall and 98 pounds, she probably wasn't too hard to spot. She was allotted B.I. Number 7. Since she was from Kansas, her "sentence", as recorded on the card, was to be " taken to Wichita". Reading the card, one suspects we have just learned the 1910 method for dealing with runaways.

Mayor Scales resigned on October 17, 1910, and Daniel V. Lackey was appointed to succeed him. One of Lackey's first orders was to instruct Assistant Chief Joe Burnett and Shirley Dyer of the Secret Service to "clean up the town". Taking axes to the gambling houses and joints, the officers soon left a wreckage in their wake that a reporter said "looked like Sherman's march to the sea". The next month, the citizens had their first attempt at repealing the state prohibition law, actually the second attempt if you count the fact that they had their chance to defeat it in the original election in 1907. The Women's Christian Temperance Union, the Anti-Saloon League and their followers prevailed again, however, and the effort met with defeat. Oklahoma County again voted futilely for repeal but the margins were getting consistently closer.

The first prisoner thrown into the City Jail in 1911 was an old favorite. Old Zulu, the "giant negress equal in point of muscular strength to any bluecoat" and the most arrested person in the City's last decade, was back in again, spurred on to ever-rising heights of frenzy by her cocaine addiction.

*OCPD officers on January 9, 1911-Second from the left is future Chief Rolley Organ.*

The simplest, least complicated fighting going on in Oklahoma City in 1911 was done by Jess Willard. A rough-hewn 6-foot-7-inch, 240-pound giant who had been a laborer on the construction of the Lake Overholser Dam and also employed his talents at the Turf Exchange Club (presumably as a bouncer), he began his boxing career training at the Oklahoma City Athletic Club on West Main Street. Dubbed "The Great White Hope" after he turned professional, Willard won the Heavyweight Championship in 1915 by defeating the controversial black champion Jack Johnson. He held his championship for four years before losing it to Jack Dempsey in 1919.

THE DAILY OKLAHOMAN
March 10, 1911

STRUCK BY CHIEF

W.H. Good, an employee of the Oklahoma Portrait Company, who, according to Chief of Police John Hubatka, was trying to incite trouble this afternoon, was struck in the head by Chief Hubatka with a cane he was carrying. A slight wound was inflicted on his head...The man was not a striker, or one of the carmen, according to Chief Hubatka, but was merely in the crowd for the excitement.

ALL OF THEM RELEASED

Eleven men arrested by Gordon and Palmer of the Secret Service Department early Thursday morning, thought by them to be strike breakers, and who were all armed with pistols, were released by Police Judge Highley Thursday evening and their guns returned to them. It was thought at the time that the strike had been settled.

Two other, more complex types of conflict were brewing in the city during the first week in March of 1911. One was political. The citizens were preparing to vote on whether to abandon the Council form of government for a commission form. The other was a labor conflict. Oklahoma City was on the verge of its first strike.

A newly formed union of streetcar workers was at serious odds with the Oklahoma Railway Company. In his autobiography, Charles Colcord alleges that this discord was fomented by a group of labor activists brought in from out of the state, "imported thugs" in his words. He compared them to the activists who had set off a bomb in the Los Angeles Times building five months earlier when the paper refused to unionize. Twelve people were killed outright in that explosion and the death toll eventually reached 21.

Besides his account of personal involvement, Colcord's estimate of the situation would seem to receive some confirmation from the fact that the labor dispute was not about wages. It was about forcing management into official recognition of the union and job protection for the workers. The company had a graduated pay scale between 20 and 30 cents an hour. They alleged that management was in the habit of saving money by firing people when they were due for a pay raise.

In an interview with the press on that first Saturday in March, Anton H. Classen, the President of the Oklahoma Railway Company, stated that a strike "was impossible" because he had received signed agreements from 179 of his employees that they would stay on the job. But at noon the next day, none of his streetcars were moving. A non-violent but effective crowd of between 7,000 and 10,000 people were congregated at the streetcar barn on Grand Avenue, where the cars were turned around on a revolving platform, to keep the cars from moving out. In another indication of organized labor planning, the timing was impeccable for getting the immediate attention of the citizenry. Thousands of churchgoers had to walk home that day.

Mayor Lackey instructed Night Chief of Police Joe Burnett to send a squad of officers to each car barn at 4 A.M. on Monday morning. Lackey later said the officers were told not to interfere with the strike activities because he realized "there were not enough bluecoats in the city" to oppose the number of strike supporters. So, damned if you do, damned if you don't.

The railway company's vice-president, John W. Shartel, made some blistering indictments of the local officers. He issued statements that this was not a strike but an intimidation of his workers by labor activists. He said his men had been forced off of their streetcars and had been given no protection by city or county officers. The next day, another attempt to get the cars running was made, again unsuccessfully. Shartel expanded his accusation, saying he had seen city officers assist strikers in ejecting his motormen and conductors from the streetcars. Mayor Lackey admitted that his officers had made no effort to stop the strikers and had not deterred some instances of violence. In an outstanding display of leadership, Lackey said he had told one patrolman that "there's not a man on the force worth ten cents".

Some local businessmen, including former Chiefs Oscar Lee and Charles Colcord, made overtures to Governor Cruce to send in the National Guard because control of the situation was beyond the ability of local officers. Cruce advised that he would send the State Adjutant General, Brigadier General Frank Canton, to observe the situation and he would have three companies of soldiers on call. A meeting was held on Thursday evening between the officials. During this meeting, Night Chief of the Secret Service Shirley Dyer told Mayor Lackey that "90 percent of the force was in sympathy with the strikers". Ongoing negotiations between the strikers and the company management were stalled. Demands were that all the strikers be rehired with no retaliation from management and the executives were refusing to hire back 14 of them. Over the weekend, they relented and agreed to hire all the men back.

On Sunday, Sheriff Jack Spain deputized nearly 500 special deputies (including Lee and Colcord) and formed them into several companies commanded by "captains". Two of the company captains were Chief John Hubatka and former Deputy U.S. Marshal Ransom Payne. The next afternoon, all the streetcars came out of their barns, each one surrounded by cars full of special deputies armed with Winchesters and shotguns with buckshot loads. Other men with rifles were stationed on selected rooftops along the routes. Seven men were arrested but the strike was over.

Summer came early in 1911. It was almost 90 degrees when, on March 9, after several aborted attempts and in the midst of the streetcar strike, a vote of the citizens decided by almost a four to one margin to modify the City Charter and adopt a commission form of government. The City Council, elected by wards, was out. The now-defunct Council passed a resolution declaring the election illegal and void, and petitioned the superior court to back them up on a number of similar contentions.

On May 9, elections were held. The new Mayor was Whitaker M. Grant, a former Iowa legislator and U.S. Attorney in Alaska who was very active in national Democratic politics. The last week in May, the superior court failed to support the old City Council and the new officers were formally installed. Henceforth the City would be run by five officials elected at large—a mayor and four commissioners over departments of Public Works, Public Property, Public Safety and Accounting and Finance. No longer would the Chief of Police or the Municipal Counselor (city attorney) be elected, they would be appointed by the Mayor and commissioners.

On March 31, 1911, after a delay of nearly two years, the District Court decided that the ordinances taking the control of the Police Department away from Chief Hubatka were void and rendered judgement placing him in absolute control of the Department. One of the lasting innovations Hubatka made in the last few months of his term as Chief was the formation of the first motorcycle squad. Six Harley-Davidson motorcycles were acquired, odd-looking contraptions that looked more like bicycles with a small motor between the wheels. The OCPD's first six motorcycle officers were Joe Baum, Ollie Estes, Ernest J. Helm, Jack Johnson, Marvin M. Murray and Lloyd Petit.

That same Spring, Oklahoma City also annexed an area south of the North Canadian River that had been a separate municipality named Capitol Hill. This boosted the city population up to nearly 70,000. The state capital had been relocated to Oklahoma City from Guthrie

*OCPD Motorcycle Squad-1912.*

the previous summer, the new mayor and commissioners were looking for a new Chief of Police and they came up with a dandy.

Bill Tilghman, the legendary frontier lawman, accepted the post on July 4, 1911, his fifty-seventh birthday. The blue-eyed six-footer was truly a living legend with a reputation that didn't have to be exaggerated. Tilghman was born on July 4, 1854, coincidentally the twenty-fourth birthday of his father who had been born on Independence Day in 1830. Moving to Kansas from his birthplace in Fort Dodge, Iowa, Tilghman began his adventurous life as a buffalo hunter during the time when a man risked his scalp doing that work. He risked it further as an Army scout battling hostile Cheyennes, Arapahoes and Comanches. By the age of 23, he was in Dodge City, Kansas, where he served both as Deputy to Sheriff Bat Masterson and as City Marshal.

Because of television and movies, most people are aware of the law against carrying guns in early Dodge City. Less well known is the fact that it was enforced by Bill Tilghman whose law enforcement experience in Dodge City predated that of both the Earps and the Mastersons. The fact that he made a reputation in the Queen of the Cowtowns in the 1870's that even allowed his name to be mentioned in the same breath with the Earps and Mastersons says all that needs to be said about his courage and firearms skills. His reputation was in some ways more pristine to that of the Earps and

*OCPD officer of the early 1910s.*

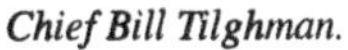

*Chief Bill Tilghman.*

*Two of the Three Guardsmen-Deputy U.S. Marshal Chris Madsen and OCPD Chief Bill Tilghman.*

Mastersons which was somewhat sullied by their gambling habits, partnerships in saloons and personal relationships with less-than-respectable citizens ranging from Doc Holliday to assorted prostitutes. If Tilghman was more of the straight-arrow family man type than his peers, he could be allowed some small vanities. His Dodge City Marshal's badge was widely known as an artistic piece fashioned from two $20 gold pieces. Moving on to Oklahoma Territory as a Deputy U.S. Marshal, Tilghman was as widely known for his fairness and integrity as for his fearlessness. That sense of fairness would eventually cost him his life. While Old West chivalry is another concept that has probably been exaggerated by movies and television, Tilghman was the beneficiary of it on at least one occasion.

Bill Doolin was another man whose reputation didn't have to be exaggerated although on the opposite side of the law. While on the trail of the Doolin gang, one frigid day in January of 1895, Tilghman ventured into a farmhouse where some of the gang was hiding. When the hidden gang members wanted to gun Tilghman down from their hiding places, Doolin stopped them, explaining his actions later on the grounds that "Bill Tilghman is too good a man to shoot in the back". Doolin's courtesy was repaid when Tilghman later captured Doolin singlehandedly without firing a shot in Eureka Springs, Arkansas. Most lawmen of the day would probably have shot Doolin down on sight as Heck Thomas eventually did. Another example of his character was that after almost fatally shooting "Little Bill" Raidler during his arrest, Tilghman nursed him back to health while bringing him in and, years later, was responsible for his parole. Following his time as a federal deputy, Tilghman was elected Sheriff of Lincoln County and, after statehood, as an Oklahoma State Sentaor.

Resigning his legislative position to take the new job, Tilghman was officially appointed as Chief of Police on July 15 by Mayor Whitaker M. Grant. His new badge was less flamboyant that its Dodge City counterpart. It was a silver eagle with outspread wings from which was suspended a three-quarter moon crescent inscribed "Wm. Tilghman", surrounding a five-pointed star with "Chief of Police" on it. He received $200 a month ($75 more than the previous Chief) to take over a department of 87 men to police the 17 1/2 square mile city with a population of 64,205.

It was a significant departure from tradition. All 15 of the men who had served as Chief before Tilghman had been "[Oklahoma] City men", men established and known in business, politics or law enforcement in Oklahoma City. Bill Tilghman became the first "outsider" to get the top job. Although none of the new mayor's constituents would go so far as to find fault with the man he chose for the job, many did fault the choice of an outsider as "the wrong kind of politics". Conversely, the Daily Oklahoman greeted him with a glowing editorial, prophesying that "Oklahoma City now has a real Chief of Police".

Tilghman's Department consisted of an Assistant Chief, 3 Captains, 2 Sergeants, 56 Patrolmen, 3 patrol drivers, 4 motorcycle officers and a Secret Service Department consisting of 1 Chief, 2 Sergeants and 12 Detectives. He also inherited four men involved in the infancy of two major law enforcement advancements. One was the first bertillon man employed by the city, Peter Biewer, heralding the scientific investigation of crime. The others were 3 Gamewell operators for 30 Gamewell electric call-boxes. Recently installed on strategic street corners, beat officers were to report in on them at least once every hour.

In some ways, Bill Tilghman the man contradicted the "lone gunman of the Old West" image that had become attached to him. One way was in his domestic life. After fathering four children, he was divorced from his first wife, Flora, in times when it was much less commonplace than it is today. His second wife, Zoe, was 27 years his junior but thoroughly devoted to him. Tilghman originally moved Zoe, their 3-year-old son Richard and his widowed 81-year-old mother into a home at 108 East 9th Street. The next year, however, he moved them into more fashionable digs in keeping with his position at 924 West 12th Street. This home would stay in the family for the next three decades until it was razed after World War II to make room for what would become another Oklahoma City landmark, Fuzzy's Lounge and Supper Club.

Belying his image in another way, Tilghman immediately began making motions like an experienced police administrator. If he was to contradict one part of his image, he was to reinforce another part of it—his personal integrity and courage, both moral and physical. These qualities were not image, they were facts and a part of the man who embodied them.

He immediately began holding meetings with the entire force, telling them that he was divorcing himself philosophically and politically from the previous Mayors, and intended to emphasize police efficiency over political maneuvering. He told them he wasn't interested in past sins and they all had his trust until they proved him wrong. He expected them to be physically fit and conduct themselves professionally. He also told them "you don't have to make a lot of arrests to prove yourselves. I'll rate you higher if your beat is kept orderly and without trouble".

Next he confronted the nemesis of every police administrator, the budget. He retained both Joe Burnett, another man who had proven his grit, as his Assistant Chief and the police matron. He cut the uniformed force from 65 men to 54, dismissed two men from the Bureau of Identification and did away with Mayor Scales' Secret Service Bureau, replacing it with a six-man Detective Division of plainclothesmen directly under his control. The laughable old Police Court was also replaced with a Municipal Court to be operated under more professional legal standards.

Everyone was curious about what Tilghman's mandate on vice enforcement would be. It didn't take long to find out. Three days after his appointment, the new Chief gave his terse mandate; "Close 'em up". Twenty-five bootleggers went to jail the first night, posting more than $600 in bonds. The newspapers lauded the Department for "the biggest day's work done in more than two years". The pressure didn't subside. Officers worked around the clock. The next 75 raids netted only 7 arrests, many places having closed in the face of Tilghman's relentless pursuit. Lookouts went to jail for vagrancy.

When some of the malefactors expressed an intent to open joints outside the City limits, Tilghman fostered an uncharacteristic spate of city-county cooperation by asking the Sheriff to give some of his officers county commissions to defeat this tactic. The city and county officers continued to go through the vice barons like fat through a goose. Fifty-seven went to jail from the Southern Club. Six wagonloads of booze came out of the Olympic Club, Billingsley's Night & Day, the Red Onion and others.

Later that month, the newspaper listed the physical standards for employment by the city's public safety departments. Applicants had to be between the ages of 25 and 45, those younger than that being considered to have "not enough judgement" for the responsibilities of the position. Firemen had to be a minimum of 5- feet-8-inches in height and weigh 140 pounds. Policemen were required to be at least 5-feet-9 1/2-inches and 150 pounds because "bigger men were needed for the police force".

Within his first six months, Tilghman faced two major cases. The first was a series of safe burglaries in Oklahoma and Texas including three in Oklahoma City. Since the safes weren't damaged, officers began by looking for an expert safecracker until Tilghman took a different approach.

Tilghman learned that all the safes had been Moslers and Oklahoma City was the company's regional headquarters. He also learned that a book containing all the combinations of all the safes they sold or serviced was missing. Deciding that the burglaries were "inside jobs", he put his best plainclothesman, 35-year-old Johnny Cassidy, on the case.

Within a week, the four-year veteran Cassidy had identified all the gang members and observed them casing their next job, a grocery store. After planting some marked money in the store's safe, Cassidy, his partner and Tilghman staked it out the next night. After patiently watching the burglars accomplish their task in the early morning hours, they arrested the Mosler Company's best safe man and his two accomplices. They also recovered all of the marked money as well as the missing book of combinations. Perhaps embarrassed by the complicity of their employee or concerned about the effect of the publicity on their company's image, the Mosler Company's executives refused to prosecute and received a scathing chastisement from Chief Tilghman for their timidity. The gang was later tried in Shawnee for murdering a night watchman during one of their jobs there.

The second major case was the murder of Thomas J. Gentry, a local dry cleaner, in January of 1912. The new year of 1912 opened with record-setting cold temperatures. One of those records was set on January 7 when the mercury dipped to a bitter 3 degrees below zero. Shortly after 9 A.M. that morning, police were summoned to 1518 Linwood where Alverta Bess Gentry had discovered her husband shot in the back of the head in their ransacked house.

Chief Tilghman soon arrived with Detectives Martin C. Binion, J.W. Morris and Sam Bartell. Their investigation rapidly turned up some inconsistencies. Although there were appearances of a burglary, the man was shot while reading his paper in a chair in his living room. There had not been a struggle. Very quiet burglars? Or someone behind him he knew and trusted? Although a diamond stud was missing from the victim's shirt, there was cash and a gold watch in his pockets. Sloppy, hurried burglars? There was also evidence of a party with whiskey and cigarettes around. But the victim didn't drink or smoke. A very quiet party? The neighbors didn't hear anything. And the widow wasn't at home last night?

A very rapid but professional investigation ensued. In a development that can be appreciated by any era's homicide investigators, the victim's brother-in-law, Maurice Weightman, fainted while being questioned by Tilghman. Within 24 hours, he had Gentry's wife, her lover Jess Mackey and her brother (Weightman) in jail with their conflicting but guilt-drenched statements on his desk. Not bad detective work for the 1990s much less 1912. Mrs. Gentry was later sentenced to life in prison, Weightman got five years and Mackey earned his freedom as a state's witness.

Tilghman solved another murder the next week. A bootlegger's girlfriend was shot in the breast but told officers she had shot herself. Significantly, the bootlegger was present when she made this statement and she had fresh bruises on her face. Transported to the hospital, she died the next day. Tilghman had a more than passing familiarity with gunshot wounds. Because the girl's dress had no powder burns or stippling around the wound, he knew the bootlegger had shot her from a distance but couldn't prove it because of the girl's statement that she had shot herself. So, with the help of an enterprising county attorney, the bootlegger was prosecuted for aiding and abetting a suicide.

Considering his background, Bill Tilghman must have been particularly bemused by the 1912 Oklahoma County elections. One of the candidates for county attorney was the bumbling former outlaw and current city attorney Al Jennings. Jennings presented himself to the voters with the prosaic attitude that "When I was a train robber and outlaw, I was a good train robber and outlaw. If you choose me as prosecuting attorney, I'll be a good prosecuting attorney".

Although some reporters and publicists would make the comparison (notably without objection from Jennings), Tilghman used to jeer at the mere suggestion that the Jennings gang was in any way comparable to those of the Daltons or Bill Doolin. Although the voters gave the reformed outlaw the Democratic nomination, he was defeated by the Republican in the general election. Not to be deterred, Jennings then entered into the venture of making a grossly exaggerated and self-serving motion picture about his outlaw career.

The only thing more objectionable to some people than a policeman who doesn't do his job is one who does it too well. During the first month of 1912, Tilghman's OCPD had made 851 arrests, assessed fines of over $7,000 and had 395 people in jail, 212 of them serving sentences.

The Chief's love affair with the citizens, the press and the city fathers couldn't last. Business owners and vice lords losing money berated him for being too strict in his enforcement efforts, the sanctimonious criticized him for not being strict enough and everybody whined to the city administration. Mayor Grant had hired Tilghman with the understanding that he would have "full control" of his police force but that promise, too, had eroded with time. The Mayor began issuing Tilghman edicts to "close this joint" and "raid that joint" without respect for legal fine points like witnesses or evidence. When Tilghman followed the law and common sense instead of instructions, relations became strained. When the Mayor wrote letters to 18 officers, bypassing their Chief, saying he was watching their performance and intended to fire them if it didn't get better, relations didn't get any better.

Detective Martin C. Binion ran for Oklahoma County Sheriff and, when elected, resigned from the OCPD to take his new office in January of 1913. Tilghman resigned on the eleventh day of the next month, possibly suffering from a common affliction of police administrators of all generations, fecal exhaustion, more colloquially known as "tired of the bullshit". He also intended to attempt to fulfill his dream of two decades, to close his law enforcement career with an appointment as U.S. Marshal for the Western District of Oklahoma. Tilghman intended to seek the post from the newly elected Democratic President. Such was his admiration for the man that when his and Zoe's third son was born in October of 1912, the 58-year-old father named him Woodrow Wilson Tilghman. Unfortunately, his credentials, experience, enthusiasm and many endorsements aside, Tilghman's efforts to achieve that goal were destined to be unsuccessful. Caught up in the miasma of national and state politics, the appointment went to another man. Double-crossed, in his own opinion, Tilghman had given up the Chief's job for nothing. When he left, unfortunately, he took much of the integrity he had lent to the position with him.

Another event of early 1913 was to have an impact upon the city's near future. This was the formation of the Central One Hundred. This was a committee of 100 men and women members of the city's churches, militant crusaders against commercialized vice in the City. They were led by their President, John Embry, a crime-busting former United States Attorney, and he was ably seconded by a phalanx of local Baptist, Methodist and Christian ministers. They intended to stridently spread their message of morals, decency, law and order, and be a constant thorn in the sides of elected and appointed officials who didn't combat these evils as stringently as they thought they should. Twice they tried to have Mayor Grant recalled. Although unsuccessful on both occasions, their time was coming. But not yet.

Larry Reedy was to make his presence felt again in the city elections of 1913. In spite of having lost his position as an "election inspector", he was still a force to be reckoned with in Ward Four. Not surprisingly, that Ward's ballots elected Reedy's friend and benefactor Judge J.T. Highley as Commissioner of Public Safety over former Mayor O.A. Mitscher.

Tilghman was followed into the Chief's office by Jerome D. Jones. He managed to survive a year in the job but just barely and it was touch and go all the way. Finally, in February of 1914, Mayor Grant ordered him to resign, calling him "a tool of the bootleggers and gamblers". In a classic case of men in glass houses throwing rocks, the Mayor was himself the subject of a recall petition at the time. Chief Jones, therefore, refused to leave office, utilizing a strategy known to craps players as "betting on the come". Maybe the citizens would get the Mayor before the Mayor got him. On February 10, Grant appointed Shirley E. Dyer as Chief and ordered him to relieve Jones. Jones still refused to yield so the two Chiefs spent a week sitting in opposite ends of the Police Station, each trying to pretend that the other didn't exist. After eight days, four days before his forty-seventh birthday, Dyer resigned, telling the Mayor in his letter that he "never wanted the job and don't want it now". Finally, seeing the writing on the wall, Jones left also. Grant immediately appointed F. Webb Jones, the brother of the slain Chief Milton Jones, as Chief. The paper publicly lauded Jones's 26 years as a Deputy U.S. Marshal, Deputy Sheriff, County jailer and detective. Jones returned some semblance of order to the troubled city and its' Police Department.

You could get a room with a bath for $2.50 at the new Lee-Huckins Hotel on Broadway and three sumptuous meals for another $1.40. Life was good. Too good to be totally placid.

When the University of Oklahoma graduated their class from the College of Law in the Spring of 1914, one young man walked down the aisle who was to make a name for himself, albeit a checkered one, in Oklahoma City history. Orban Chester Patterson immediately went into practice in Oklahoma City with Moman Pruiett, purported to be the most famous criminal defense attorney in the Southwest at that time.

While Pruiett reserved the lucrative, headline-splashing felonies for himself, he allowed

*Chief F. Webb Jones.*

*An OCPD officer directs traffic in downtown Oklahoma City as cars begin to outnumber horses.*

his junior partner to handle all of the misdemeanor police court cases. Patterson quickly recognized what a boon this could become in a city with a flourishing vice trade in a dry state. He quickly established himself as the pre-eminent attorney-cum-bondsman for the hundreds of small-time, big-profit denizens of the city's underworld.

Another local attorney returned to the front pages in the elections of 1914. Al Jennings, having made his movie touting himself as the "last of the great Oklahoma outlaws", ran for Governor. Defeated once again, he moved to California to go into "the picture business". The first month of Chief Jones' administration, he got a taste of what it was going to be like. True, it was a problem he had inherited, had been in the planning stages for at least two months and he probably couldn't have foreseen it anyway. Nevertheless, he took the criticism when the story broke.

In March, the Panhandle and Southwestern Stockmen's Association held their annual convention in the City. Since Big Anne had left town, the organizers decided to come up with some special entertainment. The special entertainment was Theo Buchanan, better known by her nom de guerre of "Queenie" in her home base of Chicago and she was to be the highlight of a "smoker" on the night of March 5. The Stockmen provided the food, 5 bands, 10,000 bottles of illegal beer and 3,000 delegates. The City Auditorium on the northwest corner of California and Walker, later to become the Ritz and Trianon Ballrooms, provided seating for 4,000 on two floors, circulating air and a stage. Queenie provided garters, feathered boas, beads, fans, seven veils and other ladies finery not usually publicly displayed. Her entrance that night was preceded by the showing of an obscene 6-reel movie, also illegal. Finally, with the rowdy audience thus primed, it was Queenie's turn to strut her stuff.

Queenie launched into her "Little Eva" dance and, slowly but surely, all of the aforementioned finery fluttered out into the reveling crowd until she was down to a single, skimpy garment secured to her person by a single string. According to later reports, Queenie continued her writhing and grinding, toying with the string until "a man of affairs whose name it would shock you to know" (as the newspaper put it) rose from the crowd and implored "For God's sake, pull the string". And she did, finishing her act wearing nothing but a smile. For a finale, she danced up and down the aisles with "a prominent local banker". Needless to say, she was a big hit.

There's an old cop's saying that says "If two people know it, it's not a secret". The Hells Angels biker gang had a similar but somewhat more stringent credo that says "Three people can keep a secret if two of them are dead". So it was with the tale of Queenie. Newspapers statewide reported it, either with detached amusement or bitterly denouncing the beer and striptease. The Ministerial Alliance raised hell as did the WCTU, the Oklahoma City Federation of Women's Clubs and the Central Hundred. The latter organization promptly started their second attempt at a recall petition against Mayor Grant. Charges of "procuring indecent exposure" were eventually filed against 3 men whose bonds were posted by a coalition of 27 city bankers and businessmen. Like many other "show" charges, they withered away on the books, unprosecuted but not forgotten.

All the wrangling over which city would be the state capital had been settled with the election in June of 1910. Oklahoma politics being what it is, the wrangling then began over where the capitol building would be built in Oklahoma City. The first site seriously considered was proposed by land developer I.M. Putnam, developer of Putnam City, and John Shartel, President of the Oklahoma Railway Company. It was a section on the El Reno interurban route where N.W. 39th is today. Naturally, another committee contested it.

Charles Colcord was serving as President of the Oklahoma City Chamber of Commerce in 1914. He led a committee that included former mayor C.G. Jones and Daily Oklahoman publisher E.K. Gaylord among others. Their proposal was a section of land at N.E. 23rd and Lincoln, about two miles northeast of the downtown area. The Colcord group eventually prevailed, arranged financing and the cornerstone was laid on November 16, 1915, the eighth anniversary of Statehood.

Larry Reedy put the "fix" in again during the County elections of 1914 but it was to be his last one in Oklahoma City. First, his machinations in Ward Four managed to defeat the Central

Hundred's crusading candidate for County Attorney. Then Reedy was called to court. Not for something as inventive as election fraud but something viewed much more seriously—assaulting a policeman.

The chain of events started several months earlier while Reedy was doing a 30-day stretch in the County Jail for another assault. His talents being too valuable to waste, Reedy rapidly became a "trusty" and was occasionally let out of jail to "attend to business matters". One day an occasion arose that called for his special talents and the jailer sent him out with an officer in a patrol car. Apparently the officer wasn't fully informed of the circumstances because when they neared Reedy's club room and Reedy jumped out of the moving patrol car, the officer gave chase as he would any escaping prisoner. As the officer followed Reedy up the alley ladder to the club room, Reedy kicked him off the ladder. The officer fell to the ground and Reedy immediately decided to leave town, deciding it would not be in his best interests to run into any OCPD officers in the near future.

Several months later, Detective (and former Chief) Charles Post arrested him in a bar on Reno with pockets full of election ballots from the town he had been hiding out in since his escape. Brought to court after doing his damage in the County election, he was fined $50. Unable to pay and unwilling to serve the time in an unsympathetic City Jail staffed by the brother officers of the officer he had assaulted, Reedy promised to leave town and the fine was cancelled.

Toward the end of Mayor Grant's administration, the Central One Hundred banded together with the Womens Christian Temperance Union and other groups of church activists and set out to have a major effect upon the spring elections of 1915.

All the mayoral candidates in 1915 ran on strong law enforcement platforms. Ten Democrats, one Independent Presbyterian minister and one Republican vied for the office. The lone Republican, Ed Overholser, and his father, City pioneer Henry Overholser, had long been foes of prohibition. As businessmen and devout capitalists, they felt it would be bad for the City and favored a more open town policy. When approached by the Central One Hundred representatives, he pledged himself to a program of strict law enforcement and won them over. Overholser was elected by defeating Will Gault, the son of the man who had defeated his father, Henry Overholser, in the City's first legal mayoral election in 1890.

*The driver is Chief W.B. Nichols. The front seat passenger is Carry Cane and the rear seat passengers are Captains D. Dunham and Mike Conners.*

True to his word, Overholser's first official act was the appointment of William B. Nichols, "the fighting Deacon" of the First Baptist Church, as Chief of Police. The new Chief immediately provided some choice quotes for the local papers that portended impending doom and gloom for the bootleggers, gamblers generally and the Big Four syndicate in particular. Since Clint Stout, one of the original Big Four, had gone to his Great Reward in 1913, Red Cameron had been one of the major pretenders to the throne. In a near replay of the scenario in the 1904 county attorney election, Red was sent by the syndicate to visit the new Chief to see if he had been quoted accurately. Chief Nichols assured him that he had been and Red delivered the message to the boys. But this was not to be an exact replay of the 1904 case. This time the Chief had the Mayor solidly behind him along with groups of vocal, organized, influential church goers who backed their principles with votes, secure in the knowledge that God was on their side. Out came the axes again. Things were looking bleak for the city's professional sinners.

Then they rapidly got bleaker. The new Democratic County Attorney, H.Y. Thompson, died during Chief Nichols' first week in office. A solid front of the Mayor, Chief and the church groups nominated the most nightmarish choice they could have under the circumstances; John Embry, former U.S. Attorney and current President of the Central One Hundred. Although the bootleggers, gamblers, prostitutes, the Daily Oklahoman and the entire Democratic machine all the way up to Governor Williams fought it tooth and nail, Embry was appointed by the County Commissioners. For the next four years, Mayor Overholser, Chief Nichols and County Attorney Embry were to be the Father, Son and Holy Ghost of anti-vice righteousness in Oklahoma City, liberally dispensing hellfire and brimstone upon the blue interests.

The crusading triumvirate sprang into action immediately with the precise persistence of a military campaign. While Overholser and Nichols conducted frontal assaults on the gamblers and bootleggers, Embry began an imaginative series of assaults on the liquor supply lines. He began by asking for the cooperation of the landlords of the bootleggers and liquor joints. While this may seem like hopeless naivete on the order of asking a madam to keep her girls chaste, it turned out that the new county attorney was asking for something he fully intended to take if it wasn't given. Within a few weeks, Embry had engineered several raids that produced significant seizures of liquor. He then promptly filed six-figure lawsuits against the property owners, seeking penalties of $1,000 a day against them for allowing their buildings to be used for these illegal activities.

Even while making these inroads into the enemy supply lines, Embry was planning something even more ambitious; a stealthy envelopment of the enemy supply base far behind the front lines.

William J. Creekmore had spent over two decades earning his position as "King of the Bootleggers" in Oklahoma, well back into the Territorial days and had become a millionaire in the process. State Attorney General Charles West declared that there were nearly 1,000 bootleggers in Oklahoma City and most of them were working for Creekmore. Pulling the strings from shifting bases of operations in Sapulpa, Tulsa, Oklahoma City and eventually Joplin, Missouri, Creekmore had always seen to it that his competitors lost more liquor than he did to the liquor raiders up to that time.

Evidently a man ahead of his time, Embry silently pursued Creekmore with a patience and astuteness worthy of the organized crime conspiracy and RICO investigations of over half a century later. He told no one in his office what he was doing. He hired two investigators he trusted from his time as a U.S. Attorney, paying them personally out of his own funds. They were never seen at his office and never had telephone conversations with him. All reports were made at his home and all meetings were set up by third parties.

Embry had his men scour the telegraph offices for messages between Creekmore and his lieutenants. Hesitancy to supply the messages by the telegraph offices was met with offers of indictment as co-conspirators and thus encouraged cooperation. Using these uncensored messages, Embry was able to obtain court orders from a county judge against all the railroad and express companies transporting goods into the city. They were henceforth to be held accountable for bringing any liquor shipments into the city without defending the importation in writing to the authorities. Within six months, Embry had indictments against Creekmore, his primary Oklahoma City lieutenant and a Wells Fargo Express employee. On December 20, 1915, they were convicted of conspiracy to violate the State's prohibition statutes, receiving the maximum sentences of one year in jail and a $500 fine. While this may not seem like much by today's standards, that along with the promise of continued vigilance was enough to break the back of Creekmore's organization.

Simultaneously, Embry and allies were pursuing the Big Four into their gambling dens. The Big Four now consisted of Jake Barnes, Cecil Proctor, Jim Dupree and the deceased Clint Stout's position was being wrestled over between Red Cameron and William Monnahan. Two men from the Oklahoma City Secret Service were assigned full time to investigate their clubs.

Twenty-eight arrests, including the "Big Four" gambling syndicate, and total demolition of the plush fixtures finished The Southern Club. The Olympic, Monte Carlo and others soon followed. Another saloon and gambling house that fell under this onslaught was Robert D. Kerr's Sasaric where he had killed George Burton six years earlier. Nichols personally led many of the raids and conducted some of them alone, as he did one night catching some prominent citizens in one of the City's more affluent houses of joy. When several of them complained that they were too important to go to jail because they "had friends downtown", Nichols lambasted them as though he were still in the pulpit. His comments merit repeating; "My best friends in this town have double-crossed me time and time again since I've been Chief. I may not be Chief longer than tomorrow night but while I am Chief, I'm going to be one. And it doesn't make any difference if I catch my own brother in one of these raids, he'll have to come to jail. Millionaires and hod carriers all look alike to me. I've started to do something and I'm going to carry it through".

While that kind of integrity is admirable, it isn't bulletproof. Nichols didn't make it six months before he was shot down....by one of his own officers. Shortly after noon on October 1, 1915, the Chief observed Patrolman John O. Lung on duty at the police station and apparently drunk. Nichols and Lung stepped into the Captain's office and witnesses soon heard loud words coming from behind the closed door. As they opened the door, they observed Officer Lung standing over a prostrate Chief Nichols, beating him over the head with a pistol.

Driver Del Bruce pulled Lung off of the Chief and Assistant County Attorney Harold Lee began leading Nichols out of the door. Lung, frustrated at no longer being able to use his gun for a club, decided to use it for its primary purpose. He fired three times at the retreating Chief. Two bullets hit Nichols in the left leg and one penetrated his right hand, going on to strike Assistant Jailer J.R. Bittle in the left arm while he was standing in the hallway outside the office. Nichols collapsed to the floor. Lung was brandishing a gun in each hand when he was rushed and subdued by Patrolman Bill Slayton, Traffic Officer Otto A. Cargill and Sergeant T.D. Brandon. In the melee, Lung was trying to draw still a third gun from his hip pocket before they got him under control.Lung was booked into the City Jail "crazed with anger and in a highly nervous condition from drinking". Sheriff M.C. Binion arrived shortly to transport the weeping patrolman to the County Jail. Charges of Assault with Intent to Kill were filed against Lung.

Both Nichols and Bittle recovered from their wounds but the incident was a precursor of changing times for law enforcement. During the next year, 105 law enforcement officers would be killed in the line of duty nationwide, the first time the number had escalated to three digits. The annual number would continue to rise for the next quarter century until the World War II era. Maybe the Wild West hadn't been that wild after all.

After that inauspicious start, Nichols' administration was to become the longest in the Department's history to that time. He took the city through the time when cars finally outnumbered horses on city streets and through World War I. The increase in vehicular traffic in the city had necessitated the creation of the first OCPD Traffic Division. Among the first traffic officers were future Chief Jerry Smith and future Mayor O.A. Cargill.

In early February of 1916, officers raided the local lodgehall of the Loyal Order of Moose at 211 1/2 N.W. First. The occupants were found to be drinking and were arrested, their beer and liquor supplies confiscated. On February 17, Mayor Ed Overholser ordered all officers who were members of the organization to resign or be dismissed by March 1. Captain John Hubatka

*The OCPD 1916-left to right,Top Row-R. Wilkerson, Ray Frazier, unknown, unknown, George Merriman, George Page and Henry 'Deacon' Powers.Row Two-John McCarty, Joe Nay, Officer Brady, Ed Veasey and Jim Pryor.Row Three-Unknown, unknown, W.E. Snelson, Rolley Organ, unknown and Henry Meter.Row Four-Marvin Murray, unknown, Ollie Estes, unknown, Redge Brandon and Tommy*

*Brandon.Row Five-Jerry Smith, Officer Fowler, C.T. Linville, unknown, Officer J. F. Milam, unknown, Charlie Wilkey and O.A. Cargill.Bottom Row-Chief W.B. Nichols, D. Dunham, John Hubatka and unknown.*

and six patrolmen, including Ike Ashburn, were listed as members. The incident eventually blew over but the officers were ordered to testify at their lodge brothers' trials.

An article in The Daily Oklahoman in April of 1916 ran the pictures of 36 uniformed officers, 21 plainclothesmen and noted the absence of 3 patrolmen who were "camera shy". It noted that there were 64 people on the Police payroll now including 27 Patrolmen and 11 Detectives. Notable faces in the crowd were Chief Nichols, Captain John Hubatka, Traffic Officer Jerry M. Smith, Patrolmen C.T. Linville, W.E. Snelson, Rolley Organ, Joe Burnett and Ray Frazier. The Department had four Traffic officers, three cars, three motorcycles and one Paddy Wagon, the infamous "Black Maria". Providing supervision were three Captains and three Sergeants. Support staff included the Superintendent of Identification, four drivers, three jailers, a matron, a prison guard, a secretary, and a custodian.

The entry of the United States into World War I was to effect the civil liberties of German citizens in a manner similar to, if less drastic than, the Nisei in World War II. Oklahoma succumbed to the temper of the times along with the rest of the nation. It was forbidden to use the German language in conversations, private or telephone, or church services. German businesses were vandalized and individuals of German extraction were attacked on the streets. German aliens were prohibited from living near military installations or transportation systems. Anti-German sentiment even reached the point that the Oklahoma City Board of Education banned the use of the word "kindergarten" in classrooms. Chief Nichols added to his notoriety as the leader of a raid on the International Bible Students Association, where books were burned for the first time in the city's history.

The target was "The Finished Mystery", a novel that the U.S. Justice Department had decreed contained seditious and pro-German sentiments. The raiders seized and burned 5,000 copies of the book. Nichols also placed himself firmly on the side of the city's patriotic faction which had the slogan "Go to work, go to war or go to jail". Accordingly, his officers were ordered to increase vagrancy arrests in cooperation with Selective Service officials seeking draft evaders. One of the first effected by the new edict was Larry Reedy. Having been gone for over two years after his conviction for assaulting a policeman, he decided to come back and "test the waters". The waters had changed and Mayor Overholser saw to it that Larry Reedy got the message. Within a week, Reedy had explored his options, joined the U.S. Navy and left for Boston.

A short time later, Boston papers carried articles about a "tremendous meeting on the Common, addressed by an Oklahoma blacksmith who stirred thousands to a high pitch of patriotic fervor, as he called upon every red-blooded American to enlist in the service at once...hundreds flocked to the recruiting stations".

The *coup de grace* was delivered to the William Creekmore bootlegging empire and organization in May of 1917. Again it was a precursor of the tactics used in later years against organized crime. After Creekmore's conviction in Oklahoma County District Court, the Feds got into the act. He was in Federal Court in February for conspiracy to violate Federal Prohibition statutes. Always the scheming manipulator, this time he didn't handle it well at all. This led to a second bout in Federal Court in May for bribery and jury tampering. All told, he ended up with a $3,000 fine and over 3 years in the Federal Pen in Leavenworth, Kansas. When released, he became a hog farmer, supplying swill to pigs. The Prohibitionists would have considered it poetic. Exit Creekmore.

On June 30, 1917, the Oklahoma State Capitol building was completed. The $5 million structure was special in two ways. First, it was the only state capitol that had producing oil wells on the capitol grounds. Second, although it had been originally designed to have a dome, it remained domeless due to the high costs and scarcity of materials because of World War I. The following January, new Governor Lee Cruce hedged his bets in typical Oklahoma political fashion. He was first sworn in at Oklahoma City, then went to Guthrie and did it all over again. They weren't going to get him out of office by changing the capital site unexpectedly.

One of the legends of Oklahoma City law enforcement passed away prematurely in 1917. During the early morning hours of July 20, Officer Joseph Grant Burnett died at Saint Anthony's Hospital while being treated for a "stroke of paralysis" (probably a cerebral hemorrhage). His obituary noted that he was the longest serving officer on the force, having been a member (on and off) for 16 years. He was 49 years old.

Burnett was first listed as an officer in 1897 under Chief Frank Cochran. In January of 1904, he had become "the man who had killed the man who killed the man who killed Jesse James" when he shot Ed Kelly to death during their epic battle on First Street. Within the year he had been promoted to Captain.

In 1909 he was appointed Assistant Chief by Mayor Henry Scales, primarily in an attempt to challenge and circumvent Chief John Hubatka's authority. He had walked this political tightrope successfully and continued as Assistant Chief under Bill Tilghman, quite an endorsement in itself. With his rise in rank, Burnett had not lost either the instincts or the inclinations of a policeman. He was one of the officers who arrested the killer of Officer Morris Reagan in 1910. Burnett got caught up in the tumult after Bill Tilghman resigned and reverted to his old rank of Patrolman, still serving in that capacity at the time of his death. Burnett's funeral services at 2:30 P.M. that Sunday afternoon two days later were conducted at the Capitol Hill Catholic Church and were lauded as "among the most impressive in the City". The city's livery drivers provided 20 automobiles for the transportation of his surviving wife, their six children and virtually the entire police force led by Chief Nichols. Only two officers, Sergeant Tom Brandon and Ted Blakeley, were left on duty to cover the entire city between 2 P.M. and 5 P.M. that day. Even the criminals seemed to cooperate and it was necessary for them to make only one arrest.

The six officers who acted as pallbearers were Harry Thompson, J.F. Milan, John McCarty, Charles Wilkie, J.E. Veazey and future Chief Rolley Organ. Joe Burnett was laid to rest with pomp and ceremony in Fairlawn Cemetery where, 13 years before, Ed Kelly's unclaimed body had been buried in an unmarked grave.

A year-long feud reached its culmination in downtown Oklahoma City on the morning of September 28, 1917. Exactly one year before, the feud had begun on the streets of Maysville, a small town about 45 miles south of the city. On that day, the father of Oklahoma City attorney Orban Chester Patterson had been shot to death by the son of S.L. Williams, a Purcell banker and rancher. The Williams boy was later acquitted of the killing. The next year, Patterson's daughter (Orban's sister) committed suicide in an Oklahoma City hotel, allegedly despondent over her father's death. In the ensuing months, the elder Williams was occasionally in the city on business and had a couple of run-ins with Orban Patterson that only served to exacerbate the bad blood between them. Williams had allegedly threatened to shoot Patterson on sight on the last occasion.

They next saw each other at about 10:45 A.M. on September 28, 1917. Mr. Williams was standing about 20 feet north of Main Street on North Robinson when Patterson came out of a nearby building. Williams allegedly reached for his back pocket when Patterson drew a gun from his waistband and fired at Williams five times, striking him with four of the shots. Williams fell immediately, mortally wounded. Traffic Officer Jerry Smith ran to the scene from his post directing traffic in the intersection. A pistol, undrawn and unfired, was found in William's hip pocket. Patterson, calmly standing next to body and lighting a cigar, was arrested. Patterson spent the next few days openly joking with his cellmates about his confidence in his case and his legal representation, his law partner Moman Pruiett. His confidence was well founded. In his trial two weeks later, Patterson was acquitted on the grounds of self defense.

On April 22, 1918, the city's twenty-ninth anniversary, the water reservoir west of the city was dedicated as Lake Overholser in honor of the out-going Mayor. The end of Overholser's term also signalled the beginning of the end for Chief Nichols and his strict vice enforcement policies.

Armistice Day, 1918, was the end of the Great War and the beginning of the hometown boys coming home. One who returned, in full uniform with a Distinguished Service Medal on it, was Larry Reedy. Besides his strengths in boxing, conniving and manipulating, Reedy was also a strong swimmer. When his ship had been torpedoed in the Atlantic, Reedy had saved over 20 of his shipmates from drowning.

But if he thought he could waltz into town as the conquering hero while the band played "All Is Forgiven", he was quickly set straight. He was carrying far too much political baggage from his past sins. The Mayor gave him two days and then sent word to him that he'd be in jail for vagrancy every day beyond that grace period. Larry took a train for Denver that night, where he remained in the Navy Recruiting Service. He was escorted to the train by his old pals Judge Highley and Luther Langston, President of the Oklahoma Federation of Labor, who had helped him get a pardon from the Governor more than a decade earlier.

On January 2, 1919, former Chief Shirley Dyer died at the premature age of 51. Five days later, something of an efficiency record was set by the Oklahoma Legislature. That day the Eighteenth Amendment to the U.S. Constitution came before them. The Prohibition movement had been rolling like a juggernaut in spite of the fact that the experiment had already been tried and proved unsuccessful in Iceland and Russia. When Oklahoma had entered the Union less than 12 years earlier, its' Prohibition clause had made it one of only 5 dry states. Now there were over 30 dry states. Setting something of a speed record for Oklahoma politics, the amendment was ratified the same day by a vote of 96 to 8 in the House and unanimously in the Senate. Oklahoma was the eighteenth state to ratify it and nine days later prohibition became the law of the land. Oddly, the law did not ban the buying, possession or drinking of liquor, just the manufacture, sale or transportation of it. Federal law enforcement officers would now join municipal, county and state officers in their raiding.

In April of 1919, John Calloway "Jack" Walton was elected Mayor. Walton was to prove himself to be a political opportunist and demagogue of the first order. Chief Nichols, "the terror of the vice world", immediately resigned to enter the oil business and Walton promoted Jerry M. Smith from Patrolman to Chief. Described as "genial, handsome [and] gigantic", the 6-foot-6-inch tall Smith was a ten-year veteran traffic officer, having spent the last seven of them directing traffic from his post at Main and Robinson. John Hubatka was promoted to Captain of Detectives and four-year veteran Lee Mullinex was placed in charge of the Bertillon Department.

Walton's election also provided a signal opportunity for Orban Chester Patterson. No less an opportunist than the new Mayor, the shyster would prove to have the brains and vision Walton ultimately lacked. Patterson's business had suffered under the vice crackdowns of Chief Nichols and a short stint in the Army toward the end of the Great War had temporarily taken him "out of the loop". But now things were changing. Public backlash against four years of

*Mayor Jack Walton and his Mounted Patrol.*

the Overholser-Nichols vice wars and the restraints imposed by World War had elected Walton. The Big Four were all dead, in jail or retired. "King" William J. Creekmore's bootlegging empire was broken up and His Majesty was doing time, his minions leaderless. Chief Nichols was gone to the oil fields and the new Mayor was agreeable to a deal similar to the one Patterson originally had with his mentor Moman Pruiett; leave the felonies and "the big ones" to the administration and he could have all the misdemeanors and city cases. In this friendly atmosphere, Patterson made the most of this treasure trove. It wasn't long before the majority of the city's petty crooks depended upon him for more than criminal defenses and bail bonds; Patterson became their "fixer". His shady clientele paid him regular retainers which he openly called "protection".

Ensconced in his office on the fifth floor of the distinctively narrow Majestic Building on the northwest corner of Main and Harvey, Patterson wasn't narrow enough to devote his attentions only to his underworld denizens. To keep his fingers on the political and financial pulse of the community, he also had to have input to and output from the manor-born. He had agents of influence and sources of information infiltrated into many organizations of the city's social, cultural, financial and political elite. He would eventually reach a position of influence where he would end the careers of police commanders and City Managers, and probably instigate more 5-4 decisions on the City Council than the U.S. Supreme Court can claim. For the next two decades he would hold undisputed claim to the title of "King of the Underworld" in Oklahoma City. For 90 percent of that time, he would have an alternate office at the police station to be close to the crossroads most of his clientele passed through frequently.

Walton created his own Mounted Patrol Unit on August 1, 1919. It was initially two shifts of five officers each, each shift commanded by a Lieutenant. One of the original officers was John J. Jerkins. Both humor and tragedy were to become associated with the beginnings of this unit.

Walton began exercising his control over the Police Department (and showing his eccentricities) when he ordered that all the police horses would be equipped with rubber horseshoes so that criminals wouldn't hear them approaching. Smoking while in uniform was prohibited as was the pursuit of another job, even while off duty. Following the old political tradition of playing both ends against the middle, Walton also began issuing "courtesy cards" that exempted the bearer from misdemeanor arrest by the city police.

Tragedy struck the Mounted Patrol Unit on its second day in existence. On the evening of August 2, 1919, Officer William F. Byrd was patrolling on the east side of town when he heard gunshots coming from behind the house at 509 N. Rhode Island. As Byrd rounded the corner of the house to investigate, a black man named Bill Roberts opened fire on him for unknown reasons. Officer Byrd was struck in the heart but still managed to return fire, hitting Roberts four times before the officer fell dead. Chief of Police Jerry Smith was the first officer to respond to the scene. Roberts died from his wounds the next day. Byrd was described as being "about 35 years old" and had been an officer "for several months" in the obituary telling of his body being returned to Broken Bow for burial. With both participants dead and no apparent witnesses, no one knew what had caused it. John Hubatka advanced the theory that it was due to Roberts "drinking that choc beer".

It was a sign of changing times that the mounted patrol was created as a novelty fairly contemporarily with the creation of the Traffic Division. This unit was a prerequisite for what was increasingly becoming a city and a nation on wheels. In the first year of the next decade, traffic signals would be introduced by Detroit Police officer William Potts. He would adopt the red, yellow and green lights because the railroads already used them for traffic control. The post-war increase in motor vehicle registrations preceded a rise in accidents, many of them fatal. A special campaign against speeders resulted in 550 arrests in one week.

# IV — THE TURBULENT TWENTIES 1920-1929

Chief Jerry Smith, the "genial, handsome, gigantic traffic officer", lasted less than a year before the Mayor decided he should move on to bigger and better things in Walton's scheme of governmental control. Smith was replaced on August 6, 1920, by Calvin T. Linville, a Traffic Officer with eight years of service, and Smith became Walton's candidate for Oklahoma County Sheriff in the Fall of 1920. Smith was defeated, possibly as a result of the growing public dissatisfaction with Walton's turning the Police Department into his personal tool and the resulting unrest. Smith returned to the force as a patrolman in Traffic once again.

By 1921, the Walton Department had swollen to almost 150 officers to serve 92,000 citizens. Walton's critics deemed it bloated with political appointments and hampered by the resulting inefficiency. The budget had grown from a fairly steady $90,000 annually in the pre-war era to $300,000. The ornate Criterion

*Chief Calvin T. Linville.*

*Early 1920s officers in front of the police station on Maiden Lane.*

*Chief's Secretaries Clarence O. Hurt and Charles W. Kunc-1920.*

Theater opened at 118 West Main, Will Rogers was performing in the Shriner's Temple (now the Journal-Record Building) at N.W. 6th and Robinson, John Phillip Sousa's band and Heavyweight Champion Jack Dempsey were performing demonstrations in the new Stockyards Coliseum.

The Police Department had a Traffic Squad, a Detective Division, Motorcycle Squad, Mounted Patrol Unit, a bertillon department that was the forerunner of the Records Bureau and Crime Laboratory, and a plainclothes force assigned primarily to vice enforcement. Uniformed officers worked three shifts of eight hours each under a Captain's supervision. Traffic officers were all assigned to a day shift and the mounted patrolmen, who rode their horses in the outlying residential districts (such as Heritage Hills north of Northwest 13th), worked a modified evening shift.

Another interesting sidebar of Oklahoma politics involving the OCPD occurred on April 1, 1921. A movement was under way in the State Capitol to impeach Governor Robertson in a bank scandal. A number of legislators were absent for the deciding vote. One of those was Oklahoma City Police Captain John J. Jerkins, on a leave of absence to represent his district.

Jerkins was at home ill when the anti-impeachment forces dispatched an ambulance to bring him to the Capitol to cast his vote. On the way, the ambulance crashed and Jerkins was injured. He nonetheless continued on to the Capitol, bleeding from a head wound, and cast the deciding vote in a 42-42 tie that prevented impeachment. After 7 years on the OCPD, the 52-year-old Jerkins died from his injuries a few weeks later on May 24, 1921. A grateful Governor Robertson ordered that all State flags be flown at half-staff in his honor. Officer Joe F. Jerkins would carry on his father's legacy in the OCPD, also rising to the rank of Captain in later years while serving from 1919 to 1952.

The city elections of 1921 became an anti-Walton battle. Two pro-Walton commissioners were voted out and their replacements decided to wrest the Police Department's control out of Walton's hands. The new commissioners voted to dissolve Walton's pet Mounted Police Unit on April 7, 1921, on the grounds that it was inefficient and too expensive to maintain. The city was spending $25,000 a year on maintenance. The commissioners said that the disbanding was nothing against the records of the officers involved but the unit was "more ornamental than practical". Oklahoma City was a city on wheels now.

A miffed Mayor Walton refused to be photographed with the commissioners but agreed to stand in one "with the boys". Gracing the front page of the next day's Times, it listed the members of the unit as Lieutenants W.J. Kelly and Joe Campbell, Officers J.F. Jerkins, R.J. Bogard, Jim Kelly, James M. Walcott, Guy Mitchell and W.I. Eads. The officers in the unit resigned in a body immediately after the vote.

On April 12, 1921, the OCPD was placed under Commissioner Mike Donnelly, who immediately invalidated the thousands of Walton-issued "courtesy cards" (special police commissions). In what had become a time-honored tradition of the Mayor naming his own Chief of Police, Donnelly also replaced Calvin T. Linville with Martin C. Binion. Linville remained on the force as a Patrolman and Rolley Organ was promoted to Captain.

Binion, a native of Alabama, had come to the City 25 years earlier. He had begun his multi-faceted law enforcement career in 1903 as an Oklahoma County Deputy Sheriff. He served two years, 1911-12, on the OCPD under Bill Tilghman. He resigned from the OCPD upon being elected Oklahoma County Sheriff in January of 1913. After holding that office for four years, he returned to the OCPD in 1917. Seven months earlier, he had been appointed the Federal Prohibition Agent in charge of Oklahoma. He would do double duty in both offices until a replacement was found.

The City Commissioners also began the process of disbanding the Policemen's Union that had been fostered and encouraged by the pro-labor Walton. In the first three days after taking office, Binion discharged 36 officers and rehired 6. The rehires were the members of the Mounted Patrol who had resigned a week earlier. Among the discharged officers (some temporarily) were Jess Sosbee, C.C. York, Captain Frank Haefner (who had been promoted from Patrolman to Captain by Walton) and both of the Department's colored officers, W.R. Parker and W.D. Fuller. Patrolman W.W. "Big Bill" Slaton, who had been demoted from Captain by Walton to promote Haefner, was made a Captain again.

*Chief Carl Glitsch.*

A week later, another Captain and five more Patrolmen were fired. Former Chief Calvin Linville was promoted to Captain after a week as a Patrolman. Chief Binion said this brought the Department's strength down to 110 men, which is where he wanted it. This was definitely going to be the decade for the doctrine of changing fortunes.

Walton challenged the commissioners in court, the State Supreme Court reversed the decision and, after three months, Walton got control of the Department back. He immediately replaced Binion with Carl Glitsch on July 6. Glitsch was a 46-year-old lawyer from Forsyth, Missouri. Coming to Oklahoma at the turn of the century, he first practiced law in Anadarko before moving on to become the Vice President and General Manager of the New

State Ice Company in Oklahoma City. This was the position he held when he was appointed Chief.

In his first interview with the press, Chief Glitsch declared "this Department will be entirely free from politics". Nice try, Carl. It is unknown if Chief Glitsch was truly that naive and idealistic or if he was merely mouthing the platitudes the press expected.

On the last day of July, Glitsch appointed former Chief and current Patrolman Jerry Smith a Lieutenant in charge of all police traffic functions. C.T. Linville was made a Lieutenant of Detectives. Ralph Young and Waller J. Clark were also appointed Lieutenants. One would suspect the Mayor had a hand in the promotions.

Apparently ill-suited to his role as Walton's puppet and having exhausted his supply of platitudes (or the forbearance to mouth them), Glitsch stayed barely three months before falling from grace. In another interview with the press, he stated that the police were "powerless to check the liquor traffic" and that he personally "was not in sympathy with prohibition". Although it is problematical whether he had ever really relinquished it, Mayor Walton rapidly took back control of "his" police department. On October 1, a Walton-led OCPD began yet another crackdown on vice, gambling and prohibition violations in the city. The next eight days garnered 313 arrests and another press interview with Chief Glitsch. This time he said that the Mayor's recent raids, many of them on private residences, were illegal and if he were still practicing law, he could "knock most of them into a cocked hat". Glitsch promptly returned to running the New State Ice Company, his resignation becoming effective at midnight on October 15. Captain Rolley Organ was appointed Acting Chief for the next two months while Walton decided on his next appointment. Apparently Walton had learned a lesson from Glitsch about giving control of the department, even nominally, to an appointee who could become a publicly uncontrollable wild card. The day after Glitsch's resignation, Walton cut the command legs out from under Organ immediately. In a typically contradictory press interview, in one breath Walton appointed Organ as Acting Chief of Police and in the next, stated unequivocally that "I am the Chief of Police" until he decided otherwise.

Organ, a former carpenter, had been hired as an officer on May 13, 1907, at the age of 45. Although he came to the OCPD late in life, he began his law enforcement career as a youth as the town marshal of Lebanon, Tennessee. He had progressed through the ranks of Patrolman, Detective and Sergeant over the next 14 years until Commissioner Mike Donnelly had promoted him to Captain a week after temporarily wresting control of the Department from Mayor Walton.

During all this turmoil in the police department, it is possible some of the traditional police services to the public were impacted. If so, the law firm of Pruiett and Patterson didn't miss them. They took care of their own business. At 9 P.M. on the evening of October 9, 1921, 45-year-old Joe Patterson was found shot to death in front of his residence at 615 East 1st Street. As she cradled his head in her lap, the last words he spoke to his wife were "Orban Patterson shot me".

Joe Patterson was hardly a great loss to the city. His civic credentials were listed in the press as "bootlegger, gambler, stick-up man and dope peddler". Given the temper of the times, it also probably didn't help Patterson's case that he was black. The next few hours brought the voluntary surrenders of Moman Pruiett, Orban Patterson and Rush McGaffey in the incident. Although none of the men were falling down drunk, all had been drinking recently.

McGaffey, a black bootlegger and gambler, had been bonded out of jail earlier that evening by Pruiett and Orban Patterson. They had then gone to Joe Patterson's home on East 1st Street where [Orban] Patterson and McGaffey got involved in a dispute which was punctuated by Patterson taking a shot at McGaffey's head, missing his target by an estimated 18 inches. The two then began struggling when Joe Patterson came out carrying his own gun and threatening to shoot both men. When Joe Patterson began to point his weapon toward the men, one of the men shot him fatally. The paper noted that Orban Patterson had been involved in another "shooting scrape" in the negro section of the city a few weeks earlier but the victim's dying statement to his wife was contradicted when Moman Pruiett said that he had shot Patterson. After giving their statements, the three men were released on $1500 bond

*Chief Waller J. Clark.*

each. Before the week ended, a coroner's jury had accepted the three statements without questioning the men and Moman Pruiett was acquitted on the grounds of self defense.

The hypocritical attitudes and lackadaisical enforcement efforts toward Prohibition was hardly restricted to Oklahoma City or its Police Department. Former Governor Robert L. Williams had benefited from the support of the Prohibition faction while he was in office. Now, as a Federal Judge, he made no secret of the fact that he was personally opposed to Prohibition and was known to be markedly lenient with his sentencing in Prohibition cases in his court. He was certainly not the only case of an Oklahoma politician who politically lauded Prohibition while personally rejecting it or vice versa. This was also not restricted to politicians, Oklahoman or otherwise. Although bribery and corruption no doubt played a part in it, both in the political and law enforcement arenas, an increasingly pervasive attitude among the citizenry was exemplified in a letter from an Oklahoma citizen to the U.S. Justice Department which stated that "no lawman but a fanatic or a fool would enforce a law just because it appears on the books".

Shortly before Christmas, Walton installed Waller J. Clark as Chief and Rolley Organ reverted to the position of Assistant Chief. Clark said he was going to put together a "purity squad" and turn Oklahoma City into "a second Zion City". Six feet, six inches tall and weighing three hundred pounds, Clark was a former Kansas City policeman. Although he didn't last too long as Chief in the politically uncertain times, he started a long lineage in the Oklahoma City Police Department.

His son, Ray S. Clark Sr., became an officer during his father's term as Chief and remained one until his death in a traffic accident in 1936. Ray Senior's brother-in-law was Reese Galyon, who retired as a Captain. Ray's son, Ray S. Clark Jr., was an officer from 1948 to 1968. His cousin, Reese Galyon Jr., was killed in a traffic accident while a motorcycle officer in 1951. Ray Junior also had a nephew, Gil Gothard, who was an officer from 1957 to 1977. The deceased Reese Galyon Jr. also had a son, Justin Brent Galyon, who became an officer in 1971 and is still on active duty as of this writing.

The first crisis on Chief Clark's agenda was an anti-labor movement that led to strikes at the meat packing plants in the Stockyards area. This was termed the Open Shop War and was to resurface periodically, if more peacefully, for years as the Right To Work movement.

Two days after Christmas, 500 anti-open shop strikers held a parade through downtown. Emotions running high, it degenerated into a riot in "Packing Town". The riot wasn't the end of the violence. Two weeks later, nine white union men dragged Jake Brooks, a black scabbing at one of the packing plants, out of his home and lynched him. Amid clamoring for martial law and lots of "blame-laying and finger-pointing", the nine men were arrested. Three plead guilty to life sentences and the rest were released.

Early in 1922, over 2,000 Ku Klux Klansmen paraded through downtown Oklahoma City unchallenged and, in the Fall elections, their candidates won a majority of the Oklahoma County offices. One of the candidates for Oklahoma County Sheriff their influence defeated that year was Bill Tilghman. On October 5, 1,500 Klansmen openly initiated 400 new members at the State Fairgrounds in front of a crowd of 20,000.

Jack Walton ran for Governor and was elected. A man of many contradictions, Walton had been a consulting engineer before he began his political career. In that capacity, he had designed the electric chair for the State Penitentiary in McAlester. A staunch opponent of capital punishment, he had accepted no fee for his design. As Governor, Walton's electric chair would never be used, Walton commuting all death sentences to life imprisonment or less.

John Lung, the officer who had shot Chief W.B. Nichols in the Chief's office in 1915, was back in the law enforcement business in the summer of 1922. In fact, he hadn't been out of it for long. The 48-year-old native of Van Buren, Arkansas, had been a law enforcement officer in either private or public service since he was 17. The charges against him from the Nichols shooting were dismissed after having "hung on the dockets of the courts for several years".

Leaving Oklahoma City after the Nichols shooting, Lung had moved to Okmulgee and joined their police department. Still enjoying a few drinks occasionally and still combative when in his cups, Lung was arrested by his fellow officers once while walking down the street shooting out street lights. Nevertheless, he was apparently a good man to have around when the going got rough so he survived to serve several years as the Chief of the Okmulgee P.D. and then became an Okmulgee County Deputy Sheriff.

The term "law enforcement officer" fits him better than "peace officer" because there wasn't much peaceful about John Lung. Newspaper accounts of his adventures describe him as a man "of iron nerve, fearless heart and a dead shot". He was known to carry at least two guns at all times, was said to be equally proficient with them with either hand and wasn't the least bit hesitant to use them. He was lauded for killing the Poe-Hart gang at the Nuyaka Mission in 1917 and known to have killed "several bad Negroes".

Lung made an unsuccessful bid for the Sheriff's job and then opened a private security firm, Oil Field Detective Service, with a partner, although still holding his Deputy's commission. In the summer of 1922, he was investigating the burglary of a grocery store that had occurred in Okmulgee on August 28 in which more than $2000 worth of merchandise was taken. The investigation led him to suspect a man named Roy Pomeroy and the trail led him to Sapulpa.

On the night of September 15, 1922, Lung and Sapulpa Chief of Police Ralph Morey saw two men and a woman drive a car into the Continental Garage in Sapulpa. Lung recognized one of the men as Roy Pomeroy. As the two officers entered the darkened garage, one of the men and the woman were walking out toward them. From the shadows behind one of the cars in the garage, the other man opened fire on the officers, shooting twice at Lung and once at Chief Morey. Morey was uninjured but Lung was hit in the left side, the bullet passing through a lung and his heart. He fell with an unfired pistol in his left hand. The two male suspects escaped through the rear of the garage but the woman was arrested nearby.

Lung was put in a car to be taken to the hospital but the car wrecked two blocks away. Transferred to another car, he was dead on arrival at the hospital. He was buried in Okmulgee, survived by his father, widow and five children.

About 2:00 A.M. on December 1, 1922, the day after Thanksgiving, Officers Jess Sosbee and Clarence Hurt were returning from a call at 709 East 1st Street when they were shot at from ambush in the 400 block of East Grand. Sosbee was hit in the back and died the next day.

The 35-year-old officer's funeral services were held at the Washington Avenue Baptist Church. The entire uniformed force marched there from the Police Station wearing black crepe on their badges in memory of their fallen comrade. Sosbee's widow and 14-year-old daughter were joined at the church by more than 1,500 mourners including the Firemen's Band, Mayor Walton and all the City Commissioners. Following the services, the entire procession moved on to the burial site in Fairlawn Cemetery. Sosbee's pallbearers were his partner, Clarence Hurt, Briggs Chumley, J.B. Ryan, Walter Acord, Frank Baker and Dick Miller.

Three black men, Tim Smith, Herb Parker and Matt Worthey were arrested. Parker was a former policeman. The newspaper speculated that the shooting was the result of an "old grudge stimulated by corn liquor". Smith and Parker were later convicted for the crime. Their stated motive was simply that they had "wanted to kill an officer". Smith was sentenced to five years and Parker to seven years. When they were transported from the City Jail to the State Prison, they were dressed in women's clothing to keep them from being recognized and lynched.

Oklahoma Cityans were experiencing the warmest January in their history during the first month of 1923. Inauguration Day was a balmy 71 degrees. On January 8, 1923, former Mayor Jack Walton was sworn in as Governor. It was just as well that he get used to the unseasonable heat. It would get a lot hotter for the Governor before long.

Orban Patterson felt his position secure enough to leave his partnership with Moman Pruiett and open his own law office. Walton had been telling his supporters that he was going to celebrate with great style and he tried to keep his word. The next day, a parade of over 25,000 people began organizing at the Stockyards and wound its way through the downtown area until it reach the State Fairgrounds on N. Eastern where Douglass High School is now. There, former mayor Daniel V. Lackey had set up a Texas-size barbecue for "Our Jack". Barbecue for 160,000 people was cooked in over a mile of trenches. Steam fire engines had started percolating coffee the day before in three 10-by-20-foot oil tanks the size of railroad boxcars. Each urn supposedly could serve 50,000 people. It was to be a gigantic celebration for a short administration.

Mike Donnelly took over as Mayor for the remainder of the unexpired term. He was the Chief Clerk of the Water Department and had been Mayor of Capitol Hill when that near-southside area had been annexed into the city in 1911. One week after Walton's inauguration, Chief Clark was out. Clark's fortunes were to decline even further. He would end the year in jail. Donnelly again appointed Martin Binion as Chief but, as in 1921, it was only to last for three months. The Acting Mayor also promoted Briggs Chumley to Captain.

The Spring elections of 1923 were fairly tame by Oklahoma City standards except for mayoral candidate Warren Gill, who stated he was "for everybody makin' his own whiskey" and campaigned on the platform of "a still in every home". His lack of hypocrisy, though amusing, was not unique. That same year the U.S. Congress defeated an attempt to make it a crime to buy alcoholic beverages and a judge ruled that medical prescriptions for liquor were not limited under Prohibition. The nation's understanding doctors produced an average of ten million such prescriptions annually for the next ten years.

Gill's candor was not rewarded. Former OCPD officer Otto Arthur Cargill was elected Mayor, took office on April 4 and appointed Ray Frazier as Chief. Frazier wanted William E. Snelson as his Assistant Chief and, to make room for that appointment, Assistant Chief Rolley Organ became a 61-year-old Patrolman. The day after 89'ers Day, Martin Binion was demoted to Inspector, a position created especially for him. While it is not clear where this rank fit in the chain of command, he wasn't to hold it long enough for it to matter much. Three days later, Binion and Captain Briggs Chumley were unceremoniously fired. Traffic Officer James Morris would succeed Chumley as a Captain. Binion would have no successor since the position created for him would be abolished.

*Chief Ray Frazier.*

Both men would be back on the force before long, Chumley in plenty of time to give his life for it. The shakeups had become another tradition that came with every new Mayor and Chief. The tradition continues to the present day, though in a much watered down version usually marked by departmental reorganization, creation of new units, shifting or redecorating offices and some personnel transfers. It has been sarcastically referred to as a new Chief's chance to "mark his territory and get their attention". For the first few months of every early administration, it was an almost weekly occurrence to fire some officers, hire new ones, then reinstate some of the previously fired ones. Mayor Cargill stated that the reason for these particular machinations was to forcefully point out that he would not tolerate his officers soliciting business for attorneys. One of the new officers hired during this period was Frank Cissne.

The day after his appointment, Frazier erased another vestige of the Walton administration when he ordered 300 newly designed badges to replace the ones Walton had designed with a lion on top of them. The new badge was a six-pointed star backed by a wreath and surmounted by an eagle.

As usual, the 89'ers Day issue of the Daily Oklahoman carried a number of articles on city history. This year one of them profiled Ike Ashburn as the city's most senior police officer. The article noted that Ashburn had served the OCPD for over 23 years not including a two-year "break in service". Although there were older officers on the force, none had served longer. Therefore Ashburn was to be issued Badge Number 1 by the new Mayor. In spite of the fact that the honor was undoubtedly deserved, it probably didn't hurt any that Ashburn had been the training officer who "broke in" rookie officer O.A. Cargill some years earlier. Ashburn reminisced about the days when the only recognizable items of uniforms officers wore were broad-brimmed white hats. He also had fond memories of a time of enforcing the law primarily against killers and robbers. Serving as a plainclothesman now, Ashburn said today's officers spent most of their time chasing down petty thieves and dope peddlers which he considered "quite a comedown for the officers".

*The Walton badge of the early 1920s.*

*OCPD Badge 1923-1929.*

Also under Cargill, Chief Frazier and Sheriff Cavnar started another of the city's interminable wars on the bootleggers. During the first week, some 2,650 gallons of whiskey were seized and 141 vagrants and bootleggers were arrested. But the vice cleanup was recessed for the great Klan Wars and the political turmoil that followed——this time on the state government level.

*Another public whiskey destruction. A popular spectator sport in Oklahoma City during the Roaring Twenties.*

The next month another vestige of the Wild West passed when James T. Brown died at the age of 57. Jim Brown was serving as a plainclothesman on the OCPD and had been Assistant Chief for two years under Chief Emrick in 1903-05. He had also been a Prohibition Agent in half a dozen states as well as a special officer for the Anti-Saloon League. An old-time gunfighter in the mold of Bill Tilghman, he had once been questioned by a reporter about his reputation. The reporter said that he had been able to document that Brown had killed at least nine men in gunfights and asked him if that total was accurate. A reticent Brown replied that there had been " more but refused to elaborate". Associates of Brown told the reporter that the quiet but crusty old lawman had killed "at least 20 men", starting with his first gunfight in Sallisaw when he was 17 years old. Barely six months earlier, a local reporter had talked to several OCPD veterans about their first arrests as law enforcement officers. Brown's had been a horse thief holed up in a shack south of Muskogee. The horse thief decided to shoot it out with the 20-year-old Deputy Brown and lost.

At the end of June, former Chief Jerry Smith returned from his latest break in service. Smith had been fired three days after Martin Binion had been appointed Chief in January. Now he was back, this time as a Captain again.

Jack Walton had begun his political career a mere four years before as the Commissioner of Public Works for Oklahoma City. A totally unqualified political opportunist, he had bankrolled an ability to appeal to the emotions and prejudices of the masses into a career of rising stardom. A stormy term as Mayor of Oklahoma City was followed by his election as Governor and "Our Jack" began to have delusions of grandeur. He desired a future in the U.S. Senate and possibly even the Vice Presidency of the nation. One way to acquire a quick reputation has always been to pick a fight with the biggest kid on the block. Jack decided to declare war on the powerful Ku Klux Klan movement in Oklahoma, probably less in defense of any personal principles than to help achieve the national prominence necessary to achieve his dreams of higher office.

He had definitely selected the biggest kid on the block. The Klan had begun a nationwide resurgence at the beginning of the decade. Their greatest gains, both in numbers and political power, were made in the Midwest. Their membership in Oklahoma has been estimated anywhere from 90,000 to 200,000, as many as 1 in every 20 Oklahomans. Just as the state's population base was shifting from the rural to the urban areas, there also was the Klan's power base including many men in prominent positions. The first Oklahoma Grand

Dragon of the Klan was a Vice President of the University of Oklahoma. Mayors, judges, county attorneys, sheriffs and police officers were counted on their membership rolls. At one time, fully half of the OCPD's officers were rumored to be members. In the 1926 gubernatorial race, when the Klan's power was subsiding, both Oklahoma City Mayor O.A. Cargill and State Senator Elmer Thomas confessed past membership in the organization. Cargill had already made his amends by then by purging the OCPD of its overt Klan affiliations and integrating the Department.

Walton had finally gotten in over his head. His political rhetoric and showmanship that had worked so well with the citizens didn't cut much ice with the professional politicians he was dealing with now and his political naivete was working against him.The resurgent Klan had a controlling faction in the State Legislature and plans were being made for them to meet to consider his impeachment. A U.S. District Judge had ordered a grand jury to convene to investigate him. The Oklahoma News was headlining every edition "We Want Neither King Nor Klan". The Governor's enemies were circling the wagons and Walton was desperate.

On August 4, 1923, former Chief F. Webb Jones died at the age of 61 in his home at 1629 N.W. 7. Coming to Oklahoma Territory in 1890 from his home in Bowling Green, Kentucky, Jones had been one of the first Deputy U.S. Marshals in the Territory. He later served as a Deputy under Sheriff Mike O'Brien and Chief of the OCPD in 1913-14. For the last six years, he had been a truant officer for the Oklahoma City Public Schools. Jones was buried in Fairlawn Cemetery near his brother Milton, who had been killed in 1895 during his tenure in the Chief's office. Former Chief Rolley Organ led a contingent of over 50 uniformed OCPD officers.

Walton had to do something fast in an attempt to divert the voters attention from his malfeasance and neuter his political enemies. In August of 1923, using Klan violence in Tulsa as an excuse, Walton called out the National Guard and declared martial law in Tulsa County. When this didn't turn out to be enough of a diversion, Walton placed the entire state under martial law to become effective at midnight on September 15. Oklahoma, Tulsa and Creek counties were placed under "absolute martial law", totally usurping the authority of local officials. The bold morning headlines trumpeted "ARMY LAW FOR STATE".

National Guardsmen, with loaded rifles and fixed bayonets, were stationed at the State Capitol, county courthouses and police stations. Barring the doors to the Senate chambers, they received orders from Walton to "shoot to kill" to prevent the State Legislature from meeting and the grand jury from convening. It was a desperately transparent ploy to avert his impeachment proceedings. A midnight curfew was instituted and all sales of firearms or ammunition was forbidden. Machine guns were placed on the roof of a building overlooking the Oklahoma County courthouse on William Couch's old claim at Main and Walker and the police station on Maiden Lane, trained on the City jail entrance.

At 2:30 A.M. on Sunday, September 16, Colonel William S. Key of the 160th Field Artillery relieved Chief Ray Frazier and Assistant Chief William E. Snelson of command of the Oklahoma City Police Department and placed it under military rule. Key placed Captain Nelson J. Moore of the 180th Infantry in charge of the OCPD. Moore was a veteran of World War I and, in his civilian life, was a Captain on the Tulsa Police Department. There was an irony to Governor Walton being responsible for Moore overseeing the OCPD while Walton also had Tulsa P.D. under martial law and was prosecuting Tulsa officers for participating in Klan violence.

On the surface, everything was somewhat tense but peaceful. Grasping the political realities of the situation, there were few hard feelings in evidence and even some degree of fraternization between the troops and officers. Calls for police service were lower than normal and a fairly peaceful Sunday passed.

Behind the scenes, things were different. Members of the State Legislature were meeting at the Skirvin Hotel in downtown Oklahoma City. They obviously intended to go forth with impeachment proceedings against the Governor come what may. Walton claimed he had 22,000 "secret police" available to stop any vote on the subject if necessary. Mayor Cargill retaliated by deputizing 2,000 men as "special officers" to remove the state forces from local control. The County Sheriff was issuing another 2,000 special commissions to assist.

Walton's "secret police" did not materialize and, nose to nose with his opposition, the Governor blinked. Early Monday morning on September 17, Ray Frazier was reinstated as Chief and later that night the machine guns were removed from covering the County courthouse and the city jail. The military "advisor" stayed on for a short time. In fact, the following Friday Captain Moore was replaced by Major Joe Campbell of the 179th Infantry. Campbell was a former OCPD officer, had been a member of then-Mayor Walton's Mounted Patrol in 1919 and was one of the officers who resigned when it was disbanded.

The legislators arranged for a vote for an impeachment hearing to occur on October 2. All three OCPD shifts were on duty as well as the 4,000 newly commissioned city and county officers. Again, Walton's secret police were not to be found and the citizens voted 3 to 1 for the legislature to hold an impeachment session. Three days later, the military "advisors" were relieved of their duties and the Oklahoma National Guard ended their 20-day "occupation" of the OCPD.

October of 1923 saw record amounts of rainfall in the City. On October 16, the swollen North Canadian River overflowed its banks with crest waters twenty-five feet high, flooding everything up to California Avenue. Nearby neighborhoods were inundated leaving 15,000 homeless, washing out railroad tracks and creating general havoc. Also deluged was Wheeler Park which had contained the City Zoo since 1902, all of it on land that had been donated to the city by banker and land Developer James B. Wheeler. The massive damages sustained by the zoo during these floods would later become the impetus for moving the zoo to its current location north of Lincoln Park.

Mayor Cargill issued a proclamation stating "for the protection of property within the flood district, police and soldiers on duty have been ordered to shoot to kill any person found looting or breaking into any abandoned house or store building". Property owners were required to get passes from the police station or the Mayor's office to get to their damaged homes or businesses. This was in response to a Daily Oklahoman article that said that a roving mob of 75 to 100 hoboes began looting at the area around S.W. 10th and Robinson.

One of the truisms of police work is that not all the heroes get medals or their names engraved on monuments. Ten days after the flooding began, Officer A.L. Walton died of pneumonia. Earlier in the week, Walton had spent 36 hours rescuing stranded children from the flooded areas. Although Mayor Cargill had ordered him to go off duty at one point, the officer continued his rescues until he collapsed with fever. Although his death three days later was obviously due to these exertions, his death did not qualify as being in the line of duty. Nevertheless, his widow received $500 from the Police Fund.

The Walton fiasco finally ended when the Governor was impeached on 11 charges of abuse of power. Walton was removed from office on November 19, 1923, after slightly more than ten months in office. Walton would not stop seeking the people's mandate, however. He ran for the U.S. Senate in 1924 and was defeated. He campaigned for the same post in 1930 but withdrew before the election. He ran for his old job as Mayor of Oklahoma City in 1931 but was again defeated. In 1932, amazingly, he was elected to the State Corporation Commission and held the post until 1939, the only full term he ever completed in any elected office. In 1934 and 1938 he ran again for Governor, ran twice for Oklahoma County Sheriff and ran again for the Corporation Commission but was defeated in all of them.

Five days after Walton was impeached, former Chief Waller J. Clark suffered an even worse setback. While Walton had lost his job, he had managed to stay out of jail. A resident of the City since 1905, Clark had a total of 26 years of service with the police departments in Kansas City and Oklahoma City. When he had lost his job as Chief to Martin Binion the previous January, Clark had become an Inspector for the State Health Department. While serving an eviction order in that capacity, Clark had pistol-whipped a man who evidently didn't want to be evicted. On November 24, Clark was convicted of Assault with a Deadly Weapon in an El Reno court and was sentenced to serve a year and a day in the State Penitentiary.

## THE DAILY OKLAHOMAN
November 27, 1923

### IT JUST HAPPENED THAT BUCKSHOT WASN'T USED

A slight error committed Monday afternoon by Harry Wolfe, head of the police stolen automobile department, has made it necessary for the city detective to invest in a feather cushion to use in his car. Wolfe and Fred Smith went Monday to a farmhouse near Choctaw where they learned that a stolen auto had been located. Attempting to open the door of a barn, Wolfe was discovered by a woman in the house. She didn't recognize him as an officer. The shotgun she used happened to be loaded with birdshot. The car had been found by the woman's son in the road near their home and had been put in the barn. No arrests were made.

The Cargill-Frazier administration produced a 1923 Police Annual of 42 pages, 23 of them advertisements for local merchants. The City covered 17 square miles, had 150 miles of paved streets, Springlake Amusement Park had just opened and WKY had just begun operating as the first radio station west of the Mississippi River.

The 1923 Annual began with pictures of Mayor O.A. Cargill, his staff and legal department. Then followed photos of Frazier as Chief, William E. Snelson as Night Chief and John Hubatka as Captain of Detectives. Hubatka was shown in a business suit but Frazier and Snelson were wearing identical uniforms. They wore high-collared, single-breasted uniform coats with three stars on either side of the collar, gold-trimmed shoulder epaulets reminiscent of those on Army officer's dress uniforms and round, dark blue uniform caps. The cap had a gold expansion band above the visor, three gold stars on each side and a gold wreath surrounding the word "Chief" on the front. The new badges are displayed on their left breasts.

After a page devoted to the Chief's staff, the four Captains (James Morris, J.B. Ryan, Jerry Smith and Jack Carey) are pictured in uniforms identical to the Chief's except they wore two stars and the word "Captain" embroidered on the cap. Ex-Chief Carl Glitsch is pictured in a business suit on the next page, probably because he wasn't around long enough to acquire a uniform.

The Annual contained no narrative, just photographs and ads. It pictured 141 commissioned officers and 10 civilians. The eight-man Motorcycle Squad is shown under the command of Lieutenant Grover Gaines, his insignia of rank being a single star. Among the squad members are Reese F. Galyon, H.V. Wilder, Ray S. Clark, Clarence Hurt and future Captain Tom Webb. The ten men of the Traffic Squad, wearing their distinctive white caps, were shown under the command of Lieutenant Sam Ginn. Plainclothesmen pictured include Ike Ashburn, Briggs Chumley, Frank Cissne, Luther Bishop, T.J. Tellegen and Ray "Red" Robinson. Half a century later, Robinson would operate a snack bar on the second floor of the old jail building. Another page is devoted to the mayors of the nine largest cities in the state.

Also pictured in the book are the four "colored officers", the first in the Department's history to have any permanence about them. Mayor Walton had hired two black officers over two years earlier, W.R. Parker and W.D. Fuller, but they had probably been token "show horses" in his battles with the Ku Klux Klan. Both of them had been dismissed soon after control of the Department had been taken from Walton and they had not been rehired. But now the Department had been truly integrated by Mayor Cargill and Chief Frazier. Even so, these men had an uphill battle for years to come. As an example, at the 1924 Democratic Convention, a proposal to denounce the Klan was defeated by one vote. Indicative of the times, the photos of the colored officers were on the last pages in the back of the book.

*1923 OCPD officers with new Ford Patrol Cars.*

*May 1924 raid on East 23rd Street. Left to right are Captain Jerry Smith, Detective Red Robinson, Chief Ray Frazier and Officer Tyler.*

Pictured were Charles Stewart, William Washington, James House and a wide-eyed rookie named Henry McMullen, whom we will hear more about later.

Mayor Cargill gave his officers an early Christmas present on December 22. He awarded the first medals under his new merit system. Jailer James Whitehill, an Englishman by birth, received a badge for distinguished service. The previous month, Whitehill had prevented a jailbreak by fighting off half a dozen members of the Al Spencer gang by vigorously swinging a set of the heavy jail keys. Traffic Officer R.Q. Melson was given a hand-made gold medal for courtesy. The officer had never received a complaint of discourtesy from his post at Main and Robinson and was commended for his consideration of the weak and aged.

The year ended with Mayor Cargill's war on vice back in full swing and, on New Year's Eve, the rich and poor went to jail together. The Department had 13 cars and they stayed busy all night long. More than a hundred people were arrested in raids on clubs and the next morning, several long black limousines arrived at the City Jail to pick up the embarrassed sons of some prominent local leaders.

On May 28, 1924, the city lost one of her original 89'ers albeit not one of the nobler ones. John Burgess died at the age of 60, having outlived most of the lawmen who had opposed him. Bill Tilghman, Frank Cochran, John Hubatka and Ike Ashburn comprised most of the small handful of officers who could still remember dealing with Burgess in his heyday. Burgess had brought a buckboard full of booze into Oklahoma City from Wichita, Kansas, that first 89'er Day. He had first set up shop across Front Street from the Santa Fe Depot between Kid Bannister's faro bank and Big Anne Wynn's tent of joy. He later opened his first saloon in the 100 block of Grand next to the Folly Theater (later the Sooner Theater). He progressed from that humble beginning to the infamous Two Johns Saloon next to City Hall on Battle Row. The Two Johns had been co-owned with his partner Charles Reynolds and had derived its name from the fact that the two men, both large men, were often mistaken for each other by their patrons. Burgess had retired in 1907, his business killed by Prohibition.

Prohibition was to cause the death of much more than John Burgess's business. On the evening of November 1, 1924, former Chief Bill Tilghman was killed while serving as Chief of Police in the oil-boom town of Cromwell, Oklahoma. Since his departure from the OCPD Chief's job 11 years earlier, Tilghman had unsuccessfully sought an appointment as U.S. Marshal for the Western District of Oklahoma, toured the country with his motion picture production "The Passing of the Oklahoma Outlaws" (which he had produced partially to rectify some of the falsehoods in Al Jennings' Hollywood ventures) and served as an Oklahoma State Senator. Tilghman had allowed former Dalton/Doolin gang member Roy "Arkansas Tom" Daugherty to play himself in the movie. Daugherty had spent 17 years of his 50-year sentence in prison for the Ingalls gunfight in which he had killed two and possibly three Deputy U.S. Marshals. Falling back into his bad habits after his movie debut, Daugherty had been killed in Joplin, Missouri, by police arresting him for bank robbery less than three months earlier.

For the past year, Tilghman had been a special investigator (i.e., travelling troubleshooter) for Governor Trapp. Tilghman had taken the post in Cromwell at the Governor's behest. It had the additional advantage of a salary of $500 a month. To place the economics in perspective, that was the starting salary of an OCPD patrolman 45 years later.

Shortly after 10 P.M. that night, a drunk got out of a touring car in front of Marie Murphy's dance hall in Cromwell and fired a gun into the street. Tilghman came out of the dance hall and began struggling with the drunk. Still robust for his 70 years, Tilghman was allegedly getting the better of the much younger man. Tilghman was holding off the man's gun hand with one hand and, according to witnesses, could have drawn his own gun and shot the man at any time. But this wasn't just any lawman. This lawman had faced the toughest characters the Dalton and Doolin gangs could produce, had killed more than a few of them when they forced the issue and arrested Bill Doolin without firing a shot in a similar struggle almost three decades earlier. The veteran lawman was evidently hesitant to use his gun on a drunk if it was avoidable. A bystander stepped forward and grabbed the drunk's gun. When Tilghman relaxed his grip on the man, he pulled another gun and shot Tilghman three times in the chest. Tilghman collapsed, dead within minutes, and the drunk fled.

OCPD Night [Assistant] Chief W.E. Snelson phoned Mrs. Tilghman at her Oklahoma

Detective Briggs Chumley.

City home to deliver the message of her husband's death. Snelson and Chief of Detectives Leo W. DeCordova drove to Cromwell to return Tilghman's body and begin an investigation. Ironically, when the suspect was apprehended, he was identified as a Federal Prohibition agent, Wiley Lynn, who was later acquitted after pleading he had fired in self defense. Defensive jurors later blamed the acquittal on the intransigence of a juror who was a part-Choctaw (as was Wiley Lynn) Baptist preacher. The verdict was decried statewide as a monumental travesty of justice. As he had once predicted, Tilghman died as many of the best lawmen of his era did, with his boots on.

Two days later on November 3, about 1:00 A.M., 45-year-old Detective Briggs Chumley and his partner Elmer Miller arrested a man at N.W. 4th and Olie. The man was a suspect in the robbery of a restaurant a few minutes earlier at 1101 West Main. The officers held their guns on the man while they searched him. After finding no weapon, the detectives holstered theirs. The suspect then drew a gun from inside his coveralls and shot both officers, killing Chumley and wounding Miller.

The first suspect located and jailed for the crime was Babe Welch, a much-sought fugitive that Chumley and other officers had been after for some time. Welch was soon cleared and Earl Newton was identified as the killer. Newton was later apprehended in Waco, Texas, extradited, convicted and sentenced to life imprisonment. If the Texas officers had known that Briggs Chumley was a former Texas Ranger, Newton might not have made it back at all.

On the afternoon of November 5, 1924, downtown Oklahoma City was the scene of two lawmen's funerals occurring only one hour and two blocks apart. At 1 P.M., Bill Tilghman's services were held at the First Presbyterian Church at 9th and North Robinson with 800 mourners in attendance. Tilghman's body had lain in state in the State Capitol Building's rotunda for the last two days. Only the third person to be accorded that honor, he was also the first private citizen and the first law enforcement officer to do so.

Former pioneer Deputy U.S. Marshal Ransom Payne wrote a letter of comfort to Tilghman's family expressing his grief. In it, he listed some of the prominent men who had assisted Tilghman in enforcing the law in early Oklahoma, most prominently John Hubatka, Frank Cochran, Charles Colcord, Sam Bartell and James Koonce. He noted that, now that Tilghman was gone, there were only three survivors of the original 22 Deputy Marshals first assigned to Oklahoma Territory; Ewers White of McCloud, Jim Koonce and Payne himself.

In another unique honor, two of Tilghman's pallbearers were Governor Trapp and former Governor Robertson. Honorary pallbearers included former Deputy U.S. Marshals Chris Madsen and Charles Colcord, OCPD Chief Ray Frazier and future Chief W.E. Snelson. Tilghman was buried in Chandler, Oklahoma, the county seat of Lincoln County where he had served as Sheriff twenty years before. In later years, his Chandler home was restored and entered on the Register of National Historic Places, Tilghman Park was dedicated on land he had once owned nearby and July 4th in Chandler became as much Bill Tilghman Day as it was Independence Day. Over six decades after his death, they were still writing ballads about him and his handcuffs and other memorabilia were prominent exhibits in the Lincoln County Museum of Pioneer History.

At 2 P.M., an hour after Tilghman's services, one block north and one block east, Briggs Chumley's services were being conducted at the Marshall and Harper Funeral Parlor at 1010 North Broadway. Chumley's widow and two children were surrounded by more than 1,000 mourners including Mayor Cargill. Several of the numerous floral arrangements were inscribed simply "From A Friend" and were assumed to be from various figures in the City's underworld, tributes to a man widely considered to be "a square officer". The Police Quartet (Bill Parrish, William Sheppard, Henry Propst and Roland Cargill, the Mayor's brother) sang Rock of Ages accompanied by the Firemen's Band. The majority of the uniformed force then followed the casket to Fairlawn Cemetery. Chumley's pallbearers were Officers W.A. Parker, John Hopkins, Joe Layton, G.B. Connally, Tom O'Neil and H.C. Taylor. Less than two years earlier, Chumley had been one of the pallbearers for Officer Jess Sosbee, the last officer to have been slain in the line of duty.

Frazier's administration lasted a little more than one more year. In 1924 he had 108 police employees, 70 less than two years earlier. The force had acquired 19 vehicles including 5 motorcycles and 13 cars but only one car was dedicated to patrolling.

On April 21, 1925, 50,000 people attended the 89'ers Day parade in downtown Oklahoma City. The city would be 36 years old the next day. The parade contained all the cowboys, indians and pageantry familiar to anyone who has ever attended one of these annual events. This one, however, had something that is denied to latter-day viewers.

One of the groups riding by consisted of a group of old men whose weather-beaten countenances bespoke a life spent outdoors and whose easy grace in the saddle told of years on horseback. They were all former U.S. Marshals

*Chief W.E. Snelson.*

*Some of the OCPD's motorized police force in the early 1920s.*

and their Deputies who had policed the Territory during those first, dangerous years. Leading that group was former Deputy U.S. Marshal Ransom Payne who, with Charles Colcord, had been the only law in Oklahoma City for the first seven months of 1890.

As Payne rode by the throngs of people, he led another horse beside his own. The horse's saddle was empty but carried a Winchester rifle, a pearl-handled Colt and a belt of ammunition. Mutely symbolic of a fallen warrior, they belonged to Bill Tilghman.

William E. Snelson succeeded Frazier for a year. Born on December 30, 1870, in Missouri, he left home when he was 20 to work in the mines in California. Coming to Oklahoma City in 1910, he spent short stints working in construction and real estate before joining the OCPD in 1911 at the age of 40.

Probably the most controversial case of Snelson's short tenure was the murder of State Crime Bureau Agent Luther Bishop. Although only 41 years old, Bishop had already carved out a legendary reputation in Oklahoma law enforcement. He had served as a Deputy Sheriff in Caddo and Oklahoma Counties, the jailer for Oklahoma County and the town marshal of Britton, a small suburb north of the city that was eventually annexed into it. He had also been on the OCPD before becoming an agent for the State Crime Bureau. Earlier in the year, he had been instrumental in solving the murders in the Osage Hills Reign of Terror in the northern part of the state. He had most recently been working in Sapulpa guarding members of the Kimes gang prior to their bank robbery trials.

Bishop returned from Sapulpa on the evening of Saturday, December 4, 1926, to his home at 1515 N.W. 28 in Oklahoma City. Shortly after 2 A.M. the following morning, his neighbors were awakened by a series of gunshots. As Bishop's son and neighbors ran upstairs to the second-story bedroom Bishop shared with his wife, the found him dead on the floor, shot seven times.

The evidence indicated that Bishop had been shot while he slept in his bed. Two of the shots were in his back, three hit him in the left arm, one in his right arm and one in his chest, above the left breast area. Four of the shots had pierced his lungs. Chief Snelson, who responded to the scene, later told reporters that he observed powder burns around the wounds in Bishop's back, indicating that the gun was very close to him when fired.

Bishop had a reputation as a very aggressive, effective, unintimidatable officer. He had made plenty of enemies and hard feelings during his law enforcement career. He always carried two .44 pistols and kept them within easy reach of his bed at night. The guns were missing from the bedroom. Although most of the slugs that killed him were badly damaged, at least two were confirmed to have been .44's. The initial reports called the killing a "skillfully planned execution" and theorized that the assassin had hidden in the house until everyone went to bed and then did his deed. The newspaper noted that two windows leading into the bedroom were open with the screens unlatched that night.

Governor Trapp immediately announced a $500 reward for the killer or killers, dead or alive. An anonymous donor offered another $500. Then the inconsistencies started showing up.

There were inconsistent statements from the neighbors about whether or not they had heard a car leaving the area with gears grinding right after they heard the shots. Some said they did, most said they didn't. Some said there had been domestic strife in the Bishop household of late and the Bishops had a quarrel earlier that night. The evidence indicated Bishop had been in bed when shot but had risen and staggered to the light switch before collapsing. Mortally injured and rapidly dying, would he have gone to the light switch first, bypassing the guns at his bedside? Or were the guns already gone?

Mrs. Bishop was arrested and jailed the next day. That day, 36 hours after the shooting, Bishop's two .44's were found under some clothes in one of the upstairs closets. One gun had all six chambers fired, the other had two chambers fired. J.W. Long, Chief of the OCPD bertillon department, was fired for insubordination by Chief Snelson, allegedly stemming from the fact that Long had been vehemently insistent that the house should have been searched immediately for Bishop's guns.

Mrs. Bishop was released the next day when a coroner's jury decreed that Luther Bishop had been feloniously murdered by a "person or persons unknown".

Luther Bishop was buried on December 9 in Fairlawn Cemetery, almost exactly four blocks directly east of his home, with Chief Snelson leading a 45-man contingent of OCPD officers at the services. The $1000 reward was never claimed and no one was ever prosecuted for Bishop's slaying.

Such was Luther Bishop's notoriety at the time of his death that his grave was left unmarked in Fairlawn Cemetery for concern that any headstone would be vandalized. Over half a century later, in 1990, the slain officer's son, Dr. Leo Bishop, and OSBI Agent Dee Cordry began a move to erect a monument at the gravesite. Cordry, an historian, was also President of an organization called Oklahombres, dedicated to the research and preservation of Oklahoma lawman and outlaw history. Donations were collected and, on May 16, 1991, Luther Bishop got his grave marker. Almost exactly four blocks directly east of the house where he was slain, the pink marble marker reads;

LUTHER BISHOP
1885 - 1926
Pioneer Oklahoma Peace Officer 1916-1926 Deputy U.S. Marshal and operative of the O.S.B.I. Known for his courage, bravery and detective skills. Bishop died at the hands of unknown persons. Dedicated by Oklahombres 1991

In the first week of February, 1927, the city adopted a city manager form of government to replace the commission form that had been in place for the last 16 years. The theory was that the city would be run by a man who would be non-partisan because he wasn't elected, he was appointed. The fallacy was that he was appointed by the City Council, who were elected and who had their individual political agendas. City Managers could also be un-appointed. The Oklahoma News made the cogent observation that the City Manager system had one thing in common with the commission system it replaced; it would be only as good or as bad as the people allowed it to become. They were to find that it didn't change much.

A few weeks after the appointment of the first City Manager, Edmond M. Fry, representatives of the influential Committee of 100 complained to him that a wild drinking and gambling joint was running wide open on the northside. It was being operated by a policeman's brother and was apparently immune to enforcement efforts. The Mayor and City Manager checked it out for themselves and reported back to the influential businessmen.

The story was true. They had copied down the license numbers of the expensive automobiles in the parking lot and checked the registrations. When they provided the list to the Committee, it read like a who's who of the city's social, political and business elite. End of complaint.

*Chief Martin C. Binion.*

In April of 1927, Snelson was replaced by M.C. Binion on his third trip to occupy the Chief's Office. The highlights of 1927 were a visit to the Oklahoma State Fair by Colonel Charles Lindbergh and the advent of the council-city manager form of government.

Officer Jack Vaughn started his 34-year police career in 1928. At a Retired Officer's Association meeting almost half a century later, he would reminisce that the OCPD scout car "fleet" then consisted of four Model-T Fords with curtained windows. He also remembered that he was hired with nine other young men and their training consisted of a very short speech from a Captain—"I hope to hell you can handle yourselves". End of training.

THE NEAREST THING TO IT

An irate citizen rushed in the police headquarters recently to file a complaint against a fellow citizen. The desk sergeant asked him to state his case. The irate citizen explained that he was innocently driving west on Main Street when a man suddenly backed his car out into the street, smashed into the irate citizen's car and damaged a fender. "When I asked him to have the damage to my car repaired he told me to go to hell. I hurried to police headquarters at once."

The OCPD celebrated 1928 with a new Chief and a bigger, better Police Annual. At 100 pages, it was over twice the size of the 1923 Annual and had only 14 pages devoted to advertising. It states that the City covers 19 square miles, has a population "close to 175,000" and employed 571 persons who were paid an average of $1,780 a year.

The Annual went on to laud the City as a major center of manufacturing, marketing, distribution, education and oil development. Oil had been discovered in the Oklahoma City oil field and the City area was producing 71 percent of the oil in Oklahoma which in turn produced 29 percent of all the oil in America. Construction had begun on the 33-story Biltmore Hotel in the 200 block of West Grand and the first all-talking picture had opened at the Criterion Theater.

The Annual bid a fond farewell to Chief M.C. Binion who retired on May 15, 1928, to run for Oklahoma County Sheriff. Details were given of his peripatetic 28-year career in law enforcement. Prophetically, it included a paragraph telling of his pride in the fact that his long career had included only one instance in which he had been forced to use his gun, wounding the suspect in the heel. Ironically, two of his fellow Democrats opposing him for the Sheriff's office were also former OCPD officers. Former Chief Charles Post, now a Federal Narcotics Agent and Sam Bartell, having spent 39 of his 63 years as a federal, county and local law enforcement officer in Oklahoma County, were both candidates.

A welcome was extended to the new Chief, Benjamin B. Moore. Born on August 6, 1876, in Cloud County, Kansas, he had been a farmer near Guthrie for his first 34 years. He became an Oklahoma County Deputy Sheriff in 1910 and served eight years in that position until becoming the Federal Prohibition Agent in charge of Oklahoma. In 1920 he had become a Special Agent for the MK&T Railroad until appointed Assistant Chief of the OCPD in 1927. Thus his history in law enforcement was long but short with OCPD.

Whoever prepared the new Chief's biography for the Annual may have been a little too flattering in his praises. It stated that Moore had "participated in the arrest and conviction of many noted Oklahoma outlaws including the Dalton gang, the Littrell gang, Doolin gang, Henry Starr, Al Spencer and Ray Terrell gangs". Quite a record especially considering that, according to the previous statements in the biography, Moore was a 16-year-old high school student in Guthrie when the Dalton gang was mostly wiped out in Coffeyville, Kansas, in 1892. Even though the last vestige of the Doolin gang technically lasted until Arkansas Tom Daugherty was killed in Missouri in 1924, the rest of the gang ceased to exist more than a decade before Moore entered law enforcement in 1910.

The new Chief, as Chiefs are wont to do, had already made a number of changes and planned more. Ten veteran officers had been retired to the reserve list at half pay and he had hired 21 new men to bring Department strength up to 131. Already in place was a "show-up" system where witnesses could view suspects unobserved, a pistol range and a three-way mirror in the officer's restroom. The last two were no doubt appreciated by a young Detective named Bryce who spent hours in front of the mirror practicing his fast draw. That probably was a source of amusement for some of the older officers. That amusement would soon turn into awe.

The Chief would require every officer to engage in pistol practice twice a week and inspect his uniform in the mirror before going on duty. There would be plenty of use for the mirror since he intended the entire force to wear uniforms except Detectives. Former Chief Rolley Organ was made the "Humane Society" officer in charge of the dog pound. Captains were to be in charge of shifts and their offices were moved and remodeled along with the Sergeant's office. Future plans included putting two officers at each fire station, making them "sub-police stations", to shorten response times on calls. Also planned was the future creation of a "radio bureau", installation of more traffic signals and moving the existing signals out of the center of the intersections and onto the sidewalks to improve their visibility for pedestrians.

The OCPD of 1928 had 115 officers which included 50 patrolmen, 12 detectives and 22 traffic officers, 6 of them on motorcycles. The jail had 32 double-deck cells to accommodate 128 prisoners. There were a few lines bragging about the new electric traffic signals. But it also complained that "the City has outgrown its Police Department" and they were 60 officers short of achieving the general standard of one officer for every 1,000 citizens. The Annual bragged on the night shift of officers, saying it was "the hardest shift". The night shift was from 2:30 P.M. until 10:30 P.M. and was manned by one Captain, one Sergeant, 2 motorcycle officers (one of them H.V. Wilder), 15 Patrolmen, 6 Detectives and a jailer.

The Bureau of Criminal Identification was subdivided into criminal records, fingerprints and photography. The Annual noted that the Department had 44,664 criminal records and more than 13,000 sets of fingerprints on file. Police Court cases had increased in the past year from 11,831 to 18,919 and fines had gone up from $28,598 to $85,965. Newly appointed Assistant Chief Charles Becker was to continue to head the Stolen Goods Department as he had for the past six years, temporarily occupying both offices. Stolen Goods had recovered over $566,000 worth of property during that time. Clarence Hurt provided statistics from the Stolen Car Department for the last year, stating that of the 1,069 car stolen during that period, 921 had been recovered. The value of recoveries was $151,650, giving an average value of less than $165 per car. They had also arrested 151 car thieves.

Another paragraph bears quoting. It stated that;

"The Auxiliary Branch of the Police Department, better known as the Detective Division, is made up of men who have had years of experience in police work and the Division is called upon to ferret out cases where exceptional intelligence is required". No response from Patrol or Traffic officers is included but one can easily imagine.

The Department had just bought two steel vests as an experiment after the Chicago salesman walked into former Chief Binion's office, borrowed the Chief's gun and shot himself in the chest without injury. This demonstration was later repeated in the City Manager's Office.

The photograph of veteran Ike Ashburn in the 1928 annual was to be his last. Ashburn died on July 20 at 51 years of age. He died from injuries he received after having been struck by a car more than two weeks before at Broadway and Grand, the same intersection where Chief Milton Jones had died 33 years earlier. Ashburn had been going back to the Police Station to go off duty. The motorist, E.J. Holland, was initially arrested for reckless driving and later charged with manslaughter.

*Officer Isaac Daniel "Ike" Ashburn.*

More than three decades had passed since Ike Ashburn had been involved in the wild shootout in Traylor's Saloon on Alabaster Row in which half a dozen men were killed and more than two decades since another officer tried to shoot him in the furor surrounding the 1907 elections. After all he had survived, he was literally run over by progress. The Police Benefit Fund paid $2,000 to his widow. His death occurred too late for it to be mentioned in the annual. His funeral procession to Fairlawn Cemetery included 71 policemen.

Shown with the Detectives in the annual are the seemingly-eternal John Hubatka, nearing his fortieth year with the OCPD, and John Cassidy, Bill Tilghman's "best plainclothesman" 17 years before. Also shown are the progenitors of two multi-generation OCPD families. Plainclothes man Lee Mullinex's son Jack would become Chief of Detectives in the 1960's. Jack Mullinex's son Eric and daughter-in-law Pat would become officers in the 1970's. Desk Sergeant H.V. Wilder's son, Robert V. Wilder, would become Chief of Police 57 years later.

The Annual also spoke of a "new experiment" inaugurated on July 9, 1928, by City Manager E.M. Fry. The new experiment was dubbed Police School. Inspector, later Captain, T.J. "Jack" Tellegen was in charge. Six classes were held each week, two for each shift. The course of study began with a police manual and included a curriculum covering the state penal code, city ordinances, courtesy and detecting crime and criminals. The Police School was discontinued during the three summer months and recruit training school was conducted. Classes for the shifts resumed on October 1st.

Another experiment they tried was asking the City Manager to approve one day off a week or, failing that, two days a month as regular days off for officers. The City Manager declined. Law enforcement was a full time job every day. This dream would not be realized until World War II.

Instead of a day off, Fry gave them a new training tool....a punching bag filled with 150 pounds of sand. Fry told the press that he wanted the officers working out on the bag because they had been handling so few bad guys in the past few months that "he was afraid the copper's punches would become soft".

A former officer who was profiled in the 1928 Annual was Raymond "Red" Robinson. Born in Enid in 1895, Robinson had joined the Department in 1923. His first assignment was as a member of the "Raiding Squad" led by Claude Tyler and Luther Bishop. Together they had captured the largest still located in Oklahoma County to that time, confiscating 105 gallons of mash from the still on West Main Street. Robinson had also participated in the arrest of Earl Thayer, a well-known bank robber who was a member of the Al Spencer gang and an associate of Frank Nash, later to gain more notoriety from his death in Kansas City than in his life. Robinson said there wasn't much of a thrill in the arrest since Thayer just surrendered without protest. Following his tour with the Raiding Squad, due to his three years of education at Oklahoma A&M College (later Oklahoma State University), Robinson was assigned as the Secretary to Chief Ray Frazier and then Chief Snelson. Leaving the Department in 1926, Robinson took over the Sanitary Buffet at 107 West Grand. Almost half a century later, Robinson, then in his late seventies, was running a snack bar on the second floor of the old Jail Building, the walls covered with old historical photos of the early days of the Department.

On the afternoon of November 7, 1928, John Robinson was shopping for transportation. In town from Chicago, Robinson and a friend from New Orleans, Johnny Walker, had no intention of paying for it, however. They were shopping for a car to steal. About 3:30 they found one parked at 1st and North Walker. Walker acted as lookout while Robinson got in the car and began manipulating the wires to the ignition. But Walker evidently wasn't doing his job well. Robinson was startled when he looked up and there was a young man standing next to the car looking down at him. A fancy dresser, a little hard around the eyes maybe but still just a kid.

Robinson was partly right. Jelly Bryce was a fancy dresser and he was still a month away from his 22nd birthday but he wasn't a kid. As he explained to Mr. Robinson, he was a police officer who was arresting him for trying to steal the car. Bryce and his partner, B.D. "Chick" Faris, had been following the suspicious pair for several hours. Then Robinson made his second, and worst, misjudgment of the day. He reached for the gun he had concealed on him.

Before Robinson got his gun into action, Bryce put a bullet through his arm. Faris came hauling Johnny Walker up and they arranged for Robinson to be taken to Oklahoma City General Hospital. A little over a week later, the two very active detectives made the front pages again when they arrested a man who tried to sell Bryce a stolen car for $100.

The year ended on a note of optimism. A New York City banker addressing the Chamber of Commerce told them that due to the recent oil boom, the city should be prepared for a population of 300,000 by 1935 and over 400,000 by 1940. Unfortunately, the optimism was premature.

Contrary to the City Manager's concerns, the officers didn't have much time to become soft and sometimes they didn't have time to punch. At 7 P.M. on the evening of April 28, 1929, a call came in for help, saying there was "a wild Negro running amuck" at 12 West Pottawatomie (later Southwest 4th Street). Because of the hysteria of the caller, Captain Jerry Smith decided to send three officers instead of the usual pair. Motorcycle Officers Jake O. Robertson and Joe Jerkins headed for the call to be met there by plainclothesman Sam Ginn.

Lester Duncan was definitely running amuck, having terrorized the entire block. As the officers approached him to arrest him for drunk and disorderly conduct, he pulled a gun and started blazing away. The three officers responded in kind.

Someone once described police work as countless hours of boredom punctuated by seconds of stark terror. It is a very apt description of the job, now as then. In a few of those slow motion seconds on Pottawatomie, 25 shots were fired. One of them hit Officer Jake Robertson in the neck and eight of them hit Lester Duncan. The gunfight raged at such close quarters that Robertson's uniform coat caught on fire from the muzzle flashes and Joe Jerkins had powder burns on one cheek. Robertson recovered from his wounds, Lester Duncan didn't.

Chief Moore was also under fire but in a different way. The county attorney had been critical of the Police Department, saying the city was "wide open". Rumors of payoffs and protection abounded in the press. On April 26, the City Council interviewed the county attorney and the federal prohibition agent in charge of Oklahoma. The county attorney charged the Police Department with "indifference" in vice enforcement and said his "wide open city" statements meant the city was overrun with slot machines and punchboards. Neither witness had any information on payoffs or protection involving the police.

The investigation closed with no conclusive results but Moore was not off the hook. Rumors persisted that he was being ushered out to be replaced by Assistant Chief Charles Becker. The Women's Christian Temperance Union initially objected to Becker's appointment because he had been a salesman for a distillery. When it was determined that Becker's time as a whiskey salesman had been before Prohibition became the law of the land, they withdrew their objections.

The year 1929 brought another Annual, another Chief and another badge. Chief Moore resigned in May, saying that after "going fishing for a few days", he intended to return to his old job as a special officer for the railroad. After exactly one year as Assistant Chief, Charles A. Becker was appointed Chief on May 15, 1929. Born in Chicago on January 24, 1878, he had been a traveling salesman between Chicago and San Francisco until he moved to the city in 1898. He continued his sales career and was manager of the Bristol Hotel for four years before joining the OCPD on July 15, 1921, as a clerk in the Stolen Goods Bureau. He became head of that Bureau the following year and held that position until becoming Assistant Chief in 1928.

*Chief Charles Becker.*

When Becker became Chief, Clarence O. Hurt, Superintendent of the Auto Theft Bureau, was appointed Assistant Chief (or Night Chief) to succeed him. Hurt began his OCPD career on September 25, 1919, as a 24-year-old motorcycle officer after two years in the World War I Army. After three months on motorcycles, he began working nights in a scout car for the next 3 1/2 years. In April of 1923, Hurt began a four-year tour as a special investigator working

*1929 OCPD Traffic Officers-Centered in the front row is Frank Cissne.*

*1929 OCPD uniformed officers and administration in front of the Maiden Lane station.*

*1929 OCPD Detective Division. Left to right: (Seated) Ed Veazey, Joe Jerkins, John Hubatka, Emmett Drane, John Cassidy, Harry Jones. (Standing, first row) Dick Parker, W.V. Brown, Ed Snelson, Joe Layton, Walt Acord, John Ryan, N.V. McCollum. (Top row) Dick Strain, Reese Galyon, Grover Gaines, Chick Faris, Earl Karr, Charles York and Al Large.*

*OCPD Badge 1929-1990.*

out of the office of Chiefs Frazier and Snelson. During this period, he gained his first experience working under federal jurisdiction while working on a special assignment out of the U.S. Marshal's office on the Osage Hills murders in northeastern Oklahoma. In 1927 he became a plainclothesman in the Auto Theft Bureau and the next year was made Superintendent of the Bureau. When Becker appointed him Assistant Chief, it was with the understanding that he would also continue his duties as head of the Auto Theft Bureau.

Becker was described as consistently cheerful, courteous and good-natured. But several years before, a photo of him and a sample of his handwriting had been submitted to a handwriting expert from the Chicago Tribune. A character analysis appeared in the October 12, 1924, edition. The analyst stated that this was a man "of the strongest will whose thoughts are no sooner formed than he is ready to turn them into actions". Becker was also described as "independent, brusque and exhibiting shrewdness, excessive tenacity and stubbornness". If one accepts this analysis as accurate, these qualities no doubt contributed to his rapid rise in the Department.

Becker was generally conceded to be a far-sighted man ahead of his time. He attempted to reduce response times by introducing radios and increase anti-crime patrolling, innovations that were not realized until the next administration.

The 1929 Annual had 50 pages, 30 of which were wholly or partially devoted to advertisements. While it makes no mention of Department strength, it contains pictures of 124 commissioned officers, some repeated in several areas, and three jail matrons. These pictures indicate a complement of 45 patrolmen, 33 plainclothes men, 21 traffic officers and 11 motorcycle officers.

Becker evidently made few changes in personnel but moved many officers to positions for which he considered them more suited. The few changes he made, he made decisively and stood by them. On July 16, 1929, he demoted Captain Jerry Smith down to Sergeant for "incompetence" and promoted Tim J."Jack" Tellegen to Captain. Tellegen, a Marine veteran of World War I, would later receive a law degree from Oklahoma University and become an Assistant Oklahoma County Attorney in 1944. When taken to task before the City Council for this action, Becker stood firm, offering to give both men a test for the duties of a Captain and let the Council compare their scores. The challenge was not taken and the decision stood.

On August 7, Jerry Smith applied for and received a six month leave of absence which noted that he would return at "an undetermined rank". Evidently recognizing the doctrine of changing fortunes at work, Smith did not return.

Becker also instituted improvements in the records system including new Captain's work sheets, officer's call report blanks and individual arrest cards. These were evidently not just cosmetic changes because he used them to keep closer track of his men's activities. He would later write letters to those officers who had not made an arrest in the previous month, chastising them by saying " It is inconceivable that any officer of this Department can walk his beat for a month without being able to make any arrests".

The new badge that was adopted was a heart-shaped shield topped by an eagle with spread wings. The "Oklahoma City Police" was stamped into scrolls above and below the stamped number in the center of the badge. The fourth badge change of the decade, this one would last for the next six decades.

There were three raiding squads of two detectives each that specialized in liquor, narcotics and rooming houses. Vice, traffic and property crimes were the obvious priorities since it stated that the city was now "patrolled by 8 scout cars with 2 men in each car". As a sign of the times, each car was equipped with a sawed-off repeating shotgun. Two new scout car zones were added extending down to the Canadian River. Captain Tom Webb was in charge of 21 Traffic and 11 Motorcycle officers. Of the 23,661 arrests that year, 8,848 were motorists.

The Bureau of Criminal Identification had photographed and fingerprinted 1,223 persons during the last year. They had also added two special investigators, W.V. Brown and former Chief W.E. Snelson, covering 16 hours a day. Former rank having its privileges, Snelson had the day shift from 6:30 A.M. until 2:30 P.M. while Brown had to work until 10:30 P.M.

Another milestone was even farther in the future than the hope for a day off. The 1929 Women's Civic Council asked city officials to hire female police officers to "supervise dance halls, parks and motion picture houses...where young people meet". They felt that by adopting this measure "the lives of many girls would be salvaged". The city's response was not favorable, the general consensus being that if they recruited females as police officers, the applicants would either be "coarse, mannish types" or "snoopers". When the women followed up on their suggestion with the idea that the women should earn the same pay as the men, that did it. The idea was dead for the next quarter of a century. Women in the Police Department would continue to be jail matrons and receptionists or, eventually, secretaries, stenographers, report clerks and radio dispatchers as they gradually displaced men from those jobs.

The 1929 Annual also applauded the Auto Theft Bureau for having recovered a record 81.26 percent of the 961 cars that had been stolen that fiscal year. Sergeant G.A. Burnhame was in charge of the office as a reward for his record. Operating without a partner, Burnhame had recovered 41 stolen cars in one month including seven in one night.

Several of the car theft rings successfully broken up by the Auto Theft Bureau that year were detailed. The only team mentioned twice for their efforts were B.D. "Chick" Faris and his partner, identified as "J.A. Bryce". D.A. "Jelly" Bryce had been hired too late to be pictured in the 1928 Annual but he was identified correctly under his picture in the 1929 version. The two car theft rings Faris and Bryce were credited with breaking up that year were one led by John Hughes while the other was termed "the most desperate auto thieves apprehended by Oklahoma City police during the last year".

The latter group consisted of M.M. "Roy" Gage, H.G. "Jack" Vaughn and Earl Johnston. Faris and Bryce had arrested the 3 men after they got in a stolen car at 5th and North Hudson that the detectives had staked out. During the arrests on March 10, Faris and Bryce had removed a gun from Gage and then began transporting them to jail. Faris was sitting in the back seat of the stolen car with Johnston, Gage was driving and Vaughn was on the passenger's side of the front seat. Bryce was following them in the police car. While passing by the Liberty Theater (later the Harber Theater) on Robinson, Gage told Vaughn to grab the steering wheel and, when he did, Gage lurched over the seat and attacked Faris, trying to get his gun. Gage was shot and killed by Faris and Jack Vaughn was shot by Bryce for "offering resistance" when he refused to stop the car, ending the incident in front of the Orpheum Theater (later the Warner Theater) on Grand. Earl Johnston, evidently thinking better of it, kept his own counsel and was not injured during the melee.

Also mentioned was the annual Police Benefit Ball. It was held to raise money for the Police Benefit Fund. The primary expenditure of this fund was $6,000 a year to pay the premiums on a $2,000 life insurance policy for each police employee. The fund had been in effect for five years and, during that time, they had paid the benefits out to the survivors of 15 officers.

Another new feature was the establishment of four "sub-stations". Still without radios, this was a measure intended to reduce police response times to the "distant" quadrants of the city. They were to consist of two officers and a scout car stationed at four Fire Stations around the City. These were at N.W. 16th and Pennsylvania for the west area, N.W. 36th and Classen for the north area, N.E. 9th and Stonewall for the east area and S.W. 25th and Harvey for the south area. These units were dispatched by telephone from the Captain's desk at the central station. This was anticipated to be a considerable improvement over the previous system which had the cars reporting in to the station every five minutes, north side cars reporting on the even numbered minutes and south side cars reporting on the odd numbered ones.

One such emergency call came in on July 26, 1929. The Metropolitan Theater, on the southeast corner of Grand and Walker, was the only non-union theater in town. It had received threats that it would be blown up if they didn't unionize. The famous actor Lon Chaney had been a stage hand there in 1909. Shortly after midnight on that date, dynamite blew a four-foot hole in the rear wall and damaged the rest of the building. It was later condemned and the Mummers Theater was built there.

On July 30, 1929, the Oklahoma City Times carried the obituary of former Chief Edward F. "Frank" Cochran. Although he is listed as "Frank E. Cochran", it is undoubtedly the same man. Having come to Oklahoma in 1880 at the age of 20, he served 26 years as a Deputy under six U.S. Marshals. The article sated that he had been 69 years old when he died on the previous day at 222 1/2 West California. His career choice had cost him six gunshot wounds and the loss of a leg. He had been a Deputy U.S. Marshal under Judge Isaac Parker and was said to have been "well acquainted" with Belle Starr, Cherokee Bill, the Daltons, Doolins and others. He served two terms as Chief of the OCPD, was an Oklahoma County Deputy Sheriff between terms and then returned to the Marshal's service. In January of 1901 he had been seriously wounded in a famous gunfight with bank robbers in Bristow, Oklahoma. Cochran's left leg was amputated as a result of his wounds and he had been in declining health from them until his death. But he never strayed very far or very long from the vicinity of the only craft he knew. He had served as desk sergeant with the OCPD under his brother Ralph, Chief of Police in Bristow in 1904, Federal jailer in Muskogee and night jailer with the OCPD in the 1920's. He was a night watchman at the public market on California Avenue at the time of his death.

Two days later, Chief Becker added 21 men to the force, among them Elmer Sartor, to bring strength up to 154 men. Charles C. York was welcomed back from a ten month leave of absence and assigned to the Stolen Motor Car Department.

There is an old adage about "cop's kids and preacher's kids" having a tendency to go bad. And sometimes they do. I don't know if they're more prone to it than, say, bricklayer's kids or accountant's kids or if it's just scrutinized or publicized more. Presumably, a psychologist would say it is a rebellion against the more repressed behavior, stricter discipline and higher expectations placed upon them because of their parent's profession. While there is a strong tendency for the children of people in those professions to follow in their footsteps, there seems to be an almost equally strong tendency for them to choose a totally opposite lifestyle.

That adage was publicly exhibited three months before the end of the decade when two sons of one of Oklahoma's most respected law enforcement officers became involved in a violent robbery. On October 6, the attempted robbery of a gambling game near Minco, Oklahoma, erupted into a gunbattle that saw one man killed and four more wounded. Two of the suspects were rapidly identified as Richard and Woodie Tilghman, sons of the martyred Bill Tilghman. Both were quickly arrested at their widowed mother's home at 924 West 12th in Oklahoma City. Sixteen-year-old Woodie was unscathed but 21-year-old Richard had received serious gunshot wounds in his liver and kidneys. Taken to a local hospital for emergency treatment, Richard died on October 28. He was buried in Chandler, next to his famous but more law-abiding father.

As the Roaring Twenties closed, the OCPD finally emerged from a long period of intense political turmoil. In the past decade, a dozen men had occupied the Chief's Office and the state had impeached two successive Governors. But now Chiefs would begin to serve longer terms, the Department would be less subject to political whims and it came just in time. The OCPD was about to enter the most destructive decade of its' short existence.

One of the causes of the tumult that made The Roaring Twenties roar was gunfire. The number of law enforcement officers killed in the line of duty during the decade had almost doubled from the previous decade and had quadrupled since the turn of the century. An average of 164 officers died doing their jobs every year. It would get worse.

# V — DUST, DEPRESSION AND GANGSTERS 1930-1939

The 1930 Census showed a city population of 185,383, forty-third in the nation. A decade before it had been eightieth. The economy was reaching a point of crisis. After World War I, farm prices had collapsed. Unemployment went up, huge oil discoveries drove the price of oil down and the Sooner economy was in dire straits even before the Dust Bowl struck.

Beginning in 1930, a severe drought forced many farmers, unable to pay their mortgages, to uproot and head west in search of opportunity. "Okies" became a generic term for dispossessed migrators. Before they migrated west, however, they migrated to the urban areas of the state, mostly to the largest one, Oklahoma City. Unemployment was high as industrial plants curtailed their operations. With the coming of Roosevelt's New Deal in 1932, Public Works jobs became more attractive and the Department experienced a rapid rise in job applications. As many as 300 men at a time signed up to take the City exam for a position on a police department consisting of only slightly more than 200 officers.

Working conditions for officers were austere throughout the Depression. Patrolmen drove their rounds in cars with no climate controls. The new decade began with the coldest month in the City's history. The thermometers dipped nine degrees below zero on several days and a week passed without the temperature rising out of the teens. In the town of Watts, in the eastern part of the state near the Arkansas border, they recorded the coldest temperature in state history, 27 degrees below zero. During this and other winters of that decade, several of them with record-setting lows, officers often heated bricks on potbellied stoves, wrapped them in blankets and placed them on the floorboards of their scout cars next to their feet. Wool uniforms provided some relief from the cold but became miserable during the scorching Oklahoma summers which also set records. Still, at $100 a month, the Police Department was one of the more attractive employers in town. But they earned it. Nine of them would die earning it in the coming decade.

The earliest retrievable personnel files of OCPD personnel date from the early 1930s. Most of the files were obviously created during this period with previous information backdated in them. A few date back into the late 1920s but specific dates in the files (dates of hiring, promotion, transfer, etc.) that would indicate accurate information rarely extend back beyond the time of World War I. Nevertheless, the files are revealing about certain practices of the times.

First, it was very easy for an officer to get suspended from duty. It appears that practically the first response to virtually any complaint lodged by a citizen against an officer was the suspension of the officer. Most were reinstated within a week but many officer's files from that time have at least one such instance of suspension. Some of the letters of reinstatement specifically note that the complaint for which the officer was suspended was found to be unjustified. The letters of suspension state nothing about "with" or "without" pay and the reinstatements state nothing about retroactive pay.

Second, officers were held to a very high standard in their financial dealings. As late as the early 1970s, newly hired officers were still advised by their superiors that the quickest way to lose their jobs was "booze, broads and bad debts". That advice was not just a catchy alliteration, it was backed up with action. More than one officer was forced to resign for having a few checks for insufficient funds brought to the attention of their commanders.

The practice had deep roots. The files of the early 1930s show letters of complaint to the Chief from local merchants stating that individual officers had unpaid debts, sometimes of less than five dollars. Those letters are invariably followed by a letter from the Chief to the officer directing the prompt arrangement for payment of the debt. The consequences of noncompliance are usually left unstated but indisputably implied. In those days of the Depression, as with the suspensions, it was a rare personnel file that didn't contain at least one of those letters.

Another fairly common thread was breaks in service. It was a very rare individual that got hired and spent the next 20 years or more with the OCPD without at least one break in service. Some had three or four such breaks and it didn't reflect upon the quality or effectiveness of the officer. Sometimes he just got caught up in the fluctuating retirement plans of the day. An excellent example was Lee Mullinex.

Originally hired on April 15, 1915, Mullinex served as a motorcycle patrolman and Superintendent of the Bertillon Bureau until leaving service on January 1, 1923. He was rehired exactly five years later on the first day of 1928 and served for five months as a Detective before leaving again. He was back again on April 21, 1930, and served until he retired on April 21, 1941, at the age of 54.

Now came into play an old Oklahoma tradition known as "getting caught in the Wewoka switch", i.e. the rules sometimes change on very short notice and not to your advantage. On August 1, 1942, the City Council passed a new Pension Plan for the OCPD. The new plan stated that for officers to be eligible for retirement benefits, they must have served over 20 years and reached the age of 60 or have become totally disabled in the line of duty. Because of breaks in service, over a 26-year period Mullinex had only accumulated 19 years, 5 months and 5 days of active service at the time of his retirement. He was also under the mandatory age of 60. Thus, on August 1, 1942, Lee Mullinex reported back to active duty. He retired again on May 16, 1946, 3 days after his 60th birthday, having amassed 23 years, 9 months and 20 days of active service in a 31-year period.

The once-automatic cycle of Chiefs coming and going with each new City administration was broken. A new Mayor no longer meant a new Chief. Chief Becker saw the new decade in. Although crime was rising, as it always did in times of economic crisis, the full effects of the 1929 stock market crash were yet to be felt. In the end, the economic conditions helped spawn a national crime wave of epidemic proportions. People had believed that the 1920s was a violent decade and they were right. But they weren't prepared for the 1930s. During the first year of the new decade, 215 law enforcement officers were killed in the line of duty, the first time the figure had exceeded 200.

The decade also saw the development of the phenomenon of a series of media-created reputations for gangsters that made some of the old dime novels seem well researched. In spite of the toll paid by law enforcement, the crime wave saw some felons elevated to near folk-hero status and Oklahoma saw the worst of them.

John Dillinger was arrested once in Oklahoma City and later escaped to continue his depredations. Charles Arthur "Pretty Boy" Floyd was an Oklahoma native and learned how to rob banks here. George "Machine Gun" Kelly, Frank Nash, Bonnie Parker, Clyde and Buck Barrow, Wilbur Underhill, Vern Miller and "Ma" Barker's lawless brood were all on familiar ground in Oklahoma.

*Officer Jack D. Gates.*

Some of the less well known homegrown ones were bad enough. Two armed robbers held up the Clarence Saunders store at 1412 N. Robinson just before 9 P.M. on March 22, 1930. One of the men remained on guard outside the front door while the other one went in and confronted the manager with a .32 automatic. About 50 customers were in the store at the time. Also in the store was OCPD Officer John D. "Jack" Gates. Hired only 22 days earlier, Gates had been assigned to the store to "provide security". At that moment, Officer Gates stepped out from behind the front door and the gunman emptied his gun at him, striking the officer three times.

As the gunman ran out of the store carrying the moneybag, the gunshots that wounded Gates had attracted the attention of Officer John T. Anderson who was at the Piggly Wiggly store two doors to the south. Anderson exchanged shots with both men as they fled behind the residences on 14th Street.

Gates was taken to the Oklahoma Polyclinic Hospital. The nature of his wounds explained why he didn't return fire. One bullet entered his right arm below the shoulder, one shattered a bone in his left forearm and the third entered just over his heart, crushing a comb and fountain pen in his breast pocket. The 27-year-old officer died late the next day.

A state-wide alert was broadcast, 74 arrests were made and 27 of them were held for investigation. A few days later, H.D. Bradberry and Charlie Points were arrested in Duncan and returned to the City. Both were later sentenced to life terms.

Jack Gates' body was taken to his hometown of Fort Cobb, Oklahoma, accompanied by his older brother Douglas. The services were attended by Chief Becker, Assistant Chief Clarence Hurt (who was Gates' brother-in-law, having married his sister) and a contingent of 30 OCPD officers including pallbearers O.L. Ragland, F.P. Hill, R.S. Worthy, E.L. Drane, Jake Robertson and George Baker. On April 1, ten days after his brother's death, 29-year-old Douglas W. Gates quit his job as a checking clerk for the Rock Island Railway and joined the OCPD. He was destined to follow in his brother's footsteps in more ways than one.

Four days after Officer Gates' death, the oil market was glutted even more by a spectacular gusher in southeast Oklahoma City. The well was to gain national fame as the Wild Mary Sudik. Spewing oil and natural gas hundreds of feet in the air, the Oklahoma prairie winds spread a film of oil over a 20-mile area from Nicoma Park to Norman. Before it was capped eleven days later, nearly a quarter of a million barrels of oil settled on Oklahoma City and the surrounding area.

The Spring elections of 1931 brought another flurry of sparks to City Hall. Most of the sparks centered around the newly elected councilman from Ward Two, J.E. Taylor. Taylor was a contentious, unabashedly partisan, blatantly self-serving individual, perfectly suited to Oklahoma City politics. He would provide the Council and citizens with more entertainment or fireworks, depending upon your point of view, since the early days of the first provisional City Council.

Taylor immediately went to war with Ward One Councilman John Frank Martin. Martin nominated John McClelland for City Manager and Taylor supported Louis Abney. In a 5-4 decision, Abney won. Martin called Taylor "Oklahoma City's Judas" and Taylor went after him. Unlike the Jack Love-Abe Couch show of 1890, Taylor was escorted from the Council chambers before he could extract any pieces of silver or anything else from Martin's hide.

*Chief John Watt.*

On April 20, 1931, Abney was sworn in as City Manager. He resigned two days later and Councilman Martin's former candidate, John McClelland, was elected to the post. Chief of Police Becker retired and McClelland immediately appointed John Watt to take his place. Watt had no previous law enforcement experience and was appointed to the position directly from being a branch manager for the Miller Rubber Company. Born on August 27, 1889, Watt was a close personal friend and previous associate of the City Manager, a man McClelland said he could trust. One of Watt's first moves was to evict Orban Patterson's special interest office from the police station.

One of the first problems Watt had to confront was the budget. In mid-June, two weeks before the end of the City's fiscal year, the Police budget ran dry and Watt had to dismiss 25 men to make ends meet. Ten of the men were rookies who had been hired the previous February to combat rising crime rates but 15 were veterans. Most prominent among the veteran officers dismissed was T.J. "Jack" Tellegen. Promoted to Captain by Chief Becker, Tellegen had been made a desk sergeant when Watt first took over. Other familiar names among the unemployed veterans were two Detectives who had recently been placed in scout cars to cut costs, D.A. Bryce and Lee Mullinex. Also dismissed were G.A. Burnhame, Ray Clark, Douglas Gates and William Washington, one of the original black officers. Watt said that he expected the move to save $1,900 since the average officer's salary was $150 a month. Some survived the temporary purge with only a demotion. After two years as Assistant Chief under Becker, Clarence Hurt went back to the Auto Theft Bureau as a Detective. The dismissal of the 25 men dropped the Department strength to 185 but the Chief said he hoped to be able to raise it to 230 men after the new fiscal year started. As a temporary cost-cutting measure, it worked and later that summer, the men were rehired.

Less than two months later, on August 2, John McClelland died suddenly from influenza complications. Councilman Taylor began stumping for A.R. Losh for City Manager and he was elected by yet another 5-4 vote. Taylor began making immediate demands upon Losh to fire City employees so Taylor's political supporters could have their jobs. Losh proved less compliant than Taylor anticipated and refused. After less than a month, Taylor began trying to get rid of Losh.

It took Taylor three months to get the job done. On December 1, 1931, Losh was dismissed by, what else, a 5-4 vote and Albert McRill was appointed City Manager. McRill was an attorney, former newspaperman, municipal counselor, law professor and President of Oklahoma City University. A conservative Prohibitionist and former member of the Central One Hundred, he was also to prove to be a thorn in Taylor's side, among others. In later years, McRill was to write a book, And Satan Came Also, a fascinating social and political history of the City's first sixty-five years.

Since Chief Watt's appointment, both of the City Managers had received outside pressure for his dismissal. McRill was not to escape this either. One of his first visitors was Orban Chester Patterson. McRill quoted the attorney's statements in his book:

"I don't care who the city manager is, or under what system of government the city operates. In fact, I don't care a damn for your city government, except for what I can get out of it. This is the first time in my political career that I've been on the outside looking in and I don't like that a damn bit. The Police Department will make you or break you, Mr. Manager. You'd better take my advice and get a new Chief of Police".

McRill refused to bow to the pressure and Patterson left him with the threat that he only needed one more councilman's vote to have McRill's job. Patterson was no stranger to the 5-4 vote either.

Thusly John Watt survived his first test in office. Against the odds, he was to hold the job for six years, setting a new record for length of tenure in the top spot. During his administration, the single most vital contribution to law enforcement in the city's history became a reality......the police radio.

Since the pre-war period, officers had utilized call boxes and public telephones to call headquarters every half hour to receive messages, assignments and information. "Call 6-1" is a message familiar to generations of OCPD officers telling them to contact headquarters. Although all know what it means, most are probably unaware of its' origin. It was the first telephone number of the Oklahoma City Police Department.

As the foot patrols expanded to horse, motorcycle and finally auto patrols, the call-in procedure became bothersome and less than effective. While serving under Becker, John Watt had learned of the use of the police radio in Detroit and other cities. This use was pioneered by using commercial radio stations that broke into their programming with emergency messages. Watt finally succeeded in bringing the radios here. The OCPD's first police radio frequency went into operation on June 5, 1931.

The first police radios were one-way. Cars could receive messages but they couldn't reply or ask for further information so the call-box routine remained as standard procedure. By 1936, 40 radio-equipped scout cars were receiving 3,000 calls a month over station KGPH.

*Officer Fred Buckles and his partner pose with his 1932 OCPD patrol car.*

*On September 4, 1932, OCPD officers examine their equipment to deal with the era's gangsters.*

Chief Watt also started the first separate, specialized Homicide Squad. His day was also the day of the bootlegger as it was for his predecessors. Liquor and vice enforcement remained a prime duty for police officers and a prime headache for police administrators. Chief Watt attended to it with vigor.

A representative incident occurred in 1934 in an apartment house in the 3100 block of North Harvey. Newspaper accounts state that several women were arrested on suspicion of possessing whiskey, mash and beer. The raiders seized a 100-gallon still, a large quantity of

*Legendary OCPD officer D.A. 'Jelly' Bryce.*

mash, 165 gallons of whiskey and 30 gallons of beer. The lady proprietor of the house told officers that she had no idea how the contraband came to be in her living room.

One of the most singular individuals ever to wear an OCPD uniform served during the 1930's. Sam A. Phillips awed his friends with bizarre antics. At the Oklahoma Sheriff's and Peace Officer's Convention in Bartlesville in 1930, Phillips devoured ten pounds of flaming cotton, declaring that he was "a fire-eater, not a fire fighter". Phillips was also an accomplished guitarist, comedian and impersonator.

Perhaps the most legendary officer of them all was D. A. Bryce. Born in Mountain View, Oklahoma, on December 6, 1906, Bryce had actually cut his teeth on firearms. His sister later said that he was actually allowed to teethe on his father's unloaded pistol in his crib. Growing up in rural western Oklahoma, hunting and fishing became his favorite pastimes. He became very familiar with firearms and had plenty of wide open spaces in which to practice. He once saved over $100 he made from shining shoes. Exemplifying what would later become two of his lifelong passions, nice clothes and shooting, he used the money to buy a pair of pants and spent the rest on ammunition. His grandfather was so proud of him that he paid for part of the boy's ammunition expenses.

Blessed with extraordinary eyesight, phenomenal eye and hand coordination, and a natural talent for marksmanship, he became an incredibly accurate, instinctive shooter while still a young boy. While his talents were obviously honed by long hours of practice, that his abilities in this area were a natural talent became evident in his adult years when he transcended the need for practice with no decrease in his speed or accuracy. After graduating from high school in 1926, he attended a military camp at Fort Sill where they had firearms competitions. Bryce won first place with both pistol and rifle, and then won the national rifle competition at Camp Perry, Ohio.

After a short period of time working in a grocery store in Seminole, he became an Oklahoma State Game Ranger. Bryce began his career with the OCPD during the summer of 1928 at the age of 21. He was allegedly recruited by Clarence Hurt when the two met at a pistol competition match. Both men would more than adequately prove their shooting skills in the future and not just at paper targets. The personnel files of those years are not nearly as accurate or comprehensive as those of later times. Thus his OCPD personnel file gives conflicting dates for his date of entry, listing both June 16 and July 15. The records indicate that he entered the service as a plainclothesman in the Auto Theft Department without serving any time as a uniformed patrolman.

Bryce seemed to be surrounded with unusual names all his life. He was originally christened Jacob Adolphus Bryce, named respectively after his great-grandfather and grandfather. Many people who knew him from childhood called him "Jake" all his life. After he grew to maturity, Bryce decided he wanted his name patterned after that of his father, Fel Albert Bryce. So he had it legally changed to Delf Albert Bryce.

Perhaps due to his unusual first name, Bryce rapidly acquired another nickname. Bryce was noted for dressing with great fastidiousness, care and attention to style. Starched white shirts, fashionable ties, well-cut three-piece vested or double breasted suits, white Palm Beach suits, highly polished two-toned brown shoes and a straw or snap brim hat worn at a rakish angle were his uniform of the day. Apparently some observers felt he looked like an early 20's version of a "jellybean", a slang term for a dandy or foppish dresser. Bryce was walking past a drunk one day when the man wisecracked "Just a jellybean". The drunk rapidly entered the City Jail and Bryce eventually became known from coast to coast as "Jelly". He came to like the nickname so much that he later had it legally incorporated into his name.

Bryce rapidly earned a reputation as a gunman unequalled by any other OCPD officer with the possible exception of Bill Tilghman. He killed three men in the line of duty during his first year on the force, one trying to steal a car and the other two trying to burglarize a furniture store. All three of the men drew their weapons first and the two burglars fired at him before he killed them with one shot apiece. He was rapidly promoted to Detective in Auto Theft and is pictured as such in the 1929 Annual.

Bryce was noted for his lightning draw and accurate shooting. He developed the draw by long practice in front of a full length mirror in the patrol lineup room, sometimes for hours at a time. Veterans of that era recall that he was such a fast and accurate shot that he often performed exhibitions. One trick involved the use of a shiny ring on his left hand which he used to reflect the target from over his shoulder, circus-style. He seldom missed. Another impressive demonstration was conducted with a Thompson submachine gun loaded with tracer rounds. Bryce would write his name in the sky with the tracers, then come back and put the periods behind the D. and the A.

His firearms talents weren't only for show. As an Oklahoma City officer and later with the FBI, he killed a number of criminals and was involved in the shootings or captures of Wilbur Underhill and Alvin Karpis among others. Bryce was later said to have killed as many as 17 men in the line of duty. In later years, his draw was timed at two-fifths of a second to draw and fire accurately. It was said that if a suspect blinked at Jelly Bryce, he died in darkness. Some years later, Bryce gave Jack Mullinex, Lee Mullinex's son, his crass but realistic advice on how a police officer could best avoid getting hurt on the job; "Approach everyone with a smile on your face, murder in your heart and rape on your mind". The Boy Scouts made a motto out of roughly the same sentiment; be prepared.

Some justice was done on July 17, 1932, but at a high price. Wiley Lynn, the drunken Federal Prohibition Agent who had killed Bill Tilghman in Cromwell, Oklahoma, almost eight years earlier was now in Madill, near the Texas border. No longer a Federal officer, Lynn was again armed, drunk and nursing a grudge. This time it was against Crockett Long, former Madill Police Chief and now an Agent for the State Crime Bureau (later OSBI).

*John Hubatka-Four decades with the OCPD.*

Accosting Long in a corner drug store in Madill, Lynn pulled a gun on him. Both men were killed in the resulting gunfight along with an innocent bystander. When told of it, an unforgiving Mrs. Tilghman lambasted the jury that freed Lynn for her husband's murder, telling a reporter "I'm terribly sorry that another good man and that boy had to die but glad Wynn went the way he did. No jury on earth can acquit him now". A tough lady. She must have been a great complement to her man.

On August 16, 1932, the man died who was most identified, for better or worse, with the OCPD for its first half century. John Hubatka died at the age of 66 in the city he helped police for nearly two-thirds of his life.

A Czechoslovakian immigrant, he participated in the Land Run of 1889, settling in Oklahoma City on the opening day. "The Bohemian Bloodhound" had been one of the four original officers hired by Charles Colcord in 1890. He held every rank in the Department from patrolman to Chief except for Sergeant. While others sat on the Sergeant's desk, he was a Deputy U.S. Marshal. He served three separate, stormy terms as Chief. He declared open war on a Mayor and City Council, was suspended, sued for reinstatement charging them with graft, was indicted by a grand jury, sued a newspaper for libel, was finally vindicated, reinstated and outlasted them all.

He served four decades on the force and, for the last two years of his life, was still a reserve officer. The obituary recounted one of his innumerable "shooting scrapes", when he engaged in a face-to-face gunfight with three armed robbers, shooting one and arresting the other two. Stating that he "seemed to have a charmed life", he later found that three of the robbers bullets had gone through his coat.

In 1895, Hubatka had been one of the officers presiding at the only legal hanging in Oklahoma City. A 21-year-old multiple murderer, John Milligan, was hanged from a gallows on Main Street with a special rope borrowed from Fort Smith, Arkansas. As Hubatka was quoted, "We had a lot of lynchings but this was the only legal hanging".

Although accused of being "soft on vice", no one ever questioned his ability or courage. Had he been able to choose his own epitaph, he might have settled for what a newspaper editorial said more than twenty years earlier;

"...and John Hubatka's capability as a fearless police officer and as a detective in solving crime mysteries cannot be questioned...he cannot paint pretty word pictures in oratory...he has not the culture and the charming poise...it is hardly probable that he has ever read Shakespeare, Dickens, Carlyle, Longfellow or Tennyson...but...remember, John Hubatka has horse sense aplenty; he is not afraid of the very Devil himself; he understands the art of capturing criminals; in short, John Hubatka is a policeman".

Hubatka was buried in Fairlawn Cemetery. Two of his pallbearers were John Cassidy and M.C. Binion. Although Hubatka had not been on active duty at the time of his death, City Manager Albert McRill decreed that his funeral procession would have an escort of Oklahoma City Police officers. If anyone objected, there is no record of it.

Shortly before 2:30 P.M. on October 17, 1932, the police dispatcher broadcast a call for units to respond to a "shooting scrape" at the corner of Frisco and Robinson Streets. Car Seven, Officers Roy Bergman and J.B. McGuffin, started in that direction. So did Clarence Hurt, back on the streets as a working detective after two years as Assistant Chief under Chief Becker. Hurt had missed his shot at the top job when City Manager McClelland had appointed his friend John Watt.

When the officers arrived, they saw that a 1932 Chevrolet coupe with Kansas license plates had run up over the curb on the north side of Frisco just east of Robinson and crashed into a parked car in a used car lot. Detective George Baker was sitting in his car in the street with E.A. Peery in custody. Baker's partner, Detective Charles Gerald "Jerry" Campbell, was standing next to the wrecked car with a gun in each hand and blood all over his shirt. The blood wasn't his, however. It came from the dead man slumped in the driver's seat of the wrecked Chevy, his head and body pierced by several of Campbell's bullets.

The incident had begun a block farther south, at Choctaw and Robinson. Campbell and Baker, doing their jobs as members of the Stolen Car Department, were scouting the south part of town when they noticed the Chevy coupe with two men sitting in it. Their suspicions aroused, perhaps by the Kansas plates, the officers circled the block and parked behind the car. Approaching the car and identifying themselves as officers, they began questioning the men and examining the car. Their suspicions were justified when they discovered that the motor number had been altered. After placing both men under arrest, Baker took Peery back to the police car while Campbell got in the stolen Chevy with the driver. The two cars then started toward the police station, one suspect driving the stolen Chevy with Detective Campbell on the passenger's side followed by Baker and Peery in the police car.

The convoy had gone less than a block when Campbell noticed a lump under the rear seat floormat. Turning sideways in the seat, he lifted the floormat up and saw a sawed off shotgun.

The driver had seen his movements and took his left hand off of the steering wheel, dropping it back out of Campbell's view. Just as Campbell told the man to keep both hands on the steering wheel, the man drew a .45 pistol and shoved it into the officer's chest. Campbell batted the gun away just as it fired, leaving a powder burn on his right arm. Campbell then drew his own weapon and, before the man could fire again, fired five shots at him. Four of them struck the man in the jaw, neck, shoulder and chest. The car veered and came to a halt as it jumped the curb into a car lot, crashing into one of the used cars. Campbell grabbed the driver's .45 and jumped out of the car, still covering him with his own weapon just in case the man had somehow survived and still had some fight left in him. He hadn't and he didn't.

Later found in the car was a Remington 12 gauge automatic shotgun fully loaded with five rounds of buckshot, a .25 automatic pistol and plenty of extra shotgun ammunition. The car was determined to have been stolen out of Shawnee. Peery also had a car that proved to be stolen from Texas. The dead man was identified as Elbert "Cole" Oglesby, the newspapers began printing the story and the letters and phone calls started coming.

Oglesby came from a Texas family of outlaws and this wasn't their first contact with the OCPD. Two years earlier one of Cole's brothers, John, had been shot by OCPD Detectives J.M. Mabe and Jack Roberts while they were chasing him through one of the City's oil fields. The Oglesbys were first cousins of the Newton brothers who had masterminded a $2 million train robbery in Illinois in 1924. Cole had been involved in that enterprise and had an auto theft conviction in Texas. He had been very busy for a young man of 28 years. He was wanted for a murder that occurred in 1928 in Abilene, Texas. He was also wanted for bank robberies in Lumberton and Columbia, Mississippi, that had occurred during the first two months of this year. His brother Jerry had been killed in a gun battle with pursuing officers following the Lumberton job. He was also wanted for bank robberies in Moline, Kansas, as well as Decatur, Paradise and Canton, Texas, where he was "considered a bad man and a killer". The books were closed on a lot of crimes when Jerry Campbell closed Cole Oglesby's book permanently. Unfortunately it wasn't the end of the OCPD's dealings with the Oglesbys.

The third year of the decade was to bring national attention to the center of the country as the gangsters that dominated the first half of the decade began their sprees in earnest in early 1932. Missouri had earned the title "Mother of Bandits" for birthing three generations of outlaws ranging from the families of Jesse James to that of Ma Barker. Missouri may have been the mother of bandits but mother brought her hellions to Oklahoma to train them.

While Bonnie Parker and Clyde Barrow were becoming locally notorious in Texas, the first one to captivate the national press's attention was an Oklahoma boy. Charles Arthur Floyd was Georgia-born but considered Sallisaw and nearby Akins, his home since early childhood, his hometowns. Floyd was causing bank insurance rates to double (literally) all over Oklahoma for three years when the only people who had heard of John Dillinger were his fellow inmates in the Indiana State Penitentiary. In fact, Dillinger had been out of the joint less than a month when Floyd conducted his piece de resistance at Kansas City's Union Station.

He had acquired the nickname "Choc" from his fondness for home-brewed Choctaw beer but he was to become more famous by his other nickname, "Pretty Boy". One of the stories that circulated about how he acquired the flamboyant nickname was that some of the local hometown gentry dubbed him that because of his slicked-back hairstyle and the constant presence of a comb in his pocket. Another possibility is the fact that at the time of the arrest that led to his first prison term, in St. Louis in 1925, he was originally confused with a local hoodlum known as Pretty Boy Smith. In fact, that continued to be listed on his wanted posters as one of his aliases right up to the time of his death. He despised the more pretentious and what was to become the more famous nickname. Due to the attitude that was to lead him to kill at least ten people during his depredations, half of them lawmen, he was not usually called by it.

He began 1932 by successfully hitting two banks in the same day, a coup that had spelled the doom of both the Dalton and Bill Cook gangs in territorial days. After robbing Paden and Castle, 60 miles east of Oklahoma City, he completed the hat trick by robbing the bank in Dover north of Kingfisher the next day. He and his partner George Birdwell also lavished their attentions on financial institutions in Shamrock, Stonewall, Henryetta and even his hometown of Sallisaw. It was during these forays that Floyd made attempts to earn his reputation as a "Robin Hood", just a "good old boy" down on his luck. When accosted on the street by people who had known him since childhood with a "Whatcha doin' in town, Choc?", he amiably told them he was going to rob the bank and then proceeded to do it. While inside, Floyd took extra time to destroy as many of the bank's mortgage papers as he could find to make it harder for the bank to foreclose on his impoverished rural brethren. When leaving, he sprinkled handfuls of money out of the car window to the citizens standing in his dusty wake. Despite this public relations flair, Floyd was a very good shot, favored a Thompson submachine gun and was a cold-blooded killer when someone got in his way. He once wrote a letter to the sheriff of Sequoyah County, Oklahoma, telling him that he was coming home to visit his mother and the sheriff would be wise to leave him alone. The sheriff left him alone.

The careers of Bonnie Parker and Clyde Barrow took a decided turn for the worse when they decided to branch out of their usual stomping grounds of Texas and ventured north across the Red River. They became federal fugitives when they drove a stolen car from Texas into Oklahoma. They also killed their first law enforcement officers in Oklahoma during the summer of 1932 when they killed the Atoka County sheriff and his deputy in a gunbattle in Stringtown.

It took some doing to stand out in this crowd but one who achieved that status was Raymond Hamilton. He started his outlaw career in January of 1932 at the age of 19. Bonnie and Clyde broke him out of prison in Texas and he became Bonnie's lover since Clyde was homosexual. This situation caused some friction among the trio during their travels. Over the next three years, with and without the more famous pair, Hamilton committed at least two dozen robberies including seven banks, two oil refineries, a packing plant, a post office and the Fort Worth National Guard Armory, where he loaded up on shotguns and machine guns. His primary quality being meanness and not genius, he was frequently captured but escaped four times including once when he single-handedly disarmed a 20-man posse, taking the leader hostage when he left.

Ma Barker raised her brood of hellions in Tulsa. Her son Arthur, known as "Doc", was the hardest case of the four. He was sentenced to life in the Oklahoma State Prison in 1920 for murdering a night watchman in Tulsa. Eccentric Governor Alfalfa Bill Murray granted Doc a "banishment pardon" in 1932. He could go free if he would leave Oklahoma. Doc jumped at the chance and the family reputation took off.

The year 1933 was to be the blackest in the Department's history. In accordance with the doctrine of changing fortunes, former Chief Martin C. Binion was again serving with the OCPD as a Detective (at 66 years of age!). Perhaps the old saying that "there's no such thing as a retired cop" was invented for him.

It was bitterly cold on February 8, 1933, with the temperature sitting at five degrees below zero. On that day, Martin C. Binion and his partner, 50-year-old Charles C. York, went to a rooming house at 6 South Geary to arrest Otis Tillman. The black man, three times an inmate of Granite Reformatory, was wanted for bogus checks and mortgaging stock that didn't belong to him.

Binion and York located Tillman in a room in the apartments. After determining that he was the man they were looking for, Binion told Tillman to come along and turned to leave. Tillman drew a gun and shot at York three times, one of the rounds piercing his heart, killing the 11-year veteran.

Martin Binion was justifiably proud of his 32-year career in law enforcement. After two

*Detective Charles York.*

*Officer John Harold Beasley.*

terms as Oklahoma County Sheriff, three terms as OCPD's Chief of Police and separate tours as a Deputy U.S. Marshal and Federal Prohibition Agent, the venerable old warhorse was back on the OCPD as a Detective at the age of 66. One of the points he was most proud of in his career was the fact that he had never had to kill anyone in the line of duty. A gunfight with burglars years before had resulted in Binion being wounded in the leg and his return fire had hit the man in the heel of one foot. He was about to end that record. As York fell, Binion turned around and shot Otis Tillman once in the head, killing him instantly. Charles York died in the arms of his partner. Survived by his wife and two children, York was interred in Rose Hill Cemetery attended by an honor guard of 34 officers. His pallbearers were Officers Bert Shaffer, R.A. Nelson, Sam Phillips, W.L. Shirley, C.M. Shepherd and Lee Mullinex.

The slaying of Officer John H. Beasley by "The Human Bomb" on the morning of May 18, 1933, was perhaps the most spectacular in departmental history. Beasley had been sent with other officers to an alley at N.W. 4th and Hudson to arrest a drunk. As they were searching the drunk, an unemployed carpenter named James Ferguson, a pistol was found. Ferguson then revealed to the officers that he had a box containing 24 sticks of dynamite strapped to his body and threatened to detonate it if the gun was taken from him. With Sergeant Lloyd F. White and Officer J.M. Mabe in the front seat and Beasley and Ferguson in the back seat, they drove to a parking lot east of the First National Bank building in the 100 block of N.W. 1st. They were followed by Officer John Reading in another scout car.

Ferguson ordered Officer Mabe to go to the nearby Pettee's Hardware Store and get him some more dynamite. While Mabe went in the store, Sergeant White got out of the car and began trying to talk Ferguson into surrendering peacefully. While Ferguson was momentarily distracted by White, Officer Beasley began struggling with Ferguson in the back seat and Beasley was shot twice in the chest. White and Reading began firing at Ferguson from opposite sides of the car. The wounded man jumped out of the car as Officer Mabe exited the store firing at him. Ferguson fell dead in the street, hit a total of 13 times in the head and shoulders.

The dynamite was taken to an oil lease by personnel from the Fire Department and explosives experts from the Tex-Okla Torpedo Corporation and detonated harmlessly. Beasley, meanwhile, was rushed to the hospital where he was initially reported as "holding his own". Rapidly taking a turn for the worse, he received four blood transfusions from his fellow officers but died four days later on May 22 after losing the battle with the wounds in his chest and liver. Newspaper accounts said that the officer told his wife, "I'm going to live" just seconds before he expired, causing the 40-year-old officer to be elevated to hero status for months after the slaying.

Ferguson's relatives stated that he had been brooding about his inability to find work for the last year. His children said he had been working on the mysterious box for about ten years and he had told them it was "an egg separator". They speculated that he had chosen a gun battle with police as an indirect means of suicide because he had sold $150 worth of his tools a few days earlier for $10.

At midnight on the day of Beasley's death, Chief Watt read a citation for his bravery and gallantry over the air on the city-county radio station KGPH. The next day, in what was to become a tradition for the remainder of the decade, Officer Beasley's services were held in the Shrine Auditorium (later the Municipal Auditorium and Civic Center Music Hall). The regular Tuesday City Council meeting was adjourned so all the councilmen could attend as well as

Mayor Blinn and City Manager McRill. A large number of officers and firemen were also present. The hymns In The Garden and The Old Rugged Cross were sung by the OCPD quartet, the Flatfoot Four, consisting of Officers W.C. "Red" Elliott, J.D. Walker, Johnny Whalen and Jack Roberts. As the solemn procession continued to the burial site in Memorial Park Cemetery, three of Beasley's six pallbearers were the officers who had killed his assailant, Officers Mabe, Reading and Sergeant White.

During the summer of 1933, Orban Chester Patterson was finally able to make good on his threats to City Manager McRill of 18 months before. McRill had alienated the perverse Councilman J. E. Taylor and Taylor had gotten a new Councilman in his pocket with his support during the elections. Patterson had his 5-4 majority and told McRill so on June 13, the morning of the Council meeting. Given the same message by Taylor, McRill resigned. W.A. Quinn was elected, 5 to 4, to replace McRill. Quinn would only last 47 days before being replaced by Orval Mosier. Orban Patterson, after more than two years of banishment, was reinstated in his office in the police station. The new City Manager's first order to Chief Watt was to inform his force to show "a more liberal attitude to those who violate our ordinances".

In July of 1933, a referendum to legalize the sale of beer was finally presented to the citizens of Oklahoma after the normal tortuous, protracted process of tug of war between the wet and dry factions. The national mood had turned against the dry viewpoint in the last 13 years. Prohibition was a national joke, the pot of gold at the end of the rainbow for organized crime and generally cost more to enforce than it was worth. The bootleggers and brewers picked up in local raids were assessed small fines and/or short jail terms and could delay those by appealing for jury trials at the County level. Even if these didn't totally abrogate the fines and jail terms, the counties usually spent two to six times more on the prosecutions then they had any hope of recovering. A few counties managed to make more in fines than they lost in financing the prosecutions but they were a distinct minority.

The Prohibitionists may have felt that even God was against them this time, trying to lower voter turnout. More likely they interpreted it as God giving the sinners a little taste of what hell is like. On July 10, thermometers in Oklahoma City reached a record of 104 degrees. On election day, July 11, they went to another record of 107 degrees. Whether it was the heat, lower voter turnouts or the national mood, it worked. Almost two-thirds of the voters legalized 3.2 beer in Oklahoma, classifying it as a "non-intoxicating liquor". It was a decidedly urban victory. The voters in Oklahoma City were for it by a 4 to 1 margin. Only 20 of the State's 77 counties were against repeal, most of them in the rural western part of the State. Eccentric Governor "Alfalfa Bill" Murray petulantly declared martial law, called out the National Guard to keep the trainloads of beer from being raided prematurely by the thirsty citizenry but finally relented the next morning. On July 12, 1933, the first legal foam was blown off of beers in the 25-year-old State of Oklahoma.

DAILY OKLAHOMAN
JULY 27, 1933

REAL ESTATE-FARMS FOR SALE
160 acres land, good five-room house, deep well, also cows, tools, tractor, corn and hay. $3,750 for quick sale. Terms. Write Box H-807, Oklahoman and Times.

When the above advertisement appeared in the Daily Oklahoman, it had nothing to do with selling a farm. It was a signal to a group of kidnappers that E.E. Kirkpatrick had a suitcase containing 10,000 $20 bills ready for delivery. It was the largest ransom demand in history, double that demanded by the Ma Barker gang for Minnesota brewer William Hamm the previous month and four times the amount paid for the Lindbergh baby the year before. The advertisement was also a graduation announcement of sorts—George "Machine Gun" Kelly had finally entered the major leagues of crime.

Five days earlier, on the evening of July 22, oil millionaire Charles F. Urschel was playing bridge with his wife and neighbors, Mr. and Mrs. Walter Jarrett, on the screened sunporch of his Heritage Hills mansion at 327 N.W. 18 in Oklahoma City. They didn't pay much attention when they heard a car pull into the driveway a little after 11 P.M., thinking it may have been one of their children returning home. Moments later, they knew better. The screen door burst open and two men carrying submachine guns walked in. Covering both men with his tommygun, George Kelly said "Which one's Urschel?", which gives some indication of the amount of planning that George Kelly had put into this. Receiving no answer, Kelly and his accomplice, Albert Bates, abducted both men. On a rural road somewhere south of Norman, one of them got the ingenious idea to check both men's wallets for their identification. Identifying their prey in this manner, they let Mr. Jarrett out minus the $51 in his wallet.

Prior to this, his big night in crime, George Kelly had been a small-time, somewhat dimwitted Oklahoma City bootlegger with a bad heart, a "good-natured slob...who spilled more than he delivered". Born George Kelly Barnes in Memphis, Tennessee, he had celebrated his thirty-eighth birthday four days before the Urschel kidnapping. Scion of a respectable if not wealthy family, he had endured one substandard semester and part of another at Mississippi A&M College (now Mississippi State University) before giving up and dropping out. He tried his hand as a taxi driver for a while but soon discovered that in the early 1920s, there were more profits in delivering booze than passengers. Following several altercations with the Memphis PD that resulted in bootlegging arrests, Barnes decided to ply his trade farther west and stopped using his last name.

After being arrested for bootlegging in Santa Fe, New Mexico, he relocated to Tulsa where he was promptly arrested for vagrancy but he soon found gainful employment. Unfortunately, it was smuggling liquor onto an Indian reservation, for which vigilant Federal Prohibition agents treated him to three years in Leavenworth Penitentiary. There he tried to expand his horizons by associating with a better class of criminal, Frank "Jelly" Nash among others.

When Kelly got out in 1930, he drifted into Oklahoma City where he affiliated himself with a local rumrunner named "Little Steve" Anderson. Kelly soon developed a yen for Anderson's mistress, Kathryn Thorne, and the couple soon left for Minneapolis where they were married in September of 1930. From this union would spring the legend of "Machine Gun" Kelly.

Kathryn Kelly was a real piece of work. Born Cleo Brooks in Mississippi 26 years earlier, she started calling herself Kathryn because she thought the name had more *je ne sais quoi* than her real one. "Kathryn" would spend the rest of her unincarcerated years always pretending to something better. By the time she met Kelly, she already had three marriages behind her, the first one at age fifteen and the last one to a Texas bootlegger named Charlie Thorne. Charlie Thorne had died from a gunshot wound that an inquest ruled was self-inflicted in spite of the fact that Kathryn had told a witness she was on her way "to kill that God-damned Charlie Thorne" the day before his "suicide".

Kathryn Kelly was an ambitious, single-minded woman with bigger plans for her man than peddling booze. George embarked on a series of bank robberies with some of the more experienced associates he had met in Leavenworth. He even tried an early foray into kidnapping. Unfortunately, then as later, George's brains couldn't keep up with Kathryn's ambitions. On January 27, 1932, Kelly and a not-any-brighter associate named Eddie Doll abducted Mr. and Mrs. Howard Woolverton in South Bend, Indiana, after running their car off the road. Mrs. Woolverton was released with a $50,000 ransom demand. Over the course of the next two days, Woolverton evidently talked his kidnappers into believing that he didn't have the money but could raise it and send it to them if they would release him. Incredibly, they did. Naturally, Woolverton didn't send the money. Naturally, he got threatening letters and phone calls from the stiffed kidnappers but summarily ignored them. Kelly and Doll may have been the only kidnappers in history stupid enough to take a verbal IOU for ransom.

Kathryn Kelly bought her hubby a Thompson submachine gun at a pawnshop in Fort Worth, Texas, in February of 1933. J. Edgar Hoover and other sources credit Kathryn with launching an intensive reverse public relations campaign on Kelly's behalf, trying to improve his standing in the criminal community. She allegedly had Kelly practice with the weapon, bragged that he could shoot walnuts off of fence poles and handed out the spent casings as souvenirs of "Machine Gun" Kelly. Hoover also credited her with giving her husband his nickname although the name never appeared in the press until after he was identified as a suspect in the Urschel kidnapping.

Hoover also contributed to the legend. He picked up the story that Kelly was an "expert machine gunner" and listed him as such on his wanted posters. After all, his agents' successes would be measured against the quality of their opposition. It behooved his agency's reputation to be catching the toughest, cleverest desperadoes in the country, thus proving themselves tougher and more clever. "Expert machine gunner" looked more impressive on the posters (and in the headlines) than "buffoon" or "oaf".

A few days later, Urschel was released after family friend E.E. Kirkpatrick delivered the $200,000 ransom in marked bills. Kathryn had wanted to kill Urschel instead of setting him free but Kelly refused, incorrigibly more non-violent than the reputation she had manufactured for him. It proved to be his downfall. Urschel provided so many clues that the Feds had little trouble rounding up more than a dozen accomplices in a few weeks. Arrested in Memphis, Tennessee, two months later, Kelly was allegedly the one who gave the FBI their most famous nickname when he surrendered by yelling "Don't shoot, G-Men!". The legend has since been debunked by many sources, not the least of which are numerous career law enforcement officers who said they never heard the term used outside of a movie theater. They insist that the generic term used for the agents by the gangsters, then as now, was "Feds". A more specific counter-claim that sounds much more realistic is that the arrest was actually made by three Memphis PD officers and Kelly's only statement when a shotgun was shoved in his belly was "I've been waiting for you all night".

Kelly and his accomplices went to trial in Federal Court in Oklahoma City and, in spite of Kathryn's attempts to make him a bad man, the truth came out. Kelly played cards amiably with Urschel while holding him hostage. Kathryn wanted to kill him instead of releasing him but for once Kelly stood up to her and Urschel was released unharmed.

All were convicted and Kelly went to Alcatraz, the toughest prison in the country, a testament to the reputation Kathryn had built for him. There, his easy-going attitude earned him the nickname "Pop-gun" Kelly from the hardcase cons and guards and he was eventually transferred to Leavenworth. He died there on July 18, 1954, his fifty-ninth birthday, having never killed anyone and apparently never fired a gun in anger. Albert Bates died in Alcatraz in 1948. Kathryn Kelly was released from prison in 1958 and faded into obscurity. Charles Urschel died in 1970 at the age of 80.

The political climate was just as chaotic as the rest of the decade. On November 7, Mayor Clarence J. Blinn was ejected from office by a recall petition and Thomas Bennett McGee was selectedto finish his unexpired term.

On December 3, 1933, Scout Car Officers Douglas Gates and Webb Campbell became involved in a chase with a stolen car. Unbeknownst to them, the stage was being set for a final clash between two families, one of them dedicated to upholding the law, the other dedicated to breaking it. The situation was fraught with coincidence, not the least of which was that the car they were chasing had been stolen several weeks earlier from Jack's Chevrolet Garage in Fort Cobb, Oklahoma. Fort Cobb was Officer Gates' hometown and the burial site of his brother, Jack, who had been killed three years earlier while serving as an OCPD officer.

*Officer Douglas W. Gates.*

Gates was driving the scout car when the chase began shortly before 7:45 A.M. north of the State Capitol and continued west on N.E. 23rd. When the vehicle stopped at the traffic light at the intersection of N.W. 23rd and Robinson, Gates stopped the scout car beside and slightly to the rear of the stolen car. Campbell got out of the passenger's side and went around to the passenger's side of the other car, checking the tag again. He leaned down and asked the driver if the car was his.

It wasn't. The driver was Ernest Oglesby and he wasn't in the mood to discuss it. Two of his brothers had already been shot down by OCPD officers. John Oglesby had been shot trying to escape from OCPD Detectives J.M. Mabe and Jack Roberts three years earlier. Only a little over a year before, his brother Cole had been killed by OCPD Detective Jerry Campbell. Ernest must have realized how close he was to sharing their fate.

Oglesby told the officer it was his car, trying to gain time. As Campbell walked back behind the car to come around to the driver's side, Oglesby started driving off. Campbell, a former football star at Oklahoma University, jumped on the rear spare tire carrier of the accelerating vehicle, drawing his gun and yelling for the driver to stop. The driver drew his own gun and, pointing it backwards over his shoulder, fired through the rear window at Campbell. With splinters of glass driven into his eyes and blood streaming down his face, Campbell fired two shots blindly into the car, hitting Oglesby once in the left forearm. The car swerved into the path of an oncoming car and Campbell was thrown to the ground when they collided.

Gates, following in the scout car, pulled up at the scene of the accident and got out. Oglesby was out of his car first and fired several times at Gates, hitting him twice. One of the bullets was deflected by Gates' badge but the other broke his left collarbone and veered into his neck. Oglesby jumped on the running board of a passing car and escaped as Campbell ran after the retreating car, wiping blood from his eyes and trying to get a clear shot. Campbell saw children in the commandeered vehicle and held his fire.

Officer Gates died in the hospital that afternoon. The bullet in his neck had severed an artery. His younger brother, Officer Jack D. Gates, had been killed in the line of duty three years earlier ten blocks south of the intersection where Douglas sustained his fatal wound. Their sister was married to Clarence Hurt, who had been Night Chief under Charles Becker several years before. A Medal of Merit for valiant service was awarded to both Officers Gates and Campbell, Gates' award being posthumous. Oglesby was arrested two hours later at a house in the 2900 block of N.W. 12th. Four spent shell casings were recovered from his pockets and a gun was found hidden in the bathroom stove. Ballistics tests proved that the gun had fired the bullets that killed Douglas Gates. Oglesby was tried, sentenced to death and later electrocuted in McAlester's State Prison.

On December 5, a morose contingent of 75 officers accompanied Douglas Gates' body to be buried near that of his slain brother in Fort Cobb. The OCPD quartet "The Flatfoot Four", now comprised of Officers Red Elliott, Johnny Whalen, Jack Roberts and Bill West, sang hymns at the services. The pallbearers were Officers Emmett L. Drane, Dwight F. Brown, Roy J. Bergman, J.B. McGuffin, C.M. Shepherd and R.K. McKim. In future years, Brown would become Chief of Detectives and Bergman would become Chief of Police. Emmett Drane's career would end somewhat more ignominiously.

Douglas Gates' widow was given the proceeds of her husband's $2,000 group insurance policy and the City Council voted to give her a stipend of $1,000 in payments of $50 a month.

Two days after the Gates murder, the Twenty-First Amendment to the U.S. Constitution was ratified, repealing national prohibition. The State Legislature petulantly procrastinated to the point that the amendment went unratified by Oklahoma. The state law, however, remained intact. For over a quarter of a century now, as Will Rogers quipped, Oklahomans had been "staggering to the polls and voting dry". It wouldn't make much difference.

Two of the City's pioneer law officers and the worst of the decade's gangsters passed from the scene in 1934. The first one began his exit two days before the beginning of the New Year. Wilbur Underhill had been raising hell for almost half of his 32 years since his first two-year stretch in the Missouri State Penitentiary for attempted robbery while still a teenager. When he got out, Wilbur worked very hard on the "attempted" part of it and eventually got better at it. In fact, he eventually robbed more banks than his Cookson Hills neighbor, Pretty Boy Floyd, becoming known as the Tri-State Terror from his depredations in Oklahoma, Kansas and Arkansas.

But he had developed a short temper along the way. Underhill allegedly killed a drug store employee during a robbery for not getting his hands up fast enough. After a murder in Okmulgee in 1927, he was sentenced to life in the Oklahoma State Penitentiary. Having developed a talent for getting caught, he developed a talent for getting uncaught second only to Ray Hamilton. Underhill escaped on July 14, 1931. One year to the day later, he was arrested in Wichita, Kansas, for killing a policeman during a robbery, establishing his reputation as "a crazy killer who would rather shoot a cop than eat".

Sentenced to life imprisonment again, he escaped from the Kansas State Penitentiary on Memorial Day of 1933. He lived up to his nickname for the next six months until he decided he needed a new wife to help celebrate the holidays. Unfortunately, when he married Hazel Hudson in Coalgate, Wilbur used his real name. Federal agents under R.H. Colvin began tracing him and finally located him in a cottage at 606 West Dewey in Shawnee.

Colvin had picked up a posse along the way. One of them was FBI Agent Frank Smith, who had survived the Kansas City Massacre six months earlier and would later become Chief of the OCPD. Three others were OCPD Detectives Clarence Hurt, Mickey Ryan and D.A."Jelly" Bryce.

At 2 A.M. on the cold, rainy morning of December 30, the heavily armed officers surrounded the cottage under the cover of a dense fog. Seeing Underhill through a bedroom window, one of them called out for his surrender. Underhill responded by grabbing a gun in each hand and emptying them through the window. The officers answered with a fusillade from machine guns and shotguns. A half- hour gun battle followed that saw over 1,000 rounds fired. Finally, in the best traditions of Bogart and Cagney, Wilbur tried to shoot his way out. Wielding a shotgun and wearing only his long underwear, he blazed his way out of the cottage and through the cordon of officers. He made it 10 blocks before he collapsed in a furniture store after being hit 13 times. Although he was guarded around the clock by officers with machine guns at Shawnee Municipal Hospital, the Feds were still nervous about Wilbur's escape talents plus the fact that his old gang had shot up the small town of Vian the night after his capture. He had also enhanced his already considerable reputation by running 10 blocks with that much lead in him. On January 6, 1934, they moved him to the more secure surroundings of the State Pen at McAlester where he died later that night. Although suspected of complicity in the Kansas City Massacre, Underhill denied it convincingly until the last.

Gun battles between police officers and felons usually happen very quickly and at very close range, usually only a few feet. Police work is often described as months of boring tedium interspersed with seconds of stark terror. Those are the seconds they mean. They are compressed instants of incredible violence second only to explosions in their suddenness. The noise is horrendous for any bystanders but doesn't seem to be noticed much by the participants.

They try to train for it. In the beginning, officers practicing with their weapons was an individual matter for their own self- protection. In later years, regularly scheduled qualifications and modern practice ranges were instituted. Automated targets, moving targets, adjustable lighting and special combat courses increased the rigors and realism. Technology would eventually provide sophisticated video games programmed with "shoot-don't shoot" scenarios that could move training indoors without the noise, smoke or safety concerns of using live ammunition.

But it is very difficult to train officers for combat situations. Too many things change when the target isn't made out of paper and is shooting back. Winston Churchill once said that the most exhilarating experience in life is to be shot at and missed. He was right. He would probably have agreed with the Irish Republican Army member who noted that "a bit of shooting...takes your mind off of the cost of living". But it affects different people in different ways. The idea of killing or trying to kill another human being is a very momentous decision to make for all but psychopaths and sociopaths. But the time to make that decision is not during one of those compressed instants of violence. It's too late to think then, just time to react.

There is a classic western movie in which some farmers try to get a gunfighter to buy them guns to defend their town against bandidos. He tells them they should use their money to hire gunmen instead of buying guns. The farmers figure that should be easy because all the men in town carry guns. The gunfighter remarks that all the men wear guns for the same reason that they all wear pants, because it's expected of them. The men he recommends are not chosen so much for their fast draw or their marksmanship as for their willingness to use their guns while voluntarily placing themselves in harm's way.

All men may be created equal but they don't stay that way. Some police officers have been known to carry their weapons with the first chamber empty or loaded with low-powered target ammunition because they felt that if they were to get shot, it would probably be with their own gun. There are some statistics to bolster that theory. They figure if the hammer falls on an empty chamber or they get shot with a wadcutter target round, it might give them an extra second to get to their backup weapon and save their life. Other officers have been known to have such an aversion to the possibility of taking a human life that they have carried unloaded weapons. Some officers in plain clothes have even been known to carry no weapon at all. Commendable personal values but an odd choice of professions to choose to exercise them in especially if you get down to the nuts and bolts of it. Your grandmother can arrest people who respect authority and won't resist it. It takes something more for the others.

It is a truism of police work that most officers, even if they complete careers of 20 years or more, never fire their weapons except on the firing range. The vast majority of officers never have to face a combat situation. Of the small percentage who do, they seem to primarily fall into two main categories; those who are involved in a single combat situation and those whose are involved in more than two. Not many seem to become involved in only two situations. Anyone can get involved in one by being in the right place at the right time, or the wrong place at the wrong time, depending upon how you look at it. But the odds are very high against stumbling into two of these types of situations. So the ones who are involved in more than two don't just stumble into them. They have a talent for seeking out situations, suspects or both that have that potential for violence and a willingness to place themselves in harm's way. They are usually termed "active, aggressive officers".

They might do this for a number of reasons. Some might characterize it as being crazy, macho, fearless or having a death wish. I doubt these for the following reasons. In my experience, no one is fearless except perhaps the truly insane and it is unlikely they could function as a police officer most of the time. If they really have a death wish, they are usually able to fulfill it themselves without help from others. And macho alone doesn't stand up long under gunfire. The real reasons are probably more closely allied to the adrenaline rush Churchill was alluding to in his statement. Another reason sounds awfully trite when written down or spoken. That is the old saw that "Somebody's got to do it". Some people just won't be arrested without a fight, with or without weapons. These are often the type of people who hurt other people including cops. Most cops, no matter how hard or cold or cynical they have become, don't like to see that happen. Perhaps it could be summarized in another old saw; "Those that can, do. Those that can't, teach.".

Ultimately, the gangsters of the '30's would leave us one abiding legacy besides the film careers of Bogart, Raft, Cagney and Edward G. Robinson—the monolith we know as the Federal Bureau of Investigation. When the Floyds and Barkers started their marauding, J. Edgar Hoover ran the Justice Department's obscure little Bureau of Investigation consisting of accountants and lawyers who investigated violations of federal statutes against white slavery, interstate auto theft, bankruptcy and antitrust laws. Their primary duty was as investigators, not law enforcement officers, with a very definite line drawn between the two distinctions. They weren't authorized to make arrests unless they were accompanied by a law enforcement officer with local jurisdiction or carry weapons except on specially authorized occasions. In fact, the government men were sarcastically known as "briefcase agents" because they weren't allowed to carry much more equipment than that. Hoover, a masterful if somewhat flawed organizer, wanted a much larger piece of the American law enforcement pie than that; he wanted an "American Scotland Yard". The gangsters had been at bat since Prohibition began but the Lindbergh kidnapping was strike one. Hoover took the first step when he got a federal kidnapping law passed after the Lindbergh kidnapping in March of 1932.

When FDR took office a year later, Hoover found his strongest ally in the new Attorney General, Homer Cummings. The Hamm kidnapping by Ma Barker's boys in June of 1933 added fuel to the fire. Strike two. Machine Gun Kelly's grabbing Charles Urschel was the last straw. Strike three. The bloodbath at Kansas City's Union Station the next month was icing on the cake.

The Urschel case was a godsend for Hoover's ambitions for himself and his bureau. The record ransom demand and the interstate nature of the case made all of Hoover's points for him forcefully; kidnapped in Oklahoma, hidden out in Texas, ransom note mailed from Missouri, ransom money recovered in Minnesota and Oregon, the investigation covered 17 states with arrests made in 5 of them. It was tailor-made for Federal jurisdiction. By June of 1934, Hoover had authority to arm his agents and make arrests for a whole new battery of federal crimes like bank robbery, interstate flight, assaulting federal officers and a tougher, amended kidnapping law. In late 1933, it had been renamed the Division of Investigation and, on July 1, 1935, they would become the Federal Bureau of Investigation. Oddly enough, in later years Hoover would consider the FBI's Oklahoma City Field Office as one of his "disciplinary offices" where wayward agents were sent for punishment.

Although Hoover now had the means and the authority to arm his agents, he didn't have a lot of time to grant them for training with their new guns much less the time to acquire gradual experience in arresting the more violent public enemies. So he turned to a readily available force of men who had already acquired that proficiency with firearms and the experience in using them...local police officers, sheriffs and deputies. Preference was given to current and former pistol team members but the best credentials available were a few gunfights to your credit.

In May of 1934, Jerry Campbell and Clarence Hurt were granted a one-year leave of absence by Chief Watt to "go hunting" with the FBI. The 30-year-old Campbell had just under four years on the force while Hurt, a 15-year veteran, had been promoted to Lieutenant of Detectives slightly more than 6 months earlier. In spite of the fact that this was the man whose appointment had probably cost him the Chief's job, Hurt had become good friends with Chief John Watt. He promised to stay in touch and he did.

Hurt wrote Watt from Washington, D.C., on June 18 while attending the FBI school. He noted that they had completed their last test of the school that day and that he and Campbell were the only ones in the school who weren't lawyers. He mentioned that the rainy capital weather was a nice change from a typical Oklahoma June and that it was fortunate there was plenty of cheap seafood available because "steak is worth forty cents a pound and a one- room apartment rents for $60 per month". He also mentioned that crime in Oklahoma City was mild compared to the nation's capital. As an example he told Watt of a recent case where three hijackers had robbed a policeman, stolen his car, robbed everyone they came across for the next ten days and killed a filling station operator, listening to police broadcasts about them on the stolen police car's radio all the way. Watt's reply a few days later was encouraging, telling Hurt that he and Campbell would get through the FBI school just fine because they already had what the lawyers would need years to acquire, "practical experience". He also congratulated them on the news that they were being transferred to "a regular territory".

The regular territory was Chicago. Campbell was issued FBI Badge Number 278 and Hurt received Badge Number 365. On July 10, Hurt and Campbell got a letter from the Secretary of the Employee's Benefit Fund, telling them about some changes in their insurance. The Secretary also mentioned "I understand that you are out looking for "Bad Boy" Dillinger. The whole Department is pulling for you....".

He understood correctly. Hurt and Campbell had been assigned to J. Edgar Hoover's newly created "Flying Squad". They got their name from the fact that they were intended to fly, literally in airplanes and figuratively in time, all over the country, knowing no jurisdictional boundaries in their relentless pursuit of leads to track down the top public enemies. The squad was led by Inspector Sam Cowley and consisted of a core group of eight agents, including Hurt and Campbell, to be supplemented as needed by local agents and police officers wherever they were operating at the time. The name incontestably at the top of their list was John Herbert Dillinger.

Twelve days later, a promising lead came up in the squad's home base of Chicago. Dillinger was supposed to attend a movie on the night of July 22 at one of two theaters.

Cowley worked out a plan with Melvin Purvis, the Special Agent in Charge of the FBI's Chicago office. Both theaters were staked out until Dillinger was seen entering the Biograph Theater on Lincoln Avenue with two women about 8:30 P.M. The observing agents must have enjoyed the irony—the feature was a gangster movie with a "crime doesn't pay" theme.

The agents were summoned from the other theater while Cowley notified Hoover in Washington, D.C.. Hoover instructed him to arrest Dillinger when he left the theater to minimize the danger to innocent bystanders. Very quickly, 21 FBI agents and 4 East Chicago Police officers were stationed within half a block of the theater entrance on both sides of the street in both directions. Two uniformed Chicago officers who answered a call to check on the "suspicious subjects" around the theater were hurriedly shown badges and told to leave the area.

If adrenaline could be converted to electricity, those 25 men could probably have lit the theater's bright marquee during the two hours Manhattan Melodrama was playing inside that night. Any officer who has spent time on an armed robbery stakeout can appreciate a little of the tension of those two hours. In the last 11 months, this man and his gang had robbed almost 20 banks and 3 police arsenals, engaged in 3 spectacular jail escapes, killed 10 men and wounded 7 others including police officers and federal agents.

About 10:30 P.M., Dillinger and the two women left the theater. As they strolled past the first doorway adjacent to the theater entrance, a man standing in the doorway unobtrusively lit a cigar and sealed John Dillinger's fate. The smoker was Melvin Purvis and his flaring match in the darkened doorway was a signal to the agents that he had positively identified the fugitive. The adrenaline must have been practically flowing into the street.

As Dillinger and his companions continued down the sidewalk leisurely, three men turned from their positions and fell in behind the trio. After a few more steps, the two women stopped. When Dillinger noticed after a few more paces that his girls had fallen behind, he looked around for them. Seeing the three men in suits behind him, he instantly figured out the situation. He reached into his right pants pocket for a Colt .380 automatic pistol as he darted into a nearby alley. The three pursuing agents fired five shots, two of them hitting Dillinger in the chest and head. Two women were slightly wounded by ricochets but Dillinger was dying. Some of the gathering crowd dipped handkerchiefs in the blood pooling in the alley for souvenirs.

The names of the men who surrounded the Biograph Theater that night slowly became known to the public. For decades afterward, J. Edgar Hoover refused to publicly identify the three agents who had shot Dillinger. He wanted the Bureau as a whole to receive the credit instead of glorifying individual agents. The legend began circulating that Melvin Purvis had killed Dillinger, probably because Purvis disagreed with the Director's policy and had a penchant for seeking personal publicity. When Purvis's fame began to rival that of the almighty Director, it would eventually lead to Purvis's resignation from the Bureau but the legend continued. Purvis committed suicide in 1957 without disputing the legend.

After Hoover's death in 1972, the truth was acknowledged. The legend was wrong. Melvin Purvis never fired his weapon that night. Agent Jerry Campbell had been stationed across the street from the theater in the opposite direction, in what he would probably have considered an unlucky position. Dillinger walked away from his area. The three men who shot John Dillinger in that alley were Agents Clarence O. Hurt, Herman E. Hollis and Charles B. Winstead. There was some speculation that Winstead's bullets had been the ones that hit Dillinger because he was using a .45 automatic while Hurt and Hollis were believed to be using .38 revolvers but it was never resolved what caliber the fatal bullets had been.

Agent Hollis and Inspector Cowley were killed four months later in a gun battle with the remnants of Dillinger's gang. Baby Face Nelson was killed in the same shootout. The work apparently to their liking, Clarence Hurt and Jerry Campbell went on to long careers with the FBI.

The big names were dropping like flies in 1934. On May 23, Bonnie Parker and Clyde Barrow were machine gunned into mince meat by Texas and Louisiana officers near Arcadia, Louisiana. When the smoke cleared, the stolen 1934 Ford Clyde was driving had 107 bullet holes in it. Clyde personally absorbed 27 of those bullets while Bonnie was hit over 50 times. One day short of two months later, Dillinger was killed in Chicago. That same day, Ray Hamilton of Bonnie and Clyde's gang escaped from the Death House in Huntsville, Texas. He would soon be recaptured and executed the following year. In the same week, Earl Thayer died in Leavenworth. The old member of Al Spencer's gang, after being arrested by a group of OCPD officers including Red Robinson in 1926, had broken out of Leavenworth two years earlier by taking the warden hostage. He kept his freedom for only three days but that exposure to a Kansas December broke his health.

On June 13, Oscar Grant Lee died in Kansas City from stomach cancer at the age of 70. After his ten months as the OCPD's third Chief, Lee had created a building empire that had lent his name to the Lee and Lee-Huckins Hotels before moving his headquarters to Kansas City. Lee had obtained some of the financing for his first hotel from Charles Colcord in 1900. Lee was buried in the family mausoleum in Fairlawn Cemetery.

If Hoover was looking for another OCPD recruit, he found him a few days before Clarence Hurt and Jerry Campbell helped end Dillinger's career. Jelly Bryce already had a notation on the first page of his OCPD personnel file that said " This officer has worked in Auto Theft Dept., Raiding and Vice Dept., Detective Bureau on general and special cases-Always selected when rounding up badly wanted men-Is a crack pistol shot. Has been instrumental in assisting State and Federal officers in apprehending notorious characters including Wilbur Underhill ". On July 18, 1934, he put an exclamation point behind it.

That morning, OCPD officers learned that Harvey Pugh was in town. An associate of Clyde Barrow and wanted for the murder of a police officer in McPherson, Kansas, Pugh and two other gangsters, Tom Walton and J. Ray O'Donnell, were supposed to be at the Wren Hotel at 408 1/2 West Main. Detectives Jelly Bryce, Charles Ryan and C.D. Pierce went to arrest them.

Bryce was carrying his "lucky" gun with him that morning. It was a .44 revolver with ivory handle grips. A steer's head was embossed on one side of the grips and a black cat and the number "13" on the other side. He would need both the revolver and the luck today.

Arriving at the hotel about 8 A.M., they asked the clerk, Nora Bingaman, to see the owner. She said her daughter, Mrs. Merle Bolen, was the owner and offered to take the officers up to her daughter's room. Knocking and opening the door, she started in and then backed out of the door, looking surprised. Bryce, nearest to the door, blocked it from closing and opened it. Mrs. Bolen was laying in bed with J. Ray O'Donnell who was holding a pistol with both hands, pointing it directly at Bryce. Before O'Donnell could fire, Bryce drew his revolver from under his suit coat and fired five times. All five shots hit O'Donnell in the head and he was probably dead before his gun hit the floor, unfired.

Both women were arrested along with Tom Walton. Harvey Pugh was picked up later when he came back to get his car. A little over three months later, on November 1, Jelly Bryce was given a six-month leave of absence to work with the FBI. It wouldn't be long enough. He remained with them for the next 23 years.

*Officer Elmer Lee Sartor.*

One of the first axioms that new motorcycle cops hear from the veterans is "Don't brag about having never gone down on the bike. If you ride them long enough, you will". As much driving as police officers do, much of it at high speeds and in dangerous situations like pursuits, it is a dangerous enough task when surrounded by several thousand pounds of steel on four wheels. Another factor they bear in mind is that, like the military, "always remember that all of your equipment was supplied by the lowest bidder". Many officers feel their chances of being injured in their vehicles is much greater than being shot or stabbed. Motorcycle officers accept the additional risks of the vulnerability of riding what is essentially a bicycle with the power of a car.

Losses to the community continued in 1934 when, on August 20, Motorcycle Officer Elmer Sartor died from injuries sustained in a traffic accident. Sartor was one of a group of officers escorting Postmaster General James H. Farley to Wichita, Kansas, when the accident occurred about 10 A.M. on Highway 77 south of Ponca City, Oklahoma, near the famous 101 Ranch.. It was reported that a wheel on his motorcycle locked which caused the accident. Rushed to a Ponca City hospital, Sartor had a fractured skull. Chief Watt tried to get Sartor's wife to Ponca City before he expired but it was in vain as they had not arrived when the officer died less than three hours later.

A 28-year-old, five-year veteran, Sartor had been involved in one previous accident on his motorcycle but not at highway speeds. Sartor was lauded as one of the most popular officers, both with his colleagues and motorists, due to "his unfailing good nature". An orphan, the officer had been raised in the home of Mr. and Mrs. J.G. Street, parents of future Oklahoma City mayor Allen Street and proprietor of the Street and Draper Funeral Home. Ironically, it was a Street and Draper ambulance that had transported the officer's body back to Oklahoma City for burial.

Sartor was laid to rest in Memorial Park Cemetery two days later. His pallbearers were Chief John Watt, Captains Tom Webb, R.W. Cantrell and W.G. Lloyd, Lieutenant G.P. Harrison and Sergeant John H. Reading. To compound the tragedy, Sartor's widow was six months pregnant. Three months after her husband's death, on November 23, she gave birth to a baby boy who would never have the chance to know his father.

As is often the case, comedy followed close on the heels of tragedy. On the same day as Officer Sartor's death, the OCPD again made the front page, albeit with a little less dignity. This time it was under the headline "Police Recover Own Car Amid Shots and Shouts". Sergeant Lee Mullinex and Officer J.G. Muse were called to a disturbance at the St. Nicholas Hotel at N.W. 8th and Broadway. Chief John Watt and another car stopped to assist. When they officers came out, they discovered Mullinex's and Muse's police car gone.

The stolen police car was reported on the radio. Lieutenant G.P. Harrison and Officer Robert Steffey saw the car at N.E. 23rd and Lincoln and "the race was on". With Harrison firing an automatic shotgun and Steffey a rifle at the fleeing car, the suspects abandoned it at N.E. 21st and Walnut, running into a field to hide. Rapidly surrounded by officers, the two men were hauled out of the field and charged with larceny of an auto. The only casualty of the affair was the police car. The paper noted that "The police car's windshield and rear glass were shattered and the car was riddled with bullets".

*Charles F. Colcord-1859-1934.*

John Dillinger had been shot down outside the Biograph Theater in Chicago on July 22. Three months later Charles Arthur "Pretty Boy" Floyd was killed in a gunfight with FBI agents in an Ohio cornfield. Never fond of his highly publicized nickname, he allegedly even repudiated it with his dying breaths. When asked by an FBI agent if he was Pretty Boy Floyd, the mortally wounded man corrected him by stating "I'm Charles Arthur Floyd". His body was returned to his hometown of Sallisaw, Oklahoma, for burial in the Akins Cemetery eight miles to the northeast. Nearly 40,000 people attended the funeral from 15 states, his headstone all but destroyed by souvenir hunters knocking chips off of it. In a typical Oklahoma paradox, Floyd was buried near three relatives who were all former lawmen.

On December 20, Charles Francis Colcord

died in his seventy-fifth year. He had resigned as Oklahoma City's first Chief of Police when he was elected as Oklahoma County's first Sheriff. He was to become a major community leader for most of its first half century. Branching out into the real estate, banking, insurance and oil businesses, he constructed the building named for him as the City's first "skyscraper" of twelve stories in 1910. Colcord was interred in Fairlawn Cemetery.

On the up side, Mayor McGee said the City was "in great shape". The City had no tax levy, $3 million cash in the bank, owned $80 million in property and the Water Department had just put another million dollars in the City Treasury. He stated that the Depression was over in Oklahoma City. Not all of the citizens agreed with him.

During the first week of January, 1935, Ma and Freddie Barker were killed in a four-hour gunbattle with the FBI in Florida. According to one account "They died in an old Oklahoma tradition, [with] empty guns in their hands". A gentleman to the end, Freddie had allegedly been chivalrous enough to give Ma the machine gun with the 100-round magazine while he took the one with the 50-round clip. The Feds were equally considerate. Ma was felled by three slugs while Freddie absorbed fourteen. Rumor had it that Jelly Bryce was one of the officers involved.

The Barkers were buried in the Williams Timber Hill Cemetery east of the small town of Welch in far northeastern Oklahoma. Herman Barker had passed from the scene in 1927 after being shot up so bad by Wichita, Kansas, police following an armed robbery that he shot himself in the head just to get some relief. Arthur "Doc" Barker would survive another four years before being killed during an escape attempt from Alcatraz. Lloyd, the last surviving brother, would be killed by his wife during a domestic argument in 1949. Thus was the ignominious end of the outlaw Barker family.

Also during that week, the City Council started yet another investigation into allegations of police payoffs by gamblers. When it was all said and done, the only evidence they said they were able to come up with was the fact that two Detectives had not been making their inspections of cigar stores. Their investigative report cleared both Chief Watt and the City Manager of any malfeasance, stating that the Police Department was "cleaner than it has been for years".

The spring elections of 1935 marked the beginning of the end for the irascible City Councilman J.E. Taylor. The man had been raising unmitigated hell at City Hall for the last four years with his belligerence, nepotism, and alternating crusading and hypocrisy. After being instrumental in "liberalizing" law enforcement under Chief Watt and the resulting return to power of Orban Patterson, the man had the gall to start screaming for public investigations of vice and bribery of police officers. While there is little doubt that both were occurring, it was anticlimactic and nothing came of his investigations.

The leading candidates for Mayor that year were Taylor and his old nemesis, Councilman J. Frank Martin. If one thing could be said for Taylor's bad judgement, it was that it was consistent. Taylor's Baptist preacher wrote a public letter criticizing Martin's Catholicism. In addition, Taylor was supported by many Ku Klux Klan members from the Walton years. Martin's followers made the most of it in the black areas. Martin was elected, Taylor ejected. Nevertheless, it was still very plain that the City Council, not the City Manager, ran the city. Emphasizing that fact, the city was to have eight City Managers during Mayor Martin's two two-year terms.

By 1935, Oklahoma City had grown into a major metropolis with a population approaching 200,000. Severe droughts of 1934, 1935 and 1936 kept the Depression spiralling downwards. Symbols of that Depression, squatter camps sprang up all around the City. One of the worst ones was the May Avenue Camp, near that street's intersection with the North Canadian River. Hundreds of families lived in horrible squalor for miles up and down the river bed. Typhoid, spinal meningitis and others calamities reached epidemic proportions. Progress, however, was being made in the form of heavy industry and agriculture. Central to it all was the automobile.

When the decade started, there were 550,000 vehicles registered in Oklahoma, 10 percent of them in Oklahoma City. In the downtown area, parking and traffic congestion were causing innumerable problems for police and commuters. Traffic officers worked diligently to monitor cars parked in time zones by chalking tires, a process of making chalk marks on the tires of parked cars so the officer could tell if the car had moved since his last round but many flagrant violations occurred. A new system was needed.

In 1932, Carl C. Magee had been appointed Chairman of the Traffic Committee of the Chamber of Commerce. As a solution to the parking problem, he suggested the installation of a series of automated, self-policing meters. A contest was sponsored by the Chamber of Commerce and Oklahoma A&M College (now Oklahoma State University) offered a prize for the first working model. One year later, two A&M professors submitted the winning entry. Magee patented it and had it produced in Sand Springs.

On July 16, 1935, the world's first Park-O-Meter was installed in downtown Oklahoma City on the southwest corner of Park Avenue and Robinson. That parking meter is now on display at the Oklahoma Historical Society.

A testing plan called for the installation of 200 meters on the 14 most congested downtown blocks. The parking fee was set at a nickel an hour with a $20 fine for violations.

Public reaction to the new device was mixed. While some citizens welcomed it as the solution to the parking problem and the City viewed it as a new source of revenue, others took a more comic approach. At one meter, two couples inserted a nickel, set up a folding table and proceeded to play bridge. On another occasion, a rancher tied his horse to a meter, claiming it was cheaper than using a livery stable.

For the first few weeks after the first installation, Chief Watt ordered his men not to issue tickets to violators, giving the public a chance to adapt to the new program. The response among officers on the street was enthusiastic. The automated system made it much easier to identify violators and to defend police summonses in court. By Christmas of 1935, there were 600 parking meters on the streets of Oklahoma City.

Another year of triumph and tragedy came with 1936. Government WPA building projects included the Municipal Auditorium (now the Civic Center Music Hall) and Taft Stadium. Another attempt was made to repeal the state prohibition law but was defeated again. Oklahoma became the only state to have producing oil wells on the grounds of the State Capitol and construction began on a new police station a block north of Main Street on Shartel. The city's homicide rate was 30 percent higher than the national rate. The OCPD had 40 cars, evenly divided between Patrol and Detectives, and 23 motorcycles. All Department vehicles were equipped with one-way radios. The Traffic Division comprised 41 of the 222 officers along with 18 "corner men" directing traffic at major intersections.

There was a deadly rainstorm in Oklahoma City on the night of Saturday, May 23, 1936.

*The OCPD Scout Car Division of the mid-1930s posing in front of their offices at 2121 Westwood.*

In two traffic accidents that night, thirteen people were injured and two were killed. The first accident occurred at 10:25 P.M. at S.W. 17th and Robinson. Two cars collided, one containing ten people and the other three people. A nine-year-old boy was killed.

Officers J.A. McRee and Ray S. Clark, leaving the police garage at 2121 S. Westwood, went on duty five minutes later. As they crossed the Exchange Avenue viaduct with McRee driving, they were dispatched to investigate the other accident. At the eastern end of the viaduct the street jogs to the right. As McRee attempted to make the turn, the police car skidded on the rain-slick street. The right front door of the car came open and Officer Clark fell partially out of the car. The car skidded across the street, striking a telephone pole and crushing Clark between them.

*Officer Ray S. Clark.*

Clark was the 45-year-old son of former Chief Waller J. Clark. His funeral procession to Fairlawn Cemetery was accompanied by his parents, his wife, two daughters and son Ray Jr., who would begin his own 20-year career with the OCPD in 1948. Typically of the officers of the day, his employment dates were misleading. Although he had begun his career with the OCPD in November of 1920, he had two breaks in service and had thus totalled a little less than 11 years of active service during the preceding 15 and 1/2 years.

The Police Department had been suffering another seesawing period since their last political castration in the summer of 1933 and the "liberalizing" of vice ordinance enforcement. Mayor Martin had been trying to restore his previous enforcement power to Chief Watt but was stymied by City Manager Mosier and a disunited City Council.

In September of 1936, reporters from the Oklahoma City Times bought illegal liquor at 22 places in 3 hours. Their paper listed another 42 places where the evil spirits was easily available. The article featured some undiplomatic quotes from Lieutenant George P. Harrison, whose prior claim to fame had been shooting up Lee Mullinex's police car two years earlier. Lt. Harrison told the reporters that the Scout Car officers had been ordered to discontinue liquor raids for the last two years. He also told them that Chief Watt was "a figurehead" and the Department was actually being run by City Manager Mosier and Inspector L.O. Bogstie.

Some anonymous soul once listed the traditional phases of all governmental projects as;1. Great expectations 2. Disillusionment 3. Panic 4. Search for the guilty 5. Punishment of the innocent 6. Reward of the non-participants.

This situation certainly followed the pattern. As Albert McRill stated it in his book And Satan Came Also, "Lieutenant Harrison at once joined the ranks of the unemployed". City Manager Mosier resigned the next month and the City Council cranked up another investigation which resulted in a report the following month. The report made the startling revelation that there was "one, and possibly several, organized liquor rings or syndicates operating in the city, headed and operated by men who held themselves invulnerable to the law by their methods of operation". This example of investigative perspicacity was followed by blaming it all on apathetic citizens and officers. The report promptly sank faster than the Titanic.

After the severe droughts of the past several years, 1937 turned out to be a year of floods. Oddly enough, the floods probably caused a greater

*Captain Frank Cissne.*

exodus from the State that the Dust Bowl or the Depression. It is estimated that as many as 300,000 people migrated to California during this period, mostly from Oklahoma.

One who was still around was Orban Patterson. In the early morning hours of January 10, 1937, police were called to Patterson's luxurious apartment in the Sieber Hotel at 1305 N. Hudson. A female companion, Ethel Shively, had been shot once in the left breast. The weapon was a .380 automatic belonging to Patterson. Police were called and the lady said she had fired the shot herself before she was removed to the hospital. No further explanation was given. Both Patterson and the lady had been drinking but were not drunk, according to the responding officers. Patterson was not arrested and no charges were filed.

Over the next few days, there were recriminations and finger-pointing all around. Chief Watt stated there were no charges to be leveled against Patterson in connection with the shooting. There were charges in the City Council of a botched investigation. A councilman censured Captain Marvin Murray, the officer who answered the original call, for not bringing Patterson's gun in for fingerprinting or arresting him. Watt said that Captain Joe Jerkins, the desk supervisor that night, was at fault for not notifying the Detective Bureau. Governor Marland publicly branded Patterson as "Public Enemy Number One", said Patterson had been doing as he pleased for years with impunity from the Police Department and he was starting his own investigation. The City Manager and Chief Watt wished him good luck. Councilman Moore, the one who censured Captain Murray, began calling for Chief Watt's dismissal and replacement with a stronger Chief.

On the morning of April 1, 1937, 50-year-old night shift Captain Frank Cissne was involved in a three-car collision at N.W. 4th and Broadway. The 14-year veteran had spent his first two years on the force in scout cars before transferring to the Motorcycle Squad in 1925. Promoted to Lieutenant in 1930, he had remained on motorcycles until 1936. That year he had been involved in his sixth motorcycle accident and, oddly enough, vowed to do the rest of his travelling in automobiles. He had served as night shift Captain since his promotion the previous January.

Ted Bried, the 22-year-old motorist who had struck Cissne's scout car, paid a $1 fine for having no State Driver's License and posted three $20 bonds on charges of reckless driving, possessing whiskey and transporting whiskey. Cissne was taken to Oklahoma City General Hospital with five broken ribs. His condition worsened as pneumonia and internal paralysis set in over the next few days. Belatedly, he received a blood transfusion from his son, Ralph, but died a few hours later on the afternoon of April 5.

The Ohio native had come to the City in 1907 from Coffeyville, Kansas. Before joining the OCPD in 1923, he had managed an apartment house, ran several restaurants and was at one time the head chef at the posh Huckins Hotel. His death was counted as the fourteenth traffic fatality in Oklahoma County in 1937. He was buried in Rose Hill Cemetery in services attended by all off-duty officers. His pallbearers were five OCPD Captains (Tom Webb, Lloyd White, R.W. Cantrell, Joe Jerkins and Charles Ryan) and Oklahoma County Deputy Sheriff George Kerr.

One of the major keys to Oklahoma City's initial success in exploiting its central location had been the railroads. By the time of statehood, more than half a dozen separate rail lines bisected the city. Though causing little trouble to a small town that moved by horses, wagons and buggies, as the central business district grew and the city became more motorized, the grade crossings of the multiple railways traversing the downtown area caused massive traffic jams. The problems finally became unmanageable as the decade of the 1930s began and an effort began for relocation of the railroads.

The Rock Island passenger depot just north of the Skirvin Hotel and their freight depot to the west would be vacated and moved to the location of the new Rock Island Depot west of S.W. 6th and Robinson. A new Santa Fe station would be constructed on its original site with the tracks elevated and industrial tracks located a couple of miles north at N.W. 24th and Santa Fe Avenue. The Frisco depot and freight shed, between First and Second Streets, would also be vacated. This project opened up a strip of land several blocks long through the very center of the business district. In a movement led by City Manager Orval "Red" Mosier, the City Chamber of Commerce raised a bond issue and, in concert with the federal government's work relief agencies, the current Civic Center was born. The mid-30's saw the construction of a new County Courthouse, City Hall, Municipal Auditorium (now the Civic Center Music Hall) and Police Headquarters.

On April 18, 1937, the new Police Headquarters building was opened to accommodate the growing force. Located at 200 North Shartel, what is now the City Jail Building was originally only five stories tall but a sixth story was added some years later. The other three streets surrounding the block were named Couch Drive on the north, Colcord Drive on the south and Lee Street on the east.

The building was divided by two large steel doors to isolate incoming prisoners from the general public or, as the officers put it, "to separate the sheep from the goats". An assembly-recreation room was included, offering off-duty officers a place to eat and relax. Bathing facilities were also available.

The Jail was on the third and fifth floors and featured a newly-developed gear system for operating the cell doors. In the fourth floor kitchen, former Detective Ray "Red" Robinson prepared meals for the prisoners. In making the move, the Department vacated the old building at Maiden Lane and Wall Street that it had occupied since the turn of the century.

The day after the new building opened, Chief John Watt retired and was replaced by Granville Scanland. Born in Randall, Kansas, on June 5, 1896, Scanland was a World War I Marine veteran with no prior law enforcement

*Chief Granville Scanland.*

*The new Police Headquarters at 200 North Shartel-1937.*

experience. A graduate of the University of Kansas law school, he had been a practicing attorney in Oklahoma City for the past 16 years. He took the Chief's job at less than half the salary he had been making as a lawyer.

An observer of the day recalls that Scanland was really a "figurehead Chief. Mickey Ryan, the Chief of Detectives, really ran the Department. Granville was a fine fellow, though, and the men liked him alright". By 1937, 228 officers worked to enforce the law including 53 Detectives and 17 special liquor raiders.

Chief Scanland stirred up some controversy during his first year in office by shaking up the Vice Squad, still a publicly prominent part of the Department because of the nearly constant whiskey raids. Within a two-week period, three men commanded the unit. Lt. Walter Acord had been in charge of it during Chief Watt's administration. Lt. Hank Reid was promoted from narcotics detective when Acord was transferred. He was rapidly replaced with Lt. Roy Bergman (later a Chief). Publicly, all three said they were "tickled to death" with their new assignments. The vice shakeups were a symptom of the disease that seemed to grip every new Chief after he took office as long as prohibition was in effect.

*OCPD Vice Lt. Walter Acord illustrates the OCPD's pursuit policy of the 1930s.*

"Everybody went raiding," W.A. "Ace" Williams, later an Assistant Chief, remembered. "We would get the old Black Maria, the wagon, and go down to those joints on Reno and take everybody in there to jail for disorderly house violations". Similar raids, but in modern black and white vans, would continue fairly frequently well into the 1970s, usually for open saloon violations, serving minors or dealing in narcotics.

In 1940, when the Department acquired brand new Fords, the lettering on the doors of the solid black cruisers proudly stated "Radio Patrol-OCPD", advertising the conversion of the entire Patrol

*OCPD Accident Squad car of the late 1930s.*

Division to two-way radios. Ten years later, the first OCPD radio frequency would carry the call letters KKC374 and be transferred to the Oklahoma County Sheriff's Office.

The police pursuit became more commonplace also, as higherpowered cars were developed. Bootleggers made a deadly game out of trying to elude the pursuing police cars and the spectacular high-speed chases often ended in wild crashes. Booze, the transient criminal displaced by the Depression, glamorous policemen and equally glamorous bank robbers——all were an integral part of the era.

*Officer Fred B. Counts.*

Former Chief William B. Hendrey died at Paris, Arkansas, on June 1, 1938, at the age of 75. Hendrey had been Chief of the OCPD from 1899-1901. He had then moved to Trinidad, Colorado, and been on the police force there for the next 12 years. For the last 25 years, he had been a stock farmer at Adona and Bigelow, Arkansas. Hendrey's obituary noted that he had come to Oklahoma Territory with his father in the Run of '89 and had settled on a farm in the Tecumseh area. His 98-year-old father survived him.

Chief Scanland's administration was destined to be saddened by the loss of two more officers. The summer of 1938 was a relatively mild one by Oklahoma standards. It was dry, as usual, but it wasn't until the third week of August that the thermometer finally hit 100 degrees. Late on the afternoon of August 22, a report came in of a fire in a barn at 706 N.E. 6th. As usual, fire and police units began responding Code Three with red lights and sirens. Most people don't think about the fact that if you're in a vehicle with a siren on, you can't hear another vehicle's siren. That afternoon, it would have tragic consequences.

A fire truck from the station at Park and Hudson was speeding east on 10th Street, Code Three. Simultaneously, a police scout car was southbound on Durland, also running Code Three at a high rate of speed. Officer L.R. Puett was driving and his partner, Officer Fred Counts, was "riding shotgun". The two vehicles entered the intersection of N.E. 10th and Durland almost simultaneously, the fire truck slightly ahead of the scout car.

The scout car plowed into the side of the heavy fire truck, turning it over and littering the intersection with firehose, chemical extinguishers, inhalators and other equipment, in addition to the two firemen who had been hanging on the back of the truck. The two firemen riding in the truck's cab were also injured but not to the extent of the two police officers. Virtually everything forward of the firewall on the 1937 Ford two-door sedan scout car was totally demolished, the front wheels lying nearly flat on the ground. Puett was taken to Oklahoma City General Hospital with severe chest injuries and shock. Counts was taken to Polyclinic Hospital but was dead on arrival. A 27-year-old Virginia native, Counts had been an officer for slightly more than two years.

The next day, Chief Scanland announced a plan to revise the OCPD's system for answering emergency calls. Firemen would instruct officers in the location of the City's fire stations and their established fire lanes so the officers would know what equipment the firemen usually dispatched to fires and the normal routes they took. Police policy for emergency runs called for officers to "slow down and proceed with caution".

Shortly before 10:30 P.M. on October 29, Detectives Webb Campbell and I.L. McCurdy responded to a general radio broadcast of a prowler in the 500 block of N.W. 24th. In those times, "prowler" was held to be synonymous with "burglar" and that was in fact the case in this instance. A citizen had seen a man reaching in the window of a residence and a woman's purse had been stolen off of a bed while the family played cards in the living room. As the two Detectives arrived at the location, Detective Campbell, a very athletic officer and a former

*Detective Webb L. Campbell.*

football player at the University of Oklahoma, jumped out of the car before it fully stopped and began running around to the rear of the house.

Two-way radios were relatively new. Officers who were used to listening to the police radio weren't necessarily used to talking on it. Procedures that were ingrained in later-day officers were absent. Procedures like announcing arrival at a call or advising that plainclothes officers were in the area. Unknown to Campbell and McCurdy, a pair of Stolen Goods Detectives had already arrived, began pursuing the burglar and had already fired shots at him.

As Campbell ran around the corner of the residence in the darkness and wearing a dark suit, Detective Lawrence Bush fired a shot at the shadowy figure with his .38. Seeing the figure fall, he began calling for his partner, thinking he had shot the burglar. When McCurdy arrived moments later, they discovered it was Campbell, hit once in the left side. He was immediately taken to the hospital but died from his wound about three hours later.

It was the first instance of an officer's death as a result of "friendly fire". Unfortunately, it would not be the last. Although exonerated for his part in the tragedy, Detective Lawrence Bush resigned from the Police Department eight months later. Campbell, a 35-year-old, 7-year veteran, had been Officer Douglas Gates' partner when Gates had been slain five years earlier only four blocks from the site of Campbell's death and had received a Medal of Merit for his actions that day. Campbell's funeral services were held in the Municipal Auditorium with more than 1,000 in attendance. As he was laid to rest in Memorial Park Cemetery, there was already a collection being taken up among his fellow officers to pay off the $1,600 mortgage on his widow's home.

Two years later, both widows of the last two officers to die in the line of duty, Vida Campbell and Lucille Counts, would be employed by the OCPD as secretaries and go on to fulfill their own 20-year careers, serving from 1940 to 1960.

As the OCPD closed its' first half century, over 200 men comprised a motorized, radio-dispatched police force headquartered in a new, five-story building. In that 50 years, 29 men had served 35 separate terms as Chief of Police. Only four of them, however, had been during the last decade, a sign of the depoliticization and stability of the new OCPD. Seventeen men had died in the line of duty to help achieve that stability, nine of them in the last ten years. Mercifully, more tranquil times were coming for the Police Department but only by comparison to what the entire nation was preparing to suffer.

As though to verify that the new stability was not an illusion, the OCPD was to have only two Chiefs in the next fifteen years. The first one was the perfect symbol of the 1930's to finish that lawless decade and begin the 1940's.

When Granville Scanland retired in October of 1939, his apparent intent to use the office as a political stepping stone was fulfilled when he was appointed an Assistant County Attorney. He would later be elected Oklahoma County Attorney in 1948 and serve four two-year terms before being defeated by Bill Berry in 1956.

Scanland was replaced with 59-year old Frank S. Smith. A native of Houston, Texas, as a young man he had served on both the Houston and Dallas police forces. In 1915, Smith had been wounded five times during a shootout with a man named Red Kelly in Dallas. Leaving local law enforcement to join the FBI, Smith had been credited with solving the Osage Hills murder cases in the mid-1920s and the capture of Barker gang member Alvin Karpis. He was one of the first Chiefs to come from outside the Department not as a purely political appointment. Smith was best known and remembered for having survived the infamous Kansas City Massacre. Less well known was the fact that Smith was the man who had started the chain of events that led up to it.

In the summer of 1933, Smith was a Bureau of Investigation (FBI) Special Agent stationed in Oklahoma City. On June 16, he and Special Agent F.J. "Joe" Lackey drove to Hot Springs, Arkansas, to attempt to locate and arrest the fugitive mobster Frank Nash. To help them identify Nash if and when they found him, they brought with them a man who knew Nash intimately, McAlester Chief of Police Otto Reed. Although he would be far out of his legal jurisdiction, by the unique rules of the day, Reed's presence was what allowed the federal agents to make the arrest and carry weapons.

*Chief Frank S. Smith.*

Nash was a native of Hobart, Oklahoma, a former member of the Al Spencer gang and a veteran burglar, bank robber and murderer with heavy mob connections. He had served two stretches in the Oklahoma State Penitentiary in McAlester and was currently an escapee from the federal pen in Leavenworth, Kansas. Locating Nash in a mob-owned cigar store, Smith arrested him while Lackey and Reed covered their exit from the store. The officers then rapidly drove out of the heavily mob-infiltrated town.

In Russellville, Arkansas, Smith called R.H. Colvin, the Special Agent in Charge of the Oklahoma City office, for instructions. Colvin ordered them to proceed to Fort Smith and take a train to Kansas City where they would be met by other officers to return Nash to Leavenworth Federal Penitentiary. If Colvin had chosen to have Nash returned to the home office first, what was to go down in history as the Kansas City Massacre could well have been the Oklahoma City Massacre.

Shortly after 7 A.M. on June 17, 1933, four local and Federal officers met Agents Smith, Lackey and Chief Reed at Kansas City's Union Station. As Nash got in the front seat of FBI Agent Raymond Caffrey's Chevrolet, Smith, Lackey and Reed got in the back seat. As the officers got in the car, three men opened up on them with shotguns and Thompson submachine guns. Killed in the holocaust were Nash, Agent Caffrey, Chief Reed and two Kansas City detectives, W.J. "Red" Grooms and Frank Hermanson. FBI Agents Joe Lackey and Reed Vetterli were wounded. Of the seven lawmen, only Agent Frank Smith was miraculously uninjured. Charles Arthur "Pretty Boy" Floyd, Vern Miller and Adam Richetti were suspected of the ambush but none of them lived to confess. Floyd and Richetti publicly denied their complicity but, in the outrage following the carnage, no one listened. Miller was murdered by the mob five months later in Detroit, Floyd died under the guns of the FBI the next year and Richetti was executed in 1938.

Smith was a reminder of the past decade and a look forward to the new one. Smith was apparently forewarned of the City's vice situation that was a thorn in every Chief's side and the chaos that had reigned in the Vice Bureau since Chief Scanland had given it three commanders in a two-week period at the beginning of his administration. Smith immediately tried to restore some stability to the Vice Bureau by promoting Walter Acord to Captain and placing him back in charge of the unit he had commanded under Chief Watt.

Acord came out of the gate running. In the last three months of the decade, his men conducted 624 gambling investigations resulting in 45 raids and 291 arrests. They also made 18 narcotics arrests, 13 of them turned over to Federal prosecution.

# VI — WAR AND PEACE 1940-1949

In our pre-war innocence, an old Department tradition achieved its' ultimate success. The "Flatfoot Four" was originated by O.A. Cargill soon after he became Mayor in 1923. The barbershop quartet made its initial public appearance at a meeting of the Oklahoma City Chamber of Commerce and it was at this meeting that Mayor Cargill first introduced them as "The Flatfoot Four". The original quartet consisted of Officers Frank Sheppard, lead; Bill Parrish, bass; Roland Cargill, the Mayor's brother, baritone; and Johnny Whalen, tenor.

This foursome remained intact until 1927 when all of them but Whalen left the Department. In 1929, the quartet was reorganized with W.C. "Red" Elliott as lead singer, Ralph Kaylor as baritone, Bill West as bass and Whalen in the tenor slot he was to continually occupy. The quartet soon began the tradition of singing hymns at the funeral services of deceased officers.

In 1930, Jack Roberts became the lead and Elliott the baritone, replacing Kaylor. West was soon replaced with J.D. "Lefty" Walker. The group stabilized until 1933 when Elliott went to the Oklahoma State Bureau of Criminal Identification. In 1936, Roberts followed him.

When Granville Scanland became Chief in 1937, he reorganized the group at the suggestion of Whalen. Personnel changes continued with Whalen the one constant factor. National attention finally began to catch up with the local interest.

The Society for the Preservation and Encouragement of Barbershop Quartet Singing in America, Inc. formed its first chapter in Tulsa in 1938. Oklahoma City and Kansas City promptly formed chapters the same year. The organization's first annual competition was held in Tulsa in June of 1939. In competition with twenty other groups, the Flatfoot Four placed third with Chief Scanland singing baritone.

*Chief Frank Smith shows off his new police headquarters and his new Radio Patrol fleet of 1940 Fords on July 31, 1940.*

*The Flatfoot Four of 1940-left to right, Lt. Johnny Whalen, Officers Britt Stegall, Sam Barnes and Red Elliott.*

In the summer of 1940, the second annual contest was held in New York City. The quartet now consisted of Whalen, Britt Stegall, Sam Barnes and Red Elliott. This time the group won the National Championship. On July 25, they took time out from the World's Fair to appear on the Major Bowes Original Amateur Hour radio show, singing "Annie Laurie".

During the last four years of their existence, the quartet made hundreds of public appearances from New York City to Mexico City. For their last five years, they were the official quartet for the American Legion of the State of Oklahoma.

The last engagement of the "Flatfoot Four" was on September 6, 1941, at the Phillips Petroleum Community House southeast of the City. The last song they sang was the "Four-Way Song", in which four different songs are sung simultaneously in harmony.

In July of 1938, a new U.S. Attorney was appointed for the Western District of Oklahoma. His name was Charles Dierker and he told the press he was going to go after some of the "big ones". Dierker was as good as his word. During the first month of 1940, Orban Chester Patterson again ended up in front of a jury as a defendant instead of as a defense attorney. After all of his shooting, bribing, conniving, conspiring, wheeling and dealing for the last two and one-half decades, they went after him the same way they went after Capone. Dierker filed five counts of income tax evasion against Patterson after an 18-month investigation that had started soon after his appointment. The government said that Patterson had filed false tax returns for four consecutive years in the mid-1930's, claiming an income of less than $15,000 while they could prove he had earned almost $90,000.

On January 31, 1940, the first of the 54 witnesses against Patterson was sworn in. He was Seth Stone, a car thief currently serving his fourth term in the State Pen at McAlester. Stone testified he had given Patterson $16,150 in three of those years as "protection" payments for his stolen car racket. In 1935, the price had gone up $50 per stolen car. The extra $50 was for Jake Strickler, the Chief of the DPS Auto Theft Bureau. Strickler had already been tried for providing the false titles for the stolen cars and was currently serving five years.

Patterson had reported his 1933 income as $8,500. The government had evidence that he had purchased a ranch in New Mexico that year for $11,000 and had expenditures for that year alone totalling over $41,000. The prosecutor then started detailing Patterson's profits from his system for importing liquor into the City from Joplin, Missouri, not coincidentally the last base of operations of "King" William Creekmore. The figures were not lost on twelve jurors who had just lived through a decade of depression in Oklahoma.

The next day, Patterson's attorney changed his plea to nolo contendere, no contest. That did not shut Dierker up, however. He wanted the judge to consider the rest of his evidence when it came to determining Patterson's sentence. He showed that Patterson had invested over $90,000 in his New Mexico "ranch" in slightly over three years and that it had actually been used as a safe house for Patterson's fugitive clients. He detailed the renegade lawyer's profits from car theft, liquor, gambling, prostitution and speculated about unverified profits from narcotics. In fact, the only absolutely legitimate income they could prove Patterson had earned in seven years was less than $4,000. Patterson received five concurrent five-year sentences and a $25,000 fine.

That summer, Dierker stated that Oklahoma was drier than anytime in the State's history. That didn't prevent another vote on the repeal of prohibition that fall. The dry faction won again, although by smaller numbers, and prohibition remained.

With all the foot beat patrolmen eliminated and placed in scout cars with two-way radios, the Black Maria patrol wagon was retired and scrapped for junk toward the end of 1940. Purchased in 1928, the black Ford appeared to be a modified pickup with the bed enclosed with steel plate and wire mesh, "Police Patrol" painted boldly on the sides. Twelve-spoke

*The infamous Black Maria near the end of its career on November 14, 1940.*

wheels almost waist-high to a man, solid steel plate bumpers meant for ramming instead of the chrome ornaments on commercial models and a special brace fitted over the radiator with an old firebell big enough for a man to stick his head in were some of the wagon's special features. Chief Frank Smith decided to retire the old warhorse because she was just about worn out and also because the new Chief decided that "there's no use adding insult to injury by making a man ride in that old cart, with the bell clanging, so everyone can see he is jailhouse-bound". Among the officers bidding her a fond farewell was the wagon's long-time driver, W.F. "Bill" Falwell. He told of how he had been able to pack 20 gamblers into the rear at once and his only accident in the wagon. A motorist, apparently disoriented by the clanging furor the wagon caused, ran into his rear at California and Walker, scratching the Black Maria's rear bumper and destroying the other car. When sold for salvage, the old wagon was taken to her last known resting place at a salvage yard at 1000 South Robinson.

Former Chief and widely diverse lawman Martin C. Binion passed away on February 8, 1941, at 74 years of age, ending a 40-year career in law enforcement. Born on April 19, 1866, in Pickens County, Alabama, he had lived in Texas and Mississippi before moving to a ranch near Chickasha in Indian Territory in 1884. He later moved to Luther and became an Oklahoma County Deputy Sheriff there in 1901. He remained in that position for ten years except for a five-month period in 1910 when he was the acting Sheriff when the incumbent was removed from office. He had been with the OCPD in 1911-12 and was elected Oklahoma County Sheriff from 1913 until 1917. He then rejoined the OCPD until he became a Deputy U.S. Marshal in 1919. The next year he was the Federal Prohibition Agent in charge of Oklahoma until appointed Chief of the OCPD for four months. When deposed, he worked for the Commissioner of Public Property on the City dam until 1923 when he was again a Deputy Sheriff and also the sergeant-at-arms of the House of Representatives in the Ninth Legislature. Chief for another four months in 1923, he was again replaced and worked for an insurance company until appointed Chief again in 1927. Ending his term in 1928, he was defeated in a reelection bid for Sheriff and back on the force as a Detective four months later. After killing the man who killed his partner, Charles York, in 1933, Binion served as a Detective, Warrant Officer and Jailer until finally retiring on June 1, 1939, at the age of 73. He was laid to rest in Fairlawn Cemetery with six retired officers acting as pallbearers including John Cassidy and W.E. Snelson.

The decade began with the strain of international tensions and, in spite of a national mood of pacifism, preparations to meet those tensions. During the second month of the new decade, the Oklahoma National Guard was activated as the 45th Infantry Division and stationed at Fort Sill. On July 30, 1941, ground was broken for the construction of the Midwest Air Depot, a $21 million facility on 1,500 acres five miles east of the City.

Like the rest of the nation, Oklahoma City was caught completely by surprise when the Japanese bombed Pearl Harbor on the morning of December 7, 1941. The first torpedo strikes that morning were on the battleship USS Oklahoma. It rapidly capsized, losing 415 men, a loss of life that day second only to that of the USS Arizona. The battleship's anchor would eventually become a memorial on Oklahoma City's previous " Battle Row".

With their surprise attack, the Japanese inadvertently caused a major transition in the OCPD. Many of the younger officers went off to war and the Department suffered a severe shortage of manpower for the duration. To alleviate the problem, hiring standards were lowered and a favorite pool of manpower for new officers was the ranks of those taxi cab drivers who had been declared unfit for military service. Their mastery of city geography was seen as an immediate advantage. Some veteran officers were over the military age limit and formed a core group of experienced, able officers to train the newcomers and maintain efficiency.

As it was at the beginning of the other World War, the temper of the times was different after Pearl Harbor. Fear and fury brought out the citizen's baser instincts which manifested themselves as hatred and prejudice. Gunji Tada and his wife had lived in this country for 43 years and had operated The Japanese Bazaar at 115 N.W. 1st for 13 years. After receiving some threats, they decided to close their shop in spite of the two officers Chief Smith sent down there to protect them.

During the Smith years, the first influx of women into the Department in positions other

*Pictured in (and over) the west front door of the Police Station is the OCPD's tallest officer. Roy 'Pat' Patterson, all six feet ten inches of him, holds the door for Captain John McManus in the early 1940s.*

than jail matrons took place. This was largely because of the general replacement of men in many civilian occupations as the war effort expanded. Prior to that time, police work and all its facets had been considered "man's work". Even the stenographers and secretaries, with few exceptions, were male. Fewer than a dozen women worked in the Police Department in any capacity but that all changed when the fellows went to war.

The patrolman's lot was basically the same though. His pay was $135 a month in 1941, no longevity or other benefits and the only hope of a raise was a promotion. Cars were notoriously untrustworthy and the rationing system of the war years resulted in some patrol vehicles registering up to 300,000 miles before they were retired. Crime and disorder flourished as the turbulence of war replaced the turmoil of depression.

On the positive side, in 1942 an OCPD officer was able for the first time to enjoy the luxury of a day off from work. Prior to that time, if an officer desired a day of rest, he was required to hire his own replacement from the "extra board" to work for him. The public safety of the citizens was not to be lessened for such luxuries. Future Chiefs Hilton Geer and Ed Rector started their careers with the Department as members of the extra board.

The temper of the times also had its positive aspects. If the rest of the world was getting more dangerous, America was getting a little safer, at least for the cops. During the first full year of the war, only 88 law enforcement officers were killed in the line of duty nationwide. It was the first time the figure had dropped to two digits since before the first World War. As evidence that it wasn't happenstance, the figure would not climb back over 100 per year until 1946.

On April 11, 1942, 80-year-old former Chief Rolley Organ applied for and received a commission as a reserve officer. Although the records are incomplete, it is assumed this is the date he retired since it seemed to be the practice of the times to issue these commissions upon retirement.

On July 16, 1942, the extra board system was abolished. All officers who were currently on the extra board were made probationary patrolmen. The six-month probation period was extended to one year when, if they survived it, they gained a $33 raise to $165 a month.

Former Detective George Hawks, who left the Department after 12 years service in 1953, was interviewed about his experiences more than two decades later for the 1975 OCPD Yearbook. He recalled the raucous days of the war when servicemen flooded the City, necessitating the addition of Military Police and Shore Patrol personnel to the manpower pool. There were 13 patrol districts then, no more than 9 of which were filled on any given night. Pennsylvania Street was the western city limits and everyone operated on one radio channel.

"Reno Street was still the wildest part of town", Hawks remembers, "but when they put up the white way lights down there toward the end of the war, the people started to move north to Grand. That was the beginning of the end for Reno".

Travelling criminals, joining in the national mobility of the war years, were a special headache. So were the servicemen driven to wildness and revelry by the pressures of war and the local citizens who took advantage of the general unrest. Frequently military personnel on leave would bust loose after having a few beers at a local bar. Local industry, restrained by the economic conditions of the 1930s, fired up their machinery and attracted jobseekers to Oklahoma by the thousands. So did the new Tinker Air Force Base in suburban Midwest City.

While the rest of the country went to war with Japan and Germany, Oklahoma City was still half-heartedly at war with its' vice and the official criticism thereof. The Federal Security Agency criticized the City for allowing legions of prostitutes to operate, spreading venereal infections rampantly among our boys in uniform. Too many were becoming casualties of their revelry in Oklahoma City before they ever got close to combat. The State Health Commissioner backed the Feds up, identifying 143 houses of prostitution in the City. Fort Sill, the Army's largest artillery training center, was conveniently located a mere hundred miles southwest of the City in Lawton. The Commanding General announced that seven city blocks south of Grand Avenue were off-limits to his troops and threatened to extend the restriction to the entire city. The city administration protested but lamely. It was probably just as well, considering the statistics that would be soon forthcoming. The military off-limits restrictions stood for the duration of the war.

In February of 1943, the city was acclaimed first in the nation for the lowest traffic fatality rate of cities between 100,000 and 250,000 persons. No doubt this was assisted by the wartime rationing of gas, tires and an increased public reliance upon mass transportation.

In March of 1943, Chief Smith resigned to return to the FBI. He was replaced by Lawrence J. "Smokey" Hilbert, yet another OCPD officer who had taken a leave of absence to serve with the FBI and then returned to the Department. Six months away from his fortieth birthday, Hilbert was the first OCPD Chief to have been born in this century and the youngest man to occupy the office since Statehood. Hilbert was to serve in that office longer than any other man and earn a public popularity rivalled by few of his predecessors. A confident, colorful police administrator, Hilbert led vice raids, made public appearances and generally impressed the officers, citizens and City officials.

Born in Marceline, Missouri, on September 20, 1903, Hilbert had been a licensed embalmer and ambulance driver before joining the Department on September 17, 1929. In slightly over eight months, he became a Detective in the Stolen Car Department, later serving also in Vice, Narcotics, Intelligence and Robbery. When Chief Frank Smith took office, he promoted Hilbert to Lieutenant in the Detective Bureau.

Hilbert took an indefinite leave of absence three weeks after Pearl Harbor, having been "called to wartime service by the FBI". He returned to the OCPD on February 5, 1943, and, skipping the rank of Captain, was immediately promoted to Inspector, the number two job in the Department. Slightly over a month later, he was appointed Chief. His nickname "Smokey" was derived from (depending upon who you asked) his chain-smoking habit, the way his gun smoked on the pistol range, his "road-burning" driving habits as an ambulance driver or his fastball delivery as a baseball pitcher during his days as a student athlete at Capitol Hill High School.

The first chapter of the Fraternal Order of Police was formed by 23 officers in Pittsburg, Pennsylvania, in 1915. Formed as a fraternity to protect its members from retribution for discussing their grievances, the organization went to great pains to avoid being labeled as a union. Nevertheless, that is exactly the label rapidly stamped on it by police administrators. Furthermore, they said the union had "secrets" and couldn't be trusted. Regardless of what the organization started out as, a union is what it eventually became.

The first "crisis" Chief Hilbert was forced to deal with was another attempt on the part of Oklahoma City Police officers to unionize. The first such attempt had occurred 18 months earlier in the month before Pearl Harbor. A group of Tulsa Police officers had come to the City and tried to help Oklahoma City officers form a local chapter of the Fraternal Order of Police.

*Chief Smokey Hilbert and staff during the early part of his administration. The two men in business suits are, left to right, Inspector Roy Bergman and Chief of Detectives Dwight Brown.*

City Manager H.E. Bailey (for whom the Oklahoma City-Lawton Turnpike was later named) quashed the movement immediately. He ordered the officers to disband or be summarily fired. They complied and the attempt was over but not forgotten.

This time without outside leadership, 80 OCPD officers formed a Lodge of the Fraternal Order of Police and elected officers. Dispatcher Frank J. Goodwin was elected President and the Executive Board consisted of C.G. Pulliam, James Miskovsky, Clyde D. Denniston, Carl Snook, Oscar Lair and John J. Whittle.

On April 15, 1943, the FOP President and Executive Board members were summoned to the office of City Manager H.E. Bailey and again ordered to disband the Lodge. This time they refused and, true to his word, Bailey fired all seven on the spot. The group was unrepentant, stating that "after firing us, he's got 73 more to go". Unfortunately, they didn't have that kind of solidarity. An eighth officer, Patrolman Joe Taylor, was dismissed the next day and the rest decided discretion was the better part of valor. They yielded to the City administration and the movement was over.

On June 14, an Oklahoma County District Court Judge affirmed that the City had a right to fire employees who did not obey orders not to join the union. The case was appealed to the State Supreme Court but at least one of the discharged officers would not live to see it through. Clyde Denniston died early the next year after falling from a train while employed as a switchman for a railroad.

On July 1, 1943, Captain Walter Acord reported to Chief Hilbert on the activities of the OCPD Vice Bureau. Unfortunately, his figures verified the accusations of the Federal Security Agency, the State Health Department and Fort Sill's commander. In the previous year, 2,489 women had been treated in the Jail VD Clinic. A startling 56 percent of them had venereal diseases, almost a third of them had syphilis, over a third had gonorrhea and over 10 percent were infected with both diseases.

Acord's report also detailed his unit's activities for the 45 months he had been in charge since October 1, 1939. Although vice was obviously still present in Oklahoma City, it was also obvious that Acord's men had been busy. The report listed nearly 20,000 arrests including

*OCPD's first Accident Squad. Left to right, front row; J. Wayne Rankin, Lucille Counts, John McManus, Louise Waller and V.L. Connell. Rear row, Fred Neal, Danny Daniels, W.A. 'Ace' Williams and Tommy Wilson.*

5,287 for liquor, 6,655 for vice and 3,427 for gambling. Almost 135,000 pints of liquor and over 33,000 pints of beer had been confiscated. Although busy, the nature of this city's vice prevented much efficiency. On the average, it took two vice raids to produce five arrests and even this looked good compared to the other standards. It took almost two liquor raids to produce an arrest and almost five gambling investigations to put one person in jail. Nevertheless, the wars continued.

On December 28, 1943, after serving nearly four years of his sentence, Orban Chester Patterson was released from Fort Leavenworth Federal Penitentiary. He moved to Utah and died there after less than eight months of freedom.

The summer of 1944 saw another attempt at a strike by the City's garbage workers. A previous attempt three years before had been routed when the City Manager had fired the ringleaders. Just the threat of similar action this time was enough to do the job. This was another problem that wouldn't go away forever, however.

Relations between the City and County were still oscillating between tolerant and adversarial. In the last week of July, County Attorney George Miskovsky demanded of the City Council that Chief Hilbert's department turn over more than 20,000 pints of whiskey the City Police had seized. This haul was valued at over $120,000 and represented all the liquor seizures between January 1942 and January 1943. Miskovsky, himself a former OCPD officer for four years in the mid-1930s, stated that all contraband liquor should be stored and destroyed by the County Sheriff. It didn't matter that the Sheriff stated that the City Police were storing the booze because he didn't have any place to put it. After a couple of weeks of sending nasty letters back and forth, some of which naturally got leaked and quoted in the papers, the city and county were finally in agreement for the Police to turn the booze over to the Sheriff.

Not all of the stash survived the red tape. On August 3, Captain Walter Acord of the Vice Bureau was inventorying some of the booze on the fourth floor of Police Headquarters (now the old Jail Building) when a stack of loosely stacked pints fell over. Breaking as they scattered over the concrete floors, a lot of the illegal spirits spilled over into the floor air vents, running down them to the third floor jail. In a repeat of the sights of the advent of Prohibition in 1907, the current inmates grabbed tin cups, caps and anything available to catch some of the manna from above. One of the long time regulars, who had almost sobered up, was particularly industrious. One of the jailers remarked "He drank about a pint—and quick!", thus extending his stay in the house of many doors.

After agreeing that the county should legally have the booze, they then spent a couple of weeks arguing over whether the Sheriff should come get it or the City Police should deliver it. After almost a month of this bureaucratic folderol, the transfer was finally completed on August 19. On that date, the Sheriff took final possession of 22,777 half-pints of contraband spirits including over 1,500 pints of non-tax paid liquor and 2,600 pints of choc beer. The destruction party wasn't quite the equal of the Statehood bash but it was enough to put a tear in many a bootlegger's eye. It is doubtful if any went out of business as a result, however. When arrested, they were still back on the streets after paying a fine equal to the sale of a couple of pints of whiskey.

The front pages of the newspapers, like many other things, changed with wartime. The headlines every day were updates on the war now. Entire pages inside were devoted to local boys with lists of reassignments, promotions, medals and, of course, casualties. By mid-1944, the casualties numbered over 5,200 of Oklahoma's sons and some daughters. Not all of the casualties were overseas. On July 27, an overwrought military policeman from Tinker accosted his girlfriend in Lucille's Tavern at 204 West Reno. The argument culminated with him using his .45 Automatic on her and then on himself, both with fatal results.

Despite all of the efforts of Captain Acord and his men of the Vice Bureau, the town wasn't getting any "cleaner". The monthly report from the Jail's VD Clinic told a woeful tale for September of 1944. Of the 160 women who went through the clinic that month, 61 percent were infected, 28 percent with syphilis, 47 percent with gonorrhea and 13 percent with both. Of the 64 ladies going through the clinic for the first time, 31 of them were infected. Over half of the first-timers were under 21 years old.

Two old lawmen died in March of 1945, one retired and one still on duty. On the second day of that month, H.A. "Hi" Thompson left his job in the OCPD's Records Bureau early, not feeling well. For the last three years, the 74-year-old officer had received yearly extensions of his commission as required for all officers on active duty over the age of 70. Shortly after 6 P.M. that evening, Hi had a fatal heart attack.

Many of the officers of the OCPD knew old Hi Thompson only as a fingerprint man and statistician in the Records Bureau for the last 15 years. But the old man was more than that, much more.

Hiram Albert Thompson had been born in Michigan City, Indiana, on April 22, 1870. It was oddly coincidental that he would celebrate his birthday on the day that would become 89er's Day, the founding day of the state he would spend much of his adult life serving. His parents moved to Kansas during his childhood and he came to Oklahoma Territory that first year of 1889, settling in Stillwater. He served as undersheriff of Payne County and as a Deputy U.S. Marshal. In 1893, Thompson had been one of the 13 marshals involved in the gunfight with the Dalton/Doolin gang in Ingalls that had seen three of the officers killed. He had been one of the surviving marshals who had transported Arkansas Tom Daugherty to jail in Stillwater after that battle. Four years later, Thompson had moved to Tulsa, still a Federal deputy. In 1904, he went to work for the "Frisco", the St. Louis and San Francisco Railway, to guard their trains during the World's Fair. In 1909, he became Chief of Police in Tulsa for two years. He then worked for the U.S. Justice Department, the Frisco railroad again and as a Deputy U.S. Marshal again.

On January 20, 1930, nearing his sixtieth birthday, Thompson was hired as a fingerprint man and statistician in the Records Bureau of the OCPD where he remained until his death. The Records Bureau was closed on March 6th when Thompson was interred in Rose Hill Cemetery.

On March 19, 1945, Chief Hilbert distributed a memo that retired officer John Cassidy had passed away at the age of sixty-nine. Chief Bill Tilghman's "best plainclothesman" in 1911, Cassidy had served during the first three decades of Statehood before retiring in 1937. He was interred near many of his fellow officers in Fairlawn Cemetery.

As two old officers left the scene, another returned. Former OCPD Detective D.A. "Jelly" Bryce was named as the new Special Agent in Charge of the Oklahoma City field office of the FBI in April. In the 11 years since he had left the OCPD to join the FBI, Bryce had built his local reputation into a nationwide legend. He had served as a field agent in the FBI offices in Kansas City, Chicago, Washington, D.C., Aberdeen, South Dakota, St. Paul, Minnesota, and Oklahoma City. He had also been selected by J. Edgar Hoover to teach the Bureau's firearms tactics. He developed the Bureau's concealed fast-draw holster as well as the draw and crouched firing stance that was eventually adopted by most police agencies in the country. A feature of the stance is that the officer's weight is shifted forward so if he is wounded, he will fall forward so he can continue to see and fire at his assailant.

One retired OCPD officer of those days later scoffed at the idea that Bryce was hired by the FBI as a firearms instructor. He believes that Bryce was hired as "a killer, pure and simple. They had too many gangsters to go up against in those days and they were losing too many lawyers and accountants doing it. They needed some gunmen".

Bryce's firearms talents had become legendary and he frequently put on exhibitions. The November after he was appointed SAC in Oklahoma City, Life Magazine ran an article about him showing a series of time-lapse photos of him drawing and firing in less than half a second. The purpose of the time-lapse photos was to illustrate that the motion was faster than the human eye could follow. Because of his speed and skill with firearms, Look magazine nominated him as "the FBI agent most likely to live the longest". Bryce had a bagful of impressive tricks that he used for his demonstrations. What was most impressive about them was that they obviously weren't tricks, they were the result of extraordinary vision, eye-hand coordination and endless hours of practice. One trick was dropping a silver dollar from shoulder height, drawing with the same hand and shooting the coin before it fell below his waist. He also had a trick with a .22 rifle and a Mexican peso, a coin about the size of a quarter. He would tell his audience that he would shoot the coin after throwing it in the air but he would shoot it close to the edge so it would make a good watch fob. Then he would do exactly that, time after time. He would also shoot clay pigeons with his .357 Magnum, sometimes holding the gun upside down. He would write his name in the sky with tracers from a submachine gun, coming back to put the periods behind the "D" and the "A". He would have an assistant hold three clay pigeons and put two more on the stock of his shotgun. Throwing them all up in the air simultaneously, he would shoot all five before they hit the ground. One of his favorite tricks was to lie on his back with a mirror held between his knees, fire at a target behind him by sighting in the mirror with the pistol upside down and the sight covered with cardboard. He would also tease his audiences occasionally by asking someone in the audience to loan him their watch. He said he wanted them to see how close he could put a bullet to the watch without actually hitting it. By sleight of hand, he would replace the spectator's watch with a cheap one that looked similar and then blow the watch to bits with the first shot. After a few moments of stunned silence, he would return the spectator's watch to him, unscratched.

Perhaps not as well known to the audiences at his exhibitions was the practical use Bryce had made of his firearms talents although it was alluded to in one of his demonstrations. Bryce would have a volunteer from the audience point an unloaded, cocked revolver at him. When a signal was given, Bryce would draw his gun and fire two shots into a target before the volunteer could pull the trigger. Largely unknown to his audiences, Bryce had already proven the practical value of this "trick" many times. The proof was the fact that he was alive.

Although he was hesitant to discuss it at length except with close friends and colleagues, by the time of his return to Oklahoma City near the end of World War II, Bryce had killed at least ten men in the line of duty as an OCPD officer and an FBI agent. He was rumored to have been involved in the arrests or killings of Baby Face Nelson, the Ma Barker gang, Alvin Karpis and others. These rumors went unconfirmed due to the emphasis on "We" instead of "I" in Hoover's Bureau and the sanctity of Bureau files. In later years he told future OCPD Chief Bob Wilder, with whose father he had served on the OCPD, that he had been involved in 19 shootings. He didn't elaborate but Wilder surmised (incorrectly) that none of the suspects survived.

In 1941, Bryce had been appointed as Special Agent in Charge of the El Paso office. After three years there, he became the SAC in San Antonio until he was transferred to the Oklahoma City office.

On the morning of July 17, 1945, an innocuous little article appeared at the bottom of the front page of the Daily Oklahoman. Very nearly the smallest article on the page, it was easy to overlook on a front page with blaring headlines about the massive fire bombing raids on Tokyo and other Japanese cities;

DAILY OKLAHOMAN
July 17, 1945

AMMUNITION MAGAZINE EXPLODES AT AIRFIELD
Alamogordo, July 16 (AP)———————
A remotely located ammunition magazine exploded Monday at Alamogordo air base reservation but there was no loss of life or injury to anyone, Col. William O. Eareckson, commandant, announced. The blast was reported heard and seen for more than 100 miles. Eareckson reported that "weather conditions affecting the content of gas shells exploded by the blast may make it desirable for the army to evacuate temporarily a few civilians from their homes."

There wasn't any ammunition magazine and there weren't any "gas shells". It was just a few pounds of plutonium doing a very brief imitation of the Sun in the early morning New Mexico desert and preparing to change the history of the world.

By early 1945, the former Midwest Air Depot was the largest, busiest air logistics and repair facility in the world. At its wartime peak, it employed over 15,000 people. It had been renamed Tinker Field after Pawhuska native Brigadier General Clarence Tinker was killed in 1942. Dozens of aircraft flew in and out daily, none meriting any more attention than the others unless they had massive battle damage. One day shortly after the war, a B-29 Superfortress landed at Tinker and was wheeled into a hanger by itself for some very special modifications. As was the wartime custom, it had a name painted on its nose...Enola Gay.

When news of the Japanese surrender arrived late in the afternoon of August 14, 1945, the town exploded in celebration. Weary police officers, themselves honking horns and cheering, stood witness to a city gone wild.

Tons of paper cascaded out of the office windows in downtown's skyscrapers. Downtown hotel guests slit pillows and dumped the feathers out of the windows. Traffic Officer J.W. Rankin held his police motorcycle stationary with the throttle wide open in the middle of the unit block of North Broadway, rear wheel smoking and siren wailing. The downtown fire station added their siren to the din. People poured out of the high-rises and into the streets. Customers in downtown theaters climbed over their seats and started conga dances in the aisles. All the theaters closed at 6:30 P.M. A sailor and a Marine, both decorated veterans, sat on the curb at Main and Robinson, splitting a liberated case of beer as an audience of hundreds cheered them on.

All police officers and deputy sheriffs were called to report for duty. The police station was bedlam for two hours as 150 men received special assignments for patrol duty downtown and in the suburban areas. By 8 P.M., traffic was so thick in the downtown area that it was totally unmoving. The streets looked like parking lots. One man exited a downtown building, calmly walked out to the curb, solemnly fired six shots in the air from a revolver and then went back inside, his part in the celebration duly accomplished.

Near midnight, as the crowds were thinning, a woman collapsed at Main and Broadway. When Traffic Officer John Flynn ran over and picked her up, she wrapped her arms around his neck and kissed him enthusiastically. Thus assured of her health and welfare, Flynn handed her over to a passing sailor, claiming "That's out of my line of duty". The bootleggers announced they had run dry by midnight and would remain so for several days.

Twenty-two arrests were made, mostly for public drunkenness and brawling. One woman complained to police that her car had been dented when a heavy paper sack full of water had been dropped from a window on North Robinson. A 19-year-old boy went to jail after taking a swing at Officer L.H. Bailey. Anyone who was there will never forget the electricity of the celebration.

The best of the Hilbert years coincided with the end of the war and the return of many former officers from the military. For several years after the war ended, a flood of old and new applicants marched into Police Headquarters, replacing the taxi drivers of the decade's first five years with an improved manpower pool.

Hilbert himself set the tone for the revival of the Department. He was a former partner of the renowned D.A. "Jelly" Bryce, had a younger brother on the force and another brother who was an unbeaten prize fighter. Hilbert was well-liked, respected and personable. Ace Williams recalled "The men liked him. He could get tough when he needed to but he was the kind of guy who could eat your rear and make you like it. You'd come out of his office smiling and thinking he was a great fellow".

Hilbert was a pioneer as well as a leader. He was the first Chief to submit OCPD officers for enrollment in the nation's two most prestigious law enforcement schools, the FBI National Academy and the Northwestern University Traffic Institute. He also promoted the beginning steps toward a full-scale police training academy although, for another 15 years, officers had to attend rookie classes at night or during the day after working a full tour of duty on the streets with senior partners.

The end of the war wasn't the end of everyone's troubles. On the evening of December 31, 1945, Traffic Lieutenant J.W. Neuffer showed up at the police station. Saying he had forgotten his gun and had to go on duty shortly, the nine-year veteran tried to borrow a gun from several officers. Finally, Officer Henry McMullen gave Neuffer his .38, saying he would use his other gun for duty that night.

At 3:44 A.M. on New Year's morning, officers received a call to 2231 1/2 N.W. 12. When they arrived, they found Neuffer's 40-year-old ex-wife Grace, dead. Neuffer's 21-year-old daughter, Beverly, was hysterical and his son-in-law, Neal Beard, had been shot in the side. Neuffer was lying dead in the doorway, shot once in the right temple, McMullen's .38 lying at his feet.

Divorced the previous February, Neuffer had been severely depressed ever since. He had arrived at the house intent upon killing his ex-wife. When his son-in-law tried to shield Mrs. Neuffer by jumping in front of her, Neuffer shot him and then his ex-wife. He then pointed the gun at his daughter and pulled the trigger. It misfired. Then he put the gun to his own head and pulled the trigger again. That time it didn't misfire.

In mid-April of 1946, the City witnessed a phenomenon that came to be known as "The Bootlegger's War" and what one author termed "a side-splitting comedy". It had various roots as its cause.

When Orban Chester Patterson finally took his leave, no one of equal talents existed to take over his organization. It thereby fragmented into multiple factions with individuals all vying for supremacy over various pieces of the pie. Naturally, one of the biggest pieces was the bootlegging concession. This occurred on the eve of World War II which eventually distracted everyone temporarily.

However, when the war ended, a number of other factors started the pot bubbling toward an eruption. There was an over-abundance of whiskey available. Thousands of GI's were coming home, flooding the colleges and job markets. Having been surviving by their wits and found themselves capable of many things they wouldn't have previously believed in the past few years, some would inevitably seek out easier ways to make a buck in the land of free enterprise.

It was a simple matter to purchase a load of booze in neighboring Texas or Missouri, bring it back to Oklahoma City and start undercutting the local prices until it was all sold, still at a worthwhile profit. A police spokesman that April estimated that there were 25 percent more bootleggers in town than there had been six months before. The competition was heating up. The author who termed it a "side-splitting comedy" described it thusly;

"....bootleggers were hijacking each other, stealing each other's whiskey and out gunning for each other. Never before had local officers been so disturbed over broken noses, cracked heads and stolen whiskey. Scout cars dashed frantically about, not to confiscate whiskey or close up illicit joints, but to stop bootleggers from hurting each other while they carried on their illegal business. Bootleggers cars were wrecked by competitors, whiskey-venders chased each other with sawed-off shotguns and a formidable "bootlegger's ring', organized by rum-runners from California fell apart when the members of the 'ring' started hijacking and beating each other." It was to continue escalating, not reaching its peak until the next year.

DAILY OKLAHOMAN
June 3, 1946

OFFICER, BANDIT SUSPECT WOUNDED
IN GUN DUEL AFTER THEATER ROBBERY

(Photo of an alley and a small tin building)
This is the alley and parking lot in which William Peter Somet, 40, of New York City, was shot 5 times and George Leech, police detective, was wounded twice. Leech and George Hawks, police detective, accosted Somet in the alley....Somet opened fire, hitting Leech twice, and then fell with 2 bullets in his body. Leaving Somet for dead, Hawks drove Leech to the hospital...other officers arrived at the parking lot, they found Somet sitting against a building on the west boundary of the parking lot. Officers shot him three more times.

The drama described in this article began about 2:30 on the previous afternoon when the persistent Mr. Somet had stolen $350 from the Warner Theater, the site of the old Overholser Opera House at 213 West Grand. Less than half an hour later, Detectives Leech and Hawks saw a man fitting the description of the hijacker entering the lobby of the Marquette Hotel at Grand and Dewey. A search of the lobby and coffee shop was fruitless but as they drove off, the officers saw the man leaving the hotel carrying a small bag.

They pulled up beside him in the alley and identified themselves as police officers. Somet immediately drew his .38 and fired three times at the officers, still seated in their car. Both officers emptied their guns at Somet, striking him twice.

Assuming Somet to be dead, Hawks, his coat pierced by two bullet holes, immediately drove his partner to the hospital to be treated for his wounds in the hip and abdomen. Scout car officers L.R. Puett and E.B. "Salty" Meals went to the shooting scene, finding that Somet had stumbled and crawled about 25 yards to prop himself up against a building.

Snapping the gun on empty chambers at the officers, Somet yelled "Either kill me or I'll shoot you". Somet then placed the gun to his head and pulled the trigger on yet another empty chamber. The two officers then shot him three more times. Welcome to Oklahoma City.

Stubborn Bill Somet recovered from his wounds as did George Leech. Somet got a free trip to McAlester, Oklahoma and George Leech retired from the OCPD in 1961 after 20 years of service.

To wind up the year, the county attorney decided to call a crime conference to see if law enforcement had any ideas about dealing with the increases in crime. Scheduled on December 30, those invited included a private detective, a railroad detective, assistant county attorneys, both the incoming and outgoing Sheriffs, the Chief of the Oklahoma Highway Patrol, the City Manager and the Commissioner of Public Safety. Rounding out the group were OCPD Chief Smokey Hilbert and the local FBI Special-Agent-In-Charge, D.A. "Jelly" Bryce.

The conference rapidly degenerated into a pointless session of what one police administrator calls "finger-pointing and blame-laying". The City Manager criticized the County Attorney, the County Attorney criticized the City Police and so forth, ad nauseam. Smokey Hilbert eventually mediated, causing everyone to agree that this was just a temporary flare-up and they adjourned to their respective bailiwicks, doubtlessly to continue privately with their "finger-pointing and blame-laying".

The Bootleggers War reached its zenith in early 1947. The star of the episode was Willie Joe Kelly. Willie Joe had been "banished" to Oklahoma from California 16 months earlier and had been raising hell ever since. First he set up a bootlegging business in a hotel at 900 North Broadway. Competitors had taken a few poorly-aimed shots at him there which brought him into direct conflict with the hotel management. They felt it hurt their business image when their tenants had to duck bullets Willie Joe was attracting and would prefer he moved. Willie Joe preferred to stay. If they tried to lock him out, he broke in. This situation degenerated to the point of Willie Joe throwing a gas bomb into the hotel's grille and a fist fight with the manager.

Looking for a new base of operations, Willie Joe decided to build his own club. He started the San Diego Club on N.E. 23rd outside of the city limits and ordered 41 cases of booze from a Chicago bootlegger to start his business. He neglected, however, to pay the $4,500 he owed for the booze. Big mistake.

At 2 A.M. on the morning of February 12, 1947, Willie Joe Kelly and his telephone operator, Claudie Jo Sams, were abducted from his home at 105 N.W. 25 by four men. They took them to a motel court at N.W. 39th and Portland where they were to be held for $4,500 ransom, not coincidentally the amount owed on the 41 cases of liquor. It isn't entirely clear who they thought was going to pay them the ransom. Willie Joe only had $700 on him, proved it and was soundly thrashed for his trouble.

The next day, the kidnappers heard on the radio that the abduction had been reported and police were investigating. Panicking at this unexpected development, the two Chicago "muscle" men and their two local "guides" called the County Sheriff's office and arranged to surrender to Deputies at N.W. 23rd and Walker with their hostages. All were arrested and proved an interesting lot.

The two tourists were Patrick J. Kelly, a Chicago bootlegger and Charles Cliff Stanton, a Chicago cab driver. Their local tour guides were even more interesting.

Harold Byford, 31, was a local bootlegger who likened himself to be the heir to Orban Patterson's throne. His original career choice had been as a car thief which resulted in his first arrest in 1932 in Texas at age 16. There had been 23 more arrests since then, his career in Oklahoma City beginning in 1937 when he was arrested in possession of a 200-gallon still and 1,400 gallons of mash. His compatriot was Harold Shimley, a small-time but ambitious local gambler. Shimley had accumulated 25 arrests in the last 8 years from Houston to Chicago for everything from running con games to "general principles".

The Daily Oklahoman, knowing a good thing when they saw one, started a series of articles sure to sell papers. Called Who's Who In The Whiskey Trade, it offered daily profiles of some of the City's more interesting, if not upstanding, citizens. Kelly, Byford and Shimley started the series off.

It continued with William Harold Quick, who had forced a man to sign his car over to him to pay a debt, Lloyd Albert Taylor, with 51 arrests in 5 years, "Pink" McCann, with over 100 arrests in 7 years, Charles Piper, whose OCPD record was 46 pages long, a man known only as "Rufus", whose customers bought from him while looking down the barrel of his gun and Kenneth Sleeper, a former minion of the deposed Orban Patterson.

Smokey Hilbert knew a good thing when he saw one, too. If there was ever a time for management by crisis, this was it. Two days later, a dozen bootleggers went to jail.

Officer G.W. Glazner, like many others, had recently returned from fighting overseas and was back to fighting the domestic war on the home front. Discharged as a Captain, Glazner had put his wartime experiences behind him as much as he could——most of them, anyway. But on June 18, 1947, he experienced every ex-GI's dream.

Glazner and his partner received a call to a fight in a bar in the 100 block of North Broadway. One of the contestants was in uniform. Upon breaking up the fight, Glazner and the soldier recognized each other at once. It was Glazner's former First Sergeant.

The Sergeant greeted him with "Well, if it isn't my old buck private". Officer Glazner immediately informed the Sergeant that he wasn't a buck private anymore, he wasn't "his" anymore and the First Sergeant was under arrest. The officer then asked him something to the effect of "Are you COMING with me or are you GOING with me?". The First Sergeant decided he was coming and, unable to pay his $20 bond, stayed in jail until his buddies could raise it. When he was released, he decided to forego any further reunion with "his old buck private".

Late in 1946, the Oklahoma Supreme Court affirmed the District Court's ruling in the 1943 case of the fired FOP officers. Similar opinions recently issued by the U.S. Supreme Court made further appeals pointless. For the time being, attempts by OCPD officers to form their own union was effectively quashed. Those efforts would not cease but it would be nearly a quarter of a century before their dreams reached fruition.

Late 1946 saw another newspaper in town, The Oklahoma County Intelligencer. Some would say that the journal exhibited less intelligence than it did crusading. Exhibiting the decidedly leftist leanings of its publisher, Joe E. Brown alias Dr. Richard Kingsley, the paper raised hell about the vice conditions in the City and encouraged all citizens to "keep and bear arms at all times". Kingsley supported the eventual winner of the 1946 Sheriff's campaign, Dick Strain, and then turned on him when Strain didn't enforce the vice and liquor laws to Kingsley's satisfaction. The summer of 1947 saw Kingsley start yet another paper, The Oklahoma County Register. This organ also took the Sheriff and County Attorney to task weekly, railing that the "elite" clubs of the City were rolling in whiskey and gambling, immune to law enforcement. It all came to a head on the night of June 4, 1947, in what one author called "The Beacon Club Massacre".

On that evening, Kingsley went to Justice of the Peace Ross Cunningham with four friends and believers. Cunningham deputized all five as "special constables" and provided them with several search warrants including one for the Beacon Club. On the top floor of the First National Bank building, the Beacon Club was one of the most exclusive clubs in the City, if not the ultimate. The membership read like a who's who of the City's political, industrial and financial mighty.

The "officers" served their warrant on the Beacon Club with relish, forcing their way in both the front door and the private lockers inside. Their haul netted 648 fifths and 127 pints of the finest liquors available. They then rolled on to a Beacon Club employee's home, looking for gambling equipment from the club but succeeded only in disrupting a birthday party for the employee's two-year-old grandson. Their bonanza at the Beacon Club kept them so busy that they failed to use their warrants for the Jefferson Club, The Oklahoma Club and The Oklahoma City Golf and Country Club.

A grand jury was hastily impanelled. Kingsley testified before it, stating that his ultimate goal had been to achieve repeal of prohibition by enforcing it strictly and impartially. Not a bad idea, just about a decade ahead of its time. On June 23, the grand jury indicted all five raiders for conspiracy and impersonating officers as well as Justice of the Peace Cunningham for illegally deputizing them. The Beacon Club was "censured" for violating state liquor and slot machine laws. The Grand Jurors commended the OCPD for their "honest, efficient conduct". After almost a year and a half, the charges were silently dismissed.

Some things changed back to business as usual after the war. On the night of December 30, 1947, two grocery stores and a cafeteria were robbed at gunpoint for a total of $680. A few hours later, Officers J.R. Skaggs and W.C. Flurry were driving south on Walker when they tried to stop a car fitting the suspect vehicle description. The car took off in the opposite direction. As the officers pursued, three bullets shattered their windshield. Radioing for assistance, they returned fire.

As the suspects crossed the South Walker bridge, they sideswiped one car and collided with another. When the officers arrived, he found the female driver injured from the collision, one male passenger shot in the hip and the other man shot five times. Neither officer was injured.

1948 started with allegations made to a District Judge and the City Manager about payoffs from bootleggers to police officers. The City Manager had Chief Hilbert, Chief of Detectives Dwight Brown and their vice officers interview a dozen known bootleggers. Some said that officers had taken whiskey from them for their personal use and one said he'd paid $2,000 in protection to an officer and then got raided anyway. The first action was not long in coming.

On January 8, Detective Emmett L. Drane was fired for "conduct unbecoming an officer". There was no more elaboration on the charges except to say that he was not the officer suspected of taking the $2,000 bribe. Drane, an 18 1/2 year veteran, didn't exactly have a spotless record, having been demoted from Lieutenant two years before.

Two days later, Patrolmen O.E. Higginbotham and C.D. Scott were suspended for allegedly having extorted six pints of whiskey from a bootlegger to take on one of their hunting trips. A few days later, Detective Barney Burnett was fired "for the good of the service". A 15-year veteran, Burnett was Drane's partner on the Whiskey Squad. This was all followed by a vice drive on Grand, Reno and California that netted 200 arrests in 6 days.

A grand jury was convened on March 29 to investigate the vice situation in Oklahoma County. A little over three weeks later, they presented their report. The essence of it was that "Due to the efforts of the Police Department, County Sheriff's Office and County Attorneys Office, things aren't as bad as they could be". Encouraged, the bootleggers decided to try to make it worse.

The Daily Oklahoman of April 29 ran a front page story that the Internal Revenue Office had issued 180 Federal liquor stamps to "wholesalers" compared to 6 for the same period the previous year. Implied was the fact that the grand jury's recent verdict had set all this off. Also on the front page were pictures of a gas station and three residences, the addresses given for some of the liquor "wholesalers". It noted that none of the four displayed a sign identifying the locations as a liquor wholesaler as required by Federal law. One of the residences was 3700 N. Kelly, listed to Harold Byford.

Farther back in the same issue was the obituary of Charles Carl Post. The former Chief had died at the age of 77. The article noted that Post had been elected Chief in 1907. When he was defeated for re-election in 1909 by John Hubatka, Post had reverted to being Chief of Detectives and was in charge of the Detective and Identification Bureaus for the next nine years. After 12 years with the OCPD, he became a Federal Prohibition Agent in charge of the Kansas City office responsible for their efforts in five states and then a Federal Narcotics Agent in Missouri and Iowa. Returning to Oklahoma City in 1929, he had been in the real estate business until his retirement in 1938.

In conjunction with the publishing of the latest grand jury's findings, the Oklahoma City Times ran a series of articles on law enforcement in Oklahoma City and County. While the articles agreed that liquor, gambling, prostitution, burglary and robbery were reaching new highs in the county, they blamed the situation on public apathy and official (i.e. City Hall) neglect. They pointed this out by a comparison of the current OCPD with the Department of 1935. Thirteen years earlier, the Department had 65 scout car officers and no beat officers. Today they had 52 scout car officers and 12 beat officers. In 1935, they had enough cars to mount two full shifts and as of the previous week, there weren't enough dependable cars to staff one full shift. In the past 13 years, the City had grown by 125,000 people, the number of businesses had more than doubled and police calls had gone from 2,000 to 5,000 a month. A 1935 officer's pay had been $155 monthly and his uniform equipment required an investment of $175. Today's officer made $175 monthly and his equipment cost about $400. They pointed out that, with all these inequities, the current rift between the city and county wasn't helping anyone but the criminals.

There had been dissension between the city's and county's raiding squads, off and on, since the beginning of the century. Another period of bad feelings had started around the first of the year during the city's corruption investigation. On May 12th, Chief Hilbert personally led a raid on some gamblers. The information had come from a rival faction.

Accompanied by Inspector Roy Bergman and five Detectives, they broke in on a crap game in progress, the table covered with $100, $500 and $1,000 bills. Thirteen arrests were made, who were taken downtown and promptly paid their $12 fines. The officers did not confiscate the $25,000 cash involved in the game. So much for deterrence.

Two days later, the county attorney's raiding squad hit the Jungle Club at 101 S. May. Four arrests were made, slot machines and $110 in cash were confiscated. In publicizing their raid, the county attorney criticized the city officers for not confiscating the $25,000 from the crap game. The City Attorney's Office countered by citing a 1915 case that stated that money was not gambling apparatus and, if it had been confiscated as such, it would have to have been destroyed. Such are the vagaries of the law.

*New 1948 Ford Accident cars parked in front of the station at 200 North Shartel.*

The same month, the Oklahoma City Times noted that Captain Jimmy Godfrey was supervising 65 scout car officers and trying to make sure that they all completed the 254-hour (six and one-half weeks) training course. Their average age was 30 and they earned $205 a month after serving a one year apprenticeship, 2 percent of which went to the Police Pension Fund. They had to make an initial investment of over $400 for uniforms, gun and ammunition since the city furnished them with nothing but a police car and opportunity.

On November 9, 1948, Officer V.L. Connell switched on his siren and pulled Wilford Schmidt over. As Schmidt rolled down his window, he wondered what he had done wrong. Imagine his amazement when Connell presented him with a box of cigars.

That morning, the OCPD had inaugurated the "Golden Rules Driver" awards program. "The weakest point of any traffic safety program is the fact that we do not recognize drivers who, day after day, do a good job behind the wheel.", explained Safety Council Manager and future Chief of Police Dan Hollingsworth. For some time afterwards, one good driver was chosen each day for recognition for driving "with a smile instead of a snarl". The ladies chosen for the award received an orchid.

On May 27, 1949, Oklahoma's last Civil War veteran died. Joshua T. Jones passed away at the age of 102 at his home in Tulsa. Jones had joined General Nathan Bedford Forrest's Light Artillery battery at the age of 15 in 1862. Eleven of his half-brothers died fighting for the Confederacy.

September of 1949 included an event both familiar and unusual. What was familiar was that it was an election to try to repeal prohibition. What was unusual was that it was a special election for that purpose and not held in conjunction with elections of officials. When all the dust and ballots settled, prohibition still remained but by the smallest margin yet.

On October 5, 1949, a very simple traffic accident at N.W. 10th and Francis drew a lot of attention. The 18-year-old girl who had bumped into the rear of the other car certainly didn't think it merited the attention of 20 cops. Officers Harold Loyd and J.W. Rankin arrived to investigate the accident. Then Captain Clay Scheid showed up with 17 rookies from the police training school. The two bemused motorists waited patiently while the rookies were instructed in the fine points of skidmarks, points of impact and completing a traffic accident investigation.

On November 25, 1949, an old man had a heart attack and died while riding on a City bus. Widowed two years before, he was living alone with two old dogs. He was identified as John Calloway Walton, "Our Jack", the former Mayor and Governor who had instigated statewide battles against the Ku Klux Klan a quarter of a century earlier. If the old man have lived another five weeks, he would have lived through the first year in the State's history in which no black men had been lynched.

As the decade came to a close, another city manager was sacrificed on the altar of political reality or, perhaps, just "tired of the bullshit". Serving since mid-1946, William Gill Jr. had been through the Bootleggers War, investigations of police corruption and two county

*1949 OCPD Accident Squad.*

grand jury investigations. Predictably, none of these hastened his exit. What shortened his tenure was doing his job.

Gill went about his duties as though he actually believed that the city operated under a city manager system instead of a "Councilmanic" system. Ignoring the fact that for over two decades, the City Council decided the agendas for all city department heads including the city manager, Gill had the temerity to personally give orders to the Chief of Police regarding vice cleanups. As Albert McRill succinctly put it;

"From the time of the adoption of the City Manager charter, the police department, with the exception of a short period, had been controlled within the City Council and by forces backstage working through councilmen....[City manager Gill] soon learned that powerful forces, not alone from the underworld but from the upperworld as well, would not tolerate strict law enforcement in Oklahoma City if they could prevent it".

Even worse, he was impudent enough to tell City employees that they were "working for the City Manager and not any individual councilman".

Well, that did it. A heretic of the first order. The man acted like he actually thought his job was like the charter mandated. He had to go. The search for a successor was on. Gill found another job before the Council found a successor. He resigned on December 6, 1949.

The decade ended with a promise of peace, prosperity and progress. The City's new Bluff Creek water reservoir was named for Mayor Robert Hefner and, in June of 1949, WKY-TV began broadcasting from the Municipal Auditorium. Citizens who could afford one of the new inventions began getting three hours of television programming every day except Saturday.

# VII — GROWTH AND SPECIALIZATION 1950-1959

It was a time of peace, prosperity and national tranquility for the 243,504 citizens who lived in the 56.31 square miles of Oklahoma City. The metropolitan area population was over 325,000. Depression followed by war had Oklahoma City booming again. The decade wasn't even six months old before another war loomed in Korea. Not really a war, they were told, but a "limited police action". A small name for an investment that would last three years and cost almost 60,000 American lives.

It wasn't much of a war by the standards of what they had just been through. You probably wouldn't get much agreement on that from someone who was in Korea but that's how the folks back home felt and the good times were not to be deterred. The previous year, OCPD officers made over 2,300 arrests for liquor law violations. It was estimated that over 500 people in Oklahoma City made all or part of their income from bootlegging. This fact was emphasized, to the Department's embarrassment, on January 14, 1950. Eight Baptist and Nazarene ministers, accompanied by special constables, conducted raids in the city that netted seven arrests and confiscated 148 pints of liquor.

As World War II ended, the returning men married, enrolled in college on the GI Bill or got jobs and began raising families. It all required money and the economic boom of the period fostered a business and population explosion that in turn caused greater wealth and prosperity. All those new people and businesses required police service. As City officials began an annexation program in anticipation of the population growth, there was more area to be patrolled as well.

Another direction of growth was in specialization and, to a lesser degree, professionalization. No longer could a man be given a badge, a gun, a blue uniform and be expected to perform all the duties of police work with equal expertise. The fingerprint technician, the traffic accident investigator, the burglary detective, the polygraph examiner, the training officer and others all had to be recruited, trained, promoted and compensated. Some of the newer officers even had college training, a new development that flew in the face of tradition.

With the increasing professionalism came a rising status in the community. Safety education efforts, a more cooperative and candid policy toward the press, public relations and appearances by officers all helped raise the policeman's image in the eyes of his employers, the citizens. It was not until the next decade that the new trend took the form of the police-community relations premise but the groundwork was being laid.

Police officers learn to expect the unexpected. Nevertheless, a unique call for assistance came in on February 25, 1950. "Leapy the Leopard" had disappeared from his "escape-proof" pit at the Lincoln Park Zoo. The wild cat had been brought to the zoo from India only a week before. The ensuing three day search involved not only the OCPD but also zoo officials, big game hunters, wildlife experts and U.S. Marines equipped with M-1 rifles and walkie-talkie radios. Two days later, the New York Daily Mirror boasted the bold headline "KILLER LEOPARD ELUDES MARINES-JUNGLE CAT TERRORIZES OKLAHOMA CITY".

Of course the only thing he had probably ever killed was what he had eaten to stay alive on the Indian steppes and the only thing he had done to terrorize anyone was to escape and stay hidden. His incredible strength and agility was intimidating, however. After bounding out of his 20-foot-deep pit, he "hurled himself across a 22-foot moat, hit the side wall and bounced from there over the front of the pit". A zoo official said "It was just like a billiard player shooting against a cushion. I've never seen such a leap".

The 175-pound leopard was described as "fast as greased lightning" and capable of killing for pleasure. A little anthropomorphic, perhaps, but it sold papers. For 61 hours, the search continued from the woods and grasslands of a closed Lincoln Park to east of Edmond.

Finally it was the animal's own hunger that was its downfall. During a rainstorm, the animal sought food and shelter near the very pit from which he had escaped. "Leapy" was back in custody on February 28. Unfortunately, he died from an overdose of the tranquilizer in the horsemeat bait left out for him.

The summer of 1950 was another typically hot one. In another typical move in what had become an annual battle, the officers began surreptitiously removing their ties and opening their collars when out of sight of their supervisors. Smokey Hilbert, out conducting whiskey raids, also removed his and authorized his men to as well. The Traffic and Patrol commanders, Clay Schied and Jimmy Godfrey, rebelled. They lamented to the Chief " We work all winter impressing the public. Summer comes, the boys throw away their ties and look like apes!". They presented the argument to the Chief about the heritage of the years officers had spent wearing ties and blue serge uniforms year round. Hilbert didn't respond to the argument that we should do it that way "because we've always done it that way". The ties stayed off and the collars were allowed to be opened...one button.

*The view looking north on Robinson from Grand Avenue in the early 1950s.*

A desperate criminal can be much more dangerous than a desperate animal. On September 2, 1950, Accident Investigator W.A. "Ace" Williams was admitted to Mercy Hospital following a wild shootout with a pair of armed robbers. With his partner, F.C. "Danny" Daniels, Ace spotted an armed robbery in progress at the Safeway Store at N.W. 13th and Robinson. As the officers drove by and glanced in the front windows, they noticed that "everybody was standing real still and that wasn't right". As the robbers ran out the front door, they were confronted by the officers who told them to drop their guns and surrender. They responded with a hail of bullets. Williams was hit and fell to the sidewalk but continued to return fire along with Daniels. His assailant was fatally struck with seven bullets. The second man was disarmed by a store employee and lived to face trial. Ace Williams recovered from his wounds, later rising to become Assistant Chief.

Former Chief W.E. Snelson passed away on May 4, 1951, at the age of 80. Snelson had begun his career walking a beat on East Grand in 1911, 40 years old at the time. Four years later, he had been promoted to Detective and, in April of 1919, Mayor Jack Walton had promoted him to Captain. He had become Ray Frazier's Assistant Chief in 1923 and replaced him when Frazier left in 1926. Snelson had been Chief only slightly more than a year when he was replaced by M.C. Binion. Binion made him a Captain in charge of the Detective Bureau, the position he held until his retirement in 1933. He had brought the slain Bill Tilghman's body back from Cromwell in 1924 and had been in charge of the investigation into the murder of Detective Briggs Chumley later the same year. The following year he had been involved in the fatal shooting of train robber Dutch Webber. Snelson was buried in Fairlawn Cemetery.

On November 1, 1951, a young man of Ukrainian extraction named Walter G. Kostiuk was hired as a patrolman by the OCPD. By the end of his first week, he must have wondered what he had gotten himself into. The next night, officers were called to Stockton's Grocery Store at 1912 N.E. 23rd on a burglary in progress. As they surrounded the store and began searching the building, they discovered first one, then two burglars hiding inside. Continuing their search, they found the third burglar crouched behind some shelves......wearing an Oklahoma City police uniform including badge and gun.

Surrendering docilely and not attempting to use his weapon against his fellow officers, Patrolman Wayne Henry Johnson was placed under arrest. The 38-year-old had been on the force for 3 1/2 years and in trouble for most of it. He had been suspended twice for drinking on duty, his last suspension having ended just the day before his arrest. Johnson confessed that he was seriously overburdened with debts and worked several extra jobs but his "$80 every two weeks just wouldn't spread around".

After leaving an extra job earlier that evening, he had been drinking in a downtown bar with two former convicts he had known since childhood. One of them suggested committing the burglary as a quick way for all of them to get well financially. Chief Hilbert made the statement that "this is the most embarrassing thing that has ever happened in my law enforcement career". The rest of the week didn't get any better.

Officer S.M. Billings was fired for having constant financial difficulties with local merchants. Vice Detective Chester V. Raper was arrested for drunk driving in Hugo, Oklahoma, and later resigned. Officers H.L. Brogdon, J.V. Birdsong and Nat Marshall resigned to keep from being fired. Brogdon and Birdsong were partners and were destined for dismissal due to their "bad associations". A known bootlegger had co-signed on a loan for Brogdon. Marshall, a probationary officer with less than a year's service, was going to be fired because "his superiors did not have confidence in him". As they say in the trade, we all took a beating that week.

In 1951, the Department won the First Place award in Traffic Law Enforcement given annually by the International Association of Chiefs of Police. It was the second time in the last three years that the OCPD had won it.

Not all of the events of 1951 were as lighthearted. On September 12, Officers J.E. "Gene" Goold and J.L.Doyle received a call to assist a citizen in the 1400 block of North Robinson. When they met Wayne Webb at that location, Mr. Webb told the officers that two women were trying to kill him. From Bristow, Oklahoma, Mr. Webb was also trying to locate his sister who lived somewhere in the City. The officers offered to give him a ride to the police station to try to help him find the sister's address.

Unknown to the officers, Mr. Webb was a mental patient. They figured it out when Webb began identifying the women in every car they passed and tried to jump out of the moving patrol car. This was before the days when security screens shielded officers from their rear seat passengers but was to become an excellent example of why they were needed. When the officers realized what they were dealing with, Goold pulled over in the 800 block of North Hudson to let Doyle get in the rear seat with their disturbed passenger. As the car pulled to a stop, Webb reached over the seat, grabbed Doyle's pistol and placed it to the back of the officer's head. Goold turned and fired three rounds into Webb before Webb could kill Doyle. Statements from several witnesses exonerated Goold in the following investigation. Gene Goold would later advance to the rank of Captain and retire as the Director of Training in 1968.

*Officer Reese F. Galyon Jr.*

As the 1951 Annual Report was being prepared, stating that there had been no marked increase in crime, tragedy struck. The death of Reese Galyon Jr., son of a retired OCPD Captain, shortly after 10 P.M. on December 22,

1951, ended the longest period on record during which no OCPD officer had been killed in the line of duty. His was the first fatality in over 13 years.

Galyon, a motorcycle officer, was pursuing a motorist speeding in a black Mercury convertible with a brown top on North Lincoln Boulevard near the State Capitol. Evidence at the scene indicated that the motorist crowded Galyon into the curb, causing him to crash at more than 80 miles per hour. The motorcycle's crash guard gouged scars in the pavement for 60 feet before it turned over and slid another 50 feet. Galyon perished from a broken neck and massive head injuries. His partner, H.A. McGill, had been chasing another speeder in a different direction when Galyon engaged in his fatal pursuit. Magill told reporters "[Galyon] mentioned something about how tragic it was that 23 people had died in traffic accidents in Oklahoma City this year. He told me he would personally give anything to save the life of an innocent traffic victim". In his four short years on the force, Galyon's commitment to purpose and exceptional diligence had been well recognized by more people than just his supervisors. One wouldn't think that motorcycle officers and taxi cab drivers would normally get along very well. Nevertheless, a group of the cabbies called the police station, offering to be pallbearers for Galyon as a mark of their respect for him, saying " his only fault was a soft heart".

The 34-year-old, 4-year veteran officer had been in the U.S. Navy Seabees during World War II. On Christmas Eve, his funeral at Fairlawn Cemetery was led by a procession of six police motorcycles and eight scout cars ahead of 50 other cars. Three hundred people and over 100 officers attended. Oklahoma Highway Patrol troopers took traffic calls in the City so that the entire OCPD Traffic Division could attend. Galyon's service revolver, the same gun that his father had carried during his police career, was to be handed down to his eldest son, 12-year -old Reese F. Galyon III.

At the time of his father's death, Justin Brent Galyon was 16 months old. In 1971, he would join the OCPD, become an attorney after graduating from law school and is still on active duty at the time of this writing.

Perhaps spurred into action somewhat by Galyon's death, the Department announced plans to equip half of the motorcycle force with two-way radios. The commander of the Traffic Division said that they were only going to install them on half the cycles because "they ride in pairs so one will do".

In spite of checking over 500 cars fitting the description of the suspect vehicle and citizens offering over $1,100 in rewards for his capture, Galyon's assailant was never identified. But cops have long memories. The last active lead in the case was investigated in 1977, almost 26 years after Galyon's death.

The Department was growing in 1952 but slowly. The hiring standards that had been lowered during World War II had been raised again, making it harder to attract and keep qualified men. In the prosperous 1950's, the $175 monthly salary was not that attractive for a job with only four days off a month. As a result, the force started the year with 284 men and ended it with 309 although the authorized strength was 317.

In light of the manpower issue, an old suggestion came up again when the City was asked to hire women as traffic officers. Polled by the press, the all-male body of officers reacted typically for the times, their comments tailor-made to make feminists grow faint with apoplexy. "Motorists won't have a chance. You can't argue with a woman, much less a woman cop", one officer responded. Another said "A woman's place is in the home doling out biscuits. Not on a police motorcycle doling out parking tickets. It just ain't ladylike". There was also concern about female officers violating the sanctity of the police game room where the men played pool and dominoes, conversed in their typically coarse street language, compared their sexual escapades, scratched their private parts, engaged in flatulence contests and did many other things that were frowned upon in mixed company. The idea was nixed for the time being. Women would get their foot in the door within a few years but two more decades would pass before a fully commissioned, trained female officer would hit the streets of Oklahoma City as a full equal to her male counterparts.

While some things refused to change, some did as a sixth floor was added to the Police Headquarters building to house the women's jail and venereal disease clinic. A new Municipal Court building was built on Couch Drive to be occupied by the city courts and their employees.

*The new Municipal Court building on Couch Drive flanked by Police Headquarters with its newly added sixth story.*

This vacated the first floor of the police building which was remodeled to house the Accident, Motorcycle, Bicycle and Juvenile Units. With the addition of the sixth floor, the Bureau of Records on the fourth floor and the Police School on the fifth floor were enlarged. The manual switchboard was replaced with "the latest dial-type board".

Two new ranks were created in 1952. The heads of the Radio Patrol and Traffic Divisions were given the rank of Major and Sergeants were added to both divisions.

The assignments of the 91 personnel of the Detective Division illustrate the increasing trend toward specialization. Although there was still a General Assignment section, the Division had separate units for Homicide/Robbery, Stolen Cars, Stolen Goods/Burglary/Theft, Forgery/Bogus Checks, Juvenile, Stolen Bicycles and the ever-present Vice. The Bureau of Records and Identification was also included under this Division.

The 58 men of the Traffic Division were divided into 8 specialties including 17 motorcycle officers and, in an interesting throwback, 14 "corner men" for directing traffic at downtown intersections.

The personnel of the Training School and Intelligence Division conducted three 144-hour schools for 44 new officers as well as 6 in-service training schools for 65 officers. While the 144-hour recruit training may sound impressive, that only computes out to 18 eight-hour days. The duties of the Intelligence Division corresponded more to reference and research, like a modern Planning and Research Unit, than those of what is now thought of as a police intelligence unit.

The 102 officers of the Radio Patrol Division were divided among 3 8-hour shifts to cover the City's 56.31 square miles, divided into 12 patrol districts and 5 walking beats. Traditionally the Department's largest unit, they proudly wore their new round shoulder patch emblazoned

*Accident Squad lineup on May 19, 1952. Left to right, Officers Daniels, Albertson, Rankin, Loyd, Williams, Real and Schmidt.*

with a winged wheel over the words "Radio Patrol". Ironically, this emblem would be adopted in later years by the Traffic Division, of which it was actually more symbolic.

A small article in the Daily Oklahoma on February 19, 1952, noted that the Department had graduated another 17 officers from Recruit School and was putting them to work on the streets. This was to raise the number of scout cars available to 7 on day shift, 10 on swing shift and 11 on graveyard. Department spokesman Roy Bergman stated that this would put more police manpower on the streets than they'd had in the last decade. They would rapidly find a use for it.

The next week, an issue of Look Magazine listed Oklahoma City as "one of the 10 most vice-ridden cities in the U.S.". Immediately, wails of protest emanated from City Hall. Chief Hilbert was allegedly looking into the possibility of a libel suit against the national publication. Then the knee jerked.

Coincidentally, Chief of Detectives Dwight Brown ordered a three-day vice "cleanup" the very next weekend. A special six-man detail of four plainclothesmen (including Gene Goold and Jack Mullinex) and two uniformed officers went into action. Friday, February 22, netted 10 arrests. Saturday, 25 went to jail and Sunday, 10 more followed. One of the veteran bootleggers caught up in the drive was 47-year-old James Franklin Perry. Mr. Perry had been arrested 108 times in the last 12 years but had served no jail time. This time he was caught at N.W. 11th and May with 1,085 pints of whiskey valued at $4,900.

The last day of February provided the citizens with some comic relief. Lieutenant George T. "Pike" Newton and his patrol car were involved in a four-car collision in the 4800 block of N.W. 10th. Since the wreck occurred about half a mile outside what was then city limits, the Highway Patrol investigated the accident. When asked for his driver's license, the 21-year veteran officer couldn't produce one. He said he though it might be "laying around the house somewhere" but he wasn't sure if he had renewed it when he came home from the military in 1946. Anyone familiar with bureaucracies can predict what happened next; driver's license inspections during shift lineups. The first shift inspected turned up three more officers with expired licenses and two others claiming they "left it at home". Those officers without licenses were ordered to ride, not drive, for that shift and to present a valid driver's license before the beginning of their next shift.

*Inspector Roy Bergman inspects a Radio Patrol lineup in front of the station on February 18, 1952.*

*Captain John McManus explains his new radar unit to an errant motorist on May 26, 1953.*

In April of 1953, former City officer and legendary gunman D.A. "Jelly" Bryce was completing his eighth year as the Special Agent in Charge of the Oklahoma City FBI office. Although the SAC was primarily a supervisory and administrative position, Bryce was a different kind of SAC. He delegated administrative responsibilities to other agents. Besides commuting between the office and his ranch in Mountain View, he frequently gave firearms demonstrations and assisted in firearms training for law enforcement officers. But nobody accused Bryce of avoiding his duties. One of the agents who served under him noted that there wasn't an unsolved bank robbery in Oklahoma during Bryce's tenure. He insisted on being involved in every dangerous arrest in his agents jurisdiction. Bryce was usually the first one to the door. In hostage situations, Bryce functioned as the "negotiator" who would go in and talk to the man. The suspect had the option to surrender or die. Some agents even began to believe in a phenomenon they called "the Bryce effect". Suspects were known to surrender as soon as Bryce showed up at a situation even though the suspects didn't know he had arrived, who he was or what he represented. It was almost as if he carried a tangible presence of death with him that the suspects sensed instinctively.

That month it was announced that he was being transferred to a similar position in Albuquerque, New Mexico. Bryce would later tell an amusing story about his new assignment. They were trailing a bank robber through the New Mexico mountains and the local officers insisted on using a bloodhound. Bryce was openly derisive about the value of the dog but the local officers used him anyway. Bryce would amusingly relate how it took them only 27 hours to find the bank robber but it took 47 hours to find the bloodhound. It seems the dog came across the scent of a mountain lion and headed the other way posthaste.

Another weapon was added to the traffic officer's arsenal on May 26, 1953. Captain John McManus, commander of the Accident and Motorcycle Divisions, stopped Robert William Voss at N.W. 46th and Classen. Mr. Voss had just gone past the Captain's new radar unit at 43 miles per hour. Mr. Voss then became the first Oklahoma City resident to receive a traffic citation as a result of this new technology. Fittingly, it was a warning ticket.

On the evening of July 22, 1953, Tommy Dean Henderson and Charles Ray Becker went to the Northeast 66 Drive-In Theater at N.E. 58th and Eastern but not to see the movie. They robbed the ticket booth at gunpoint, netting a whole $20 for their trouble. Shortly before 10 P.M. on the next night, they decided to try their luck at the Del Drive-In at 5000 S.E. 29th. This time they did better....and worse. They got $154 this time but the ticket taker got their tag number. He called the police and they broadcast it over the radio to all cars. A short time later, a newspaper reporter with a police radio in his car reported seeing the stolen 1951 Mercury going north from Reno and Eastern. Officers G.P. Tucker and Walter G. Kostiuk stopped the suspects car a few minutes later at N.E. 10th and Eastern.

The officers approached the car, calling to the two men to get out. As Tommy Dean Henderson got out of the car, he drew a gun from his waistband. Officer Kostiuk grabbed him and the two began wrestling over the gun. The gun went off, hitting Kostiuk in the leg just prior to his partner giving Henderson a pistol-whipping worthy of Charles Colcord. Becker offered no resistance. The two small-time desperados went to jail and Kostiuk went to the hospital. He would recover from his wound to serve more than three more decades.

Smokey Hilbert wasn't having a good time in June of 1953. The heat was stifling in what would become the City's hottest June on record. Seven of the month's 30 days set all-time temperature records, baking the City for almost two weeks at up to 106 degrees. Two weeks earlier, the Chief had fired Captain Dwight F. Brown for accepting a $5,000 "loan" from a Packing Town gambler. Hilbert had replaced Brown by promoting Wayne Harbolt but then had to defend himself against claims that the choice was mandated by certain members of the City Council. He declared he was reorganizing the Vice Bureau and placing it under his personal control, aiming to "stamp out politics at police headquarters". Again.

The first week of the month, a local dentist accomplished what the Council had been trying to do with varying degrees of success for years—he removed all the Chief's teeth. On the morning of June 9, Hilbert was admitted to Mercy Hospital when his tender gums began hemorrhaging. But he wasn't to get much respite there either.

The next day, allegations surfaced of black officers shaking down east side tavern owners for money and whiskey. Inspector Roy Bergman, Major Frank Thurston and Captain Wayne Harbolt began a series of interviews with 25 alleged victims. Late that night, Bergman suspended 10 of the Department's 18 black officers, 9 Patrolmen and 1 Vice Detective. Bergman said that some of the officers were nearing their retirement dates but most of them had been hired three years previously when the City decided "to give the Negroes their own officers". Allegations indicated that the shakedowns had been going on for as long as two years.

The Chief came back to work but the complainants kept coming forward and the interviews continued. The black tavern owners alleged that the black officers extorted money from them by threatening to raid them incessantly and run them out of business if they didn't pay.

Some of the payments were as paltry a $5 and a pint of whiskey every week to each district scout car while some went as high as $60 to $80 a month. More allegations surfaced that a black Lieutenant, E.E. Jones, who was known on the east side as the "Negro Police Chief" had ordered other officers to "lay off" of the 419 Club at 419 N. Stiles.

If Smokey didn't have enough irons in the fire, the same week he had to suspend two other officers for misconduct. One was a Traffic officer who had been drinking on duty while working at the stock car races at Taft Stadium and the other was a Vice Detective accused of beating a 65-year-old black man. Then Roscoe Dungee showed up at City Hall with a contingent of black civic leaders demanding a public hearing on the case of the suspended black officers. The City Manager made a public statement refusing the public hearings, stating (in what may have been a poor choice of words) that this investigation was not going to be "whitewashed".

No sooner had the investigation's six-inch thick file landed on the desk of County Attorney (and former OCPD Chief) Granville Scanland than allegations started up of a jail food scandal. Former officer Raymond "Red" Robinson had maintained a contract with the City for feeding jail prisoners since 1927, shortly after he left the force. The newspapers were crying foul over the fact that Red had charged the City for more meals than the jail had prisoners to eat them. That one died down fairly rapidly when Red calmly explained that the discrepancies were because trusties received meals with larger portions which cost more and they also had the option of coming back for second helpings which constituted another meal. The best that came out of that one was enlightening some sloppy accounting procedures and creating some new forms dealing with feeding prisoners. County Attorney Scanland shelved the corruption investigation report on the black officers, calling for a grand jury to investigate it in the fall.

Former Chief Frank Smith died at St. Anthony's Hospital on August 12, 1953, following his third stroke. He had been 75 years old. Smith had been described as "short, paunchy around the middle, wearing horn-rimmed glasses" and more reminiscent of a country store-keeper than one of the country's top lawmen.

Smith had joined his hometown Houston Police Department at age 20 and then served with the Dallas Police. It was during his service in Dallas in 1915 that he had been shot five times during the capture of robber Red Kelly. Kelly got 137 years in prison and Smith joined the FBI.

As an FBI Agent, Smith was credited with solving the Osage insurance murders in northeastern Oklahoma in 1925, had been the first FBI Agent on the scene of Machine Gun Kelly's kidnapping of Charles Urschel in 1933 and had captured then-Public Enemy Number One Alvin Karpis in New Orleans. This was a capture that achieved a great deal of notoriety, then and later.

Then it was widely publicized that FBI Director J. Edgar Hoover had personally arrested Karpis. When it was discovered in later years that Hoover's title was probably more accurately termed Dictator than Director, authors discovered that the arrest was set up because Hoover's ego had been stung by criticism that he had never personally arrested anyone. When his agents located Karpis in New Orleans, they were told to keep him under surveillance until Hoover arrived. When Hoover got there, he personally arrested Karpis, both of them surrounded by armed agents.

Smith had said he felt his closest call had been the Kansas City Massacre in 1933, "the longest 15 seconds of my life". Smith said he had ducked down in the car's seat when the shooting started. When the shooting stopped, he cautiously peeked out the window and a Kansas City policeman stuck a gun in his face, pulling the trigger. The gun misfired. "Thought I was one of the gangsters, I guess", Smith said laconically. Smith left the FBI to become Chief of the OCPD in 1939. He felt that his primary achievement there had been the first efficiently organized police school, modeled after the FBI schools that were so familiar to him. He returned to the FBI in 1943 to teach until he retired again in 1948 to enter the real estate business in Midwest City. Smith had been a third-generation lawman, both his father and grandfather having been peace officers in Texas.

What was to be the last two years of Smokey Hilbert's administration were incredibly stormy. His City had been branded by a popular national magazine as a hotbed of vice activity, riddled with "organized vice and prostitution openly operating with bought-and-paid-for connivance of the local officials....threatening an entire generation with disease and disgrace".

The County elections in the Fall of 1952 were relatively peaceful with former Chief Granville Scanland being elected as County Attorney. The City elections in the Spring of 1953 were another matter. The problems occurred in Precinct Three where Larry Reedy had fixed elections during the first part of the century. Two City employees who were not residents of that Ward had voted there. They were convicted of fraud and the State Court of Criminal Appeals criticized the registrar's apathy and negligence.

On October 8, 1953, a grand jury was convened to investigate crime and official corruption. In their final report, they said the voting practices in Ward Three "smelled to high heaven". Newspaper reporters were still making their rounds buying illegal whiskey and reporting the results on the front pages. Thus the Police Department was criticized by the grand jury for its vice enforcement practices. In a remarkable precedent, the grand jury not only recommended a sweeping reorganization of the Police Department's Vice Bureau, they even dictated the plan and specific personnel changes.

The grand jury recommended that control of the Vice Bureau be removed from the control of Chief Hilbert and placed solely under the control of Captain Wayne Harbolt, Chief of Detectives. Harbolt appointed 22-year veteran Captain John Butler to lead the new Vice Bureau. Butler immediately increased the Whiskey Squad from four men to six and lit a fire under them. He also began a policy where half of the Bureau was reassigned to other duties every six months. It was felt that this would reduce the opportunity for corruption and the "new blood" would provide a rotating supply of fresh faces, fresh attitudes and reduce "burn-out". Amid much resentment, this was implemented causing an uproar in the Department and vice community as well.

1953 ended with the promise of pay raises for officers. Patrolmen would go from $263 to $300 monthly. Smokey Hilbert's monthly wage would go from $600 to $700.

Tragedy and upheaval beset the Department in 1954. On June 3, Officer Lewis H. Swindler responded to a disturbance in the Far East Cafe at 17 North Broadway. When he tried to arrest Jack Raymond Harris, Harris resisted violently. Harris grabbed for the officer's gun and the two went down fighting for possession of the weapon. As the two struggled on the floor, Harris got the officer's .38 and shot him once in the chest. Finally subduing Harris, Swindler would survive his wound, live to retire from the force and serve for many years as the Chaplain of the local Lodge of the FOP.

Nearly a week of scorching temperatures up to 107 degrees in mid-July of 1954 made it a pleasure to work nights when it dropped down into the 80's. On the evening of July 16, good detective work and questionable tactics cost another officer his life. What was to evolve into a convoluted armed robbery and kidnapping started when the assistant manager of the Jones Boys Supermarket at S.E. 44th and Shields was closing up for the night. Two men approached him at gunpoint and demanded that he open the store's safe. Telling them he didn't know the combination, they forced him to take them to the home of the bookkeeper, Fanny Ransom. On the way, they picked up a third accomplice. Arriving at Mrs. Ransom's home, they tied her family up and took her back to the store to open the safe for them.

*Detective Ben Cravatt.*

Meanwhile, witnesses had noticed the abduction of the assistant manager and had called police. Detectives Bennie Cravatt and Bill Rackley responded. Smokey Hilbert later eulogized Cravatt as "the kind of officer the Chief didn't worry about" because he could just give him an assignment and then forget about it because he knew it would be handled right. Tonight, not everything would go right. Finding the store unoccupied and nothing apparently disturbed, they reasoned that the suspects might return to try to get in the safe. Cravatt, a ten-year veteran, waited inside the store with Rackley maintaining surveillance outside.

When the suspects returned, two of the men went in the store with Mrs. Ransom. Cravatt called to them to surrender but one of the suspects jumped him. Rackley, approaching the store from his cruiser, heard shots and saw one suspect run outside. Rackley traded shots with the running man, wounding him but not stopping his escape. Entering the store, Rackley found the 45-year-old Cravatt dead on the floor, shot once through the heart.

Nearby, wounded in the leg, was Raymond Carrol Price. The next day, a wounded Hurbie Franklin Fairris Jr. was arrested in Shawnee. Further investigation led to the arrest of James Edward Skinner. Tried and convicted, Price and Skinner were each given two life sentences for attempted robbery with firearms and murder. Fairris, convicted of being the trigger man, was sentenced to death.

The Immanuel Baptist Church was filled to overflowing and 200 more people stood outside for Cravatt's funeral services. His grieving widow told reporters about how she and her husband had completed his funeral arrangements two days before their son had been born 13 years before. Cravatt had been diagnosed with Hodgkin's Disease (lymphatic cancer) but, miraculously, became one of the few to survive the malignancy.

Since the grand jury reorganization of the previous Fall, the revitalized Vice Bureau had taken the town by storm. The new unit had seized 11,703 pints of illegal liquor compared to the 6,994 seized by the old unit in a comparable time period. Liquor arrests had risen from 755 to 1,134. Gambling arrests were up from 250 to 883. Prostitution and narcotics enforcement statistics were also up. The new whiskey unit was also markedly more efficient. The number of raids were down but arrests were up. The pre-grandjury unit had conducted 295 raids but only netted 87 arrests. The new unit had only conducted 51 raids but accomplished 163 arrests. As is the eternal nature of police work, this didn't stop the complaints, it just changed their direction.

Whereas the old Vice Bureau had been criticized for being too lax in its enforcement efforts, the new one was now criticized for being too strict. Captain John Butler had been in charge for eight months now and, in a mood that anyone who has been a middle-level police commander in any era can sympathize with, was undoubtedly "tired of the bullshit". He publicly stated that he felt that vice enforcement in the City was much improved, on the right track and he felt that it would be appropriate to return control of the Vice Bureau to the Chief. Butler also said he felt it would be appropriate to reassign him in November after a year in charge of Vice.

After almost 11 1/2 years as Chief, a record that may never be broken, Smokey Hilbert finally called it quits in 1954. City Hall was decidedly unhappy with the Chief. The last straw was a "bad judgement" arrest by one of his officers that resulted in a Tinker Field officer getting his jaw broken. Smokey, never seen as a stickler for discipline, delivered what was considered a "wrist-slap" to the offending officer. On June 25, six of the eight City Council members held a secret meeting at the Skirvin Hotel and drafted a letter to the City Manager requesting Chief Hilbert's dismissal. The next day, a Saturday, Hilbert sent City Manager Ross Taylor a letter asking to be relieved of his duties as Chief and reassigned. This request was approved.

The following Tuesday, Ward One Councilman James Norick, one of the two Councilmen not invited to the star chamber meeting in the Skirvin, read a statement during the weekly council meeting lambasting the other council members for their improper interference in the internal workings of the Police Department. Norick would become Mayor five years later, serve a second term from 1967-71 and his son, Ron, would become Mayor in 1987. In spite of Norick's protests and doubtlessly influenced by the majority faction on the council, City Manager Taylor later reconsidered his previous decision. With truly dismal timing, Taylor dismissed Hilbert on July 17, the day after Bennie Cravatt's murder, stating that the Chief would be removed from the payroll at midnight on July 20.

The next week, the Oklahoma City Times published a series of articles based on a secret poll they had taken of OCPD officers on the internal problems of the Department. Low pay was cited, naturally. They said that morale had plummeted since Chief Hilbert's dismissal and they were sick of the political influence in the Department. Opinions were advanced that the councilmen calling for Hilbert's dismissal was a violation of the City Charter. Officers were also of the opinion that council members influenced promotions as an "old boy network" without respect for qualifications or merit. They were also off balance from the stirrings that were undoing the dictates of the previous year's grand jury reorganization. Control of the Vice Squad had been returned to the Chief and half of the personnel were being changed. Lieutenants Jack Caldwell and R.S. Grimes had taken over Vice supervision from Captain John Butler. Reassigned to other investigative duties were Detectives Jack Mullinex, C.C. Miller, R.L. Tettleton, W.N. Brown, Walt Gates and Gene Goold. Newly assigned to the Vice Squad were Detectives Jim Reading, Bill Mead, Leonard Bailey and Fred Neal along with black Detectives H.V. Gaines and Ben Hart.

*Chief Roy Bergman.*

Hilbert was replaced by Roy Bergman, a well respected 24-year veteran. Bergman has been described in three words—"quiet, strict and fair". Officers say he was generally well-liked by the men. One of the major changes that took place was a change in basic philosophy. The daily duties of fighting crime seemed to take greater precedence than ever before over the Department's internal and external political squabbles.

On December 11, 1954, Officers Eugene H. Mills and Kenneth R. Dunlap responded to a disturbance call in the 3200 block of North Shartel. The officers found two men, Billy Don Spradlin and John Calvin Copeland, embroiled in a raging domestic with their wives. Unable to mediate the dispute, the officers arrested the men. At that point, Mills became involved in a fight with Copeland. As the two fell to the ground, Copeland began trying to get Mills' gun away from him.

*Officer Eugene Henry Mills.*

As the men wrestled on the ground, Officer Dunlap leaned over them, drew his .38 and pointed it at Copeland. Copeland slapped at the gun, causing it to discharge, hitting Mills fatally in the chest. Spradlin and Copeland were charged with First Degree Manslaughter. Officer Mills was buried in Sunnylane Cemetery with his widow and three daughters in attendance.

An instructor in a police training school 15 years later would remark that when a cop got killed in Oklahoma City, "there's lots of loud singing and slow driving for a while". What he meant was that such incidents gave all officers a whiff of their own mortality, made them edgy, put them all in a bad mood and usually resulted in an unofficial declaration of martial law against anyone even remotely responsible. There was a similar aftermath to the death of the two-year veteran Mills.

Spradlin and Copeland had been drinking after hours at Jeep O'Neal's cafe/bar at S.W. 15th and Western that night. The week after Mills death, O'Neal's was raided. Four people were arrested, 22 pints of liquor were confiscated and the joint was padlocked as a disorderly house. For weeks thereafter, the curfew laws for "Loitering On The Streets After Midnight" were rigidly enforced.

The Department had 277 officers now. As a result of a new raise at the end of the year, a new officer's base pay was now $280 a month.

The summer of 1955 saw a new racket on the City's east side. A numbers racket called the "policy wheel" was becoming big business. Allegedly more than 100 people made their livings selling numbers slips for as little as a dime apiece and the racket was producing as much as $5,000 a day. As many as 10,000 of the City's black residents were wagering on the numbers, many bets based on the interpretation of their dreams. Supposedly a person could win as much as $50 for a $1 bet during the twice-daily secret drawings but the odds were 3300 to 1 against you. Chief Bergman said that the evidence to make arrests was hard to find, being small slips of paper with confusing columns of random numbers printed on them. Even when officers did manage to find the slips in people's possession, they just paid their $40 fines and went right back to their operations.

That summer also saw the biggest step taken to date toward having female police officers in the City. A "Meter maid" program was instituted and females were recruited to walk beats in the downtown area enforcing parking regulations. The city officials decided this would free some male police officers for other duties. Six women were hired from the initial field of 21 applicants, Jean Linn, Lois Moore, Iona Chapman, Mildred Jones, Ina Mae Miller and Jean Latham.

The local newspapers ran pictures of them (in the Fashion section!) in their new "coronation blue" uniform jackets and skirts, calling them "copettes" and "women policemen". Although they had arrest powers, they were not issued weapons. They went through the police academy and rode with patrol officers for two weeks before they were due to begin patrolling their downtown beats on September 19, 1955. Eventually their usefulness broadened their

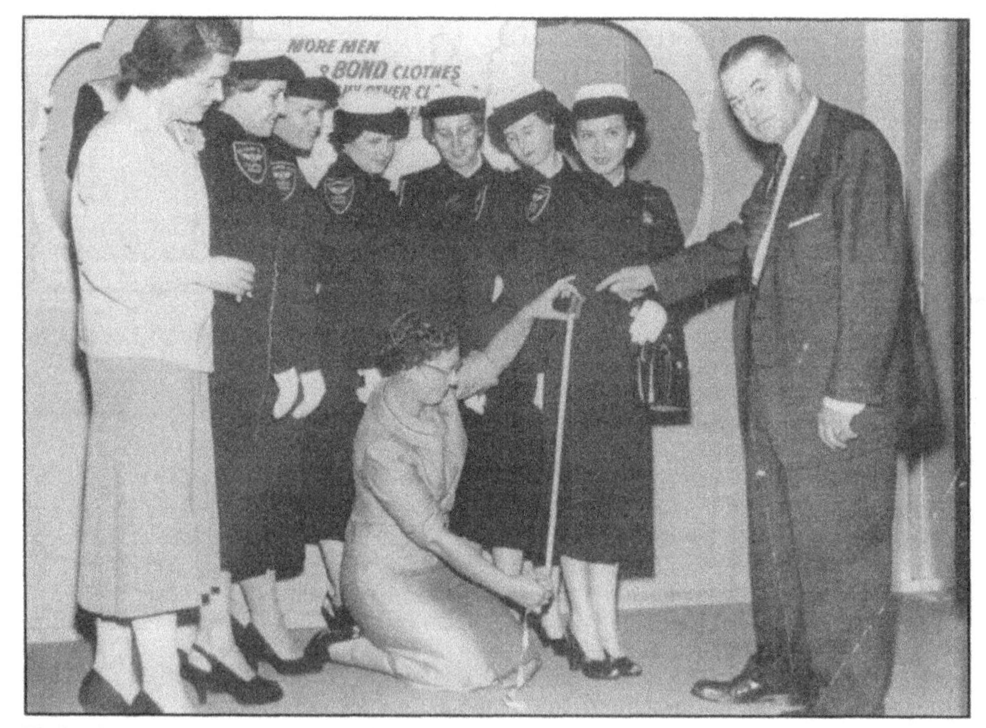


*The local newspaper was more concerned with the hemline of the 'Coronation Blue' uniforms of the OCPD's first female officers than their assignments. Note the 'Traffic Police' shoulder patch.*

*The first six-September 1955. Left to right are Jean Latham, Ina Mae 'Tiny' Miller, Jean Linn, Iona Chapman, Lois Moore and Mildred Jones.*

responsibilities. Since there were no female Deputy U.S. Marshals, they were occasionally assigned to transport female prisoners to federal prisons and were used to provide security for the Governor's wife on some occasions. When the cold weather arrived, they asked Chief Bergman for permission to wear slacks instead of their skirts but he refused to allow it.

The novelty of it didn't last long. Within a few years, only two of the original six were still around. Lois Moore left in 1959, moved to Georgia and eventually returned to go to work for the State Welfare Department. Iona Chapman married Officer Don Braswell in 1959 and worked in Traffic Court until 1961. Mildred Jones Sanders left in 1963 to work for the Water Department. Jean Linn Stewart left in 1958 to become a cosmetologist but her son, Ken Linn, joined the OCPD in 1970 and retired as a Lieutenant in 1991. Having graduated from law school while an officer, Linn then became an Oklahoma County Assistant District Attorney. The two who remained set precedents in their careers. Jean Latham would become the first female Detective and retire in 1983 after 28 years. Ina Mae "Tiny" Miller would become the first female Sergeant in 1977 and retire in 1987 after 32 years of service.

A few minutes after midnight on January 18, 1956, Hurbie Franklin Fairris Jr. was electrocuted at the Oklahoma State Penitentiary in McAlester for the murder of Detective Bennie Cravatt in 1954. He had constantly protested his innocence and even got one 60-day stay of execution by trying to blame the murder on one of his accomplices. On the second eve of his execution, he tried another ploy by saying he wanted to take a lie detector test to prove his innocence. After his execution, it was revealed that he had confessed his guilt to two people, one a priest, while on death row.

The 22-year-old Fairris may have been the model for the proverbial "kid who never had a chance". His brother was serving a ten-year sentence in Huntsville Penitentiary, Texas, for a Houston robbery. Both his parents were also in Huntsville, his mother doing time for murdering a former husband, the second husband she had killed. His mother's brother, his uncle, had been Raymond Hamilton, one of the Bonnie and Clyde gang in the 1930's. Hamilton had been executed in Texas's electric chair in 1935.

Unfortunately some people just can't learn from others mistakes. The week after Hurbie Fairris kept his date with "Old Sparky" in McAlester, two guys who should have used him as an object lesson decided to try their luck. It wasn't good to begin with and it was only going to get worse. On the afternoon of January 27, 1956, Harold Lee Kersey and Harry Eugene Bush tried to hold up a grocery store in Tulsa but it didn't work out. So they decided to try their luck about a hundred miles down Highway 66.

About 8:30 that night, they burst into Scott's Supermarket at S.E. 25th and Central. Brandishing their pistols at 50 customers, they began yelling for everyone to get down on the floor and not to look at their faces. As the men collected almost $1,500 from 3 cash registers and began to make their exit, the owner and another employee ran up from the rear of the store. The other employee was the store's security guard, off-duty OCPD Patrolman James H. "Jack" Garrette.

Drawing his weapon, the five-year veteran officer yelled at the two men to stop. Harry Bush bolted out the front door but Harry Kersey stopped and turned toward the officer with a cocked .38 revolver in his hand. Garrette, a crack marksman, fired one shot, striking Kersey in the heart and killing the 28-year-old Los Angeles native almost instantly. Over $1,000 of the loot was recovered from his body. A shaken and disoriented Harry Bush spent the next hour driving around trying to find his way out of town. He finally did but it was only a short reprieve. Five hours later, Bush was arrested in his Tulsa apartment where officers recovered the other $400 taken in the robbery. Bush went to jail and Jack Garrette went on to complete a 27-year career. Later promoted to Sergeant, Garrette spent over a decade as the Rangemaster of the OCPD Firearms Range, training another generation of officers to defend themselves until he retired in 1978.

In the last week of July, 1956, Chief Bergman requested $160,000 from the City administrators to man and equip a "mobile crime fighting squad". Some new scout cars would be purchased with it but the majority of the money would be used to hire 30 new men. Five new beat officers, a clerk and a fingerprint officer would be hired and the other 23 would be for the new squad. The new uniformed squad would be used to target specific problem areas ranging from traffic enforcement to vice crackdowns. It would be the largest increase in police manpower in a decade.

DAILY OKLAHOMAN
August 15, 1956

POLICE RADAR CAR STOLEN AT STATION

Oklahoma City Police blushed a crimson red early Wednesday and reported someone had swiped a police car from in front of the police station. The car, a black 1954 Ford, carried the police department's mobile traffic radar equipment. The equipment had been checked [out] to Sgt. E.W. Lawson of the Traffic Division. He said he searched an hour for the car before "I could get up the nerve to report it stolen". The car was taken from its parking place on the north side of the station shortly after midnight. Lawson said the thief "must have wired around the switch to get it started because my partner (J.T. Byrd) and I have the only keys to it".

In a sense, every person who puts on a badge and a gun, makes a career out of it and does it honorably sets themselves apart from those who don't make those choices. But every once in a while, a very special person comes along in law enforcement, so unique that even their peers recognize them for it. They become renowned for their courage, calmness under extreme pressures, tenacity, professional competence, single-minded pursuit of their chosen profession and a very low tolerance for taking any crap from anyone, anytime.

In the old days, they were described in terms like "a tall man" (which had nothing to do with height) or "a hard man". More contemporaneously, they are usually known by the generic term "street cop". They disdain sitting behind desks and shuffling papers. They prefer mobile desks with four legs (then) or four wheels (now). They don't like writing manuals or conducting studies or sitting on committees. They wear uniforms, answering calls, or suits, investigating crimes. They solve crimes, put people in jail and love every minute of it. In the old days, they were known by their reputations. In more modern times, they tend to have the thickest personnel files. While they may approach their work with a sardonic, fatalistic, even morbid sense of humor, basically they are dead serious about it. In modern parlance, they are "active" officers. They make things happen and see to it that they are there when they happen. Sometimes their names are chiseled into stone monuments, sometimes they survive the hazards they seek out.

Charles Colcord was such a man. So was Bill Tilghman. So were Milt Jones, W.B. Nichols, Joe Burnett, Frank Cochran, Frank Smith, Lee Mullinex, Jelly Bryce and many more than can be listed here. Such men are not as rare as hen's teeth in the law enforcement profession but they do form a distinct minority. If they could be counted, they would probably conform fairly closely to anthropologist Robert Ardrey's theory of the "Dominant 5 percent".

A very special man applied to become an Oklahoma City Police officer on November 3, 1956, two days after his 23rd birthday. Darrell Dean Pierce had just finished two years in the United States Army. Before that, the Oklahoma City native had a minor flirtation with minor league baseball. Six feet tall, weighing 180 pounds with a thick, muscular neck, Pierce was probably the epitome of some Army drill instructor's definition of "lean and mean". A prematurely receding hairline over penetrating brown eyes made him appear somewhat older than his actual age.

Pierce was hired on December 4. While waiting for the next recruit class to start, he was placed in a scout car was an experienced partner, Officer C.E. "Ed" Waggoner. They worked

*OCPD Detectives Jim Reading, left, and Bill Mead count 4,000 recovered dollars on December 8, 1956.*

*OCPD's Black officers in the mid-1950s. Standing on the far right is Officer Henry McMullen Sr.*

well together. It took them less than a month to garner their first commendation together for arresting an armed robber on New Year's Eve. It was the first of many, both armed robbers and commendations, to come for Pierce. It also wasn't the last armed robber Pierce and Waggoner would encounter together.

On January 31, 1957, Officer Henry McMullen, who had been pictured as a rookie in the back of the 1923 Police Annual, mandatorily retired at the age of 70. He had served for 34 years and walked a beat on N.E. 2nd for his last five years. Fittingly, an hour and a half before he ended his last shift, he caught a burglar and recovered a television set. Five years later, his son would join the force. Henry McMullen Jr. would retire in 1977 as a Lieutenant.

During the first week of June, 1957, Chief Bergman and the Fire Chief were called upon to defend their new merit system for promotions. Complaining about this erosion of the "good old boy" system, City councilmen said there had been complaints from a number of personnel from both departments. One councilman said that he had over a hundred letters from firemen, about one-third of the entire department. Firemen were threatening to meet with Teamsters Union officials about the new system. Bergman, speaking from his department's perspective, said the complaints about the new merit system and evaluation tests were coming from a few disgruntled officers while the majority supported it. The Chief said he was attempting to raise the caliber of officers selected for supervisory positions and trying to "take the political element out of promotions and demotions". Bergman noted that all the officers who had taken a recent Sergeant's exam had passed it and a Lieutenant's exam was scheduled for mid-June.

The Council grumbled but finally shut up in the light of public scrutiny. The Chief got to keep his merit system and the Council's "spoils" system rapidly declined. For decades, the fastest way to a position on the police department or a promotion within it had been the sponsorship of a City Councilman. Although the council's influence over and in the Department was far from eradicated, the amount they stuck their noses into the Department's internal affairs was dwindling.

After a decade of dividing the Detective Bureau into specialized areas like Robbery/Homicide, Stolen Goods and Auto Theft, Chief Bergman decided to try something new to begin 1958. In response to a 20 percent rise in crime the previous year, he decided to despecialize, at least temporarily. The Vice Bureau was renamed the Special Services Bureau and the Detective Bureau would now cover 24 hours a day. Previously there had been no Detectives on duty between midnight and 7 A.M. The Chief announced how proud he was of the advances he had made in the area of police training. Recruit schools had increased to seven weeks now under the tutelage of Lt. Ed Clark. Four had been conducted during the last year, all with a 50 percent increase in human relations training. The 361-man force was also being put through regular in-service training, officers and administrators alike.

The summer of 1958 was a racially tense period in the United States. Arkansas Governor Orville Faubus mobilized his state's National Guard to prevent the integration of the schools in Little Rock. He and President Dwight Eisenhower were at odds on the front pages every day. Oklahoma City wasn't exempt from these tensions.

Since the City's beginnings almost seven decades earlier, the City had been racially segregated; the school system, housing, restaurants, bathrooms, everything. The northeastern quadrant of the City became an exclusively black enclave, although slowly expanding westward. The publicly accepted euphemisms for it got progressively less inflammatory and it progressed from "Niggertown" to "Dark Town" to "the east side". But "east side" didn't mean southeast, it meant northeast and it was synonymous with "black".

Dining facilities, waiting areas, bathrooms and water fountains carried "White Only" and "Colored" signs publicly displayed. The restaurants and lunch counters in the fashionable downtown stores didn't have those signs because they weren't needed. It was understood that colored patrons could order food to go at these establishments but they couldn't be seated or served. This was the point of attack chosen by the local NAACP that summer.

On August 19, 1958, 35 negro children ranging in age from 6 to 17 seated themselves at the lunch counter in Katz Drug Store on the southwest corner of Main and Robinson. Forewarned, Chief Roy Bergman had issued a memo to his officers, telling them about this upcoming "controversial and explosive situation". Telling his officers to "blank out" any personal feelings, the Chief reminded them that they were to protect the public, keep the peace and urged them to use "common sense".

After occupying their seats all day without being served, the children left ten minutes before closing time. The next day, they were back. After two days, Katz relented and allowed

*In September of 1957, four of the original six female officers celebrate their two-year anniversary. Left to right, Jean Latham, Ina Mae Miller,Iona Chapman and Jean Linn.*

them service. The group then moved on to Kress's variety store and, moving progressively farther west on fashionable Main Street, John A. Brown's luncheonette.

The group grew from 35 to 66, then to 90. Supervised by adults and with police officers always nearby, there was no violence and no arrests. Kress's allowed them service after a few days but Brown's did not. Arriving at Brown's one day, they discovered all of the chairs removed and the tops of the stools taken off. The next day they found all the seats back but occupied by white customers.

The "sit-ins" ended on September 1 and the children went back to school. Thanks to a sensible group of protesters and professional conduct by the police officers, a model non-violent demonstration ended peacefully. The protesters would achieve all of their goals but not until the next decade.

A timely article on the front page during the demonstrations noted that the Police Department consisted of 312 officers whose pay started at $325 a month and increases in both were sorely needed.

If you listened closely during the 1958 gubernatorial election, you could hear the death knell of prohibition. Both of the major candidates, Tulsa County Democrat J. Howard Edmondson and Woodward County Republican Phil Ferguson, were for repealing the law or at least bringing it rapidly to a vote of the people. The increasing urbanization of the State and the decreasing rural population made it seem the best opportunity for the wet forces in years.

Another familiar name surfaced during the election. D.A. Jelly Bryce, former Oklahoma City Police officer and F.B.I. agent, having legally incorporated his nickname into his legal name, threw his hat in the ring. Now retired from the F.B.I. and living in his hometown of Mountain View, Bryce filed as an Independent candidate. He was advocating overhauling state law enforcement, the continuation of prohibition and received the backing of dry forces disenchanted with the repeal stands of the two major party candidates.

In November of 1958, Oklahoma voters went to the polls and overwhelmingly elected J. Howard Edmondson as their new Governor, setting several records in the process. The 33-year old former Tulsa prosecuting attorney was the youngest man to ever hold the office and was also elected by the biggest majority. The fact that a major plank in his platform was bringing the prohibition question to a statewide vote yet again was indicative. Although to no avail, the protest candidacy of dry advocate D.A. "Jelly" Bryce netted him over 31,000 votes, the largest in the history of the State for an independent candidate.

Edmondson's plan for bringing the pot to a quick boil was simple; stringent enforcement of the prohibition laws. His attitude was that the citizens voted for the law, let them live by it or suffer the consequences. A similar attack had ended prohibition in Kansas a decade earlier. The majority of citizens were not going to be totally deprived of their liquor, have it strictly enforced on them and pay the resulting exorbitant prices for the illegal stuff. Five times in the last 52 years, state elections had reaffirmed prohibition but by smaller margins each time.

State Commissioner of Public Safety Joe Cannon, later to become a controversial and idiosyncratic Oklahoma County Judge, became the head of the Governor's hammer. Only a year older than the new Governor, the new Commissioner went about his new duties so enthusiastically that the press dubbed him "the crew-cut commando". Threatening to usurp county sheriff's authority statewide if they didn't cooperate and enlisting the Highway Patrol to his cause, Cannon organized a deafening symphony of roadblocks, raids, searches and mass arrests. The only thing more deafening were the wails of protest and the gnashing of teeth from all echelons of the vice world, the money barons of the business world and the halls of government.

The beginning of 1959 was the end of a 40-year law enforcement career. W.I."Bill" Eads retired as the City Marshal of the wealthy suburb of Nichols Hills. The 72-year-old Eads had been one of the original members of Mayor Jack Walton's pet Mounted Patrol in 1919. When it was disbanded, he resigned, was reinstated and was an OCPD Detective for the next four years. He then served five years as head of the Federal Narcotics Bureau office in Kansas City and a decade as an Oklahoma County Deputy Sheriff. Brief forays as a private detective and chief of plant protection at the McAlester Naval Ammunition Depot preceded his tenure as the marshal in Nichols Hills at the end of World War II. His retirement may have been hastened by three unsolved burglaries of posh Nichols Hills residences a few months earlier that netted over $21,000 in lost jewelry and other valuables.

Finally, on April 7, 1959, the citizens got their vote on prohibition. After more than half a century and half a dozen elections, statewide prohibition was defeated. Repeal was approved by a small margin but it was big enough. The local option question failed however, by more than 2 to 1. Oklahoma would have liquor but not by the drink. The acronym BYOB (Bring Your Own Bottle or Booze) would become as familiar to the citizens as the phrases "open saloon" and "disorderly house" would become to the police. On July 1, the Alcoholic Beverage Control Board would be created to enforce the state's new liquor laws.

At 7:21 A.M. on September 3, 1959, the Police Department was plunged into darkness. A bolt of lightning struck a power pole at N.W. 3rd and Lee, instantly shutting off all power within a square mile. Zealous Prohibitionists probably thought it was a sign of God's displeasure. If so, He was only mildly peeved. A 1958 Ford scout car was pulled up on the sidewalk with its headlights shining in the front door of Police Headquarters until power was restored two hours later.

The decade would end with promotions and changes for the OCPD. Chief of Detectives Wayne Harbolt retired in July to become an inspector for the alcoholic beverage control board. He was replaced by 31-year veteran R.S. Worthy who was promoted to Major. Jack Mullinex became Captain in the Detective Bureau and Jim Reading was made Captain in charge of Special Services. Two Detectives were promoted to Lieutenant, Hilton Geer and I.G. Purser. Both would become Chief in the future. Geer, lauded for the talents he had shown for catching armed robbers during his last six years, wouldenjoy the most spectacular rise in fortunes in modern times. He would ascend from Detective to Chief of Police in less than three years.

# VIII — EXPANSION AND MODERNIZATION 1960-1969

Although the City had been striving toward a "600,000 in '60" goal, the census showed only 534,902 people in the metropolitan area. The first OCPD Pistol Range was constructed north of Lake Hefner just west of the Water Treatment Plant. Built with donated materials and trusty labor, it also featured the Department's first full-time rangemaster, Lt. Chris Walker. Lt. Walker expanded the range to 37 firing positions during the next 8 years.

On the evening of February 14, 1960, Officers Darrell Pierce and Larry Hannah were called to investigate a hit and run accident on N.E. 10th east of Grand Boulevard. A young Midwest City man nursing a bloody mouth told them he had been rammed head-on by a car that then left the scene. He offered to show the officers where the car went.

After being seated in the back seat of the scout car, he led them to a house in the 3200 block of N.E. 10th, about half a mile east of the accident scene. Locating the damaged suspect vehicle in the front yard, Officer Pierce knocked on the house's front door. Getting no answer, Pierce got back in the driver's seat of the scout car to call in a registration on the license number.

Just as the police car started backing out of the driveway, a black man appeared out of the darkness on the passenger's side of the scout car. Yelling incoherently, he was pointing a shotgun at Officer Hannah on the front passenger's side and the civilian witness on the rear passenger's side. Hannah yelled "He has a rifle" and ducked down in the front seat just as the man brought the shotgun up to a firing position on his shoulder.

Officer Pierce put the gearshift in neutral and, with the car still rolling backwards, got out of the driver's door, drew his revolver and shot the man once in the forehead.

Albert Scott was dead before he fell. Besides the loaded shotgun, a loaded pistol was also recovered from his body. City and State authorities cleared Officer Pierce of any charges in the shooting but the racially troubled times wouldn't let it go at that.

Ten days after Albert Scott's death, the local branch of the NAACP sent a letter to Chief Bergman, comparing the OCPD to the Ku Klux Klan and demanding that the Chief "take action", claiming Officer Pierce had "lynched" Albert Scott. Two days later, the letter was published in The Black Dispatch newspaper with accompanying editorial comments.

Often, all too often, police administrators get into an appeasing and apologizing mode when dealing with complaints against their officers. The justness or unjustness of the complaint is not as material as making it go away. This was not Roy Bergman's way.

Chief Bergman took action on March 2. He sent a letter to the officials of the local NAACP advising them that they had always received courteous and interested treatment by his office, no reports had been withheld from them but they had not acquainted themselves with all the facts in the case. He went on to accuse them of being "recklessly critical" and irresponsible in publicizing their unjust criticisms. He ended the letter accusing them of "police baiting", said they owed the officers an apology and left no doubt that this letter was the last action he intended taking in this case. VERY truly yours.

Pierce began receiving threatening phone calls at his home. Perhaps with the fate of Albert Scott in mind, no real attempts were made to make good on the threats. The calls stopped when Pierce got an unlisted phone number.

That might have been the end of it if they had been dealing with someone other than Darrell Pierce. He was not in the habit of bowing his head or turning his back on injustice, whether to others or himself. On August 30, 1960, Pierce filed a $100,000 libel suit against three officers of the local NAACP and four members of The Black Dispatch. To put this in the proper perspective, Pierce's annual salary at the time was about $4,000. He got their attention. A correction and apology appeared on the front page of The Black Dispatch.

Two days after the Pierce-Scott shooting, a new rookie went to work on the OCPD two days after his 21st birthday. Robert V. Wilder, the son of retired Major H.V. Wilder, worked in a patrol car with a senior partner until the next recruit school started in May.

Although the school was 12 weeks long, that time frame is deceptive. Four days each week were spent in the classroom. Every Friday, the rookies spent half a day on the pistol range. They then spent the other half day riding in patrol cars with senior partners on the evening shift on Friday and Saturday nights.

*Chief Ed Rector.*

Mid-1960 brought another series of newspaper interviews with disgruntled officers. They said morale was low and discipline was lax, all related to attrition rate and low pay. There had been a 75 percent turnover in Department personnel since 1953. Of the 294 officers who had left during that time, 56 had been fired or resigned under pressure and 64 others had cited better paying jobs as their reason for leaving. Half of the 20 who had left in the first half of this year cited the same reason. A third of all current officers held outside jobs as diverse as night watchmen, grocery checkers, truck drivers and car salesmen. Officers felt this situation could be alleviated by an organization of officers but the administration was adamantly opposed.

Roy Bergman retired on January 1, 1961, to become an investigator for the Oklahoma County District Attorney's Office and Patrol Division Major Ed E. Rector was made Chief. Nearing his fifty-third birthday, the Marietta, Oklahoma, native had been born on January 28, 1908, the first OCPD Chief born in the State of Oklahoma. A smallish man (5'8", 146 pounds) in comparison to his peers when he had been hired by the extra board six days after the Pearl Harbor attack, he was promoted to Detective in the Juvenile Division on January 8, 1947. Serving in Stolen Goods also, he became a Lieutenant in Patrol on June 5, 1949 and returned to his primary area of expertise when he became the Captain in charge of Juvenile on May 16, 1955. Promoted to Major on April 1, 1959, he was in command of the Patrol Division when selected for the Chief's job. He was to be a short-lived Chief whose major role seemed to be as a quick reorganizer of the 361-man force. Some would consider the term "quick reorganizer" to be a euphemism for hatchet man.

Rector immediately "requested" the Majors in command of the Patrol, Traffic and Detective Divisions to retire since they all had over 24 years of service and "their services will not be required under [the OCPD's] long-range plans". Traffic Major Clayton Scheid and Patrol Major Frank Thurston, both 25-year veterans, and the Chief of Detectives, Major R.S. Worthy, a 33-year veteran, all complied. There followed a mass of transfers and promotions. Ace Williams, Hilton Geer and Gene Goold were promoted to Major. Williams took over the Patrol Division and Geer became Chief of Detectives. Geer's first action as the new Chief of Detectives, for reasons he refused to publicly disclose, was to demote Captain Jim Reading, the commander of the Vice Squad, to Lieutenant. As the changes continued, the number of Sergeants almost doubled, the number of Detectives was reduced from 67 to 60, one Lieutenant's position was eliminated and one Captain's position was created. Gene Goold was placed in charge of the Bureau of Services and Administration. Five months later, he wrote a letter to Chief Hollingsworth, stating that he had accomplished the objectives set for him at the time of his transfer and, with refreshing candor, that his current duties did not merit the rank of Major. Goold was reduced to Captain and made the Director of Training.

Rector lasted barely six months in the top job. In a move reminiscent of the 1920's, Chief Rector was fired on July 15, 1961, by City Manager Robert Luttrell for "causing low morale

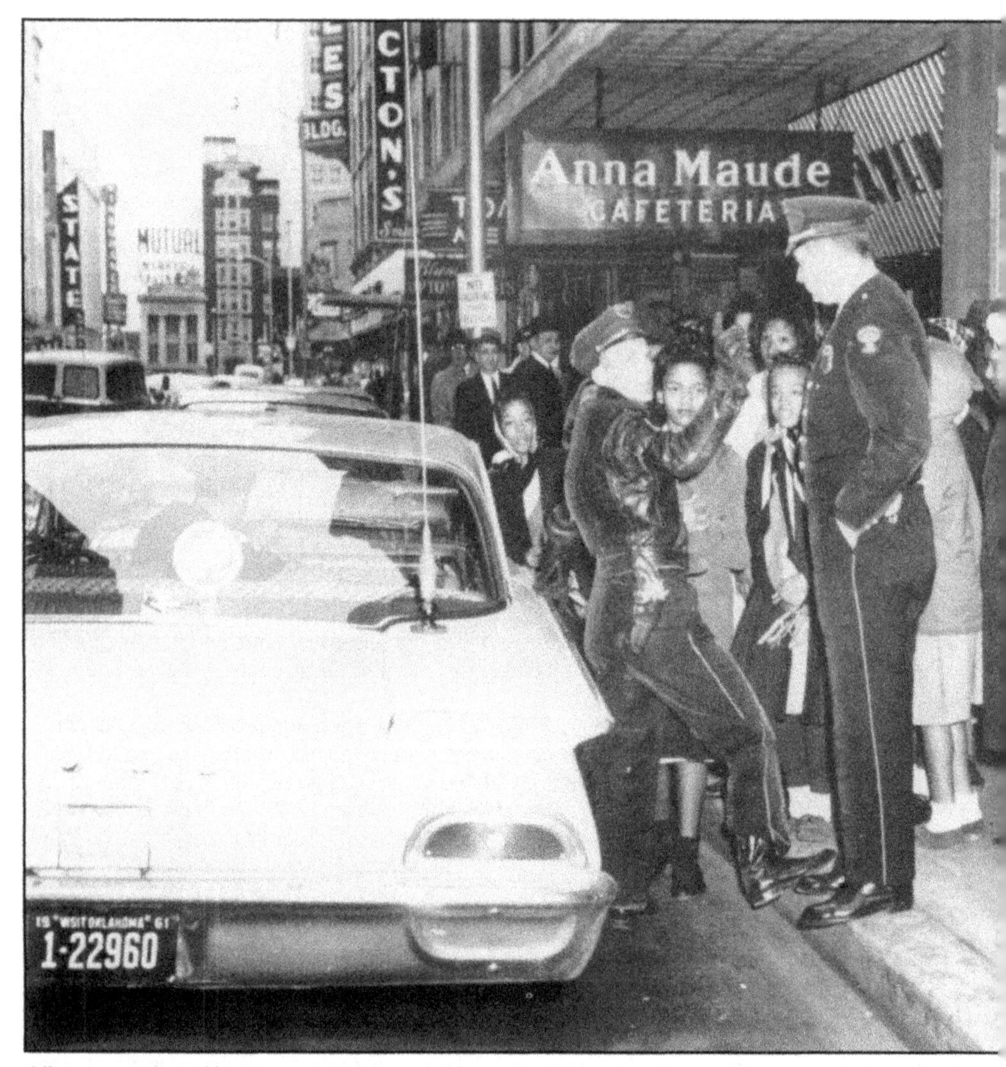


*Officers await the paddy wagon to transport racial demonstrators to jail on January 13, 1961, at the Anna Maude Cafeteria on North Robinson. Standing on the curb is Officer Ben Caswell.*

and inefficient administration". He was allowed to return to duty as a Captain a short time later, writing a manual on juvenile delinquency until he reached his 20-year anniversary and retired in December of 1961.

At the City Council meeting on Tuesday, October 31, 1961, the Council annexed 42.7 square miles of land. That acquisition gave Oklahoma City an area of 475.5 square miles, making it the largest city in the United States in land area, nearly 20 square miles larger than Los Angeles.

Also in 1961, a group of more than 350 influential politicians, businessmen and civic leaders formed the Citizens for Police Improvement Inc. (CPI). Quickly recognizable names among the incorporators included former City Managers H.E. Bailey and William Gill Jr. as well as future Mayor George Shirk. The group provided moral support, political influence and financial aid for police-related causes. They also began giving an annual CPI Police Recognition Dinner that included awards of commendations, watches, silver trays, plaques and cash to officers in a system that pre-dated the current system of medals.

The CPI Committee held their first banquet on November 19, 1961, in the Persian Room

of the Skirvin Tower. Some 800 guests heard Charles L. Bennett, Chairman of the Board, state their intent "to help improve the Department, to help the public understand the problems of the Department and to serve as a channel for community recognition of the Department". Thirteen awards would be presented annually, starting the next year; three from the CPI, five from CPI in cooperation with city businesses and five by CPI in cooperation with associations. The only award presented at this first banquet was a Distinguished Service Citation presented to E.L. "Jim" Roederer for his assistance in passing a city bond issue of $2 million for improvement of police facilities. This money would be used to construct a new police headquarters building adjacent to the current one.

Officers were nominated for the awards by police supervisors and commanders through the Chief of Police. Selection of the winners was to be made annually by a committee consisting of executives of the CPI, the City Manager and two members of the Police Department of the rank of Sergeant or below.

The three top CPI awards were named for political offices. The City Council Award was analogous to the current Medal of Honor, being for "distinguishing himself above and beyond the call of duty in the performance of an act of gallantry at imminent personal risk of his own life, with the knowledge of the risk assumed".

The Mayor's Award was a combination of the current Medal of Valor and Lifesaving award. While it called for bravery and imminent personal risk, it also involved the saving of life. The City Manager's Commendation Award was for exceptionally meritorious service, similar to the current Medal for Meritorious Service.

While the top three awards were reserved for members of the OCPD, in later years the County Commissioners Award was made available to any law enforcement officer in Oklahoma County for "contributions to law enforcement", like the current Certificate of Achievement. In addition, there were 10 lesser awards sponsored by various local businesses or associations. The initial sponsors were the Oklahoma Transportation Company, Oklahoma Gas and Electric, Dolese Concrete, the Oklahoma Publishing Company, Macklanburg-Duncan Company, Oklahoma City Downtown Association, the Chamber of Commerce, the Community Council and the Association of Independent Insurance Agents. Their awards were presented for training, juvenile enforcement, accident and criminal investigations, police leadership, traffic safety, outstanding service, administration of justice, police planning and general contributions to the community. Besides the recognition, the awards were particularly popular with officers because most of them included cash awards ranging from $50 to $2,500. While the top three awards stayed constant throughout the decade of their existence, the remainder fluctuated with changes, additions and deletions. Of the 15 business-sponsored awards given during the decade, only 3 existed for the full duration with the same sponsors and award criteria.

The day after Christmas in 1961, an old man died peacefully at his home in Tarzana, California. Attorney, motion picture producer and actor, former gubernatorial candidate and "the last of the Oklahoma outlaws", Al Jennings had been 97 years old.

Rector was followed into office by Chief Dan Hollingsworth. Born in Ector, Texas, on February 3, 1907, Hollingsworth had originally joined the Department on December 1, 1930. Originally a motorcycle officer, after seven months he transferred to scout cars but eight months later went back to motorcycles. In 1931, he had been the first officer to have his wedding in the police station and he and his bride, June Degrush, became the first husband and wife to work together in the OCPD.

On October 25, 1937, Chief Scanland had created the first dedicated Accident Squad and promoted Hollingsworth to Sergeant in charge of it. He attended the nine-month course at the

Northwestern University Traffic Institute and upon returning on June 1, 1939, he was made a Lieutenant. Less than six months later, he became a Captain, still in the Accident Squad. On June 1, 1940, he was moved to the Intelligence Unit to investigate subversives in response to the escalating international tensions.

*Chief Dan Hollingsworth.*

On March 9, 1941, he was chosen to fill the newly-created position of Director of Traffic in charge of all police traffic functions. Six days before the Pearl Harbor attack, Chief Frank Smith created the FBI-inspired position of Inspector as the Department's second-in-command, essentially the old Assistant Chief's position. Hollingsworth was the first man selected for it.

He held the new post for less than a year when, on October 24, 1942, he was given an indefinite leave of absence to serve in the wartime U.S. Navy. He returned to the OCPD on January 1, 1946, and was reinstated as a Captain but not for long. On August 13, 1946, he was given another leave of absence to become the Manager of the newly-organized Greater Oklahoma City Safety Council. It was quite a leave of absence. He didn't return until selected for the Chief's job almost 15 years later.

In 1961, just 26 years after the first Park-O-Meter was installed in downtown Oklahoma City, parking meters and fines placed over $400,000 in the City's coffers.

On March 15, 1962, Chief Hollingsworth issued a memo to his officers listing 50 changes he had made in his first 8 months. From the somewhat cynical perspective of the street officer, they could probably be broken down into three general categories; public relations changes, administrative changes and operational changes that directly affected the guys doing the police work. When tallied, the final score was Public Relations 17, Administrative 22 and Operations 11.

The public relations group ranged from establishing a weekly management group breakfast to creating a lounge for officer's wives waiting to pick up their husbands after their shift ended. Reservations were automatically made at the breakfasts for all officers of the supervisory ranks of Sergeant and above. If they didn't attend and didn't cancel their "reservation" far enough in advance, they got a brusque letter from the Chief, billing them for half a dollar for their missed breakfast. If they missed several in a row, their letter pointed this out, letting them know that heads were being counted and names taken. The letters also mentioned that while their attendance was not mandatory, it might be in their best interests to attend.

Administrative changes ranged from the formation of 14 committees to creating new incident report forms. Even though some of these changes would doubtlessly have been met with derision from the street cops, some of them are interesting from an historic point of view.

During this time period, the Police Blotter kept at the Information Desk was discontinued, the Records Bureau began charging citizens for copies of reports and the communications codes Signal 11, 12 and 13 were created. The memo stated that creating these codes "saves air time without disclosing too much information". For the uninitiated, Signal 11 meant "Call your wife at home", Signal 12 meant "Call your wife at work" and Signal 13 was a request to get out of the car to eat.

Some of the changes, however, had an operational impact. For the first time, officers were allowed to inspect their own personnel files. A disciplinary advisory board was created consisting of three Patrolmen, three Detectives and one each from the ranks of Sergeant, Lieutenant and Captain. A waiting room was created for officers waiting to testify in criminal and traffic court. An Intelligence Unit was created under Lieutenant Jim Reading. Fingerprint kits were placed in all scout cars and training provided in their use. The experimental use of 50

*Chief Hilton Geer.*

officers as a roving burglary squad brought the burglary rate down. An expanded Alias Warrant Squad covering 16 hours a day succeeded in collecting record amounts on unpaid traffic tickets. It became possible for officers to borrow against future sick leave instead of just going off of the payroll if it was exhausted. The number of telephones in the dispatchers office was increased from 2 to 7 with 30-button call directors, capable of receiving 7 calls at once. Finally the memo noted that three police dogs had been ordered for the Department. Officers to handle them would be selected the following month and it was anticipated that the dogs would be in action by July 1. Hollingsworth, however, would not be there to see it.

Hollingsworth's short administration was marked by unfortunate bickering and turmoil. It climaxed with the retirement of Chief of Detectives Hilton Geer over the use of two detective cruisers equipped with complete arsenals. They were to be on the streets at least 16 hours a day and the keys left with the Station Captain at the Information Desk the rest of the time so they were available rapidly around the clock. The impetus for this tactic was apparently an incident occurring several months before when a Parks Department employee fell into the lion's pit at the Lincoln Park Zoo and no one had a rifle available to shoot the lion. The newspaper reports of the dispute between the commanders noted that it was highly unusual for a man as young as the 43-year-old Geer to be retiring from the police service.

Hollingsworth resigned on June 1, 1962, to accept a job as a traffic consultant with the Washington, D.C.-based Insurance Institute for Highway Safety. In a first, he was replaced by Hilton Geer, who returned from retirement to accept the Chief's job.

After yet another turbulent year that saw three Chiefs come and go, a little stability finally returned. The Hilton Geer administration was to become the second longest in the Department's history—seven years—and see some of the greatest developments in its 79 years of existence. The growth trends seen in the 1950s accelerated and a massive modernization program was instituted.

A police administrator I once knew had a marble paperweight on his desk embellished with the words "When in doubt, do what's right". Although that particular administrator violated that precept more than enough times to forfeit his right to display the motto, Chief Geer created some heat during his first summer by trying to do what was right. In mid-August, yet another series of newspaper articles chronicled alleged payoffs to a group of black officers on the City's east side. Their informant was Edward Lewis Hudson, the owner of Goldie's Switch-a-roo Club at N.E. 2nd and Stiles. An investigation was begun.

The next day Geer suspended six black officers, Detectives H.V. Gear and E.B. Ackerson as well as Patrolmen H.B. Gaines, C.S. Parker, W.W. Rucker and R.C. Scobey. Some of them were no strangers to Departmental discipline.

Gaines, a 15-year veteran, had resigned once and been rehired, promoted to Detective twice and demoted twice. He had also been called on the carpet for drinking on duty and striking a woman without justification. Parker, in his nine-year career, had one brutality complaint against him as well as one complaint from a woman who said he "took liberties with her in the rear seat of a scout car". For a brutality complaint to be sustained in those days, the use of force usually had to be far out of line and policemen were expected to be able to conduct their personal affairs with women without the use of force. Parker had been suspended for three days the previous year for "being out of his district with a woman in the front seat of the car". Rucker had also been demoted from Detective once.

The newspaper's informant lost a little of his credibility when forgery charges were filed against him in Oklahoma County the day after the suspensions. The NAACP began complaining in spite of the fact that all the principles were black, victims, witnesses, informants and suspects alike. The matter was settled within the week. Gaines, Parker and Rucker were fired by City Manager Robert Luttrell, Gaines for accepting money from a gambler, Parker for taking money from a prostitute and Rucker for getting money and whiskey from a gambler. The other three officers were reinstated.

On October 28, 1962, the Citizens for Police Improvement hosted their second annual Police Recognition Dinner in the plush Persian Room of the Skirvin Tower. Fourteen Oklahoma City officers and one Bethany officer were presented awards by Bob Eastman, manager of the Oklahoma Safety Council. Sergeant Cecil W. Pierce received the City Council Award for disarming a man threatening to kill himself and his family. Officer James Myers was given the Mayor's Award for valor for entering a burning building three times to carry occupants to safety. Officer James G. Jackson was given the City Manager's Award for capturing a jail escapee without using firearms when the use of deadly force may have been warranted.

J.E Grist, Jerry G. Landreth and Bill A. Stubbs were honored as the three top police trainees of the year. Traffic Officers Ulo Kasenurm and C.S. McLaughlin were honored for the best job of accident investigation while the best criminal investigation honors went to Detective E.B. "Salty" Meals. Captain S.W. Stephens, a Marine veteran of World War II who had been captured by the Japanese on Corregidor and was a POW for over three years, won the award for police leadership while Lt. Jim G. Perdue won an award for safety education. Perdue was to gain recognition in later years as the "Red Rover" mobile traffic watch for the local KTOK radio station.

The Chamber of Commerce Award for police planning was given to Captain Kenneth A. Nash, Sgt. Lloyd Gramling was honored for his selection to attend the nine-month course at the Northwestern University Traffic Institute and Lt. Sam Watson won the Community Council Award for his development of the Canine Unit. Officer Jerry Legg of the suburban Bethany Police was given a special Award of Merit for exhibiting alertness in spotting a vehicle carrying $2 million worth of narcotics.

*One of the OCPD's first Canine units performs a demonstration in the early 1960s.*

Under Geer's direction, the new position of Assistant Chief was established. The first man chosen to fill the post, on the first day of 1963, was William A. "Ace" Williams, exactly 26 years after his first day on the job. New innovations in 1962 included the creation of a full-time Canine Unit. The unit's first commander, Sergeant Bill McDonald, had been using police dogs on various special assignments since 1954.

A Criminal Intelligence Unit was started in February and began distributing Known Offender Bulletins. The year's 29 murders, 39 rapes, 388 robberies, 3,772 burglaries and 1,926 auto thefts seem placid by current standards but actually reflected decreases in rape and burglary for that year. The year ended with a Department strength of 320 officers and 49 civilians.

There was nothing special about Friday, February 15, 1963, in the Robbery-Homicide Division of the Dallas, Texas, Police Department. If Captain Will Fritz had known that in a little more than nine months, he would be investigating the murder of the President of the United States, he might have been considering his retirement options. But he didn't so it was just business as usual.

They had received some information on an armed robbery committed in Dallas the previous month. Three people leaving church had been robbed by two black men, taking their money and checks. One of the checks had been used to buy a 1962 Chevy convertible from a Dallas car lot. The information was that the car and suspects were in Oklahoma City. Captain Fritz called Lieutenant D.C. Mosshart in OCPD Robbery-Homicide.

Lieutenant Mosshart put his men on it. For the rest of the day, records were checked, east side officers were consulted and informants were canvassed. By midnight the suspects had been traced to an apartment at 719 N.E. 9th Street. The informant said the suspects were armed and had stated they wouldn't be taken alive. A fairly common boast among bad guys until they are faced with the alternative, as it turned out these guys meant it. One suspect was Leroy A. Price Jr. and the other was known as "Big Bad Johnny Lee Parker" because that was what was stenciled on his suitcase.

Shortly after midnight, two detective cruisers with their lights out met in the alley behind the suspect's address. Lt. Jim Reading and Sgt. Bill Mead of the Intelligence Unit were met by Detectives Dale Harbolt (son of former Chief of Detectives Wayne Harbolt) and John Rowden of Robbery-Homicide. Accompanying Rowden was Lt. Jerry Legg of the Bethany Police Department. Some officers from suburban departments had a habit of hanging around in Oklahoma City, where the action was, when they weren't occupied in their own jurisdictions, where the action wasn't. The action was definitely in Oklahoma City tonight.

It was decided that Rowden and Legg would go to the front of the apartment building while the other three would watch the rear. Legg, armed with a shotgun, went up the east side of the building while Rowden, armed with a fully automatic Thompson submachine gun, went up the west side. As Legg approached the front of the building, he saw two men fitting the suspect's descriptions walking away and he yelled at them to stop. Both men turned and opened fire on him. Legg returned fire with the shotgun and Leroy A. Price Jr. went down. The other suspect ran down the west side of the building, straight into John Rowden.

Instantly face to face, they were too close to each other for Rowden's machine gun to be of much use. Rowden threw up his left hand in an instinctive reaction just as Parker fired one round from his .45 pistol. Hit in the head and stunned, Rowden reflexively squeezed off a 19-round burst from the machine gun as he fell. Parker, unhit, ran on down the alley.

Legg and Harbolt, running to Rowden, found him bleeding from a head wound but alive. They called an ambulance and started down the alley looking for Parker. They didn't have far to go. Parker was crouched behind a porch two houses away. The hesitation factor gone, both officers fired when they spotted Parker and he fell.

Big Bad Johnny Lee Parker, whose real name was Samuel Jackson, and Leroy A. Price Jr. went to the morgue while John Rowden went to the hospital. Once there, Rowden discovered just how close he'd come. Jackson's .45 slug had struck his left forefinger, ricocheted off the bone and hit him in the right side of the head, tearing a three-inch gash in his scalp before exiting. Later investigation proved that the two suspects had committed at least four armed robberies in Oklahoma City during the previous week.

John Rowden recovered and returned to duty. He was given a commendation by Chief of Detectives Jack Mullinex. A few years later, both John Rowden and Dale Harbolt resigned from the OCPD to become U.S. Treasury Agents for the Alcohol, Tobacco and Firearms Bureau. Rowden retired from ATF over 20 years later but Dale Harbolt was killed in the line of duty in an Oklahoma City suburb in the 1970's. Jerry Legg transferred to the OCPD and retired as a Detective in 1979.

*Officer Ronald Lynn Haggard.*

On March 21, 1963, a Mrs. Cantrell contacted Lt. I.G. Purser at Police Headquarters. She wanted to commend a motorcycle officer named Haggard for his actions while investigating a traffic accident near her home two days earlier. The commendation would be placed in the officer's personnel file but he would never know it. Officer Ronald Lynn Haggard had died earlier that morning from injuries received the night before.

The 22-year-old officer had apparently been pursuing a speeder in the 7300 block of South High when he lost control of his motorcycle at high speed. He had been thrown 130 feet, sustaining multiple injuries. A passing motorist found him and notified police. Haggard was taken to Mercy Hospital but died a little later. He left behind a widow and three-year-old daughter to mourn over his grave in Resthaven Cemetery. The car he was chasing was never located. Haggard had only been on the force for 15 months, the last 3 on motorcycles. His was the twenty-first traffic fatality in the City that year compared to nine for the same period the previous year. He was also the twenty-first OCPD officer to be killed in the line of duty, ending the second longest period in recent history without an officer's death.

On April 4, 1963, former Chief Roy Bergman died unexpectedly from a heart attack at age 58. Born in Oklahoma City on April 24, 1904, he had joined the Department on March 15, 1930. Promoted to Detective in 1935, he went into the Vice Squad at that rank on November 10, 1937. Eighteen days later he was the Lieutenant in charge of it. When Chief Frank Smith came, Bergman was transferred to Patrol where he became a Captain on April 18, 1941. He became the Chief's executive secretary on October 1, 1942.

A week later he received a draft deferment at the request of City Manager H.E. Bailey. Bailey stated in his letter to the Selective Service System that in the first 10 months of the war, 90 OCPD officers had left the Department to enter the military or defense-related jobs. Bergman was elevated to the position of Inspector on April 17, 1943, and finished his 31-year career serving as Chief for the last 6 1/2 years.

One of the achievements he was proudest of was installing a merit system of competitive promotional examinations. Described as "a tall, important-looking man in dark horn-rimmed glasses", his obituary noted that he had the distinction of being one of the few to retire "on his own" as Chief.

In August, Patrol Division Major Wayne Lawson started shift training on a weekly basis in his lineups and Training Bulletins became familiar handouts. In October, the arrival of 14 new 1963 Ford scout cars allowed Lawson to reorganize his Division from 15 to 24 patrol districts.

On November 1, 1963, another officer's career almost ended prematurely. Officer Rex Barrett, with only five months on the force, arrested Eugene W. Walters at his home at 608 N. Walnut for misdemeanor assault and battery. As they were on their way to jail in the 500 block of N. Dewey, Walters pulled a .25 automatic pistol and struck the officer in the head. As the scout car swerved to the curb, the suspect jumped out and ran. Barrett pursued, caught him and both men began struggling on the ground.

In the struggle, the suspect ripped Barrett's gunbelt off, gained control of the officer's .38

and shot him once in the stomach. Although seriously wounded, Barrett continued fighting the suspect until another officer arrived to help subdue him.

Assistant Chief Ace Williams said that, contrary to the officers' opinions, one-man cars were not to blame for the incident because they had been in effect for seven years on day shift. Eugene Walters was sentenced to ten years in prison. Rex Barrett recovered from his wound to complete another three decades with the OCPD.

The Third Annual CPI Awards Dinner was conducted at the Skirvin Hotel on the afternoon of November 10, 1963. Detective John Rowden was awarded the City Council Award for heroism for his gun battle with armed robbers the previous February. The Mayor's Award for valor was presented to motorcycle Officer Polk White for saving his partner's life on May 10. White shot an 18-year-old armed robbery suspect he had stopped when the youth pulled a gun and pointed it at White's partner, Officer A.W. Cathey. Officers Rex Barrett and Mike Huckaby received the City Manager's Award for evacuating 35 people from the area of a fire in the 200 block of N.E. 11th on July 3. Barrett was unable to attend since he was still recovering from his wound nine days earlier but the award was presented to his wife.

Officers Henry McMullen Jr., Joe Hughston and Jim Willis received awards as the top-ranking rookies. Captain Gene Goold received two awards; one was a marksmanship trophy and the other was for his work with the Ident-i-kit, a device for constructing composite pictures of suspects from fragmentary descriptions of witnesses. Officer Joe Wright was commended for the best accident investigation and Detective C.E. "Ed" Waggoner won the award for the best criminal investigation for breaking up a major car theft ring. Waggoner's month-long investigation culminated in the arrest of several suspects and clearing up the thefts of 30 late model cars.

Captain Tom Wilson shared the police leadership award with Sergeant John R. Donnell. Wilson was in charge of the Jail and Donnell had supervised a kidnapping investigation that rescued a two-year-old girl an hour after her abduction. The Community Council Award for the "health, welfare and betterment of the citizens" was changed to the Cains Coffee Award when it gained the sponsorship of that company. It consisted of a $300 cash grant and this year was given to Officer W.L. Williams for safety education efforts with schools and young people. Sergeant Jim Watson won the Safety Council award. Cash grants were awarded to Jim Nutter ($2,500) to attend the Northwestern Traffic Institute and Major Jack Mullinex ($750) to attend the FBI National Academy.

Two new awards were added this year. The County Commissioners Award was to be a silver tray given to the uniformed law enforcement officer serving in any capacity in Oklahoma County who contributed the most to law enforcement in the county. The first recipient of the award was Warr Acres Police Chief Nelson Beckett, cited for his activities in civic clubs, schools and safety programs.

*Officer Mark Henry Zelewski.*

The second new award was the County Bar Association Award. It was a cash grant of $100 to be awarded to the member of any regularly organized or constituted law enforcement body who had made the greatest contribution to the orderly and efficient administration of justice and the furtherance of jurisprudence in Oklahoma County. The first honoree was Midwest City Police Chief Carl Tyler for his work in helping standardize law and ordinances in Oklahoma County municipalities.

An improbable, almost incredible series of events took a tragic turn in late July of 1964. An informant notified OCPD officers that four black men were planning to rob the Safeway store at N.E. 23 and Eastern. The men were arming themselves with a number of weapons including a sawed off shotgun. The robbery was to occur between 9 and 10 P.M. on Thursday, July 23. The informant said the last names of three of the four men were Barnett, Crigler and Taylor.

The officers staked the store out, one concealed inside and the rest hiding outside. Trying to minimize the danger to citizens, the plan was to allow the robbery to occur, then confront the men after they left the store. So they waited, in vain, as it happened. They would later learn that the car the men were going to use for the robbery had broken down. Friday and Saturday were spent trying to repair the car. Saturday night, July 25, they tried again.

This time the officers allowed a Daily Oklahoman reporter and photographer to accompany them on the stakeout. They even borrowed some of the newspapermen's radios which were better than the Police Department's. The car drove by the Safeway store slowly with all four men inside. It circled the block several times as the officers watched and waited tensely. But then the men apparently decided the car still wasn't up to a getaway and they drove off into the night as the officers heard the engine chugging pathetically.

The officers set the stakeout up again on the night of Sunday, July 26. This time the men never showed up. Disappointed, the officers called the stakeout off about 10:30 P.M., about half an hour before Officer Mark Zelewski came on duty to ride Car 5 on the graveyard shift. The four men would be in jail by the next morning...but Mark Zelewski would be dead.

Zelewski, riding alone in Car 5, was a rookie with only seven months on the force but he was not as much a novice as it seems. Twenty-eight years old, he had been a policeman in the Air Force for eight years, the last part of it at Clinton-Sherman Air Force Base in western Oklahoma. Clinton-Sherman was a Strategic Air Command base then, the runways lined with B-52 bombers loaded with nuclear weapons and, in the cold war years of the late '50s and early 60's, security was taken very seriously on SAC bases. Married with three children, all preschool age, he joined the OCPD the previous November after his discharge.

Zelewski had already impressed a number of his fellow officers and supervisors with the business-like maturity he brought to his job. He made friends easily with a ready sense of humor and the Wisconsin native was good natured about the ribbing he took for being a "yankee". He was also aware of the dangers of his chosen profession. One of the friends he had made in his short time on the job was Rex Barrett who had been shot only two weeks before Zelewski was hired.

This morning, Zelewski received a radio call shortly after 1 A.M. on a burglar alarm on the 7-11 store at N.E. 36 and Prospect. Officer Karl Richter, in Car 6, volunteered to back him. One man cars were the rule rather than the exception at the time. After checking out the false alarm, the officers went their separate ways, Zelewski heading south of Prospect and Richter going west on 36th Street.

Richter had gone only three blocks when Zelewski called him on the radio. Directing him to the block east of N.E. 34 and Prospect, Zelewski said "I've got some traffic stopped here. I think I need your help". Immediately making a U-turn, Richter was at the corner of 34th and Prospect when he heard a shot. As he turned the corner, he saw a man running east, disappearing into the darkness.

Zelewski's scout car was parked in the street in front of 1520 N.E. 34, motor running, headlights and red light on. At 1:23 A.M., Richter's frenzied voice startled all the dispatchers out of their early morning complacency; "Six to headquarters, emergency traffic! Zelewski's been shot! Get an ambulance up here right away!"

Officer Mark Zelewski was lying face down in the street, his holster empty and his flashlight beside him. He had been shot three times in the chest with a .25 automatic and once in the back of the head with a .38, powder burns showing all the shots had been at very close range. A nickel plated .38 was laying near his body but it wasn't his. It was a cheap off-brand with stag horn grips and black tape around the grips. The shot to the head was from Zelewski's own .38 service revolver which had been taken by the suspects. An ambulance raced him to the hospital but he was dead on arrival.

Detectives, lab units, and patrol cars responded to the scene en masse. Among the detectives was a brand new homicide detective named Ted Gregory, responding to his first homicide under the tutelage of his partner, Charlie Greeson. Might as well start at the top because it doesn't get any rougher than this. The first witness interviewed was a man who lived across the street and had his own connections to Oklahoma law enforcement. Charles Owens was a former Tulsa police officer, an assistant state attorney and would become an Oklahoma County District Judge. Owens had heard several shots and saw several men driving away in an old car. Another witness had seen Zelewski looking into the rear seat of the car when three men jumped out and surrounded him.

All Detectives reported for duty immediately including those who had just gone off duty at midnight. The day shift came in at 3 A.M., four hours early. Officers came in from their days off and vacations without being called. One dispatcher was rumored to have walked off of an extra job to come to work. Detectives paired with scout car officers covering the entire northeast quadrant of the city. If anyone had wondered where the old TV show "Dragnet" got its' name, they were provided a good example that night. By daylight, 77 suspects were in jail for vagrancy, loitering on the streets after midnight, carrying concealed weapons or just "investigation", a valid charge at the time. A hundred more were jailed during the day. Every infamous name on the east side appeared on the booking sheets that night, names familiar to every officer who had policed the area for a generation, like Ernest Dean Sanders, Joe Ben Webb, Joe Willie Orange, et al. The media began speculating on a racial motivation for the killing but Chief Geer defused them by declaring that the case didn't have a racial angle, just a criminal angle.

More information developed. The nickel plated .38 was traced to a pawn shop. Informants talked, names surfaced, detectives interviewed suspects and tossed them out as they were eliminated although some were kept as many ancillary crimes were cleared. Priorities change under stress. Confessing to burglaries, robberies, rapes and thefts isn't such a big deal when they're talking to you about killing The Man. There's a big difference between a few years in the joint and 2,300 volts of alternating current.

On August 8, Zelewski's stolen .38 was found in a vacant lot between N.E. 19th and 20th in the 1100 block. The .25 automatic was found also. Charges were filed against 26-year-old Robert Charles Barnett, his 24-year-old brother Marvin and Harold Clevis Taylor, 24. Kenneth Crigler, 27, was held on $10,000 bond as a material witness.

Mark Zelewski was buried in Fairlawn Cemetery, not the one in Oklahoma City but the one in Elk City near his old Air Force base. Seventeen officers, most with prior military experience, hastily formed the first OCPD Honor Guard, performing for the first time at Zelewski's funeral.

Officers complained about the one-man cars and so did Mrs. Zelewski, blasting the police

*The first OCPD Honor Guard on the front steps of the new headquarters in 1965. Front row, left to right, Sergeant Bob Hutton, Officers Jeff Venard, Norman Wilkerson, Emmett Douglas, E.L. Bardtrief, Ken E. Smith, Bill Hooten, Richard Boyd and R. Keith Brown. Back row, Officers Elroy Kroeker, Marvin Doherty, Tommy Vernon, Frank Abernathy, Jack Powell, Bill Burke, D. Fillips and John Graham. An extraordinarily dedicated group, only 3 of the original 17 men (Venard, Fillips and Bardtrief) did not complete police careers of 20 years or more.*

administrators and city council, saying that her husband would be alive if he had another officer with him. Chief Geer gently contradicted her, saying "we might have two dead officers" if that had been the case. Less than six months after Mark Zelewski's death, Officer Karl Richter resigned. He found a better job.

Just over three weeks later, on August 18th, Officer Jerry R. Martin, also in a one-man unit, attempted to arrest a man for bogus checks in the 1900 block of N.E. 30th, less than a mile from the location of Mark Zelewski's murder. The suspect, Lloyd Bell, attempted to get Martin's gun away from him and in the struggle, Martin was shot. The bullet went through the officer's arm, entered his chest, pierced one lung and lodged near his spine. Although critically wounded, Officer Martin managed to regain control of his weapon and emptied it at his assailant, striking him twice. Both men would survive their wounds and Jerry Martin would continue his career, most notably in the Selective Enforcement Unit and as a homicide investigator, retiring in 1987. Both of his sons, Brian and Paul, would later become officers.

Three officers had been shot, one of them fatally, in less than ten months while riding in one-man cars. These incidents and the resulting clamor put an end, except under extraordinary circumstances, to one-man units in the high crime areas of northeast Oklahoma City.

The Citizens for Police Improvement held their awards dinner on November 8. The City Council Award went to Officer Bruce Shaw for capturing 23 burglars in a 54-day period. The last two had been arrested inside the Linwood Drug Store at 3040 N.W. 16 on September 22 when Shaw observed them commit the burglary while he was off duty. Officers Lindell W. Gay and Michael H. Morrison received the Mayor's Award for valor for their actions on the previous May 14. The two officers had evacuated residents from an area of fires started by a broken high pressure gas line in the 2700 block of N.W. 63rd. The City Manager's Award went to Officer Irven R. Box, who was to later become an attorney.

Officers Bill R. Vetter, R. Neill Griffith and John J. LeMaster received the awards as the top police trainees. Oklahoma Gas and Electric Company had sponsored an award for distinguished service for the past two years but no awards had been given. This year they altered their criteria to make the award a plaque and a $250 grant for the greatest contribution to juvenile law enforcement. Detective Herbert Booker won the first award given. A.T. Brixey won the accident investigation award and Detectives Ben Satterfield and Don Schimmels were cited for the best criminal investigation. Police leadership awards went to Major Wayne Lawson

*Mid-1960s Patrol Division line-up.*

and Sergeant Jim Watson. The Safety Council cited Sgt. Lloyd Gramling and Miss Louise Waller. The Chamber of Commerce Award for police planning changed sponsors to become the Oklahoma County Medical Society Award. The first honoree under the new sponsor was Captain Weldon Davis. Grants were given to Dale Harbolt to attend the FBI National Academy and R.S. Pierce to attend the Northwestern Traffic Institute. The CPI also presented the Department with a large plaque containing the names of all the OCPD officers who had been killed in the line of duty. The new plaque would be installed in the main lobby of the new Police Headquarters building then under construction, remaining there for over two decades until replaced with the stone monuments built in the 1980s.

Due to retirements and resignations in 1965, Department strength decreased slightly to 355 officers and 50 civilians. With a few exceptions, it was a banner year for OCPD.

Homicides increased by 33 percent to 28 that year but all other major crime categories were down. Overall, crime was reduced by 12 percent over the previous year. The City population was 382,082 citizens spread out over 649 square miles, an area that had increased by 50 percent in the last four years.

The Patrol Division consisted of 146 officers. Even though fielding a night shift of 11 two-man cars and 13 one-man cars, rarely was there a car in every district. Each shift rotated monthly in a counter-clockwise manner; that is, a month of day shift (7 A.M.-3 P.M.) followed by a month of graveyard shift (11 P.M.-7 A.M.) followed by a month of swing shift (3 P.M.-11 P.M.). In keeping with the civil rights advances of the time, two-man cars in racially mixed neighborhoods were integrated with excellent results, both from the officers and the public. Shotguns were placed in each car and each officer was issued a baton or "nightstick".

The 72 Traffic officers managed to raise the number of traffic arrests and lower the number of accidents but fatalities still went up by a third. The downtown traffic foot beat officers, whose primary task was parking enforcement, were all mobilized when they were transferred into a new three-wheel motorcycle unit. The starting pay for a patrolman was $405 a month. Things were getting better but slowly.

Just before closing time, 2:30 P.M., on March 10, 1965, William Alton Smith walked in the Northwest National Bank at N.W. 22 and May Avenue. The 40-year-old Shreveport, Louisiana, native had a 13-year history of bank robbery convictions, had been paroled from Leavenworth Federal Penitentiary less than two years before and he was in Oklahoma City to

*The OCPD's new three-wheel motorcycle unit in 1965. Standing behind them is Traffic Division Major S.W. Stephens.*

make a withdrawal, albeit unauthorized. When he ran out of the bank a few minutes later, he was carrying $45,000 and trading shots with a bank vice-president. This was the second time in the last 18 months Northwest National had been so victimized and the banker, apparently tired of it, resorted to the use of "one of several guns in the bank" to try to stop the man. Although he wasn't able to hit him, the banker called police with his car description.

Thirteen minutes later, Officer Rex Norton was sitting at the intersection of N.W. 14th and Classen when he saw the car cross Classen in front of him. Turning behind the car, Norton turned on his red light and a 75 mile-per-hour chase ensued. As they two cars careened around a corner north of 15th and Shartel, Officer R.G. Hendricks fired several shots at the fleeing robber. Although again missed by all the bullets, Smith was unnerved enough to ram the car into a tree at N.W. 18th and Francis, breaking a leg and a finger. Accident Investigator Bob McKittrick arrived on the scene almost immediately and later reported that when he approached Smith in the crumpled car, Smith blurted out "You won't find no money in my car. I didn't rob that bank!". Contrary to the brilliant Mr. Smith's assertion, over $40,000 was found in the car.

On March 30, 1965, a small racial incident (compared with past experiences) occurred and an attempt to make it bigger than it was failed. Freshman State Senator E. Melvin Porter complained to City, Police and media officials about a "vicious beating" that had been inflicted upon a black woman while being arrested by a white Oklahoma City Detective, Ken Liles. Porter said that these things wouldn't be happening if the police force were thoroughly integrated.

Investigations began and culminated about three weeks later. Chief Geer stated that the lady involved weighed over 200 pounds, was being legally arrested, was not "viciously beaten" and, in fact, would not have been injured at all if she hadn't resisted arrest so vehemently. The City Manager cleared the Police Department of any wrongdoing on April 20. Mayor George Shirk stated that the Police Department was open to all applicants who were qualified but that "the Chief can't manufacture negro policemen". Senator Porter wasn't satisfied and began a protest march but it only consisted of about 100 people and rapidly fizzled out.

On May 4, 1965, the murder case of Officer Mark Zelewski went to the jury. One of the defense attorneys, Archibald Hill, a state representative and local official of the Congress of Racial Equality (CORE), tried to prove that Robert Charles Barnett was at a family reunion when he was supposed to have shot Zelewski. Harold Clevis Taylor testified that he saw Robert Charles Barnett shoot Zelewski three times with the .25 automatic and Marvin Barnett deliver the *coup de grace* with the officer's own sidearm. Prosecutor (and former OCPD Chief) Granville Scanland destroyed whatever was left of the defense's arguments and made an impassioned plea for the imposition of the death penalty. After five hours, the jury rendered a guilty verdict and sentenced both Barnetts to life imprisonment.

Police radio calls that start out with the words "Man with a gun..." usually cause an immediate rise in the adrenaline levels of most police officers. This is especially true in those areas of the country, usually southern and western, where the laws, customs and public temperament create a climate where there are a lot of men with guns.

People who make public displays of guns usually use them to threaten and intimidate. They tend to get rid of them rapidly when other people in uniforms with guns show up. Sometimes, however, they really mean to use them.

Officer R.J. Melton received one of those calls to S.W. 63rd and Youngs on June 24. When he got there, he was relieved to discover that there was no disturbance there. Fatefully, he turned back north on Youngs. As he was approached S.W. 53rd, he was flagged down by three teenaged boys. They were the source of the previous call which had mistakenly been read as 63rd instead of 53rd. They directed him to the house at 2229 S.W. 53rd, saying a man at that address had shot at them.

Marvin Nowlin, a 42-year-old accountant, had been drinking and walking up and down his block carrying a shotgun. He had also been stopping cars in front of his residence and ordering them to take another route. When the teenagers drove in front of his house, Nowlin had fired an ineffectual shot at them.

Just as Melton pulled up in front of the house, Lt. Sam Pierce pulled up behind him as a backup unit. Just then, Nowlin burst out of the front door, yelling, cursing and pointing the shotgun at the officers. Pierce, still sitting behind the wheel of his cruiser, later said it all happened so fast that he was considering firing through the windshield of his scout car at Nowlin. Before Pierce could react, however, Melton grabbed his 12-gauge shotgun out of his scout car and shot Nowlin once, fatally.

On July 18, 1965, the new 40,000 square foot Police Headquarters Building at 701 Colcord was formally dedicated and opened to the public. Constructed directly east of the old jail building, which had been built in 1937, the two were connected by a hallway from the third floor of the old building to the second floor of the new building. The ultra-modern, three-story air conditioned structure was a luxurious, $2 million workplace for those accustomed to the old building. A rotunda rose from the first floor all the way to the roof through the center of the building.

*The OCPD's new Headquarters Building under construction at 701 Colcord Drive on January 1, 1965.*

An attached, double-deck parking facility provided additional parking and shelter for the Department's 134 vehicles. The gasoline pumps, tire shop and two car wash bays were in an underground level.

The new, spacious Records Bureau on the second floor had three mechanized filers and dozens of yards of open shelving for more than 100,000 criminal records, 150,000 case files, nearly a quarter of a million traffic records and numerous other files.

The new Communications Unit, universally referred to as "Dispatch", adjoined the Records Bureau on the second floor. Glass

*New Ford Scout Cars leave the new Headquarter's upper parking level for a night shift in 1965.*

panels separating it from the central rotunda area gave everyone a view, inside and out. One entire wall was covered with a large map of the City's patrol districts with colored lights showing unit availability. Two radio consoles on a lower level were served by seven elevated telephone positions behind them, each station having 60 lines and 10 emergency straight lines. Wreckers, ambulances, hospitals, taxis and other agencies could be contacted instantly by pushing a single button. Calls were assigned and dispatched from IBM complaint cards. All the radios were automatically tape recorded as were all the incoming phone lines. This last feature was hard to remember and get used to for most officers. Virtually every veteran of the times can recount several amusing anecdotes about citizens who didn't know (or officers who forgot) their conversations on these lines were being recorded.

Other reorganizations included a new Headquarters Division to contain all support services, moving the Canine Unit from Traffic to Patrol, a new community relations program and a Safety Education Detail. The first official OCPD Crime Laboratory was formed as a separate entity under Sergeant Don Rodgers. Recruit training was eight weeks long now and standards remained high with only eight percent of applicants being hired.

Officers of the Patrol Division formed a permanent 20-man Honor Guard under the command of Sergeant Bob Hutton assisted by Officer Elroy Kroeker. They were to be utilized for funerals, parades and other appropriate functions.

On the night of October 20, 1965, two old partners were back together again. Little did they know that Halloween was coming early this year. Darrell Pierce and C.E. "Ed" Waggoner, now Vice Detectives, were checking downtown hotels for prostitution violations. About 10 P.M. they pulled up in front of the Jefferson Hotel at 105 S. Robinson. Before they could get out of the car, they saw a man wearing a molded plastic Halloween mask cross the street in front of them. Stopping to eject a round into a chrome .45 automatic pistol, he entered the Harris Liquor Store next door to the hotel. Not wanting to

*Officer Roscoe Scobey at the new Headquarter's Communications console.*

cause a hostage situation or confront the hijacker inside around bystanders, the officers positioned themselves outside.

Inside, William Earl Potts Jr. confronted Irene Harris, the 58-year-old owner, with the .45 and the greeting "Trick or Treat". Mrs. Harris, very un-grandmotherly, greeted Mr. Potts with a fusillade of shots from a .38 before he shot her in the right shoulder. As the front plate glass window disintegrated from Mrs. Harris's shots, Potts ran out in the street only to be confronted by Pierce and Waggoner telling him to stop.

Making a career-ending decision, he didn't. The two Detectives fired ten shots at him before he fell dead in the street. Later investigation explained why he hadn't returned the officers' fire. One of the eight bullets that struck him went through his right hand, struck the .45 automatic and jammed it.

This time there were no nasty letters, threatening phone calls or editorial condemnations. The homicide of William Earl Potts Jr. was ruled to be justifiable. The following year, the Citizens for Police Improvement would award Detectives Pierce and Waggoner the City Council Award, the highest award available for gallantry at the imminent risk of their own lives. It was the municipal equivalent of the Medal of Honor. While it was a high honor, it may have been somewhat anticlimactic for Detective Pierce. Three months before the Potts shooting, Darrell Pierce had been diagnosed with chronic granulocytic leukemia. He was 31 years old.

On November 8, the CPI Police Recognition Dinner was presided over by Mayor George Shirk. The fifth such annual event drew over 575 law enforcement officers and their wives to the Skirvin Tower's Persian Room to witness the awards. Rex Norton and R.G. Hendricks won the City Council Award for their March 10 bout with the bank robber and R.J. Melton won the Mayor's Award for his incident in June. Motorcycle Officers Harold Campbell and Larry Upchurch won the City Manager's Award for alertness beyond their traffic duties that resulted in the apprehension of several armed robbers. The awards for top police trainees went to Art Smith and Richard Boyd. The top juvenile enforcement award went to Midwest City Sergeant Billy J. Hopkins. Accident investigation honors went to OCPD's James G. Jackson and criminal investigation honors were awarded to Detectives Ted Gregory and C.E. Stanfill for solving a series of rapes and robberies in August of 1964. Police leadership awards were given to Sgt. Chris Walker of the OCPD, Warr Acres Captain Jerry Landsberger and Midwest City Captain Frank Brady. Officers Henry Jones and Robert L. Gallamore received the Safety Council Award while Sgt. Bob Hutton was recognized for his organization of the OCPD Honor Guard.

Two changes were made this year. The Independent Insurance Agents Association had previously provided cash grants for two officers to attend the FBI National Academy and the Northwestern University Traffic Institute. This year they were bringing two instructors from Northwestern to Oklahoma City to teach two-week long schools in traffic law enforcement. The change would allow 80 officers from OCPD and the suburban departments to attend. A new award was initiated by the Citizens for Street Improvement Association. It was a $250 cash grant for outstanding performance in police support services. The first two awards went to dispatcher D.C. Bowen and technical investigator Nathan L. Barber. The County Commissioners Award went to Bethany Chief O.F. McLain and the Bar Association Award went to Oklahoma County District Attorney Curtis Harris.

In the 1920s, Mayor Jack Walton had given the OCPD their first unit emblem, a shoulder patch with a rearing lion on it. Since that time, officers had worn a series of emblems, round, triangular and semicircular but always stating their assignment or Division.

A major step toward Department unification was taken on January 18, 1966. As of that day, the only shoulder patches reading "Radio Patrol", "Scout Car", "Accident Investigations" or "Solo Motorcycle Squad" would be in collections. A new triangular shoulder patch was adopted. It had a black background with a yellow border, the red, white and blue City Seal located in the center and stated simply "Police-Oklahoma City". It was to be worn on both shoulders of the short-sleeved summer shirts but not on the long-sleeved winter shirts.

Cap badges on the white soft caps stating "Patrol" or "Traffic" would be stubbornly clung to for a few years but, in the early 1970's, gave way to an identical one that just said "Police". The shoulder patch, with a minor change in the City Seal, is the same one worn today.

In 1966, OCPD Stolen Goods Detectives Burke Lemay and Gerald Moore served an innocuous search warrant that was destined to have some far-reaching effects. The ensuing investigation brought to light the presence of a criminal organization operating in Oklahoma City; an organization that would be described two decades later as "a confederation of drug smugglers, pimps, pornography peddlers, burglars, car thieves and killers". The organization would acquire the nickname "The Dixie Mafia" or "Little Dixie Mafia" since their operations were detected from Oklahoma to Virginia and from Florida to Kentucky, based largely in the southern belt of the country that had been the Confederacy a century earlier.

By the mid-1970s, law enforcement intelligence units across the south were describing them as a loose-knit group of professional criminals with few apparent ties to national organized crime alliances. They also claimed to have been able to tie at least 35 inter-gang slayings to the members and their associates. By that time, they didn't have to try to convince people to take the Dixie Mafia seriously. Hollywood had done that for them.

When the motion picture Walking Tall came out in 1973, it met with huge success. It would eventually inspire two sequels, a television movie and a television series. Through these depictions, most of America became aware of Sheriff Buford Pusser's struggles against organized crime in McNairy County, Tennessee. Although I don't recall the name being used in the movie, that was the Dixie Mafia. The movie tended to portray the organization as primarily localized in Tennessee when that was not the case. In fact, when Pusser's wife was killed in his attempted assassination, one of the suspected killers was an Oklahoma City man reputed to be the leader of the organization, Kirksey McCord Nix Jr.

Remember the old saying about cop's kid's and preacher's kids? Sometimes it reached into the higher echelons of law enforcement. The son of a presiding judge of the Oklahoma State Court of Criminal Appeals, Kirksey McCord Nix Jr. had a record with the OCPD that started with a larceny charge in 1962 when he was still a teenager. By the time he was in his middle 20's, it included burglary, armed robbery and multiple murder charges. The locations of his arrests sound like the Dixie Mafia Highway, stretching from Oklahoma to Arkansas, Texas, Louisiana and Georgia.

During the investigation into the death of his wife, Buford Pusser came to Oklahoma City and was escorted by OCPD Detectives to try to identify Nix as one of the assassins but was unable to make a positive identification. Pusser was later killed in a one-car accident in Tennessee in 1974 as he was preparing to play himself in a sequel to the hit movie about his adventures. Many people would have you believe it wasn't an accident at all, it was the Dixie Mafia finally finishing what they started.

Another local figure with ties to the Dixie Mafia was a transplanted Texan named Jerry Ray James. Nicknamed "Fatman" because he packed some 250 pounds onto a 5-foot-11-inch frame, James had his own gang that specialized, for a time at least, in the armed robberies of exclusive residences where the residents were handcuffed, pistol-whipped and thoroughly terrorized until they were stripped of their jewelry, cash and other valuables. He and his associates were also suspected of firebombing a liquor store at N.W. 23rd and Broadway in 1965 but it was never proven. Another associate of the James gang who would figure in later Oklahoma City history was a man named Clifford Henry Bowen.

The Sixth Annual CPI Police Recognition Dinner was held on November 7. The principal speaker was Earl Sneed, banker and former dean of the University of Oklahoma Law School. Darrell Pierce and Ed Waggoner received the City Council Award for their gun battle with William Potts over a year earlier. Juvenile officer Bill C. Baldwin won the Mayor's Award for saving the life of a two-year-old girl a week after the Pierce-Waggoner incident. He had pulled the girl from a swimming pool and administered artificial respiration. Officers Homer O. Barnett and Charlie Hill won the City Manager's Award and Chief Hilton Geer won the County Commissioner's engraved silver tray.

Detective Herbert Booker won his second award for juvenile enforcement. The City Bus Company/Oklahoma Transportation Company awards given annually to the top police trainees changed sponsors with Lee Way Motor Freight taking over the helm. The trainee awards went to F.D. Gunther and Melvin E. Hodges. William R. Chambless won the accident investigation award while Detective W.W. Harrison was honored for the best criminal investigation.

Robert Lester, State DPS Director, won the leadership award and Sgt. Cecil Posey won the Safety Council Award. Irven Box won his second award while Sgt. Don Rodgers got the police planning award for his organization of the new OCPD Crime Lab. Two of Rodger's technical investigators, Neal Blount and Doyle Connelly, won the support service awards which also changed sponsorship this year. The new award became the Oklahoma City Retailers Association Award. The Bar Association Award went to retired OCPD Lieutenant M.B. Cooper, now the chief investigator in the District Attorney's Office. The Independent Insurance Agents Association dropped their sponsorship this year and no grants were given to attend the FBI National Academy or the Northwestern University Traffic Institute.

The need for police officers to organize for their collective welfare had been recognized and even attempted by Oklahoma City officers since World War II. The first attempt in March of 1943 met stiff resistance and culminated with the firing of the newly elected FOP President and the entire Executive Board. Court appeals were denied and the message was clear; Oklahoma City Police would not unionize, at least for the foreseeable future, and if you tried, your job was at risk. The movement did not die but it definitely went underground.

Twenty-five years of clandestine meetings, discussions and conspiracy finally boiled over in the summer of 1967. Another generation of officers decided to try to organize a police union. Survivors of the previous generation tried to dissuade them to no avail. Secret contacts were made with other chapters of the FOP, requesting information, literature and guidance regarding organization. In these pre-UPS/Federal Express days, this information was sent to the Union Bus Station and picked up by the organizers. The initial group, of activists, mostly younger officers with little seniority, met secretly at Officer Jim Parsons home to develop a plan, regardless of the consequences. This initial group consisted of Parsons, Robert Thompson, John Veccia, Homer Barnett, Don Spence, Charlie Owen, John LeMaster, Jim Burrow, Lyndell Gay, Harold Neal, Truman Coe, Glenn Christian, Richard Boyd and Darrell Pierce.

The pressing issues of 1967 were pay, condition of automobiles, clothing allowance allotment, mandatory wearing of uniform caps in police cars and living outside the City limits. On December 11, 1967, 150 officers met at the Carpenters Union Hall in the 900 block of West California. Over 100 of them joined the fledgling union and on January 8, 1968, Shepherd Lodge #123 was chartered. By the end of the month, the membership rolls included over three- quarters of the Department. The new Lodge was named in honor of the Shepherd sisters, owners of the tract of land north of N.W. 23rd Street between Pennsylvania and Villa that eventually developed into Shepherd Mall. They had recently donated money for the Department to purchase new shotguns for the officers safety.

The man elected as the first President of the fledgling organization was a Patrol Division Captain, Weldon Davis. It was his job to break the ice with the City administration to recognize the FOP as the voice of the majority of their police officers. Davis, by the use and threat of the initiative petition, brought the power of the FOP to bear on City Hall. Within 13 months of the FOP's beginnings, salaries went up $75 a month, uniform allowances were increased, officers were no longer required to wear their hats in patrol cars, air conditioned police cars became a reality and officers no longer had to reside within the City limits.

This time the organization would survive and prosper without retaliation. Three of the original 14 officers involved in the secret meetings at Jim Parsons' home would eventually become Presidents of the local chapter of the FOP. Others would later hold office in the State and National FOP. After putting their jobs on the line to achieve this organization, all but 3 of the original 14 would eventually complete 20 years of service and qualify for retirement pensions. As a measure of the City's acceptance of the inevitability of the union, 8 of the 14 would eventually be promoted to supervisory ranks including 6 to Lieutenant and 1 to Captain. Future Presidents of the local Lodge would include a Police Major and a future Chief of Police.

The seventh edition of the CPI awards drew over 700 guests and the crowd had finally outgrown the Persian Room. This year's event was moved to the Skirvin Tower's Imperial Ball Room. Officer Kenneth Buettner won the City Council Award by averting a hostage situation during a pharmacy robbery. Waiting until the suspect left his captive, Buettner subdued him without using his weapon. The Mayor's Award for valor and an engraved watch was presented to Detective G.A. "Buddy" Burns for resuscitating a drunken prisoner who collapsed in the court clerk's office. Sgt. John D. Lewis received the City Manager's Award and Assistant Chief Ace Williams was given the County Commissioner's Award.

The top trainee awards went to James E. Jones and Wallace E. Moore. Detective G.P. Tucker was honored for juvenile enforcement, Ulo Kasenurm won his second award for accident investigation, and Detectives Darrell Pierce and Bill Minor shared the award for best criminal investigation. Pierce was honored for breaking up a major narcotics and prostitution ring while Minor won for his persistence in obtaining a shotgun as evidence that led to the conviction of persons involved in armed robberies in Kansas City, Missouri.

Captain Weldon Davis won an award for assisting in the rehabilitation of 95 juveniles and raising $5,000 for the local Big Brothers program, much of it during his off-duty time. Sgt. Tom Heggy won the Medical Society Award for a study he performed on civil disorders.

One of the more amusing incidents of the later 1960's involved the Department's flagpole. After the new Police Headquarters opened in 1965, Assistant Chief Ace Williams noticed that the flagpole in front of the old jail building, facing Shartel, was rusted, pitted and had become very unattractive in the last 30 years. Upon checking for prices on a new flagpole, he came up with an initial cost of $500. After considerable shopping around, he was able to get the cost down to $165. So a shiny new flagpole went up in front of the new building facing Colcord Drive.

Chief Hilton Geer then called the Parks Department and told them to come over and cut down the old flagpole. Bureaucracies being what they are, they told the Chief that they would write up a work order and get around to it as soon as they could.

They got around to it just as the new year of 1968 began. Parks Department employees showed up with a work order to cut down the flagpole in front of Police Headquarters and promptly cut down the new flagpole.

The newspaper article telling about the 1968 CPI Awards started with the statement "Sometimes a policeman must wonder if 'hell is full and backing up on me'". The Daily Oklahoman reporter who wrote that article, Jim Rogers, evidently became fascinated with his subject matter. A few years later, he would quit the journalism business, join the OCPD and retire as a Detective after 20 years that included long stints in Special Projects and Burglary. But, for now, he just reported the awards.

Robbery-Homicide Detectives Denver Kirby and Bob Jackson won the City Council Award for their arrest of an escaped convict and armed robber from California. Confronting each other with drawn weapons after answering a robbery alarm, the officers held their fire and the suspect surrendered. The Mayor's Award for valor went to Wallace Moore and Simon Torres for quelling a mob estimated at 100 persons when a bar fight at N.E. 23rd and Eastern turned into a gunfight. After Torres shot one armed patron in the hip, both officers held off the crowd while backed against a wall until other officers arrived. Detectives Charles Hinderliter and W.W. Harrison won the City Manager's Award for cracking a national stolen car ring that recovered 36 stolen cars valued at $120,000.

Top trainee awards went to W.B. Smith and Geraldon Canary. Three officers shared the award for juvenile enforcement; Lt. Jim Reading and Detective C.O. Williams of the OCPD along with Midwest City Officer Johnny E. West. OCPD Homicide Detective Rex Norton won the criminal investigation award for undercover work that aborted the burglary of a Warr Acres bank and caught three men in the act. Cain's Coffee Company cited the entire 20-man Burglary Squad for their record-setting arrests and high felony clearance rate. The unit commander, Lt. Jim Pierce, accepted the award for the unit.

The award for police leadership was shared between Chief Ed Clark of the Nichols Hills Police, OCPD Traffic Lieutenant O.W. Ardery and Captain J.D. Sharp of the Bethany Police (who would become the Oklahoma County Sheriff in the 1980s). Officer E.W. Stevenson won the accident investigation award and technical investigator Bruce Knox won the support services award. The Medical Society Award went to Bob Coffia.

Two new awards were added this year, one was deleted and another changed sponsors. The Northwest Kiwanis Club presented awards consisting of a $100 cash grant and a plaque for dedication, conduct and achievement to Dispatcher Bob Coleman and jailer D.S. Morse. The Mercy Hospital Award of a $100 cash grant was instituted for life saving actions. The first

*OCPD Rangemaster Sergeant Jack Garrette in the late 1960s. Thirty shots, fired from distances ranging from 7 to 50 yards away, all within an area of one-half of a square foot.*

awards were presented to Officers C.J. Booe and W.R. Chambless for saving a boy's life who was choking in a restaurant where they were taking a lunch break. The officers gave him mouth to mouth resuscitation, saving his life. The Independent Insurance Agents Association, absent from the awards for the past two years, took over the sponsorship of the former Oklahoma City Safety Council Award for traffic safety contributions. This year's winners were Traffic Officers L.T. Brown and W.L. Williams. The County Commissioners Award was deleted. In a sign of the changing times, a special award was given to Jerry Marx, the DPS Public Information Officer, for public relations achievements.

One of the progenitors of one of OCPD's family dynasties died in 1969. Lee Mullinex passed away on May 5 at the age of 82. Beginning his career in 1915, Mullinex had become a Detective and was promoted to Sergeant in 1933. He served more than 31 years before retiring in 1946. He had been the Department's first fingerprint expert and had been in charge of the Bertillon Department at one time. He had also participated in the Osage Indian murder investigations in northeastern Oklahoma on a special assignment from Governor Walton.

Ace Williams reminisced about how Mullinex had been his first partner in a scout car. Williams remembered making his first arrest, a car thief, while Mullinex sat in the scout car yelling directions at him. Mullinex's son, Jack, had joined the Department the same year his dad retired and became a Major of Detectives before retiring himself in 1966. Jack's son, Eric, joined the Department in the early 1970s, serving as a Detective in Narcotics and Homicide into the 1990s.

In 1969 Hilton Geer and Ace Williams both retired, ending long and distinguished police careers. Geer, a 51-year-old from rural Gracemont, Oklahoma, joined the Department on June 24, 1941, as a member of the extra board. He was promoted to Detective in 1943 before taking a leave of absence to serve in the Navy in World War II. Returning from active duty, he continued to rise in the ranks, becoming a Lieutenant in 1959. In 1961 Ed Rector promoted him to become the Major in charge of the Detective Division. Following his dispute with Chief Hollingsworth, Geer retired on October 31, 1961. Slightly over six months later, he returned as Chief.

The OCPD grew from 312 officers to 476 officers under his administration. An officer's monthly salary increased from $357 to $500 and their number of monthly days off doubled from four to eight. Officers were also now being paid four dollars for their court appearances. Also credited to his administration was the acquisition of air conditioned patrol cars, two mobile crime lab units and the construction of a new police headquarters. He also had created a canine corps, a night-time pistol range, and a modus operandi section in the Records Bureau.

W.A."Ace" Williams also ended his 32-year career the same day as his Chief, ending speculation that he might become the top man.Williams began walking a beat for the Department on July 1, 1937. After two months he began a 19-year stretch in the Traffic Division. Becoming a Major in the Patrol Division, Williams had been elevated to Assistant Chief when Geer became Chief in 1962.

The choice of the new Chief and Assistant Chief remained a mystery for several weeks until it was announced that Patrol Major E. Wayne Lawson and Patrol Captain Weldon Davis would rise into the two top jobs. Lawson was a 47-year-old World War II Navy veteran of the campaigns against Iwo Jima and Okinawa. After returning from the service, he had served as a security officer at Tinker Air Force Base and with the State Capitol Police before joining the OCPD in April of 1947.

Davis, a 17-year veteran, skipped the rank of Major entirely and resigned his position as President of the FOP to take the Assistant Chief's job. Captain I.G. Purser was promoted to Major to take Lawson's position in Patrol and Bill Peterman became his assistant commander. Sam Watson became the first Major of the newly formed Special Services Division and Tom Heggy became his Captain and the new Director of Training. The new division also contained the Intelligence Unit under Sergeant Bruce Shaw and the Internal Affairs Unit under Sergeant Bill Vetter. Lieutenant Lloyd Gramling was promoted to Captain in the Records Bureau.

Lee Brown, a Patrol Sergeant, was Vice President of the FOP when Davis resigned and maintained the organization for six months until the next elections. The next President of the FOP was Patrolman Richard Boyd, the first member of the lowest rank to hold the position. An active participant in the affairs of City Hall, Boyd was to serve two terms as President. His most outstanding accomplishment was the introduction and passage of police bargaining legislation. Police officers needed an equal basis for meeting with City officials to discuss pay and benefits. A State law was the best solution.

FOP recognition by the public was another important accomplishment by the Boyd administration. FOP involvement in civic affairs and providing summer employment for students helped to show that the FOP was interested in the welfare of the community as well as police officers.

*Chief E. Wayne Lawson.*

Chief Lawson's administration faced a major crisis situation soon after it was installed. Eleven years to the day after black demonstrators began having "sit-down" protests at downtown lunch counters, racial tensions went up again. This time is was the predominantly black City Sanitation workers. Martin Luther King Jr. had been in Memphis, Tennessee, dealing with a similar situation when he had been assassinated the previous year. It was a volatile situation.

The City Administration had been wrangling with their garbagemen since before World War II about wages, working conditions and unionization. Their last big headlines had been in 1955 when the garbage workers joined the Teamster's Union and told the City Manager he had to bargain with the union about their wages. Maintaining the City's policy since the war, the City Manager refused to recognize the union as their bargaining agent and fired 200 garbage workers. That was followed by garbage workers attacking three garbage trucks and beating four City employees with baseball bats and soda pop bottles. Convictions followed arrests and once again the City had prevailed.

Now another 200 garbage workers had walked off of the job. The next day, they tried to blockade the City Garage at 2121 Westwood to prevent the non-strikers from taking the garbage trucks out on their rounds. Clara Luper and several other NAACP officials were arrested but there was no violence.

The strike continued with off and on negotiations through October. The Police Department went to two 12-hour shifts and scout cars were assigned to follow the garbage trucks on their rounds to prevent incidents. Progress with the City Administration would ebb and flow over wages, working conditions and the re-hiring of the strike leaders.

Finally, the NAACP declared Friday, October 31, as "Black Friday". The Police Department was ready, in force, complete with riot helmets, face shields, batons, canine units, shotguns and tear gas. Evincing the same passive but stolid stance that had worked with the 1950s demonstrators, they hoped it would be equally successful with what developed this time.

What developed was a march by 1,500 demonstrators through the downtown area to City Hall and the Police Department. The march to the Police Department was led by Theodore G.X., the local leader of the militant Black Muslims. Nevertheless, it was peaceful and orderly

*Officers peacefully disperse a gathering during the Garbage Workers Strike on August 21, 1969.*

*City garbage workers mass at OCPD Headquarters on October 31, 1969. They are met by officers led by Lt. W. Lee Brown (wearing the soft uniform cap at lower right).*

with no violence or arrests. The strike was settled on November 6 and another racial crisis was averted.

In many ways, the 1969 "garbage strike" was a turning point for the OCPD. The restraint and obvious professionalism displayed by the officers earned them wide praise, marking the Department's maturing into a truly professional big city law enforcement agency. The challenge was met by organization, the judicious use of manpower and careful planning that was to characterize the Department of the 1970s.

In the fall of 1969, the OCPD began issuing handguns to their new officers. Prior to that time, each officer had to furnish his own weapon. Now the new arrivals were each issued a brand new blue steel Smith & Wesson Model 15 .38 Special revolver with a 4-inch barrel. After recruit school, most still opted to purchase a higher powered .357 Magnum for street duty. One reason for this occurred in mid-October.

About 6:00 P.M. on October 13, 1969, Warrant Officer Don Braswell located a vehicle in southwest Oklahoma City that was wanted in connection with a bank robbery and murder in Texas. Braswell staked the vehicle out from his unmarked car and called for backups to stand by in the area. Sergeants Ben Caswell and Bob Hicks, along with Officers Jim Winter, Dave McBride, Bob Tash, Ron McKinney and Jerry Tune stationed themselves at various locations a short distance away.

A short time later, four suspects left the location in three vehicles. As officers deployed to stop the cars, Sergeant Ben Caswell stopped one of them containing a man and woman at S.W. 29th and McKinley. Caswell had them get out of the car and searched the man, who identified himself as Donald Richardson. In those days of all-male patrol officers, a very good reason was needed for a male officer to search a female. Caswell had the two start back to his patrol car. On the way, the woman produced a .38 revolver which she gave to Richardson. Richardson and Caswell then started shooting at each other. Caswell was struck once in the right shoulder and emptied his gun at Richardson without hitting him. Caswell was faced with the precarious position of being on one side of a car with an empty gun, wounded and unable to reload with an armed assailant on the other side of the car, getting ready to finish him off. Then, just like in the movies, help arrived in the nick of time.

Officer Jim Winter, first at the scene of Caswell's shooting, exposed himself to Richardson's fire to divert his attention from his wounded Sergeant. Seeing the odds rapidly worsening against him, Richardson fled in his car. Wrecking it a short distance away, he quickly got a ride from an unsuspecting citizen but was soon captured a few blocks away.

Ben Caswell recovered to retire as a Captain in 1979. Jim Winter received a CPI award for his actions that probably saved Caswell's life. Officer Dave McBride became the Chief of Police in 1990. Donald Richardson was convicted and sentenced to the Oklahoma State Penitentiary but he still wasn't through shooting Oklahoma City policemen.

Geer's term saw an increasing number of retirements of senior officers, some of whom had served since the 1920s. They were replaced with an infusion of younger blood. The World War II "baby boomers" were coming of age. Many Vietnam veterans, returning home to increasing anti-war sentiment, found the Police Department to be one employer where their military experiences counted in their favor rather than against them. The average age of the Department declined rapidly.

Buried deep in the back of the Daily Oklahoman issue of November 10, 1969, was an article indicative of the times. The City of New Orleans, Louisiana, was having problems with their Police Department. One fourth of New Orleans P.D.'s 1,400 officers had called in sick with what was termed the "blue flu", a work slowdown in response to a wage dispute with the city administrators. It would have implications for the coming decade and not just in New Orleans.

The Ninth Annual CPI Police Recognition Dinner was held on December 7, 1969, at the Skirvin Tower. Some 500 guests attended to see 34 officers honored. Officer Gary Scott received the City Council Award for his apprehension of two armed robbers. The Mayor's Award was shared between Officers Theophilus Martin, Jimmy Lee Taylor and Sergeant Cecil W. Pierce. They won it for apprehending a gunman who had barricaded himself in a house after shooting a woman. The City Manager's Award went to Officers O.V. Donwerth and Jack Montgomery. In the past year, the pair of scout car officers had recovered 78 stolen cars, arrested 13 burglars and 25 other felons.

The three top trainees of the year were Bob Tash, Tim W. Stinson and Hollis W. Harper. James Winter and Richard Jerman won the Mercy Hospital Award for successfully resuscitating a choking baby the previous January. Detective Henry McMullen Jr. won the juvenile enforcement award for a rape investigation and Harold G. Mann won the accident investigation award. OPUBCO's award for the best criminal investigation went to Officer Troy Withey, Detectives Dennis Berglan and Jerry Guinn for a homicide investigation.

Leadership awards went to Assistant Chief Weldon Davis and Major C.C. Miller. Officer John Kane won the Cain's Coffee award for serving five months undercover in the Paseo area. He had made 95 purchases of illegal narcotics during this time from 45 drug dealers. The Insurance Agents award went to Captain Bill Luttrell of the suburban Warr Acres PD and Captain Lloyd Gramling of OCPD.

The Medical Society Award went to Detectives Bill Wolf and Jim Anthony for providing counseling to persons who attempted suicide. The support services award went to Bill Burke and Doyle Connelly. The Bar Association award went to Detectives Charlie Acox and Don Schimmels for a homicide investigation. Larry Wright won the Northwest Kiwanis award for apprehending several burglary suspects. A special CPI President's Award was presented to four Midwest City Detectives and two Oklahoma City Detectives for a joint double homicide investigation. They were Steve Cummings, Roy Cook, Jack Hill and Eddie Thomason of MWCPD and Bill Baldwin and J.K. Harrison of OCPD.

# IX — UNIONS, WOMEN AND COMPUTERS 1970-1979

The OCPD began the new decade with a $5.5 million budget to pay and equip 554 officers and 67 civilians to serve a city of 368,164 citizens in a metropolitan area of almost 700,000. The starting pay was $525 a month.

A young man applying for a job with the OCPD quickly got the impression he was entering a merciless selection procedure. The rigorous selection process couldn't help but make him feel like he had been allowed to join an elite group if he made it all the way through it. It started with a Lieutenant in Recruiting tossing him an application form (misnamed because it was actually a booklet a dozen pages thick), sometimes with the admonition "...and don't lie about any of it!"

After filling out the booklet with every place he had ever lived, worked, gone to school and a miscellany of other information, it was turned in and he heard no more about it for over a month. He would later discover that during these intervening weeks, Internal Security Detectives were talking to all of his friends, relatives, former teachers, employers and neighbors they could find. Teletypes were being sent to law enforcement agencies in every jurisdiction he had ever lived in to discover every arrest, traffic accident, ticket or other negative contact he had ever had with the law. His credit, marital history, military and educational backgrounds were being examined. His fingerprints had been checked through the OCPD and FBI files. If all of this information was satisfactory, by the time they called him back to schedule him for a polygraph test, the Internal Security officers knew more about him than his mother did.

The polygraph test, commonly called the lie detector, was the second major hurdle. Every applicant went into that test thinking that its' purpose was to discover if he was a basically honest, truthful person. It was that and a lot more. Since he was asking them for a job, he had forfeited all of his rights when he agreed to that test. Tactics and strategies would be used on him that a murder suspect didn't have to endure. Every lie he had ever told since childhood, every pencil he had picked up that didn't belong to him, every aspect of his sexual behavior would be ruthlessly, frankly questioned. The applicant was not allowed to smoke while the polygraph examiner puffed on his pipe whenever he wasn't pounding it into the ashtray on his desk for emphasis. The blood pressure cuff on the applicant's arm was inflated until there was no hope of a drop of blood circulating in that arm. The slightest twitch of a finger or tremor of the machine's needle brought forth a stream of accusations, profanity and personal rebukes from the examiner. Very few people walked out of that test without thinking they had failed miserably and were probably facing imminent arrest. Only much later would he realize that part of the object of the test had been to see how difficult it was to confuse, irritate or enrage him. Most selected applicants were surprised when told they had passed the test. An oral review board and physical exam completed the process.

If he survived all these challenges and was hired, a new officer was immediately issued three complete uniforms compatible with the season; gray poplin shirts (long or short sleeved), dark blue trousers, a dark blue clip-on tie for wear with the long sleeved shirts, a badge, commission card, a blue steel Smith & Wesson Model 15 Combat Magnum .38 with a 4" barrel, one pair of handcuffs and key, a baton, a dark blue "Ike" jacket for dress wear, a black foul weather jacket with a fur collar for winter wear, a black plastic name tag, a whistle and chain.

He had a little choice in a few of the items but some were dictated by tradition. The rookie didn't have to worry about the correct placement of any gold stars (denoting five years service) or bars (denoting one year of service) on the right sleeve of his Ike jacket yet. Issued both a soft white uniform cap and a black and white fiberglass helmet, he could wear either in any uniformed assignment but tradition held that the white cap was usually worn by Traffic officers or Accident Investigators and the helmet by Patrol officers. Black calf-high Wellington boots were usually preferred for all street assignments over the new Corfam shoes with a permanent shine. They provided more ankle support for running and, occasionally, kicking. The knee-high Wellingtons were reserved for motorcycle officers as were the jodhpur style pants. The thin yellow stripe down the pants legs of the '50s and early '60s was gone. Patrol officers pants were plain, Traffic officers wore a two-inch light blue stripe and supervisors (Sergeants and higher) had a one-half-inch black "command braid" sewn down the outer seam. The old Sam Browne belt was retained but without the shoulder strap. The shoulder strap had been deleted for the same reasons that the ties were clip-ons now, so an opponent had two fewer things to grab and jerk an officer around with. The belt, holster, 12-round loop loader and handcuff strap completed the ensemble and usually indicated the relative seniority of the wearer. The "old hands" generally preferred a basket-weave pattern while the newer guys were getting the shiny Corfam type.

Two more items were available that most officers opted for. One was a "sap" or "slapper". It was a flat, black leather flexible truncheon about ten inches long with a strap on the handle and loaded with several ounces of lead on the other end. It slipped easily in a hip pocket and was flexible enough to stay there during an eight-hour shift of getting in and out of the car repeatedly. It was just as effective and less troublesome than the baton.

The other item was a flashlight called a Kel-Lite. Coming in four-cell and six-cell models, depending upon the number of "D" batteries they held, it was made from a knurled aluminum alloy, anodized a non-reflective black color. While they were good flashlights, their main feature was their sturdiness. Virtually the only thing breakable in the whole unit was the small bulb in the lens. You could call an officer's night stick a baton, night stick, billy club or whatever other euphemism you like, but there was just no getting around it; it was a club and its primary use was to hit people. Kel-Lites were a light source and a baton combined without the offensive appearance of the latter. Thus outfitted, the new rookie was ready to go to work.

Unless his hiring coincided precisely with the beginning of a new Recruit School (and few did), he was placed "on rotation". He reported to work at once, usually on a night shift, and began rotating through different areas of the Department on a weekly basis. A week in Records, then the Jail, Traffic Division, Detective Division (covering several units in the week) and ending in Patrol. When he arrived in the Patrol Division, he remained there until the next recruit school started. He was assigned to ride a patrol district with a senior partner, "senior" meaning someone who had completed recruit school and had over one year on the force.

Since recruit school was ten weeks long (eight weeks of classes and two weeks on the pistol range), most officers of that period had from one to six months patrol experience before they ever received any formal training. When he reported to his first lineup, he was quickly informed that rookies stood on the front row and the back rows were reserved for veteran officers.

Although he would be introduced to the shift by the Lieutenant in command, the only people he could expect to speak to him were his Sergeant (to introduce his partner) and the partner. Most of the senior partners introduced themselves with the "Keep your eyes open, mouth shut, stay right with me no matter what, don't touch the shotgun or the radio and, no, you can't drive" speech or some variation of it.

There was no formal training, testing, grading or evaluations. As in years past, "street school" preceded recruit school. The only "evaluation" came at the end of his rotation period just before he was scheduled to attend the next recruit school and it was equally informal. It was usually a series of questions from the Sergeant to the senior partner along the order of "Is he worth keeping?", "Has he got any sense?", "Do you trust him?" and "Will he fight?". Sometimes those questions were asked in front of the rookie with both the Sergeant and senior partner acting like he was invisible.

An affirmative answer to those questions would allow the rookie to begin eight weeks of classroom training on the third floor of Police Headquarters, where the Chief's reception area is now. Successful completion of that phase allowed him to move on to the Firearms Range, west of the Lake Hefner Water Treatment Plant at Hefner Road and Portland, for two weeks. Passing scores on the range meant graduation and a return to one of the 27 patrol districts unless he volunteered for Traffic, Motorcycles, the Crime Lab or another specialty.

The morality of the times was different as well. At a time when many of America's young men were smoking marijuana, dropping acid and availing themselves of the advantages of the free love generation, it was pointed out to new police recruits that these and many other options were now forever closed to them. They were informed immediately that the three quickest ways to get into trouble in their new jobs were "women, whiskey and bad debts". In these days before wrongful discharge lawsuits and complaints of discriminatory practices, it was made very plain to officers that their private lives were held to a higher standard of behavior as much as their professional conduct. One veteran officer was discovered to be living with a woman and they weren't married. Supervisors approached him with three options; leave her, marry her or resign. He resigned. Other officers were forced to resign after commanders received several complaints of their personal checks bouncing or creditors called complaining about overdue bills. One veteran motorcycle officer was forced to resign in a bizarre situation involving bigamy. His previous wife had left him some years before, saying she was going out of the state to divorce him. As time passed, he heard no more from his former wife and assumed she had gone through with her plans. He met another lady and they got married. Then, after an absence of several years, his former wife came back to town. As it turned out, she had not gone through with the divorce. When she discovered that he had remarried, she contacted police commanders, informed them of the situation and the officer was forced to resign.

Homicides, assaults and robberies decreased in 1970 but all other crimes were on the rise. The Paseo district west of N.W. 30th and Walker was the last stronghold of the "hippies" of the '60s. The area was full of clubs like The Yellow Submarine that didn't agree with closing or licensing statutes. Free love communes, crash pads and dope houses abounded as well. Narcotics, hallucinogens and runaway juveniles were everywhere. If they weren't dying from overdoses or trying to fly off the buildings while high on LSD, they were demonstrating against the Vietnam war, the establishment, narcotics laws, motorcycle helmet laws or "the pigs". The fourth shift put two officers walking a beat in the area from 6 P.M. until 2 A.M. along with undercover narcotics officers to try to calm the situation. Some of the situations were tragic, like those when kids died because their latest chemical experiment convinced them they could fly and gravity proved they couldn't. On the other hand, some situations were comical.

One of the local rebels sewed an OCPD shoulder patch on the seat of his ragged bell-bottom jeans in a mute protest. The beat officers were not amused. Neither was he when he went to jail charged with impersonating a police officer. Nor was the young man who was arrested for using a United States flag for window curtains in his Volkswagen bus.

A significant traffic problem developed when some of the impromptu demonstrations moved into Paseo Street, blocking the vehicular traffic with dozens, sometimes hundreds of long-haired young people. Several nights of the beat officers and the district car issuing citations to pedestrians for Failure To Yield The Right Of Way To A Moving Vehicle restored the normal traffic flow. The neighborhood denizens grudgingly moved back to the sidewalks.

A few nights later, everybody got a lesson in the impartiality implied by lady justice's blindfold. Officer Mike Ratikan was cruising down Paseo when he saw another car coming straight at him northbound on the one-way southbound street. Turning on his red overhead light, Ratikan stopped the conservative sedan in the middle of the street. After a short conversation with the short-haired, clean-shaven motorist in a business suit, Ratikan began writing him a citation for going the wrong way on a one way street. As he did so, several hundred "flower children" lining both sides of the street spontaneously gave him a standing ovation.

As Paseo was being calmed, other improvements were underway. Some of the aging fleet of Plymouths and Fords, some as much as five years old and with hundreds of thousands of miles on them, were being replaced with new 1970 Chevrolets. Two of them were special. They were equipped with 454 cubic-inch interceptor engines, steel belted radial tires and were capable of 145 miles per hour. One was assigned to patrol district 2, covering the N.W. 39th Street "raceway" west of May Avenue and the other was used by the Traffic Division as the Northeast Expressway radar car. The two cars became legendary to the surprised owners of many Corvettes, Cobras, Panteras and other low flying missiles. In a break with tradition and a harbinger of things to come, the Traffic car was solid white.

Police officers, when forced to use their weapons, are always concerned with "stopping power". When they have to shoot, they would like to be able to shoot one time and disable the suspect, stopping him immediately. That way the suspect is instantly no longer a threat to them or anyone else. Oklahoma City officers felt that they had discovered a new, more effective tool toward that end in the new decade.

*1970 Chevrolet Accident Squad cars.*

The new rage among the street officers was "Super Vels", a high velocity hollow-point bullet. Demonstrations were performed at the pistol range with one-gallon milk containers filled with water. When shot with .38 military ball ammunition, which was relatively slow, they just punched a hole through the jug and the water dribbled out. When shot with a Super Vel, the jug exploded in a shower of water. The theory was that "hydrostatic shock", the instantaneous compression of a fluid-filled container (i.e. a human body) when struck by one of these rounds, would immediately incapacitate the wounded party. Everybody was carrying them.

At 10:25 P.M. on the evening of April 27, Officers Paul D. Taylor and Carey Gilbert got a call on a domestic disturbance at 1601 N.E. 27th. They were due to go off duty in less than an hour. They would be late getting off tonight.

When they arrived at the house, screams drew them inside. L.C. Green had broken into the home of his estranged wife Shirlene. While their seven-year-old daughter Michele screamed in terror, Green slashed his wife on the arm with a knife and fell to the floor struggling with her. This was the scene Officers Taylor and Gilbert walked in on. Taylor struck Green several times in the back to get his attention away from the wounded woman writhing under him on the floor. It worked.

Green got up and started toward the two officers holding the bloody knife in front of him. Both officers drew their weapons and yelled at him to stop and put the knife down. Green kept coming. From a distance of only a few feet, Taylor shot Green once in the chest. The man stopped, hesitated for a moment and then continued advancing toward them, still holding the knife. Taylor fired three more times, hitting him in the chest with each shot. Gilbert was pointing his cocked revolver at the man although he had not fired yet. The man stopped again, looked slowly down at his bloody chest and, looking up at Taylor, asked "Are you through?". He then sank slowly to the ground, the knife clattering on the floor at his feet.

Green was taken to Mercy Hospital where surgery was performed. Although initially surviving his wounds, he died on May 12. After that, you couldn't give away a box of Super Vels.

When the Oklahoma City Airport Trust was formed in 1956, they had contracted with the OCPD for security at Will Rogers Field. After a few years, the Trust decided to hire their own personnel and created the Oklahoma City Airport Police as a separate entity. Although they wore OCPD badges and attended OCPD training, they were not part of the Department. They had their own distinctive dark brown and tan uniforms similar to those of the Oklahoma Highway Patrol.

On July 1, 1970, the Will Rogers Airport Police came under the jurisdiction of the OCPD. Although they would retain their own distinctive uniform and duty station (for the time being), Airport officers were offered the opportunity to transfer to the OCPD. Several applied and were accepted. Regular OCPD officers were also given the opportunity to transfer to the Airport Police and several were granted.

Also in 1970, the Department utilized the first large grant of Federal funds from the Law Enforcement Assistance Administration (LEAA) to start the Community Service Officer (CSO) program. The CSO's were 18-to-20 year old cadets who joined the force before they could become fully commissioned officers at age 21. This was necessitated by a State Law that required someone to be 21 or older to own or possess a handgun. Until that time, they rode in specially equipped trucks accompanied by a commissioned officer. The CSO's took crime reports, assisted motorists, searched for lost children and performed many other duties that were compatible with their uncommissioned, unarmed status. Most of the CSO's eventually achieved fully commissioned status and some have over 20 years of service now. The highest ranking former CSO to date is Deputy Chief M.T. Berry.

Chief Lawson officially formed the Forgery Unit in response to keen interest from the business community. Its lineage could be traced to the end of World War II. In 1945, Harold Hooper, owner of Stores Protective Services, offered to help the OCPD with "bad checks" which had become a common problem for Detectives. Detective Herb Mesigh began working with Hooper, locating suspects while Mrs. Hooper drew up the charges Mesigh filed against them.

In the mid-1950s, Detective Don Cochran began working with Mesigh and they became known as the "Check Detail". When Chief Lawson formalized the unit in 1970, Lt. Don Cochran was placed in charge of it. The next year, after training with the U.S. Secret Service and OSBI, Detective George Englebretson was added to the unit as the Department's first document examiner.

The Citizens for Police Improvement celebrated their first decade of existence with their Tenth Annual Police Recognition Dinner on November 9, 1970. This time the crowd exceeded 800 and was moved to the Top of the Mall Restaurant in Shepherd Mall at N.W. 23rd and Villa. Twenty OCPD officers were honored for their service during the previous year. One of the speakers called the police officers "the leash holders of society". He didn't say what this made society by comparison.

Officer Claude Shobert received the City Council Award of $100 and a watch for capturing an armed robber following a high-speed chase. The arrest also led to the arrest of two other suspects in the robbery. Paul D. Taylor and Carey D. Gilbert received the Mayor's Award for valor for saving the woman and child in their incident and James Winter won the City Manager's Award for his actions in the gunfight with bank robbers when Ben Caswell was wounded.

The top trainee awards for the year's three recruit schools went to Michael Hatch, Don Pennington and William E. Lewis. Kenneth Shockley won the Mercy Hospital Award for rushing a woman who was eight months pregnant and hemorrhaging to the hospital. The juvenile enforcement award went to Lt. B. J. Anderson and the best accident investigation award was shared between C.E. Dozier and W.B. Smith. The criminal investigation award was shared by Lt. Jim Watson, Detectives Bill Hooten and Tony Hyde for their investigation of the stabbing deaths of a woman and her seven-year-old daughter. Chief Lawson won the police leadership award for his Department's actions during the garbage strike. Detectives Bennie Lovett and Harold Neal were honored for narcotics investigations and Sergeant Walt Wilhelm won for his supervision of traffic direction in the downtown urban renewal construction area. Sgt. Ted Gregory won the Northwest Kiwanis award for his services in the Internal Security Unit that resulted in 73 new officers being hired. One of those 73 is the author of this book.

Two awards were deleted this year. The Chamber of Commerce Award and the County Bar Association Award were not to be given again. Carolyn Geckler, a Records Bureau clerk, was given an award for her development of a Modus Operandi section to help identify suspects by cataloging them by their physical characteristics and their criminal preferences. Special awards were given to Major Kenneth Nash who had received his Juris Doctor degree and become a member of the Oklahoma Bar Association, Judge Clarence Mills for his efforts to bring defendants to a speedy trial and Sgt. Phil Kennedy, who had recently won the National Pistol Championship.

In 1971, the citizens of Oklahoma City elected their first female Mayor, Patience Latting. Having served on the City Council for the past four years, she had been the first woman elected to the Council in the City's history. Sworn in on April 13, Mrs. Latting became the first woman in the nation to become the chief executive of a city with over 200,000 population. She was immediately greeted by a spiraling crime rate.

In an attempt to combat it, the Patrol Division realigned the City into 36 patrol districts and a prefix was added to the numerical call signs designating the quadrant of City. The northwest cars became Adam 1 through 15, northeast cars were Baker 1 through 7, southeast cars were Charlie 1 through 4 and the 10 southwest cars answered to Delta. A number preceding the call sign designated which shift they were on; 1 for day shift, 2 for swing shift, 3 for graveyard shift and 4 for the permanent 6 P.M.-2 A.M. shift. The "4-shift" kept those hours permanently and did not rotate like the other shifts. That shift was made up primarily of officers attending college with Federal assistance during the day. Over half of the Department's 600 officers had some college hours.

Like the rest of the country, Oklahoma City suffered racial unrest in the early 1970s. Several attempted snipings of officers on calls luckily were unsuccessful due only to poor marksmanship. Incidents where scout cars and officers were pelted with bricks and bottles became commonplace in the primarily black northeast sector. Assigning backup units became automatic on all calls, no matter how innocuous the call. Sometimes the backup unit was necessary if only to guard the vacated scout car while the officers were away from it to prevent it from being stolen, vandalized, having the shotgun stolen out of it or, worse, used against the officers when they came out of the call. Fire trucks and firemen were shot at on several fire calls and there were several housing projects that the Fire Department would not enter without waiting for a police escort. One fireman, a former police officer, began carrying his .38 revolver in the pocket of his overcoat on fire calls. Conflicts with local members of the militant Black Muslims and Black Panthers became more serious and frequent. Statistics on assaults on police officers and resisting arrest charges were skyrocketing. Every traffic stop rapidly drew large, violent, abusive crowds.

These tensions exploded on Easter Sunday, April 11, 1971. About 1,500 black people rioted at Springlake Amusement Park, allegedly inspired by a white youth throwing a black youth off of the park's roller coaster. The first pair of responding officers walked into the midst of the milling crowd while Sergeant Henry McMullen kept Communications advised over his portable radio. As he was talking, the crowd closed around the officers and suddenly, both white heads disappeared in the mass of black faces while a black and white patrol helmet spiraled up out of the melee. Hearing the supervisor on the radio would have been almost comical if the situation hadn't been so serious.

"Headquarters, I think we got everything under control here...uh...send me...uh....send me two...HEADQUARTERS, SEND ME THREE AMBULANCES CODE 3!"

The entire shift responded as did the 4th Shift. Very shortly, the 1,500 rioters were confronted by half a dozen canine officers and 60 others armed with carbines, shotguns, hunting rifles and every caliber of handgun from .38 up. The Patrol Division commander, Major I.G. Purser arrived and took charge. He had the officers form a line abreast and they began moving the crowd south toward N.E. 36th Street.

Occasionally, one of the bolder rioters decided to stop and confront the line converging on him. Invariably, he went down immediately, the line passed over him and he was scooped up by the second wave of officers, handcuffed and hustled back to one of the waiting vans.

The canine officers were interspersed between every dozen officers or so. The German Shepherds, most of them weighing over 100 pounds, were specially selected for their size and aggressiveness. Trained to react to even mildly threatening glances or gestures, they were driven wild by the pandemonium confronting them. Held at bay by their trainers on 12-foot leashes, most of them spent much of the time on their hind legs, front legs windmilling and foaming jaws gnashing, trying to get at the crowd.

Several of the younger rioters, confident of their speed and judgement of the length of the dog's leashes, decided it would be good sport to tease them by lunging at them while staying just out of their range. One girl made a serious misjudgment when she failed to notice the officer holding the dog on about eight feet of leash with another four feet coiled in his hand. When he got tired of the girl lunging at his dog, he merely dropped the remaining four feet of leash in mid-lunge. The dog, already on his hind legs and straining forward with all his might, shot forward, snapping jaws first. The girl shrieked in terror, skidded to a stop and spun around in one motion and raced back into the crowd. As she did, the shepherd's jaws snapped shut on her dress mere inches behind her rapidly pumping buttocks. As the vengeful shepherd snarled and shook his head like a shark trying to rip out the chunks of meat he almost tasted, the girl ran completely out of the shredded dress, trampling several of her compatriots in her wake.

As they were backed into the apartment complex at N.E. 36th and Prospect, the crowd

*Officer Michael J. Ratikan.*

gradually dispersed while committing small, random, defiant acts of vandalism in their wake. As he tried to reach the scene, Chief Wayne Lawson had a brick hurled through the windshield of his unmarked cruiser. Nearly 30 people were arrested and a dozen more received minor injuries including four officers.

The spontaneity of the riot and the source of the false rumor that started it were brought into question when one of the arrested persons was later identified as the "Defense Minister" of the Tulsa chapter of the Black Panthers.

The April 1971 edition of the Criminal Intelligence Unit's Known Offender Bulletin contained a picture of an obscure, small-time armed robber and car thief named Jerry Lewis Fowler. He wasn't wanted for anything currently but Intelligence wanted the officers to know that he was out and about, probably up to no good. He was.

Mike Ratikan had just been through a very stressful nine months. He had been riding as a relief officer in various district cars, mostly in the northwest sector, on Lieutenant Walter Kostiuk's shift when he had transferred to the 4th Shift the previous September after enrolling in college. In that ensuing nine months, he had been trying to maintain some semblance of family life with his wife and nine-year-old son when he wasn't attending classes during the day or working 22 nights a month in volatile northeast Oklahoma City. He had been among the first officers on the scene at the Springlake riot two months earlier. He had been the officer who had arrested the man later identified as the Defense Minister of the Tulsa chapter of the Black Panthers. Answering hundreds of police calls, making scores of reports, making dozens of arrests, filling out the attendant paperwork and making court appearances meant very few of those nights were only eight hours long. A brief respite had been provided when he and his partner were drafted to work undercover vice for a few nights, busting bootleggers and prostitutes. It was a nice break to arrest people you didn't have to fight every time but, even then, he got a shotgun shoved in his face one night by an irate bootlegger.

Mike was pushing his luck. He needed a break. As the college semester ended in late May, he was considering transferring back to his old shift as his former partner had done when the 4th Shift supervisors decided he needed a break also. Returning from a few relaxing days off, when he reported for duty at 6 P.M. on the evening of Monday, June 14, 1971, he was scheduled to ride alone in Patrol One, the downtown paddy wagon that patrolled primarily for drunks, hookers and vagrants in the business district. But, as they say, the best laid plans...one of the officers assigned to Unit 4-Baker-4 that night called in sick. They couldn't put a one-man car northeast in the prevailing climate. Patrol One was scratched from the lineup and Mike Ratikan was assigned to ride in 4-Baker-4 with Officer Charlie Shelden.

Shortly before midnight that night, Officers Mike Ratikan and Charlie Shelden stopped a Cadillac containing eight suspects at N.E. 14th and Kelly as they were leaving University Hospital. A security guard at the hospital had told them that the car had been prowling the parking lots acting suspiciously. As Ratikan approached the driver's side of the car, Shelden covered his partner from the traditional position at the right rear. While being questioned by Ratikan, the driver, Raymond Fowler, bolted and ran west across the street. Giving chase, Shelden caught him in a grassy area near the entrance to the Veteran's Administration Hospital parking lot, where they began struggling. As Ratikan went to help his partner, Jerry Lewis Fowler, Raymond's brother, emerged from the passenger's side of the vehicle. Drawing a .25 automatic pistol, Fowler leaned across the roof of the car and fired three shots at the two officers struggling on the ground with his brother.

Ratikan, struck in the side, fell instantly. The bullet had traversed his chest from side to side puncturing his aorta, the largest artery in the human body. Through this massive vessel, freshly oxygenated blood is pumped under great pressure out of the top of the heart to the rest of the body. It was the kind of wound that doctors say is virtually unsurvivable even if it were to happen in an operating room in front of a prepared surgical team.

Shelden, still wrestling Raymond Fowler on the ground, turned and returned fire as the other passengers scattered. One shot in the leg felled Johnny Lee Washington while the rest got away unscathed, Jerry Fowler among them. Shelden crossed the street to the scout car, dragging a kicking and screaming Raymond Fowler with him. Grabbing the microphone, he breathlessly broadcast the call that any officer who has ever heard it will ever forget their reaction to it..."Shots fired, my partner's been shot, need backup!"

Among the first responding backup officers was Lieutenant Darrell Pierce, the night Detective Supervisor. As the news spread, the entire Department mobilized. A command post was set up in a restaurant at N.E. 30th and Lincoln. Dozens of officers and detectives came in off duty, checked out cars and hit the streets. Martial law was instituted if not declared that night. Informants, snitches, bootleggers, gamblers, prostitutes were all pressed for information. Dozens of informal search warrants were executed. More than a few conversations were carried on through holes kicked in hollow core doors. Officers stopping cars all over the city, calling in their location and the tag number, immediately drew several backup units.

One of the stories that came out of that night, possibly apocryphal, concerned one traffic stop. A black man called in to complain the next day. He said that he had been pulled over in an area about half a mile from the officer's shooting. He was stopped by a plain, unmarked sedan with red lights in the grille. A man in a three-piece suit, wearing a straw hat and carrying a Thompson submachine gun approached him. The man said he was a police officer, asked for his driver's license and began questioning him while resting the muzzle of the machine gun on the car door. The motorist became somewhat indignant, stating that he couldn't be treated like this because he "had friends downtown". The unknown officer reached into a back pocket,

*Lt. W. Lee Brown and Sgt. Bill Gillespie examine new riot control gas equipment on September 20, 1971.*

pulled out a black leather wallet and flipped it open under the driver's nose. It contained a gold badge with "Major" engraved on it. The man then tersely stated "Motherfucker, you're talking to downtown". And the questions got answered.

An all night search led to Jerry Fowler's arrest the following morning in the Kerr Village housing project at S.W. 17th and Independence.

Fowler's trial was moved to Pauls Valley, a small town some 50 miles south of Oklahoma City. He was defended by Stephen Jones, a noted civil liberties lawyer from Enid. During his trial, Fowler tried to justify his actions by saying that he shot Ratikan when he saw the officer's right hand reaching back for his gun and he thought the officer was going to shoot his brother. The District Attorney didn't have too much trouble with that "defense". Mike Ratikan was left handed. He was reaching for his handcuffs. Fowler was sentenced to life imprisonment.

Advancements of 1971 included the formation of an eight-man Bomb Squad complete with specialized truck and bomb disposal trailer as well as a Youth Counselor's Office staffed with four civilian counselors. Additional riot control equipment in the form of gas guns, gas grenades and projectiles were placed in supervisors cruisers. While Elvis Presley was in town giving a concert, Chief Lawson presented OCPD badge number 0833 to him since Presley was a big law enforcement buff and collector of police memorabilia. The badge was put on display with the rest of his collection at his home in Memphis, Tennessee.

Officer Charlie Owen, the local FOP's fourth President, presided over negotiations that enacted the first official collective bargaining agreement between the City and Police Department.

What was to become the last CPI Awards Dinner was held on November 8, 1971. Officer Charlie Shelden was given the City Council Award for his actions the previous June when his partner, Mike Ratikan, was killed. The Mayor's Award was given to Glen DeSpain for saving a woman from a burning house on March 4th. Officer W.T. Jackson was given the City Manager's Award for his undercover investigation of a moonshine operation that netted seven arrests.

The top trainee awards went to James Gallegly and Michael Heath, both of whom would become Majors two decades later. Officer Don Landes of the Canine Unit was given the Mercy Hospital Award for helping locate the bodies of three men buried in the May 6, 1971, collapse of the Empire Building. The juvenile enforcement award went to Russell Rigsby for his organization of the Youth Counselor section in the Youth Bureau. Officer Conrad Nelson won the accident investigation award and the criminal investigation award went to Detective Richard Mullins for an investigation in September of 1970 that led to the discovery of a missing person's body in a shallow grave in Dibble. The killer was later arrested and convicted.

Lt. John Donnell won the police leadership award for his organization of a task force that led to the arrest of a man who had burglarized 84 residences in the City. Warr Acres Officer Richard Cravens was honored for his anti-drug programs among the youth. Safety Education awards went to L.T. Brown, Robert L. Gallamore and W.L. Williams. OSBI Agent Ernie Smith received an award for his work as a handwriting expert.

The Northwest Kiwanis award went to Officer Mike Hoover for recovering 129 stolen vehicles, arresting 17 burglars and 69 other felons in the past year. Special awards went to Oklahoma County Sheriff Bob Turner for his 35 years in law enforcement and the OCPD Intelligence Unit for a year's activity that included 805 investigations as well as large numbers of arrests. Lt. Bill Vetter accepted the award for the Intelligence Unit. A special citation was given to Mrs. Michael Ratikan, praising her as a "person of high courage in her action and faith following the slaying of her husband."

On January 25, 1972, a man died who had set a standard of personal and professional courage for 15 years. After almost seven years, Lt. Darrell Pierce succumbed to his battle with leukemia. He was 38 years old.

Most people never know how they would respond after being diagnosed with a terminal illness. We know how Darrell Pierce responded. First, he volunteered to become an experimental outpatient for the Oklahoma Medical Research Foundation. For over six years, he would receive blood transfusions and other procedures to help medical science learn more about his affliction. The receding hairline receded further, the complexion got paler but the piercing stare didn't waver and he kept on gnawing on the ever-present cigar stub.

Second, he went back to work. I don't mean he kept reporting for duty, I mean he went back to work. In the first two years after his diagnosis, he received two CPI awards. The first was the City Council Award for heroism during a gunfight with an armed robber. The following year he received the Oklahoma Publishing Company Award for the best criminal investigation of the year, a four-month investigation of a narcotics and prostitution ring that resulted in Federal convictions.

Rewarded for his continuing efforts, Pierce was promoted to Sergeant in 1968 and Lieutenant in 1970. As the night Detective Division supervisor, he continued supervising crime scenes, making investigations, stopping cars and making arrests. He continued these duties until three weeks before his death when he went to the Mayo Clinic in a last attempt to beat the disease. His obituary contained eulogies from the Chief and the Governor, punctuated with words like "vigorous", "dedicated", "honor" and "integrity". The obituary also stated he had been awarded 17 commendations in his 15-year career. It was either a misprint or a miscount. There were 27 commendations in his personnel file.

With the continuing success of the CSO program, the staff found additional uses for Federal funds in 1972. The Alcohol Safety Action Program (ASAP) was formed in the Traffic Division. It was to eventually grow to over 30 officers and account for more than 70 percent of the force's DUI arrests.

The Selective Enforcement Unit (SEU) was formed with one Sergeant and six patrolmen operating in plain clothes and unmarked vans. Working under both Patrol and Detective command for the next three years, the unit would create an impressive record in patrolling high crime areas, conducting burglary and robbery stakeouts as well as assisting in many narcotics, homicide and intelligence investigations. In the next decade, it would evolve into the FAST (Felony Apprehension and Surveillance Team) Unit while the name Selective Enforcement would be attached to a specialized Traffic unit.

The OCPD Tactical Team was created under the leadership of Sergeants Richard DeLaughter and Robert Hicks. It would evolve into a precision team including officers on every shift, trained hostage negotiators, an armored car and three vans full of specialized equipment. An entire book could be written about successful hostage rescues, barricaded suspect arrests, narcotics raids and other operations by this unit.

At 6:08 A.M. on April 5, 1972, Airport Unit 475 radioed the dispatcher requesting a homicide unit and the medical examiner to come to a pond in a remote area of the Will Rogers Airport grounds near S.W. 74th and MacArthur. What was unusual about the call was that the officer was calling the units for himself.

When Unit 475 didn't respond to other calls from the dispatcher, other officers were sent to the area to check on his welfare. When they arrived, they found the body of 26-year-old Joe McArthur lying at the edge of the pond, dead from a single gunshot wound behind his right ear. His service revolver was lying in the water next to the body with one expended round in it. The officer was in full uniform but his scout car was parked nearby with all of his brass uniform buttons, badge and gunbelt lying in the front seat.

As Homicide investigated, a series of events from the past few months began to fall into an ominous pattern. With slightly over two years on the force, McArthur had transferred to the Airport the previous September. Shortly before that, he had changed the beneficiary on his insurance. He had been acting nervous and highly-strung lately but his co-workers didn't consider that unusual. He had been giving away clothing and paying off debts. He had sent $345 to his mother in Louisiana. He had a conversation with another officer earlier that night asking about the officer's experiences investigating homicides, suicides and fatal gunshot wounds. While they discussed the fact that a gunshot wound to the head with a 125-grain hollow point bullet is usually instantly fatal, this wasn't unusual shop talk for cops. As he left the police station less than half an hour before his last radio call, McArthur said "See you in hell, boys".

On April 20, 1972, Chief Wayne Lawson retired to become the Assistant Director of the State Department of Corrections . An officer since April 19, 1947, the 51-year-old Lawson spent 11 years as a motorcycle officer and stories still occasionally surfaced about "Cotton" Lawson. One of the more entertaining ones, whether it was true or not, concerned Lawson taking an "unauthorized" break in the downtown area near the railroad tracks. To prevent

*Chief Sam Watson.*

being caught by the supervisor, Lawson allegedly hid his motorcycle in an empty boxcar on the railroad tracks. When he returned from his break, the boxcar was gone. A train had hooked it up and left. Lawson supposedly had to go to El Reno to retrieve his motorcycle.

Promoted to Captain in 1959, he was in charge of the Headquarters Division. The next year he moved back to Traffic until he became Major of Patrol in 1963. He had become Chief in 1969 upon Hilton Geer's retirement.

A dozen new units and programs had been added to the Department during his administration including the Special Services Division.

Lawson was replaced by Assistant Chief Sam Watson. Born on January 22, 1932, Watson had been hired as a booking desk clerk at the age of 20 before becoming a probationary patrolman on July 16, 1953. Remaining in Scout Car through promotions to Sergeant in 1958 and Lieutenant in 1960, he had become a special assistant to Chief Hollingsworth the next year. On June 4, 1962, Watson had been transferred to the Traffic Division to supervise the Warrant Office and the creation of the new Canine Unit. He and Sergeant Bill McDonald had made several trips to Missouri for training and selecting dogs. On July 1, 1965, Lt. Watson became the OCPD's first Community Relations Officer. Promotions to Captain in 1967 and Major of the Special Services Division in 1969 preceded his being selected as Assistant Chief by Lawson. Six days after Watson became Chief, Captain Gerald Emmett, good naturedly known as "Captain Midnight", was promoted to Major and became the first black officer to achieve a position on the Department's administrative staff.

Three months later, Chief Watson created the first Firearms Review Board to investigate all instances of officers firing their weapons in the line of duty. This creation may have been hastened somewhat by a newspaper article that appeared that summer. The article noted that in the year since Officer Mike Ratikan had been killed, Oklahoma City officers had shot eight suspects, killing six of them. Another patrolman, Officer Steve Upchurch, had narrowly missed death when a shot grazed his right cheek while trying to make an arrest in the Hamilton Courts housing projects on S.E. 15th the previous December. Interviews with Chief Watson, Captain Tom Heggy of the Training Division and a notably liberal attorney debated the question. The implication was that since Ratikan's murder, officers were more inclined to shoot than risk personal injury by hesitating to shoot or by pursuing escaping suspects. The officers were not necessarily vengeful or adopting a "take no prisoners" attitude, just one of "take fewer prisoners". That wasn't accurate either. It was more complicated than that.

The Oklahoma City Police Department of that time was still a relatively small fraternity. A little over 500 officers, virtually everyone knew everyone else on a first-name basis. They usually saw each other every few days, either working together or coming on or off duty. The "brotherhood" attitude surrounding the creation of the FOP was still relatively fresh. The core of that group was the Patrol Division, an even smaller fraternity of slightly over 200 officers.

Fraternity is the right word because, at that time, they were all men. No females enforced the law on Oklahoma City's streets yet. The mentality was that if criminal laws were enforced in the City, if crimes were prevented or solved, if bad guys went to jail and justice was served, this was the group that was responsible for 99 percent of it. Besides being the prevailing mentality, it was also the reality of the situation.

An even smaller group within the Patrol Division were those officers who worked in the northeast sectors, colloquially known as the "combat zone". This predominantly black quadrant of the City was the focal point for the militant black organizations that typified the racial divisiveness of the times. Often the police in these areas were looked upon as an occupying military force. The last two officers who had been killed in the line of duty had been slain in this area. More shootings, stabbings, assaults on officers and instances of resisting arrest occurred in this area than anywhere else in the City. Mike Ratikan was a member of this group when he died and so was Mark Zelewski.

So there were no attitudes of "revenge" for Mike Ratikan. That was done when Jerry and Raymond Fowler went to jail. There was also no attitude of "take no prisoners" or "take fewer prisoners". Ratikan was shot in the back while pursuing an escaping prisoner. So there was an attitude that officers were hesitant to risk their lives by not resorting to using deadly force when the laws allowed them to do so. At least one officer expressed this as "if you're going to run, you better be able to run faster than 1300 feet per second", referring to the velocity of a .357 Magnum bullet. Nevertheless, the time was right for Chief Watson's Firearms Review Board.

Prior to that time, procedures existed that would be considered incomprehensibly lax to the officer of today but they were in line with the times. A public hue and cry or lawsuits against the City or Police Department over an officer-involved shooting were rare.

If an officer fired his weapon in the line of duty and no one was injured, many times there was no report made. His sergeant might make a followup investigation and counsel him if his shooting had been grossly inappropriate. If someone was injured, Homicide and the officer's Sergeant both made reports on their investigations and copies went to the Chief. He had the option to intervene but rarely exercised it. When he did, in grossly inappropriate cases, the usual form of discipline was the removal of the officer from enforcement or "street" duties. Usually this was a transfer to the Information Desk, Jail, Communications, Records or some other place where the offender would never again have to decide whether or not to shoot.

When an officer killed someone in the line of duty, the standard practice was that Homicide completed their investigation by taking statements from everyone involved and gave the District Attorney a synopsis of it. The D.A. would usually file First Degree Murder or Manslaughter charges against the officer and he would be arraigned before a District Judge. Since he was a resident of the community, gainfully employed and of previous good character, the officer would be OR'ed by the Judge; that is, released on his own recognizance without having to post a bond.

Usually within three days, the officer would appear in District Court, sometimes before the same Judge, and waive his right to a jury trial. The Judge would then hear the facts of the case as presented by the D.A.'s Office and, in light of the fleeing felon statutes of the day, rule it as a justifiable homicide. At that point, the double jeopardy rule would come into force and the officer could not be charged or tried in that case ever again.

Chief Watson's Firearms Review Board has evolved into today's thorough, detailed investigations of officer involved shootings, special training for Homicide and Internal Affairs investigators specializing in these types of cases, automatic preparations for forthcoming lawsuits and screening committees.

After two years under the aegis of the OCPD, the Airport Police became a separate organization again. This time the separation was emphasized by a uniform change. Airport Officers' shirts, trousers and caps were solid navy blue. Although the shoulder patches were similar, the new Airport badge was a distinctive seven-pointed star with the City Seal in the center.

The Fall of 1972 saw the creation of two new ranks for the first time in twenty years. Specific promotional tests were offered to all officers with three years of service or more and they were ranked according to their scores. On September 22, 1972, 73 Patrolmen were promoted to become 56 Master Patrolmen and 17 Specialists. They were the equivalent in rank and pay to Detectives. The Master Patrolman rank also became known as Senior Police Officer and they were utilized as training officers for new officers, the forerunners of the future FTO's. The Specialist rank was granted to technicians in the Crime Lab, helicopter pilots and others in support services. By now, 76 percent of the 591 officers had some college training.

In the last month of 1972, the sexual revolution hit the OCPD with full force. It had been a long time coming. The Women's Civic Council had asked the city in 1929 to hire female officers to police movie theaters, parks and dance halls to keep young girls from "going astray",

*Officer Jewell (Julie) Black [Smith] receives instruction from Master Patrolman Ron McKinney on her first day on patrol.*

sort of a 1920s juvenile officer-cum-social worker. The suggestion that they should earn the same pay as men had killed that idea. A group of "Meter-maids" had been hired in the mid-1950s but the novelty had rapidly worn off and within a few years only two of the original six were still on active duty and were now approaching their 20-year anniversaries, Ina Mae [Faldo] "Tiny" Miller and Jean Latham. Male Traffic officers on three-wheel motorcycles had taken over the parking enforcement function in the mid-1960s and the commissioned women had been transferred to jobs as jail matrons or other headquarters duties. They had never been asked or expected to function as "real cops".

A 1972 Supreme Court ruling mandated that women must be allowed to work on all public jobs. The Equal Employment Opportunity Commission said that women should be hired and given the same pay, training and treatment as men. Of the first 100 who applied, 16 passed the initial testing and background checks, moving on to take physical and polygraph examinations. On December 7, 1972, Sherry Lynn Hamman became the first woman hired as a fully commissioned Oklahoma City Police officer, equal in all respects to her male counterparts. Eventually, five women from the first group were hired and assigned to patrol duties. In the previous 82 years, women in the OCPD had been assigned duties as jail matrons or given training and public relations duties. But now they would be expected to function just like their male counterparts. Same uniform, same training, same duties, same hours, same dangers and the same stresses.

The first stress test was the Police Academy. The Academy stressed semi-military discipline with formal uniform inspections, marching, standing at attention, "yes sir and no sir", all of the rigid discipline placed upon recruits to try to infuse in them the self-discipline that would be required of them on the streets. This was a uniquely different environment for the women who, unlike many of the men, brought no military experience with them to the job. Simultaneously other stresses were applied from outside. Some officers wives picketed City Hall, protesting the intent to assign the new female officers to patrol duty. Some of the wives felt that, with female partners, their husbands safety would be compromised. Others were doubtlessly more worried about their husbands chastity being compromised when confronted with the challenge of spending all night in a scout car with a partner who wore earrings and smelled of perfume. Nevertheless, the ladies completed their training, asking no favors and receiving none.

Once assigned to patrol duty, the new recruits were subjected to the usual pranks and initiations perpetrated on all rookies but, due to their gender, some of them took unusual forms. Street cops are relentlessly traditional and ruthlessly inventive. One Master Patrolman, knowing that he would be assigned to train one of the new female recruits, bragged to his fellow officers about making a sexual conquest of his new partner the first night. A renowned practical joker, he brought one of his wife's bras to work in his briefcase that night. The shift passed uneventfully and the next morning, as he drove into the gas line at the end of the shift, the officer dangled the brassiere out of the window like a captured trophy for all the shift to see. Naturally he was careful to hold it above the top of the car window so his female partner couldn't see it. No doubt she was puzzled as to why the officers standing around in the bay gave them a standing ovation as they drove by.

Julie Smith tells another story about one of her first training officers. Part of his training program was to have his rookie arrest drunks who were known to fight officers, just to see how they could handle themselves. He directed Smith to arrest a drunk he knew was a former golden gloves boxer who always resisted arrest. Smith told the man he was under arrest, searched him for weapons and he meekly got in the back seat of the scout car. On their way to jail, the drunk tapped on the screen separating the seats and said "Little lady, if you hadn't been a lady, I would have kicked your butt!". Perhaps her speechless partner began to see some of the advantages of female officers.

It was also a tradition that whichever officer was driving when the scout car had a flat tire had to change it. One summer, Smith's car had a flat in front of Mercy Hospital. As the driver, she changed the flat while her partner relaxed under the shade of a nearby tree. The tradition was upheld but the male officer got the cold shoulder treatment from some of the nurses who witnessed the event.

Overcoming a great deal of protest, predictions of doom and gloom, male posturing and sometimes incredible sexual harassment, some of it very inventive, they made it work and were the vanguard of the female officers of today. Like true police officers, they have had their peaks and valleys, made their own legends and changed spouses a few times. However, over 20 years later, all of the first five are still on duty; Shirley (Cox) Conners, Sherry (Hamman) Garcia and Norma (Bowerman) Hutchcroft are Sergeants in Investigations and Gladys (Burns) Loflin is a Lieutenant in Patrol. The one who has set the pace however, then and now, was 22-year-old Julie (Black) Smith. Serving several years in Patrol in some of the roughest areas of the City, with partners of both sexes, she measured up to all of them. As a Detective, she withstood the dangers of working undercover narcotics, the emotional trauma of investigating sex crimes and excelled. But this is just the beginning of her story.

In 1973, "Helicopter One" took off and the OCPD became airborne. Acquired under a trial lease program, it has been hailed almost unanimously as the greatest law enforcement tool since the two-way radio. Initially manned by Police Specialists Manuel Beck, John Bohan, J.J. Young and Don Ayers, the unit was supervised by Sergeant Jim Jackson who doubled as an observer. Initially based out of Wiley Post Airport in far northwest Oklahoma City, the Hughes 300C chopper was equipped with a powerful searchlight and immediately began compiling an impressive record of assistance in pursuits, surveillances, searches and suspect apprehensions.

Racial tensions still plagued the nation in 1973. The Black Panthers, Black Muslims, Black Liberation Army and numerous other militant organizations were declaring war on white society and its police. A gun stolen from the body of a slain New York City policeman was recovered during the attempted murder of a San Francisco officer. Record numbers of officers were being slain nationwide in racially motivated incidents, some in planned assassinations and ambushes. In 1970, over 200 law enforcement officers had been killed in the line of duty, the first time the number had exceeded 200 since 1930. Although the worst problems were in the larger cities like New York, Detroit and Los Angeles, Oklahoma City was having their share of the troubles. Many officers believed it was partially due to the more severe restrictions placed on the officers in those larger jurisdictions.

Officers in many of the larger or more liberal cities, usually in the north and far west, were only allowed to carry .38 caliber pistols and use slow, military ball-type ammunition. Even in some cities where officers were allowed to carry .357 Magnums, they were only allowed to use the less powerful .38 bullets. High-speed hollow point ammunition was specifically forbidden in many cities, detractors claiming it was "cruel" and comparing it to the use of dum-dum ammo in war. The farther south you looked, however, the more preponderance of large caliber Magnum handguns and hollow point ammunition you found.

A recent series of homicides and arsons had occurred that indicated the involvement of Black Muslims and possible racial motivation. The FBI was entering the investigations to see if they might be a part of a nationwide campaign of black terrorism. Tempers were short, nerves were frayed and officers were still displaying an attitude of taking no unnecessary chances whenever possible. One of the summer's incidents was illustrative.

Police were summoned to a violent domestic call in the northeast sector one day. A black man was in town from Oakland, California, visiting his relatives. Oakland, the home base of the Black Panthers and the activists at the university in neighboring Berkeley, had a reputation with police at that time as a national hotbed of liberalism. Officers joked that was what helped California become "the vacationland for the criminally insane".

Drunk, doped up or mentally unbalanced, for whatever reason, the man had gone into a towering rage. Slashing at them with knives, he had chased his two sisters out of the house. When the two officers arrived, they found the man isolated in the house with a knife in each hand. When they tried to talk him into dropping the six-inch butcher knife and two-inch paring knife, he began cursing them roundly and waving the knives threateningly in their direction. Backing off, the officers decided to call their supervisor.

When the Sergeant arrived, they advised him of the circumstances. All three officers went back in the house with the Sergeant in the lead. Approaching to within eight feet of the man, the Sergeant said "I'm going to tell you one time. Drop the knives". The man responded with a profanely negative response consisting of two words but he only got the first one out before the Sergeant drew his .357 Magnum and carefully put a 158-grain hollow point round through the man's right knee. The knives clattered to the floor and the man collapsed instantly, howling in agony as two inches of his femur and kneecap turned into minute bone chips.

The Sergeant used his portable radio to call for an ambulance as the man berated him for shooting him. Between screams of pain and comments about the Sergeant's mother, the man said he was going back to Oakland as soon as he could because the Oakland Police wouldn't have shot him just for threatening them with the knives, Oakland Police couldn't fire unless

*Early 1970s Patrol Division lineup.*

they were actually attacked. The Sergeant laconically informed him "You ain't in Oakland now, asshole". Thus was born the legend of the man who brought a knife to a gunfight.

On July 27, 1973, the Oklahoma State Penitentiary in McAlester exploded in one of the worst prison riots in the country's history. With fires being set and hostages taken, the guard force at the prison and the McAlester Police were rapidly outnumbered by the 1,800 inmates. The National Guard was dispatched as a containing force but were under orders not to load their weapons or confront the prisoners.

Later that night, over 60 OCPD officers were sent to McAlester in a convoy of black and white scout cars. A force of Oklahoma Highway Patrol troopers was also sent by former Chief Wayne Lawson, now the Commissioner of the Oklahoma Department of Public Safety. The next day, this group of officers combined with the troopers and entered the prison, armed with shotguns and automatic weapons. The rioting prisoners had shown no fear of the National Guard troops once the word got around that they had not been allowed to load their weapons. When the convicts figured out that they were only a containing force and not a potential assault force, they began taunting the reservists. This attitude changed rapidly when the OCPD and OHP forces entered the prison. Many of the prisoners had prior experience with members of these two agencies. No longer was there any doubt that these guns were loaded. Nor was there any doubt that it would be unwise to taunt them. In fact, three of the prisoners went to great pains to stay close to each other, be on good behavior and try to stay in front of news cameras at all times. They were Robert Barnett, convicted killer of OCPD officer Mark Zelewski in 1964, Jerry Fowler, convicted killer of OCPD officer Mike Ratikan in 1971, and Jerry Cudjo, convicted killer of OHP Trooper Robert Ake in 1972. Supposedly, they feared that if the show of force turned violent, they were fairly certain to be among the first casualties. This show of force brought about negotiations that ended the crisis.

Aerial surveillance throughout the riot was provided by the OCPD helicopter. The record it had achieved so rapidly led to its purchase in 1974 and an OCPD helicopter became a permanent fixture in the skies over Oklahoma City.

The word "laconic" is defined as meaning brief, terse, concise, or using few words. The word's origin allegedly stems from a legend about the King of Laconia, a province in ancient Greece. The Laconians were evidently more spiritually akin to their bellicose Spartan countrymen than their gentler Athenian brothers. As a warlike horde of Huns approached Laconia, their leader sent a message to the Laconian king, calling for him to surrender without resistance. It said something like "If we conquer you by force, everyone will be put to the sword". In declining the offer, the King of Laconia sent back a one-word reply: "If".

There was a scene in one of Clint Eastwood's spaghetti westerns of the mid-1960s in which a gunman was threatening another gunman, telling him all the horrible things he was going to do to him. While the man was threatening him, the other man shot him down. The survivor expressed his philosophy of the situation by saying "When it's time to talk, talk. When it's time to shoot, shoot". This maxim was proven again in the early morning hours of September 17, 1973.

Officer Sam Sealy was something of an anachronism in a number of ways. Because of his fair complexion, blond hair, green eyes and Caucasian features, only his closest friends usually knew he was a half-blood American Indian. He wasn't hiding his Indian heritage, he just didn't talk a lot about it. In fact, he didn't talk a lot about anything to anyone he didn't know well and trust. In a profession that sometimes encouraged macho and bravado, he was quiet, laconic, reticent and calm. While most policemen's hobbies leaned towards hunting and guns, Sealy was an accomplished artist. Professionally, he did composite drawings of suspects for the Detective Division and later collaborated with Detective Bill Harrison to draw the first portrait of the sardonic vulture that became the symbol of the OCPD Homicide Unit. Personally, he did precise, detailed, beautiful scrimshaw work that many officers commissioned from him for knife and gun handles. Perhaps the reason the six-year-veteran preferred art to hunting was because he had already satisfied his hunting instincts as a "Lurp" (Long Range Recon Patrol) Team Leader for a year in Vietnam with the 101st Airborne Division before joining the OCPD in 1967. Even though he was quiet, laid back and carved pretty pictures, Sam Sealy was not a man to be taken lightly.

Shortly after midnight on September 17, Officers Sealy and G.W. Davis received a call on a silent burglar alarm on Walt Durham's TV Store at 3101 N. May Avenue. Also responding to the call were Officers Joe Poe and the rookie partner he was training, Officer Julie Black. Approaching quietly with the lights out, Sealy got out to cover the rear of the store while Davis drove the car around to cover the front. When Poe and Black arrived, Poe remained at the front while Julie Black went to the rear.

The rear of the building was enclosed by a stockade fence,separating it from a parking area on the south side. At one point near a tree, there was an open space in the fence leading to the rear of the building. As Officer Black made her way down the fenceline, as she approached the break in the fence, she froze in her tracks as she heard a chillingly cold voice on the other side of the fence say "Die, motherfucker!". This menacing statement was instantly followed by a shot. Stepping through the hole in the fenceline, she saw a man lying on the ground holding a gun. A spreading bloodstain showed that he had been shot in what officer's referred to as the "ten-ring", referring to the area in the center of the paper targets used on the Police firearms range. A score of ten points, the highest possible, was awarded for a hit in the "center of body mass", that area of the chest over a person's heart. Sam Sealy was holstering his sidearm. Black looked at a calm, composed Sealy and asked "What happened?" In his normal, quiet method of understatement, Sealy laconically said "Man was talking when he should've been shooting."

As Sealy had approached the rear of the building through the space in the stockade fence along the side, he saw George Wright crouched by a parked van in the darkness. Arresting him, Sealy holstered his revolver as he leaned Wright against the fence to search and handcuff him.

That accomplished, Sealy began taking Wright around to the front of the store to put him in the scout car. As Sealy approached the space in the fence, George Wright's accomplice, Sammy Jon Rhodes stepped out from the shadows near the tree. Rhodes, with a leveled pistol pointed at Sealy's chest, apparently wanted Sealy to know he was going to die an instant before he shot him and said the words that had stopped Julie Black in her tracks. In the time it took Rhodes to say those two words, Sealy drew his weapon and shot Rhodes once in the chest. Rhodes died before he could fire. A third burglar was arrested as he came out of the building. For public consumption, Sammy Rhodes' last words were published in the newspaper as "Right now, man". Contrary of Mr. Rhodes' intentions, Sam Sealy went on to complete a 20-year career as a Master Patrolman, Homicide Detective and Technical Investigator before retiring in 1988.

On January 18, 1974, Chief Watson retired to become Director of the Oklahoma State Bureau of Investigation. A good example of the standards Chief Watson held himself and his Department to is illustrated by a minor traffic accident that occurred at S.W. 36 and Pennsylvania in May of 1973. When motorcycle Officer Danny Mercer arrived on the scene, he had to be somewhat dismayed to find that one of the drivers involved was the Chief of Police. Nevertheless, the accident was investigated like any other and the Chief appeared to have been at fault. The Accident Review Board held the next month agreed that it was a preventable accident. Assistant Chief I.G. Purser was then placed in the unenviable position of writing a reprimand to his Chief, cautioning him to drive more cautiously in the future. That was the policy and that's what was done. Watson had also maintained the Department's high hiring standards. The previous year 1,226 people had

*Chief I.G. Purser.*

*Officer James Dewey Chamblin.*

applied to become Oklahoma City officers and only 120 had been accepted, less than 10 percent.

Assistant Chief I.G. (initials only) Purser took Watson's place. Born on December 29, 1926, the Non, Oklahoma, native had grown up in Geary. Don't bother trying to find the town of Non on a current Oklahoma map. It is one of Oklahoma's "ghost towns" now. Originally located eight and one-half miles east of Holdenville in Hughes County, the post office closed the same month Purser joined the OCPD and, by the time he became Chief, the town consisted of a church, a cemetery and five homes. Prior to joining the OCPD on October 1, 1954, Purser had been a Staff Sergeant in the U.S. Army and a policeman at Tinker Air Force Base from 1950 to 1953. After six months in the Patrol Division, Purser transferred to Traffic, spending the next four years on motorcycles and in accident cars.

In 1958, Purser was promoted to Detective and, a year and a half later, to Lieutenant in Traffic. On July 1, 1965, he became a Captain in the Records Bureau and, four years later, the Major of the Patrol Division. On April 22, 1972, Chief Watson had named him Assistant Chief.

Purser immediately reorganized the Department into two bureaus, Operations and Administration. These were to be presided over by two Assistant Chiefs, Tom Heggy and Gerald Emmett. With this reorganization, Emmett became the first black officer to rise to the number two position in the Department.

In the early morning hours of April 16, 1974, Officers James Dewey Chamblin and John C. Campbell were conducting a routine bar check at Tom's Tiptoe Inn at N.E. 6th and Harrison and made some routine arrests for public drunkenness. The incident became a perfect example of why the hackles should rise on the back of every police officer's neck whenever he is doing anything with people that he considers "routine".

James Dewey Chamblin was a 31-year-old rookie who had been on the force for ten and one-half months. As with most officers who come into law enforcement in their late 20's or beyond, he was more worldly-wise than the term "rookie" would indicate. Married with a son and two daughters, Chamblin had already served three years as a U.S. Army paratrooper and nearly a year as a police officer in the western suburb of Yukon before joining the OCPD. He had completed his military obligations before the time when he would have seen combat in Vietnam. His combat experience would be in northeast Oklahoma City. Earning his high school diploma in the service, he had already completed a couple of semesters of college and was well on his way to establishing his new career. His brother-in-law, John Hauck Jr., was an officer with the Airport Police.

Chamblin's partner that night was John C. Campbell, a five-year veteran who had been promoted in the first group of Master Patrolmen in 1972. Campbell was a Vietnam veteran who had earned a Purple Heart and a Bronze Star for Valor during his service in the Army.

Tom's Tiptoe Inn was a sleazy little bar located at the triple intersection of North Walnut, N.E. 6th and Harrison Street, which ran diagonally from southwest to northeast from the downtown area to the most disadvantaged area of the near northeast quadrant. The entranceway was a narrow hallway only wide enough to accommodate a single person's width. Any group of people entering or leaving had to do so in single file. Situated on the borderline between the skid row area of downtown and the "Deep Deuce" area of the volatile eastside, the joint drew its' multiracial clientele from both areas. The two officers reflected the variety of their patrol district since Chamblin was white and  Campbell was black.

Under Oklahoma law, beer taverns had to close at midnight and private clubs that served liquor had to close at 2 A.M. But Tom's had a small grill which gave them the ability to serve food, thus making them, legally, a restaurant and giving them the ability to stay open 24 hours a day. They weren't supposed to serve beer after midnight or liquor after 2 A.M. but then, a lot of people frequently did things they weren't supposed to in this part of town. That made the Tiptoe one of the regular stops for the area scout cars. A four-square-mile circuit also covered the Fun Club, the Fish Fry Club, Luster's Hotel, Elwood's Doin' It To Death Cafe, the Masters Club with its electronic locks, The Spider Web, the Cavalier Club, Dude's, the Ram's Inn, the Trevas Club, the Moonlight, the "Hole" and Columbus Jackson's place where the night Homicide car usually stopped every night so the Detectives could circle, date and initial the fresh bullet holes in the walls. It simplified their shooting and homicide scene investigations.

Shortly after 3 A.M., the two partners decided to check the Tiptoe for drunks and other violations. Checking identification, relative sobriety and attitude, they made their way from table to table inside. Stopping at one for longer than usual, they checked the identification of a white man and an Indian couple. They soon arrested all three for being drunk in public. The three prisoners meekly got up and led the way out of the bar with the two officers following. As a police supervisor later pointed out, it was not common practice to search prisoners arrested for misdemeanor violations on the premises if they weren't causing problems or resisting arrest. They were normally taken out to the scout car and searched before they were placed in the car for transportation to jail. None of the prisoners were physically or verbally resisting their arrest so the officers treated it "routinely".

The Indian man and woman were just what they appeared to be, a little too intoxicated to be in public. The white man was something more. The name and identification he had given the officers were not his. The name, identification and much of the over $1,600 in the wallet belonged to an armed robbery victim in Kentucky. Their public drunk was a desperate interstate fugitive.

Michael Wayne Green had packed a lot of activity into his 31 years, much of it illegal. Six weeks earlier, he had been imprisoned in North Carolina's Central Prison for robbery and burglary charges. On March 4, he and Larry Keith Somerset, also 31, were being transported to testify in court when they overpowered their guards. Taking both of the corrections officers' .38 pistols, they handcuffed them to a tree and escaped, stealing the state car in the process. The corrections officers should have been more careful. Green had escaped from prison twice before and Somerset once.

The two then went on a crime spree across half the country. An armed robbery and kidnapping in South Carolina, another armed robbery in North Carolina, a stolen car in New Jersey and armed robberies in Ohio and Kentucky led them to Bowling Green. There they bonded Sue Evelyn Craft, 25, out of jail and continued their adventures.

Escaping a police pursuit in Excelsior Springs, Missouri, led them to abandon their stolen car in the small town of Liberty, where they abducted a couple and stole their car. Liberty, Missouri, holds the distinction of being the location of the first daylight bank robbery in the United States, committed by the Jesse James gang almost a century before. Leaving the couple tied up in a motel room in Kansas City, they switched cars again in Emporia, Kansas, stealing a replacement vehicle. Distancing themselves from prior problems led them to the Tradewinds Motor Inn at Reno and Eastern in Oklahoma City. Then Michael Wayne Green decided to go have a few drinks at Tom's Tiptoe Inn.

As the prisoners walked into the parking lot followed by the officers, Michael Wayne Green was a teletype and a fingerprint away from spending the rest of his natural life in jail and he knew it. Reaching into his waistband and drawing the .38 Colt revolver he had taken from the North Carolina corrections officer, he turned rapidly and fired five times. Four of the rounds hit flesh.

Chamblin was wounded twice in the abdomen and groin, one of the rounds puncturing his aorta, virtually an unsurvivable wound. As he fell on his back, he drew his sidearm and fired at Green in the last moments of his life. Two more bullets hit John Campbell in the upper left thigh and the small of his back. Campbell emptied all six rounds from his sidearm at Green, reloaded and fired three more at his assailant. Green was hit five times with a combination of

.38 and .357 Magnum hollow point rounds, twice in the abdomen, once in the buttocks and in both forearms.

At 3:20 A.M., a female voice came over the police radio—"Police, get an ambulance to 6th and Walnut, please. Two policemen are injured...I think one of them's dead!". Martha Henson, a taxi driver who had been celebrating her 42nd birthday in Tom's Tiptoe Inn, knew how to use the police radio in the scout car and did. She and others that had come outside after hearing the flurry of gunshots found Officer Chamblin laying on his back, covered with blood and breathing his last breaths. Campbell, refusing to go down, was leaning against a car in the parking lot. Green had crawled away.

Officers Eddie Hoklotubbe and Ed Bradway were less than six blocks away. Racing to the scene, they drove up on the carnage in the Tiptoe's parking lot. Ed Bradway had graduated from the Police Academy with Dewey Chamblin less than five months earlier. Another member of their Academy class had been Eric Mullinex, son of former Chief of Detectives Jack Mullinex and grandson of Lee Mullinex. Searching the area, the officers found Michael Wayne Green laying in an alley half a block away in the 100 block of Harrison, his .38 beside him.

While officers swarmed over the crime scene, separate ambulances rushed Officer Chamblin and his assailant to Mercy Hospital's emergency room. Chamblin was pronounced dead on arrival. Officer Chris Eulberg dragged Officer John Campbell into his scout car and took him to the hospital.

The Detectives took over. A few hours later, a door was kicked in at the Tradewinds Motor Inn. The other .38 stolen from the North Carolina corrections officers was knocked out of Larry Somerset's hand and he was arrested with Sue Craft.

John Campbell would survive his wounds, return to light duty in five weeks and full duty within three months. Michael Wayne Green would also survive his wounds. After weeks in critical condition, he would finally be transferred to the City jail on July 31. Charged with murdering Officer Chamblin and the deadly assault on Officer Campbell, he was convicted and sentenced to death. Two years later, when Oklahoma's death penalty law was declared unconstitutional, Green's sentence was commuted to life in prison.

James Dewey Chamblin was buried in Yukon Cemetery with over 800 people in attendance, nearly 500 of them police officers from more than a dozen cities. His funeral procession had more than 150 cars in it.

The recent deaths brought attention to bear upon the Department's firearms training program and the emphasis on marksmanship. Later in the year, two OCPD Sergeants, Phil Kennedy and Jack Garrette, won the two-man competition at the National Pistol Championships.

A group of retired FBI agents held a reunion in May of 1974 at the Shangri-La Lodge on the shores of Grand Lake near Afton, Oklahoma. One of those attending was D.A. "Jelly" Bryce who had come to be known as "Mr. FBI". Retired for the last 15 years after 23 years in the FBI, Bryce was 67 now and feeling his years. With an old cop's instincts, he still carried a gun everywhere he went and never sat with his back to an open room or doorway. After a failed bid but a good showing in the 1958 Oklahoma governor's race, Bryce had settled down to a peaceful existence of hunting and fishing in his hometown of Mountain View in Kiowa County.

Thirteen months earlier, however, his wife of nearly 29 years had died. Since then he smoked too much, grieved for his wife and complained of being tired all the time. On the evening of Saturday, May 11, he went to bed soon after

*D.A. Jelly Bryce.*

*Shift change in 'the bay', May 13, 1974.*

dinner. He missed his check-out time the next day and didn't respond to friends knocking at his door. His body was discovered the next morning. After a life of unparalleled violence, he had died in his sleep from a heart attack. His body was returned to Mountain View for burial next to his beloved wife Shirley. He was survived by his two sons, a sister, five grandchildren and his parents including his ninety-year-old father.

Shortly after 5 P.M. on May 17, 1974, many Oklahoma City citizens were listening to news updates on a massive gun battle between the Los Angeles Police and members of the radical Symbionese Liberation Army, the suspected kidnappers of Patty Hearst. One Oklahoma City citizen, however, was not. He was witnessing the aftermath of another tragedy closer to home.

The passerby called police to tell them that he had just seen a Lake Ranger's boat adrift and empty in Lake Hefner. Officers responded and found the Ranger's boat grounded on the northeastern shore with the engine still running. The Lake Ranger, William L. Stewart Jr., had last checked in by radio shortly before 5 P.M. but could not be located now. Lake Rangers, police officers, firefighters and two National Guard helicopters began a thorough search of the lake area.

Winds on the lake were gusting over 40 miles per hour and waves were running a foot high. Some disquieting evidence was soon found on a weather island about half a mile away from the beached boat—the Ranger's gun, gunbelt, boots and hat. The search intensified even further, with 20 men keeping at it all night long and fearing the worst.

The following morning, Fire Department divers began dragging that area of the lake with grappling hooks. After three hours, their fears were realized. The Ranger's body was recovered about 11 A.M. some 50 yards north of the weather island.

Investigating officers hypothesized that the Ranger had been making a routine check of the weather island when the high winds had set his boat adrift. The rope was found still attached where he had tied it up. The 26-year-old Stewart apparently stripped off his boots, hat and gunbelt, tried to swim out and retrieve the boat but drowned in the churning waters. Seattle-born, Stewart had been a Ranger for about a year following his discharge from the Navy. Relatives stated that he had "loved his job". He left a widow and four-year-old son.

Stewart was interred in uniform in Arlington Memory Gardens attended by half a dozen Lake Rangers for pallbearers.

Since the OCPD first became a motorized force, they had gone through a series of cars, usually Fords, Chevrolets, Plymouths and Dodges. Being a bureaucracy, it depended upon who made the lowest bid at any given time. One of the constants was, at first, the solid black color and later, what became the traditional black and white. The black and white paint job cost a little extra on each car. In 1974, City planners decided that a solid white fleet would be easier and cheaper to maintain and repair. That year the OCPD received their first shipment of solid white Rambler Matadors.

Another tradition broken at the same time was the single rotating red light on top of the cars. The "bubble gum machine" was replaced by clear plastic visibars mounted on the car roof. With alternating red and clear lenses reflected through a series of mirrors, they were much more visible. The siren speaker was also contained in the unit instead of being mounted under the hood. Visibility and audibility were much improved but the veteran officers groused interminably about the solid white cars.

Another white car was about to become involved in the history of the Oklahoma City Police Department, although by a much longer, more circuitous and, some would say, devious route. Shortly after 7:30 P.M. on the evening of Wednesday, November 13, 1974, the Oklahoma Highway Patrol received a call to investigate a traffic accident south of Crescent, about 30 miles north of Oklahoma City. A white 1973 Honda Civic had run off the road and struck a concrete culvert. A young woman was dead.

The first OHP Trooper on the scene found the car lying on its left side in the ditch, the young woman crushed and pinned inside the car. Lying in the mud near the car was a paycheck from the Kerr-McGee plutonium processing plant in Crescent. The name on the paycheck was Karen Silkwood.

The year 1975 was destined to become unique in OCPD history. The Selective Enforcement Unit started it off with a bang, literally, on January 11th while trying to serve a narcotics search warrant at a secluded house on the southeast corner of N.E. 50th and Interstate 35. Several future commanders were involved including Sergeant Bill Jackson, Patrolmen Roger Winborn, Don Pennington, Larry Allen, Jack Wells, Ron Owens and Jerry Martin.

Since they saw only three cars parked at the house, four of the officers were going to

*Aerial view of downtown Oklahoma City looking north across Interstate 40 on November 22, 1974. The massive Myriad Convention Center, lower right, covers the area of the old 'Hell's Half Acre'.*

approach the house on foot while the rest remained in vehicles a half block away in case it was necessary to pursue escaping vehicles. Unknown to the officers, the house contained eighteen suspects. Also unknown to the officers was the existence of armed lookouts posted in the shadows outside the house. As the officers started moving up the 50-yard gravel driveway, the lookouts opened fire on them. What had started as a routine dope raid became a wild 15-minute gun battle with over a dozen suspects. Over a hundred officers responded to the melee. Miraculously, none of the officers were hurt and only one of the suspects was injured. At least two suspects escaped through the woods. Ultimately it ended with thirteen arrested and the confiscation of heroin, marijuana, and a collection of shotguns, rifles and handguns.

The SEU's luck was still holding. Less than a month earlier, during a stakeout at a shopping mall the week before Christmas, one of the unit's officers had become involved in a foot chase with a man trying to steal a car from the parking lot. During the chase, the man drew a .38 automatic pistol, pointed it at the officer's face and pulled the trigger. Fortunately, he had neglected to chamber a round before he tried to fire and the hammer fell on an empty chamber. Next came the drug raid. It was only the prelude to a long, hot summer and a stormy autumn.

On January 23, one of the most popular and respected commanders in the Department's history retired. Major Bill Peterman ended his 21-year career as the commander of the Patrol Division after having had open heart surgery the previous year. Of average height but seemingly shorter because of his stockiness, his swarthy complexion and usually impassive expression bespoke his Chickasaw Indian blood while his calm, unblinking gaze radiated the quiet self-confidence of a man who had earned three Bronze Stars and the Combat Infantryman's Badge in Europe in World War II. When relaxed, he also showed some of the fatalistic sadness of someone who had seen too many of the bad things and bad people the world has to offer. However, that dour countenance also masked a dry, impish sense of humor much appreciated by his officers. It was well known that his sympathies lay with the officers on the street who got the job done. Known as "a policeman's policeman", his officers had given him an all-time high number of arrests the previous year.

Hired on January 18, 1954, Peterman had served as a scout car officer in the Patrol Division and remained in that Division throughout his career. Promoted to Sergeant in 1961 and Lieutenant in 1966, he became the Assistant Division Commander when promoted to Captain in 1969. The day after becoming Chief, Sam Watson chose Peterman to be the Major over his largest Division.

Many officers riding alone had the experience of making calls on busy nights, coming out of a building at all hours of the night after making a domestic or disturbance call and seeing a dark, unmarked cruiser idling across the street. Nothing was said on the radio, just an unsummoned backup unit sitting there, waiting, watching, just in case. A wave of the hand when he saw that one of his boys was all right and "Pete" would drive off. One officer remembered "That man would show up on a call at midnight and then ask us if we knew what businesses were open in our districts, how often they were robbed and were we watching for such and such police character".

Since it is very difficult to be a police officer for very long without getting complained on, most officers have had the experience of having been summoned to a commander's office to defend and explain their actions on a call or traffic stop. Most officers, whether they like to admit it or not, know when they've got a reprimand coming and will accept it maturely. It's the ones given just to be politically expedient or to pacify a complainant, right or wrong be damned, that they find objectionable. If that ever happened under Bill Peterman, the word never got around.

Peterman was known to be brusque with citizens who came to his office with frivolous, petty or unjustified complaints on his officers. More than one officer has been seated in the waiting area outside of the Major's office when they saw a citizen leaving hurriedly followed by Pete's voice trailing them ".....outta here or I'll put your ass in jail myself". The Major would then stroll out with his hands in his pockets, look down at the waiting officer and say "Go back to work". Major Peterman would occasionally come in shift lineups and give them his philosophy of police work; "Know your old thieves and dopeheads. Hassle them whenever you can. Put 'em in jail where they belong."

He was speaking from experience. He had 32 commendations in his record, most of them for catching burglars, for which he seemed to have a special knack. The last commendation he earned was dated only nine days before his retirement. It was from the Chief of a small suburban police department whose family had been robbed in Oklahoma City. The suburban officer complimented Peterman, his officers and Detectives for their professionalism, thoroughness and compassion. Most Majors do not go to armed robbery scenes especially nine days before they are retiring but Bill Peterman wasn't most Majors. The suburban officer made the statement in his letter that "policemen aren't easily impressed by other policemen". Bill Peterman was the kind of policeman who had been impressing other policemen for a long time.

Peterman would have been concerned as the rest of the year abounded in close calls for his troops. On June 2, Officer Ted Carlton was wounded in the cheek by a bullet ricocheting off his rear view mirror in a shooting chase with armed robbers. The suspect escaped but was identified as Donald Richardson, the same man who had shot Sergeant Ben Caswell in 1969. Richardson had escaped from the State Pen and had gone back to his old trade, armed robbery. He was arrested several months later in Chicago by the F.B.I.

Officers John Clark and Mike McCall ducked flying glass and buckshot in a confrontation with a drunk suspect in a domestic fight. The officers were standing on the suspect's porch on either side of the door when the suspect fired through one of the windows beside the door. The blast was just above Officer McCall's head. McCall was 5 feet 8 inches tall, Clark was 6 feet 6 inches. If their positions had been reversed, Clark would probably have been killed by the shotgun blast.

Officer Bob Woods killed a residential burglar in far northwest Oklahoma City. Officers Charlie Gooch and Gary Ward traded shots in a chase with a former convict on South Pennsylvania. Officers Dennis Prater and Gary Damron arrested an armed patron in a bar at N.W. 30th and Pennsylvania after he pulled the trigger on his pistol, only to have it misfire inches in front of their faces.

Officers Doug Phipps and Ron Owens faced down an armed drunk after responding to a reported sniper incident a few blocks north of Police Headquarters. It wasn't a sniper, just a drunk who shot through his own front door and hit a neighbor in the foot. When he opened his front door pointing the gun at the officers, both drew their weapons. Some tense moments of negotiation followed until the drunk surrendered after being convinced of the folly of confronting a .357 Magnum and a 12-gauge shotgun with his .22 revolver at a range of less than six feet.

Over 100 officers surrounded three trapped armed robbers in a supermarket at N.E. 36th and Springlake Drive. Negotiations, some conducted by Chief Purser, resulted in a tense but peaceful conclusion. Chief Purser was interviewed by a local reporter and stated that "for some reason a lot of people seem to be suddenly interested in shooting our officers".

The pattern was still intact on September 17. Three-wheel motorcycle officer Ben Bridges was talking to a woman about a parking complaint across from City Hall near Colcord and Walker. As Bridges was debating with the woman, 20-year-old Roy L. Campbell of Chickasha walked up behind him and grabbed the officer's .38 revolver out of his holster. As Bridges ran for cover, Campbell fired four shots at him, fortunately missing with all of them. Campbell then stuck the officer's gun in his belt and began nonchalantly strolling toward the police station two blocks away.

A parking lot owner who had witnessed the incident jumped in his car and drove the two blocks to the police station. In front of the station, he began telling his story to the first officer he found, who happened to be Patrol Lieutenant Dennis Berglan. As he was telling it, he saw Campbell coming across the street toward the station and told Berglan "There he is!".

Berglan observed the gun stuck in the man's waistband and, drawing his own weapon, yelled at the man not to draw the gun. Campbell went for the gun anyway and got off one shot before Berglan shot him. The shots must have been almost simultaneous because Berglan did not initially realize that Campbell had fired at him.

In the midst of all this, the FOP and the City were at odds over pay. Studies showed that City police pay was behind that of comparably sized cities and police departments. The FOP wanted a 10 percent raise and the City offered 7 1/2 percent. The City Administration, led by Mayor Patience Latting, City Manager Howard McMahan and Personnel Director Dave Falk, refused and the issue was presented to a neutral arbitration panel. The arbitrators recommended the 10 percent raise. Since the arbitrator's decision was not binding upon the City, they again refused.

*The first FOP Lodge #123 Hall—'Old Blue'—at 715 West Sheridan.*

Through the first week in October, there had been 30 officer-involved shooting incidents that year. In the last one of those, on October 7, Officers Byron Woods and Hollis Harper had become involved in a domestic call that escalated to gunfire when the suspect opened up on them with a shotgun. The suspect was killed and Officer Woods was hospitalized with serious wounds. It was going to be hard to convince the officers that they didn't deserve that extra 2 1/2 percent. But the City negotiators were intransigent and tempers were growing short.

On October 22, most of the nearly 600 officers began a "work slowdown". There was no clause in the City's contract with the Police Department prohibiting such work actions, slowdowns, stoppages or even strikes. At the time of the first contract in 1971, it never occurred to anyone such a clause would be needed. Teamsters went on strike, auto workers struck, garbagemen, bus drivers, garment workers but cops?.......never! Never say never.

On the contrary, police strikes were not unheard of. Almost 75 percent of the Boston Police had gone on strike in 1919, leading to chaos and a callout of the state militia. Less than half a dozen years before, New Orleans had suffered a similar, though not as drastic, labor problem. Astute politicians had even been able to use the disharmony to their benefit on occasion. His settlement of the 1919 Boston Police strike became a significant political stepping stone for the then-Governor of Massachusetts. Calvin Coolidge became the vice-presidential nominee the next year and, three years later, President of the United States. In 1975, there were no Calvin Coolidges in Oklahoma City government.

Few tickets were written and most officers would not respond to dispatcher's calls. Dispatchers began broadcasting priority calls without expecting an answer and just hoping someone would show up. On the serious ones, someone usually did but you couldn't tell it by listening to the police radio. For the citizens, it was a bad time to have a traffic accident or need a police report taken.

Officers of all ranks and assignments had been discussing, debating and arguing the issues for the last three days. Between scout cars parked side by side on street corners, Detectives standing in the halls, supervisors and commanders in offices and coffee shops, the debate raged. Sarcastic statements like "Let's have Patience", a pun on the Mayor's name, began circulating as a derisive comment on the City's intransigence. The citizens were suffering from the neglect, the public image and reputation of both City and Police was being smudged. The general opinion of the rank and file was that they were stuck between a rock and a hard place. The work slowdown was not having any effect except to hurt everyone involved and would have to continue for an indeterminate period of time to effect any real change. Rumors of escalating to a full fledged strike began circulating.

Since the union had been organized, their headquarters had been a tin building at 715 West Sheridan. Nicknamed "Old Blue" because of its pale blue color, its main accommodations for the members were a pool table and a soda pop machine that dispensed canned beer. Crammed to full capacity with the folding metal chairs provided for meetings, the building probably could comfortably hold 150 people at most. On the afternoon of October 24, a meeting was called by FOP President Jim Parsons at the Lodge Hall. What followed has been described by some who witnessed it as "a police riot". A non-violent one but a riot nonetheless.

*October 24, 1975. Dozens of OCPD badges litter a conference table in City Hall, surrounded by City Councilmen and Mayor Patience Latting (lower right). Hundreds more have already been removed.*

The small building was jammed with officers, on and off duty, shoulder to shoulder and spilling out into the street. The parking lot was full of scout cars from the swing shift that had just come on duty. Fiery oratory from a number of officers, some of them supervisors, inflamed already shortened tempers. Officers got on their radios in their scout cars in the parking lot and transmitted on all frequencies "All officers 10-19 City Hall". The signal "10-19" actually means return to the station. By adding "City Hall" to it, it left no doubt in anyone's mind who heard it what was going to happen.

As an emergency meeting of the Finance Committee was in progress in City Hall, the front steps and grounds filled with hundreds of officers along with some wives and girlfriends. The area around the building became clogged with black and white police cars, three wheelers and motorcycles. They were parked at every angle on the sidewalks, on the lawn, in the gardens

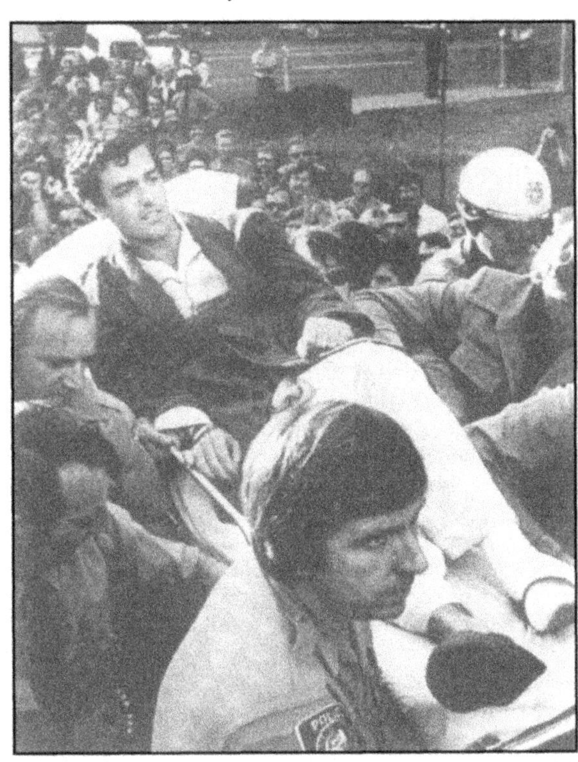

*Led by Officer Paul D. Taylor, OCPD officers carry a wounded Byron Wood into City Hall to add his badge to the growing pile on the City Council's conference table.*

and some were left sitting in the middle of the streets. They were blocking streets, sidewalks, fire hydrants and bus stops. Some officers, of a mindset to burn bridges behind them, removed the keys from their vehicles and threw them into the storm drains.

The mass then stormed into City Hall and into the conference room. Parsons made a short statement to the assembled City administrators that could have been summed up simply as "I told you so". The officers then formed a single line and, with relative silence and orderliness, filed through the room. As each passed the conference table, they unpinned the gold and silver badges from their chests or removed them from badge cases and tossed them into an ever-growing pile in the middle of the conference table.

Psychological warfare was employed as well. Some officers went to the hospital where Officer Byron Woods was still recovering from the shotgun wounds he had received earlier in the month. An ambulance was summoned and directed to City Hall. As the line of officers was still filing through the conference room, a group of officers carried Woods on his gurney up the front steps of City Hall and to the front of the line, where Woods added his badge to the pile. Eventually, that pile was to contain all but 16 of the 599 badges carried by active duty officers...and one more.

A 12-year-old boy suffering from leukemia in a local hospital had been unofficially adopted by the officers. They had donated 75 pints of blood to him. The officers also brought him souvenirs, not toys, like a real police whistle, a cap and a badge. According to the newspaper reports, the boy asked his mother to take his badge down and turn it in with the others.

A force of Oklahoma Highway Patrol troopers and Oklahoma County Sheriff's units responded quickly to try to maintain order in the City. They had been alerted to this possibility since the beginning of the slow down several days earlier. OCPD commanders, some of whom had been performing administrative duties for years, began manning scout cars and taking calls.

For the next three days, the newspapers and newscasts had a heyday. The media waited outside as officers met in the abandoned Center Theater across the street from City Hall. They eagerly filmed as officers came in from their days off, vacations and sick leave to pin their badges on the huge curtain over the stage. The editorial page was filled with scolding articles from officer's wives, letters criticizing the strikers, letters supporting the strikers, letters supporting the 16 who didn't strike and so forth.

The news made the cartoon page, too. One showed Mayor Latting screaming after a retreating shadow "Help, purse snatcher, call a cop!". The next frame showed her saying "Wait a minute. That WAS a cop!". Another took advantage of the proximity of Halloween. It showed a uniformed officer holding a trick or treat bag in one hand and a smoking gun in the other. The officer was standing in front of a doorway with a prostrate body labelled "John Q. Citizen" lying dead. The cartoon was captioned "I told you so!".

Stories and photo spreads also documented the State Troopers getting used to the City Police cars with their multiple frequency radios tuned according to which area of the City they were assigned and the shotgun mounted prominently standing straight up between the driver and passenger sides of the front seat. The steel mesh screens between the front and rear seats were also new to them.

The stories told of troopers checking out City maps and street guides. Response time to calls was slow if they were off of the main arteries as troopers called headquarters for directions in the residential areas. The state officers, used to dealing primarily with traffic violations and accidents, found the profusion of misdemeanor and felony criminal activity somewhat unusual but managed to muddle through. Some stories, possibly apocryphal, began circulating about frustrated troopers firing in the air to break up domestic quarrels and feisty crowds.

In spite of the tensions, they apparently did not extend to the relations between the drafted state officers and the striking City officers. Both groups understood the respective situations they were in and troopers told of being invited down to the FOP Lodge for coffee after their shifts were over. Shortly into the strike, two troopers were interviewed in a coffee shop. Asked for their opinions after a few days of doing the City officer's jobs, one was quoted as saying "Whatever it is they're paying them, it's not enough."

Finally, after three days of offers and counter-offers, the strike was settled. A nine percent raise and additional benefits were agreed upon. The officers agreed to accept no pay for the three days they didn't work in return for a guarantee of no retaliation against the strikers. Thus a very unpleasant chapter for all concerned was closed.

The next year, and in every succeeding year, one of the first clauses in the contract between the City and the Police was one prohibiting strikes, slowdowns or work actions of any kind.

This year of great divisiveness also saw the production of the most comprehensive yearbook to date as well as a new Policy and Procedures Manual. Both City and Police administrators were beginning to get the idea. There was a need to write down the responses to every potential situation, how it should and should not be handled, and why it should be that way. The old days of depending upon "common sense", unwritten rules, implied understandings and the tried and true "because we've always done it that way" were gone. No longer did the boss have unlimited power, no longer could things be done with a handshake and a promise.

The 1975 Oklahoma City Police Yearbook was by far the most ambitious, comprehensive and professional effort thus far. This was primarily due to the editorial assistance of Mike Brake, a police reporter for The Oklahoma Journal. Nearly 200 pages long, the book had a durable dark blue binding with a chrome OCPD Patrolman's badge stamped into the front cover. The Administrative section profiled the sorely-tried Chief I.G. Purser and his Assistants Tom Heggy and Gerald Emmett. A twelve-page section was devoted to photographs and articles on the 24 OCPD officers that had been killed in the line of duty to that point.

The first Division profiled, as befitted its status as the largest, was Major Bill Peterman's Patrol Division. The 299 photos of Patrol personnel were followed by articles on special units in the Division including the Selective Enforcement Unit, Bomb Squad, Canine Unit, Community Service Officers and Helicopter Unit. The photos of the 109 members of Major Lloyd Gramling's Traffic Division was next with unit histories on Traffic Law Enforcement (motorcycles and radar cars), Traffic Direction and Control (three wheeled motorcycles), Hit and Run, Ambulance and Taxi Inspectors, Accident Investigation, Safety Education and the Alcohol Safety Action Project.

The photos of the 119 personnel of the Detective Division preceded profiles of the Youth Counselors, Stolen Goods, Homicide-Robbery, Forgery, Youth Bureau, Vice and the Polygraph Examiners. Next came the photos of the 153 personnel assigned to Major Bob Wilder's Headquarters Division to staff Communications, the Jail, Property Room, Crime Laboratory, Records Bureau and Administrative Services Unit. Major Jim Nutter's Special Services Division pictured 29 officers who staffed the Firing Range, Internal Security, Community Relations and the Training Academy.

A section picturing 48 retired officers preceded a 51-page retrospective of the history of the Department that contained many rare and unique photos. Small sections on the history of the Honor Guard and the FOP preceded several pages of humorous snapshots of officers.

## McALESTER NEWS-CAPITAL
## November 5, 1975

### RITES FRIDAY FOR LAST OF FBI'S EARLY DAY 'GANGBUSTERS'

The article under this headline at the top of the front page told of the career of the late Clarence O. Hurt. Hurt died from cancer the day before at the hospital in McAlester, Oklahoma, at the age of 80. Born in Springfield, Illinois, on March 14, 1895, his parents had come to Oklahoma during his infancy. He joined the OCPD on September 25, 1919, after serving in the Army during World War I.

He served as a motorcycle officer and in scout cars for several years. He had been Jess Sosbee's partner the night Sosbee was shot to death from ambush just before Christmas of 1922. Hurt later was a special investigator assigned to the Osage Hills murders in the mid-1920s. He then became a Detective in the Auto Theft Bureau before becoming Superintendent of the Bureau in 1928. The next year, he was named Assistant Chief by Chief Charles Becker. He held this position until being returned to the rank of Detective by Chief Watt in

1931. Two of his wife's brothers, Jack and Douglas Gates, were killed while serving as OCPD officers in the early 1930s.

At the end of 1933, Hurt had been one of a group of officers that included Jelly Bryce who were involved in the shootout in Shawnee that killed Wilbur Underhill, known as the "Tri-State Terror" for his violent activities in Missouri, Kansas, Oklahoma and his alleged participation in the Kansas City Massacre. Less than six months later, Hurt took a "leave of absence" to join the FBI. He remained with the Bureau until he resigned in 1944 for personal reasons. Rejoining them the next year, Hurt retired from the FBI in 1955 to run his ranch six miles east of McAlester in Pittsburg County, Oklahoma. Three years later, Hurt was elected Sheriff of Pittsburg County, completing two terms in that office before fully retiring in 1966.

The anecdotes and legends about Hurt abounded. Some of the stories can be disproven and marked down to the enthusiasm of the storytellers. With a man of Clarence Hurt's accomplishments, the false legends can be debunked without reflecting upon the man. As with most stories about famous (and infamous) people, some were probably apocryphal, some overstated, some understated but there had to be at least a grain of truth in each. People don't tell these kinds of stories about people if no one would believe them. Some were told by Hurt to his children. As one homespun philosopher remarked once about false modesty, "If you done it, it ain't braggin'".

Hurt was alleged to have been the first to drive an auto for the OCPD. This is doubtful since the OCPD had automobiles almost a decade before Hurt joined the force, while he was still a teenager. Photos exist of Chief W.B. Nichols behind the wheel of an OCPD scout car. Chief Nichols had come and gone before Hurt ever joined the force.

He was also alleged to have been the first lawman to carry a machine gun which would seem to be very difficult to substantiate. He was also supposed to have been the first local police officer hired by the FBI to protect their agents when they couldn't carry weapons. Hurt was definitely one of the first two OCPD officers hired by the Bureau. When he was hired, however, the federal agents had just been given Congressional authority to arm themselves. The Feds could carry guns, they just didn't have the practical experience of using them against targets that shot back like Jerry Campbell, Clarence Hurt and Jelly Bryce did.

He allegedly cradled John Dillinger in his arms while the bank robber died. Some stories were even told that Hurt carried Dillinger to a Catholic church for the last rites. I find both tales a little farfetched. But Hurt was definitely the last survivor of the trio of agents who actually shot Dillinger. Agent Herman Hollis had been killed in a gunfight with Baby Face Nelson a few months after Dillinger's death and Agent Charles B. Winstead had passed away on August 3, 1973.

Hurt had allegedly been involved in the cases of Pretty Boy Floyd, Ma Barker's gang, Machine Gun Kelley, Bonnie and Clyde, Matt Kimes and Alvin Karpis. Several tales were told that countered the old tale about J. Edgar Hoover personally arresting Karpis in New Orleans in 1936. Karpis himself said in an interview in 1971 that Hoover had been present at his arrest but only after a number of other agents had him covered. Another of the stories had it that Hurt was escorting Hoover away from the area for his safety when they accidentally ran into Karpis. Hurt allegedly took Karpis into custody, tying the man's hands together by knotting his necktie around them.

During World War II, Hurt was sent to Pearl Harbor to investigate reported leaks in top secret military information. He remained to work with Naval Intelligence for the rest of the war.

Another story concerned how Hurt decided to run for Sheriff in Pittsburg County after leaving the Bureau. Allegedly an inmate of the Oklahoma State Prison, which is also in McAlester, sent word to Hurt that he wanted to see him about something important. When Hurt went to see the man, he was told about an impending prison break being planned with guns to be smuggled into the prison in books with the pages cut out. Hurt alerted the authorities, the books were confiscated with the guns inside and the escape attempt was foiled.

Just two years before his death, Hurt had been a technical advisor to a motion picture about the life and death of Dillinger that had been filmed in Oklahoma City. The movie's producers had used the Midwest Theater as a double for the Biograph Theater because of the similarities between them. Bemused OCPD officers had provided traffic control and security around the set during the filming.

Violent crime was rising and changing in nature as well. There were only 76 homicides in the City in 1976 but the clearance rate was only 75 percent. The homicide unit was used to clearing over 90 percent of their cases. Murders were becoming more random, more vicious, more bizarre and more difficult to solve. The worst was yet to come.

In July of 1976, Assistant Chief Gerald Emmett introduced the Department newsletter, The Cosmopolitan. Later that year, the newly constructed Police/Fire Training Center at 800 N. Portland became the new home of the Police Academy. In December of 1976, Class #76 became the first class to graduate from the new facility.

Also that month the OCPD acquired its first Police Chaplain. Dalton Barnes, a retired Army Chaplain, became the first man to hold the new position, his salary paid by grants from the Home Mission Board and the Oklahoma Baptist Convention. In accordance with the philosophy that a cop sees more misery, bloodshed, trouble and sunrises than the average person, Chaplain Barnes immediately began providing a sympathetic ear to the problems of the officers.

An incident on November 17 illustrated that those who intend to survive in this world need to pay closer attention to the details, especially if you are a fleeing felon. Larry Dale Lemmons was a resident of the area near N.W. 1st Terrace and Pennsylvania, known as the "Flats". An area of run-down shacks and seedy bars bisected by railroad tracks, it was one of the more notorious white combat zones in the City where felons were a little thicker and life was a little cheaper.

Five days earlier, Lemmons had delivered a vicious beating to his girlfriend that resulted in her being hospitalized with a broken jaw and him dodging a felony charge. Shortly before 4 P.M. on the afternoon of the 17th, some neighbors saw Lemmons enter his residence and called police. They reported that Lemmons had left his house carrying a suitcase and walking south towards Interstate 40.

Responding to the radio broadcast, Sgt. John LeMaster spotted Lemmons near Reno and Pennsylvania. Jumping out of his scout car, LeMaster chased him toward the railroad tracks. As Lemmons hotfooted it down the tracks, LeMaster fired a warning shot from his service revolver, yelling at him to stop or he would shoot again. Lemmons stopped, turned toward the officer and said "Go ahead and shoot me. I want to die". As Lemmons turned to run again, LeMaster fired again. At 4:37 P.M., Lemmons was dead on arrival at Saint Anthony's Hospital.

The events of the previous year had pointed out that the FOP needed a larger building for their meetings. During this year, the FOP began sponsoring bingo games at N.W. 16th and Indiana to raise money for a new Lodge Hall. A number of buildings were surveyed and a selection was finally made. At 1624 S. Agnew was the old Black Angus Restaurant and the attached Maverick Club. Easily several times larger than "Old Blue", the old Lodge Hall, the members moved their bingo games down there and began remodeling as they went. Two years of bingo games paid the building off. Shortly afterwards the bingo games were discontinued.

On January 18, 1977, Chief I.G. Purser retired and was replaced by Assistant Chief Tom Heggy. Although 45 years old, Heggy only had slightly over 16 1/2 years on the Department when he took the Chief's job. This meant he would have to last almost 3 1/2 years in a position with an average tenure of 2 years before he became eligible for retirement. Long nicknamed "Von Heggy", he was a personable man of German extraction who was popular with the line officers. He affected a somewhat Prussian bearing that was offset by a dry sense of humor. When exasperated, he usually muttered to himself, presumably swearing, in German. He had

*Chief Tom Heggy.*

*Sergeant Terry G. Lawson.*

been pictured in the 1975 Annual wearing a black suit with white stitching that field officers jokingly said resembled an SS uniform.

With half a dozen college degrees himself, Heggy's emphasis on education was reflected in his Department. Over 90 percent of his 669 officers had some college and 43 percent of them had degrees. Heggy was also a proponent of "civilianization", the process of freeing as many officers as possible for enforcement functions by replacing them with civilians. He had 184 of them to prove it.

As a matter of course, police officers see senseless tragedies on a daily basis. On April 19, one of those senseless tragedies involved one of their own. During the early morning hours, veteran officers were conducting a night field problem for police recruits. The problem chosen was a simulated gangfight in a parking lot in the 3900 block of N.W. 3rd, about half a mile from the Police Academy. Captain Bruce Shaw, the Director of Training, had them using blank ammunition to increase the realism of the situation. It was a mistake.

During the exercise, 15-year veteran Sergeant Terry Lawson was portraying an armed felon. As Lawson drew his weapon during the scenario, Recruit Jim Hatfield drew his and fired twice at close range into Lawson's right side. While harmless beyond a few yards, at extremely close range blank ammunition fires wadding that can be just as dangerous as a bullet.

Lawson was quickly placed in a scout car and rushed to the hospital. In spite of surgery to repair his damaged liver, the 38-year-old recipient of 15 commendations died on April 21st. Due to his easy-going manner and dry sense of humor, Lawson was a popular supervisor. An Explosive Ordinance Disposal expert, he had been one of the original members of the Bomb Squad when it had been organized four years earlier. The officers on his shift immediately began taking up contributions. The result was a bronze bust displayed on a pedestal under a plaque in the newly opened Police Training Center on Portland Avenue.

The day after Lawson died, the class of 33 police recruits he had helped train graduated. The class spokesman, Officer Charles Allen, delivered an emotional eulogy to Lawson. In an unintended irony, Recruit Jim Hatfield was presented the class trophy for marksmanship. Hatfield remained on the Department and went on to become a highly decorated officer. The use of blank ammunition in training exercises was immediately discontinued.

There is an old cop's superstition that bad things usually happen in patterns of threes. The superstition was to gain more credence during a three-week period this April. Not long before Terry Lawson's tragic death, OHP Trooper Larry Crabtree was shot and killed during a traffic stop. On April 27, two days after Lawson's funeral, OHP Lieutenant Cell Howell was killed in a hit- and-run traffic accident in southwest Oklahoma City.

Heggy wasted no time in earning his reputation as an innovator. The homicide rate was almost doubling and, being assigned to the same unit, lesser assaults and sex crimes were going uninvestigated. Heggy formed a separate Sex Crimes Unit with five Detectives and a Sergeant. The Robbery-Homicide Unit was separated into two separate units. A Crime Analysis Unit was created with civilian analysts to study crime patterns and collate street intelligence into useful information. Computers began making gradual inroads into the Department. Heggy also utilized the first assessment center for staff promotions and, as a result, Captain Marvin Maxwell was promoted to Major.

Almost three years after her death, Karen Silkwood's shadow still loomed large. By now, it had cast itself from Crescent, Oklahoma to Washington, D.C. It had also fallen on the steps of the OCPD.

When she died in her crumpled Honda Civic that evening in November of 1974, Silkwood had been on her way to a clandestine meeting at the Holiday Inn Northwest in Oklahoma City. She had been less than half an hour away from a meeting with an official of the Oil, Chemical and Atomic Workers Union from Washington, D.C. and a reporter from the New York Times. Herself contaminated with plutonium, she was supposed to provide them with documentation that defective plutonium fuel rods were being produced by Kerr-McGee.

Much had transpired in that three years. The security director for Kerr-McGee was Jim Reading, a retired OCPD Captain of Detectives; the same Jim Reading who had organized Chief Hollingsworth's Intelligence Unit in 1962, had helped trace the hijackers that shot John Rowden the following year and later commanded the Robbery/Homicide Unit.

The FBI had instituted an investigation that had been decried as a coverup. Inconsistencies had turned up. Lawyers, private investigators, Federal agents and God only knows who else was running from coast to coast with their noses to the ground. Lawyers had been hired and lawsuits had been filed. Theories, accusations and speculations about murder, conspiracies and involvement of intelligence agencies were rampant. Confidential informants and code names were blossoming faster than John Le Carre' and Ian Fleming together could have cranked them out; Echo, White House, White House II, Fairy Godfather, Sierra and others. Reports were being made that indicated that Karen Silkwood had been under both physical and electronic surveillance before her death. One of "Echo's" allegations was that the OCPD had "[Central Intelligence Agency] or [National Security Agency] undercover personnel either in the Intelligence Unit or the Department's upper ranks". In a back-handed compliment, "Echo" also said that the OCPD "had a wiretapping and bugging unit equipped with the best electronic gear in the central United States". It was neither the first nor the last insinuation of CIA and/or NSA involvement with the OCPD and the Silkwood case.

The information about the case became even more ethereal. A psychic had visions of three cars following Silkwood immediately before her crash, even describing the men in the cars and that they "seemed to be in radio contact" with each other.

Then the credibility of the informants improved somewhat. One was Trudy Preston. She had been the secretary of the OCPD Intelligence Unit in 1969-70 and told of typing reports concerning illegal entries, lock-picking, wiretapping and bugging. She brought up the names of Lt. Bill Vetter and Sgt. Larry Upchurch.

Following a lead obtained at the Don Quixote Club, a night club in the Holiday Inn Northwest (where Silkwood's last meeting had been scheduled), one of the private investigators located an unnamed homosexual former Intelligence Detective who had been fired from the OCPD in 1975. He said that OCPD Intelligence officers had the best training available and the best equipment on the market. He alleged that he had been involved in numerous incidents of illegal entries, bugging and wiretapping. Some of the unverified incidents he mentioned included officers surreptitiously entering Black Muslim headquarters and photographing their mailing lists, bugging the hotel room of radical leader Abbie Hoffman and wiretapping the phone of an Iranian student suspected of smuggling guns. He also portrayed Detective Larry Baker as the "King of Wiretapping" for OCPD and said that Lt. Bill Vetter maintained close ties with Kerr-McGee security director Jim Reading.

During the first five months of 1978, nearly a dozen former and current OCPD officers were subpoenaed to give testimony in depositions. Jim Reading was asked about Kerr-McGee's security measures and his knowledge of Karen Silkwood. Officer Bill Byler, an OCPD Crime Lab photographer, had allegedly met Silkwood at one point, reported to ATF about seeing some M-16 automatic rifles in the possession of one of her associates and had photographed portions of a diary involved in the case. Two former commanders of the OCPD Intelligence Unit, Lieutenants Bill Vetter and Bob Hicks, were deposed along with the current commander of the unit (since renamed the Organized Crime Unit) , Lt. Ken R. Smith. Sergeant Larry Upchurch was questioned about his lock-picking skills and Detectives Larry Baker and Dave McBride about their wiretapping experiences. Questions were raised about whether OCPD officers received training at the National Intelligence Academy or used electronic devices purchased from Audio Intelligences Devices Corporation, both in Florida. Lastly, Chief Heggy discussed his orders to Lt. Smith to discontinue use of the equipment and his refusal to start an administrative investigation within his department while the court proceedings were in progress. The civil trial of Silkwood vs. Kerr-McGee would roll on for another year.

Between August of 1977 and March of 1978, the Department conducted their first "sting" operation. Funded with $76,000 from the Law Enforcement Assistance Administration, "Operation Easy Money" recovered over $1,250,000 in stolen property and resulted in the arrest of over 200 defendants.

Major Robert V. Wilder, grandson of H.V. Wilder, was transferred to command the Detective Division in mid-July of 1978. His first day in the job was greeted by Oklahoma City's crime of the century.

On the evening of July 16, 1978, an armed robbery occurred at the Sirloin Stockade restaurant at 1620 S.W. 74 after closing. Six employees, four of them teenagers, were found executed in the walk-in freezer. Assistant manager Louis Zacarias, 43, cook David Lindsey, 17, janitor Isaac Freeman, 56, and busboys Anthony Tew, 17, and David Salsman, 15, were found dead at the scene. The only female, waitress Terri Horst, 16, was still alive when discovered but died before reaching the hospital. The City's entire force of a dozen homicide investigators was mobilized.

Hardened Detectives who thought they had seen everything walked into a mind-boggling crime scene; dozens of tables, hundreds of dishes, thousands of knives, forks and spoons to be fingerprinted; bullets and fragments to be cut out of boxes of frozen steaks while walking on a sheet of frozen blood several inches thick. The investigation mushroomed rapidly to include over 40 Detectives and other officers on special assignment.

A suspect vehicle described as a green Oldsmobile Vista Cruiser station wagon was received from a witness on the nearby interstate highway. Massive computer print-outs listing this type of vehicle were checked out, hundreds of possible witnesses and suspects were interviewed, thousands of telephone tips were screened and prioritized.

The jurisdiction expanded when connections were made between the Stockade killings and the executions of the three members of the Lorenz family near Purcell a month earlier. A contingent of detectives, officers and OSBI agents covered Purcell like a blanket, some almost living there for two months.

After almost a year, Roger Dale and Verna Stafford were arrested in Chicago, Illinois. The

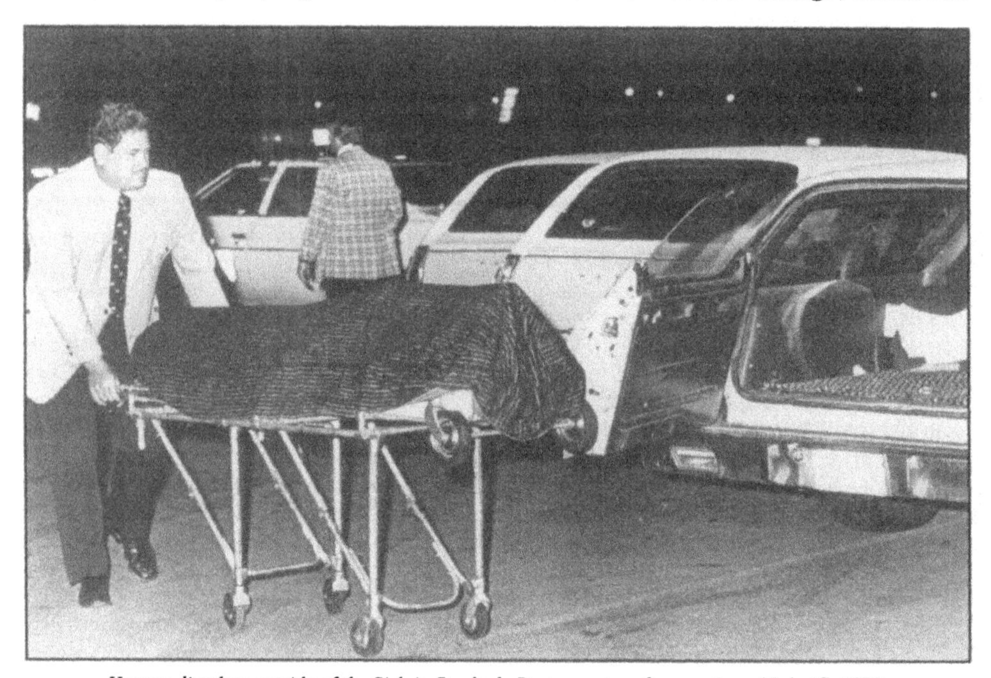

*Hearses lined up outside of the Sirloin Stockade Restaurant on the morning of July 17, 1978.*

third suspect in the crimes, Roger's brother Harold, had already been killed in a motorcycle crash. Tried the following year, Verna was allowed to plead guilty to a ten-year armed robbery sentence in return for her testimony. Roger Dale Stafford went to Death Row under nine death sentences for the family at Purcell as well as the Sirloin Stockade murders.

The previous year, the Sex Crimes Unit had been created because the Homicide Unit didn't have the proper time and personnel to devote to the investigations. The Stockade investigation pointed out that they also didn't have the time or personnel for non-fatal assault cases. On August 1, 1978, Chief Heggy created an Assault Squad. Four officers were given a one step pay raise to "assignment pay", placed under a Sergeant in the Detective Division and assigned all non-fatal assaults. Originally, the officers so assigned were those on the Detective's promotion list and assignment to the Assault Squad was implied as a virtual guarantee that the officer would be promoted in the near future.

As the decade neared its end, Oklahoma City was firmly entrenched in the big leagues. The Forensic Laboratory had just completed their new facility on the second floor of headquarters. The police budget was almost $20 million annually. For the first time, the Department achieved a ratio of two officers for every 1,000 citizens, still below the national average but improving. A force of 761 officers and 197 civilians utilized 352 vehicles to serve 384,000 citizens over 629 square miles.

One of the newest vehicles was a brand new Chevrolet 3/4 ton Metro Van purchased by the Independent Insurance Agents of Oklahoma City for the Crime Prevention Unit. The unit used the van to transport displays and hand-out materials to teach crime prevention and safety education. The bicycle safety program was the most popular.

Two traditions were broken in 1978 and another was reinstated. First, the Department ordered Kawasaki 1000 motorcycles to replace the aging fleet of Harley Davidsons. The high pitched whine of the accelerating Japanese bikes was irritating to the old timers who missed the rumble and thunder of the Harleys.

Second, Major Bob Wilder was able to get approval to issue his Detectives gold badges. Prior to that time, gold badges were reserved for supervisors of the ranks of Sergeant and above. All other badges were silver. Detectives were issued small, silver wallet-sized badges with "Detective" stamped into it. When they were promoted, they kept their patrolman's badge since it was the only full sized badge they had to wear with a uniform. The new Detective badges were full-sized in the same style as the other badges but they were slightly curved instead of flat. The "Oklahoma City Police-Detective" and the badge number were embossed on the surface in black instead of stamped into it. The Detectives loved them. Wilder even had the Division's entrance hall redone in dark brown wallpaper with a pattern of rows of the new gold badges.

The tradition reinstated was the cars. After the white Ramblers, that experiment was dropped. Police cars were once again Fords, Chevrolets, Plymouths and Dodges. Best of all, they were black and white again.

Citizen assistance in solving crimes was solicited through the implementation of the Crimestoppers program. Actual crime scenes were recreated on video tape, narrated by police personnel and broadcast on local television channels. In its first year, the program would be responsible for clearing 147 felony crimes and the arrests of 91 felony suspects for an expenditure of $14,250 in privately funded rewards. A system of victim notification letters began showing more concern for crime victims.

The north and south briefing stations, named the Will Rogers and Santa Fe Divisions respectively, were occupied on April 2, 1979. The Department was decentralizing. For the first time, officers would come to work and never come to the central police headquarters except to book prisoners.

The Silkwood vs. Kerr-McGee case ended on May 18. A number of conclusions were reached, officially and unofficially; Kerr-McGee was found to have been negligent in allowing Karen Silkwood to become contaminated with plutonium and a judgement of over ten and a half million dollars was rendered against them; conspiracy charges against Kerr-McGee and the FBI had been dismissed; there was insufficient evidence to legally proceed with any of the murder theories; and apparently the OCPD had considerably more extensive and sophisticated intelligence-gathering capabilities than expected.

*Will Rogers Briefing Station under construction on August 14, 1978.*

June 1, 1979, saw the presentation of the first Departmental medals under a new system of awards that Chief Heggy had introduced the previous summer. The medals were awarded in conjunction with the graduation ceremonies of Class 83 at the Training Center. The new system augmented the former practice of written commendations and letters of appreciation from supervisors, citizens and civic groups. The first OCPD Medals of Valor, the third-highest award behind the Medal of Honor and the Police Cross, were awarded to Officers Beau James and Jim Hatfield. On October 2 of the previous year, the two officers were eating lunch in an oriental restaurant next to a gun store. A mentally deranged man entered the gun store, grabbed an AR-15 assault rifle (the semi-automatic version of the M-16) and began shooting randomly. The officers ran outside and became involved in a running gunbattle with the suspect for two blocks before the suspect committed suicide.

The first Life Saving Awards were presented to Officers John Windle and Ray Ledford for rescuing residents from a fire in a South Robinson hotel the previous November, and to Officers Jay Einhorn and John Kane for resuscitating a woman who had a heart attack in March. The first Meritorious Service Award was not awarded until several months later in conjunction with the graduation of the next recruit class. It was presented to Officer J.J. Young, one of the Department's helicopter pilots, for rescuing motorists stranded in snow drifts during a blizzard the previous February. Young had airlifted the people out in extremely hazardous flying conditions.

Four days after the awards ceremony, former Chief Wayne Lawson died from cancer prematurely at the age of 57. Lawson had been the Chief who created the Special Services Division in 1969. After retiring, Lawson had served a year as the Assistant Director of the State Department of Corrections and had then become the Commissioner of the Department of Public Safety until his health began failing.

The Technical Investigations Unit attained several firsts for the year. Sergeant Tom Bevel became the first OCPD officer to qualify as an expert in blood splatter interpretation. Bevel and another of the unit's Sergeants, Gary James, became the first American police officers to be invited to attend a six-week school of specialized training conducted by London's Scotland Yard. In addition, a new Forensic Laboratory was created with six chemists divided into Drugs and Serology sections. Prior to this time, all drug and serological evidence had been sent to the OSBI Laboratory. The City's burgeoning homicide rate and drug seizures pointed out the necessity of the Department having their own laboratory. With the acquisition of a color photo processor, officers had access to color mug shots replacing the old black and white ones.

An official OCPD flag was designed and adopted. Blue with a gold border, it displayed the logo "Trust in the Force", a phrase Heggy adopted from the currently popular movie Star Wars.

In August, the Detective Division hosted the 41st National Robbery and Homicide Conference for over 700 investigators from all over the nation. Homicide detectives went to Houston, Atlanta, Minneapolis and other major cities to compare techniques and learn new ones. The lessons were not wasted.

Homicide was becoming an increasingly popular pastime in the city. For the previous decade, the city's number of yearly homicides had hovered around 50, had dipped as low as 35 and had not been out of the 60s. In 1976, the final count had been 46. The next year, there were 71 homicides. The next year, the rate increased again to 76. This, coupled with the magnitude of the Sirloin Stockade slaughter, led to the formation of the Sex Crimes and Assault Units to investigate the crimes against persons that Sergeant Mike Heath's "Dirty Dozen" homicide detectives didn't have time to do justice.

Since its inception, the Homicide Unit had operated as other detective units, with two-man teams of partners. With the increase in activity, the homicides were assigned to individual detectives so each of the partners might be investigating a separate homicide at the same time. In April of 1978, they decided to try a new attack. The "Dirty Dozen" were formed into three four-man teams. Modern homicide investigations often presented more things that needed to be done immediately than two men could handle. The theory was to dump double the manpower on the case at once. It worked. The team concept plus the formation of the new units allowed the clearance rate to exceed 90 percent, far above the national average. Then, as they say, cometh the deluge.

Mike Heath began the new year with 12 homicide detectives; Bill Harrison, Les McCaleb, Ron Chambers, Don Pennington, Bill Cook, Bill Lewis, Ron Owens, Steve Upchurch, Larry Andrews, Bob Tash, Larry Baldwin and Roy Sellers. The transfer of Tash and the promotions of McCaleb and Baldwin to Sergeant in February were replaced with Detectives Steve Pacheco, Larry Koonce and Rick Logan. In September, the unit's size was increased to 15 with the addition of Detectives Jerry Martin, Bob Thompson and Bob Horn to allow the formation of four teams. They needed the help.

During the first half of 1979, Oklahoma City's murder rate almost doubled compared to the year before and it didn't slow down much. The rates in cities of the same size increased by 17 percent; Oklahoma City's increased 95 percent. The homicide rate and clearance rate set records in 1979 that have not been equalled yet. There were 102 homicides in the City that year and 99 of them were solved for a 97 percent clearance rate. Even while setting the new record, the detectives returning from Houston, Atlanta, New York, Los Angeles and Kansas City were well aware that this wasn't a drop in the bucket compared to other cities problems. That suited them just fine.

Oklahoma City was changing and yet it was the same. The Karen Silkwood case had drawn dozens of people into town from both coasts and even foreign countries, defense attorneys, private investigators, journalists and others with somewhat liberal attitudes that they soon found were distinctly out of place.

A lady who was in town to assist with the Silkwood case was offended by what she considered to be the blatant sexism of a sign over a local pancake house showing a well-endowed waitress carrying pancakes over the logo "THEY'RE STACKED BETTER". Having once organized waitresses into a union in California, she decided to recruit the restaurant's employees into a picket protest. Receiving no cooperation from the employees, in the words of the author who recounted the story, "then she remembered where she was". As was pointed out to a young man from Oakland with a shattered kneecap a few years before, Oklahoma City isn't in California.

A journalist from Rolling Stone magazine who was researching a book about the Silkwood case was also surprised by the ambience of the City. While he acknowledged that the crime was not as bad as in the nation's capital, he noted that "...there was a different feeling in

Oklahoma City, a feeling of violence merely in the way men opened a door...grab, shove, slam...violence was part of the landscape". He said that Urban America met the Wild West here. As evidence of his contention he cited two of the City's more spectacular crimes in the last nine months; the six executions in the Sirloin Stockade and a woman whose dismembered body was recovered over a period of several days spread over a half-square-mile area near the State Capitol. While he got a few of the details wrong, his analysis of the environment was right. Violence was part of the landscape.

On September 19, the Airport Police received a call about a woman with a young boy acting strangely, walking down one of the roads bordering the airport and throwing clothes away on the roadside. Officers Garland Garrison and Teresa Wells were sent to investigate. Garrison, a seven-year veteran at 50 years of age, had retired from the Air Force as a Master Sergeant after tours of duty in Korea and Viet Nam before joining the OCPD. Wells, 24, had been an officer for two years.

Shortly after 8:30 A.M., when the officers located Rita Nauni, a 31-year-old American Indian, and her ten-year-old son walking in the 5400 block of South Meridian, they began questioning her. They noted that she had arrived on a 6:30 A.M. flight from California and her behavior was becoming increasingly erratic. As Officer Garrison was putting the boy in the scout car, Nauni attacked Officer Wells, taking control of her sidearm. She then shot both officers, hitting Wells in the leg and fatally wounding Garrison in the chest. Taking the officer's scout car, she left the scene. After an 8-mile chase with other officers, she was finally apprehended at N.W. 39 and I-240 when Officer Brian Joyce rammed her with his pursuing scout car. Joyce received a broken hand and ruptured spleen from the crash.

Planning was progressing on a new pistol range, a Police/Courts Criminal Justice complex and a Computer Aided Dispatch system to replace the manual card system.

The 1970s had been a time of transition for Oklahoma City. Much was for the better, some was for the worse, some was a little of both. It had been a time of major change involving one of the more ambivalent programs, the Urban Renewal Authority.

Created in 1962, the Urban Renewal Authority had been a master plan to bring the downtown area back to a position of prominence in City life. After over half a century as the literal and figurative center of the City, that prominence had begun to erode. The beginning was in 1953 when Sears had opened their new store at N.W. 23rd and Pennsylvania. The erosion became more rapid when Penn Square Shopping Mall opened in 1960, the first major commercial development outside of the downtown area.

The Urban Renewal plan called for the removal of many old buildings and the building of a new downtown. Many of the old buildings slated for destruction were mere brick edifices and commercial establishments that needed to be replaced with more modern structures. Also caught up in this plan, however, were a great many unique, ornate, architecturally or historically significant structures.

A few were saved by the City's power structure, seemingly haphazardly. The city's first skyscraper, the Colcord Building at Sheridan and Robinson, and the Daily Oklahoman building at N.W. 4th and Broadway were spared by being placed on the National Register of Historical Places in 1976 and 1978, respectively. Although they saved Colcord's skyscraper, they couldn't seem to do the same for his home. The elegant 1903 mansion at 421 N.W. 13 was razed in January of 1965 and the new headquarters for the Standard Life Insurance Company was built on the spot. A few others were saved by private firms or individuals, most notably Central High School, the Black Hotel, the Hightower Building and the Perrine/Cravens building. The Medical Arts Building and the State National Bank Building were incorporated into the First National Center. The Skirvin Hotel still stands vacant and unused today but at least it still stands.

The Herskowitz Building fell to demolition in 1970, the Roberts Hotel and the Baum Building in 1973. The Roberts was on the site of the old Two Johns Saloon on Battle Row. The Huckins Hotel, the Kingkade Hotel, the Hudson Hotel, and the Oklahoma Club Building all came down. In 1973, the Midwest Theater had been used in the filming of the movie "Dillinger" because the ornate, neon-flooded facade was a close approximation of Chicago's Biograph Theater where Dillinger met his end in 1934. The Midwest was gone before long as well as the Warner, the State, the Criterion and the Harber/Cooper and the site of the old

Oklahoma City Athletic Club, where Jess Willard started boxing and Jake Barnes gambled with The Big Four.

The year 1977 was particularly destructive. On April 17, the Halliburton Building was brought down. The same month saw the fall of the slim Majestic Building, where Orban Patterson's office had been. In October, the 33-story Biltmore Hotel was dynamited down.

Many of these buildings could have been renovated, remodeled and saved. At great expense, no doubt, considering the outmoded plumbing, heating and electrical systems but they could have been saved. Many other cities seem to manage to successfully preserve, renovate and utilize their historic buildings for modern purposes. But it was not to be. The Myriad Convention Center was being constructed, covering almost a million square feet from Reno to Sheridan, Santa Fe to Robinson. It was ironic that the location of most of the Police Department's Awards Banquets would be built directly over Bunco Alley, Hop Boulevard and Alabaster Row. Indeed, the Myriad's Great Hall is situated almost directly over the old Hell's Half Acre. Some of the leveled buildings did not sacrifice themselves in such a worthy cause. Far too many ended up as parking lots. But a new City was going up.

As the decade ended, the term "Selective Enforcement" became not a unit but a concept and actually two units, one in the Traffic Division and one in the Patrol Division. The Traffic unit, made up of a Sergeant and six officers, targeted high accident locations for traffic enforcement while the Patrol unit would provide undercover saturation patrols for areas, usually one square mile, experiencing high burglary rates.

The decade had also set a record for violence against the nation's police officers. It had begun with over 200 officers being slain in the line of duty for the first time since 1930. It got progressively worse until a new record was set in 1974. An American law enforcement officer died in the line of duty on the average of every 33 hours that year, totalling 268 of them at year's end. For the entire ten year period, the annual average was 215. After the passage of another two decades, those records have still not been surpassed, thankfully. The next decade would be less costly but only slightly.

# X — GROWTH, PROFESSIONALISM AND MORE COMPUTERS 1980-1989

The 1980s brought a rapid growth in population and industrialization to the "Sun Belt" as well as a dramatic increase in the challenges to be met by the OCPD. In the first year, crime increased in Oklahoma City as well as nationwide. Property crimes went up nine percent, lower than the national average, and a small but significant increase was noted in violent crimes. Clearance rates for both types of crimes were above the national average. Traffic accidents went down by 6 percent, fatalities by 4 percent and, not coincidentally, drinking driver arrests went up 33 percent.

The Cosmopolitan newsletter published a cartoon during the second week of the new year. The first frame showed an old lady standing under a tree with a cat in it and asking a Philadelphia Police officer if he could get her cat out of the tree. In the second frame, the officer replied "Sure!", drew his gun and shot the cat out of the tree. Another cartoon showed a Houston Police officer approaching a car for running a stop sign, swearing, threatening and berating the occupants while his partner waited in the scout car. It then showed the Houston officer on his knees next to the driver's window apologizing and pleading for mercy. As he unsteadily stumbled back to the police car, his partner started yelling at him about why he hadn't written them a ticket, arrested them and so forth. The other officer replied shakily "Philadelphia cops!".

The publication was satirizing a recent series of nationally publicized problems the Houston and Philadelphia forces were having. Both forces were gaining a national reputation for corruption and brutality by renegade officers. Within the last year, Houston had several officers charged with shooting a young man during a pursuit and trying to cover it up by planting a gun on him. A Houston Deputy Chief was in the Federal Penitentiary for income tax evasion charges, several more officers were being tried for handcuffing a suspect and throwing him in a bayou to drown, a black officer was booked into the Houston jail in full uniform for trying to extort sex from white women with phony traffic charges and a litany of other embarrassments.

Philadelphia's officers weren't faring any better. Their homicide officers seemed to bear the brunt of the problems. They were accused of falsifying their overtime records to the point that some detectives were making more than high ranking commanders. There was also a problem with extracting confessions from homicide suspects under extreme coercion. One suspect had allegedly been suspended out of an upper story window during his interrogation and fell to his death. Other stories surfaced of placing the Philadelphia yellow pages on top of suspects' heads (to minimize bruising) and beating on them with hammers to encourage confessions. Another story started making the rounds about the officers of a Philadelphia suburb department learning from their neighbors in their inventive and less violent interrogation of an unsophisticated suspect. Telling him they were going to give him a lie detector test, they placed a colander on his head with wires running from it to a copy machine. They had placed a piece of paper in the copy machine with "He's lying!" written on it. They would ask the suspect a question and when he answered, they would punch the "Copy" button and a sheet would come out of the machine that said "He's lying!". This continued until they got their confession. The officers of the OCPD should have known better than to make light of the public troubles of other departments, cities and states. They were due to have a plethora of their own in the near future.

The previous summer, the initial reports had surfaced of what at first appeared to be just another one of those periodic scandals involving Oklahoma politicians. This investigation would mushroom into an expose' of one of the nation's largest political corruption scandals. Dubbed OKSCAM, over the next 5 years, 220 people would be convicted from 60 of the state's 77 counties. Most would be local county commissioners taking bribes and kickbacks from funds intended to purchase supplies and services to build county roads.

The allegations of criminal behavior would soon invade the ranks of the OCPD. Reputations and public perceptions, of the Department and individuals, would be touched by the allegations. Some would be true, some would be false and others would be misrepresented until it would be hard to tell the distinction between the two. All would suffer in an atmosphere of pervasive malfeasance by public officials, creating a climate in which the accusation of wrongdoing could be as damning as actual wrongdoing.

As the new decade opened, the OCPD's female officers had proven themselves an unqualified success. A few die-hards among the men still grumbled under their breath about the ladies but the grumbling was about individual officers or instances. Overall, the change was for the better. During the first month of the new decade, the supervisors and commanders rewarded them by breaking new ground.

Officers Marcella Joy Raymond and Terri McKinney had joined the Department as dispatchers, Raymond in July of 1974 and McKinney in June of 1975. In 1976, both had become officers and been assigned to the Patrol Division. Now they were applying for new assignments. Marcella Raymond became the first woman to be assigned to the OCPD Motorcycle Squad while Terri McKinney became the Department's first female canine officer.

A new sign began appearing on desks around Police Headquarters; "There are three kinds of people; those who make things happen, those who watch things happen and those who wonder what happened." Chief Heggy's administration continued to make things happen at a record pace.

On February 1, the Firearm and Toolmark Examiner's Unit was established with Specialist Roy Golightly. A year's training with OSBI and at the Smith & Wesson school made him one of only three such qualified specialists in Oklahoma. The next month, Specialist Gene Fansler began using the Inforex computer to build a data base of coded information on fingerprints of known burglars and began matching suspect's prints to them. The Technical Investigations Unit also acquired a new $28,000 Mobile Evidence Van for on-site investigations at major crime scenes.

One of those crime scenes occurred at the La Plaza Apartments in the 700 block of North MacArthur on the evening of March 26, 1980. About 7:30 that evening, Officers John Clark and Allan Garlitz were at the apartments trying to serve an arrest warrant on a child abuse suspect. The apartment manager called the apartment's security guard, OCPD Officer Greg Turner, to assist them. Upon checking the suspect's apartment, they were unable to locate him. Meanwhile the manager told the officers about several complaints he had received about a loud drinking party going on in Apartment 202 and asked them to quiet it down while they were there.

When the officers went to the apartment, they found it occupied by ten people who had been, in the words of one witness, "drunk, throwing beer cans and raising hell" for several hours.

The main problem seemed to be Clyde Keith Edwards, a 29-year-old maintenance man for the complex. Drunk, irate and aggressive, the 6-foot-2-inch, 185-pound convicted felon came out of the apartment, began swearing at the officers and threatening them. Initially, they tried to calm him down and quieten the party. Edwards' girlfriend came out of the apartment, giving him an audience that aggravated his macho posturing and the situation rapidly went from bad to worse. Officer Garlitz arrested her for interfering, removed her to the scout car and called for backup units while Clark continued to try to negotiate with Edwards.

Edwards ignored repeated requests from Clark and Garlitz to go back in the apartment and quieten down. In retrospect, their attempts to reason with Edwards may have deluded his alcohol-fogged brain into thinking the officers were afraid of him. As backup Officers Brian Joyce and Joel Franks arrived, it evidently became obvious to Edwards that they were going to arrest him. The odds had improved somewhat but the officers were still outnumbered and, still unsure of the exact situation, Franks approached carrying his shotgun.

Edwards began hyperventilating and flexing his abundant muscles, evidently trying to intimidate the officers. When they told him he was under arrest, Edwards tried to kick Clark in the groin and the fight was on. Edwards fought with such strength and ferocity that the officers would later speculate that he had been under the influence of something more than just alcohol. All experienced officers, they were familiar with the superhuman strength that could be exhibited by the mentally deranged or those under the influence of certain drugs, most notably PCP.

As the officers wrestled with Edwards on the floor trying to handcuff him, managing to get only one cuff fastened, he bit one of Joyce's thumbs almost to the bone. During the melee, Edwards was hit in the head several times with Kel-Lite flashlights, adding his blood to Officer Joyce's in what was becoming an increasingly bloody arena.

Finally overpowered, about half an hour later Edwards was admitted to Saint Anthony's Hospital with head injuries. After lingering for 19 hours, he died the next afternoon.

The Homicide Unit began an investigation. If Edwards had been shot by the officers, the investigation would have been accorded the same thorough treatment as any other homicide. But, because of the nature of Edward's death, Detective Division commanders overreacted. The initial orders given were that the witnesses from the apartment, who could logically be considered to be hostile witnesses, were to have their statements taken without being confronted or questioned about any possible biases they might harbor. They were not to be questioned about their criminal backgrounds, any possible grudges they might hold against the police or confronted with any inconsistencies in their statements that might indicate lying or exaggeration. This led to some serious disagreement between Homicide commanders and the brass but the Detectives basically ignored the orders and did it the right way anyway. The apartment complex was canvassed, dozens of witnesses were interviewed and statements taken. An autopsy of Edwards' body concluded that he had died from blunt force trauma to the head, i.e. the blows from a Kel-Lite. Some of the witnesses in the apartment alleged that they had seen Officer Clark hit Edwards several times with his Kel-Lite.

The investigative package was presented to the D.A.'s Office and District Attorney Andy Coats made a momentous decision. Charges of Second Degree Murder were filed against eight-year veteran Master Patrolman John Clark. He would be the first OCPD officer to go to court as a defendant against criminal charges in the death of a suspect in the line of duty. Clark was placed on administrative suspension without pay.

On March 7, 1980, Chief Heggy presented four life saving awards to officers in conjunction with the graduation ceremonies of Recruit Class Number 85. Officer David Haney was honored for saving a 12-year-old girl from a burning house and resuscitating her from smoke inhalation the previous November 19. Officers Richard Aytes and Jim Hatfield received awards for having saved a man choking on his food on January 19. Officer John George won the award for kicking in the door of a burning house and rescuing a resident. Tragically, barely a year after his act of heroism, Officer George would be killed in a motorcycle accident while off duty.

In May the Helicopter Unit moved into a new hanger at Northeast Airpark. Moving with them was a new master mechanic and a $290,000 five-seat Bell 206 Jet Ranger helicopter. Two of the pilot officers were now certified flight instructors.

On July 1, the Training Academy was designated the Central U.S. Police Institute. It was now accredited by Oklahoma State University. OCPD instructors began teaching a month-long Technical Investigations school, Geometric Blood Stain Interpretation seminars and other specialized schools in criminal, traffic and forensic investigation. These classes attracted students from all over the nation and some foreign countries. These classes were conducted in addition to maintaining the Police Academy recruit training which was now 720 hours of instruction over a 19-week period. Recruits earned 15 college credit hours for completing this training. The Academy was preparing to schedule all veteran officers for 40 hours of in-service training annually.

In the early morning hours after midnight on Sunday, July 6, 1980, three men were sitting around a table next to the swimming pool at the Guest House Inn at 5200 N. Classen Boulevard in Oklahoma City. Lawrence A. Evans, 29, was a roofer from North Carolina in town for a temporary job. Marvin F. Nowlin Jr., 28, was a petty felon and a disabled Vietnam veteran. He had recently been adjudged mentally incompetent and his attorney had been appointed as his guardian. The attorney had been paying his rent at the motel for the last two months. Having a few beers and passing the time having some sociable conversation with another of the motel's transient residents, they weren't bothering anyone but they were unknowingly keeping some dangerous company. Their companion was Raymond Leroy Peters, 39.

Webster's Dictionary defines the word entrepreneur as "one who launches or manages a business venture, often assuming risks". Ray Peters was an entrepreneur whose primary occupation was selling narcotics. In the process of conducting his enterprise, Ray Peters dealt with some very dangerous people. These were not the kind of people who sued you for damages if they caught you cheating them out of money. If you damaged them, they damaged you. Ray Peters cheated them. That was a mistake. The only mistake Lawrence Evans and Marvin Nowlin made that night was being in the wrong place at the wrong time having a beer with the wrong guy.

Until shortly before 2 A.M., two other men had been with the group at the table. One of them was tall, slim and nervously hyperactive with nearly shoulder length hair. As they rose to leave, the man spoke briefly with Peters, touching him on the shoulder before leaving. As they departed down the hallway, they walked past a vending machine area. Fifteen yards behind Ray Peters, leaning against a candy machine in the shadows, a tall, heavyset man with graying hair and wearing a red baseball cap took note of which man had been touched on the shoulder by the man who had just departed. The man might as well have hung a target on Ray Peters' back. He had, in fact, done just that.

Stepping out of the shadows, the large man took only seconds to cover the few yards to the table. Pointing his .45 automatic pistol at the back of Ray Peters' head, he fired twice at a range of less than three feet. Peters never knew what hit him. Two more shots at Evans struck him in the arm and chest, two more hit the fleeing Nowlin in the back. Six shots, six hits. Three men up, three men down. Very efficient.

Coming on the heels of a normal Independence Day, most of the motel's other residents thought the popping sounds coming from the courtyard were just another string of firecrackers going off. A few saw a man running down the motel breezeway.

Ray Peters was technically alive when he arrived at Baptist Hospital but it was hopeless and he died soon afterwards. OCPD Homicide Detectives Roy Sellers, Bill Harrison, Bob Horn and Bill Cook arrived at the crime scene. Evans and Nowlin were what the detectives classified as "D.R.T.", "Dead Right There". With a real "whodunit" on their hands, they went through the whole drill on this one—canvasses of the motel's 44 rooms, interviews, photographs, measurements, ballistics, blood types, autopsies, teletypes, informants, everything. They even tried the relatively new technique of asking key witnesses to undergo hypnosis to draw out their subconscious memories. They came up with a rough description and a composite drawing of their suspect.

Professional assassinations were not unknown in Oklahoma City but they were a relative rarity mixed in with the majority of cases that were motivated by sex, rage, jealousy, profit and a thousand other more petty reasons. The group in Homicide, sometimes considered strange even by other cops' standards, many times considered compiling a list of the multitude of frivolous reasons for taking lives in Oklahoma City. One man was killed because he refused to yield the right of way to another motorist at an intersection. Another died because he picked the wrong quarter up off of a pool table in a bar. Another because he coughed on a man seated next to him at a bar, accidentally getting phlegm on the man's sleeve—the killer said the man "harked" on him. Another was killed by his roommate because his feet stunk and he refused to change his socks. Another man honked at a double-parked car and was shot in the face for his trouble.

But this kind of killing required the kind of suspect that was outside of the ordinary. As the description and composite drawing of the killer spread around the Department, different officers began making suggestions about people who could be considered as suspects. Detective Sergeant Dave McBride suggested the investigators might look into the activities of a man named Clifford Henry Bowen, a member of the Jerry Ray James gang of the Dixie Mafia. Bowen, a 49-year-old Oklahoman from Lawton, was a long time associate of the James gang.

Six feet tall, well over 200 pounds with a pronounced potbelly and graying hair, police intelligence units in Oklahoma and Texas said his criminal specialties were "burglary, bank burglary, residential robbery and hit man".

Harold Dean Behrens had a short but unusual career with the OCPD. Hired on April 16, 1968, he was 22 years old, had just completed three years in the U.S. Army and had just returned from a year's service in Vietnam. Six feet tall, 170 pounds lean, he graduated from Recruit School on Christmas Eve of 1968. Two of his fellow recruits in that class were Larry Gramling, younger brother of then-Captain Lloyd Gramling, and future Chief Dave McBride. Less than eight months later, on August 14, 1969, he voluntarily resigned, stating he "was young and had some running around to do". He got it done fast because only three months later he applied for reinstatement and on December 1, 1969, was reemployed by the OCPD.

He was assigned to the Patrol Division, riding a scout car, usually in the Packing Town area around the Stockyards. In the late 60's and early 70's, this area was heavily frequented by many of the old time, hardcore thieves, burglars, bootleggers and dope peddlers left over from the 40's and 50's...Billy Fields, Frankie Turner, Bugs Raines, Kiplinger, Beasley, Henager, the names were familiar to all officers in the area. These men came from an era when they played rough and they expected the cops to play rough, too.

Behrens developed a reputation as an active, aggressive officer who preferred chasing crooks to writing traffic tickets. In dealing with his felonious constituents, Behrens also developed a reputation for being "scrappy", not brutal or sadistic but quite ready, willing and able to meet the physical challenges of his prisoners. Behrens qualified as an officer who, to use the street phrase, would "kick your ass in a heartbeat". The street people in his district called him "Mister Behrens". Personally, he was very hyperactive, quick and nervous in his movements and speech. Since he was that way all the time, no one thought much about it, that was just his manner. Many officers just assumed he was another transplanted "yankee" and that accounted for it. Actually he was from a small town in southern Oklahoma just east of Ardmore but that wasn't generally known. He was single, had never been married and no one knew much about his personal life but that wasn't considered unusual for a man in his early 20's. Behrens gave every indication of being the type of officer who allowed his profession to dominate his life, day and night, on and off duty. That, also, was not particularly unusual for relatively new officers.

His activeness paid off. Two years was the minimum time to qualify for Detective rank at that time. Behrens was promoted to Detective in June of 1972, only six months after he had served the minimum period. He was assigned to Robbery-Homicide and started collecting commendations, mostly for arresting armed robbers. After a little over a year in Robbery-Homicide, he transferred to the Organized Crime Unit, the renamed Intelligence Unit. There he grew his hair down almost to his shoulders and, with his bellbottom jeans, paisley shirts and hyperactive manner, developed an expertise for undercover narcotics work. The commendations kept coming including one for an 11-week investigation during which he worked 220 hours of overtime and eventually netted 23 arrests. Harold always seemed to be working, seen around the clock in the sleaziest joints with the sleaziest people, nights, weekends, holidays, all the time. But then, that was his job.

In the summer of 1975, the Organized Crime Unit discovered that some notorious members of the Dixie Mafia were in town. They were staying in an apartment near N.W. 16th and Portland, barely half a mile north of the Police Academy. Keeping them under surveillance, the unit had an undercover detective move into an apartment near them. The detective got to know both men and began associating with them but then, that was his job. The two men were Jerry Ray James and Clifford Henry Bowen. The detective was Harold Behrens. His supervisor was Sergeant Fred Weed.

In late 1975, an internal investigation started concerning an allegation that an undercover police officer was involved in a homosexual relationship with a juvenile boy. Slowly the details leaked out. Harold Behrens was the suspect. Before the investigation culminated, on November 5, 1975, Harold Behrens resigned from the OCPD "for personal and financial reasons".

As a civilian, Harold not only remained mired in Oklahoma City's underworld, he got into it even deeper. He entered into a partnership with another man in the old Chieftain movie theater on S.W. 29 that specialized in showing pornographic movies downstairs and providing prostitutes upstairs. His partner was Carl Eugene "Geno" Hines, a well-known felon in his own right.

There is evidence that Behrens became involved with narcotics purchases, sales and usage personally while he was supposed to be doing it professionally while still a police officer. Once he resigned, it became his livelihood. His primary product was Dilaudid, a pharmaceutical narcotic and semi-synthetic form of morphine, usually prescribed for the intense pain of terminal cancer patients. Behrens recruited Ray Peters to sell the dope for him. Peters' police record with narcotics stretched back to age 17.

Harold Behrens' name had been one of the first to come up the night of the homicides. He was sought out and was among the first to be interviewed but they didn't have enough evidence to hold him. Harold knew how to play the game. By the summer of 1980, Harold Behrens had been the subject of a narcotics investigation being conducted by OCPD Detective Eric Mullinex for over a year. Homicide brought Mullinex into the investigation. For the next month the investigation ranged all over the state and into Texas, centering around Bowen's home in Tyler. Behrens' drug connections were discovered to be a doctor, pharmacist and the owners of a trucking company in Stigler, Oklahoma. By the week before the homicides, Ray Peters had become a big problem for Harold Behrens. Peters was using more Dilaudid than he was delivering, costing Behrens as much as $3,000 a week in potential profits and he talked too much. He had also been arrested for Driving Under the Influence by the OHP. He had been in Behren's car transporting a load of Behren's dope while stoned on Behren's dope. Strike one, two and three. Peters had to go.

August of 1980 was a busy month. Electrophoresis equipment for blood analyses was added to the Forensic Laboratory. A new $332,000 firearms range began going up at 8500 S. Air Depot Boulevard. Located on seven acres just west of Tinker Air Force Base, it was to have two range towers, a concrete blockhouse, 60 firing positions, the latest electrical target system, a 200-yard rifle range with 8 firing positions, a competition trap and skeet range and a night lighting system. It would later come to be utilized by over 40 different law enforcement agencies.

On August 4, the Communications Unit vacated the time-honored "dispatch" area on the second floor of Headquarters. It moved to a new 4,800 square foot location in the Central Fire Station complex at N.W. 4th and Shartel. Computer Aided Dispatching (CAD) became a reality and the manual card system died forever except, of course, when the computers went down. A dozen telephone positions relayed calls by way of computer terminals to radio consoles broadcasting on 15 frequencies. These innovations brought with them another change, the now-familiar incident number. Each call was assigned a unique nine-digit number to be listed on all reports relative to that incident.

The recently vacated communications area in the Headquarters Building was rebuilt into a work area for the report clerks as well as offices for the Headquarters Division commander and his staff. As part of a $246,000 remodeling project, the third floor administrative offices were remodeled with tinted glass and new carpet.

On Wednesday, August 27, after seven and one-half weeks, the detectives assigned to the Guest House triple murder case were trying to bring it all together. That was easier said than done since it was now spread over two states. Clifford Henry Bowen was under surveillance at his home in Tyler, Texas, and Harold Behrens had gone to Tulsa. Detectives Bill Harrison and Roy Sellers had made arrangements to meet Behrens that afternoon at the Midway Restaurant, so named because it was halfway between Oklahoma City and Tulsa on the Turner Turnpike. Behrens had been showing increasing interest in the investigation's progress and the officers thought he was preparing to run as soon as he thought charges were about to be filed against him. There was no guarantee that Behrens would keep his appointment with Harrison and Sellers if he though he was about to be arrested. As a precaution, Narcotics Detective Eric Mullinex was trying to follow Behrens. Since this was all real and not a movie, it would be a tossup as to which would be more difficult; a lone officer trying to follow a suspicious man a hundred miles on a barren turnpike or trying to keep up with him in a busy metropolitan area without being observed. The fact that the suspect was an ex-cop who was himself proficient at following people just complicated it further. Mullinex tailed Behrens to Tulsa but then lost him.

Behrens' instincts were right but his timing was a little off. Detectives Bill Cook and Bob Horn were at the Oklahoma County Courthouse getting an arrest warrant for him on three counts of First Degree Murder. When they got the warrant, they notified two plainclothes troopers of the Oklahoma Highway Patrol's Internal Affairs Division since they had statewide jurisdiction.

Other than rest areas, there wasn't anyplace else to stop on the Turner Turnpike between Oklahoma's two largest cities except the Midway Restaurant. Everyone began converging there since it seemed to be the best bet since no one was certain of Behrens' location. Eric Mullinex got there first. Walking in and looking around trying to spot Behrens, the two recognized each other simultaneously. Mullinex sat down with Behrens since to do anything else would have made him even more suspicious.

Although empowered to enforce all state and federal laws, Oklahoma's Highway Patrol troopers primary duties usually consist of enforcing traffic laws. They don't get called upon to arrest many armed ex-cops in crowded restaurants who are wanted for multiple murders. It is therefore understandable if their adrenaline was flowing freely. Shortly after 1 P.M., the two OHP Internal Affairs troopers arrived at the restaurant. Unfortunately, they had been warned that Behrens might be in the company of another dope dealer who was usually armed. Even more unfortunately, the description they had been given fit the long-haired, unshaven man seated with Behrens. That is how Eric Mullinex sustained a couple of broken ribs from having .357 Magnums rammed into them. The next night, Clifford Henry Bowen was arrested by officers in Tyler, Texas.

Just as the Police Academy was making such advances in training, an incident was to occur within sight of the Academy that would question the Department's training standards. About 8:00 on the evening of October 4, 1980, a call came into Police Communications reporting an armed robbery in progress at the We'll Do Club on the northeast corner of N.W. 10 and Portland, two blocks north of the Police Training Center. The anonymous caller gave a description of the white male suspect, telling the dispatcher that the man was still there.

Officer Julian Rotramel, 24 years old and 10 months out of the Academy, was sitting at a stop light 6 blocks north of the club when the call came out. He was there in seconds. Pulling into the parking lot, Rotramel got out of his scout car and cautiously entered the windowless, one-story cinder block tavern. As he scanned the patrons sitting at the bar, his gaze froze on a man who exactly fit the description the dispatcher had broadcast.

The man, William Adam Tuttle, a 35-year-old from Bartlesville, avoided looking at the uniformed officer, immediately left his seat and started to walk past him to the exit. Neither the other people at the bar or the waitress standing behind it moved but all eyes were on the two men converging on each other at the front door. Rotramel reached out, stopping him and telling him he wanted to talk to him. Tuttle bent down, starting to reach inside one of his cowboy boots. Even in his short experience, Rotramel had seen more than one handgun taken out of a cowboy boot. The officer grabbed Tuttle and pushed him upright against the wall. He then turned around and asked the barmaid if she had called the police. She turned around and ran toward the other end of the room behind the bar. When Rotramel's attention was diverted for that moment, Tuttle reached down toward his boot again. Rotramel again pushed him up against the wall but the man pushed his way past him, running out the front door.

As the officer went out the door behind him, drawing his weapon and yelling for him to stop, the man stopped in the parking lot. In the shadows of the neon lights, the man crouched and reached into his cowboy boot for the third time, turning toward the officer. Rotramel fired one shot and the man fell, fatally wounded.

The homicide investigation turned up some unusual facts. A toy gun was removed from the cowboy boot Tuttle had reached for three times. It was discovered that he had been arrested the previous February for unsuccessfully attempting suicide. Finally, it was determined that no robbery had been attempted at the bar but Tuttle himself had made the call to police, giving his own description. Officer Rotramel was absolved of criminal responsibility in the shooting by the District Attorney's Office and an OCPD Firearms Review Board. Presumably, it was over. It wasn't.

On October 7, 1980, a federal grand jury in Oklahoma City indicted seven men for a drug distribution conspiracy. Five of the names didn't mean much to most of the people in the OCPD. They were a doctor, pharmacist, drug store manager and two trucking company operators from Stigler, a small town 125 miles east of Oklahoma City. The other two names, however, were more familiar. Harold Dean Behrens, former OCPD Detective, had been indicted along with his former supervisor in the Organized Crime Unit, Fred Weed. Weed had retired as a Lieutenant in 1977 after 20 years with the Department and was now working as a security guard at Children's Memorial Hospital. Assistant U.S. Attorney Jim Robinson, a former Oklahoma County prosecutor, said that the indictments were the direct result of the homicide investigation at the Guest House Inn.

Dilaudid tablets were usually sold to pharmacies for about 20 cents apiece. The investigation indicated that Weed and Behrens had obtained as many as 400 pills a week from their Stigler connection, paying $17.50 apiece for them. They then resold them in Oklahoma City for $30 each and street dealers ended up getting as much as $60 apiece for them. The pay was a lot better than police work...until now. You don't get paid anything in jail. Weed was released on $30,000 bond. Behrens was returned to the County Jail where he was being held without bond on the murder charges.

The federal drug conspiracy trial began on December 8. Assistant U.S. Attorney Jim Robinson had to walk something of a tightrope during his prosecution because no mention of the Guest House murders could be made because it would prejudice the jury. The trial was further shortened because the doctor and pharmacist were awarded separate trials. Charges were dismissed against the Stigler drug store manager. Eight days later, it was over. Harold Behrens and Fred Weed were both convicted.

As Officer Julian Rotramel's professional troubles were just beginning, Officer John Clark's were coming to a head. Although District Attorney Andy Coats had filed charges of Second Degree Murder against Clark in the death of Clyde Edwards almost nine months earlier, he had not stayed around to prosecute him. Coats had gone back into private law practice and the new District Attorney was Bob Macy who had been an OCPD officer for four years in the late 1950s. Macy set out to prosecute the case he had inherited.

The trial in Judge Charles Owens' court on the eighth floor of the Oklahoma County Courthouse was held under very tight security. Clark's attorney was D.C. Thomas, one of the most prestigious and effective in the city. He had received death threats saying if Clark was acquitted , Thomas was "a dead man". The extra Deputy Sheriffs were watching for Edwards' brother, Milford Wayne Edwards, believing he might cause some disruption in the trial. He didn't show up, possibly because there were seven felony warrants out for his arrest at the time. The FOP, which was vocally supporting Clark, received a bomb threat at their Lodge. All spectators at the trial were searched.

Several prosecution witnesses, some of whom had themselves been arrested during the incident, testified that they had seen Clark strike Edwards in the head with his flashlight "4 or 5 times" while dragging him to the police car after he had been handcuffed. Clark testified that he had been striking Edwards' hand which was pulling on the baton ring on his gunbelt.

On December 22, the jury gave John Clark and his family an early Christmas present. After deliberating for only 45 minutes, they came back with a unanimous verdict of not guilty. They also declined to convict the officer on the lesser charges of First Degree Manslaughter or Assault & Battery with a Dangerous Weapon.

When questioned about their decision, the jurors said that they had concentrated on the events that had occurred outside of the apartment. They considered what had occurred inside the apartment to be totally within the officer's line of duty responsibilities. The jurors said that they acquitted him because "no juror was convinced that any possible hitting that did occur was not in keeping with acceptable police behavior" under the circumstances. They also stated that their actual deliberations had only taken about half of the 45 minutes they were out.

Officer Clark, "very happy" with the vindication, would return to work and collect almost $13,000 in back pay. Former District Attorney Andy Coats would be elected Mayor in 1983. John Clark would stay with the OCPD because "the job is worth it". As of this writing, he is still serving as a Lieutenant in the Operations Bureau.

A Patrol Services Section was created the next year that combined all specialized patrol support services including Canine, Helicopter, Bomb Squad, Tactical/Hostage Negotiator Unit, Foot Patrol officers and the Selective Enforcement Unit. The new firearms range opened and the Training Division stayed very busy. In addition to the recruit schools and in-service training, another Technical Investigations school was held, a Police Motorcycle Competition was hosted and the Department co-sponsored the Southwest Association of Forensic Scientists Convention with the OSBI.

Public relations moved forward as well. A Ride-Along Program was established for the spouses and fiancees of officers. It was intended to help them adjust to and acquaint themselves with their spouse's duties. A Jewelry I.D. Program was begun in an attempt to register precious items in the hope of decreasing thefts and improving recovery rates.

On January 16, 1981, Chief Heggy awarded two more life saving awards at the graduation of Recruit Class Number 87. Officers Nick Pittman and Patricia Norman were decorated for saving a customer at a cafe from choking by applying the Heimlich maneuver successfully.

Three days later, Harold Behrens murder trial began in Oklahoma County District Court. District Attorney Bob Macy had charged Behrens with all three murders, saying that Ray Peters had developed a large dope habit and was threatening to expose Behrens' drug operation. Behren's defense attorney, Irven Box, gave the case an unusual angle. This may have been the first case in which the prosecuting attorney, the defense attorney and the defendant were all former OCPD officers.

A homosexual former roommate of Behrens testified that Behrens had told him that he arranged for Peters' murder with an associate who "owed him". Three witnesses from the motel testified they saw Behrens leave the courtyard only minutes before the shots were fired. The case went to the jury after five days. They acquitted Behrens of the murders of Evans and Nowlin, saying they were done by the hitman just to eliminate witnesses. They found him guilty, however, of hiring a hitman to kill Ray Peters and recommended life imprisonment.

One way or another, the Guest House murders were still not through causing casualties. On February 6, Clifford Henry Bowen was given his third bond hearing since his arrest the previous August. The first one in Texas and the second one, held only ten days earlier in front of Oklahoma County Judge Raymond Naifeh, had both resulted in him being denied bond. But his attorney kept trying. This time it was held in front of Judge Stewart Hunter. After much wrangling and testimony from witnesses, including Bowen, that he was at a rodeo in Tyler, Texas, at the time of the killings, Judge Hunter set bond at $75,000. Bowen immediately posted it, saying he was "going to Texas to build some witnesses".

District Attorney Macy strenuously objected. This was a triple homicide, murder for hire. One person had already been convicted in this case. Two other judges had denied bond. Judge Hunter's bond order allowed Bowen to leave Oklahoma. Twelve days later, Judge Hunter was relieved of his duties in the Civil-Criminal Division and reassigned as the head of the Domestic Relations Division. He would henceforth preside over divorce cases and child custody hearings.

Later in the month, sentencing was handed down in the federal drug case. Federal District Judge Ralph Thompson sentenced Harold Behrens to 15 years and Fred Weed to 7 years. The Judge noted that "while Weed had only a peripheral connection to the drug conspiracy...a career police officer who made the conscious decision to traffic in narcotics did not deserve probation". Yet another irony was to be attached to this case. Since wrongdoing cannot legally be made retroactive, Fred Weed continued receiving his retirement check from the Oklahoma Police Pension Fund while he was incarcerated at the El Reno Federal Correctional Institute.

The second week in March, Clifford Bowen's murder trial opened under Judge Joe Cannon but he soon assigned it to Judge Naifeh. Several witnesses from the motel identified Bowen as the gunman. They also identified Behrens, one of them demonstrating the way Behrens had touched Ray Peters on the shoulder as he was leaving. Bowen insisted he was at a rodeo in Tyler, Texas, that night. In rebuttal, the police chief of Tyler testified that the rodeo grounds were located four minutes away from an airstrip. A private jet could have brought Bowen to Oklahoma City in half an hour and this apparent luxury was well within the means of a man who had posted $225,000 in bond, no mean feat for a man who made his living "playing poker", as he said. Detective Bill Cook testified it took 13 minutes to go from the Downtown Airpark to the Guest House Inn obeying all the traffic laws. Sergeant Dave McBride testified to Harold Behrens' former association with Jerry Ray James and Bowen while McBride had been in the Organized Crime Unit. The jury returned verdicts of guilty on all counts and recommended three death sentences.

In April of 1981, Officer Julian Rotramel resigned from the OCPD to go to work for a petroleum exploration company. He would maintain years later that the shooting of William Tuttle did not influence his decision. What did influence his decision was the long hours, rotating shifts and low pay. The next month, William Tuttle's widow, Rose Marie, filed a federal lawsuit against Rotramel, the Police Department and the City asking for $4 million for the "wrongful death" of her husband.

In the summer of 1981, even while construction was being completed, police units began moving into a new 53,000 square foot Criminal Justice Center. Covering the southwest corner of Couch and Lee (built over the old "bay" parking lot), the four-story facility connected the Police and Courts buildings. The two lower floors were occupied by the Municipal Courts and provided secure internal passages for the movement of prisoners between the courts and the jail. The two upper floors provided expanded office space for Detective units, the Forensic Laboratory, Technical Investigations, Crime Analysis, Traffic and Patrol operations.

On September 25, Chief Heggy presented two more life saving awards. Officer Jerry Flowers won his award for rescuing an unconscious man from a burning residence the previous July 26. Officer Larry VanSchuyver, while off duty, had encountered an 8-year-old girl who had collapsed unconscious in a restaurant parking lot. He had resuscitated the girl using cardiopulmonary resuscitation.

When Jack Vaughn began his career in 1928, the OCPD had four Model T Fords, a few motorcycles and the Black Maria wagon. Half a century later the Department had hundreds of scout cars, detective cruisers, motorcycles and motor scooters as well as dozens of specialized vehicles including undercover cars, a recreational vehicle converted into a Command Post, station wagons, pickup trucks, Tactical Team vans, a bomb truck and an armored car. A new Transportation Unit was created in the Chief's Office to be responsible for monitoring the repairs and maintenance to this fleet.

The August 21 edition of the OCPD Cosmopolitan carried a cautionary tale of police stress. A 37-year-old Cleveland, Ohio, officer had gone berserk, barricaded himself in his home and held 40 of his fellow officers at bay for 14 hours. During that time he had fired 52 shots at them with his .357 Magnum, not hitting anyone, and thrown his burning police uniform out of the window. The four-year veteran, who was assigned to investigating applicant's backgrounds for the recruiting section, was twice divorced and beset with personal problems. His home eventually caught on fire and he was burned to death. No one else was injured during the standoff.

One of the officers who was on the staff of the Cosmopolitan at the time that story was published was Officer Ben Mize. Highly intelligent but iconoclastic, he had a Bachelors Degree from Arkansas State University and a Masters Degree from Oklahoma City University. Having served as an interpreter for four years in the U.S. Army, Mize was fluent in German, Korean and nearly as familiar with Spanish. Having served almost ten years with the OCPD, he was now assigned to the Training Center.

On Christmas morning, Officer Mize's body was discovered in his private vehicle on the Oklahoma State Fairgrounds about half a mile from the Police Training Center. He had evidently committed suicide with his service revolver which was lying next to him in the car seat. A partially empty liquor bottle was also present. The investigation turned up a journal he had been keeping for some time. It indicated an increasing pattern of domestic problems with his Korean spouse, job dissatisfaction and frustration. Some of the frustration was with some of his Police commanders at the Training Center. He even touched upon the possibility of killing several of his commanders before taking his own life. Investigators speculated that if his frustration and depression hadn't been exacerbated by alcohol and peaked over the Christmas holidays, when the Training Center was closed, he might have done just that.

Over sixty years after Mayor Jack Walton's Mounted Police Unit was disbanded, history repeated itself. On December 5, 1981, the Patrol Division initiated an experimental public relations program using three mounted horse patrols in the Stockyards area. Merchants in the area donated the horses, tack and stable space. The first three officers, Ron McKinney, G.W. Davis and Sam Chesnut, received two weeks of training with the Albuquerque, New Mexico, Police mounted unit. A pickup truck and horse trailer was added to the fleet of specialized vehicles.

THE OKLAHOMA JOURNAL
December 21, 1981

'PHANTOM' STALKS POLICE STATION

**Every now and then, the "phantom" at Oklahoma City police headquarters mysteriously—and anonymously—appears, offering a colorful, caustic and satirical interpretation of what is going on in the department.**

Another Department legend was born during the summer of 1981. Since 1976, the Department had been publishing The Cosmopolitan as the official Department newsletter. Published on paydays every other week, the newsletter featured columns such as "The Chief's Corner" and "The Chaplain Says", classified ads, notices on upcoming events and stories on happenings within the Department. During the summer, a counterfeited version started being distributed around the Department. The counterfeit version contained pointed barbs, ribald wisecracks and sarcastic comments on some of the events not covered in the official version. One of the first issues took some serious jabs at the newly formed Black Officers Association, taking the organization to task for causing divisiveness. The issue featured a drawing of a black background with white eyes and mouths representing the black officers. Another listed the Department's fictitious basketball team, giving a list of notably short officers. A somewhat hefty female officer nicknamed "Crisco" was advertised as competing for the World Sumo Championship. A psychological exam was announced, the exam being forced to ride one night each with two of the Department's more "eccentric" officers. The publication listed a group of officers with reputations for being somewhat dim-witted, stating they would be enrolled in a "Career Development School" that was designed for officers who scored lower than dolphins on intelligence tests.

The "Underground Cosmo", as it was dubbed, started showing up even more frequently than the official version. One copy surreptitiously laid on a vacant desk or taped to the inside of a restroom stall door caused an immediate run on Department copy machines. Copies passed from hand to hand and even through Department mail as the distribution network mushroomed. An anonymously interviewed officer admitted that there was at least a grain of truth in all the items in the Underground, even though some of the comments were a little too caustic for the administration's liking. As he put it, "They take lighthearted shots at various people. Some are really shots, though".

Later issues featured an advice column by "Police Polly" and formed an "I Got Caught" Club for officers being disciplined for various infractions. It also featured "OCPD Trivia Pursuit". Various questions would be posed about some of the wider known escapades, sexual and otherwise, of various officers, both male and female. A similar column had appeared in the official publication but always gave the answers in the next issue. The Underground never published the answers to its' trivia questions, letting its' readers run the answers down for themselves if they didn't already know them. Some active criminal investigations were temporarily placed on hold while dozens of officers sought to answer trivia questions like "Which female officer used to faint at climax? (Multiple answers)".

The newsletter knew no limits, taking to task Chiefs, City Council members, City Managers, Mayors, fellow officers and high ranking commanders equally fearlessly. While it lampooned Mayor Latting occasionally ("Let's have more Patience"), one of its favorite targets in the City Administration was Scott Johnson. Johnson was appointed City Manager on the last day of November 1981. A previous City Manager had allegedly once said that you could do anything you wanted in that job "as long as you don't screw around with the State Fairgrounds or the Police Department". Johnson didn't heed the warning. He rapidly alienated the PD's affections by adopting a distinct management vs. labor bent, recommending magnanimous pay raises for management while favoring more chintzy ones for police and, probably, not giving the officers the respect they felt they were due and the deference to which they had become accustomed. There were still some old hands on the job who could remember when "contempt of cop" was a good enough reason to put someone in jail and, in any time, the quickest way to get on someone's bad side is to start messing around with their pay. Johnson rapidly became the most unpopular City Manager since Howard McMahan. Following his resignation in February of 1984 to become the City Manager in Cincinnati, Ohio, an issue of The Underground prominently featured a picture of the smiling former City Manager under the salutation "Goodbye Asshole!". A story circulated that the local lodge of the FOP had sent a black wreath to the Cincinnati FOP lodge with their condolences upon Johnson's appointment.

There eventually developed several different versions of the newsletter, marked by different writing styles and typing. Some were barely literate and particularly venomous, obviously targeting personal attacks against certain individuals on one particular Patrol shift. Others were more comprehensive and bitingly satirical in the tradition of Saturday Night Live and The National Lampoon.

The Underground went on for years, amid various attempts to stop it and discover the identities of its' publishers, all to no avail. Most police administrators, like Chief Heggy, didn't pay much attention to it except to officially condemn it as unprofessional while privately chuckling at some of its more poignant barbs. Even the mightily offended ones decided it was hopeless to search for suspects among the 722 commissioned officers and 204 civilians. Some however, like Investigations Bureau Major (later Deputy Chief) Walt Wilhelm, went to greater lengths.

Wilhelm, a proud but not particularly personable man with a primarily Traffic Division background, was particularly defensive about heading a bureau of Detectives while he had no experience himself in that area of police work. He also came from an era when promotional tests were not very difficult or selective, the order of promotion was not mandated by union agreements and was done for the most part by the "old boy network". He was thus plagued by persistent rumors that his rise in rank was due solely to his personal friendship with Bob Wilder. Stories circulated of supervisors being ordered to stake out copy machines on paydays trying to catch people copying the Underground or getting examples of typing from various department typewriters, trying to compare them with the latest issue.

Major Wilhelm had a special ax to grind with the editors since he acquired a nickname from the publication. The motion picture E.T., The Extraterrestrial was sweeping the box offices of the country at the time. One of the Undergrounds stated that Wilhelm, who had a large head with a florid face, "looked like E.T. in a cheap suit". Wilhelm became universally known as "E.T." after that issue and became the highest ranking member of a small group of unpopular, usually dictatorial commanders most frequently pilloried in the publication. Some of the others were a Lieutenant who gained the nickname "Moon" after ripping his uniform trousers one day revealed that he was wearing no underwear, another Lieutenant nicknamed "Mickey Mouse" because of his unachieved desire for martinet-like discipline from his officers and his attention to relatively unimportant details, and his fawning Sergeant "Donald Duck". "Mickey Mouse" and another unpopular Lieutenant, "Chicken Hawk", had their legends permanently memorialized when some enterprising rebel scratched their nicknames in the wet concrete near the gas pumps at the Will Rogers briefing station.

The Underground Cosmo was a regular Department tradition into 1987 when it began to fade into infrequent publication, although certainly not for lack of material. Speculations have been ventured that the various editors had resigned, retired, been fired or promoted beyond the point where it was convenient to continue their clandestine involvement in the publication. Various police reporters, officers, supervisors and even commanders were suspected of being editors of various versions. There was even some speculation at one time that Chief Heggy, not unknown for his sometimes sardonic sense of humor, had contributed a few issues himself as a means of bolstering morale. Nevertheless, the identity of an Underground Cosmo editor has never been positively established. People waited for years for someone to be caught copy-

*Chief Lloyd Gramling.*

ing an original proof or for one of the official investigations to develop a suspect. It never happened. Now they have been waiting for years for a confession at a retirement party. They are still waiting. The mystery may never be solved.

Chief Tom Heggy retired in April of 1982 to become head of the State Bureau of Narcotics and later to direct the Criminal Justice program at Oklahoma City University. His farewell in the real Department newsletter was headlined "AUFWIEDERSEHEN" and ended, in typical Heggy style, with "you vill do it and you vill enjoy it!". Lloyd Gramling, the 53-year-old Assistant Chief, was promoted to fill the position. A tall, white-haired, distinguished looking veteran of the Korean War and 28 years on the OCPD, his three years in the office were typified by a strict adherence to the code that a police officer's conduct, personal and professional, should be above reproach. Although he seemed to be cordial, polite and a genuinely good man, Chief Gramling did not enjoy popularity with the majority of his officers. Most felt that his Traffic background and genuine good-heartedness contributed to a naivete that prevented him from understanding the true hazards and hardships of their duties. Conduct that would have once marked an officer as a "hard nose" and drawn a few words of advice from the Sergeant about insensitivity was now met with official reprimands or time off without pay. Behavior that would once have been dubbed as "pranks" or "extreme aggressiveness" was met with terminations. Chief Gramling's habit of signing his initials "LAG" started some officers to applying the word's definition to his administration. General morale plummeted, underscored by a curious statistic. Not a single Medal of Valor was awarded for actions that occurred during Chief Gramling's three-year administration. The general feeling at the time was not that the heroism was absent, just the rewards.

Although morale initially suffered, progress continued. Some lower priority crime reports were now taken over the telephone and no officer was dispatched. A private firm was contracted with to provide psychological services to the Department. The Records Bureau began microfilming records and training records were computerized. The uniformed officers began working permanent, non-rotating ten-hour shifts.

In conjunction with the new shifts and a patrol realignment that increased the number of districts from 23 to 35, a Field Training Officer (FTO) Program was initiated. The old methods of "breaking in rookies" were gone forever. The old informal format for breaking in rookies was designed to (1) examine their heterosexuality, (2) their physical courage and (3) their ability to impose their will on a suspect. The old saying that went with this style was "Get him laid, get him in a fight and get him a felony arrest". Even if this outdated hit-and-miss methodology had been acceptable in the 1980s, it wouldn't have passed muster under Lloyd Gramling.

Senior, experienced, interested officers could apply to become an FTO. If accepted on the basis of their record, they received specialized training, insignia and (eventually) incentive pay for training new officers in the field.

After graduating from the Police Academy, new officers would ride with several different FTO's in a three-to-six month period. During this time, they would be graded daily on everything from appearance to the practical application of what they were supposed to have learned. Probation periods were extended to allow time to properly evaluate new officers and their transition from theoretical classroom situations to real street situations. The termination rates went up. So did the quality of the officers who remained.

On May 1, 1982, the OCPD's First Annual Awards and Appreciation Banquet was held at the Holiday Inn West at I-40 and Meridian. Ed Sossen of KTOK radio acted as the Master of

Ceremonies while the guest speaker was Mike Turpen, the District Attorney of Muskogee County. About 235 officers and their guests paid $20 a couple to see four officers honored with the Medal of Valor, all decorated for rescuing citizens from burning buildings. Officers Phil Carr and Mike Goodspeed had rescued six men from the burning Herriman Hotel at 911 N. Broadway the previous January 3. Officers James Linam and Jerry Mauk were decorated for saving an elderly man from his burning house at 3132 N.W. 45 on December 3, 1981. Officer Don Hull was awarded the Life Saving Bar for saving a traffic accident victim. Specialist Don Cravens, Officer John Cave, Detectives Julie Smith and Andy Cain and Forensic Chemist Joyce Gilchrist were awarded Certificates of Achievement for outstanding performance of duties under unusual, complicated or hazardous conditions.

The day before the first awards banquet, the FOP formed the Oklahoma chapter of a charitable organization called Make A Wish Inc. It was patterned after a program begun in Phoenix, Arizona, to grant the wishes of terminally ill children. The OCPD was represented on the Board of Directors by Officer John Clark, Detective Royce Robison and the current President of the local FOP Lodge, Lieutenant Dave McBride.

During that summer of 1982, the lawsuit against the City for Officer Julian Rotramel's shooting of William Adam Tuttle went to trial in federal court. Attorneys Mike Gassaway and Carl Hughes prosecuted the argument that the OCPD's training program had been "grossly negligent" in preparing Officer Rotramel (and, by inference, all its other officers) to deal with those types of situations. They contended that he had not been trained in how to enter a one-story cinder block building with a front and rear exit and no windows. They faulted him for not waiting for a backup unit to arrive before entering the building alone. They faulted him for firing before he actually saw a gun. On June 4, the jury rendered their verdict. Officer Rotramel was not held liable for his actions but the OCPD's training program was heavily criticized. Mrs. Tuttle was awarded $1.5 million in damages. Assistant Chief Bob Wilder and the President of the FOP, Lieutenant Dave McBride, among many others, disagreed vehemently. The advances in the police training program were discussed. Also discussed was the vast difference between spending days, weeks and months debating in a court room over circumstances that occurred in fractions of a second in the neon-lit parking lot of a bar. Just because it is not uncommon to take guns out of prisoner's cowboy boots, can the officer assume the man wasn't reaching for his wallet...for the third time? Do you have to see the gun? Do you have to wait until the suspect points the gun at you? Do you have to wait until he fires to make sure it isn't just a realistic looking water pistol? How many shots is the suspect allowed before you can fire? The City appealed the verdict.

Toward the end of 1982, Bob Wilder made a bad decision. Although the ultimate fault was Chief Gramling's because it had to be done with his authorization and approval, responsibility is sometimes hard to fix in the upper echelons. For the last two decades, the identifying decals on the doors of OCPD scout cars had been black lettering on reflective silver backgrounds. They were stark, contrasting and easily visible when light struck them at night. Before them, the decals had been a gold OCPD badge. But now a change was being contemplated.

A committee was formed, chaired by Assistant Chief Wilder. After some wrangling, a new design was chosen. It had been created by Carol Walsh, the wife of one of the committee members, Sgt. Eldon Walsh. Someone once said that a horse that was designed by a committee would come out looking like a camel. The die was cast.

The new logo was a somewhat stylized depiction of an OCPD badge with "Oklahoma City Police" on it. Across the top of the badge was an eagle in full flight with outspread wings. Written on a ribbon clutched in the eagle's beak was the new Department motto "Trust in the Force". It was all done in color and therein was the rub. The badge was a pale blue.

The logo was approved, the decals ordered and were applied to the doors of the 170 new 1983 Ford LTD black and whites, the first Fords the Department had ordered since 1968. The officers who had been assigned the 51 Plymouth Grand Furys purchased earlier in the year were thankful they had the old door emblems but the officers slated to get the new cars moped and most joined in the bitching.

The new design was castigated in the Underground Cosmopolitan. Cartoons about the dissension even began appearing in the Daily Oklahoman. One showed a cute bunny rabbit standing next to an OCPD scout car pointing to the new logo on the door. An obviously chagrined officer driving the car was telling the bunny "I don't care what you think it looks like, I'm NOT a Game Ranger!". Things were not cheery in Mudville.

Naturally the logos stayed until the cars wore out but they did precipitate a new design toward the end of the decade. This one was much more to the officers' liking. It featured a colored City Seal underscored with the City motto "We Serve With Pride" followed by "POLICE" in large, black, block letters under a smaller logo "The City of Oklahoma City".

On December 29, officers received a complaint of a man having threatened another man with a gun at Bosco's Club at 2829 W. California. Checking the tag registration produced the name of Danny Ray Barbo, a 33-year-old outlaw biker wanted for weapons and assault charges in Beaumont, Texas. Prowling their districts, officers soon found the car parked in front of a trailer at the Sands Motel at 721 S. Rockwell, the type of rest stop usually favored by travelling felons.

As Officers Jerry Gates and Ron Houck positioned themselves outside the trailer, Officer Steve Helmer knocked on the door. Barbo must have realized what the situation was as soon as he opened the door and saw the uniform. He had his dog attack Helmer and ducked back into the trailer. Reappearing a moment later, Barbo charged out of the trailer with a .223 caliber assault rifle with a 20-round clip, spraying bullets. While Officer Helmer was dealing with the dog, Houck took cover under Barbo's car while Gates ran back to his scout car to get on the radio. Evidently considering Gates' proximity to the radio and shotgun in the police car the greatest threat, Barbo pursued him, firing all the while. When Barbo got within five feet, Gates rose up and fired once, killing him instantly. There were 14 bullet holes in the scout car.

*OCPD Mounted Patrol Officer G.W. Davis-1983.*

The new year began with a 4 percent increase in personnel. There were now 751 commissioned officers and 215 civilians. In January of 1983, the OCPD formed "The Bridge", a minority public relations program to "bridge" the gap between the Police Department and the black and Hispanic communities. In March, a separate Missing Persons Unit was established in the Detective Bureau. A Burglary Task Force was formed targeting daytime burglaries and the Helicopter Unit moved back to Wiley Post Airport.

The ultimate recognition came for Oklahoma City FOP Lodge No. 123 in 1983. OCPD Lieutenant Richard Boyd was elected President of the National FOP to serve from 1983 to 1987. Boyd had been the local lodge President in 1969-70, the State President from 1972-76 and the National Treasurer from 1979-83. He was the first president of the national organization from a state west of the Mississippi River. With over 216,000 members, the FOP now represented over a third of all American law enforcement officers.

Retiring in 1984, Richard

Boyd can take no small measure of the credit for the stature that the Fraternal Order of Police gained in the OCPD. He also left behind a more obscure and humorous legacy. During the period when Lieutenants were shift commanders and the times allowed them more authoritarian control over their men, Boyd developed a progressive feud with a few of his more rebellious officers.

At the time, the shift commanders' cars were identified by reflective silver decals, over a foot long and several inches wide, embossed in large black letters with the word "Lieutenant". The decals were held in place on the car doors by a very strong adhesive, designed to withstand years of exposure to heat, cold, rain and snow. As the hard feelings escalated, the insubordination became more clandestine and pointed. A plan was hatched to give everyone a constant reminder of what they would like to do to their Lieutenant every day, in effigy if not in fact.

Someone obtained one of the reflective silver decals from the City Garage and, one morning, it was found applied around the inside of the toilet bowl in the center stall of the men's room nearest to the Patrol lineup room on the third floor of Police Headquarters. The strong adhesive and the curvature of the inside of the toilet bowl made it virtually impossible to scrape off. It remains firmly fixed there as of this writing, survivor of thousands of flushes. Thus was born the legend of the "Richard Boyd Memorial Crapper".

On May 7, the Department hosted their Second Annual Awards and Appreciation Banquet. This time it was held at the Hilton Inn West, across the interstate from the previous location. Some 230 officers and their guests paid $12.50 apiece for their tickets. Ed Sossen of KTOK radio repeated as the Master of Ceremonies. Mike Turpen was the guest speaker again, having become the State Attorney General in the past year. Officer Jerry Gates was awarded the Medal of Valor for his gunfight with Danny Ray Barbo. Medals for Meritorious Service were awarded to Detectives Larry Andrews and Bill Tays. Andrews received his award for a seven-month investigation into the disappearance of a local woman. His investigation uncovered evidence that the woman had been slain and flown to the Gulf of Mexico in a small airplane, leading to the filing of the first murder charge in the state in which the victim's body was never found. Tays award was for his investigation which led to the arrest of the "ad bandit", a man who used classified ads to lure his victims into a series of robberies and rapes. The Chief also awarded six Life Saving awards, seven Certificates of Achievement to officers and ten Certificates of Appreciation to citizens.

Since its' inception a decade earlier, the OCPD Aviation Unit had maintained an enviable safety record over more than 15,000 flying hours. There had been some engine failures during that time but they had always landed safely. That record came crashing to the ground about 2:30 P.M. on the afternoon of Wednesday, July 6, 1983, along with the OCPD's Bell Jet Ranger III.

Specialist J.J. Young, a 19-year veteran officer and one of the original pilots in the unit, was preparing to start his evening shift from the unit's hangar in Northeast Airpark at N.E. 63rd and Bryant. Although normally accompanied by an observer, today the observer was staying behind to take a sick child to the doctor. A ground-based auxiliary power unit had been connected to the helicopter's front end to start the engine. Young started the engine and went through the warm-up procedures with everything operating normally.

The observer normally disconnected the auxiliary power line but today wasn't normal. The observer was not there and the pilot was going up alone. Young applied the power and began lifting off of the pad on the north end of the runway. When the helicopter was between 10 and 20 feet in the air, it reached the limit of the length of the power line still hooked to the aircraft's nose. The line pulled the nose down, the tail went up and the spinning rotors sliced off the tail rotor section. Having lost its only method of controlling sideways movement, the helicopter spun around several times out of control before crashing on its right side, the side the pilot's seat is on.

Young, bruised but without any major injuries, was trapped in the fallen aircraft for a few minutes. A small fire started but luckily went out rapidly. Pieces of the broken rotor blades were later recovered as much as 250 yards away from the crash site. Helped out of the aircraft by the observer, who was still in the hangar, Young was rushed to South Community Hospital for observation but was released shortly with only minor bruises. Young said that while he was trapped in the crash, the thought kept running through his head that he "only had 90 days to retirement" if he could just make it through this. He said he kept remembering the stories about cops completing most of their 20 years and then getting blown away three days before their were due to retire. Having made it through this, apparently J.J. thought the worst must be over because he completed 25 years of service before retiring in 1988.

On December 1, the Aviation Unit received a new five-seat Bell Jet Ranger 206B to replace the helicopter that had crashed the previous July. The unit now consisted of three helicopters including a pair of two-seat Hughes 300C's and a Cessna 206 airplane. Stricter safety and pre-flight guidelines were now in force.

The last week of February 1984 was another one of those violent weeks for OCPD. The first incident occurred on the evening of February 23. Officer Ralph Courtney was working as an off-duty security officer in the Reding Shopping Center at S.W. 44th and Western. Shortly before 8:30 P.M. he was approached by the manager of the C.R. Anthony store in the shopping center. The manager told Courtney he had been contacted at home by their alarm company and requested him to go along to check the alarm.

The two men entered the darkened store and proceeded toward the rear when Courtney saw some movement behind a table stacked with shoe boxes. A man leaned out from behind the table and started firing at Courtney, hitting him in the chest and right arm. Courtney returned fire but the man ran out the rear door.Courtney, a foot-beat officer, had his portable radio and called for assistance, telling the dispatcher "I've been hit". Sgt. Danny Cochran responded quickly and assessed the situation even quicker. As a patrolman almost 13 years earlier, Cochran had been one of the first officers on the scene of Officer Mike Ratikan's shooting. Courtney was quickly transported to South Community Hospital, only a few blocks away. Later taken to St. Anthony's Hospital for surgery, he would survive his wounds. The suspect, Larry Louis Gilbert, was arrested several weeks later by an alert detective in Tallahassee, Florida.

Two nights after Courtney was shot, Officers Terry Harrison and Don Hull responded to an armed robbery in progress at the Gas N' Go convenience store at 944 S.W. 29. The store's clerk had passed a note to a customer during the robbery and the customer coolly left and called the police. As the officers arrived, they began trading shots with Everett Carr who opened fire on them through the plate glass window of the store. Officer Hull was showered with shattered glass and Harrison was hit in the left hand. Carr was also hit and was arrested. All three survived their injuries.

During his administration, a number of instances occurred that resulted in Chief Gramling firing officers for infractions that would have met with lesser discipline in the past. Some officers agreed that some of the firings were justified and, even at that, some of the terminated officers got their jobs back later through labor negotiations, lawsuits or arbitration hearings. Even so, some light-hearted officers began wearing some T-shirts made up with the logo "I survived the Purge of '84". Chief Gramling's oft-convened Disciplinary Review Board gained the nickname of "The Firing Squad". The Underground Cosmo had a field day.

One who would not survive the "purges" of the Gramling administration was 1965 CPI Award winner R.J. Melton. Now a Lieutenant, Melton had gotten himself embroiled in a federal investigation of Oklahoma County District Judge William C. Page. Page had been investigated for his dealings with Richard Riley. Riley was a former informant of Melton's and was involved in counterfeiting drugs, i.e. selling "turkey dope". Melton's name had come up a number of times in conversations between Page and Riley that had been taped by the FBI. A long time friend of Page, Melton had secretly tape recorded conversations he had with Assistant U.S. Attorney Wesley Fredenburg, the lead federal prosecutor in Page's trial. Melton had then turned the tape recording over to the attorneys defending Page, Mike Gassaway and Carl Hughes. The tape had been used to attempt to charge federal prosecutors with misconduct.

Page was convicted on July 29, 1983, on two counts each of interstate racketeering and extortion, facing a penalty of 90 years in jail and $70,000 in fines. An internal investigation brought it all to light. Another veteran officer, Captain Don Schimmels, was investigated for "fraternizing with known criminals" but retired after testifying in Page's behalf. Melton was brought before a departmental disciplinary board. Chaired by Assistant Chief Gerald Emmett, the board of Lieutenant Bob Taylor, Majors Marvin Maxwell and William R. Chambless recommended that Melton be dismissed for violating the Department's code of ethics. Chief Gramling agreed and fired Melton on September 13, 17 days before he completed 21 years on the force.

Melton had not been widely popular on the force as an officer, detective or supervisor. Even so, a number of the officers fired for various infractions by Chief Gramling had the sympathies and support of their fellow officers. R.J. Melton was not among them. The general attitude was that Melton had "crossed over the line", violated that invisible demarcation of behavior that police officers will and will not tolerate from their colleagues. But it wasn't over. Melton sued.

The annual Awards Banquet was held on May 5, moving back to the Holiday Inn West this time. Tickets were still $12.50 each and over 250 officers attended. Ed Sossen of KTOK radio returned for his third year as emcee and the speaker was Federal District Judge Ralph Thompson. The Medal for Meritorious Service was awarded to Officer Howard Barnes for spending over an hour talking an armed man out of suicide. Also awarded were one Life Saving award, ten Certificates of Achievement and seven Certificates of Appreciation to citizens.

On June 1, 1984, Assistant Chief Gerald Emmett retired after 30 years of service. He had become the first black staff officer on the Department and the highest ranking black officer to that time. Patrolman Paul D. Taylor was elected President of the local FOP Lodge. He was to serve in this office longer than any other person, remaining in that position for the next decade.

The Forgery Unit's name was changed to White Collar Crime to reflect the changing responsibilities. The implementation of the Bogus Check Restitution Program in the District Attorney's Office allowed the unit to spend more time on the rising rates of fraud and computer crimes.

The night of Saturday, February 2, 1985, was a frigid one in Oklahoma City. A recent winter storm had blanketed the city in snow. Shortly before 11 P.M., a young black man approached the main desk at the Holiday Inn Northwest at 3535 N.W. 39th Street. He told the night clerk that he wanted to rent a room but he wanted to look at it first. He registered in what turned out to be a false name and the clerk gave him the key to Room 108, a ground floor room on the north side of the motel. He left and, after thinking about how unusual his request had been, the clerk contacted their security guard and asked him to check the man's suspicious behavior.

OCPD Auto Theft Detective Gary Ward was working the off-duty job as security guard that night. The 44-year-old, 14-year veteran officer had been working the job for the past three weeks, standingin for his brother-in-law, Homicide supervisor Sergeant Les McCaleb. McCaleb was hospitalized for stomach surgery, the first round in a battle with cancer that would claim his life little more than a year later.

*Detective Gary Lee Ward.*

Gary Ward was a good police officer; bright, courageous, direct, forceful when he had to be. More than that, Gary Ward was a good man; a placid, gentle, caring, peaceful man. He didn't want to hurt anyone. In his early years on the force, he had received a call on a shooting in a residential neighborhood. When he and backup officers had arrived, a car was overturned in the street and shots could still be heard in the area. All of the responding officers drew their weapons as they got out of their cars, preparing to return fire if they were fired upon. Gary Ward never drew his gun. It takes an extraordinary man to hear gunfire around him, see a bullet-punctured car lying on its top with the wheels still spinning and not draw his weapon because no one has directly threatened him yet. Gary Ward was such a man.

Alerted by the motel's desk clerk, Ward went to check the man out. Minutes later, Ward's body was found lying in the snow in a breezeway on the northwest corner of the motel's central courtyard. He had been shot in the left side of the chest with his own .357 Magnum service revolver which was missing. A shattered color television was lying in the snow near his lifeless body.

Officers and Homicide Detectives swarmed to the scene in response to the call. The courtyard and west parking lot were cordoned off. A search was begun of every room in the motel and every car in the parking lot. Slowly, the facts surfaced. The broken television had been removed from Room 108. A witness had seen Ward approach a black man stealing the television in the central courtyard. The man had dropped the television as Ward grappled with him. Gaining control of his prisoner, Ward had forced him up against a wall and began searching him. The man was heard to say "You're not taking me to jail", knock Ward down and run away. Ward got up, pursued and caught the suspect and they went down fighting again. Three shots were heard and the black man was seen to flee again, leaving Ward motionless in the snow.

Registration checks were run on all of the cars in the parking lot. One of them checked to a 28-year-old black man named Glen Briggs. Briggs, a twice-convicted burglar, had not been a guest in the motel. Questioning him increased the detectives' suspicions. A handwriting sample was taken from Briggs and it matched the false registration of the man who had been given the key to Room 108. The rest of the story soon followed. Briggs' partner, and Ward's killer, was Alvin Parker, 26. They had tried the same scam before. Briggs would con a desk clerk out of a room key with a false registration and Parker would steal the television out of the room. They had tried it at the Pebbletree Inn, a mile and a half east of the Holiday Inn, an hour before hitting Room 108. Parker was a convicted armed robber, having served four years of a ten-year sentence for a robbery committed in May of 1979. He had been paroled in July of 1983.

Detective Gary Lee Ward was buried on Wednesday, February 6, mourned by his wife and three children. The services were held at the First Southern Baptist Church of Del City, a suburb east of the city. The pastor told nearly 700 mourners that Gary Ward had been "a man of peace who may have given someone a second chance that cost him his life".

During the early morning darkness of the next day, officers surrounded two houses in eastern Oklahoma City; the houses of the parents and the girlfriend of Alvin Parker. About 9:30 A.M., officers entered the parent's house at 5319 N.E. 71. Alvin Parker was found hiding in a crawlspace under the house. A foot away from him was a small box. Inside the box, wrapped in plastic, was Gary Ward's .357 Magnum service revolver. Parker was convicted and sentenced to 199 years in prison.

Two days after Gary Ward's death, the jury rendered a verdict in former OCPD Lieutenant R.J. Melton's federal lawsuit against the City and Police Department. Melton had been fired 17 months earlier after a disciplinary board had found that Melton had violated the Department's code of ethics by secretly tape recording statements of a federal prosecutor investigating District Judge William C. Page and giving the tape to Page's defense attorneys.

The jury awarded Melton over $1.3 million in actual and punitive damages. His lawsuit had alleged that he should have been allowed representation by an attorney and allowed to confront his accusers before the disciplinary board. The jurors agreed that his First Amendment right to talk to Page's defense lawyers had been infringed upon, he had been denied due process of law and that he was denied a hearing to clear the stigma from his reputation. The jury rejected an allegation that the police command and the board conspired against Melton. The City was held liable for $1,272,000 in actual damages. Another $28,200 in punitive damages was awarded against Chief Gramling, OCPD Public Information Officer Lieutenant Dave McBride, board members Assistant Chief Gerald Emmett, Major Marvin Maxwell, Major Bill Chambless, Lieutenant Bob Taylor and Assistant City Manager Paula Hearn. Only Internal Affairs Lieutenant Carl Smith was not found in complicity by the jury.

Melton's attorneys said that they had no intention of trying to collect the awards of punitive damages from the individual defendants. Chief Gramling had already announced his impending retirement. Carl Hughes said that the OCPD's command staff was "inbred like a bunch of beagle pups" and the retiring Chief should be replaced with "someone from outside with an objective attitude who can analyze their policies and procedures". A lot of people would remember these remarks a few years later.

*Chief Robert V. Wilder.*

Chief Gramling retired on February 14 after 30 years of service and was replaced by a 25-year veteran, Assistant Chief Robert V. Wilder, who celebrated his 46th birthday the next day. Chief Wilder was the son of Houston V. Wilder who had served from 1915 to 1950, retiring as a Major. His mother served for 26 years with the Oklahoma County Sheriff's Office. Chief Wilder was to become the most popular, charismatic Chief since Smokey Hilbert. His sense of humor and love of harmless practical jokes gave him an approachability rarely associated with the office.

In April, the Make A Wish program recognized its third anniversary. In the past three years, the program had been able to grant trips to Disneyland and other wishes of 36 terminally ill children, an average of one a month. Twenty-two of those children had not survived to see this anniversary. A major uniform change was made that Spring when the white uniform caps were retired. Dark blue caps were adopted with silver trim for officers and gold trim for Sergeants and higher ranks.

On May 3, in spite of the fact that the Annual Awards Banquet had moved to larger quarters in the Myriad Convention Center and, for the first time, officers were not charged for their tickets, the atmosphere was somewhat subdued. It was the first occasion since its inception that necessitated the award of the Police Cross to an officer slain in the line of duty. Over 650 officers and their guests attended to watch Detective Gary Ward's widow accept his medal. KWTV news anchor Patti Suarez acted as emcee while the keynote speaker was Sir Kenneth Newman of New Scotland Yard. One Medal for Meritorious Service was awarded along with 4 Life Saving awards and 18 Certificates of Achievement, 12 to officers and 6 to civilians.

As the summer of 1985 approached, former officer Julian Rotramel had been gone from the OCPD for over four years and William Adam Tuttle had been dead for almost five years. Finally, the U.S. Supreme Court had reversed the decisions of two lower courts that had held the City liable for a $1.5 million judgement and challenged the OCPD's training methods.

The lawsuit had produced some positive results both on a local and State level. Training was much better documented, instructors were certified and the outlines of police training topics were completely updated. The 42-page decision centered on the main question, which was "whether a single isolated incident of the use of excessive force by a police officer establishes an official policy or practice". The Supreme Court pointed out a number of errors including instructions given to the jury that they " could infer that City policies [on Police procedures] were deliberately indifferent thus, inadequate training was provided in a grossly negligent manner". In a seven to one decision, the Justices said "this inference is unwarranted. It is therefore difficult to accept a theory that someone pursues a policy of 'inadequate training'...". Delivering the majority opinion, Justice William H. Rehnquist said the jury's instruction improperly created an assumption that the officer's actions were linked to some "official" policy. The City's lawyers noted that the idea that the Police Department had deliberately implemented a policy of insufficient training as "totally preposterous".

A new trial was ordered. In the second trial, Officer Rotramel was again found not liable. This time, so was the City, the OCPD and their training program. But a precedent had been set. People had always been hesitant to sue police officers because of the limited amount of money that could be awarded. It would be tough to get enough out of a cop's pockets to pay lawyer's fees. But now it became common to only incidentally sue individual officers. The main target became the Police Departments and, more importantly, the cities themselves. The big bureaucracies had the big budgets and the deep pockets that could pay the multi-million dollar settlements sought after. Money and publicity-hungry shysters could file nuisance lawsuits to their hearts content, finding misconduct in almost every arrest or use of force if they just put the right interpretation on it. Municipal attorneys would have a new kind of job security.

In June of 1985, the Department lost 58 years of experience with only two retirements. Sue Brunts was more than the Chief's secretary, she was THE Chief's secretary. Retiring after 25 years of service, she had served the last 16 years as secretary to the last six Chiefs. A few days later, Lieutenant Walter Kostiuk retired after more than 33 years of service. Hired on November 1, 1951, almost 32 years had passed since he had been shot by an armed robber at N.E. 10th and Eastern. The stocky, muscular Ukrainian had survived that to become a supervisor and commander in both the Patrol and Detective Divisions. Renowned for his jovial demeanor, military-short haircut and blunt speech, Kostiuk was the epitome of a "redneck 1950s cop", proud of it and prized by his men for it. He was also renowned for being a nightmare to television news media reporters trying to interview him at crime scenes. Police departments were now providing polished Public Information Officers with college degrees, some former journalists, schooled in providing the news media with 30-second sound bites and film clips. When they chose to interview Lieutenant Kostiuk at a crime scene, it was different. Kostiuk usually interspersed his commentary with vividly descriptive phrases in a cop's "street language" that usually rendered the interview unusable without violating FCC standards, always with a mischievous twinkle in his eye.

Formal retirements, for those officers who wished it, were usually held in the old Patrol Division lineup room on the third floor of Police Headquarters. Cake and punch were served following a few appropriate remarks by the representatives of the administration and friends, if any, of the retiree. Prior to many of those ceremonies, it was not uncommon for commanders to scour the halls and offices of the building, ordering people to come to the ceremony. This was not the case when Walt Kostiuk retired. The lineup room was jammed with officers shoulder to shoulder and spilling out into the halls. The room was hot and stuffy, the speeches long, and the tokens of respect and appreciation many. A "policeman's policeman" in the mold of Bill Peterman and widely popular, Kostiuk's retirement ceremony was marred when he suffered a heart attack during the emotional parting. Luckily, his son Stefan was a physician and was present at the ceremony. Due to his presence, Kostiuk happily survived to enjoy his retirement.

In July of 1985, at the beginning of the City's fiscal year, Chief Wilder reorganized the Department into three bureaus and created a new rank. Three majors were promoted to Deputy Chief. Marvin Maxwell was placed in charge of the Special Services Bureau, W.R. "Bill" Chambless took over the Uniform Bureau and Walt Wilhelm headed the Investigations Bureau. The newly created Uniform Bureau contained both the old Patrol and Traffic Divisions. On August 30, the Helicopter Unit placed two new Hughes 500E helicopters in service.

September of 1985 saw the fruition of a major narcotics investigation. Special Projects Detectives, Customs and Drug Enforcement Administration agents were conducting a joint surveillance of persons suspected of smuggling large quantities of cocaine into the City from Colombia. Officers followed the suspects to the Downtown Airpark in the 1700 block of S. Western.

The illicit shipment had been flown in and left parked in a twin-engine Cessna 421. Three days of around-the-clock surveillance followed before the suspects began unloading the aircraft. Officers moved in and arrested pilot George Crenshaw and his accomplice William Pickering. A total of 726 pounds of cocaine were seized. The case led to convictions in Oklahoma, Texas and California. It also provided leads that started further investigations of drug and money laundering organizations in Mexico, Panama and Colombia.

At 8:59 P.M. on the evening of Tuesday, January 7, 1986, a broadcast went over the police radio of an armed robbery occurring at the Tom's Market convenience store at 1000

N.E. 36th Street. The dispatcher also broadcast the description of a van and several people involved. Two of the officers that heard that broadcast were spending their first night together as partners. Thirty-two-year-old Master Patrolman Richard Riggs was an eight-year veteran, popular with his peers and respected by his supervisors. His personnel file already contained a number of commendations, letters of appreciation and several superior performance evaluations. He had been selected as "Officer of the Month" the previous March and was promoted to Senior Police Officer shortly afterwards. As large men have a tendency to do, Riggs had recently been gaining weight, straining the limits of his tailored uniforms. As a result, he had stopped wearing his bulletproof vest under his uniform shirt about a week earlier. It was tragic timing.

*Officer Richard O. Riggs.*

Riggs was also a Field Training Officer and was expected to train new officers. In that capacity, his new partner that night was 29-year-old rookie Ronnie Craig Gravel. Gravel had been an officer less than nine months and had recently completed the Police Academy. Tonight he would start learning about the streets. The first lesson would be a harsh, unforgiving one.Interstate Highway 35 runs along the eastern edge of Oklahoma City about two miles east of the Tom's Market on N.E. 36th Street. As in most large, sprawling cities, the system of high-speed, non-stop, multi-lane interstate highways that surround and bisect Oklahoma City are the fastest way to cover a lot of ground in a little time. Most armed robbery alerts that are broadcast are for robberies that have already occurred, not in progress. One nearby car is assigned along with a backup unit just in case it is in progress. Most of the other experienced officers who hear the broadcast do not head for the scene. They usually allow a little travel time for the information to have been relayed to police communications so they start checking the major streets for a few miles around the armed robbery location.

Shortly after 9 P.M., Officers Riggs and Gravel saw a van that fitted the description of the armed robbery vehicle parked by a gas station at N.E. 36th and I-35. As the officers drove up in the lot, they saw several people in the van. A black man was standing next to the filling station talking on a pay phone. Officer Riggs got out of the car and, flashlight in hand, began approaching the van. Officer Gravel got out, his attention switching between the dual threats of the people in the van and the man on the pay phone. Suddenly the man on the phone turned around and fired two shots at Riggs with a .38 revolver. Riggs, mortally wounded in the stomach and chest, drew his weapon as he fell and returned the fire but missed the man. Officer Gravel took cover behind the nearby gas pumps and emptied his weapon at the now fleeing man. His fire also missed its target.

The frantic radio call for help brought swarms of scout cars and an ambulance rapidly. Riggs was rushed to Oklahoma Memorial Hospital but died less than an hour later. Two black men and a black woman were arrested out of the van. The escaped suspect, soon identified as Ronald Keith Boyd, was not located but throngs of officers and detectives began the process of working around the clock until he was.

Oddly enough, it was soon discovered that Officer Riggs had arrested Boyd several months earlier for another armed robbery and had been forced to fight him during the arrest. Boyd had not been identified by the victim in that robbery and had been released.

Fourteen hours after the search began, Boyd was traced to the house of a friend at 2108 S.W. 65th, almost as far on the opposite side of town from the shooting scene as he could get and still be in the city. The Tactical and Hostage Negotiations Team was notified and quickly surrounded the residence. After isolating the telephone line, negotiator Steve Pacheco called the residence to try to talk Boyd out peacefully. He listened to the telephone ring unanswered for the next three and one-half hours while the surrounding Tac Team members listened to the two dogs barking in the garage. During this time, an assault team taped off a scale layout of the residence in a nearby church's parking lot and began practicing an assault on the residence in case negotiations failed.

As the phone continued to ring, negotiations never got started. Finally, shortly before 4 P.M., Tactical Commander Captain Mike Heath approved the assault. An instant of blinding light and a concussion wave from a flashbang grenade tossed in the garage stunned and disoriented the dogs as the assault team rushed in. The officers, quickly crisscrossing the residence while covering each other, cleared one room at a time. In seconds they had worked their way back to a rear bedroom. Covered by Sergeant Bobby Tidwell, Officer Steve Carson rushed into the apparently empty room, jumping on the bed. As he did, the bed collapsed. Ronald Keith Boyd was hiding under the bed. Boyd was arrested without further incident.

Boyd was charged with First Degree Murder and his other accomplices in the van were charged with Robbery with Firearms. Since Boyd had killed a police officer and had barricaded himself in a residence, the Tactical Team received high praise from the local media for their professionalism in capturing him alive.

The next morning, the .38 revolver that Boyd had used to kill Officer Riggs was found by a golfer on one of the fairways of the Twin Hills Country Club east of the shooting scene across I-35. When he was arraigned on the murder charge, the judge asked Boyd if he had a lawyer. Boyd replied that he did but his lawyer was also in jail. The attorney who had defended Boyd on the previous robbery charge had been arrested for DUI. Boyd was later tried and sentenced to life imprisonment.

The following Saturday, services were held for Officer Riggs at the First Presbyterian Church on the northern border of Fairlawn Cemetery. The huge church was selected for its capacity since, in addition to Riggs' widow, daughter and stepson, the services were attended by over 1,500 officers and friends including an honor guard of more than 100 officers from cities as far away as Broken Arrow and Woodward. Following the services, a cortege of more than 100 cars and two police helicopters led the funeral procession to the burial site in the small town of Wellston north of the city that Richard Riggs had died protecting.

On April 25, the Fifth Annual Awards and Appreciation Banquet at the Myriad Convention Center started on a somber note since it was the second consecutive occasion when the Police Cross was awarded to a slain officer. KWTV's Patti Suarez hosted again. The occasion was becoming a bigger success with the officers since they didn't have to pay for their tickets and more than 900 attended.

The family of Officer Riggs received his Police Cross award. One of the four Medals for Meritorious Service awarded that night went to Julie Smith, who had been promoted to Sergeant in 1983. She received the award for the wide recognition of her expertise in the field of sex crimes and her organization of a highly effective burglary task force. Ten Life Saving awards were given along with 17 Certificates of Achievement.

On the Police Memorial Day of May 11, 1986, a new monument was dedicated in front of Police Headquarters. A slab of dark gray marble was mounted in a central plaza surrounded by three flagpoles flying the City, State and National flags. Engraved on the stone were the names of the 27 OCPD officers who had given their lives in the performance of their duty in the previous 97 years.

Exactly one week later, another OCPD officer came close to having his name on the memorial. It all began when a man was abducted from a shopping center at S.W. 89th and Western, robbed and had his car stolen by two white male suspects. At 4:11 P.M. that afternoon, the same car was used in the armed robbery of a McDonald's restaurant at S.W. 74th and Western. After a radio broadcast of the description of the suspects and car involved, Officer Mike Hampton was checking a residential area a few blocks south of the robbery. Seeing the car in a driveway at 1113 Straka Terrace, Hampton got out to check the car. As he approached, the two suspects who had been laying down in the front seat rose up and started firing at him. Drawing his weapon, Hampton returned fire, hitting both suspects. Steven Keith

Shoup, wounded in the right leg, was arrested at the scene. Jesse D. Jacobs temporarily escaped to a house at 7901 S. Douglas, where he forced the residents to bandage his wound and drive him to S.W. 89th and Western, letting him out in the same shopping center where the chain of events had begun earlier that day. Jacobs was later apprehended.

A bizarre incident occurred in the early morning hours of October 24, 1986, that proved to have an odd connection with the history of the OCPD. Thieves broke into two tombs in Fairlawn Cemetery and stole the skulls from three human bodies. One of the tombs was the Lee family vault and one of the skulls was that of former Chief of Police Oscar G. Lee. As an investigation commenced the next day, word came in of someone trying to sell a human skull in the area. The tip led officers to an apartment at 501 N.W. 24th, barely half a mile from the cemetery. A 21-year-old woman answered the door and told Officer Mark Wenthold and Sergeant Andy Cain that she knew nothing about the incident and no one else was there. As the officers looked past the woman, they saw something that caused them to decide to come in and look around for themselves....two human skulls sitting on the fireplace mantle.

Two men in their twenties were located inside the apartment and arrested for unlawfully removing a body. The third skull was found sitting on top of a stereo cabinet. Because of the proximity of Halloween, the idea of occult involvement or satanism occurred to some people but officers felt the crime was strictly one for profit because some gold teeth had been pried out of the skulls. After an examination by the Medical Examiner's Office, the skulls were returned to the cemetery and reinterred in their former tombs.

OCPD COSMOPOLITAN
February 23, 1987

> Two policemen were eating lunch in a cafe and heard a woman seated nearby tell her son loudly, "Jimmy, if you don't eat all your peas, I'll have those policemen come over and talk to you". One of the policemen promptly got up and walked over to the five-year-old who was being scolded. "Jimmy," he said, just as loudly, "I'm six- foot-two and I weigh 200 pounds. And I never ate a pea in my life!". As the two policemen left the cafe, the other patrons were laughing, Jimmy's mother was absolutely silent and a smiling Jimmy was no longer afraid of policemen.

The next summer saw two major innovations. The first was a new take-home car program. Previously, marked units had been assigned to districts just like individual officers. In many cases, it was not uncommon for one officer to get out his car at the end of his shift, the next officer assigned to that district to put gas in the car and go to work without even turning the engine off.

Planners decided to experiment with a program that would assign marked units to individual officers. These vehicles would be kept all the time by the assigned officer including being driven to and from their homes. The reasoning was that this would not only increase the visibility of marked police units on the street but would also reduce maintenance costs due to the vehicles receiving better care. Officers operating the vehicles while off duty were required to carry weapons, identification and report forms so they could respond to any calls they were close to or crimes they witnessed. The program became a resounding success and was expanded greatly in the next few years.

On May 1, the annual Awards and Appreciation Banquet was held, this time at the State Fairgrounds Arena. Officer Mike Hampton was awarded the Medal of Valor for his shootout with the two armed robbers the previous May. Officer Riley Lenex also received the award for rescuing an elderly resident from a fire in the Prince Hall Apartments on December 27, 1986. Three Medals for Meritorious Service were awarded; to Detective David Hodges for arresting an armed robber and avoiding a hostage situation, to Officer Michael D. Taylor for arresting a murder suspect and shooting him when he tried to take the officer's gun and to Officer Elroy Kroeker for his two decades of leadership in the Honor Guard.

Two Life Saving awards were given out along with 43 Certificates of Achievement, 31 to officers and 12 to citizens.

Remember when Ace Williams was reminiscing about the 1930s when "everybody got in the Black Maria and went raiding"? Well, times change but only slightly. Now the "Black Maria" was a non-descript Special Projects van with blacked out windows and the raiders, equipped with body armor and shotguns, weren't hunting illegal booze but narcotics. Shortly before 11 P.M. on June 15th, such a raid was planned for a house at 2115 S.W. 15th. Undercover officers had received a search warrant based on previous purchases of "speed", the poor man's cocaine. Ten officers, five undercover Detectives wearing raid jackets and ball caps with badges and "POLICE" stenciled on them and five uniformed officers, prepared to serve the warrant.

One of the Detectives selected for the entry team was Clyde Ray Bowling. It wasn't hard to figure out why. At 6 feet 3 inches and 240 pounds, Bowling hadn't received the nicknames "Animal" and "Bear" for nothing. When he wanted in somewhere, not many doors could resist him for long. His 15-year career also included long service with the Tactical Team and experience in a number of combat situations in the past so his reaction time to danger was reliable. That helps when you present that big a target. His reaction time would come in handy this night.

As the officers made entry into the house, Douglas Capps grabbed his gun and turned toward them. To coin a phrase, he shouldn't'a hadda oughta done it. Three blasts from Detective Bowling's 12-gauge shotgun in his right side and left arm pointed that out with crystal clarity. Mr. Capps great fortune in surviving his wounds was offset by the four ounces of methamphetamine confiscated from his residence.

On July 1, 1987, the Airport Police at Will Rogers World Airport and the Lake Rangers officially became a part of the OCPD. While these units had been placed under the authority and control of the Department in the past, they had always been separate entities. They had their own distinctive uniforms, insignia and duty areas. They were not interchangeable with OCPD officers and, at various times, were not even fully commissioned with police powers.

*Oklahoma City Airport Police officers in their dark blue uniforms and seven-pointed stars before being assimilated into the OCPD.*

*Oklahoma City Lake Rangers in their pre-OCPD uniforms.*

This time was different. The Airport Police were placed under the Uniform Bureau and the Lake Rangers under the Traffic and Support Division. All of these officers became fully commissioned OCPD officers if they were willing to stay. They were to be subject to the same duties, transfers and interchangeability, no longer to be guaranteed that they would work at the airport or lakes exclusively. Some resigned but most stayed and welcomed the change.

Two civilian employees and 24 Lake Rangers made the changeover along with 25 Airport officers, 4 dispatchers and 1 civilian. The navy blue uniforms and seven-pointed stars of the Airport Police were phased out as were the tan and gray uniforms of the Lake Rangers. All would be standardized in the gray shirts and blue trousers of the OCPD now. The new officers were afforded all of the same rights and benefits of OCPD officers including the capability of transferring between various areas of the Department after they completed in-service training.

In accordance with the absorption of the new units, an addition was made to the monument in front of Police Headquarters to honor Lake Ranger William Stewart Jr. and Airport Officer Garland Garrison who had died in the line of duty during the 1970's.

During the summer of 1987, the Guest House murder case came unravelled. The practice of hypnotizing witnesses had fallen into disrepute after several years of being challenged in court. Clifford Henry Bowen's attorney presented an argument that one of the key witnesses had been improperly hypnotized during the investigation. State courts agreed, overturned the conviction and said Bowen should be retried. The preliminary hearings took place in front of Judge Joe Cannon. More than a quarter of a century after his rampages as Governor Edmondson's "crew-cut commando" prohibition enforcer, Cannon was becoming infamous for his courtroom eccentricities, temper tantrums and scathing diatribes when things didn't go as expected in his court. When the hypnosis evidence came up and Cannon began bitter denunciations of detectives, prosecutors and the previous trial judge alike, it became obvious that the case was doomed. After six years on McAlester's Death Row, Clifford Henry Bowen was released. Harold Behrens, his case unaffected by the hypnoses, remained in federal prison.

Prior to 1969, OCPD officers had to purchase their own sidearms for duty purposes. In late 1969, the Department began issuing Smith & Wesson Model 15 .38 Special revolvers with four-inch barrels to new officers. During the 1980s, the Department began issuing stainless steel Smith & Wesson Model 65 .357 Magnums and, in the next decade, would convert to

Glock 9 mm automatics. In the summer of 1987, when the last officers who had to purchase their own weapons were nearing retirement, Chief Wilder endeared himself to his officers again by obtaining the City Council's approval to allow retiring officers to keep their service weapons. Under the new policy, officers who died prior to retirement would have their weapons passed on to their heirs. Officers who were disabled prior to retirement could keep their weapons subject to the Chief's approval. Besides being a memento from the City for police service,the Council cited a State statute that said retired officers retained their peace officer status, could legally carry arms and could even be called back to active duty in an emergency.

The Major Violators Unit was formed in the Special Projects Group to investigate and prosecute high level narcotics organizations and effect large scale asset seizures. Initially formed with six Detectives under Sergeant Steve Upchurch, the group was to apply special skills to the anti-drug effort. These techniques included extensive electronic surveillance, complex financial investigations and coordinating with State and Federal agencies to utilize RICO (Racketeering Influenced and Corrupt Organizations) statutes against major narcotics conspiracies.

Keeping pace with the expanding, modernizing force, a new Police Operations Manual made its debut. Hundreds of pages longer than any of its predecessors, it was by far the most comprehensive manual to date.

The year ended with the death, on December 17, of another former Chief. Dan Hollingsworth passed away at the age of 80. As an officer from 1930-46, he had risen from motorcycle officer to Inspector. He had been Director of Training from 1939-42 and again in 1946, when he left to manage the Greater Oklahoma City Safety Council. After less than a year as Chief in 1961-62, he had been a consultant in traffic safety for several agencies including the Oklahoma Department of Public Safety. He had written a number of books on traffic safety including Rocks In The Roadway, a standard police training manual.

The Oklahoma City Police Academy marked a milestone on February 12, 1988, when the forty-six officers who made up Class Number 100 graduated. It was the largest graduating class in Department history to that time. The winner of the top Firearms Award was a young officer named Delmar Warren Tooman.

On May 6, the Awards Banquet was hosted by Jane Jayroe. Ms. Jayroe had been Miss America in 1967 and was now a news anchor with the local ABC affiliate, KOCO-TV. The Medal of Valor was awarded to Detective Clyde Bowling for the drug raid eleven months earlier. The coveted award was also given to Officer Doug Northrup for his actions during a robbery at the American Home Savings and Loan three weeks before Bowling's incident. The suspect had been behind the counter sacking the money when Northrup walked in. Northrup shot the man, who was being sought for a dozen other bank robberies, after the suspect pointed his weapon at him. Two Meritorious Service Medals, two Certificates of Achievement and a Life Saving award were bestowed along with nine Certificates of Achievement to citizens.

The year 1988 also saw the fruition of what was sometimes not so affectionately called "The Big Hummer". A massive, City-wide computer system, it placed an incredible amount of information literally at the fingertips of every officer. Operations that once would have necessitated dozens of teletypes, phone calls and trips to several different agencies as well as different areas of the Department could now be accomplished in minutes at a single terminal.

Shortly before 3 P.M. on November 4, 1988, a large woman entered the Continental Federal Savings and Loan at 7500 S. Western. Officer Ed Moore Jr., working an extra job as a security guard a the bank, noticed her for a couple of reasons. First, she was carrying a shoebox which isn't usual in a bank and can raise lots of curiosity in suspicious people like police officers. Second, at 6 feet tall and about 170 pounds, she was a pretty good sized gal. You can only disguise so much with a black wig and a pair of earrings. Approaching a female bank employee, "she" inquired about safety deposit boxes and asked to be shown where they were kept. When they got back to the safety deposit box area, Harold J. Sigman pulled a .25 automatic pistol on the female employee and forced her back to the front counters. As they approached the teller's windows, he put the shoebox on the counter.

As Sigman was demanding the money be placed in a plastic bag, Officer Moore was approaching with drawn weapon. Aiming his .357 Magnum at Sigman's head, Moore yelled at him to drop the gun. Sigman tried to spin around but Moore shot him once in the head before he could fire.

The Bomb Squad was called to examine the shoebox but it was found to contain only a can of green beans. Sigman was taken to the hospital and survived his wound.

The summer of 1989 saw the City host two major events. The 1989 Olympic Festival covered the last two weeks of July. The OCPD provided security for 14 events held at 11 locations in the City. On the first day of August the City began hosting the 49th National Conference of the Fraternal Order of Police. Six thousand people including 2,100 delegates poured an estimated $6 million into the local economy.

The Centennial year of 1990 marked even more radical progress. On March 1, a 911 emergency communications system became operative and, in a radical departure from tradition, was taken out of the Police chain of command. The unit was moved to the underground Emergency Operations Center near the Lincoln Park Zoo and was placed under a civilian manager.

The annual Awards Banquet was held on May 12. Bill Mitchell, news reporter for the local ABC affiliate, KOCO-TV, hosted. Officer Ed Moore Jr. was awarded the Medal of Valor for aborting the savings and loan robbery six months earlier. His father must have been especially proud that night. Officer Ed Moore Sr. had retired from the OCPD two years earlier after twenty years of service. Two Meritorious Service awards, four Life Saving awards and five Certificates of Achievement were given along with two certificates to citizens.

On July 1, the Animal Welfare Division was placed under Departmental control but it was overshadowed by a more drastic restructuring of the rank system. The ranks of Master Patrolman, Specialist and (amidst some furor) Detective were eliminated. All officers of those ranks were reclassified to Sergeants. Higher ranking officers were also reclassified one rank higher. The only officers not affected by the restructuring were those with less than six and one-half years of service, the Chief, the three Deputy Chiefs and the three existing Majors.

In spite of the fact that salaries were rising, extra jobs were still a part of many police officer's lives. Whether it was in plain clothes trying to catch shoplifters or in uniform, sometimes it was a pretty tough way to earn ten bucks an hour. Ed Moore Jr. could testify to that. It got pretty tough on the morning of August 3rd, too.

At 11:10 A.M., Martin Vernon Stamps walked into the Communications Federal Credit Union at 427 N.W. 6th in downtown Oklahoma City. A resident of a local so-called "half-way house", the 36-year-old convict was on a house arrest program for a 14-year sentence for burglary.Instead of a check in his hand, he was carrying a gun.

It's a big career step up from burglary to armed robbery and an even higher step to bank robbery. Mr. Stamps wasn't ready for the graduation yet. He committed one of the cardinal sins of survivability before he even got in the door. He wasn't paying attention. He never saw Lt. Norman Cook sitting at a desk at the far end of the lobby, although Cook was in full uniform and not doing anything to hide his presence. On the contrary, this was one of those "scarecrow" jobs where the visibility of a uniformed police officer is usually enough of a deterrent to would-be robbers.

Cook, on the other hand, was paying attention. The 19-year veteran didn't need all that experience to deduce Mr. Stamps' intentions when he saw him approach a teller's window with the pistol raised. Drawing his nine-millimeter automatic, Cook covered the dozen steps to the teller's window quickly. Covering his suspect with the weapon, Cook used his free hand to push a customer out of the way as he yelled "Stop!" at the gunman. When Stamps didn't respond to the warning, Cook fired once, fatally wounding him.

Later proven to be the suspect in two other recent robberies, Stamps had committed another mistake that decreased his chances of survivability down to nil. During the crime scene examination, his gun was discovered not be a gun at all but a very realistic toy gun made of plastic. Thus another maxim was born. Never try robbing a bank with a kid's toy and a burglar's heart.

Sometimes the bad guys' survivability is harder to overcome. George Aebischer's was. At 52 years of age, he had a 35-year history of state and federal convictions for burglary, robbery, manslaughter, larceny and drugs. Now on parole for a Postal burglary, Aebischer had been released from Leavenworth Federal Penitentiary only three months earlier. As a condition of his parole, he had to submit to periodic drug tests. In perfect harmony with his past history of being unsuccessful at anything that didn't have a statute number attached to it, George failed his first test. That resulted in a warrant being issued for his arrest in late July of 1989.

Sgt. Phil Davis was intimately familiar with George Aebischer and his past history. When he saw the familiar name on the wanted list, he immediately started using his resources to locate Aebischer. At 8:30 P.M. on the evening of August 19, those resources led him and Sgt. David Ellis to the Southern Oaks Apartments at 4525 S. Woodward.

When the door of Apartment Four opened in response to their knocking, the two officers saw several men inside. As they entered, one of the men got up from a dining room table and walked out of their sight into the kitchen and another left the couch, turning into a hallway. As Davis watched the remaining men, Ellis retrieved the one heading for a rear bedroom, had him sit at a table in the dinette attached to the living room and began questioning the man who had ducked into the small kitchen. Davis began checking the identities of the others.

Just then, there was a knock at the door. Sgt. Davis, standing just inside, opened it. Seeing the shadowy figure of a man in the dimly lit vestibule, Davis asked him for some identification. George Aebischer evidently had already decided that he was tired of running but he wasn't going back to jail again. He had to walk past the marked black and white scout car to enter the building and, seeing the two uniformed officers inside the apartment, decided to confront the situation head on. Reaching behind his back as though for his wallet, he drew a gun stuck in the rear of his waistband.

Firing once at a range little more than arm's length, he hit Sgt. Davis in the chest. As Davis fell, Aebischer ran past him into the apartment, apparently intent upon taking on Sgt. Ellis next because Aebischer fired a second round toward the kitchen area which hit one of the men sitting in the dinette in the ankle. Drawing his nine-millimeter automatic and returning fire even as he fell, Davis hit Aebischer four times in the chest. Sgt. Ellis stepped out of the kitchen to find both Aebischer and his partner down. Holding the other men at bay, he summoned help.

*Technical Investigations Sergeant Ron Wortham demonstrating the use of the new Automated Fingerprint Identification System (AFIS).*

*OCPD Aviation Unit Officer Jamison demonstrating the Forward Looking Infra-red Radar (FLIR) thermal imaging system.*

*Matching wits with the "Big Hummer."*

Davis was wearing a bulletproof vest. Although he sustained a large bruise on his chest and was temporarily admitted to the hospital because the force of the shot had thrown his heart into an irregular beat pattern, he survived without any disability. George Aebischer, however, was not wearing a vest. He died where he fell.

In the Fall, two new acronyms entered the OCPD vocabulary, AFIS and FLIR. AFIS was the Automated Fingerprint Identification System, a new multi-million dollar tool in the Technical Investigations Unit. It is a computerized system for comparing fingerprints somewhat similar to the Inforex System developed almost a decade earlier but much faster and more sophisticated. Checking an unknown suspect fingerprint against a massive data base, the computer produces a prioritized list of similar prints on file with the most similar listed first. Police fingerprint technicians then visually compare the prints in order. During the testing phase at the first of 1989, the computer solved a murder that had occurred in 1972 by matching a suspect print from the crime scene to that of a suspect already in prison for another homicide.

FLIR was the Forward-Looking Infrared Radar system installed on one of the Department's two Hughes 500E helicopters. The new FLIR unit is basically a television camera that picks up thermal or heat images instead of visual ones. Transmitting the images to a monitor in the cockpit, it shows anything warmer than its' background standing out clearly. This included human bodies and engines that have been running recently. The OCPD Aviation Unit was now commanded by Lieutenant Manuel Beck, one of the original pilots back in 1973. Toward the end of the year, the Aviation Unit moved the helicopters and their fixed wing airplane into a new hangar specially designed and built for the unit at Downtown Airpark.

Thus ended the two most violent decades in the history of American law enforcement. The 1970s had seen more police officers slain in the line of duty than any time previously. An average of 185 officers died every year during the 1980s, making it easily the second most costly decade and continuing an escalation that had been going on for 30 years. Mercifully, only seven of the fallen had been OCPD's and the price could have been far higher but it was still far too high.

# XI — THE SECOND CENTURY 1990 —

In 1984, the citizens of Oklahoma County made pari-mutuel betting legal. The Oklahoma Horse Racing Commission was formed and began authorizing the construction of race tracks around the state. In 1988, Remington Park was opened as a showpiece race track north of the Lincoln Park Zoo.

All of the race horses had to be tested for illegal drugs. The samples were initially sent to a laboratory in Colorado under contract to the Racing Commission. At this point, Chief Wilder and Deputy Chief Dave McBride decided to set a precedent.

Entering into negotiations with the Commission, a half-million dollar contract was approved for the City to provide for the drug testing for all the race tracks in the State. Construction began in late 1989 and on January 1, 1990, the OCPD Equine Testing Laboratory became the official laboratory for all sanctioned racing in the State of Oklahoma. Attached to the Laboratory Services Division, it was the first such laboratory in the United States affiliated with a municipal police agency.

The 1990 Census listed 444,719 citizens. In March, the Springlake Division briefing station became operational. The first joint Police/Fire briefing station, it is located at N.E. 41st and Prospect, only a few blocks from the riot-torn area of 1971. The first commander was Major Lawrence Johnson.

The Ninth Annual Awards and Appreciation Banquet was staged on May 11. Linda Cavanaugh, news anchor for the local NBC affiliate, KFOR-TV, provided the opening remarks. Sgt. Phil Davis and Lt. Norm Cook were both awarded the Medal of Valor for their actions the previous August. Three Life Saving awards were received along with three Certificates of Achievement and six Certificates of Appreciation to citizens.

On June 14, Chief Bob Wilder retired after over 30 years of service, the last 5 as Chief. Only three men in the last century had managed to exceed his tenure in the top office.

Hired on February 16, 1960, the day after he became eligible on his twenty-first birthday, Wilder was the son of retired Major H.V. Wilder who had served with the OCPD's first mounted patrol unit. After serving as a motorcycle officer, like his father before him, he was promoted to Sergeant in 1964 and served as a supervisor in the Jail, another position his father had

*Chief David R. McBride.*

*Chief Bob Wilder and wife, Edy, at his retirement ceremonies, June 14, 1990.*

occupied. Three years later he became a Lieutenant and in 1970 was promoted to Captain to command the Department's first Planning and Research Unit. After achieving the rank of Major in 1972, he commanded every division in the Department over the next decade. Upon Chief Heggy's retirement in February of 1982, Wilder was appointed Assistant Chief. Having earned Bachelor's and Master's degrees from Oklahoma City University, three years later he succeeded Lloyd Gramling as Chief.

Professionally, Wilder was looked upon as a good administrator who held the welfare of his officers uppermost. Personally affable, prepossessing, unpretentious, mischievous and an inveterate practitioner of harmless practical jokes, Wilder gained the respect (and occasional reciprocation) of his officers by showing that he could take a joke just as well as he could dish one out, an ability markedly absent in most commanders. He left a legacy as one of the most personable and popular Chiefs.

Deputy Chief Dave McBride was elevated to the top spot. Two weeks later, at the beginning of the new fiscal year, the 911 system was once again brought back under the control of the Police Department. Captain Steve Upchurch, who had begun his career 21 years earlier as a civilian dispatcher, was promoted to Major and designated as the first police commander of the unit.

The next step in the evolution of police communications began as the Department began installing mobile data terminals in the fleet of patrol cars. This would give every officer the capability of checking warrants, vehicle tags, driver's licenses and all the other checks themselves. No longer would they have to radio the information in and wait their turn while civilian dispatchers checked the information.

July 5 started out as a pretty good day for Guadalupe Ruis. He didn't even have to leave his home at 209 S.W. 31st to make a profit on his first cocaine sale of the day. Without his knowledge, the day went downhill. The purchaser was an undercover police officer who immediately passed the news to his Special Projects cohorts and obtained a "no-knock" search warrant for the Ruis residence.

Shortly before 10 P.M. that night, Special Projects Detectives Tom Terhune and Randy Kirby returned to the Ruis residence to serve the warrant backed up by three uniformed officers, Sergeant Willard Edwards, Officers Scott Samuel and Bill Weaver. When the officers forced the front door open, Ruis was laying on a couch in the living room. When he saw the officers, Ruis reached under the couch and pulled out a .357 Magnum revolver. Terhune and Kirby both leapt on Ruis, struggling to disarm him. Ruis managed to fire one round during the struggle, scorching Kirby's left forearm with a powder burn and spraying powder and metal fragments into Terhune's eyes before both officers were able to return his fire, fatally wounding him.

On the 56th anniversary of John Dillinger's death, the FBI's Office of Public Affairs published a retrospective article on that night's events in their magazine The Investigator. The secretive J. Edgar Hoover would have had an apoplectic fit if he could have seen how much information his Bureau was publishing openly. A list of all the agents involved, their photos and a map showing their locations on the stakeout were included. The article noted that of the 20 agents present that night, only 2 of them still survived today. One of them was 83-year-old retired Special Agent Charles Gerald "Jerry" Campbell who, with Clarence Hurt, had been one of the first two OCPD officers recruited into the Bureau two months before Dillinger's capture in 1934. Campbell had retired from the FBI in 1965 and had evidently made the most of his retirement.

The next month the concept of assessment centers was again applied to the promotional process but this time for Lieutenants and Captains. The first promotions made under this new system were Captains Bill Citty, David Shupe and W.B. Taylor closely followed by Lieutenants David Simpson, Randy Yarbrough, Ken McDonald and Gil Hensley. Another promotion to Captain made from this promotional list was Larry Koonce, the great-grandnephew of J.B. Koonce, the first City Marshal of South Oklahoma City in 1889.

In mid-September, new commission cards and the first new badge in half a century were introduced. The new badge was a consequence of the production of a "centennial badge" the previous year.

A large number of officers had expressed a desire for a new badge to celebrate the completion of the City's first century and because the current style had been in use since 1929. In the ensuing six decades, a certain lack of uniformity had crept in as officers had their badges copied or personalized. Some were a dull tin finish and some were chrome-plated. Some gold badges were differently tinted. While most had the badge number stamped into them, some had numbers sculpted in low relief. Officers were encouraged to submit designs and many did.

*New OCPD badge-1990.*

Ultimately, the Department declined to officially sponsor the centennial badge. The design featuring a small six-pointed silver star with the City Seal in the center, the whole surmounted by a gold eagle and surrounded by a gold wreath. A gold scroll across the top of the star carried the dates "1889-1989". They were eventually privately produced and offered for sale to officers for about $50. The Department agreed that those officers who chose to purchase the badge would be authorized to wear it but only during the centennial year, reverting to the official badge after then.

In the meantime, the Department was considering a change in the official badge. This was finally decided, the badges produced and issued in mid-September. The new badges featured a City Seal in the center and several tradition-breaking features. All badges were now gold instead of only those of detectives, supervisors and commanders. No rank was displayed on the badge, only a commission number, so officers would no longer changes badges when promoted. The old commission card was replaced with dual cards, one a police commission and the other a photo identification card. A newly redesigned cap badge prominently featuring the City Seal was also issued.

The new badges and commission numbers would be issued in order by rank and seniority within rank. Therefore, Chief McBride was the recipient of badge and commission Number One. Despite being requested by several of the Department's more irreverent iconoclasts, badge number 666 was held back and not issued.

The new badges and commission cards were met with general dissatisfaction by the majority of the officers. Most felt that there had been not enough change in some ways and too much in others. While the lower-ranking "silver badges" enjoyed the status of a gold badge, the officers who already had gold badges didn't like spreading that status freely. For as long as any active officer could remember, a gold badge was symbolic of promotion, seniority and supervisory or command status. That distinction was now erased. Everybody had a gold badge.

They also didn't like the rank not being displayed on the badge, changing their commission numbers and felt that the badge hadn't changed that much. It was basically the same old badge, gold-plated and with the City Seal stuck in the center of it. The specialist ranks of Master Patrolman, Specialist and Detective especially disliked giving up the "special" status they had worked to achieve. The Detectives, in particular, raised so much hell and so many threw the new badges in a drawer to continue wearing the old ones that they were eventually officially authorized to wear their old Detective's badges.

The new commission cards were equally criticized. The two larger cards required a new badge case to display them which was too large for hip pockets and almost too large for inside jacket pockets in suit coats. Officers derisively referred to them as "FBI credentials" because of the similar size and style. It didn't help any that the new badge and commission card wallets were not provided by the Department but instead were offered for sale for $10 by the Police Benefit Committee. Not only were the officers being asked to suffer these indignities, they were being asked to pay for the privilege. Predictably, the officers boycotted them and the Benefit Committee was left with hundreds of unpurchased badge wallets.

The Major Violators Unit concluded a 3-year investigation of Johnny Lee Sanders heroin organization, ending his 15-year distribution ring with Federal convictions and significant seizures. In its first 3 years of existence, the unit had seized over a quarter of a million dollars and 50 vehicles annually. Other significant seizures had included boats, airplanes and homes of drug dealers. Capitalizing on this success, an Interdiction Group of four Detectives and a drug detector dog was added to the unit. Working in teams, they monitored the airport, bus station, freight and parcel services as well as hotels and motels to intercept drugs smuggled by common carriers.

In response to the increase in drugs and gang activities and the well-armed nature of these criminals, the Department began issuing semi-automatic Glock nine-millimeter handguns to new officers.

On the evening of September 29, 1990, the Department suffered the tragic death of Officer Delmar Warren Tooman during the armed robbery already recounted in the Introduction to this work. Within 48 hours, the tragedy was nearly compounded and the OCPD almost lost four more officers, including its' third Chief, in the line of duty.

On October 1, Chief McBride was flying in one of the police helicopters to Anadarko to meet with Officer Tooman's family. He was accompanied by pilot Sergeant Mike Jones, observer Sergeant Doug Burnett and Public Information Officer Major Bob Taylor. As they lifted off from the meeting, the Hughes 500E helicopter clipped a power line, faltered in mid-air, turned on its' side while grasping for altitude and went down in a shower of dust and broken rotor blades. Miraculously, the chopper didn't burst into flame and only minor injuries resulted. The entire incident was videotaped by Officer Tooman's brother on the ground and it was later featured on a national television show.

On October 3, as a six-mile long procession of officers followed Officer Tooman to his burial, the mourning officers felt strangely fortunate to be burying only one of their colleagues instead of five.

*Officer Delmar Warren Tooman.*

On December 6, 1990, a fourth police briefing station opened. The Hefner Station at N.W. 122nd and Portland was dedicated and Major Robert A. "Bob" Jones became the first commander. Built as a result of a 1985 bond issue, the million dollar station was staffed with 128 officers to cover a 141 square mile area of northwest Oklahoma City.

In early April of 1991, another one of those periodic outbursts of violence against the City's police officers broke out. On April 2, four officers shot and killed a barricaded mental patient who attacked them with a weeding scythe after they responded to a domestic call at his northeast residence. A week later, during the early morning hours of April 9, Officer Charles Provines was chasing a man trying to burglarize a business on the southeast side. During the chase the man stopped, drew a nine-millimeter automatic pistol, pointed it at the officer's face and pulled the trigger. In the stress of the moment, he had forgotten to load a round into the chamber. As the hammer clicked on the empty chamber, the officer shot him. The gun had been stolen in the burglary of a State Narcotics Agent's home. The forgetful burglar would survive his wound but the entire force was buzzing with the news the next morning. Older officers went around philosophizing "These things happen in threes, ya know". Some scoffed at them, some ignored them but a lot of people spent the day halfway holding their breath, waiting for the other shoe to drop. This time they were right.

Shortly before mid-afternoon that day, officers of the Oklahoma Department of Corrections contacted the OCPD, requesting assistance in recapturing an escaped robber. They had information that 42-year-old Jerry Long was at 2236 N.W. 10th. Sergeant Ed Dugan and his new recruit partner, Jeff Tanksley, joined the Corrections officers in an unmarked car to assist in the arrest.

When the officers arrived at the address on 10th Street, Long was standing outside. He saw the officers getting out of their car and immediately drew a handgun. Sgt. Dugan drew his weapon and fired three times, hitting Long in the stomach, leg and foot. Jerry Long would survive his wounds to return to prison, all the officers would breathe easier since the Department had survived three officer-involved shootings in nine days without losing an officer and the old philosophers could go around smugly pronouncing "I tole'ja so!".

A new program of Neighborhood Oriented Policing was implemented and the addition of a DNA Laboratory was being planned. The average age of officers during World War II was 41. Now it was in the mid-20s and still declining.

One of the new programs implemented as a result of the concept of Neighborhood Oriented Policing was the Bicycle Patrol. It wasn't exactly a new program. Rather it was one of those cyclical ideas that found new life like the Mounted Patrol. Teddy Roosevelt had created a bicycle patrol in New York City in 1895 to control the "steam carriages" then making pedestrian traffic unsafe by breaking the speed limit of eight miles per hour. Now it would become a means of closer contact with the public and had a practical side in that the bikes could go places where their gasoline-powered counterparts could not.

The new concept had originated in the Seattle Police Department in 1987 and had successfully been transplanted to over 50 cities. Six officers on bicycles would be assigned to transitional neighborhoods in two-man teams. They were specifically targeting enforcement efforts on daytime burglaries, vandalism, drug deals, prostitution and auto theft.

The first officers assigned to the new program were Sergeants Johnny Carroll, Jack Ballard and Willie Edwards along with Officers Glen Holcomb, Scott Wilson and Greg Johnston. Initial efforts were targeted in the Will Rogers Division area of N.W. 10th Street between Classen and Pennsylvania. The program became operational on April 15, 1991. In the first week, the officers answered 86 calls, made 6 felony arrests, a dozen other arrests, filled out 64 Field Interview Cards and created some good public relations with citizen contacts.

April 19, 1991, was the first issue of The OKC Police Review. The old Cosmopolitan had been published monthly since early 1990 but was now re-named and published on payday every other Friday.

In an unforeseen move, after less than 11 months in office, Chief McBride retired on May 3, 1991. McBride had begun his career on August 5, 1968. He had served three years in the Patrol Division and had been involved in the incident that resulted in the shooting of Sergeant Ben Caswell in October of 1969. Four years as a Detective in Narcotics, Intelligence and Burglary led to promotion to Sergeant in 1975. Serving nearly seven years in that rank, he had supervised units in Vice, Organized Crime, Communications, Burglary, and Patrol. In 1981, he served a one-year term as the President of the FOP. His promotion to Lieutenant the following year led to assignment as the Department's Public Information Officer. In 1985, he was promoted to Captain and made Administrative Assistant to Chief Bob Wilder. He ascended through the ranks of Major and Deputy Chief before becoming Chief in 1990.

Chief McBride was primarily identified with two statements he liked to quote, one publicly and one privately. The more public quote was "Police work, if done right, is the toughest job in the world". The more private quote, which was used against him more than once, was "If you always do what you've always done, you'll always be what you've always been". Innovative, iconoclastic, politically astute, ambitious and decisive were some of the kinder adjectives applied to him. His liberal political beliefs and innovative attitudes toward change had stunted his popularity in an inherently conservative organization that tolerated change frequently but grudgingly. His lack of personal popularity among the lower ranks was compounded by a managerial style in which he also tended to operate somewhat fast and loose under the governmental principle that "it's easier to obtain forgiveness than permission".

Chief McBride's retirement was effective the same day as the Tenth Annual Police Awards Banquet. Among his last official acts as Chief were the awarding of the Police Cross to the family of Delmar Warren Tooman and the Medal for Meritorious Service to Officer Barry Lanzner. In addition, five Medals of Valor were awarded. Three of them honored multi-generation OCPD families.

Sergeants Tom Terhune and Randy Kirby were given the award for their shooting struggle during a dope raid the previous July. Officer Ron Burks was honored for saving several residents of his apartment complex during a fire in which he sustained burns rescuing people on May 15, 1990.

Robert E. "Bob" Terhune had retired from the OCPD on the last day of 1984 after a 21-year career, most of it spent as a Detective working Vice, Narcotics and Intelligence, during which he garnered nearly two dozen commendations and letters of appreciation. One of his partners, Mike Huckaby, had won a CPI City Manager's Commendation award in 1963. During the years they rode together, they gained a reputation as one of the most active, aggressive teams of detectives in the city. Some detectives had reputations as being "retired on duty"; guys who became detectives only so they could get out of uniform, stop answering calls, writing traffic tickets and work day shift. Like bread and butter, "Huckaby and Terhune" was spoken and thought of as one word among the street officers in the late '60's and early 70's. They were the kind of detectives that the street officers could pass an informant's information on to and something would be done about it. Mike Huckaby later resigned from the OCPD to join ATF and eventually became the Special Agent in Charge of the Tulsa ATF office. Before his retirement, Bob Terhune created a unique specialty for himself. He began specializing in investigations of the theft and fencing of stolen oilfield equipment, a remarkably prevalent and lucrative avocation in oil-rich Oklahoma. When he retired in 1984, he became an agent for the OSBI. Tom Terhune is his oldest son. Terry Terhune is Bob's daughter. She became an OCPD dispatcher in 1977 and later married Officer Ron Burks. Thus, both Bob's son and son-in-law were awarded the Medal of Valor that year.

Randy Kirby had more in common with Tom Terhune than just receiving the Medal of Valor for the same deadly narcotics raid. He was also the son of a much-decorated retired OCPD Detective. Denver G. Kirby had retired prematurely in 1977 after an abbreviated 10-year career primarily spent as a Detective in Robbery-Homicide. His short career was due to a disability retirement necessitated by duodenal ulcers, a measure of the intensity he brought to his job. Like father, like son, awards for heroism were no stranger to Denver Kirby either. In 1968, Denver and his partner Bob Jackson were awarded the City Council CPI Award for Heroism for capturing an escaped convict from California during an armed robbery attempt. In his ten years on the job, Denver Kirby had accumulated 17 commendations.

In addition, Officer Scott Samuel was honored with the Medal of Valor for an incident that occurred the day after Burks' heroics in the burning apartments. Samuel had been fired at several times by an elderly man who appeared to be mentally incompetent. Samuel was able to apprehend the man without shooting him. The man was found incompetent to stand trial. Sergeant Glenn Ring received the medal for preventing a man from murdering his 76-year-old mother the previous October. Ring, a member of the OCPD Pistol Team, had been returning from a pistol match near Cushing in his private vehicle when he saw the man push the woman out of his car. Ring apprehended the man and gave medical assistance to the old woman.

Six Life Saving Awards were also presented along with six Certificates of Achievement to officers, eight Certificates to citizens and a special presentation was made to Oklahoma County District Attorney (and former OCPD officer) Bob Macy. In his farewell message to the Department he led, Chief McBride provided another quote; "There are a lot of things you can do to make a living, some things you do make a difference".

McBride was accepting the position of Commissioner of the State Department of Public

Safety under Governor David Walters. The OCPD's Public Information Officer, Major Bob Taylor, retired as well to become McBride's assistant at DPS.

The City administrator's, led by Mayor Ron Norick and City Manager Don Bown, announced another departure from tradition. A nation wide search and assessment center would be conducted to determine McBride's successor. Deputy Chief M.T. Berry was appointed interim Chief until a candidate could be selected, becoming the first black officer to lead the organization since Assistant Chief Gerald Emmett had served periods as Acting Chief under Chiefs Purser and Heggy.

One of interim Chief Berry's first duties was to preside over the formal opening of the Department's new $438,000 Equine and Canine Facility on June 11, 1991. Located at 1400 S. Portland, two miles south of the Training Academy, the ten-acre facility provided housing and training areas for the Mounted Patrol and Canine Units animals and officers.

The Summer of 1991 saw the publication of the largest Police yearbook yet. The 1990 Oklahoma City Police Department yearbook was the first that was directly comparable to professionally produced high school and college yearbooks. The dark blue binding was offset by one of the new gold badges inset in the front cover. At 272 pages in length, it was also the most comprehensive effort thus far.

The frontispiece of the inside cover provides an interesting historical panorama of the Department's first century. It is a wide-angle photograph taken in the Air Support Unit's new hangar at the Downtown Airpark. The hangar's interior is darkened, lit only by the lights of the half dozen vehicles inside. The dim atmosphere is made even more murky by an artificial smoke machine that produced an ethereal, foggy mist that thickened increasingly toward the rear of the hangar. The huge red, white and blue City Seal and Oklahoma City Police logo painted on the rear wall of the hangar is barely discernible through the haze.

In the left foreground, Sergeant J.D. McLaughlin of the Mounted Patrol Unit represents something of an anachronism. Dressed in the current police uniform, he is holding his horse's reins, its' saddlebags embroidered with the words "Oklahoma City Police". Facing them in the right foreground is a 1990 Chevrolet scout car with all its' lights on, the red and blue lights of the visibar frozen in mid-flash. Officers Teresa Sterling and Barry McCary flanked their car, standing directly in front of the Department's 1981 Gulfstream Aero Commander. The twin-engine turboprop, worth $538,000, had been confiscated along with two other planes and a van during a drug-money laundering investigation between the United States and Mexico. As part of the asset forfeiture program, the plane had been presented to Chief McBride by Congressman Glenn English the previous December.

Centered in the photograph are Sergeant Rick Staton and Lieutenant Norman Cook next to their Kawasaki 1000 police motorcycles, their red, white and blue lights reflecting off of the hangar's shiny floor. To their right, standing half a dozen paces behind McLaughlin's horse, Sergeant Ron Burks stands outside his Canine Unit holding his German Shepherd's leash.

Behind Burks, Sergeants Doug Burnett and David Chadwick stand in front of one of the Department's Hughes 500E helicopters, their pilot's helmets under their arms. The searchlight in the chopper's nose sends a piercing beam across the hangar, illuminating a squat, sleek black Corvette in front of it. Another drug asset seizure, the Corvette's headlights accentuate the fogginess at the extreme rear of the hangar. Standing in the open doors of the sports car are Sergeants Janice Stupka and Dexter Nelson of the Drug Enforcement Unit. Stupka is wearing a blue raid jacket and Nelson is wearing body armor, both with "Police" emblazoned across the front.

Finally, centered in the photo but at the far back of the hangar, easily overlooked at first in the thickest part of the smoke, are three members of the Tactical Team. They are the Department's "final option" in violent situations. Dressed in camouflaged fatigues and black balaclavas with only a narrow slit for their eyes, they hold their automatic rifles at port arms. Like three modern horsemen of the Apocalypse, they present an appropriately menacing picture looming out of the foggy haze.

The introductory pages listed commendatory letters from District Attorney Bob Macy (a former Oklahoma City officer), City Manager Paula Hearn, then-Chief of Police Dave McBride, Mayor Ron Norick and the City Council, including Ward One Councilman and former Chief

I.G. Purser. Profiles of Chief McBride and former Chief Wilder preceded a 96-page section on the history of the Department from its inception. It was the compilation of that history section with then-Lieutenant C.E. "Ed" Hill that was the genesis of this book. While I concentrated on the narrative, Ed composed the general layout of the volume which included arranging the myriad of photographs in the book including over 300 in the historical section, many of them rare, unique and never printed before.

Color fold-out pages paid a tribute to the 28 OCPD officers, 1 Lake Ranger and 1 Airport officer who had lost their lives in the line of duty and the 14 Medal of Valor winners. A Department organizational chart preceded the photos of the 81 personnel assigned to the Office of Administration under Deputy Chief Richard DeLaughter. These people were profiled in the articles covering Internals Affairs, Staff Inspections, Public Affairs, Community Relations, Crimestoppers, Campus Resources, Drug Abuse Resistance Education, Police Athletic League, Planning and Research, Budget, Court Liaison, Information Desk and Fleet Management.

Next came the 261 personnel assigned to the Special Services Bureau under Deputy Chief Major T. Berry. These people staffed Personnel, Recruiting, Human Resources, Polygraph, Training, the Firearms Range, Property Management, Permits and ID, Records Bureau, Detention Unit, Communications, Communications Information Unit, Technical Investigations, Fingerprint Identification, Photo Lab, Document Examiner, Firearms Lab, and the Forensic and Equine Laboratories.

The Operations Bureau, as usual the largest, was separated into its respective Divisions. The Hefner Division operated from its new (1990) briefing station at 3924 N.W. 122nd. Its lineage was traced back to when it was the original "North Briefing Station" in Will Rogers Park. When the Patrol force was decentralized, the old Central Patrol Division was moved to Will Rogers and the old Will Rogers became the new Hefner Division. The Division section pictured 130 officers assigned there under Major Bob Jones to patrol the Division's 141 square miles of far west and northwest Oklahoma City. It served about 125,000 of the City's citizens in areas that ranged from the bars and strip joints of Northwest 10th Street to wealthy neighborhoods in the far northwest areas.

The next Division pictured was the Santa Fe Division under Major Larry Gramling, younger brother of former Chief Lloyd Gramling. Located at S.E. 89th and Santa Fe, it was one of the two original briefing stations built when the Department began decentralizing in the late 1970s. Pictured were 123 officers to cover the Division's 293 square miles which encompassed much of the huge annexations of the 1950s, covering the entire southern half of the City. The narrative noted that this Division included parts of five different counties, Oklahoma, Canadian, Cleveland, Pottawatomie and McClain. This huge area completely surrounded and extended beyond Tinker Air Force Base, Stanley Draper Lake, Will Rogers Airport and the City of Mustang. It also went all the way north to Reno, encompassing the old original area of South Oklahoma City. It also included a widely variable population ranging from very expensive neighborhoods in the far southwest area to housing projects, ghetto areas and huge expanses of open land. One of the Watch Commanders pictured is Captain Charlie Shelden, Mike Ratikan's partner on that fateful night in 1971.

The Springlake Division pictured 119 officers under Major Lawrence Johnson to cover the Division's 130 square miles, primarily the northeast quadrant of the City. Operating out of the only joint Fire and Police Station at 4016 N. Prospect, it was located just east of and named for the old Springlake Amusement Park, scene of the riot of Easter Sunday in 1971. Serving about 90,000 citizens in the predominantly black area of the City, it was the first station built under the Neighborhood Oriented Policing concept. Springlake's officers were the first to exercise their imaginations in applying these concepts when several scout cars began having picnic lunches in front of the houses of known narcotics dealers. The innocuous tactic played hell with the dope business while greatly entertaining the honest neighbors.

The Will Rogers Division, the old Central Patrol Division, included photos of 129 officers under Major Tom Mundy. Occupying the other original briefing station at 3112 N.W. Grand Boulevard in Will Rogers Park (hence the name), the Division encompassed only 25 square miles in the near northwest area of the City as well as the downtown area.

Next were pictured the 137 personnel of the Uniform Support Division under Major Bill Jackson. This Division was a conglomeration of the old Traffic Division with the addition of some specialized units. These officers and civilians staffed Traffic Investigations, Parking Enforcement, Solo Motorcycles, the Horse Patrol Unit, Foot Patrol and the Air Support Unit (Helicopter). The Airport Division pictured 29 officers and 5 civilians tasked with providing police services to Will Rogers World Airport and the two municipal airfields, Wiley Post and C.E. Page. Following were photos of the Animal Welfare Division, Canine Unit, Tactical and Hostage Negotiations Unit and the Bomb Disposal Unit.

Three pages honored the 21 officers and civilian personnel that had been activated for duty in the 1990 Persian Gulf War and the members of the Honor Guard. Following were the photos of the 116 personnel assigned to the Investigations Division under Major Mike Heath. These officers and civilians staffed the Homicide, Robbery, Missing Persons, Sex Crimes, Assaults, Burglary, Larceny, Auto Theft and White Collar Crime Units. The Special Investigations Division pictured the 33 personnel in the Intelligence, Vice, Drug Enforcement and Major Violators Units.

The back pages paid tribute to civilian volunteers in the VIPS (Volunteers in Public Service) Program, the Awards Banquet, Pistol Team, the FOP and its Auxiliary, the Make-A-Wish program, Police Athletics and Explorer Scouts. Ending the book was a section on the Retired Officers Association, containing a record 143 photos under that of their President Nate Barber, a CPI award winner 25 years before. Four former Chiefs were pictured, Geer, Heggy, Gramling and Wilder. Some of the other older but distinguished historical faces shown included Ray Clark, Walt Kostiuk, Jerry Martin, Jack Mullinex, Lewis Swindler, six-foot-ten-inch Pat Patterson and the indefatigable Ace Williams.

There is an old joke about a farmer who had driven his mule and wagon into town to get supplies. After the supplies were loaded in the wagon, the farmer waved goodbye to the grocer and got in the wagon. He snapped the reins and yelled "Giddyup" but the mule didn't move. The farmer then reached back into the wagonbed and picked up a 4-foot piece of 2-by-4 lumber. Getting down from the wagon, he walked around in front of the mule, drew back and hit the mule right between the eyes with the 2-by-4 as hard as he could. The mule collapsed onto his front knees, shook his head and got back up. Tossing the club back in the wagon, the farmer was climbing back up on the wagon when the shocked grocer asked him "What'd you do that for?" The farmer said, "Gotta get his attention first". He then snapped the reins again, yelled "Giddyup" and the mule dutifully started forward.

It had been almost half a century since a person had been brought in from outside the OCPD to act as Chief. The last such Chief had been FBI Agent Frank Smith during the World War II years. With all three Deputy Chiefs and a number of Majors applying for the job, many felt that this was just an attempt by City Manager Bown and the City Council to get the attention of the Police Department staff and make them more responsive to his wishes. They thought that, ultimately, the tradition of inter-Departmental succession would prevail. This was not to be the case.

On August 24, 1991, City manager Don Bown announced the assessment center's successful candidate. The new Chief of the Oklahoma City Police Department would be Sam Gonzales. From Police Headquarters to City Hall, there echoed a resounding "WWWWHHHHOOOO?".

Gonzales had recently retired as an Assistant Chief of the Dallas, Texas, Police Department after 28 years of service there. Selected from a field of 54 applicants to become the 46th man to hold the office and appointed on his fiftieth birthday, the native Texan had no former connection with the OCPD with the exception of a rumored friendship with former Chief McBride. A large portion of the Department and virtually everyone above the rank of Captain went into an immediate tizzy. A normally reticent Deputy Chief began talking openly of retirement. Majors and Deputy Chiefs huddled over long lunch hours and drinks at out-of-the-way clubs, questioning, grousing, bitching, recriminating, threatening, and hypothesizing. What was Bown's agenda? What would be Gonzales' agenda? Where did we go wrong? Who have we pissed off? Why, why, why? The pouting and sulking was endemic for weeks among the staff of Majors and above.

*Members of OCPD's first Emergency Response Team (ERT). Left to right, Lieutanant Larry Baker, Officers Gary Youngker, Ron Thomas and Ron Gruver.*

It was announced that it would be some weeks before the new Chief could actually take office. Arrangements had to be made for the move to Oklahoma City. Awaiting Gonzales ascendancy, some of the merely interested traditionalists eventually came around to the viewpoint of "Let's see what's on his mind and what he's got". In the delaying interim, this "wait and see" attitude pervaded most of the Department. However, it didn't make any inroads among the pretenders to the throne and the staunchest traditionalists in the Department.

Sam Gonzales began his first day in residence as Chief of the Oklahoma City Police Department on Monday, October 14, 1991. Some of the more sardonic observers said the delay was to allow the assassination plots and suicide pacts among the staff to break up. He inherited a Police Department of 909 commissioned officers and 317 civilians to serve a City of nearly half a million people in a Metro area of over a million. A recruit's starting salary was now over $1,800 a month, more than 30 times Charles Colcord's first salary as Chief of Police. A budget of over $60 million annually supported the efforts of these personnel in a dozen police facilities spread over the City's 621 square miles. Gonzales stated that he didn't intend to make any changes until after the first of the year. After observing and educating himself with his new organization for the first few months, he would then decide what changes to implement.

The first change, although minor, took place the first Friday after the new Chief reported for duty. The Department newsletter, The OKC Police Review went through another name change. Now it was dubbed The Police Beat. Publication was still every other Friday and nothing in the format changed but the name.

True to his word, the first major changes the new Chief made were accomplished on January 17, 1992. The Assistant Chief's position was revived and Deputy Chief Richard DeLaughter was promoted into it. Lawrence Johnson became the second black Deputy Chief, was transferred to the Operations Bureau and Jim Gallegly was promoted to Major in the Springlake Division. In addition, he made three Captain's promotions, five Lieutenants and nineteen other transfers, mostly of command personnel.

The Department was reorganized and several new units were created. The Investigations

Bureau was re-established as a separate entity from Operations and Deputy Chief M.T. Berry was placed in charge. An Office of Professional Standards was created to include Criminal Intelligence, Staff Inspections, Internal Affairs and Public Integrity.

When violent riots had exploded at Springlake Amusement Park on Easter Sunday of 1972 and at the State Penitentiary at McAlester the following year, the officers who responded had no special training to deal with the events. But the passage of two decades had increased the numbers and types of situations that could require that kind of predetermined response. The Blazers hockey team, the OKC Cavalry basketball team, numerous sports at several local colleges and numerous music concerts that occurred all over the city year round attracted tens of thousands of fans. In addition, the metropolitan area was becoming a more popular forum for various kinds of protests and demonstrations. The time was right for an organized police unit that could be quickly assembled and deployed, specially trained and equipped to deal with this multitude of special situations.

In April of 1992, the OCPD Emergency Response Team (ERT) was formed. Major Steve Upchurch and Captain Ed Hill of the Will Rogers Division were given the responsibility for the initial selection and training of the unit. Sixty officers and six Lieutenants were chosen from a group of volunteers.

*ERT officers demonstrating shotgun-launched smoke granades.*

*ERT officers in riot formation.*

After their initial training, one squad of 15 officers commanded by a Lieutenant was in place in each of the four Operations Divisions, Will Rogers, Hefner, Springlake and Santa Fe. The Lieutenants in charge of these squads were John Clark, Larry Baker, Riley Lenex and Pat Vicsek. The unit also contained two teams of Investigations Bureau personnel for processing prisoners, filing charges and performing field services as needed.

The unit's mission is to contain and isolate dangerous or potentially critical situations. In addition to protests, civil disturbances, crowd control and riots, the ERT is also trained to assist in situations as diverse as airplane crashes, train derailments, explosions, bombings, diplomatic security, tactical team support, manhunts, hazardous material accidents and natural disasters such as tornadoes. All ERT members were issued pagers and made subject to 24-hour callout. Their training would continue on a monthly basis.

May of 1992 was one of the more violent months in recent memory in Oklahoma City. There were 14 homicides in the City that month. It could have been worse. There were almost 15.

A little before 2:00 on the afternoon of May 4, Officer Jim Duncan heard an unusual request while working his off-duty job as a security guard at the Lincoln National Bank at 1111 N. Lincoln—"I want your fucking gun!". The blunt requestor was 50-year-old Larry Maurice Little of Oologah, Will Rogers' hometown. But Little didn't have Rogers' genial disposition. Dressed in a shoddy-looking suit and tie, Little had pulled out a shotgun and pointed it at Duncan's chin to emphasize his demand. Desperately intent upon robbery, Little had decided to confront the most dangerous person in the bank first—the armed cop at the security desk.

When Duncan hesitated to give up his weapon, looking around in quick, seemingly panicky glances, Little poked the officer with the shotgun and repeated his demand. The officer returned his gaze to the man confronting him, said "No problem" and reached for his gun with two fingers as instructed.

But there was a problem and it was Little's problem. A 5-year veteran officer, 41 years old and a former U.S. Navy SEAL, Jim Duncan wasn't panicked. His quick, darting glances had been looking around to see if the man was alone or had accomplices, not looking for a place to run. After his quick scan, Duncan felt certain that the robber didn't have a partner in the bank but was alone. As he gingerly, with exaggerated slowness, reached to surrender his sidearm, with the shotgun four inches from his face, Duncan swept the gun away from his face with his other arm and grabbed Little. As the two men struggled over the shotgun, it discharged, blowing a hole in the wall and sending everyone else in the bank diving to the floor. The struggle continued across the floor until Little was subdued and handcuffed, unharmed.

In spite of Jim Duncan's restraint, it was all for naught. Eight days later, Larry Little showed everyone just how truly desperate he had been. He took the sheets off his bed in the Oklahoma County Jail and hanged himself.

Chief Gonzales hosted his first Awards Banquet on May 8, 1992. The program was emceed by Dean Blevins, a popular local sportscaster for KOCO-TV and former quarterback for the Oklahoma University football team. The guest speaker was to have been motion picture actor Wilford Brimley but he was unable to attend. A last minute substitute surfaced in the person of actor Barry Corbin, one of the stars of the popular television series Northern Exposure. In his opening remarks, Corbin began discussing a touchy subject for an audience of nearly a thousand cops when he talked of the public outcry about the recent videotaped beating of Rodney King by four Los Angeles Police officers following a pursuit. He spoke of the nationwide media blitz on the subject, the endless repetitions of playing the videotape of the beating and the media contention that the case had brought about a national distrust of police officers. Some friends of his at a party in Los Angeles had recently asked him if, as a result of the recent case, he hadn't lost faith in the LAPD. His reply, he said, was that he was disappointed and had lost faith in four LAPD officers—but he still had quite a bit of faith in and respect for the remaining 8,000. The remarks drew a very respectable ovation.

Sergeants Ed Dugan and Robert Campbell were awarded the Medal of Valor. Eleven months earlier, Campbell had been on duty alone as a lake patrol officer at Lake Hefner when violent thunderstorms erupted. Since it was a Sunday, the lake was crowded with boats. In a storm that produced 60 mile-per-hour winds and with lightning striking the surface of the lake,

Campbell towed three capsized boats to shore and rescued four people. Sgt. Ed Dugan received his award for the shooting capture of the escaped robber 13 months earlier. Six Life Saving Awards and 14 Certificates of Achievement were awarded to other officers and 5 citizens received certificates.

In a violent month, the worst day was to come eight days after the Awards Banquet. Early in the afternoon of May 16, Homicide Detectives began investigating a mass murder in the far northeast sector. The bodies of 5 women aged 14 to 40 were found in a house at N.E. 50th and Washington. Information began surfacing that the house was a "crack house", the occupants selling crack cocaine.

Later that night, officers obtained a search warrant for another drug house at 626 N.W. 28th. An old two-story brick apartment house bordering on the old Paseo district and only a block east of Fairlawn Cemetery, the contingent of officers approached it about 9 P.M. As the officers entered the residence, a flurry of shots were fired. Officer Bo Leach, in the process of climbing the stairs, was hit in the back by a shot from the upper floor. Leach and other officers returned the fire. Sean William Cain, 21, was hit in the cheek. Cain and four other men were arrested. Officer Leach was taken to the hospital and recovered from his wound.

Chief Gonzales made history with another promotion on July 31, 1992. Nineteen and one-half years after she was hired as one of the original five female officers for patrol duty in December of 1972, Julie (Black) Smith was promoted to Major and became the first female officer to achieve command staff rank in the history of the Oklahoma City Police Department.

Smith had served several years as a patrol officer and, upon being promoted to Detective, was the first woman assigned full time to the Vice and Narcotics Units. She participated in four "sting" operations that netted hundreds of felony arrests and seized millions of dollars worth of property. Smith found that she had an advantage as an undercover officer; "I could sit in a bar with these guys and they would brag about what they had stolen. They would look at me and say they could smell a cop from a mile off".

During her service as a Detective and supervisor in the Sex Crimes Unit, Smith gained a statewide reputation as an expert on sexual crimes and child abuse, teaching many classes to officers all over the state. She became a driving force in the Oklahoma Women in Law En-

*OCPD's first five fully qualified female officers celebrating their completion of 20 years service in December of 1992. Left to right, Sergeant Sherry [Hamman] Garcia, Sergeant Norma [Bowerman] Hutchcroft, Major Julie [Black] Smith, Sergeant Shirley [Cox] Conners and L:ieutenant Gladys [Burns] Loflin.*

forcement, serving as president of that organization. One of her proudest achievements was the creation of the Child Abuse Response and Evaluation Center, a special room next to the Sex Crimes Unit filled with children's toys and books to make the police station a friendlier, less dehumanizing place for these victims with tender sensibilities.

Proving her competence and adaptability at every rank, Smith also became the first woman to command the Homicide Unit and the Internal Affairs Unit. She had gained the respect and acceptance of all those she commanded, men and women alike. Upon her promotion to Major, Julie Smith was given command of the Santa Fe Division of the Operations Bureau, thus adding another first to her list of accomplishments.

She had persevered to see women come into their own in law enforcement with, like the men, both positive and negative results. Also like the men, there had been a price and they had paid it. During the next year, 10 of the 154 police officers slain in the line of duty nationwide would be females.

The Fall/Winter issue of the National FOP Journal listed the local FOP Lodge #123 among the 20 largest Lodges in the nation. When the next Police Academy class graduated and joined the union unanimously, it brought the membership to 1,147.

At 11:08 P.M. on January 28, 1993, a man called the 911 Police Communications Center. He told a dispatcher that he was the manager of the McDonald's Restaurant at 5815 N. Martin Luther King Boulevard, barely a mile straight north of the 911 Center. He said that a man with a shotgun was trying to break in his business which was closed. The dispatcher heard several shots over the telephone and then the line went dead.

The fast food restaurant manager had underestimated the gunman. Randy Radial Payne, 26, wasn't just trying to break in, he was determined to break in. After trying to gain entrance through several of the building's locked entrances, Payne used his shotgun to shoot out the window in the drive-through section and crawled in through the shattered window. Holding the manager at gunpoint, he robbed him while the other two employees bolted for safety out the back door.

One of the first officers on the scene was Mike Homan, a three and one-half year veteran.

*The Final Option-An OCPD Tactical Team sniper. Some have coffee cups labelled with the Latin phrase 'Rubicundus Nebula'. It means 'Pink Mist'.*

Getting a rundown on the situation from the two escaped employees, Homan decided to position himself at the back door on the west side of the building until more help arrived. Within moments, the back door opened. Payne had taken the manager hostage and, holding his gun on the man, was using him as a shield as he forced him out the back door. Homan reached around the opening door, grabbed the manager, pulling him out of the way and fired several rounds at Payne. He saw the man fall as the door shut again.

As officers interviewed the shaken but unharmed manager, 18 members of the Tactical Team arrived and surrounded the restaurant. Demands to surrender went unanswered and, two hours later, the Tactical Team entered the business. They found Payne lying on the floor next to a booth in the front of the business. Wounded in both arms from Homan's shots, that was as far as he had been able to drag himself. He was charged with burglary, armed robbery and pointing a firearm.

In the Spring of 1993, a sore spot was assuaged when new commission cards were issued to all officers, signed by the current Chief. They were now a two-sided laminated card and back to the old, more convenient size. Officers who had never carried the larger cards could once again formally identify themselves as police officers.

The Twelfth Annual Awards Banquet was held at the Myriad on May 14, 1993. The emcee was Jenifer Reynolds, news anchor for KWTV, the local CBS affiliate. Chief Gonzales presented the Medal of Valor to Sergeant Jim Duncan, Officers Mike Homan and Bo Leach. Six Life Saving Awards, 16 Certificates of Achievement for officers and 2 Certificates to citizens were also awarded.

The week after the Awards Banquet, Chief Gonzales created a brief flurry of activity on May 19 when it was publicized that his name was on the list of 14 finalists for the position of Chief of Police of his alma mater, the Dallas Police Department. Rumor and speculation abounded for the next couple of weeks until, on June 1, the Chief announced that he had removed his name from contention. He cited the fact that he had made a three-to-five year commitment when he accepted his current position and he intended to stand by it.

New programs continued to be implemented. IMPACT (Initiating Multiple Police Actions) Teams had been created in each of the four operations divisions. Consisting of officers assigned to each division, operating both in uniform and plainclothes according to the assignment, they were an immediate response team to specific problems within their division whether it was drug houses, prostitution or an epidemic of burglaries. In 1993, IMPACT Teams would make 1,830 arrests, recover 275 weapons, seize over $600,000 in cash and property, and confiscate more than $2.7 million worth of drugs.

Drive-by Response Teams were formed to combat the "gangbangers" new recreational activity of drive-by shootings. To complement their duties, a Gang Enforcement Unit was incorporated with them. The new unit was intended to be a proactive unit to respond to areas of known gang activity to address problems before they escalated.

On June 14, retired Major Bill Peterman had his final heart attack. His funeral three days later was extraordinary. Normally, the funeral of an officer who had been retired for over 18 years could be expected to draw a symbolic presence from the Department and a modest attendance; a scout car to lead the procession, a couple of motorcycles for escort duty, a couple of Honor Guard members to act as honorary pallbearers, a few retired contemporaries of the deceased and a smattering of active duty officers who remembered him. Bill Peterman's funeral was different.

It was a measure of the near-universal respect and affection this man had engendered that turned it into a spectacle usually reserved for officers slain in the line of duty. A dozen police motorcycles blocked the street next to the funeral home along with at least that many black and white scout cars. Over a dozen Honor Guard members standing at attention lined the entire walkway leading inside where two more stood guard at either end of the flag-draped casket. The guard contingent was changed at frequent intervals in a ceremony similar to that conducted at the Tomb of the Unknown Soldiers, the guards exchanging places with crisp military facing movements in total silence except for the clicking heels on highly polished boots while the officer in charge slowly salutes the deceased's casket.

Hundreds of officers of every rank, active and retired, filled the funeral home to overflowing. Three former Chiefs, Watson, Gramling and Purser, attended. Officers who hadn't been seen at any Departmental functions in the years since they retired showed up. Extra chairs were set up in the aisles and still there were more than the building could hold.

As the long procession wound its way to the cemetery, a black and white police helicopter, symbol of a new generation of law enforcement, hovered protectively 200 feet above the hearse. The graveside services ended with the sharp crack of .357 Magnums from the Honor Guard's 21-gun salute and, as the last mournful notes of Taps sounded, the helicopter dived low over the gravesite in a high-speed flyby as a final farewell. Pete would have been proud.

On October 7, 43 of the 50 police recruits that had started OCPD Recruit Class Number 109 22 weeks earlier graduated and entered the FTO Program. All 43 had joined the FOP, bringing Lodge 123's membership to 1,217.

During the early evening hours of Thursday, October 21, 1993, a special night session was held in Judge John Amick's courtroom in the Oklahoma County Courthouse. The defendant being accorded this special treatment was the Democratic Governor of the State of Oklahoma, David Walters.

A multi-county grand jury had been investigating charges of impropriety in Governor Walters' last election campaign for the last 14 months. They had handed down over 20 indictments, some of them sealed. Speculation had been rife for several months that the Governor was the subject of one of the sealed indictments.

Naturally the information leaked. Earlier in the week, the avidly conservative Daily Oklahoman newspaper had reported in banner headlines that the Governor's indictment was true in spite of the fact that it was still sealed.

True it was. Walters had been indicted on nine counts, eight of them felonies and six of those for perjury. That Thursday night, he was pleading guilty before Judge Amick... to a single misdemeanor count of violating the State's election laws. The other eight counts, all felonies, were dismissed. He was given a one-year deferred sentence which, under Oklahoma

*OCPD Memorial and Honor Guard.*

*The Second Century. Left to right, Canine Sergeant Nathan Pyle, Mounted Patrol Sergeant J.D. McLaughlin, Patrol Sergeant James Torres, Aviation Sergeant J.J. Young and Motorcycle Sergeant Don Dunsmore.*

law, does not count as a felony conviction on a person's record if successfully completed. The Governor was also fined $1,000 and ordered to pay $135,000 to the State Ethics Commission out of funds already collected for his next campaign.

District Attorney Bob Macy, a former OCPD officer for several years in the late 1950s, and Attorney General Susan Loving said that this fine would virtually wipe out the Governor's campaign chest for the next election. Nothing in the plea bargain prevented the Governor from completing the remaining year of his current term of office or running from another term.

The newspaper lambasted Macy for the "special deal". The D.A. went on local television defending his position, saying that the Governor should resign but could have completed this term anyway while waiting to be brought before a trial which would have been very expensive for the taxpayers. Macy also condemned the scathing editorial in the paper, inviting the anonymous writer to a public debate on the issues and indicating that 20 years earlier, he would have invited the writer to another, more physical contest. Macy also criticized the meeting between several Oklahoma County judges who had tried to find a way (unsuccessfully) to legally negate the plea bargain.

The citizens bitched, the grand jurors bitched and the State Legislature started looking for impeachable offenses. Thus Oklahoma politics, after 104 years of progress. Or, to quote another old Oklahoma saying, "Progress is a beer they don't make anymore."

# XII — THE BOMB APRIL 19, 1995

Every project like this book has to have a beginning and an ending. The beginning is usually a meaningful point in history.For this book, it was April 22, 1889, the day when a few square miles of barren prairie grassland in the center of Indian Territory became Oklahoma City overnight. That event and its unique beginnings merited worldwide attention, reported in the London [England] Times among other international publications.

The ending point is usually an arbitrarily selected date beyond which it is impractical to further update the manuscript before sending it to the publisher so they can turn it into a printed volume. For the purposes of this book, that arbitrarily selected date was July 1, 1994.

Nothing that occurred in the history of the OCPD after that date was intended to be included in this book. But that changed on Wednesday, April 19, 1995. If this chapter may seem to be somewhat out of sync between the previous chapter and the epilogue, that is the reason. I would like to point out, however, that I wrote the epilogue before this final chapter was ever envisioned or necessary. I am proud to say that I didn't change a word of the epilogue and I stand by every word in it.

That said, now the story of April 19, 1995. I can't tell it all, I can't even tell as much as needs to be told but I have to tell some of it...some that might not be told in the books and TV movies to come. On that date, the world spotlight again fell upon Oklahoma City but this time for more tragic reasons...the most cataclysmic event in the history of Oklahoma City, the OCPD and American law enforcement as a whole.

Bombs have been as uniquely deadly instruments against law enforcement as they have been against the military. They seem to be a favorite tool of anarchists, misfits who view all forms of government as oppressive and undesirable. On the night of May 4, 1886, in Haymarket Square on Randolph Street in Chicago, Illinois, a labor riot precipitated a dynamite bomb being thrown into a formation of 180 Chicago Police officers. Officer Mathias J. Degan died immediately and six of his fellow officers died later at area hospitals. Over 70 other officers were injured, two civilians were killed and another 60 injured. In a highly biased and unsatisfactory conclusion to this incident, suspicion eventually fell upon eight anarchists who may or may not have been responsible. Ultimately one was sentenced to 15 years in prison and the other seven were sentenced to death. Two had their sentences commuted to life imprisonment, one committed suicide by swallowing dynamite and four were actually hanged.

The death of those seven Chicago Police officers was, to that time, the deadliest single incident in the history of American law enforcement. That record would stand for a little over three decades. Shortly after 7 P.M. on Saturday, November 24, 1917, a boy delivered a package to the Milwaukee, Wisconsin, Police Station. The package had been left near the Italian Evangelical Church and a cleaning woman had the boy take it to the police. Some detectives were just getting out of their roll call lineup as the boy arrived and some of them began examining the package. It exploded, killing one patrolman and eight detectives.

Several weeks earlier, a riot had resulted in several anarchists being arrested and the priest of the Italian Evangelical Church had been very vocally critical of the rioters. Officers felt that the bomb had been planted at the church in retaliation for this. No suspects were ever identified or prosecuted. A tenth officer was killed that day in Columbus, Ohio, and a new record was born. That record would stand for over three quarters of the century. But like most records, it was also destined to fall.

Many banks, credit unions, savings and loans, and other financial institutions have silent holdup and intrusion alarms. Most if not all of these are wired to automatically and instantaneously notify the communications center of the local police department when they are set off. As in most large cities, such is the case in Oklahoma City.

It isn't particularly unusual for these alarms to be set off around 9 A.M. on weekday mornings. Sometimes it is a bank robber who wants to get his business done early but most often they are accidentally triggered by employees at the beginning of the banking business day. Doors are being unlocked, vaults are being opened, cash drawers are being readied for the day's business and employees don't always remember to deactivate the alarms first. Since the alarms are silent, many times the first indication they have that anything is amiss is when a police dispatcher calls and asks to speak to one of the bank officials listed on their Computer Aided Dispatch screen. When the puzzled bank officer gets on the phone, he is asked if everything is all right. If so, he is asked for his physical and clothing description and told to go out a specific exit and talk to the officers. What officers? No sirens or squealing tires have been heard.

The banker hesitantly goes to the exit and looks outside. No matter which exit he checks, he sees black and white police cars with officers behind them, usually with very serious expressions on their faces and twelve-gauge shotguns close at hand. After being assured that all is well, several of the officers will go back in with him to satisfy themselves that the alarm was an accident.

That is the usual course of events for an alarm. On the morning of April 19, 1995, the most unusual alarm in Oklahoma City's history went off.

09:02:20. Twenty seconds after 9:02 A.M. on that morning, the Oklahoma City Police Department's 9-1-1 Center received instantaneous electronic notification of a silent holdup alarm activated at the main downtown branch of Boatmen's First National Bank of Oklahoma. This time, however, it wasn't a bank robbery or a careless employee. The alarm had been set off by the shock wave from an explosion three blocks away.

Explosions aren't unheard of in Oklahoma City. Automobile gas tanks, tanker trucks, oil storage tanks, grain elevators, natural gas explosions and a bomb now and then. But that wasn't this. Alarms were set off in every quadrant of the city, areas separated by 20 to 30 miles or more. In seconds, the calls started.

The state capital and largest city in Oklahoma had just endured the worst terrorist bombing in the history of the United States. A rented Ryder truck full of explosives had been detonated while parked in front of the Alfred P. Murrah Federal Building at 200 N.W. Fifth. The explosives would later be identified as a mixture of fuel oil, detonator cord and 4800 pounds of ammonium nitrate fertilizer, approximately equal in explosive force to a ton of dynamite.

In that instant, a blast wave of superheated compressed air traveling at an estimated 6500 feet per second put almost a thousand pounds of pressure on every square inch of the nine-story building's north side which was mostly glass. The glass shattered into millions of pieces of supersonic shrapnel blowing entirely through the building and out the other side unless it struck something else first. If it was fabric or flesh, it punctured, lacerated, or shredded it. If it was something more substantial, it turned into even more deadly ricocheting missiles.

The blast wave lifted all of the eight upper floors of the building upwards momentarily, snapping two-inch thick steel reinforcing rods and destroying some of the concrete support columns at the front of the building, also compressing, rupturing and bursting more fragile eardrums and eyeballs in its path. When the blast wave passed and the floors were no longer

*The north side of the Murrah Federal Building as it once was. The Ryder truck containing the bomb was parked where the pickup is in this photo.*

supported by the scorching wave of air, concrete columns or crossbeams, they began collapsing. Multi-ton slabs of concrete honeycombed with reinforcing steel bars plummeted down, pancaking lower floors between them. Also between the crashing monoliths were desks, chairs, tables, filing cabinets, all the other furnishings of a modern office building...and people...hundreds of people including a day care center full of children on the second floor. Light fixtures and live wires swung from the ceilings, where something resembling a ceiling remained. Plumbing pipes snapped, gushing water and threatening to drown pinned survivors before they could be freed. Some of the wreckage and people collapsed into the four-level parking garage beneath the building. Cars in a parking lot across the street were lifted, thrown, twisted and burst into flame, their gas tanks exploding. Their tires, upholstery, fuel and insulation added to the boiling cloud of greasy, black smoke boiling into the sky. Bodies lay in the street, some looking like broken dolls, some charred beyond any resemblance as the remains of human beings. In less time than it takes to read this paragraph, over 160 people died. But even more survived, some miraculously.

A Deputy U.S. Marshal had just walked back in the building from a cigarette break. He forgot to close the glass door behind him. The vacuum created by the explosion sucked him 39 feet back out the same door without harming him.

The building housed the offices of a number of federal government agencies including much of the federal law enforcement contingent for central Oklahoma. The law enforcement agencies in the building employed 77 people, 40 of them commissioned federal law enforcement officers. This concentration was the reason for the demise of the existing record. Nineteen of these employees perished in the bombing, a dozen of them federal officers.

The Defense Investigative Service was housed on the third floor. Five of their employees died, four of them Special Agents. The U.S. Customs Service was on the fifth floor. Only half of their six employees were in the office. Two Special Agents died, leaving an investigative assistant as the only survivor. A criminal investigator for the Inspector General's Office as-

*The north side of the building in a photo taken from the parking lot across the street.*

signed to the Department of Housing and Urban Development also perished. The remainder of the federal law enforcement agencies had offices on the top or ninth floor.

The U.S. Secret Service lost six employees, four of them agents, the largest single loss in the agency's history. If the reader will forgive the lapse into first person, I had become friends with one of those agents, Mickey Maroney, when I was a Sergeant in Special Projects. I had known another one much longer and better. Don Leonard was an Oklahoma City native and had been an OCPD officer for three years before he joined the Secret Service in 1970. During the ten-week school of OCPD Recruit Class Number 57, Don Leonard sat on the row in front of me. We got to know each other, we practiced judo on each other because we were about the same size (he was a little bigger and that usually cost me) and we became friends. We graduated together, were assigned to the same patrol shift under Lieutenant Walter Kostiuk, answered calls together and made arrests together. I hadn't seen Don for several months, since we had run into each other at the graduation of OCPD Class Number 110. We had laughed about some of the things that had happened in the quarter-century between those 53 recruit classes and the differences between us and them. We had compared our gray hairs (he had more) and laughed about the fact that two of our classmates' sons were graduating with this class. Don intended to retire within a few months after completing 25 years service with the Secret Service. It was not to be.

The Justice Department's Drug Enforcement Administration (DEA) also had offices on the ninth floor. Just before the explosion, one of their civilian employees, six months pregnant, was blissfully showing the new sonogram of her unborn baby boy to three other civilians and an agent near the elevators. As an elevator arrived, the DEA agent got on with an ATF agent as another DEA agent got off. The bomb went off just as the elevator doors closed. The elevator plummeted in a free fall from the ninth floor to the third floor before stopping. The four civilian DEA employees and the agent who had just exited the elevator on the top floor were all killed. The two agents on the elevator survived, rushing back up the stairs to try to rescue others.

The Treasury Department's Bureau of Alcohol, Tobacco and Firearms (ATF) employed thirteen persons in the building, several of them also friends I had worked with in the past. In one of the ironic blessings of the tragedy, this time the number wasn't unlucky. ATF's location on the southeast corner of the top floor sheltered them somewhat from the devastation which chewed deepest into the east side of the north face of the building. Eight of their employees were out of the building at the time. Two agents had not arrived in the office yet, one was conducting an investigation in Pawnee, three were appearing in court out of town and two more were appearing in court in the Federal Courthouse one block to the south.

In spite of the fact that no ATF employees were killed or hospitalized with major injuries, they weren't exactly unscathed. Alex McCauley, the Special Agent in Charge of the office, had been in the elevator that fell six floors, thus narrowly escaping the fate of the DEA agent who had just gotten off on the ninth floor. Agent Luke Franey was blown out of his chair by the blast wave just before the walls and ceiling collapsed on top of him. He was trapped in the building for 90 minutes and had to kick his way through three walls before he could start assisting rescue workers.Inspector Vernon Buster had a nail blown through his arm, Inspector Jim Staggs was blown across the office and both received head injuries. Secretary Valerie Rowden-Matthews' head was blown against her desk by the blast, receiving minor injuries. Her father, John Rowden, was a former OCPD officer who had received the City's highest decoration for valor in 1963 after a gunfight with two armed robbers and was now a retired ATF agent. Her grandfather had been killed in the line of duty while serving as the Chief of Police in Cushing in 1968.

Many of the other agencies housed in the building were of a nature that encouraged much civilian traffic...Army and Marine Corps Recruiting offices, the Department of Health and Human Services, the Department of Housing and Urban Development, the Federal Employees Credit Union, the Social Security Administration, the General Services Administration, the General Accounting Office, the Department of Veterans Affairs and others.

The entire north face of the building had been sheared off. Where offices, walls and plate glass had been a second before, there was nothing but a broken concrete ledge and open space all the way to the ground. A man in a chair rolled over the edge and plummeted to the ground.

Another fell into the bomb crater, 8 feet deep and 30 feet wide, in front of the building where the truck had been parked. A U.S. Army Captain was launched from his recruiting office on the fourth floor to the first floor. Miraculously, he survived. As the inhuman rolling thunder of the explosion moved on, it was replaced by other more human sounds...cries for help, the plaintive sobbing and crying of the frightened, moans and groans of the injured, piercing shrieks and screams of the utterly terrified.

09:02:20. In OCPD Headquarters at 701 Colcord, five blocks west and four blocks south of the Federal Building, the plate glass window on the south side of Deputy Chief M.T. Berry's second-floor office shattered. On the third floor, ceiling tiles, insulation and dust cascaded down. A ceiling fan fell on the AFIS fingerprint computer. Captain Ed Hill and several other officers thought a chiller unit for the air conditioner had exploded on the roof. As they ran up the stairs to the roof area that had been a helicopter landing pad, they were greeted by an eerie specter. Black clouds of smoke and dust covered the sky, giving the area the appearance of late evening instead of what had been a bright, sunny spring morning. Cars on the streets below were turning their headlights on to see through the gloom. As the cloud wafted over the police building, they could smell the distinctive smell of burned cordite, a smell familiar to everyone who shoots on the police pistol range several times a year. As the eternal Oklahoma winds ebbed and flowed, papers started falling out of the sky. Hill picked some of the fluttering pages up from the roof and looked at the letterheads...U.S. Army Recruiting papers, Social Security Administration papers, Department of Housing and Urban Development papers.

With years of experience as a Detective, Sergeant and Lieutenant in Narcotics, Hill had worked a great deal with agents of the DEA, ATF and Customs on narcotics, RICO and conspiracy cases. He had spent many months assigned to a federal drug task force headquartered in...the Federal Building. Like many OCPD officers, he too had many friends in that building.

Automatically looking to the northeast, they saw the black cloud boiling over the Federal Building. Captain Hill and all the others bolted back down the stairs. The Investigations Bureau, largely a day shift function in the OCPD, emptied into the streets along with other headquarters officers including Forensic Laboratory Sergeant John Avera. They jumped into patrol cars, detective cruisers, lab vans, motorcycles, scooters and their personal cars. The first officers were on the scene within 90 seconds.

In addition to the alarms going off everywhere, the calls were coming into 9-1-1 from the citizens now, calls from every corner of a city spread out over more than 600 square miles. A man at N.W. 127th and Pennsylvania, more than 12 miles north of the downtown area, thought it was an earthquake. Others thought it was a sonic boom, a tornado, a gas explosion, a nearby car wreck or a plane crash. The dispatchers typed the citizens' comments into their computers..."loud boom...whole house shook...gas blowing everywhere...a lot of glass flying at Park and Rob[inson] (four blocks south of the site)". At the police radio consoles, the radio calls began coming in from the officers simultaneously with the citizens, the cold abbreviations on the computer screens not nearly communicating the controlled frenzy behind them or the controlled anxiety in the fingers that typed them..."A126 at Main & Walker...damage from Main to Park...C52 adv[ises] will need all EMSA (Emergency Medical Services) units available...6-7 people down 100 NW 6...C118 is on the e[ast] side 3rd floor fed blding has water rising and can't get them out".

09:02:20. In the Federal Courthouse, one block south of the Federal Building, OCPD Officers Casey Owens, Stanley Campbell, Steve Whitson and Sergeant Guy Valencia were sitting in a first-floor courtroom. They were the defendants in a civil rights trial that was beginning that morning. The plaintiff had filed a federal lawsuit alleging they had used excessive force while serving a search warrant. The building shook, glass broke, light fixtures fell out of the ceiling followed by the insulation and dust above them. All four officers and their chairs were shoved backwards by an invisible wall of hot air. Quickly helping jurors (and the lady who is suing them) out of the courtroom, all four officers ran outside. Seeing the windows blown out of the relatively intact south side of the Federal Building, they realized that was the target instead of the courthouse. Quickly covering the half a block, they would be the first emergency personnel on the scene.

*Closeup of the east side of the north face of the building.*

Whitson and Owens got on their portable radios, calling for assistance from all the police, fire and EMSA ambulances they could get. Whitson broadcast on the Will Rogers Division frequency (the area that covers the Federal Building) while Owens switched to the Hefner Division frequency (the division covering the far north and west areas of the city). As they ran into the building, they could hear the shifting concrete and steel creaking and groaning as though the building was a living thing anguishing from its wounds. Debris was still falling and bloody walking wounded were helping each other out of the south exits. A gnarled, grotesquely twisted tricycle was resting in a planter near the children's play area. Most of the injured mumbled something to the officers about a day care center being on the second floor. Officer Owens ran into the stairwell and looked up, seeing nothing but blue sky and thinking to himself

*A photo taken from the Regency Towers Apartments just minutes after the explosion. Looking east on N.W. 5th, the smoke from the burning cars has barely risen above the nine-story height of the Federal Building.*

"But there is no second floor!". Going to the north side, he first saw the true devastation they were dealing with. People were standing on the floors above, in offices that were now open-air balconies without railings, leaning over the jagged edges, waving down and calling for help.

09:02:20. Bicycle Patrol Officers Jim Ramsey, Jennifer Rodgers and Steven Brackeen were preparing for lineup on the headquarter's third floor. They ran for their cars with the others flooding out of headquarters. Rodgers ran to the south side of the Federal Building while Ramsey ran to the Water Resources Board building across Fifth Street. Ramsey rescued one dazed man standing inside the building and then helped another bloody victim on the sidewalk in front of it. Officer Rodgers put two victims in her patrol car and rushed them the half-mile to Saint Anthony's Hospital. Returning after leaving them with medical personnel, Rodgers climbed to the third floor where she helped rescue a man hanging over one of the precipices, his office chair tangled in the twisted steel rebar.

A federal agent on the top floor, although dazed and shaken by the blast, grabbed his portable radio and began broadcasting an alert to his fellow agents in the field while simultaneously locating the other equally dazed employees in his office. Standing in what had been an enclosed office and now looking out over collapsed walls at an unobstructed view of the skyline of downtown Oklahoma City, he was very aware that their survival was not at all assured yet. Understandably upset and fully aware it might be delivered posthumously, he closed his broadcast to the other agents with a personal message for the suspects; "Tell the motherfuckers they didn't get all of us!". He then led the other employees nine floors down the stairwell to safety.

Most police officers have to deal with the specter of violent death at some time in their careers. Some have to deal with it more often than others, depending upon the violence quotient of their patrol area. And some of them volunteer to deal with it exclusively. In cities large enough to have a police unit exclusively dedicated to criminal death investigations, there are no draftees in Homicide. It is one of those specialized areas of police investigation that is hard to get into because you have to show a talent and a strong desire for it. Conversely, because of some unique stresses, it is one of the easiest areas to get a transfer out of...all you have to do is raise your hand, say "I want out" and you're out. If they spend enough time in it to get good at it, they'll see more death than most military combat veterans and an infinitely wider variety. Because of this, they possess a unique esprit de corps because they come to realize that what they do, what they see, what they learn, makes them forever different, even among other police officers.

OCPD Lieutenant Ray Rupert was one of the right people in the right place at the right time that morning. A 21-year veteran who had spent over half of his career as a Detective and supervisor in Homicide, he was now a supervisor in the Sex Crimes Unit. At 9:02 that morning, Rupert was driving his unmarked police car on N.W. Fourth between Robinson and Broadway, a block and a half from the Federal Building. He was on his way to Police Headquarters to get some travel orders approved for some of his investigators. Suddenly there was a loud noise and his car was one lane further over in the street than it had been. To this day, he doesn't know if the car was pushed sideways or lifted up and dropped in the next lane. In the next instant, a wall of dust, smoke, broken glass and other debris passed in front of him southbound down the man-made canyon of Robinson Street.

Rupert's first thought was of a gas explosion in the Federal Courthouse. Pulling around the corner and parking his car, his first thought was reinforced when he saw the windows blown out of the courthouse's north side. Glancing toward the south side of the Federal Building, it first seemed normal until he noticed the windows blown out there also. Then another sight told him what the real target had been...people were hanging out of some of the windows, others were jumping out of the upper story windows or trying to rappel down curtains to the ground or a lower floor.

As Rupert ran into the east side of the parking garage, a woman covered in blood staggered out to meet him. As she collapsed in his arms, she kept repeating "My child's in the garage". Leaving her with two other people, Rupert entered the garage, ankle deep in water. Screams and panicked shouts echoed eerily as a building maintenance man approached him. Between them, they got the water cut off. Rupert then went to the area around the elevator shaft and worked his way toward the area where the day care center had been at the front of the building.

Finding several other officers in that area, they formed an assembly line passing the bodies of children out, many of them obviously dead. As the flow of bodies slowed somewhat and increasing amounts of debris were encountered, some of them went scrounging for materials to clear some of the debris. An OHP Trooper grabbed some rope off of a fire truck and Homicide Sergeant John Maddox, who had once worked for Rupert, obtained some cutting tools from somewhere. The dead were being carried to the south plaza area.

Police commanders were also on the scene within minutes. Deputy Chief R. Neill Griffith, commander of the Operations Bureau, and Major Larry Gramling, commander of the Will Rogers Division that encompassed the Federal Building, activated the Mobile Command Post and began coordinating officers' duties. Major Garold Spencer, commander of the Emergency Response Team, activated the ERT and directed them to their staging area. Spencer was later named the On-Site Scene Commander until after the building's final demolition. The Department's new $125,000 Mobile Command Post, not yet used, was set up under the direction of Captain Danny Cochran, initially at Eighth and North Walker. Like many others, the ERT would work 12-hour shifts for the next 17 days, some of them even longer hours. A first aid station for walking wounded was set up at Fifth and North Broadway and a triage area for more seriously injured was established at Fourth and North Harvey. All of these locations would be moved to respond to changing conditions in the ensuing hours. An Oklahoma County Deputy Sheriff told his dispatcher "We got a war zone down here". One emergency medical technician said the building and victims looked like they had all been run through a giant blender together and then dumped out.

Officer Terry Yeakey ran into the first-floor carnage of the General Services Administration. After helping a woman out with an injured leg, he went back for two men, Tom Hall and

Richard Williams. Firemen, EMSA paramedics, highway patrol troopers, deputy sheriffs, doctors, nurses and plain citizens were also helping. One of the citizens was Peter Schaffer, a downtown restaurant owner. Schaffer helped Yeakey carry a bloody mess named Richard Ledger out. On the way, some of the rubble collapsed under Yeakey and he fell three feet, injuring his back. Officer Yeakey and Richard Ledger, a carotid artery in his neck severed, were rushed to Presbyterian Hospital in the same ambulance.

Some of the first officers on the scene ran to the area that used to be the day care center, drawn by the children's cries that could be distinguished among the chaos. Two of them were Sergeant John Avera and Officer Casey Owens. Severed hands, feet, arms, legs and heads lay among the pulverized concrete rubble they clambered over. Owens passed by the bodies of half a dozen children who were obviously beyond help before he and Avera began digging debris away from one small form. Baylee Almon had been one year old the day before. Today her short life would be immortalized.

Sergeant Avera lifted the limp, bloody form and ran out of the building. As he neared the street, he met one of the firemen who had begun arriving from the downtown stations. As the officer was handing the girl's body to the fireman, a photographer was snapping pictures. The one of the fireman carrying the baby would receive worldwide publicity, coming to symbolize the tragedy and, by extension, the senseless horrors of terrorism. Somewhat less well publicized was the one of Sergeant Avera handing the baby to the fireman. Seconds after the photos were taken, the baby girl was pronounced dead at the scene by medical personnel.

Detective Sergeants Steve McCool and Rick Dunn of the White Collar Crime Unit were among the dozens of investigators that responded. On the third floor, in what had been the offices of the General Accounting Office, they rescued Steve Pruitt, a GAO evaluator who wasn't supposed to be there. Not your average bean-counter, Pruitt was fluent in four languages including Mandarin Chinese and had been due to begin his training at the FBI Academy three days earlier. Perhaps because that had been Easter Sunday, the training had been delayed until mid-May. His training would be further delayed from his injuries but he would survive. One floor below, Officer David Pennington rescued Susan Walton, a customer in the Federal Employees Credit Union. She too would survive after surgery.

Casey Owens had worked his way around to the north side of the building. The upper reaches of the shambles were no less a glimpse into hell then the wreckage at the bottom. Slabs of concrete flooring that had been separated by a dozen feet were now resting directly on one another like the huge slices of a concrete sandwich, blood seeping out from between them. A hand was sticking out from between two slabs, from another hung a leg in the red-striped bright blue trouser leg of a once-immaculate U.S. Marine dress uniform. A man in a dust-covered white T-shirt was sitting on one of the upper ledges. Appearing dazed but calm, staring straight ahead, he appeared to be trying to pull himself up. A fireman brought up a ladder long enough to reach the ledge and they started climbing it. Before his rescuers could reach him, the man toppled over sideways. Both of his legs had been severed at the thigh and blood was gushing from the stumps. He bled to death.

Mike McPherson arrived at the scene prepared to do double duty. A Detective Sergeant in Auto Theft and also a member of the OCPD Bomb Squad, McPherson immediately recognized the signs of a car bomb. From the devastation, it was obvious the vehicle it had been in had to have been a large van or truck. Most of it had probably been vaporized...most but definitely not all. He knew that hardened steel portions like the drive train were usually the most survivable parts. Those parts had numbers on them if you knew where to look and those numbers could be traced. The rear axle would almost certainly have survived like the one in the New York World Trade Center bombing in 1993. He was right.

The Ryder truck's driveshaft had been propelled like a huge bullet through several walls at the Oklahoma Water Resources Board across the street, killing a retired Air Force Major. The charred frame of the truck was found in the parking lot across the street along with many of the 74 cars that had been totally destroyed, one of which contained the burned body of a woman. The truck's engine fell through the roof of a pawn shop two blocks away.

In sharp contrast to most of the people hurrying toward the building, McPherson began walking away from the bombing site, his eyes scanning the ground. A block west, he found the twisted axle lying next to a parked car it had bounced against. Examining it, he found a VIN (Vehicle Identification Number). This number was traced to a Ryder rental truck agency in Florida and then to the location where the truck had been rented in Junction City, Kansas. Before the smoke cleared, McPherson had found that first vital piece of evidence leading to the solution of the crime.

09:22:47. Panic and misinformation reign supreme. A suspicious briefcase is reported in the Bank of Oklahoma building and the employees evacuate. OCPD Bomb Squad officers respond. False alarm. No bomb. The building remains empty for four days with the doors unlocked, the cash drawers full, the vault open, tens of thousands of dollars unsecured. When the bankers return, nothing has been disturbed, not a cent is missing.

Along with hundreds of other medical professionals, nurse Rebecca Anderson rushed to the scene from a medical center five miles south of the downtown area minutes after hearing the first news reports. A short time later, she was seen reeling in the street, apparently having been hit in the head by falling debris. She collapsed and was taken to the hospital.

Sergeant Chuck Wheeler was rummaging in the debris on the second floor. Seeing a woman's hand sticking out of the rubble, he reached down and squeezed it. The hand squeezed back. He knelt by her and asked her name. The hand belonged to Priscilla Salyers, an investigative assistant with the Customs Service. She had fallen into this pit from her fifth floor office. One of only three Customs employees in the office at the time of the explosion, she was destined to be the only survivor. Wheeler held her hand, prayed with her and began removing the debris covering her. Before he could uncover her, people began yelling to evacuate the building, another bomb had been found. Wheeler reluctantly left her side.

10:33:37. Officer Ramsey had also worked his way to the third floor where two women were trapped. While trying to excavate them, someone began yelling to evacuate the building because another bomb had been found. Ramsey decided to stay with the women when another officer reasoned "If it's a bomb and if it goes off, we'll never know anyway". Ignoring the warning, the officers led the women down the stairwell to safety.

Below them on the streets, firemen, medical personnel, victims, walking wounded, other rescuers and spectators began running away from the building. Once again moving against the

*Looking south from N.W. 63rd and Broadway Extension (over 5 miles north of the bombing), the smoke has now risen to the height of the 18-story Fidelity Plaza and has begun drifting to the west and south.*

*The car that was struck by the Ryder truck's rear axle in front of the Regency Towers Apartments. The axle, in the foreground, caused all the damage done to the car. A teenage boy was in the car at the time but was unhurt.*

flow, Sergeant Mike McPherson and three other bomb squad members passed them while running into the building to search for the device, the others looking at them like they were madmen. The word soon spread that the other bomb was an ATF training device. Actually it was an inert anti-tank missile from one of the other agencies.

The rescuers began heading back into the building, Officer Casey Owens among them. Before he could get back inside, Owens collapsed, suffering from smoke inhalation. Medical personnel examining him told him his heart rate, respiration and blood pressure were dangerously elevated. Overwhelmed by the obvious, he replied "Well, whose isn't?!" Against his will, he was taken to his personal doctor to keep from adding to the load on local hospitals. He was still coughing up black phlegm days later.

When the second bomb scare occurred, Lt. Ray Rupert saw fleeing people running over and stepping on the bodies laid out in the south plaza area. Knowing the situation would only get worse and the number of casualties would rise, he organized moving the bodies to the southwest corner of the First Methodist Church on the northeast corner of Fourth and Robinson. The building dated from 1905 but services had been held on the site since the first Sunday after the land opening on April 22, 1889.

Rupert tried to give the dead some privacy behind a short stone wall but even there the press and gawkers collected to indulge a morbid fascination with the bodies. Rupert then had the bodies moved inside the church and ejected everyone except a Chaplain from the Oklahoma County Sheriff's Office. He then called the State Medical Examiner's Office and gave them directions to the temporary morgue he had set up. As he was hanging up, his pager went off. It was his office. His detectives in the Child Abuse Unit of Sex Crimes, learning about the disaster and knowing Rupert had been going downtown, were worried about him. After calling them and telling them the situation, they came down to assist him. Arriving soon afterwards, Sergeants Joanie Townsend, Janet Hogue, Teresa Sterling and Graham Robertson spent many hours in the ensuing days staffing the morgue before they were relieved by a U.S. Army Graves Registration team. Soon a team of forensic pathologists and field investigators from Dr. Fred Jordan's State Medical Examiner's Office arrived. As they entered the church, they were confronted with a scene of sheer horror even for hardened professionals. Rows of bodies were lined up on the floor, a dozen of them children, the most horrible injuries imaginable, burned, crushed, slashed, dismembered, limbs and body parts missing, blood everywhere, some nude, some in blackened diapers, a little girl wrapped in an Army recruiter's shirt. Just then, Ray Rupert walked in carrying the body of 18-month old Blake Ryan Kennedy. Normally inured to such sights, one of the pathologists said "That looks just like my son" and began crying. No one blamed him.

Barely 90 minutes after the bombing, Oklahoma Highway Patrol Trooper Charlie Hanger made what would almost certainly become the most memorable traffic stop of his career near Perry, north of Oklahoma City. He stopped a yellow 1977 Mercury Marquis with no license plate. The driver was carrying a Glock nine millimeter pistol loaded with "Black Talon" bullets, designed for penetrating protective body armor like that worn by officers. Hanger arrested Timothy McVeigh and took him to jail in Perry.

OCPD Canine officers and their dogs were called in to search for victims as well as any other explosive devices. At least 312 buildings within one square mile of the blast sustained some damage. Ten buildings would collapse from the structural damage days later and 14 others would be condemned within a week.

Yukon ( an Oklahoma City surburb) Police Officer Daniel Coss had been involved in the rescue efforts for hours. In doing so, he had been suppressing personal motivation in favor of his duty because, like many of the rescuers, he had a very personal connection to the bombing. His sister was an employee of the Internal Revenue Service several blocks away. That morning she had left her two sons, Chase, 3, and Colton, 2, in the Federal Building's day care center. While rescuing others, Coss was simultaneously looking for his two missing nephews. Finally, by mid-afternoon, he had found them. Both were dead.

The stories of horror, heroism and happenstance go on and on. A blind snack-bar owner led a sighted man out of the dark, smoking cauldron. A 20-year-old girl was trapped in the concrete jungle. Finally determining that they could not free her trapped, crushed leg, it was amputated by a doctor lying on top of her, both of them sandwiched between concrete slabs. With only a partially effective anesthetic to deaden her pain, her screams echoed through the cavernous devastation around them. All the stories cannot be recounted here. They could easily fill a volume of their own and probably should.

Within five minutes of the explosion, it was almost impossible to make a telephone call in Oklahoma City. The lines were hopelessly clogged. All of the police, fire and federal command posts were soon moved behind the Southwestern Bell Telephone headquarters at One Bell Central, the remodeled Central High School on the National Register of Historic Buildings. Bell immediately provided 100 telephone lines and offered more if needed. They virtually turned over their lavish headquarters to emergency personnel for the next three weeks as well as providing 500 cellular phones, batteries and mobile relay sites. Bell was only one of dozens

 ***A view looking northwest on the second day shows the deceptively intact south side of the building.***

*The car struck by the truck's rear axle is still in front of the Regency Towers at the upper left of the photo.*

of businesses and governmental agencies, large and small, who volunteered anything and everything needed in the superhuman efforts in the weeks to come. At least 44 Oklahoma police and sheriff's departments sent officers to help. Many others offered help that wasn't needed because of the overwhelming response.

The local television stations immediately suspended all programming, broadcasting around the clock for the next three days. No commercials, soap operas, game shows, talk shows or network programming. Emergency messages and phones numbers, lists of the confirmed dead and missing, condition reports and locations of the injured, public service messages for donations of money, equipment and assistance were repeated continuously along with news updates. Sensitive, logical, helpful, intelligent, and informative but not intrusive, sensationalistic, or needlessly morbid, they seemed to personify broadcast journalism at its best to their local audience. Then the national and international media came. The local paper aptly said "The circus is in town".

First among them was CBS anchorwoman Connie Chung, arriving with an entourage in two limousines. Already controversial, her visit to Oklahoma City was to be her swan song. Her reputation as a "soft-news personality" and her uneasy mismatching with Dan Rather was strike one. Her infamous "Hillary is a bitch" whisper-interview about the First Lady with the mother of Speaker of the House Newt Gingrich was strike two. She had been sent to Oklahoma City from New York City instead of Rather who was much closer to the scene in Austin, Texas. In an interview with the Fire Department's Public Information Officer, she asked "Can the Oklahoma City Fire Department handle this?". Although obviously somewhat taken aback momentarily, Assistant Chief Jon Hansen handled the question quite diplomatically without pointing out that most of the city's streets were paved now, Indian attacks were relatively rare and the fact that the OCFD no longer had any horse-drawn engines. Strike three. Within a week, T-shirts were on sale. The front pictured an Oklahoma City skyline and the legend "It's their job but they're Oklahoma City's heroes" with the various categories of rescuers superimposed over it. On the back it said "Who the HELL is Connie Chung?". Another version had a somewhat more graphic and less flattering message on the back. They sold extremely well.

Then cometh the dregs, the tabloid reporters, print and electronic. One was caught dressed in a priest's vestments while trying to sneak into a local church to talk to victim's relatives. Others were caught in local hospitals trying to get into intensive care units to talk to victims, one while dressed as a doctor and another while dressed as a patient. An Illinois man claiming to be a photographer for a tabloid TV show was arrested inside the bombsite security perimeter while impersonating a Fire Department Captain. Another disguised as a rescuer was even giving interviews to other media members.

The bombing fostered an immediate and unprecedented spirit of cooperation between city, county, state and federal law enforcement, fire and medical personnel, civilian agencies, thousands of volunteers and a myriad of others. By and large, this spirit of cooperation lasted throughout the ordeal with minor exceptions. But there had to be some minor exceptions. Predictably, the first friction was between police and fire and cropped up a few hours into the rescue efforts.

The bicycle patrol and other officers were continuing their rescue efforts when a fireman announced on a bullhorn "If you're not a fireman, get out of the building now!". A fire commander was alleged to have made a comment to the effect that "...amateur hour's over". An extremely frustrated Officer Jim Ramsey expressed many officers' frustrations when he said "What gives this man the right to come in here and tell me this? I've been in here since the beginning." A bristling Officer Jennifer Rodgers agrees; "...we were there first...we should have been allowed to continue the help that we started." Another officer felt "We get life saving training too, you know. We get paid to accept certain risks also. How much training do you need to move rocks? How much training do you need not to touch sparking electric wires hanging down around you? And when you've got tons of concrete swinging by the rebar over your head, how much protection is a plastic hat and a canvas raincoat going to be? Give me a break!" It also seemed to have slipped some people's minds that this was not just a disaster scene, not just a rescue effort, it was also a crime scene. Murders had occurred here, evidence was present here and a continued police presence was more than justified, it was necessary.

Steven Brackeen was under additional stress in abandoning his rescue efforts. While helping the others, he was searching for a close personal friend from his church who was a vice-president of the Federal Credit Union. Nevertheless, he swallowed hard and left the building as directed along with the other officers. After all, a police department operates on discipline, much of it necessarily self-imposed. It's probably just as well. I wouldn't have wanted to be the one to try to remove them if they were intent on staying.

Brackeen's friend's body was recovered a week later, one of the last victims to be brought out.

In spite of the evidence of the goodness of people as exemplified by the rescuers and the outpouring of assistance from around the world, there was still plenty of evidence of an inherent baseness in the human condition and there were even worse examples than the tabloid reporters. The bombing triggered a spate of bomb threats nationwide against federal installations and other businesses. The OCPD alone received 29 bomb threats in the next week. They were directed against various hospitals, businesses including United Parcel Service and agencies like the Department of Human Services among others. One particularly vicious one was against the Federal Aviation Administration, allegedly scheduled to explode at 9:02 A.M. exactly one week after the Federal Building disaster while rescuers, City and State officials stopped their work downtown to observe a moment of silence. Mercifully, all the threats were false.

Crime statistics in the city dropped by half for a little while but it didn't stop entirely. There were several homicides in the city during the next few weeks. All of the victim's bodies had to be taken to the Tulsa office of the State Medical Examiner. There was no more room for dead bodies in Oklahoma City.

For the first 12 hours, the rescuers were painstakingly removing survivors from the wreckage. Tragically, most of the rescues were performed in the first two hours. The last living person was removed that first evening. Although they tried to remain optimistic and keep their hopes up, after that they were emptying a tomb. The decimated building was increasingly marked with areas where a rescuer had marked a pile of concrete shards with an orange spray paint can "DB" (dead body) and the date. As each day progressed, the number of orange marks increased. The distinctive stench of death was discernible from blocks away.

Two days after the bombing and just hours before he was scheduled to be released, the FBI connected Timothy McVeigh to the rented Ryder truck and located him in the Perry jail. He was transferred to El Reno Federal Correctional Center and Terry Nichols was also implicated in the investigation. Nichols was arrested in Kansas.

On Sunday, April 23, volunteer nurse Rebecca Anderson died from her head injuries without regaining consciousness. Her heart and kidneys were donated to others. The same day, a memorial service was held at the state fairgrounds. President Clinton, Attorney General Janet Reno, Reverend Billy Graham and other dignitaries attended. Secret Service Agent Don Leonard's funeral was delayed one day so his colleagues could bolster the President's protection detail.

At the City Council meeting on May 2, the leaders of the three City employee unions, the FOP, the International Firefighters Union and AFSCME, offered to forego their contract negotiations for pay raises. The FOP vote passed by 88%.

About 10 A.M. on May 4, OCPD 9-1-1 Dispatcher Betty Murphy called for a supervisor from her radio console, adding "I've got an explosion". She definitely got everyone's attention. There had been an accidental dust explosion in an Acco Feeds grain elevator at S.W. 20 and Robinson, slightly over two miles south of the Federal Building. Although the grain elevator sustained some structural damage, mercifully there were no injuries.

That night, the 164th body was removed from the rubble. Three remained but could not be reached because they were under a pile of debris that was supporting one of the remaining columns in front of the building. The next morning, the thousands of rescue workers gathered at the site for a final memorial service. In police shift lineups and roll calls all over the metropolitan area announcing a gradual return to normalcy, physically exhausted and emotionally drained police commanders tried to express the pride they felt for the equally exhausted and drained men and women in their units, more than one shedding tears in the process.

Lieutenant Ray Rupert and his Sex Crimes detectives who had staffed the temporary morgue couldn't attend the funerals of all the victims who had lain in the First Methodist Church. Nor did they want to. It would have been too much. But they made an exception for Blake Ryan Kennedy. They weren't assigned to the Child Abuse Unit by accident. Kids were special.

The 18-month old boy's mother, a Health and Human Services employee, had survived the blast. In the day care center, Blake had not. It had been his limp form in Rupert's arms that had caused one of the medical examiners to burst into tears at the horror of the slaughter of the innocents.

So many people attended the boy's funeral that it had to be moved from the small rural town of Amber to nearby Chickasha. Far back in the crowd, the plainclothes officers silently bowed their heads and paid their respects. No one else there knew who they were. They weren't interviewed or filmed by the news crews. They didn't introduce themselves to the family or friends. The story didn't appear in the newspapers, magazines or on the nightly news. They just came, said goodbye to Blake and went back to work.

Almost from the very beginning of the incident, it had been generally assumed that the Federal Building would not be rebuilt. While architects and others noted it was possible, others noted it was probably fiscally irresponsible and most agreed it would be disconcerting to survivors or future tenants to have the building remain. Suggestions were pouring in for a park and some type of memorial on the site. Many of the suggestions included as a centerpiece a statue based upon the now world famous photograph of the fireman carrying Baylee Almon. On May 8, Chief Gonzales expressed reservations about a memorial that favored any one group of rescuers over any of the others. Fire, police, EMSA, doctors, nurses, National Guard, deputy sheriffs, highway patrol troopers, the Red Cross, Salvation Army, the Federal Emergency Management Agency, civilians, and the variety of nationwide volunteers had just grown much too wide to be represented by a statue commemorating any one agency or category.

Three weeks after the bombing, Priscilla Salyers, her broken ribs and punctured lung healing, was reunited with Sergeant Chuck Wheeler. On May 12, John Youngblood, a Department of Transportation employee, became the 168th victim of the bombing when he died in Presbyterian Hospital from the effects of smoke inhalation.

On May 18, Connie Chung was informed that she had anchored her last CBS Evening News telecast and her weekly newsmagazine would not be renewed. Connie had been "eye to eye" with Oklahoma City, came away with two black ones and no job.

The next day, one month to the day from the date of their deaths, the twelve federal officers killed in the bombing were added to the Oklahoma Peace Officers Memorial during the 1995 ceremonies at DPS Headquarters in Oklahoma City. A star was chiseled into the granite next to their names to mark the deadliest incident in American law enforcement history;*Cynthia L. Brown, U.S. Secret Service*Paul Broxterman, U.S. Inspector General's Office*Harley Cottingham, Defense Investigative Service*Peter L. DeMaster, Defense Investigative Service*Paul D. Ice, U.S. Customs Service*Donald R. Leonard, U.S. Secret Service*Kenneth G. McCullough, Drug Enforcement Administration*Mickey B. Maroney, U.S. Secret Service*Claude A. Medearis, U.S. Customs Service*Larry L. Turner, Defense Investigative Service*Alan Whicher, U.S. Secret Service *Robert Westberry, Defense Investigative Service

On May 23, 26 hours and one minute short of five weeks after the bombing, the remains of the Federal Building were dynamited down by the same Maryland company that had imploded the Biltmore Hotel in the 1970s. Six days later, the last three victims were removed from the rubble, the two that were known missing and a credit union customer. While acknowledging and appreciating the invaluable assistance of the hundreds of volunteers from all over the nation, the natives took great pride in the fact that all 167 of the bodies were recovered by Oklahomans. Like the Marines, we have a tradition of taking care of our own.

On June 1, Richard Ledger bought dinner at a local restaurant for Officer Terry Yeakey, Peter Schaffer, the EMSA medic who took him to the hospital and the intern who stopped him from bleeding to death from his severed carotid artery after he had already lost two-thirds of his blood supply.

The dollar cost of the bombing has been estimated from $650 million to over a billion dollars. The human cost is incalculable.

This is the final tally, as if anything like this can ever be expressed accurately in mere numbers. When the explosion occurred, 162 people died in the Federal Building, the streets nearby or the parking lot across Fifth Street. Two more died in the Water Resources Board building across the street and two more in the Athenian Building next door. The deaths of Rebecca Anderson and John Youngblood brought the final death toll to 168 including 19 children. This figure does not take into account the unborn children of at least two of the victims who were pregnant. The last living survivor was pulled out of the building a little over 12 hours after the explosion. At least 490 people were treated for injuries in area hospitals. At least 110 more were treated later at local clinics, by their personal physicians or sought no professional treatment at all. Oklahoma Governor Frank Keating, a former FBI agent, decreed that all state flags shall remain flying at half-staff in tribute to the victims until 9:02 A.M. on July 4, 76 days after the bombing.

As I close this chapter, the news reports are providing the kind of sharp contrast that tend to harshly snap one back into reality from the euphoria of cooperation, selflessness and pride that has surfaced to deal with this tragedy. During the Waco siege in 1993, the ATF had four agents killed and justifiably had to defend their actions under national scrutiny. Now, in a unique counterpoint to the Waco incident, the ATF has been asked to publicly defend why none of its employees were killed in the bombing. A group of victim's relatives are suing the company that made the fertilizer used in the bomb. Another group is circulating a petition calling for an investigation of the FBI and ATF. And we wonder why we are the most crime-victimized society in history? A federal agent was soon seen wearing an addition to the rash of new T-shirt designs stimulated by the bombing. It showed a badge with a black ribbon across it, symbolic of officers slain in the line of duty, and bore the caption "A society that accepts criminals killing their police had better get used to living with its criminals".

This chapter must of necessity remain unfinished. The last act of this story will be played out in a federal courtroom and minutely described on the nightly newscasts and front pages of America and the world in the months to come. Things will return to normal but normal will somehow never be the same again. The citizens of Oklahoma and Oklahoma City, and the officers of the Oklahoma City Police Department will go on with their lives and work as will the rest of America. But, perhaps, with a greater appreciation for one another.

THE END ??

# EPILOGUE

It is very easy to accuse a government of imperfection, for all mortal things are full of it.
-Montaigne- Essays (1580-1588)

And so it goes. Some things change, some things don't. Some get better, some get worse. Through it all, the job gets done. That is a credit to the "lower level functionaries" I mentioned in the Preface to this work...the Officers and Sergeants who patrol the streets, respond to the crimes, document them, investigate them and solve them.

I have honestly done my best to report the facts of this history as factually as I could. Nevertheless, my sardonic sense of humor, my natural tendency toward sarcasm and the cynicism I have garnered during almost a quarter of a century in this profession have undoubtedly crept into the writing and colored it somewhat.

Lest these be misunderstood, as an afterword I would like to express some thoughts about my true feelings toward my city, profession, its members and the Oklahoma City Police Department.

The city of Oklahoma City, its' government, political leaders and Police Department have had their problems and shortcomings in the past 104 years. These have been no greater, and in many cases much less, than any other major city in this country. This city has its' ghettos, slums, skid row, homeless, substandard public housing projects and all the other defects shared by every other large urban area in this nation. While we have our share of these inequities, we don't have proportionately more than our share and, in many cases, much less. Somehow this city continues to rate relatively high on the lists of good places to live that are produced by people who rate them based upon crime rate, local economy, climate, opportunities and other variables affecting the quality of life.

I am a native of Oklahoma and Oklahoma City. I have spent the greater portion of my adult life with the OCPD. I will be forever identified with all three. It would be a gross understatement to say that I don't regret any of it for an instant. On the contrary, I take great pride in all three associations.

I have been to many other cities and towns in this country in my personal and professional travels. I always come back home and it always looks better every time. I was in a comedy club one night where a stand-up comedian was performing. He had recently moved to Oklahoma City from a much larger city in the northeastern United States. The police department in that city had been undergoing an investigation for corruption recently and he took the opportunity to do a routine involving cop jokes. He finished the routine by saying he had recently been stopped by an OCPD officer for a traffic violation. When the officer came up to his car, he handed his driver's license out the window with a $20 bill wrapped around it. He said that was when he discovered the biggest difference between his hometown cops and Oklahoma City cops..."Oklahoma City cops don't take tips".

When an organization grows to the size of the OCPD, with over a thousand employees and an $80 million annual budget, its administrators tend to view it as a large corporation. When you look at it in those terms, the whole thing boils down to two things...money and people. That's the only difference between Elm Street P.D. and New York City P.D. A lot of cities have more money and a lot of police departments have more officers, more equipment, and sometimes more sophisticated equipment that the additional money can provide. But neither Oklahoma City nor its' Police Department has to take a back seat to anyone when it comes to the people.

Remember what I said in the Prologue about this profession tending to follow bloodlines? On June 16, 1994, the first Oklahoma City Police Academy class of 1994 graduated. Thirty-four men, six women, six African-Americans, one Hispanic-American and one Asian-American. Fully twenty percent of the 40 graduates of Class #110 came from OCPD families; Lt. Manuel Beck's son, Ronnie; retired Sergeant Charlie Greeson's son, Jon; Captain Larry Kettler's wife, Jerri; Sergeant D.R. "Doc" Lanning's wife, Kristin; Lt. Sharon Pollman's husband, Patrick; Sergeant Scott Samuel's wife, Angela; Lt. Bobby Tompkins' son, Robert L. Tompkins Jr.; and one more.

Probationary Police Officer Paul R. Galyon's badge was proudly pinned on by his father, Sergeant (and attorney) J. Brent Galyon. His grandfather, Reese F. Galyon Jr., had been killed in the line of duty over four decades earlier. His great-grandfather, Reese F. Galyon, had retired from the OCPD as a Captain.

Within 24 hours of the rookies' graduation, a man's life ended that provided a counterpoint to the continuum that was law enforcement in Oklahoma City. On the night of June 17, 1994, the man who led the Department through most of the decade of the 1960's and had the second longest tenure in the top job, passed away. Former Chief Hilton Geer, who had joined the OCPD six months before the Pearl Harbor attack and had been retired for two weeks less than a quarter of a century, died two months and a week into his seventy-sixth year. And the legacy continues into the next century.

## BIBLIOGRAPHY

### BOOKS

Adams, James Truslow, Editor in Chief, THE DICTIONARY OF AMERICAN HISTORY, Seond Edition, Revised, Charles Scribners Sons, New York, N.Y., 1940.

Alexander, Charles C., THE KU KLUX KLAN IN THE SOUTHWEST, University of Kentucky Press, 1965.

Blackburn, Bobby L., OKLAHOMA COUNTY-AN ILLUSTRATED HISTORY, Windsor Pubications Inc., Woodland Hills, CA., 1982.———, OKLAHOMA LAW ENFORCEMENT SINCE 1803, unpublished doctoral dissertation, Oklahoma State University, Stillwater, OK, July 1979.

Boardman, Barrington, Isaac Asimov Presents FROM HARDING TO HIROSHIMA-AN ANECDOTAL HISTORY OF THE UNITED STATES FROM 1923-1945, Dembner Books, New York, N.Y., 1988.

Bunky, THE FIRST EIGHT MONTHS OF OKLAHOMA CITY, The McMaster Printing Company, Oklahoma City, OK., 1890.

Cannon, Devereaux D., Jr., THE FLAGS OF THE CONFEDERACY-AN ILLUSTRATED HISTORY, St. Lukes Press, Broadfoot Publishing Company, Memphis, TN, 1988.

Churchill, Winston S., A HISTORY OF THE ENGLISH-SPEAKING PEOPLES, Dodd, Mead and Company, New York, NY, 1956.

Colcord, Charles F., THE AUTOBIOGRAPHY OF CHARLES FRANCIS COLCORD 1859-1934, C.C. Helmerich, Tulsa, OK., 1970.

DeArment, Robert K., BAT MASTERSON-THE MAN AND THE LEGEND, University of Oklahoma Press, Norman, OK., 1979.

Edwards, Jim, and Hal Ottaway, THE VANISHED SPLENDOR, Abalache Book Shop Publishing Company, Oklahoma City, OK, 1982.———, THE VANISHED SPLENDOR II, Abalache Book Shop Publishing Company, Oklahoma City, OK, 1983.———, and Mitchell Oliphant, THE VANISHED SPLENDOR III, Abalache Book Shop Publishing Company, Oklahoma City, OK, 1985.

The Eighty Niners, OKLAHOMA THE BEAUTIFUL LAND, Times-Journal Publishing Company, Oklahoma City, OK, 1943.

English, Billie Joan and Sharon Cooper Calhoun, OKLAHOMA HERITAGE, Holt, Calhoun, Clark & Quaid Publishers, Oklahoma City, OK, 1989.

Fischer, Leroy H., Editor, OKLAHOMA'S GOVERNORS, 1907-1929: TURBULENT POLITICS, Oklahoma Historical Society, Oklahoma City, OK, 1981.

Franklin, Jimmie Lewis, BORN SOBER: PROHIBITION IN OKLAHOMA 1907-1959, University of Oklahoma Press, Norman, OK, 1971.

Gaines, W. Craig, THE CONFEDERATE CHEROKEES: JOHN DREW'S REGIMENT OF MOUNTED RIFLES, Louisiana State University Press, Baton Rouge, LA, 1989.

Helmer, William J., THE GUN THAT MADE THE TWENTIES ROAR, The MacMillian Com pany, New York, 1969.

Hendrickson, Kenneth B. Jr., Editor, HARD TIMES IN OKLAHOMA: THE DEPRESSION YEARS, Oklahoma State Historical Society, Oklahoma City, OK, 1983.

Hoig, Stan, THE OKLAHOMA LAND RUSH OF 1889, Oklahoma Historical Society, Oklahoma City, OK, 1984.
Holloway, Harry, with Frank S. Myers, BAD TIMES FOR GOOD OL' BOYS: The Oklahoma County Commissioner Scandal, University of Oklahoma Press, Norman, Oklahoma, 1993.
Horan, James D. and Paul Sann, PICTORIAL HISTORY OF THE WILD WEST, Crown Publishers Inc., Bonanza Books, New York, NY, 1954.
Jackson, Kenneth T., THE KU KLUX KLAN IN THE CITY 1915-1930, Oxford University Press, New York, NY, 1967.
Josephy, Alvin M., Jr., THE CIVIL WAR IN THE AMERICAN WEST, Alfred A. Knopf, Inc., New York, N.Y. 1991.
Kelly, Robert J., Editor, ORGANIZED CRIME-A GLOBAL PERSPECTIVE, Rowman and Littlefield, Totowa, N.J., 1986.
Kohn, Howard, WHO KILLED KAREN SILKWOOD?, Summit Books, New York, NY, 1981.
Long, E.B. with Barbara Long, THE CIVIL WAR DAY BY DAY-AN ALMANAC 1861-1865, Da Capo Press Inc., Plenum Publishing Corp., New York, N.Y. 1971.
Louderback, Lew, THE BAD ONES: GANGSTERS OF THE '30'S AND THEIR MOLLS, Fawcett Publications Inc., Greenwich, Conn., 1968.
McRill, Albert, AND SATAN CAME ALSO: AN INSIDE STORY OF A CITY'S SOCIAL AND POLITICAL HISTORY, Britton Publishing Company, Oklahoma City, OK, 1955. SPECIAL NOTE: I don't feel that the mere inclusion of this book in this bibliography is enough recognition. Mr. McRill's book is hardly an unbiased account, being heavily weighted with his personal values, religious views and conservatism. Whether you share them or not, it is nevertheless an invaluable account of Oklahoma City's history, politics and law enforcement, made even more entertaining by Mr. McRill's talent for using allegory and metaphor.
Morgan, H. Wayne and Anne Hodges Morgan, OKLAHOMA: A HISTORY, W.W. Norton & Company Inc., New York, NY, 1984.
Morris, John W., Editor, CITIES OF OKLAHOMA, Volume XI, Oklahoma Series, Oklahoma Historical Society, Oklahoma City, OK, 1979.
Morris, John W., GHOST TOWNS OF OKLAHOMA, University of Oklahoma Press, Norman, OK., 1978.
Nix, Evett Dumas, as told to Gordon Hines, OKLAHOMBRES: Particularly the Wilder Ones, University of Nebraska Press, Bison Book reprint, Lincoln, NE, 1993.
Pace, Denny F., and Jimmie C. Styles, ORGANIZED CRIME: CONCEPTS AND CONTROL, Prentice-Hall Inc., Englewood Cliffs, N.J., 1975.
Painter, Louise, BIOGRAPHICAL PROFILES-MAYORS OF OKLAHOMA CITY 1889-1993, Oklahoma Historical Society, Oklahoma City, OK, February 1993).
Paton, John, Managing Editor, CRIMES AND PUNISHMENT-A PICTORIAL ENCYCLOPEDIA OF ABERRANT BEHAVIOR, 20 volumes, Phoebus Publishing Company, U.S.A., 1973-1974.
Peterson, Clarence Stewart, LAST CIVIL WAR VETERAN IN FIFTY STATES, Privately printed, Baltimore, Maryland, January, 1961.
Rashke, Richard, THE KILLING OF KAREN SILKWOOD. THE STORY BEHIND THE KERR-MCGEE PLUTONIUM CASE, Penguin Books, New York, NY, 1981.
Roosevelt, Theodore, THE ROUGH RIDERS, Charles Scribner's Sons, New York, N.Y., 1920.
Rosa, Joseph, THE GUNFIGHTER-MAN OR MYTH?, Oklahoma University Press, Norman, OK, 1969.
Sabbag, Robert, TOO TOUGH TO DIE: DOWN AND DANGEROUS WITH THE U.S. MARSHALS, Simon and Schuster, New York, NY, 1992.
Scott, Angelo C., THE STORY OF OKLAHOMA CITY, Times-Journal Publishing Company, Oklahoma City, OK, 1939.
Shirk, Lucyl, OKLAHOMA CITY, CAPITAL OF SOONERLAND, Oklahoma City Board of Education, Semco Color Press, Oklahoma City, OK, 1957.
Shirley, Glenn, WEST OF HELL'S FRINGE: CRIME, CRIMINALS AND THE FEDERAL PEACE OFFICER IN OKLAHOMA TERRITORY 1889-1907, University of Oklahoma Press,

Norman, OK, 1978.
SPECIAL NOTE: This is absolutely essential reading for anyone interested in the early criminal history of Oklahoma. Many pre-Statehood incidents merely alluded to in my book are given a much more thorough treatment in this volume by a master historian.
———, GUARDIAN OF THE LAW: THE LIFE AND TIMES OF WILLIAM MATTHEW TILGHMAN (1854-1924), Eakin Press, Austin, Texas, 1988.
———, HECK THOMAS, FRONTIER MARSHAL, University of Oklahoma Press, Norman, OK., 1962.
———, LAW WEST OF FORT SMITH, University of Nebraska Press, Lincoln, NE., 1957.
Sifakis, Carl, THE ENCYCLOPEDIA OF AMERICAN CRIME, Facts on File Inc., New York, NY, 1982.
Speer, Bonnie, MOMENTS IN OKLAHOMA HISTORY, Reliance Press, Norman, OK, 1988.
Stein, Howard F. and Robert F. Hill, Editors, THE CULTURE OF OKLAHOMA, University of Oklahoma Press, Norman, Oklahoma, 1993.
Stewart, Roy P. and Pendleton Woods, BORN GROWN: AN OKLAHOMA CITY HISTORY, Fidelity Bank N.A., Oklahoma City, OK, 1974.
Thompson, John, CLOSING THE FRONTIER: RADICAL RESPONSE IN OKLAHOMA, 1889-1923, University of Oklahoma Press, Norman, OK, 1986.
Trachtman, Paul, THE GUNFIGHTERS-THE OLD WEST SERIES, Time-Life Books, New York, NY, 1974.
Ungar, Sanford J., FBI, Atlantic Monthly Press, Little, Brown and Company, Boston, Mass., 1975.
Wellman, Paul I., A DYNASTY OF WESTERN OUTLAWS, Pyramid Books, New York, NY, 1961.

ARTICLES, MAGAZINES, NEWSLETTERS, JOURNALS AND PERIODICALS:
Alley, John, CITY BEGINNINGS IN OKLAHOMA TERRITORY, Oklahoma Municipal Review, Volume IX, Number 4, April, 1935.
Chaffin, K.B., JELLY BRYCE-THE FBI'S LEGENDARY SHARPSHOOTER, Oklahombres Newsletter, Spring, 1993.
Cloud, Jim, DEAD-THE MAN, WHO KILLED THE MAN, WHO KILLED JESSE JAMES, Oklahombres Newsletter, Spring, 1992.
Cordry, Dee, STATE OPERATIVE LUTHER BISHOP, Oklahombres Newsletter, Summer, 1991.
Fraternal Order of Police Journal, multiple issues.
The Grapevine; Official Publication of the Society of Former Special Agents of the Federal Bureau of Investigation, Inc.; July 1974; February 1976.
Lamar, Howard R., THE CREATION OF OKLAHOMA: NEW MEANINGS FOR THE OKLAHOMA LAND RUN, The Culture of Oklahoma, Howard F. Stein and Robert F. Hill, Editors, University of Oklahoma Press, Norman, Oklahoma 1993.
Markardt, Stephen P., G-MEN FACT AND FICTION; AN EVENING AT THE BIO, The Investigator, Office of Public Affairs of the Federal Bureau of Investigation, July/August 1990.
Mattix, Rick, MACHINE GUN KELLY, Oklahombres Newsletter, Fall 1992.
Maxwell, Gloria, THE KANSAS CITY UNION STATION MASSACRE, Oklahombres Newsletter, Spring, Summer and Fall issues, 1991.
Oklahoma City Police Annual 1923Oklahoma City Police Annual 1928
Oklahoma City Police Annual 1929
Oklahoma City Police Beat, multiple issues.
Oklahoma City Police Cosmopolitan, multiple issues.
Oklahoma City Police Department Yearbook 1975.
Oklahoma City Police Department Yearbook 1990.
Oklahoma City Police Review, multiple issues.
Oklahoma Sheriff and Peace Officers Association Magazine, multiple issues.
Pioneering in Kiowa County, Volume 3, Kiowa County Historical Society, September 1, 1978.

"Police Notes", Oklahoma Municipal Review, Volume X, Number 10, October, 1936.
Reed, Louis A., OKLAHOMA CITY FIRE AND POLICE DEPARTMENTS 1910, Warden Printing Company, Oklahoma City, OK, 1910.
Walker, Wayne T., A 'TOO-PERFECT' ALIBI, Detective Cases magazine, October 1981 issue.

NEWSPAPERS ( all Oklahoma unless otherwise noted):

The Broken Bow News
The Mountain View News
The Cherokee Messenger
The New York (NY) Daily Mirror
The Daily Oklahoman
The Oklahoma City Times
The Edmond Sun Democrat
The Oklahoma Daily Times-Journal
The El Reno News
The Oklahoma Gazette
The Evening Gazette
The Oklahoma Journal
The Fort Cobb Express
The Oklahoma News
The Indian Chieftain
The Oklahoma State Capital
The Luther Register
The Shawnee Evening Star
The McAlester Democrat
The Shawnee Morning News
The McAlester News-Capital
The Tulsa World
The Okmulgee Daily Times

OTHER MATERIALS:

Burial records and headstone inscriptions, Fairlawn Cemetery.
The Daily Oklahoman Archives
Inactive Personnel Files-Oklahoma City Police Department
Oklahoma Christian College, newspaper clipping files.
The Oklahoma Historical Society

# APPENDICES

## ABBREVIATIONS

ATF-Bureau of Alcohol, Tobacco and Firearms. Formerly ATU, Alcohol Tax Unit. A law enforcement agency of the U.S. Treasury Department.
BPD-Bethany Police Department. Bethany is a suburb west of Oklahoma City, 1990 population 20,075.
CIA-Central Intelligence Agency
CPI-Citizens for Police Improvement
CSO-Community Service Officer. A "police cadet" program instituted for people over the age of 18 but under the age of 21.
DPS-Oklahoma State Department of Public Service.
DUI-Driving Under the Influence. Drunk driving charge under Oklahoma law.
EPD-Edmond Police Department. Edmond is a suburb north of Oklahoma City, 1990 population 52,315.
FBI-Federal Bureau of Investigation
FOP-Fraternal Order of Police
FTO-Field Training Officer. An experienced officer who trains recruits.
LEAA-Law Enforcement Assistance Administration.
MWCPD-Midwest City Police Department. Midwest City is a suburb east of Oklahoma City, 1990 population 52,267.
NAACP-National Association for the Advancement of Colored People
NHPD-Nichols Hills Police Department. Nichols Hills is a suburb north of Oklahoma City.
NSA-National Security Agency.
OCPD-Oklahoma City Police Department.
OCSO-Oklahoma County Sheriff's Office
OHP-Oklahoma Highway Patrol
OKC-Common abbreviation for Oklahoma City.
OPUBCO-Oklahoma Publishing Company, publishers of the Daily Oklahoma newspaper.

OR-Own Recognizance. To release an arrested subject without requiring him or her to post a cash bond due to his ties to the community (owning a home, children in school, long-time residence, responsible position or long-time employment).
OSBI-Oklahoma State Bureau of Investigation, originally called the State Crime Bureau.
PCP-Phencyclidine, an illegal hallucinogenic drug.
SEU-Selective Enforcement Unit
WAPD-Warr Acres Police Department. Warr Acres is a suburb west of Oklahoma City, 1990 population 9,288.
WCTU-Women's Christian Temperance Union

## OKLAHOMA CITY POLICE OFFICERS KILLED IN THE LINE OF DUTY

| | |
|---|---|
| Marshal John S. Howard | June 14, 1889 |
| Chief J. Milton Jones | June 30, 1895 |
| Assistant Chief George W. Jackson | April 12, 1898 |
| Officer Morris R. Reagan | February 25, 1910 |
| Officer William F. Byrd | August 2, 1919 |
| Officer Jesse H. Sosbee | December 1, 1922 |
| Detective Briggs Chumley | November 3, 1924 |
| Officer Isaac Daniel Ashburn | July 20, 1928 |
| Officer John D. "Jack" Gates | March 22, 1930 |
| Detective Charles Cash York | February 8, 1933 |
| Officer John Harold Beasley | May 18, 1933 |
| Officer Douglas W. Gates | December 3, 1933 |
| Officer Elmer Lee Sartor | August 20, 1934 |
| Officer Ray S. Clark | May 23, 1936 |
| Captain Frank Cissne | April 1, 1937 |
| Officer Fred Beaumont Counts | August 22, 1938 |
| Detective Webb L. Campbell | October 29, 1938 |
| Officer Reese Franklin Galyon Jr. | December 22, 1951 |
| Detective Benjamin Franklin Cravatt | July 16, 1954 |
| Officer Eugene Henry Mills | December 11, 1954 |
| Officer Ronald Lynn Haggard | March 21, 1963 |
| Officer Mark Henry Zelewski | July 27, 1964 |
| Officer Michael John Ratikan | June 14, 1971 |
| Officer James Dewey Chamblin | April 16, 1974 |
| Lake Ranger William L. Stewart Jr. | May 17, 1974 |
| Sergeant Terry Glenn Lawson | April 21, 1977 |
| Airport Officer Garland Garrison | September 19, 1979 |
| Detective Gary Lee Ward | February 2, 1985 |
| Master Patrolman Richard O. Riggs | January 7, 1986 |
| Officer Delmar Warren Tooman | September 29, 1990 |

## OKLAHOMA CITY POLICE CHIEFS

| | |
|---|---|
| 8/9/1890-2/9/1891 | Charles F. Colcord |
| 2/9/1891-4/25/1892 | Thomas J. Word |
| 4/25/1892-4/12/1893 | Oscar G. Lee |
| 4/13/1893-10/9/1893 | Willis Ivers |
| 10/9/1893-5/9/1894 | Edward Frank Cochran |
| 5/9/1894-6/30/1895 | J. Milton Jones |
| 7/4/1895-12/30/1895 | J.H. Boles |
| 12/30/1895-5/1/1896 | George W. Jackson |
| 5/1/1896-4/1/1897 | Thomas Abraham "Abe" Couch |

| | |
|---|---|
| 4/1/1897-2/7/1899 | Edward Frank Cochran |
| 2/7/1899-4/11/1899 | George W. R. Chinn |
| 4/11/1899-4/2/1901 | William B. Hendrey |
| 4/2/1901-4/13/1903 | Ralph W. Cochran |
| 4/13/1903-4/4/1905 | Orris H. Emrick |
| 4/4/1905-4/9/1907 | John Hubatka |
| 4/9/1907-4/27/1909 | Charles C. Post |
| 4/27/1909-7/15/1911 | John Hubatka |
| 7/15/1911-2/11/1913 | William M. Tilghman |
| 2/11/1913-2/18/1914 | Jerome D. Jones |
| 2/10/1914-2/18/1914 | Shirley E. Dyer |
| 2/18/1914-4/13/1915 | F. Webb Jones |
| 4/13/1915-4/5/1919 | William B. Nichols |
| 4/5/1919-5/1/1920 | Jerry M. Smith |
| 9/20/1920-4/14/1921 | Calvin T. Linville |
| 4/14/1921-7/6/1921 | Martin C. Binion |
| 7/6/1921-10/1/1921 | Carl S. Glitsch |
| 10/1/1921-12/16/1921 | Rolley Organ |
| 12/16/1921-1/15/1923 | Waller J. Clark |
| 1/15/1923-4/23/1923 | Martin C. Binion |
| 4/23/1923-3/1/1926 | Ray Frazier |
| 3/1/1926-4/14/1927 | William E. Snelson |
| 4/14/1927-5/15/1928 | Martin C. Binion |
| 5/15/1928-5/15/1929 | Benjamin B. Moore |
| 5/15/1929-4/22/1931 | Charles A. Becker |
| 4/22/1931-4/19/1937 | John Watt |
| 4/19/1937-10/1/1939 | Granville Scanland |
| 10/1/1939-3/10/1943 | Frank S. Smith |
| 3/10/1943-7/30/1954 | Lawrence J. "Smokey" Hilbert |
| 7/30/1954-1/1/1961 | Roy J. Bergman |
| 1/1/1961-7/15/1961 | Edgar E. Rector |
| 7/15/1961-6/1/1962 | Daniel A. Hollingsworth |
| 6/1/1962-7/1/1969 | Hilton J. Geer |
| 7/1/1969-4/20/1972 | Elvin Wayne Lawson |
| 4/20/1972-1/18/1974 | Samuel D. Watson Jr. |
| 1/18/1974-1/2/1977 | I.G. Purser |
| 1/2/1977-2/15/1982 | Tom L. Heggy |
| 2/15/1982-2/14/1985 | Lloyd A. Gramling |
| 2/14/1985-6/14/1990 | Robert V. Wilder |
| 6/14/1990-5/3/1991 | David R. McBride |
| 8/24/1991- | Sam Gonzales |

## MAYORS OF OKLAHOMA CITY

| | |
|---|---|
| 4/27/1889-11/11/1889 | William L. Couch |
| 11/27/1889-12/30/1889 | Dr. Andrew Jackson Beale |
| 7/15/1890-8/9/1890 | D.W. Gibbs |
| 8/12/1890-4/12/1892 | William J. Gault |
| 4/23/1892-4/9/1894 | O.A. Mitscher |
| 4/9/1894-4/13/1896 | Nelson Button |
| 4/13/1896-4/12/1897 | Charles Graham Jones |
| 4/12/1897-4/10/1899 | J.P. Allen |
| 4/10/1899-4/8/1901 | Lee Van Winkle |
| 4/8/1901-4/13/1903 | Charles Graham Jones |
| 4/13/1903-4/10/1905 | Lee Van Winkle |

| | |
|---|---|
| 4/10/1905-4/8/1907 | Dr. J.G. Messenbaugh |
| 4/8/1907-4/11/1910 | Henry M. Scales |
| 4/11/1910-6/8/1911 | Daniel V. Lackey |
| 6/8/1911-4/13/1915 | Whitaker M. Grant |
| 4/13/1915-12/24/1918 | Edward Overholser |
| 12/25/1918-4/7/1919 | Byron D. Shear |
| 4/7/1919-1/9/1923 | John Calloway Walton |
| 1/9/1923-4/4/1923 | Mike Donnelly |
| 4/4/1923-4/12/1927 | Otto Arthur Cargill |
| 4/12/1927-4/12/1931 | Walter C. Dean |
| 4/12/1931-11/7/1933 | Clarence J. Blinn |
| 11/7/1933-4/9/1935 | Tom E. McGee |
| 4/9/1935-4/11/1939 | John Frank Martin |
| 4/11/1939-4/8/1947 | Robert A. Hefner |
| 4/8/1947-4/7/1959 | Allen Street |
| 4/7/1959-4/9/1963 | James H. Norick |
| 4/9/1963-5/3/1964 | Jack S. Wilkes |
| 6/16/1964-4/11/1967 | George H. Shirk |
| 4/11/1967-4/13/1971 | James H. Norick |
| 4/13/1971-4/12/1983 | Patience Latting |
| 4/12/1983-4/14/1987 | Andrew Coats |
| 4/14/1987- | Ronald Norick |

## PRESIDENTS OF OKLAHOMA CITY LODGE #123 OF THE FRATERNAL ORDER OF POLICE

| | |
|---|---|
| 1968-1969 | Captain Weldon Davis |
| 1969 | Lieutenant Lee Brown |
| 1969-1970 | Officer Richard Boyd |
| 1971-1972 | Officer Charlie Owen |
| 1973 | Major Kenneth Nash |
| 1974 | Officer Ralph Pearce |
| 1975-1980 | Detective Jim Parsons |
| 1981 | Detective Ray Clark |
| 1982 | Lieutenant David McBride |
| 1983 | Detective Vic Colbert |
| 1984- | Officer Paul D. Taylor |

The following transcriptions of names from the OCPD Annuals of 1910, 1923, 1928 and 1929 are given exactly as they appear in the Annuals including misspellings.

## 1910 OKLAHOMA CITY POLICE & FIRE SOUVENIR BOOK

Henry M. Scales-Mayor
John Hubatka-Chief of Police
Joe C. Burnett-Assistant Chief
Frank L. Staton-Chief of Secret Service
CAPTAINS-William Slayton and Mike Conners
SERGEANTS-A. Bradford and John H. Reeh
SECRET SERVICE DEPT.-R. Burnett-A.A. Gordon-D.B. Herring-John Cassidy-F.W. Jones-C.A. Clark-Sgt. J.M. Stewart-Sgt. P.N. Biewer
PATROLMEN: 34 Patrolmen pictured, unidentified but recognizable among them are:Rolley Organ-Jerry Smith-Ed Veazey-Ike Ashburn 1923

## 1923 OKLAHOMA CITY POLICE ANNUAL

MAYOR-O.A. Cargill

SECRETARY TO THE MAYOR-John W. Tipton
MAYOR'S STENOGRAPHER-Clara B. Kelley
LEGAL DEPARTMENT-E.S. Stewart, Assistant Court Clerk Robert E. Lee, Prosecuting Attorney Joe O'Leary, Court Clerk D.B. Welty, Assistant Municipal Counselor Judge O.P. Estes, Municipal Judge John Frank Martin, Municipal Counselor R.E. Woods, Assistant Municipal Counselor Tom Harvey, Evidence Officer Vashti Hitchins, Stenographer
CHIEF OF POLICE-Ray Frazier
NIGHT CHIEF OF POLICE-W.E. Snelson
CAPTAIN OF DETECTIVES-John Hubatka
SECRETARY TO THE CHIEF-T.D. Brandom
SECRETARY TO THE NIGHT CHIEF-M.L. Austin
SECRETARY TO THE CHIEF OF DETECTIVES-Roy Hatchett - C.A. Becker-Secretary/Treasurer, Police Relief Association and Head of the Stolen Goods Department O.A. Collins
CAPTAINS-James Morris, Jerry Smith, Jack Carey and J.B. Ryan
EX-CHIEF OF POLICE-Carl Glitsch
SERGEANTS-J.B. Jeter, E.V. Stockton, C.W. Cunc and O.M. Milholland
GAMEWELL OPERATORS-Roy Cantrell and Everett Clawson Master Mechanic J.F. Martin Mechanic J.G. Eums
MATRONS-Lillian Murray, Vesta M. Glass and V.J. Boarman
BERTILLION DEPT., STOLEN GOODS DEPT., ELECTRICIANS AND JAILORS-L.C. Bowles-John Coleman-D. Dunham-W.R. Farguson-W.D. Fossett-G.L. Golding-H.D. Hahn-M.C. Hiatt-Walt Kessler-John W. Long-Walter McCoy-Matley-D. Miller-M.L. O'Rourke-Henry Powers-T.B. Roach-H.L. Sadler-Bill Slayton-Fred Smith-Carl H. Stratton-Harry Wolf-J.R. Whitehill
MOTORCYCLE SQUAD-Lt. Grover Gaines-Ray S. Clark-Reese F. Galyon Clarence Hurt-Guy Mitchell-Gay E. Sharp-Thomas Webb-H.V. WilderRalph Young
TRAFFIC SQUAD-Lt. Sam Ginn-W.D. Daniels-R.C. Jones-E.L. Littlefield W.S. McCall-John McCarty-R.I. Melson-W.E. Mitchell-J.T. Nay - M.F. Shelton-J.W. Strain
PATROLMEN-L.B. Armstrong-Sam Bartell-R.J. Bates-Sam Burnett - Thomas Busch-R.W. Cantrell-W.M. Cavnar-G.B. Conally-Ed Cothrum-Dan Crowley-M. Davis-Leo W. DeCordova-A.M. Estes-W.F. GatesTom Gray-P.C. Greenwood-Roscoe Harwell-Tom Hennessey-F.C. Hoffman-John Hopkins-James House-C.W. Hubycka-F.D. Janovy-C.L. Johnston-George D. Kerr-H.L. Lair-Henry McMullen-John Marrinan-W.N. Mitchell-T. Nangley-Lewis Nicholson-T.J. O'Neill-H.C. Overfelt-G.W. PageW.T Pemberton-S.C. Reeves-R.A. Sanders-J.B. Saunders-M.I. Shaffer-Perry Shrake-W.W. Shumate-Charles Stewart-P.B. Stinnett-George A. Stinson-J.T. Taylor-R.L. Walton-W. Washington-W.F. White-D. Wilkerson-L. Youngblood-J.T. Younger-J.F. Zerbe
PLAINCLOTHES-Ike Ashburn-C.H. Barnes-Jim Beaty-Luther Bishop-F.S. Boyd-R.F. Brandon-George Brigman-W.V. Brown-John Cassidy-C.H. Chesley-B. Chumley-F.J. Cissne-Roy Cogswell-Mike Conners-H.S. Cummings-John Davis-Tom Davis-J.H. Dees-W.O. Eads-F.O. HaneyE.S. Hardin-C.W. Kemp-E. Miller-R.D. Mitchell-W.R. Parker-S.H. Prather-R. Robinson-George J. Schuler-Joe Slayton-Clyde E. Sutton-T.J. Tellegen-C.M. Tyler-C.F. Weaver
CITY PHYSICIAN-Carey W. Townsend-O.A. Cargill-Mayor of Oklahoma City -H.F. Newblock-Mayor of Tulsa-R.A. Hefner-Mayor of Ardmore-R.O. Renfrew-Mayor of Woodward-John Carn-Mayor of Enid-W.C. McAdoo-Mayor of Okmulgee-D.D. Ruebnsthal-Mayor of Miami D.C. Youmans-City Manager of Muskogee-George H. Walker-Mayor of Muskogee

## 1928 OKLAHOMA CITY POLICE ANNUAL

CHIEF-Ben B. Moore
SECRETARY TO THE CHIEF-Charles W. Cunc
ASSISTANT CHIEF-Charles A. Becker
SUPERINTENDENT OF AUTO THEFT-Clarence Hurt
CAPTAINS-Randall W. Cantrell-John F. Milan-Jerry Smith
DESK SERGEANTS-Earl F. Cunnyngham-Timothy J. Tellegen-H.V.Wilder

JAILERS-Charles Campbell-John C. Coleman-James Whitehill
BERTILLON SUPERINTENDENT-Carl Stratton
MATRONS-Mrs. V.J.Boarman-Rosa Foster-Effie Tratchel
TRAFFIC SQUAD-Captain Tom Webb-L.B. Armstrong-G.B. Connally-J.J. Flynn-Tom Guest-E.L. Littlefield-William G. Loyd-W.S. McCall-Walter Moore-L.E. Nelson-W.N. Shumate-J.W. "Dick" Strain
MOTORCYCLE SQUAD-Frank Cissne-Joe Jerkins-Grover Gaines-Reece Galyon-George Kerr-Guy Mitchell
PATROLMEN-John T. Anderson-Ike Ashburn-Ed Barrett-John Bell-Lester Boone-Allen Brown-I.E. Burns-Mark Davis-D.D. Dougherty-W.F. Fallwell-James Hardwick-Joe Hopper-C.W. Hubycka-W.E. Jones-Ted Kangley-H.L. Lair-John T. McCarty-H.H. McClure-James M. Meads-R.Q. Melson-W.E. Mitchell-Samuel Murphy-Joe Nay-Thomas J. O'Neill-William Pemberton-H.W. Powers-J.M. Pryor-John Revels-R.A. Sanders-J.B. Saunders-M.I. Shaffer-Elzye Stewart-O.A. Vansickle-D. Wilkerson-Louis Youngblood
PLAINCLOTHES-J.E. Anderson-G.A. Barnhame-R.J. Bates-Reg F. Brandom-Sam Burnett-James Carter-John Cassidy-C.H. Chesley-Mike Conners-John Davis-Chick Faris-W.R. Ferguson-M.E. Forsyth-S.G. Ginn-P.C. Greenwood-John Hubatka-Robert Hurt-C.W. Kemp-A.C. Large-Joe Layton-F.P. McDonald-James Morris-Lee Mullinex-W.A. Parker-Charles Ryan-John Ryan-Wade Spear-W.J. Sterrett-Ed Veazey-John Von Elm-C.C. York

## 1929 OKLAHOMA CITY POLICE ANNUAL

Walter C. Dean-Mayor
E.M. Fry-City Manager
Charles A. Becker-Chief
Charles W. Cunc-Secretary to the Chief
Clarence Hurt-Night Chief
Paul Theimer-Secretary to Night Chief
CAPTAINS-R.W. Cantrell-J.F. Milam-T.J. Tellegen-M.E. Forsyth (Traffic)
DESK SERGEANTS-Ray T. Hatchett-Guy Mitchell-H.V. Wilder
PATROLMEN-C.F. Anderson-J.T. Anderson-S.B. Arrion-G.F. Baker-O.F. Barnett-E.L. Barrett-John Bell-W.C. Bolton-Lester Boone-Allen Brown-I.E. Burns-J.F. Butler-B.F. Cole-G.B. Connally-D.D. Daugherty-K.A. Davis-Mark Davis-W.F. Fallwell-G.P. Harrison-C.W. Hubycka-E.E. Jones-G.E. Kentman-H.L. Lair-H. McKim-H.H. Maynard-W.M. Moore-Joe Nay-W.R. Nelson-W.T. Pemberton-Sam Phillips-J.M. Pryor-O.L. Ragland-R.A. Sanders-C.W. Scott-A.C. Shelton-W.L. Shirley-Perry Shrake-E. Spillers-W.D. Tucker-G.C. Waldrop-W.M. Washington-L.F. White-W.A. Williams-R.S. Worthy
DETECTIVES-Walter Acord-R.C. Bradford-W.V. Brown-D.A. Bryce-Sam Burnett-E.E. Carr-Jim Carter-John Cassidy-Mike Conners-E.F. Cunnyngham-E.L. Drane-B.D. Faris-G. Gaines-R. Galyon-P.C. Greenwood-B.F. Hill-John Hopkins-John Hubatka-Joe Jerkins-H.C. Jones-A.C. Large-Joe Layton-N.V. McCollum-Marvin M. Murray-Dick Parker-Charles Ryan-John B. Ryan-W.E. Snelson-Wade Spears-J.W. Strain-J.E. Veazey-John Von Elm-L.H. Walen-C.C. York
TRAFFIC-L.B. Armstrong-M. Cragg-D.E. Ellison-J.J. Flynn-H.C. Henry-W.E. Jones-L.H. Kolb-E.L. Littlefield-A.B. Livingston-Lt. W.G. Loyd-W.S. McCall-W.L. McCoy-L.E. Nelson-H.W. Powers-Jake Robertson-W.N. Shumate-O. Silvey-E.E. Stewart-O.A. Vansickle-Jack Vaughn-Capt. Tom Webb
MOTORCYCLES-F.A. Carr-F.J. Cissne-J.W. Clingan-Roy DeShields-R.P. Finley-J.H. Gates-B.J. Gibson-H.G. Paris-E. Sartor-K.E. Treadwell-C.O. Willis
SERGEANT-AUTO THEFT-G.A. Burnhame
STOLEN GOODS-C.W. Kemp-E.F. Cunnyngham
BERTILLON SUPERINTENDENT-Carl H. Stratton
JAILERS-Charles Campbell-John Coleman
MATRONS-Virginia Boarman-Rose Foster-Elfie Tratchel
DECEASED-Ike Ashburn-Briggs Chumley-Louis D. Fowler-M.C. Hiatt-O.M. Milhollan-Earl

Rardin-S.C. Reaves-J.B. Saunders-M.E. Shelton-W.M. Slayton-A.L. Walton-C.H. White-James R. Whitehill-H.C. Wolfe

## CITIZENS FOR POLICE IMPROVEMENT INC. AWARDS 1962-1971

NOTE: Honorees are members of the Oklahoma City Police Department unless otherwise noted.

### CITY COUNCIL AWARD FOR HEROISM

CRITERIA: CPI Inc. will present in the name of the City Council, an award of honor, to the member of the Oklahoma City Police Department who, in the opinion of the CPI Wards Committee, distinguishes himself above and beyond the call of duty in the performance of an act of gallantry at imminent personal risk of his own life, with the knowledge of the risk assumed. The action will not necessarily involve an attempt to save someone's life.The award: Initially, this award consisted of a silver bowl, suitably inscribed, and a certificate. In 1964 an inscribed clock was given. From 1965-1969 an inscribed watch and a plaque was given. In 1970-1971 the award was an inscribed watch and a $100 cash grant.

WINNERS

1962-Sgt. Cecil W. Pierce
1963-Det. John Rowden
1964-Off. Bruce Shaw
1965-Off. Rex L. Norton
Off. R.G. Hendricks
1966-Det. Darrell D. Pierce
Det. C.E. Waggoner
1967-Off. Kenneth J. Buettner
1968-Det. Denver Kirby
Det. Robert Jackson
1969-Off. Gary Scott
1970-Off. Claude Shobert
1971-Off. Charles Shelden

### THE MAYOR'S AWARD FOR VALOR

CRITERIA: CPI Inc. will present in the name of the Mayor of Oklahoma City, the Mayor's Award for Valor, to be given to any member of the Oklahoma City Police Department who, in an attempt to save someone's life, distinguishes himself by the performance of an act of bravery, with the knowledge of the personal risk assumed, when such act in the opinion of the CPI Awards Committee, actually resulted in the saving of a human life, such life having been in imminent danger.
The Award: Same as the City Council Award.

WINNERS

1962-Off. Cecil W. Pierce
1963-Off. Polk A. White
1964-Off. Lindell Gay
Off. Michael H. Morrison
1965-Off. Raymond J. Melton
1966-Off. Bill C. Baldwin
1967-Off. G.A. Burns
1968-Off. Wallace Moore
Off. Simon Torres
1969-Off. Theophilus Martin
Off. Jimmy Lee Taylor
Sgt. Cecil W. Pierce
1970-Off. Paul D. Tylor
Off. Carey D. Gilbert
1971-Off. Glen DeSpain

### THE CITY MANAGER'S COMMENDATION AWARD

CRITERIA: CPI Inc. will present the City Manager's Commendation Award to one or more members of the Oklahoma City Police Department, serving in any capacity, who perform exceptional meritorious service to the Police Department or to the people of Oklahoma City.

The Award: Initially, this award was a certificate. In 1963 it was an inscribed silver bowl. From then on, the award was the same as the City Council Award and the Mayor's Award.

WINNERS

1962-Off. James G. Jackson
1963-Off. Mike Huckaby
Off. Rex Barrett
1964-Off. Irven R. Box
1965-Harold Campbell
Off. Larry K. Upchurch
1966-Off. Homer O. Barnett
Off. Charles Hill
1967-Sgt. John D. Lewis
1968-Det. W.W. Harrison
Det. C. Hinderliter
1969-Off. O.V. Donwerth
Off. Jack Montgomery
1970-Off. James Winter
1971-Off. W.T. Jackson

## THE COUNTY COMMISSIONERS AWARD

CRITERIA: CPI Inc. will present the County Commissioners of Oklahoma County Award to the member of any regularly organized or constituted law enforcement body within Oklahoma County serving in any capacity, who contributes the most to law enforcement within the County.
The Award: An inscribed silver tray.

WINNERS

1963-Chief Nelson Beckett,Warr Acres PD
1964-Chief Carl Tyler, Midwest City PD
1965-Chief O.F. McLain, Bethany PD
1966-Chief Hilton Geer, OCPD
1967-Assistant Chief W.A. Williams, OCPD

## LEE WAY MOTOR FREIGHT INC. AWARD

CRITERIA: Lee Way Motor Freight Inc., in cooperation with CPI Inc., will present to the top-ranking members of the Oklahoma City Police Department trainee group, as determined by the CPI Awards Committee, a plaque and a cash grant of $100 each, to be used for any purpose, such as tuition, book purchases or travel, to further their education in police work.
NOTE: This award was given by and known as the City Bus Company and Oklahoma Transportation Company Award prior to 1966.

WINNERS

1962-J.E. Grist
Jerry G. Landreth
Bill A. Stubbs
1963-Henry McMullan
Joe Hughston
Jim Willis
1964-Bill R. Vetter
Richard Neill Griffith
John J. LeMaster
1965-Art Smith
Richard A. Boyd
1966-Frank D. Gunter
Melvin E. Hodges
1967-James E. Jones
Wallace E. Moore
1968-Geraldon Canary
W.B. Smith
1969-Bob Tash
Tim W. Stinson
Hollis W. Harper
1970-Michael Hatch
Don Pennington
William E. Lewis
1971-Michael Heath
James Gallegly

## THE OKLAHOMA GAS AND ELECTRIC COMPANY AWARD

CRITERIA: The Oklahoma Gas and Electric Company, in cooperation with CPI Inc., will present a plaque and a cash award of $300 to be given to the officer or officers in the

Greater Oklahoma City area who make the greatest contribution during the past year in the field of juvenile enforcement.

WINNERS

1962-No award
1963-No award
1964-Det. Herbert Booker
1965-Sgt. Billy J. Hopkins, MWCPD
1966-Det. Herbert Booker, OCPD
1967-Det. G.P. Tucker, OCPD
1968-Lt. Jim Reading, OCPD
Det. C.O. Williams, OCPD
Johnny E. West, MWCPD
1969-Det. Henry McMullen Jr.
1970-Lt. B.J. Anderson
1971-Sgt. Russell Rigsby

## THE DOLESE COMPANY AWARD

CRITERIA: The Dolese Company, in cooperation with CPI Inc., will present a plaque and a cash award of $300 to the policeman or team of policemen doing the most outstanding job of accident investigation and analysis work, which contributes materially to the prevention of accidents in the City of Oklahoma City.

WINNERS

1962-Off. Ulo Kasenurm
Off. C.S. McLaughlin
1963-Off. Joe Wright
1964-Off. A.T. Brixey
1965-Off. James G. Jackson
1966-Off. William R. Chambless
1967-Off. Ulo Kasenurm
1968-Off. E.W. Stevenson
1969-Off. Harold G. Mann
1970-Off. W.B. Smith
Off. C.E. Dozier
1971-Off. Conrad Nelson

## THE OKLAHOMA PUBLISHING COMPANY AWARD

CRITERIA: The Oklahoma Publishing Company, in cooperation with CPI Inc., will present a plaque and a cash award of $300 to be given to the police officer or team of officers of the Oklahoma City Police Department who perform the best investigation job leading to the solution of a crime in Oklahoma City. The award may be in cash, or as part payment on tuition to a police school or short course.

WINNERS

1962-Det. E.B. Meals
1963-Det. C.E. Waggoner
1964-Det. Ben Satterfield
Det. Don R. Schimmels
1965-Det. Charles E. Stanfill
Det. Ted Gregory
1966-Det. W.W. Harrison
1967-Det. Darrell D. Pierce
Det. Bill M. Minor
1968-Det. Rex L. Norton
1969-Det. Jerry L. Guinn
Det. Dennis Berglan
Det. Troy L. Withey
1970-Lt. Jim Watson
Det. Anthony W. Hyde
Det. Bill L. Hooten
1971-Det. Richard Mullins

## THE MACKLANBURG-DUNCAN COMPANY AWARD

CRITERIA: The Macklanburg-Duncan Company, in cooperation with CPI Inc., will present a plaque and a cash award of $50 to command or supervisory police officers in the Greater Oklahoma City area selected for superior achievement in police leadership.
NOTE: Prior to 1965, this award was a gold or silver citation bar.

WINNERS

1962-Capt. S.W. Stephens
1963-Capt. Tom Wilson
Sgt. John R. Donnell
1964-Major E. Wayne Lawson
Sgt. Jim Watson
1965-Capt. Jerry Landsberger, WAPD
Capt. Frank Brady, MWCPD
Sgt. Chris C. Walker
1966-Robert R. Lester
Comm. of Public Safety
1967-Capt. Gordon Anderson, WAPD
1968-Capt. J.D. Sharp,BPD
Chief Ed Clark, NHPD
Lt. O.W. Ardery, OCPD
1969-Asst. Chief Weldon Davis
Major C.C. Miller
1970-Chief E. Wayne Lawson
1971-Lt. John R. Donnell

## THE CAIN'S COFFEE COMPANY AWARD

CRITERIA: Cain's Coffee Company, in cooperation with CPI Inc., will present a plaque and a cash award of $300 to the member of any police department in the Greater Oklahoma City area who, either in line of duty or extra police activity, contributes the most to the betterment, welfare and health of the people of Greater Oklahoma City during the year.

NOTE: In its' first year, this award was the Community Council Award.

WINNERS

1962-Lt. Sam Watson
1963-Off. W.L. Williams
1964-Lt. M.B. Cooper
1965-Sgt. Bob Hutton
1966-Off. Irven Box
1967-Capt. Weldon E. Davis
1968-Lt. J.C. Pierce & shift
1969-Off. John H. Kane
1970-Det. Bennie Lovett
Det. Harold Neal
1971-Off. Richard Cravens, WAPD

## GREATER OKLAHOMA CITY SAFETY COUNCIL AWARD

CRITERIA: The Greater Oklahoma City Safety Council, in cooperation with CPI Inc., will award to two members of any metropolitan area police department, a plaque and a cash award of $100 each for outstanding achievement or contribution in the field of traffic safety or traffic control.

NOTE: From 1968 through 1971, this award was known as the Independent Insurance Agents Association Award and the award was increased to $150.

WINNERS

1962-Lt. Jim G. Perdue
1963-Sgt. Jim Watson
1964-Sgt. Lloyd A. Gramling
Miss Louise Waller
1965-Off. Robert L. Gallamore
Off. Henry Jones
1966-Sgt. Cecil L. Posey
1967-Charles Jones, EPD
1968-Off. L.T. Brown
Off. W.L. Williams
1969-Capt. Bill Luttrell, WAPD
Capt. Lloyd Gramling, OCPD
1970-Sgt. Walt Wilhelm
1971-Off. Robert L. Gallamore
Off. L.T. Brown
Off. W.L. Williams

## OKLAHOMA COUNTY MEDICAL SOCIETY AWARD

CRITERIA: The Oklahoma County Medical Society, in cooperation with CPI Inc., will present an award of a $100 savings bond and a plaque to be given to the police employee who, in the judgement of the CPI Awards Committee, has contributed the most constructive plans or ideas for improvement of police operations during the past year.

NOTE: This award was originally known as the Chamber of Commerce Award prior to 1964. It was discontinued after 1969.

WINNERS

1962-Capt. Kenneth A. Nash
1963-Capt. Gene Goold
1964-Capt. Weldon Davis
1965-Det. Robert S. Pierce
1966-Sgt. Don M. Rodgers
1967-Sgt. Tom L. Heggy
1968-Sgt. B.J. Coffia
1969-Det. Jim W. Anthony
Det. William F. Wolf

## OKLAHOMA CITY RETAILER'S ASSOCIATION AWARD

CRITERIA: The Oklahoma City Retailer's Association, in cooperation with CPI Inc., will present to one or more individuals assigned to a support service in any metropolitan area police department, a cash award of $250 and a plaque for outstanding service to their department or their community.

NOTE: In 1965, this award was known as the Citizens for Street Improvement Association Award.

WINNERS

1965-Off. D.C. Bowen
Off. Nathan L. Barber
1966-Off. Neal F. Blount
Off. Doyle H. Connelly
1967-Sgt. Robert S. Pierce
1968-Off. Bruce Knox
1969-Sgt. William T. Burke
Off. Doyle H. Connelly
1970-Carolyn Geckler
1971-Ernie Smith, OSBI

## OKLAHOMA COUNTY BAR ASSOCIATION AWARD

CRITERIA: The Oklahoma County Bar Association, in cooperation with CPI Inc., will present a cash grant of $100 and a plaque to the member of any regularly organized or constituted public law enforcement body, who has made the greatest contribution to the orderly and efficient administration of justice and the furtherance of jurisprudence in Oklahoma County.

WINNERS

1963-Chief Carl Tyler, MWCPD
1964-Robert "Jim" Turner
Asst. Dist. Atty., Ok. Co.
1965-Curtis Harris, Okla. Co. D.A.
1966-M.B. Cooper
1967-Judge Hillis Sanford
1968-Jack Swidensky
1969-Det. Charlie Acox
Det. Don Schimmels

## NORTHWEST KIWANIS CLUB AWARD

CRITERIA: An award of a $100 cash grant and a plaque for superior achievement, dedication and conduct.

WINNERS

1968-Off. Doyle Morse
Off. B.J. Coleman
1969-Off. Larry Wright
1970-Det. Ted W. Gregory
1971-Off. Michael Hoover

## MERCY HOSPITAL AWARD

CRITERIA: An award of a $100 cash grant and a plaque for the saving of human life.

WINNERS

1968-Off. C.J. Booe
Off. W.R. Chambless
1969-Off. James Winter
Off. Richard Jerman
1970-Off. Kenneth Shockley
1971-Off. Don Landes

## SPECIAL AWARDS

1968-Jerry Marx,
DPS Public Information Officer
1969-Steve Cummings, MWCPD
Roy G. Cook, MWCPD
Jack Hill, MWCPD
Eddie Thomason, MWCPD
Detective Bill C. Baldwin
Detective J.K. Harrison
1970-Major Kenneth A. Nash
Judge Clarence Mills
Assistant District Attorney Kenneth Turner
1971-Oklahoma County Sheriff Bob Turner
OCPD Intelligence Unit
Mrs. Donna G. Ratikan

## OKLAHOMA CITY POLICE DEPARTMENT AWARDS

## 1979-PRESENT

(Year indicates year awarded)

NOTE: The Annual Oklahoma City Police Awards and Appreciation Banquet was instituted in 1982 as a forum for the presentation of these awards. Prior to 1982, the Medal of Valor, the Medal for Meritorious Service and the Life Saving Awards were awarded in periodic ceremonies, usually held at the Police Training Center in conjunction with the graduation ceremonies for a police recruit class.

The term "above and beyond the call of duty" in qualification for the Police Medal of Honor and the term "voluntary course of action" in the qualification for the Police Medal of Valor disqualify all acts of courage, no matter how great, performed in the course of carrying out verbal or written orders.

## THE POLICE MEDAL OF HONOR

The highest award in the Department. To be awarded to a police officer of the Oklahoma City Police Department who voluntarily distinguishes himself conspicuously by gallantry and extraordinary heroism. The act must be in excess of normal demands and of such a nature that the officer was fully aware of the imminent threat to his personal safety and acted above and beyond the call of duty at the risk of his life.

No awards

## POLICE CROSS

Ranked next in prominence to the Medal of Honor. To be awarded when an officer lost his life in performance of duty under honorable circumstances. The Police Cross may be awarded in addition to any other award to which the officer may be entitled in making the supreme sacrifice.

1985 Detective Gary Lee Ward
1986 Senior Police Officer Richard O. Riggs
1991 Officer Delmar Warren Tooman

## MEDAL OF VALOR

Ranked next in prominence to the Police Cross. To be awarded for exceptional bravery at imminent risk of serious bodily injury, the recipient demonstrating exceptional courage by performing a voluntary course of action in an extremely dangerous situation.

1979-Officer Beau James-Officer Jim Hatfield
1982-Officer Phil Carr-Officer Mike Goodspeed-Officer James Linam-Officer Jerry Mauk
1983-Senior Police Officer Jerry Gates

1987-Officer Michael J. Hampton-Senior Police Officer Riley Lenex
1988-Officer Doug Northrup-Officer Clyde Bowling
1989-Officer Ed Moore Jr.
1990-Sergeant Phil Davis-Lieutenant Norman Cook
1991-Officer Scott Samuel-Officer Ron Burks-Sergeant Tom Terhune-Sergeant Glenn Ring-Sergeant Randy Kirby
1992-Sergeant Robert Campbell-Sergeant Ed Dugan
1993-Officer Bo Leach-Officer Mike Homan-Sergeant Jim Duncan
1994-Officer David Mauck-Officer David Pennington-Officer Gerald Ritter

## MEDAL FOR MERITORIOUS SERVICE

Ranked next in prominence to the Police Medal of Valor.

a. To be awarded for a heroic deed and exceptional meritorious conduct involving exemplary courage, risk and danger to personal safety.

b. May be awarded to an officer for meritorious service in a duty of great responsibility, the duty reflecting excellence in performance, and distinguishing himself and the Department.

1979-Officer J.J. Young
1983-Detective Larry Andrews-Detective Bill Tays
1984-Officer Howard Barnes
1985-Sergeant Eddie G. Hoklotubbe
1986-Officer Harvey Allread-Sergeant Charles A. Owen-Sergeant Larry Andrews-Sergeant Julie F. Smith
1987-Officer Elroy Kroeker-Officer Michael D. Taylor-Detective David Hodges
1988-Officer Craig Gravel-Officer Dana Mitchell
1989-Detective David Hodges-Detective Mike McPherson
1991-Officer Barry Lanzner
1994-Lieutenant Jim Story

## CERTIFICATE OF ACHIEVEMENT

Ranked next in prominence to the Medal for Meritorious Service.

a. To be awarded to police officers of any rank for outstanding performance of duties under unusual, complicated or hazardous conditions over any period of time.

b. To be awarded to officers or civilian police personnel for outstanding or superior performance of any assignment over a prolonged period of time, with such performance to be clearly exceptional, placing them well above other officers or civilians of equal rank or grade.

c. May be awarded without bar to any police officer from another law enforcement agency qualifying under the above mentioned conditions if earned while aiding, assisting or working with any officer of the Oklahoma City Police Department.

d. May be awarded with or without bar to any civilian, who assists in bringing favorable recognition to the Department, through their cooperation or involvement.

1982-Detective James A. Cain-Officer John W. Cave-Forensic Chemist Joyce A. Gilchrist-Detective Julie F. Smith
1983-Forensic Chemist Janice Davis-Officer Bill Hanneman-Specialist John Hill-Detective Jerry Martin-Specialist Jim Nutt-Detective Jim Parsons-Detective David Emberling-Trooper Ricky Robinson, OHP
1984-Detective Robert Cannon-Detective Claude Martin-Detective Jim Parsons-Detective William Pierce-Detective Ken E. Smith-Officer Lloyd Smithson-Senior Jailer Kermit Ander son-Chemist Melissa Hughes-Chemist Tom Kupiec-Property Room Clerk James E. Elder
1985-Detective James A. Cain-Detective James K. Bell-Detective David Emberling-Detective Jerry L. Flowers-Detective Larry Foreman-Detective William A. Gregory-Detective Robert

A. Nash-Detective Gary Lee Ward (posthumous)-Officer James D. Digby Jr.-Officer Ed ward Heinken-Officer Mackey R. Keener-Specialist James J. Young-Neal Hightower-Gaynor Igou-Wayne H. Jackson-Ben E. Owen Sr.-Ben E. Owen Jr.-Detective David Pierce, MWCPD.

1986-Detective Jon S. Gustin-Detective Robert E. Smart-Detective David Fredrickson-Officer Byron L. Boshell-Officer Jeffrey W. Bomgaars-Officer David F. Brewer-Senior Officer Ben J. Bridges-Officer Donald R. Browning-Administrative Aide Jorge Quiroga-Chaplain Jack Poe-Captain Larry L. Jurczewsky, OCSO-Special Agent Don Kyte, FBI-SFC Phillip L. Daughtery, U.S. Army-Yolanda Leighton-Danh Van Le-District Attorney Bob Macy, Okla. Co.-State Attorney General Michael Turpin

1987-Officer Lanell White-Officer Kelly Owens-Officer Keith Simonds-Officer Pat Byrne-Officer Jim Hughes-Officer Chris Rau-Specialist E.R. Southard-Specialist Jon Smith-Detective Charles McIntyre-Detective William Cook-Detective Bob Horn-Detective Wayne Owen-Detective Sam Sealy-Detective Robert Woods-Detective Sarene Cox-Detective Nick Pittman-Detective Eric Mullinex-Detective Mike Burke-Detective William A. Pierce-Detective Jerry Flowers-Detective Robert Woods-Detective David Shupe-Detective Bill Citty-Sergeant John Windle-Sergeant Claude Shobert-Sergeant Larry Koonce-Sergeant Charles Gooch-Sergeant Gary James-Lieutenant Larry Baldwin-Forensic Chemist Joyce Gilchrist-Lake Ranger Ron Stevenson-Danny Anderson-Mike B. Williams-Richard Brown-Joy Ann Nicholson-Franklin Sisk-Bill Eastham-Rick D. Horner-Jeff Alexander-Brian Jowaisas-Billy Robertson-William F. Foster

1988-Detective Jim Rogers-Dispatcher Debra Hill-Larry Stevenson-Kenneth McKinley-Hardeman Sellers-Doug Dooly-Randy Bell-Jimmy Taylor-Mike Helderman-Mike Harrison-Steven Nash

1989-Detective William A. Pierce-Detective Marc Coffelt-Senior Officer Ben Bridges-Detective Gerald McKenna-Specialist Mel Thee-Donald Long-Linda Jackson

1990-Officer Dexter Nelson-Officer Barry McCary-Sergeant Eric Mullinex-Sergeant Mike Burke-Lieutenant Robert Woods-Clifford Manning-Curt Hockemeier-Richard Ward-Captain Ronnie Nye-Glenn Clark-Roy Baker

1991-Lieutenant John Clark-Sergeant Kelly Owens-Officer David Cook-Officer James Kennedy-Robert Hammitt-Officer Danny Fitzwilliams-Phillip McCarthey-Judith Mayfield-Todd Woods-Rhonda Kjeldgaard-Dorothy Johnson-Robert Corteway-Clifford Manning-Pat Flowers

1992-Sergeant Jimmy Hughes-Officer Lori Holland-Officer Teresa Sterling-Dispatcher Richard Robinson-Captain C.E. Hill-Lieutenant Ron Owens-Sergeant Gregory Karim-Sergeant Joe Snodgrass-Sergeant Jerry Farris-Sergeant Ron Wortham-Sergeant Tom Jester-Ser geant Jim Hatfield-Records Clerk Leroy Hammer-Records Clerk Terri Carpenter-Ruth Mitchell-David Wooten-Daniel Vu, Dept. of Corrections-Jim West, Dept. of Corrections-Russ Buchner, Crim. Just. Res. Ctr.

1993-Captain Adam Edwards-LLieutenant Bill King-Sergeant John Checotah-Sergeant Roger Frost-Sergeant Janice Guyton-Sergeant Mike Hoskins-Sergeant Jim Juniper-Sergeant Fred Kerr-Sergeant David Rivers-Sergeant Alexis Sawtelle-Sergeant Mark Wenthold-Officer M.B. Brown-Officer Britt High-Officer H. Maurice James-Dispatcher Elaine Pitts-Dispatcher Alycia Robinson-Chris Allen Horn-Andrew Dwight Moulin

1994-Sergeant Norma Adams-PST Gloria Bailey-Captain Phil Carr-Sergeant Dwight Culbertson-Sergeant Douglas Hawkins-Sergeant Paula Howard-Officer Maurice James-Sergeant Doug Kimberlin-Ms. Pam Kraker-Lieutenant Rick Logan-Sergeant Tom Looney

## LIFE SAVING AWARD

Ranked next in prominence to the Certificate of Achievement.

a. To be awarded to any officer for the saving of a human life. This award is intended for all officers directly responsible for the saving of a human life. Documentation and supporting evidence must be included to substantiate the award such as statements from witnesses, physicians and supervisors.

b. This award may also be made where evidence indicates that actions by an officer prolonged a human life to the extent of the victim being released to the care of medical authorities even though the victim might expire at a later time.

c. May be awarded in addition to the awarding of a higher medal where the facts show the recipient is entitled to such award.

1979-Officer John Windle-Officer Ray Ledford-Officer John Kane-Officer Jay Einhorn
1980-Officer David Haney-Officer John George-Officer Richard Aytes-Officer Jim Hatfield
1981-Officer Nick Pittman-Officer Patricia Norman-Officer Jerry Flowers-Officer Larry VanSchuyver
1982-Officer Don A. Hull
1983-Officer Jeff Bomgaars-Officer Patrick Byrne-Officer John Frederick-Senior Officer Gilbert Hogue-Senior Officer Robert Lakin-Senior Officer Tim Routen
1984-Officer David Griffin
1985-Officer Larry D. Hammett-Officer Michael S. Harmon-Officer Bennie L. Nichols-Specialist Nathan A. Pyle
1986-Officer Don Evans-Officer John M. Scully-Officer Aven H. Bull-Officer Kevin M. Johnson-Officer James D. Burnett-Officer Thomas F. Picchione
1987-Officer Glen Holcomb-Sen. Officer Chris Talley-Officer J. Brent Galyon-Officer Terry D. Turner-Specialist Eldridge B. Wyatt-Officer Steven W. McCool
1988-Officer Craig Gravel
1989-Officer Dana Mitchell-Senior Police Officer James Carson-Specialist David Simpson-Officer Vernon Baker
1990-Officer Ritchie Willis-Officer Douglas Kimberlin-Sergeant Robert Ardle
1991-Officer Chris Suriano-Officer Duane Bieber-Officer Ron Burks-Officer Vanessa Crocker-Officer David Cook-Sergeant Bill Swanson
1992-Sergeant Charles Wheeler-Sergeant Dan Helmuth-Sergeant Stan Moss-Sergeant Mike Cory-Sergeant Mark Gore-Sergeant Rod Hill
1993-Officer Brian Blosmo-Officer Barry Clark-Officer Jamell Shields-Officer Dennis Reedy-Officer James Wheatley-Sergeant Darrell Jameson
1994-Mr. S.R. Bryant, Jr.-Officer Allen Chute-Mrs. Donna Eddy-Sergeant Bill Farley-Sergeant David Gage-Sergeant Bill Martin-Officer Matthew McCullough-Officer Gerald Ritter-Sergeant Truman Widener-Sergeant Carl Wooten

## THE OKLAHOMA CITY POLICE DEPARTMENT as of September 1, 1995

| | |
|---|---|
| 1 Chief | 135 Lieutenants |
| 1 Assistant Chief | 511 Sergeants |
| 3 Deputy Chiefs | 274 Officers |
| 11 Majors | 79 Recruits |
| 31 Captains | 319 Civilians |

CHIEF-Sam C. Gonzales

ASSISTANT CHIEF-Richard B. DeLaughter

DEPUTY CHIEFS-Major T. Berry-Support Services Bureau
R. Neill Griffith-Operations Bureau
Lawrence Johnson-Investigations Bureau

MAJORS

| | | |
|---|---|---|
| Harold M. Campbell | William J. Jackson | Kenneth R. Smith |
| James C. Gallegly | Robert A. Jones | Garold L. Spencer |
| Larry D. Gramling | Billy Keith Mann | Stephen R. Upchurch |
| Michael C. Heath | Donald L. Pennington | |

CAPTAINS
Charles L. Allen
Howard H. Armer
Virgil T. Bevel
Ted G. Carlton
Phil M. Carr
William J. Citty
Danny L. Cochran
Emmett D. Douglas
Adam S. Edwards
James J. Fitzpatrick
Charles T. Foley
Charles E. Hill
James M. Hollier (Retired)
Larry C. Kettler
Larry D. Koonce
William E. Lewis
Theophilus T. Martin
Jerry A. McCarley
Kenneth S. McDonald
Richard E. Neaves
Ronald J. Owens
Seth C. Owsley
Billy K. Pratt
Michael W. Roach
Arthur W. Robinson
Charles H. Shelden
David L. Shupe
David L. Story
William B. Taylor
Simon Torres
Eldon R. Walsh
Jerry W. Williams (Retired)
Jimmy L. Yandell

LIEUTENANTS
Larry D. Allen
Dennis L. Asper
Richard L. Aytes
Larry P. Baker
Rex V. Barrett
Manuel R. Beck
Ronald L. Blevins
Eddy R. Blosser
William F. Booth
Byron L. Boshell
Robert C. Bowman
David F. Brewer III
Dennis R. Buckley
Michael A. Burkhart
John R. Burks
Robert E. Bybee
Patrick C. Byrne
Clinton V. Caswell
John W. Cave
John C. Clark
Norman K. Cook
Phil L. Coventon
Terry L. Cronkite
Jessica M. Cummins
Curtis W. Dick
James D. Digby
Don R. Dillard
George H. Doughty
Edward E. Dugan
David J. Duke
Robert D. Duvall
Emol R. Edwards
Chris N. Elias
David P. Ellis
Dan Evans
Don Evans
Daniel J. Flanagan
Kimberlee Flowers
Robert R. Frantz
Dennis R. Frazier
David Fredrickson
Kelly D. Garnett
Ralph K. Gibson
John D. Gonshor
Charles E. Gooch
William A. Gregory
Janice K. Guyton
Thomas E. Hart
Darrell L. Hatfield
Edward L. Heinken
Gilbert L. Hensley
Quina G. Hill
David E. Hodges
Larry D. Hodges
Phillip D. Hoile
Jerry D. Holding (Deceased)
Robert W. Holz
Bob L. Horn
Richard A. Hudson
Mike R. Hutchcroft
Keith A. Jackson
George T. Jester
George L. Johnson
Skyler S. Kays
Danny L. Keener
Jeff Kelly
Douglas M. Kimberlin
Billy B. King
Jim D. Kuchta (Retired)
Johnny L. Kuhlman
Larry D. Larimore
Riley D. Lenex
Guy S. Lindsey
Jon M. Loffi
Richard D. Logan (Retired)
Thomas M. Looney
Hardin M. Lovelace
Scott R. McCall
Raymond A. March
Dale A. Marshall
James W. Martin
Robert B. Mercer
Ronald E. Mills
Dewey F. Morse
Glenn W. Mullins
Michael T. Nard
Robert A. Nash
Howard L. Owen
Wayne F. Owen
Stephen C. Pacheco
Willard P. Paige
Thomas W. Parker
Jodie W. Perkins
Jaryl L. Phillips
Sharon A. Pollman
Dennis R. Prater
Nathan A. Pyle
Chris L. Querry
Joe Ann Randall
Jeff B. Rateliff
Nancy A. Rateliff
Chris A. Rau
Bradley B. Redemer
Larry K. Rhodes
John E. Riley
Larry D. Rodgers
Dennis P. Ross
C. Ray Rupert
Dennis L. Scott
John M. Scully
Roy L. Sellers
Larry G. Shoals
Daniel R. Shubert
David L. Simpson
Jon W. Smith
William B. Smith (Retired)
Eddie R. Southard
Bobby G. Steelman
Jimmie D. Story
Janice R. Stupka
Chris C. Talley
Gregory A. Taylor
Melvin E. Thee
Bobby W. Tidwell
Linda S. Tidwell
Bobby L. Tompkins
Jammes L. Trimble
Stan L. Van Nort
Clarence J. Vassar

Patrick S. Vicsek
Billy E. Walls
Norma L. White
David R. Williams
Richard W. Williams
David G. Wilson
John E. Windle
Chris A. Woodruff
Robert A. Woods
Ulysse R. Yarbrough

SERGEANTS
Bryan Aaron
Lorene D. Abernathy
Melissa A. Abrahamsen
Dennis B. Adams
Gary D. Adams
James L. Adams
Norma J. Adams
Susan F. Adams
Jennifer J. Aleman
Gary W. Alexander
Ann A. Ali
James R. Aliff
Richard D. Allen
Ronnie M. Allen
Vance W. Allen
Ralph G. Appleton
Latina K. Aragon
Robert E. Ardle
Ann E. Armstrong
Clyde B. Armstrong
Richard J. Armstrong
Phillip M. Arnold
Thoams E. Ashing
Robert L. Atkins
Richard K. Avants
John R. Avera
Robert L. Bach
Jeffrey A. Baecher
Terry L. Baer
Dennis L. Bailes
Vernon D. Baker
Leonard F. Baldwin
Jack S. Ballard
Howard M. Barnes
Jeff L. Barnett
Charlene Berry
Michael G. Beaucort
James K. Bell
Ronald A. Bell
Robert F. Bemo
Duane C. Bieber
Charles L. Bingham
Mike C. Black
Brian R. Blosmo
Christina L. Blosmo
Max J. Blumenthal
Thomas L. Bogle
John T. Bohan
Jeffrey W. Bomgaars
James D. Booth
Ronald K. Bradbeary
Floyd Bradford
Ronald J. Bradford
Ed L. Bradway
Roger D. Bratcher
Linda D. Bray
Crawford L. Brock
Gary D. Brock
Jack C. Brock
Alan K. Broerse
Raymond J. Brooks
Rhett A. Brotherton
Douglas C. Brown
Michael B. Brown
Michael W. Brown
Timothy S. Brown
Donald R. Browning
Aven H. Bull
Kim L. Burge
Alan H. Burgett
Michael D. Burke
Ronnie E. Burks
Paul K. Burley
Doug J. Burnett
James D. Burnett
Jimmy D. Bynum
Kathy D. Bynum-Sioux
Jerry E. Caldwell
Michael A. Calton
Brenda D. Campbell
Dal A. Campbell
Robert D. Campbell
Robert L. Cannon
John M. Carroll
Johnny B. Carroll
Dewayne L. Carruth
James S. Carson
Gary L. Carter
Gary M. Carter
Karen R. Carter
Lori E. Carter
Michael R. Casey
Randy J. Cashhion
Darin W. Cathey
David W. Chace
David L. Chadwick
Thomas A. Chaney
Randall D. Chapman
John L. Checotah
Samuel J. Chesnut
Chet D. Childs
Barry L. Clark
Glen C. Clark
Randy A. Claypool
Linda S. Cody
Marcus S. Coffelt
David W. Coffman
Steven M. Colker
Kenneth A. Conley
Shirley R. Conner
David A. Cook
William L. Cook III
Michael E. Cory
Breck R. Cotter
Kent L. Courkamp
Gerald D. Cowan
James L. Cox
James W. Cox
Sarene J. Cox
Regina Z. Craig
James K. Cravens
Dwight D. Culbertson
Tommy L. Dale
Gary L. Damron
May R. Dan
Cecil R. Daniels
Mark E. Danner
Brian L. Davenport
Bruce D. Davis
Gale W. Davis
Kenneth D. Davis
Kenneth W. Davis
Mark W. Davis
Melvin R. Davis
Michale D. Davis
Phillip M. Davis
Ricky A. Davis
Robert M. Davis
Charles E. Dawson
Wesley W. Dawson
Larry R. Deeds
Leah K. Demartra
Glen E. Despain
Terry A. Dickerson
Orville D. Dicus
Kathy L. Dodd
Ronald W. Doss
Robert C. Douglas
Samuel A. Duke
James D. Duncan
Richard L. Dunn
Donald O. Dunsmore
Robert M. Easley

Gary B. Eastridge
Kyle A. Eastridge
Tonya L. Eastridge
Willie L. Edwards
Jay M. Einhorn
Richard F. Elder
David W. Emberling
Gary L. Englebretson
Charles E. Epperly
Kathryn M. Epperson
Lonny H. Ercanbrack
Billy T. Farley
Robert I. Farrar
Jerry G. Farris
Earl L. Faubion
Robert M. Ferguson
John R. Fiely
Danny K. Fitzwilliam
Earl W. Flangan
Jacque R. Fleming
Jerry L. Flowers
Daniel E. Foreman
Darrell M. Fortune
Lorre R. Freeman
Roger E. Frost
David L. Gage
Justin Brent Galyon
Daniel Garcia
Sherry L. Garcia
Mitchell A. Gardiner
Roland E. Garrett
James B. Gibbons
Gregory D. Giltner
Larry D. Gleason
Charles V. Goforth
Mike E. Goodspeed
Mark Gore
Anthony R. Gracey
Gregory L. Gracey
Jack W. Graham
John R. Graham
Craig R. Gravel
David P. Griffin
Kenneth J. Griffin
Ray V. Grimes
Wilburn E. Grimes
Debra A. Gruver
Gilbert R. Gruver
James E. Hale
Maxwell D. Hames
Larry D. Hammett
Mike J. Hampton
William J. Hanneman
David M. Hardin
James N. Hardin
Monica C. Hardman
Mike S. Harman
Hollis G. Harper
Terry L. Harrison
Terry L. Harrison
Kent H. Harville
Dennis A. Hasklins
Jimmy W. Hatfield
Douglas G. Hawkins
Jerry A. Hawkins
Larry S. Hay
Steve L. Helmer
Daniel J. Helmuth
Marshall S. Helsel
Jerry R. Hendrick
Theodore W. Herziger
James L. Highfill
Joseph B. Hill
Rodney D. Hill
Wayne M. Hlinicky
Timothy A. Hock
Gilbert D. Hogue
Janet A. Hogue
Glen K. Holcomb
Pamela S. Holston
Ray E. Homer
Michael R. Hoskins
Ronald E. Houck
Paula K. Howard
James P. Hughes Jr.
Kim J. Hughes
Don A. Hull
John M. Hull
Mozella S. Hurte
William R. Hykes
Donald R. Isaac
Michael S. Jackson
Beau M. James
Virgil L. James
Darrell C. Jameson
Howard F. Johnson
Joe P. Johnson
Kevin M. Johnson
Patricia G. Johnson
Randall L. Johnson
Terrel L. Johnson
Gregory W. Johnston
Jeffrey L. Jones
Michael Earl Jones
Mike E. Jones
Stanley A. Jones
James R. Juniper
John H. Kane
Gregory E. Karim
Ronald E. Keef
Garland E. Keel
Mackey R. Keener
Kim D. Kelley
James O. Kennedy
Freddie R. Kerr
Randy A. Kirby
Donny R. Kidd
Kenneth W. Kidd
Edwin L. Killebrew
Roger L. Knox
Frank T. Koch
Timothy J. Kraeger
Robert W. Lakin
Rene A. Lamar
Don M. Landes (Retired)
Jack A. Lane
Delbert R. Lanning
Chris A. Larson
Jan M. Latta
Raymond A. Ledford
Richard E. Lee
Richard M. Lee Jr.
Floyd D. Lindsey
Dennis L. Lippe
Ramon H. Lira
Thomas L. Livingston
Jeffrey M. Locke
Keith B. Locklear
John W. Loflin Jr.
Phillip D. Long
Michael W. Loruse
Johnnie W. Loudermilk
Homer R. Lovell
Mark A. Lowery
Gary D. Lowrance
Russell S. Lowry
Thomas A. Maassen
Scott S. Mackelvie
John H. Maddox
John F. Mangrum
Russell R. Manuel
Teddy D. Mapes
Darl A. Marang
Brian T. Martin
Claude C. Martin
Paul R. Martin
William R. Martin
Wimford E. Martin
Nick C. Mathews
Robert Matthews
Donell Matthews
Johnny L. Matthews
Jerry L. Mauk
Pat W. Mauldin
Karen E. Maule

Cameron D. McAntire
Barry N. McCary
Robert F. McClatchie
Steven W. McCool
John L. McCornack
Kevin D. McCullough
Stafford L. McCumber
Charles M. McIntyre
Gerald K. McKenna
Terri A. McKinney
J.D. McLaughlin
Don K. McLerran
Doug K. McLerran
Mike R. McPherson
David T. Melendez
David A. Mercer
Bobby R. Merrill
Thomas O. Mills
Dana S. Mitchell
Lannie D. Mitchell
Ronald E. Mitchell
Michael D. Monahan
Roger P. Montgomery
Fred M. Moon
Calvin M. Moore
Charles O. Moore
Edward L. Moore
Michael E. Moses
James S. Moss
Earl D. Mullendore
Eric L. Mullinex
Patricia D. Mullinex
Marc A. Neifing
Joy L. Neilson
Dexter A. Nelson
Timothy D. Nelson
Earl D. Newton
Bennie L. Nichols
Barry L. Niles
Michael A. Norris
Michael F. Okonczak
Stanley C. Olive
Ernest E. Onley
Thomas N. Owen
Kelly D. Owens
Kenneth R. Park
Susan A. Parker
Timothy K. Parker
Darlena D. Patty
James A. Peck
Larry Peterson
Charles A. Phillips
Thomas F. Picchione
Jeffrey L. Pierce
Marvin J. Pierce
William A. Pierce
Gary S. Pistole
Nick C. Pittman
Joe J. Poe
Stephen W. Pollock
John L. Powell
Clarence A. Powers
Robin D. Pratt
Roger D. Price
Lisa J. Pritchard
Alan A. Prokop
Doyle F. Qualls
Jeff R. Ramsey
Paul R. Randall
Charlene K. Reed
Dale W. Reed
Jeffrey L. Reed
Eric B. Richardson
Phillip J. Richey
Kenneth W. Rickenbrode
Billy R. Ricketts
David E. Riggs
Gil R. Riggs
Glenn O. Ring
David J. Rivers
Gordon L. Robertson
Graham M. Robertson
Jimmy C. Robertson
Max R. Robinson
Ken E. Roddy
Steven M. Rodgers (Deceased)
James K. Rollins
Mary A. Rowland
William M. Rowlett
Robert O. Rusche
Tommie L. Rutledge
Scott A. Samuel
Kendall W. Satterwhite
Alexis M. Sawtelle
Michael J. Schoenberger
Randy L. Schuessler
Brenell L. Scobey
Randy K. Scott
William D. Scruggs
Jerry D. Seaton
Mark W. Sexton
Gregory A. Sharp
Michael D. Sharp
Paula J. Shaw
Lindel D. Sides
Keith W. Simonds
Max A. Sioux
Robert R. Sipe
Roger A. Skeen
David L. Skinner
Clifton L. Slopak
Jack E. Slover
Robert E. Smart
Bruce R. Smith
Donnie J. Smith
Scott P. Smith
Everett L. Smithson
Bryan C. Smythe
Dale L. Sneed
Joe H. Snodgrass
Kevin B. Southerland
Richard F. Spanbauer
Larry E. Spruill
Richard L. Spurgeon
Loyd R. Slaton
Kenneth M. Stepien
Arnold T. Sterling
Teresa W. Sterling
James L. Stone
Robert A. Story
Terry A. Stroud
Edward W. Stupka
Martin M. Stupka
Henry J. Sullentrop
William A. Swanson
Kenneth L. Tallant
Michael D. Talor
Milton W. Taylor
Paul D. Taylor
Robert D. Taylor
William T. Terhune
Thomas E. Tahrp
Ronald K. Thomas
Eric H. Thompson
Joyce M. Thompson
Kevin G. Thompson
Andrew F. Timmons
Curtis L. Timmons
Martha A. Tivis
David N. Tolbert (Deceased)
Margaret M. Tolbert
Joan M. Townsend
Robert E. Tunnell
Gregory A. Turner
Terry E. Turner
Antonio G. Valencia
Joseph J. Vanbeckum
Michael A. Veasey
Mary L. Vinson
Gordon W. Vowell
Allen L. Wade
Roger D. Wagnon
Rodger A. Wagoner
William W. Ward

Ronald D. Warren
Aaron G. Watson
Bill R. Weaver
Timmothy R. Webb
Blake A. Webster
Edward J. Weir
Jack K. Wells
Mark S. Wenthold
Denise D. Wenzel
Charles C. Wheeler
Milton F. White
Truman D. Widener
Randall D. Wiens
Kenneth D. Wilkey
James E. Williams
Jeanette A. Williams
Richard W. Williams
Robert R. Williams
Brian J. Williford
Ritchie L. Willis
Don E. Wilson
Perry A. Wilson
Scott K. Wilson
Becky A. Wolf
Byron W. Wood
Jeffrey D. Wooliver
Carl E. Wooten
Ronald G. Wortham
Richard E. Wright
Eldridge B. Wyatt
Frankie Yeahquo
Garry W. Youngker

OFFICERS
Michael D. Ables
James S. Albertson
Daimmon R. Alexander
Stephen L. Allen
Richard A. Alvarado
Patrick J. Anderson
Rochy E. Argo
Ron C. Bacy
Deborah K. Baer
Gregory S. Ballard
Kevin W. Barnes
Jay W. Barnett
David T. Baxter
Karen S. Beets
Rodney E. Bell
Roland D. Benavides
Steven R. Bennett
Kimberly J. Benson
Allen J. Bentley
Donald E. Bingham
Tyler J. Birdwell
Michael D. Black
Steven L. Blevins
James M. Boggess
Jesse N. Boring
Steven M. Brackeen
Roger D. Bratcher Jr.
Grayce Brotherton
Gregory I. Brown
David S. Brunner
Marcia L. Bull
Shelby L. Bullard
Antonio D. Bustos Jr.
Kevin A. Butler
Vashina L. Butler
J.L. Cadena
Paul Camacho
Stanley L. Campbell
Jon C. Cargill
Charles M. Case
Randy A. Castle
Joann Castle
Alvin L. Chandler
Shannon D. Childers
Allen R. Chute
Darren J. Clark
Don A. Clark
Darryl G. Coats
Brian C. Cook
Lisa A. Cook
Valari S. Cook
Steven M. Cooper
Robert W. Cornelson
Ronald G. Couch
Tamara L. Crew
Vanessa B. Crocker
Lori L. Crowcroft
Cris L. Cunningham
James M. Darter
Cecil A. Davis
John M. Dawson
Richard G. Dixon
Daniel D. Dominguez
Charles L. Douglas
Eric L. Drain
Darla L. Dugan
Robert D. Dunagan Jr.
Jeral S. Dupy
Keith A. Duroy
Drew W. Dyer
Lyndell R. Easley
Damon L. Edminsten
Bill R. Essman
David W. Evans
Lisa S. Fogle (Deceased)
Tony D. Foreman
Jay W. Freeman
James M. French
Timothy E. Frost
Roderick D. Gaymon
John D. George
Anthony D. Germany
Darrell L. Gilbert
Dwayne T. Gilliam
Ted W. Glover
Isaac A. Goodman
Wade R. Gourley
Harry L. Gray
Kevin M. Gray
George A. Guerrero
Darrin W. Guthrie
Randy L. Hall
Rose M. Heath
Priscilla A. Helm
Scott D. Helm
Ronald J. Hendricks
Britt N. High
Tessa R. Hinds
Travis D. Hinton
Donald A. Hodges
Donald L. Holland
Peggy D. Holmes
John M. Homan
Timothy E. Hovis
Ronnie D. Hurd
Percy G. Hurtado
Lance D. Hutson
Ronald C. Ison
David E. Jacobson
Thomas M. Jaha
Harold M. James
Brian D. Jennings
Angela L. Johnson
Michael R. Johnson
Michael A. Kelley
Michael S. Kelley
Danny H. Kennedy
Se Y. Kim
Kimberly A. Kimmel
Silvio R. Kimmel
Jody K. King
Michael E. Klicka
Gary R. Knight
Michael D. Knight
Patrick L. Knox
Marval A. Kreft
Vernon L. Kreithe
Thomas J. Krug
Joe P. Kysela
Kevin C. Kyte
Reubin E. Lacaze Jr.

Charles D. Lack
Bill M. Lamb
Tommy J. Lane
Barry R. Lanzner
Tyler T. Larson
Bo D. Leach
Elizabeth J. Lewis
William J. Loftis
Jodi R. Loggan
Roeliff E. Loomis
William K. Lord
Jay R. Lowery
Theresa F. Lyons
Robert B. Macy
Amer Mahmud
James E. Martin
Maurice A. Martinez
David B. Mauck
Stuart L. May
Michael V. Mayer
Mark A. McCaleb
Gregory D. McCalister
Martinus D. McConnell
Mitchell D. McCoy
Matthew C. McCullough
Joseph S. McMahon
Mark C. Meier
Matthew A. Merits
Chris C. Miller
James E. Miller
Trela C. Miller
John D. Mobley
Russell B. Minkres
Harvey L. Moore
Forrest R. Moser
Ellen M. Murdoch
Timothy A. Muzny
Leo F. Nash
Tyara D. Nash
Russell S. Neal
Jessie L. Neil
Larry R. Northcutt
Francis J. O'Brien
Michael S. O'Leary
Crockett W. Oaks III
Sharon S. Oster
Kevin W. Owen
Casey D. Owens
Michael J. Pacheco
Lonnie S. Palmer
James R. Parsons
William F. Patten
Phillip W. Paz
David M. Pennington
Kenneth W. Peters
Jeffrey L. Phelps
Ricky D. Pierce
Ronnie A. Pisano
Ronald R. Porter
Charles E. Provines
Randy W. Rable
Robert D. Raines
Christopher R. Ramming
Miguel A. Ramos
Charles E. Ramsey
James M. Ramsey
Jarrod B. Raper
Lourinda R. Rayner
Kevin T. Reagor
Tyrone R. Reece
Tammie L. Reeder
Dennis S. Reedy
Daniel T. Reeves
Stanford J. Rice
Cortez E. Richardson
Gerald R. Ritter
Jennifer D. Rodgers
Scott Z. Rodgers
Tommy B. Rutledge
Larry D. Sanders
Vanessa E. Sanders
Paul R. Schonauer
Nicky L. Schwarz
Ricky B. Schwarz
Brendan D. Sheehan
Brent D. Shetley
Jamell H. Shields
Shawn D. Shropshire
Eric S. Simmons
Lisa K. Simonson
Robert W. Skalla
David G. Smith
Kendall R. Smith
Scott A. Smith
Shauna E. Smith
Stephen F. Smith
Tamara L. Smithee
Robin L. Snavely
Dennis Stewart
Patrick W. Stewart
Randy D. Stewart
Rodney L. Strecker
Steven E. Summy
Chris P. Suriano
Khan B. Tang
Jeffrey D. Tanksley
Nathaniel R. Tarver
William W. Tays Jr.
Mark D. Teachman
Jimmy J. Thomas
Steven L. Thomas
Frankie A. Torres
Jesse C. Trillo
Steven S. Vassar
Bill B. Vetter
Peter O. Walker
Jasper K. Washa
Reginald E. Washington
Dennis N. Watts
Warden K. Webb
Robert D. Weemhoff Jr.
Julie A. Wheat
James G. Wheatley
Kenneth D. Whitebird
Jon C. Whitekiller
Steven L. Whitson
Clay E. Williams
Darren S. Williams
Donald D. Williams
Michael T. Williams
Scott G. Williams
Willie A. Williams
Suzanne E. Williford
David L. Wilson
Thomas P. Wilson
Mark D. Wood
Travis C. Woods
Kevin Woolfolk
Richard S. Worley
Terri R. Ybarra
Terrance F. Yeakley
Susan M. Yoha
Timothy A. Yoha
Kelly C. Yon

RECRUITS
Matthew W. Allen
Timothy M. Ballard
Ronnie A. Beck
Dennis J. Bueno
Jason C. Bussert
Bryn J. Carter
James K. Chiles
Jason S. Clifton
Peter Cordova
Leroy Dancy III
Michael B. Davis
Todd A. Deaton
Marvin L. Denny
Talor A. Dinh
Jonathan P. Dragus
Donald W. Drake
Bryan P. Edwards
Robert H. Ellyson
Daniel W. Evans

Nathan W. Fields
Craig A. Files
Brian S. Fowler
Dale M. Frazier
Tobias Frederick
Paul R. Galyon
Jo A. Gawlik
Christopher L. Gayheart
James A. Green
Jonathan E. Greeson
Bernard Hamilton Jr.
Robert K. Henderson
John R. High
Steven G. Johnson
Jae H. Kang
Jerri K. Kettler
Kristin J. Lanning
Jeffrey S. Lathan
Brenda L. Lemaire
William T. Lindsey
Clinton G. MacKinnon
Joe C. Marshall
Lance C. Marston
Donald L. Martin
Tracy R. McCalister
Steven C. Michael
Kevin B. Miller
Sally D. O'Neal
Jeffrey D. Padgett
Patrick O. Pollman
Jeffrey D. Pounds
Michael T. Pribble
Troy N. Rankin
James M. Ray
Vernon L. Rayburn
John W. Ricketts
Martin S. Ruscher
Angela K. Samuel
Terry V. Schofield
Mark W. Scott
Gamille I. Shockley
Kevin W. Smith
Mark A. Smith
Michael C. Smith
Steve M. Spencer
Clifton T. Stewart
Steve B. Stolz
Michael P. Stoyanoski
John P. Szymanski
Robert L. Tompkins Jr.
Jeffrey R. Treat
Kevin F. Tucker
Arnold M. Upshaw
Jeffrey M. White
Phillip A. Williams
Eric A. Wisecup
Larry E. Withrow
Mark A. Wolfe
Daril T. Yates
Jeffrey A. Yust

CIVILIANS
Dorothy C. Abberton
Cheryl L. Aitson
Wanda L. Albertson
Nicole M. Alexander
Robert N. Alexander
Jeffrey R. Allen
Jacqueline Y. Ames
Evelyn M. Anderson
Leslie T. Anderson
Marva J. Anderson
Lorie A. Ardle
Michael T. Armstrong
Alyssa L. Ashby
Jacquitta L. Baldwin
Sharon T. Baldwin
Gloria J. Baley
Lequency Barnett
Mmaxine A. Bell
Lance A. Bemo
Robert D. Benavides
Eric B. Bevenue
Tamara L. Bewley
Teresa J. Binswanger
Matthew P. Bishop
Raquel P. Bizal
Michael B. Blake
Darren J. Bohall
Marcella L. Bollenbach
Jacquleine M. Bolt
Theresa L. Bond
Rachel Booker
Doris R. Boone
Janice M. Bowen
Christi J. Bowerman
Ronnie L. Brackett
Shelli F. Bradbeary
Patricia R. Bradley
Lori A. Brewer
Donna C. Brice
Angela R. Brooks
Veronica V. Brown
Deanna J. Brunner
Dale W. Bruns
Emily J. Buchanan
Karen J. Buettner
Marilyn A. Bumgarner
Rose T. Burks
Judith A. Busch
Jessie K. Byrd
Sharon L. Caldwell
Sandi J. Carbone
Micki M. Carney
Amy S. Carrick
Genea D. Carter
Tula L. Chadwick
Lowell W. Childress
Wanda M. Christian
Traci J. Clark
Judith A. Cochran
Phyllis E. Coffey
Joe A. Cole
Wyvetta D. Conley
George F. Cooksey
Gennetta P. Cornelius
Kimberly A. Dale
Pamela A. Davis
Paula E. Davis
Richard E. Dawes
Keri L. Deaton
Laura B. Deer
William L. Dennis
Joyce M. Diggs
Marilyn J. Dillon
Russell W. Dillon
Sheryl G. Doughty
Alfredda L. Downing
Bernard J. Dresel
Dorothy J. Dunn
Jackie A. Dunsworth
Constance M. Eichler
James E. Elder
Theda B. Ellis
Betty J. English
Deloris C. English
Sharon F. English
Sandra D. Essman
Daniel W. Evans
Diana M. Evenson
Teri L. Farley
Cheryl A. Farrar
D'Esta L. Farris
Donna K. Fitzgerald
Glenn D. Fitzpatrick
Harvey R. Flowers
Jeannie A. Ford
Victoria A. Foreman
Quin E. Fortune
Marla J. Gabler
Allan N. Garlitz
Dollie R. Garrett
Joyce A. Gilchrist
Ricky P. Ginn
Paula B. Glass

Carol D. Glenn (Deceased)
Cynthia Goudeau-Jordan
Wesley E. Graf
Brian R. Graham
Sharon K. Gray
Arthur H. Gregory
Michael J. Grewell
Beverly L. Grider
Maya J. Griffin
Adam N. Griffith
Calena F. Groves
David C. Gulikers
Darlinda Hagens
Janet K. Hall
Janice G. Hall
Carlton B. Hardman
Loretta L. Hardrick
Ray A. Harrison
Cathy F. Hatcher
Kimberly K. Hatcher
Kimberlee S. Haworth
Gloria B. Haygood
Tina M. Heiskill
Don L. Helm
Tina L. Hernandez
Barbara S. Higgins
Saundra C. Higgins
Wilma Hightower
Debra D. Hill
Yvonna Hill
Sherry D. Hitchye
Jason R. Hodges
Cheryl L. Hoffman
Mary A. Hoffman
Robert B. Holland
Robin P. Holt
Delores A. Honea
Patricia A. Horn
Brett A. House
Carol D. Hughes
John P. Hughes
Kandi L. Humphries
Dena M. Hunt
Kellis J. Hurt
Cynthia L. Hutchcroft
Cheryl L. Hutchinson
Marjorie C. Irvin
Barbara J. Jackson (Retired)
Gary D. Jackson
Jackie J. Jackson
Lynne C. Jacksonbonne
Perry H. Jenkins
Mia P. Johnson
Oneta J. Johnson
Sharon A. Johnson
Sherri A. Johnson
Adam A. Joseph
Debra A. Jones
Rose M. Kalousdian
Melissa C. Keith
Burl R. Kelly
Dorothy L. Kendrix
Lawrence Klein
Freda E. Knapp
Pamela D. Kraker
Susan F. Kruta
Analinda B. Lane
Alicia E. Lawrence
Paul H. Ledbetter
Deborah K. Lewis
Debra J. Lira
Steven R. Lira
Brenda K. Long
Janice P. Lowder
Mary K. Luttrell
Darlene L. Mangum
Gary P. Mangum
Janet T. Mansfield
Carolyn S. March
Gordon L. Martin
Leslie W. Martin
Rhonda L. Martin
Shonda R. Martin
Leland E. Mason
Gary P. Massey
Edna J. Matts
Judith L. Mayfield
Karen S. McCalister
Jerri D. McCarthey
James L. McFarland
Loretta L. McGrath
Cheryl A. McKinnon
Linda E. Mitchell
Anthony W. Mitchell
Amos Mobley
Loretta Moreland
Jenney L. Morren
Beverley Moses
Pamela E. Mullendore
Michelle R. Mullins
Daniel E. Murdoch
Betty S. Murphy
Dionda L. Napoleon
Beverly K. Neifing
Elaine D. Nelson
Dau D. Nguyen
Dorothy S. Niebling
Ramona K. Norris
Penny M. Oaks
Sherry O'Bryant
Twila N. Overstreet
Deborah S. Owens
Fay Palmer
Harvena F. Pennington (Retired)
Teri L. Pennington
Joy A. Phelps
Robert P. Pickett
Warren R. Poe
Christina M. Poe
Debra K. Pollock
Deanna S. Pool
Kathhy L. Poore
Joanne Porter
Patricia L. Porter
Mary E. Powell
Warren D. Powers
Bette B. Prater
Teresa A. Price
India A. Raines
Sondra L. Remer
Billy D. Rhodes
Lillie G. Rhodes
Trena S. Riddle
Judith A. Ridley
Beverley J. Robbins
Teri J. Robertson
Alycia R. Robertson
Richard T. Robinson
Christy S. Roles
Cynthia R. Rook
Nelda S. Rose
Anita S. Ross
Cari L. Routh
Lonnie C. Runyan
Robert C. Russell
Katherine A. Ryan
Renee K. Sachau
Aaron M. Samples
Michelle V. Scalice
Matthew G. Scott
Raymond L. Seay
Darla K. Sellers
Martin A. Sharp
Paul S. Shelden
Phillip M. Shelton
Leslie D. Shores
Amy K. Simpson
Penny S. Sims
Deanna L. Sinopoli
Linda G. Slaten
Karen L. Smith
Kevin R. Smith
Leonard C.Smith Jr.
Gem E. Sorton

Jonathan P.Statum
Charity K. Stephens
Connie S. Sterling
Georgia M. Stocker
Kathy L. Stockman
Melinda K. Stuart
Burlla S. Swanson
Chris W. Swanson
Dixie L. Talkington
Elaine M. Taylor
Karen S. Teel
Cathy J. Thomas
Cyndi S. Thomas
Francene Thomas
Vicki J. Thomas
Sheri D. Thompson
Shanea L. Tilley
Joanna C. Tillinghast
Sharon L. Todd
Alice M. Troy
Irene K. Turner
Stephanie A. Turner
Vickie T. Twiggs
Claudine Vails
Debra J. Vowell
Charles A. Walker
Tracy J. Walker
Valerie K. Walker
Eldon F. Walsh
Pat R. Warme
Mary S. Watson
Teresa A. Webb
Laura F. Wells
Teresa L. Wells
Anna P. White
John R. Whitehead
Joetta L. Whitford
Janet L. Whitley
Rebecca S. Williams
Melissa A. Willis
Stephen M. Willoughby
Vikki L. Wilson-Parker
Matthew J. Winborn
Jimmy S. Wolfe
D'Angela N. Wollie
Patsy A. Woodberry
Christiena Woods
Debbie E. Wooliver
Kim A. Wright
Latresa J. Wright
Nancy K. Wygle
Sally E. Wylie
Brandon J. Yandell
Deena M. Yates
John P. Zondlo

## RETIRED POLICE OFFICERS ASSOCIATION OF OKLAHOMA MEMBERS AS OF JULY 1, 1994

(including widows [w] drawing pension benefits, the officer's years of service and highest rank held, where known.)

Off. Bobby G. Abbott (69-89)
Off. Frank P. Abernathy (64-84)
Sgt. Enos L. Ables (68-91)
Mrs. [Lt.] Walter M. Acord (w)(20-53)
Sgt. Charles R. Acox (60-78)
Det. Donald W. Acox (67-76)
Capt. Dahl R. Adams (64-88)
Off. Edward I. Ailey (69-87)
Mrs. [Det.] Tony J. Allison (w)(71-88)
Off. William H. Allread Jr. (67-88)
Maj. Billy J. Anderson (57-77)
Sgt. Larry W. Andrews (67-87)
Det. James W. Anthony (53-74)
Lt. Olen W. Ardery (51-81)
Off. Robert F. Artman (37-57)
Off. Edward A. Atkinson (59-79)
Sgt. Donald L. Ayers (65-91)
Mrs. [Off.] George E. Bailey (w)(43-64)
Off. Leonard H. Bailey (45-64)
Mrs. [Off.] Mark D. Bain (w)( -76)
Lt. Billy C. Baldwin (61-84)
Lt. Larry D. Baldwin (67-88)
Capt. Phillip G. Ballard (64-88)
Spec. Nathan L. Barber (59-79)
Spec. Donald R. Barbour (59-80)
Off. Dawson B. Barnes (67-87)
Lt. Homer O. Barnett (61-82)
Mrs. Ted D. Baughman (w)( -58)
Det. Melvin D. Beall (64-84)
Off. Kenneth R. Beatty (66-86)
Det. Donald P. Bennett (59-82)
Capt. Dennis L. Berglan (62-82)
Det. Allen F. Blackshere (47-68)
Det. Jim R. Blair (59-76)
Spec. Neal F. Blount (59-76)
Sgt. Robert Steve Bonny (72-92)
Det. Herbert Booker Sr. (57-78)
Sgt. Clyde R. Bowling (72-92)
Lt. Richard A. Boyd (64-84)
Mrs. Richard D. Bradford (w)(49-69)
Det. William P. Branum Jr. (66-86)
Det. Donald L. Braswell (57-79)
Det. Chester L. Breeden (57-77)
Off. Daniel W. Brewster (73-76)
Sgt. Ben J. Bridges (70-93)
Sgt. Abraham T. Brixey (57-78)
Off. Charles A. Brown 63-84)
Off. James W. Brown (63-93)
Off. Leo T. Brown (51-72)
Off. Ronald K. Brown (62-87)
Off. Walter L. Brown (50-74)
N. Sue Brunts (60-85)
Mrs. Fred L. Buckles (w)(31-57)
Off. Kenneth J. Buettner (60-80)

Sgt. William T. Burke (63-78)
Det. U. Leon Burnett (52-82)
Sgt. George A. Burns (61-81)
Sgt. Jimmy D. Burrow (65-85)
Janis A. Buschnell (60-82)
Off. William K. Byler (64-84)
Lt. James A. Cain (72-93)
Mrs. Jack D. Caldwell (w)(37-67)
Capt. Ronald G. Calvery (63-86)
Sgt. Kenneth E. Cambron (69-89)
Sgt. Edward L. Campbell (68-90)
Sgt. Geraldon Canary (67-87)
John W. Casady (35-59)
Patricia B. Cash (65-85)
Capt. Ben M. Caswell (57-79)
Sgt. Ron G. Chambers (66-88)
Dep. Chf. William R. Chambless (63-88)
Sgt. Roy G. Cheatham (69-89)
Off. Powell H. Chick (61-76)
Sgt. Donald M. Christian (70-91)
Sgt. Glenn R. Christian (64-84)
Sgt. Danny V. Clark (68-89)
Sgt. Jim D. Clark Sr. (59-81)
Ray S. Clark (48-68)
Det. Raymond R. Clark Sr. (66-86)
Ruben L. Clark (56-74)
Det. Tom C. Cline (67-87)
Sgt. Aaron J. Clovis (69-78)
Lt. Donald R. Cochran (51-77)
Lt. Ronald L. Cochran (51-71)
Phyllis E. Coffey (67-88)
Lt. Bob J. Coffia (56-77)
Det. Victor K. Colbert (66-86)
Sgt. Robert J. Coleman (52-73)
Mrs. [Sgt.] Doyle H. Connelly (58-78)
Det. Shirley Conner (72-94)
Mrs. Roy D. Cook (w)(26-46)
Off. Alonzo A. Cooper (52-74)
Mrs. [Lt.] M.B. Cooper (w)(36-64)
Off. Ralph D. Courtney (64-85)
Mrs. [Det.] Ben F. Cravatt (44-54)
Spec. Don F. Cravens (67-87)
Elizabeth E. Crider (60-80)
Arthur M. Cundiff (43-69)
Off. Tim L. Cunningham (72-92)
Mrs. Earl T. Cunyngham (w)(27-49)
Mrs. F.C. Daniels (w)(42-63)
Off. Paul Darragh (62-73)
Mrs. Harry S. Davidson (46-64)
Asst. Chf. Weldon Davis (50-72)
Lt. Vernon W. Demoss (70-91)
Sgt. Howard H. Divine (57-80)
Sgt. Marvin L. Doherty (64-84)
Capt. John R. Donnell (52-80)
Off. Cecil R. Douglas (54-74)
Sgt. Charles E. Douglas (66-87)
Sgt. Ronald V. Douglas (61-82)
Off. Charlton E. Dozier (66-81)
John C. Dunbar (72-91)
Mrs. S.B. East (w)(45-71)
Mrs. [Asst. Chf.] Gerald L. Emmett (w)(52-82)
Sgt. Buren D. Enger (63-85)
Det. George Englebretson (55-77)
Lt. Jack R. Evans (50-75)
Sgt. Ina M. Faldo (55-87)
Mrs. [Spec.] Wesley G. Fansler (w)(63-86)
Mrs. W.P. Faris (w)(49-65)
Lt. Robert A. Ferguson (54-76)
Det. Noel W. Fink (62-83)
Shirley A. Courts-Fisher (66-92)
Lt. David S. Ford (72-92)
J. W. Ford (50-73)
Det. Larry G. Foreman (70-90)
Mrs. [Lt.] Leon D. Fox (w)(30-65)
Off. Robert L. Gallamore (57-77)
Sgt. James H. Garrette (51-78)
Sgt. Elzy Garrison (66-90)
Off. Jerry Gates (66-86)
Lt. Lindell W. Gay (63-83)
Det. H.V. Gear II (41-62)
Off. George H. Geiger (51-73)
Lt. James L. Gibbs (67-87)
Off. Carey D. Gilbert (69-84)
Sgt. William R. Gillespie (56-76)
Sgt. Horace W. Glemboski (61-82)
Off. Vernon L. Glover (56-76)
Mrs. [Capt.] James T. Godfrey (33-61)
Off. John M. Goldenstein (68-89)
Lt. Roy L. Golightly (74-93)
Capt. John E. Goold (47-68)
Lt. Gilbert F. Gothard (57-77)
Off. Robert L. Gourley (66-87)
Off. John E. Graham (63-83)
Chief Lloyd A. Gramling (53-85)
Off. Robert L. Green Sr. (52-72)
Sgt. Curtis E. Greene (66-92)
Sgt. Charles E. Greeson (59-79)
Lt. Ted W. Gregory (61-81)
Det. Robert M. Griffis Sr. (59-81)
Mrs. Robert S. Grimes (w)(30-61)
James F. Grounds (51-59)
Lt. Jerry L. Guinn (64-84)
Sgt. Jon S. Gustin (71-91)
Off. Jesse Gutierres (66-86)
Edna R. Hackler (46-68)
Det. Bernard E. Hall (58-79)
Mrs. Charles H. Hall (w)(45-67)
Off. James E. Hall (67-87)

Mrs. [Off.] Wayne E. Hamilton (w)(50-85)
Lt. Huel I. Hamm (47-68)
Off. Grant H. Hammersburg (50-70)
Det. Henry L. Handke (57-77)
Mrs. [Major] Wayne Harbolt (w)(34-59)
Irven H. Hardgraves Jr. (51-72)
Sgt. J. Dwight Harper (66-87)
Clement A. Harris (49-70)
Lloyd J. Harris (51-71)
Det. Billy G. Harrison (66-86)
James K. Harrison (60-73)
Kenny B. Harrison (71-91)
Walker W. Harrison (48-68)
Chief Tom L. Heggy (60-82)
Sgt. Don L. Helm (62-88)
Major Larry W. Henderson (63-88)
Sgt. Robert G. Hervey (57-77)
Carolyn S. [Murray] Hicks (56-77)
Lt. Robert J. Hicks (63-83)
Mrs. [Chief] Lawrence J. Hilbert (w)(29-54)
Capt. Charles G. Hill (66-86)
Off. John G. Hill (63-83)
Mrs. [Det.] Charles M. Hinderliter (w)(51-71)
Sgt. Hershall W. Hodges (60-84)
Sgt. Eddie G. Hoklotubbe (68-88)
Off. Clayton R. Hollinger (60-80)
Capt, Bradford C. Holt (67-87)
Det. Billy L. Hooten (60-80)
Sgt. Kenneth P. Hopkins (56-79)
Maurice Hroch (77-89)
Mrs. [Det.] Lowell D. Huckabee (w)(52-74)
Mrs. Robert A. Hudson (w)(45-60)
Off. Dannie L. Hutchinson (70-80)
Sgt. Bobby E. Hutton (53-74)
Dep. Chf. Anthony W. Hyde (66-87)
Det. Haskell W. Irwin (62-84)
Barbara J. Jackson (67-88)
Mrs. J.S. Jackson (w)(50-74)
Sgt. Jimmy G. Jackson (57-79)
Det. Robert D. Jackson (66-86)
Sgt. Gary A. James (67-88)
Mrs. [Capt.] Joseph F. Jerkins (w)(19-51)
Det. Richard A. Jerman (66-89)
Albert S. Johnson (52-73)
Mrs. Vern L. Johnson (w)( -68)
Ida Gwinn Johnson (65-86)
Sgt. Jerry F. Johnson (66-88)
Sgt. Ernest J. Johnson (w)(67-82)
Mrs. Casey C. Jones (w)(45-66)
Sgt. Henry E. Jones (59-79)
Lt. James E. Jones (66-86)
Off. Joe Bob Jones (63-85)
Lt. Lucien Jones (72-90)
Margaret E. Jones (62-84)
Off. Raymond P. Jones (71-90)
Mrs. [Det.] Jack C. Jordan (w)(47-67)
Herbert C. Judkins (42-62)
Off. Ulo Kasenurm (57-78)
Det. Cecil Ray Keesee (66-89)
Sgt. Phillip G. Kennedy (61-83)
Det. Winfred L. Kerlick (57-77)
Off. Donald E. King (66-83)
Lt. Ronald S. King (63-83)
Sgt. Billy G. Kirkwood (67-87)
Off. Herman C. Kirkwood Jr. (68-88)
Lt. Adam J. Knight (67-87)
Spec. Bruce L. Knox (58-78)
Lt. Walter Kostiuk (51-85)
Off. Elroy Kroeker (63-89)
Mrs. William L. Krueger (w)(35-59)
Sgt. Richard H. Kutz (63-80)
Major Jerrald G. Landreth (61-81)
Sgt. Billy J. Larson (66-86)
Sgt. B. Jean Latham (55-83)
Mrs. [Chief] Wayne Lawson (w)(47-72)
Mrs. [Sgt.] Terry G. Lawson (w)(63-77)
Det. Clifford T. Lea (66-86)
Mrs. George D. Leech (w)(41-61)
Det. Jerry A. Legg (63-79)
Det. John N. Lehr (66-88)
Mrs. [Det.] Burke C. LeMay (w)(52-72)
Lt. John D. Lewis (49-75)
Lt. Kenneth R. Liles (56-76)
Lt. Kenneth T. Linn (70-91)
Lt. Gladys [Burns] Loflin (72-94)
Lt. Benny C. Lovett (62-84)
Lt. Harold L. Loyd (48-69)
Mrs. Dow W. Lunn (w)(47-67)
Ola B. Mangham (55-75)
Mrs. [Lt.] William A. Marcum (w)(36-71)
Off. Glen H. Marrow (76-90)
Elzie L. Martin (48-62)
Mrs. W.C. Martin (w)(42-63)
Det. Jerry R. Martin (62-87)
Capt. Melvin D. Martin (67-91)
Mrs. Maurice M. Maulding (w)(40-62)
Dep. Chf. Marvin A. Maxwell (61-86)
Chief David R. McBride (68-91)
Major James C. McCrite (52-75)
Sgt. Billy R. McDonald (51-71)
Capt. Ronald L. McEwen (62-82)
Mrs. Reid K. McKim (w)(35-57)
Off. Ronald J. McKinney (68-88)
Lt. Robert W. McKittrick (58-81)
Off. Clyde S. McLaughlin (53-76)
Mrs. [Capt.] John D. McManus (w)(36-59)
Lt. Henry McMullen Jr. (62-82)
Mrs. [Off.] Henry McMullen Sr. (w)(23-57)

Lt. C.B. Mead (48-75)
Lt. Raymond J. Melton (62-83)
Mrs. [Off.] Danny R. Mercer (w)(68-85)
O. Fred Merz (45-66)
Off. Tommy J. Metzger (63-83)
Major Clifford C. Miller (48-72)
Off. James C. Miller (70-91)
Warren A. "Doc" Miller (52-68)
Lt. Donald L. Ming (51-77)
Sgt. William M. Minor (64-93)
Capt. Bill R. Mize (52-76)
Mrs. [Capt.] Vince E. Moncrief (w)(36-57)
Off. Edward L. Moore (67-87)
Det. L. Gerald Moore (52-82)
Off. Richard L. Morgan (71-92)
Sgt. Michael H. Morrison (62-79)
Lt. Bobby R. Moses (70-90)
Capt. Dewey C. Mosshart (52-74)
Major Jack L. Mullenix (46-66)
Sgt. Richard H. Mullins (64-85)
Major Thomas G. Mundy (71-90)
Off. Jerry C. Nance (67-87)
Major Kenneth A. Nash (52-72)
Lt. Harold D. Neal (66-86)
Off. Richard A. Neal (53-73)
Off. Conrad S. Nelson (66-72)
Off. James R. Nutt (70-91)
Major Jimmy C. Nutter (58-78)
Sgt. Hayes P. Ohler (58-79)
Stenson D. Orr (53-69)
Det. James F. Osborne (78-90)
Mrs. John W. Osborne (w)(41-61)
Capt. Charles A. Owen (67-91)
Jean D. [Hogan] Parker (61-83)
Sgt. James O. Parsons (64-84)
Off. Frank E. Patton (53-73)
Off. Gerald S. Payne (64-81)
Mrs. Milton E. Peaster (w)(38-69)
Capt. Jerry C. Pendry (59-79)
Harvena F. Pennington (66-89)
Mrs. [Capt.] Jim G. Perdue (w)(46-75)
Mrs. [Major] Bill Peterman (w)(54-75)
Det. Charles E. Phelps (59-79)
Billy E. Phillips (51-72)
Off. Gary D. Phillips (58-79)
Wayne K. Phillips (46-62)
Sgt. Cecil Wayne Pierce (47-71)
Mrs. [Lt.] Jim C. Pierce (w)(55-70)
Sgt. Sammie V. Pierce (62-82)
Lt. Theodore F. Pollock (60-84)
Sgt. Kenneth R. Pool (67-88)
Lt. Cecil L. Posey (51-74)
Lt. William J. Price (64-84)
Chief I.G. Purser (53-77)
Off. Jackie R. Raines (66-88)
Joseph W. Rankin Sr. (43-61)
Mrs. [Off.] Michael J. Ratikan (w)(68-71)
Capt. James H. Reading (48-72)
Det. Billy J. Reese (71-91)
Sgt. Henry A. Reid Jr. (57-78)
Off. Billy J. Revels (47-72)
Mrs. C.R. Richards (w)(42-60)
Mrs. George W. Ridley (w)(37-70)
Lt. Russell M. Rigsby (59-80)
Sgt. K. Leroy Rinehart (68-88)
Off. Jimmy D. Robertson (64-85)
O. Jake Robertson (28-50)
Off. Robert W. Robinson (64-85)
Sgt. Royce W. Robison (69-89)
Lt. Donald M. Rodgers (48-77)
Sgt. James R. Rogers Sr. (70-90)
Det. Michael D. Rose (66-86)
Sgt. Henry R. Rowell (71-92)
Sgt. Robert O. Rusche (51-76)
Det. George Rust (53-73)
Det. Ben H. Satterfield (58-80)
Mrs. [Major] Clay Scheid (w)(36-61)
Capt. Donald R. Schimmels (59-83)
Henry J. Schmidt (46-66)
Mrs. [Off.] Kenneth W. Schoonover (w)(67-72)
Mrs. [Off.] Roscoe C. Scobey (w)(56-77)
Mrs. (Sgt.] Gary C. Scott (w)(61-87)
Mrs. Charles W. Scott (28-53)
Off. Kenneth L. Seal (51-72)
Det. Sampson H. Sealy (67-88)
Capt. Douglas F. Shaeffer (69-91)
Mrs. [Sgt.] Robert G. Shahan (w)(68-90)
Mrs. [Major] Bruce M. Shaw (w)(63-90)
Raymond C. Sheffield (36-62)
Sgt. Claude L. Shobert (68-88)
Off. Donald T. Smaistrla (64-84)
Mrs. Donald R. Smathers (w)(51-72)
Off. Arlin G. Smith (66-86)
Off. Arthur L. Smith (64-83)
Off. Billy F. Smith (63-84)
Lt. Carl D. Smith (62-89)
Carol S. [Creech] Smith (62-84)
Lt. Donald E. Smith (70-92)
Off. Douglas N. Smith (70-90)
Evelyn M. Smith (61-82)
Off. Jack W. Smith (53-74)
Major Julie F. [Black] Smith (72-94)
Det. Ken E. Smith (64-88)
Sgt. Raymond L. Smith (64-85)
Off. Robert T. Snider (71-91)
Sgt. Bill F. Snipes (67-87)
Det. Jacob J. Snook (57-78)
Sgt. Harvey D. Standridge (57-77)
Sgt. Robert W. Starr (49-72)
Calvin Stephens (48-68)
Major Shedric W. Stephens (46-72)
Connie S. Sterling (67-88)
Off. Ernest W. Stevenson Jr. (52-73)
Det. Richard D. Stickney (67-86)

Det. Donald L. Stout (57-77)
Sgt. Orvil R. Summers (59-79)
Off. David E. Swidler (57-77)
Off. Lewis H. Swindler (51-72)
Det. Bobby L. Tash (68-88)
Off. Howard T. Taylor (59-80)
Off. Jimmy L. Taylor (66-89)
Lt. Leland Don Taylor (57-77)
Major Robert H. Taylor (69-91)
Capt. William S. Taylor (54-75)
Sgt. William W. Tays (70-90)
Det. Robert E. Terhune (64-85)
Sgt. James H. Thomas (72-92)
Det. Robert W. Thompson (66-84)
Lt. Danny J. Troyer (60-80)
Mrs. Gene P. Tucker (w)(53-72)
Lt. Jerry W. Tune Sr. (67-87)
Lt. Walter M. Turner (36-70)
Lt Kenneth P. Uffen (63-85)
Lt. Larry K. Upchurch (62-82)
Dale M. Vaughn (51-63)
Off. Tommy J. Vernon (62-82)
Major Bill R. Vetter (63-87)
Det. Robert E. Vogt (63-84)
Det. Charles E. Waggoner (55-75)
Lt. Logan E. Waldrup (60-81)
Sgt. Cecil C. Walker Jr. (56-79)
Lt. Chris C. Walker (45-68)
Mrs. [Det.] Gary L. Ward (w)(70-85)
Capt. James M. Watson (54-78)
Chief Samuel D. Watson (54-74)
Sgt. Jerry J. Webb (63-83)
Mrs. Victor O. Webb (w)( -67)
Off. James R. Webster (67-75)
Lt. Fred Weed (57-77)
Thelma P. Whalen (41-62)
Off. Glenn P. White (65-88)
Lt. David Whitfill (64-87)
Off. Wayne V. Whitley (59-92)
Janice Wilbanks (58-77)
Mrs. [Major] H.V. Wilder (w)(15-50)
Chief Robert V. Wilder (60-90)
Off. D.S. "Dutch" Wiley (56-76)
Dep. Chf. Walter J. Wilhelm (63-88)
Mrs. [Off.] Norman V. Wilkerson (w)(57-80)
Mrs. William L. Williams (w)(51-72)
Mrs. Charles O. Williams (w)(51-72)
Off. Jimmy M. Williams (66-91)
Asst. Chf. W.A. "Ace" Williams (37-69)
Lt. W. Gene Williams (60-80)
Det. James H. Willis (62-82)
Off. Jerry W. Wilson (66-82)
Thomas J. Wilson (46-69)
Capt. Roger L. Winborn (71-92)
Lt. William F. Wise (65-92)
Lt. Travis W. Witcher (63-82)
Det. William F. Wolf (62-82)
Det. Lonnie H. Wood (61-82)
Capt. Jimmie D. Woodie (71-91)
Lt. Bob L. Wright (63-88)
Spec. James J. Young (63-88)

DECEASED

Tony J. Allison
S.B. East
Ernie J. Johnson
Walter M. Acord
Lawrence B. Ebeling
V.L. Johnson
Samuel Arrion
Gerald Emmett
Casey Jones
George E. Bailey
O.H. "Ezzy" Ezzell
E.E. Jones
Mark H. Bain
W.F. Fallwell
Denver G. Kirby
Ted Baughman
Wesley Gene Fansler
Wm. L. Krueger
Roy Bergman
William P. Faris
Charles W. Kunc
Joe Birdwell
Leslie L. Filson
Harvey A. Lakey
W.C. Bolton
Earl Fimple
E. Wayne Lawson
Ellis L. Bond
Wilson Flury
George Leech
Percy L. Borden
Leon Fox
Burke C. LeMay
Richard Bradford
Jess Francis
A.B. Livingston
H.C. Brisco
Sam Frazier
William Lord
R.D. Brokaw
Hilton J. Geer
William G. Loyd
Dwight F. Brown
E.B. Giddens
Dow Lunn
J. Leo Brown
James T. Godfrey
J.B. Mabe
James Brown
Giles G. Greene
John Maddox
Fred L. Buckles
Robert S. Grimes
William A. Marcum
Isaac E. Burns
Roy Grubaugh
M.M. Maulding
Tom Bush
S.E. "Pop" Gunn
Julius A. May
J.H. Butler
Charles H. Hall
Leslie McCaleb
John Byrd
Wayne E. Hamilton
N.V. McCollum
Jack Caldwell
Wayne Harbolt
J.C. McCuen
Lula Caldwell
Bennie C. Harris
Iva Lee McCurdy

Vida R. Campbell
George P. Harrison
Reid K. McKim
John W. Clingan
Ben Hart
A.D. McLendan
Frank M. Cole
Grover C. Hassell
John McManus
V.L. Connell
Manuel E. Higgs
Henry McMullen Sr.
Doyle H. Connelly
L.J. "Smokey" Hilbert
E.B. "Salty" Meals
Roy C. Cook
C.M. Hinderliter
Danny Mercer
M.B. Cooper
Roy W. Hopper
M. "Dutch" Mills
A.N. "Art" Cox
L.D. Huckabee
W.C. "Casey" Mills
William H. Culbertson
Robert Hudson
Ben Mize
Earl F. Cunyngham
Leona Hurt
Vince E. Moncrief
Danny Daniels
Arthur E. Jack
Lee Mullenix
Harry S. Davidson
J.S. Jackson
Marvin M. Murry
Roy J. DeShields
Joseph P. Jerkins
A.C. Myler
Morris Ned Jr.
Edward J. Yanish Jr.
G.T. "Pike" Newton
Jim R. Orrell
Jack W. Osborn
Roy C. Patterson
Milton Peaster
Ray L. Peddicord
Bob V. Perdue
Jim G. Perdue
Bill L. Peterman
John L. Lemaster
James Perrine
Sam A. Phillips
W.L. "Bill" Pickney
Darrell Pierce
Jim C. Pierce
Lucille Counts Price
O.L. Ragland
Fred Ramsey
Ed E. Rector
Paul Reed
Henry A. Reid Sr.
Alice Reilley
J.H. Revels
Ralph Richards
G.W. Ridley
Jack B. Ryan
John B. Ryan
Mary Ryan
John Sanderson
Clayton A. Scheid
Roscoe C. Scobey
Charles Scott
Gary C. Scott
Robert G. Shahan
Bruce M.W. Shaw
Ruby Sherman
Tom Simpson
Don Smathers
Sidney Smith
Margaret Stark
Richard A. Stevens
Bertha Stokes
William Stubbs
Joe Swofford
Jack Thorne
Frank Thurston
Gene Tucker
Van Ellis Van Scoy
Jack Vaughn
Sherman Wagoner
Tom W. Webb
Victor O. Webb
J.E. "Ed" White
Polk A. White
H.V. Wilder
Norman V. Wilkerson
C.O. Williams
W.L. Williams
James A. Wright
R.S. "Bob" Worthy

HONORARY MEMBERS

Virgil C. Black-Oklahoma County District Judge and former OCPD officer.

Irven R. Box-Attorney at Law and former OCPD officer.

Iona Chapman Braswell-Housewife and former OCPD officer.

Billy B. Cunningham-Oklahoma County Deputy Sheriff.

Jean (Linn) Deathridge-Housewife and former OCPD officer.

Stuart Earnest-United States Marshal

Bill Franklin-U.S. Department of Defense

Ken Grace Jr.-Oklahoma County Deputy Sheriff

Jean Johnson-former OCPD employee.

William A. Kerr-Oklahoma County Deputy Sheriff

Elmo Lawson-Retired and father of deceased Sergeant Terry Lawson.

Keith C. Leftwich-Oklahoma State Senator, District 44.

Robert H. Macy-Oklahoma County District Attorney and former OCPD officer.

James R. Maxey-Maxey Honda

Lois Moore-former OCPD officer.

Al Muzny-Arrow Wrecker Service

Doyle Parks-former OCPD officer.

Ralph R. Pearce-Businessman, Tulsa, and former OCPD officer.

Jim Pyle-Retired

Jack Poe-OCPD Chaplain.

Jim Strong, Del City P.D.

Frank Syke Jr.-Oklahoma Department of Corrections

Paul D. Taylor-FOP President, Lodge # 123.

Harry J. Thomas-Oklahoma County Deputy Sheriff

Harvey Lee Towler-Oklahoma County Deputy Sheriff

# DOWNTOWN OKLAHOMA CITY
# 1989

### Section A Index

1. Sycamore Square
2. 531 Couch Bldg.
3. 511 Couch Bldg.
4. Police Dept.
5. Civic Center
6. Bicentennial Park
7. 616 Colcord Bldg.
8. Downtown Baptist Church
9. Hotel
10. 500 Main Plaza
11. Sheridan-Walker Parking Garage
12. First Interstate Bank Drive-in
13. Centre Theater
14. City Hall
15. 100 Walker Bldg.
16. Hightower Bldg.
17. Main Place
18. Union Bus Station
19. Myriad Tower
20. Stage Center
21. Festival Plaza
22. Arts Council Complex
23. St. Joseph's Cathedral
24. Alfred P. Murrah Federal Bldg.
25. Federal Courthouse
26. Old Post Office
27. Oklahoma Natural Gas
28. Oklahoma Gas and Electric
29. Federal Reserve Bank
30. Bank of Oklahoma
31. Law Center
32. Metro Parking Garage
33. Oklahoma City Urban Renewal
34. Parking Garage
35. County Office Bldg.
36. Investor Capitol Bldg.
37. Court Plaza
38. County Courthouse
39. 45th Infantry Division Memorial
40. Leadership Square
41. Park Harvey Center
42. First Oklahoma Tower
43. Cravens Bldg.
44. American First Tower
45. Regency Tower

### Section B Index

1. Colcord Bldg.
2. Myriad Gardens
3. Crystal Bridge
4. Fred Jones
5. Fred Jones
6. Fred Jones
7. First Methodist Church
8. Bank of Oklahoma Drive-in
9. Metropolitan Library
10. Southwestern Bell
11. Southwestern Bell
12. Kerr McGee Parking Garage
13. Kerr McGee Tower
14. Kerr McGee Bldg.
15. Kerr McGee Bldg.
16. Midland Center
17. Globe Life Center
18. Robert S. Kerr Park
19. First City Place
20. Arts Place II
21. Continental Savings Bldg.
22. 100 Park Ave Bldg.
23. First Interstate Bank
24. Oil & Gas Bldg.
25. Main Street Parking Plaza
26. Sheraton Century Center
27. Myriad Convention Center
28. Continental Baking
29. Cotpa Transfer Terminal
30. Oklahoma Publishing Co.
31. Oklahoma Publishing Co.
32. Liberty Drive-in Bank
33. Broadway & Kerr Parking Garage
34. Continental Drive-in Bank
35. Skirvin Plaza Hotel
36. Santa Fe Plaza Parking Garage
37. Skirvin Plaza Hotel
38. Liberty Bank Tower
39. Mid-America Tower
40. Parking Garage
41. Thermal System Plant
42. Old Santa Fe Terminal
43. Community Building - YMCA
44. Journal Record Building
45. Chamber of Commerce

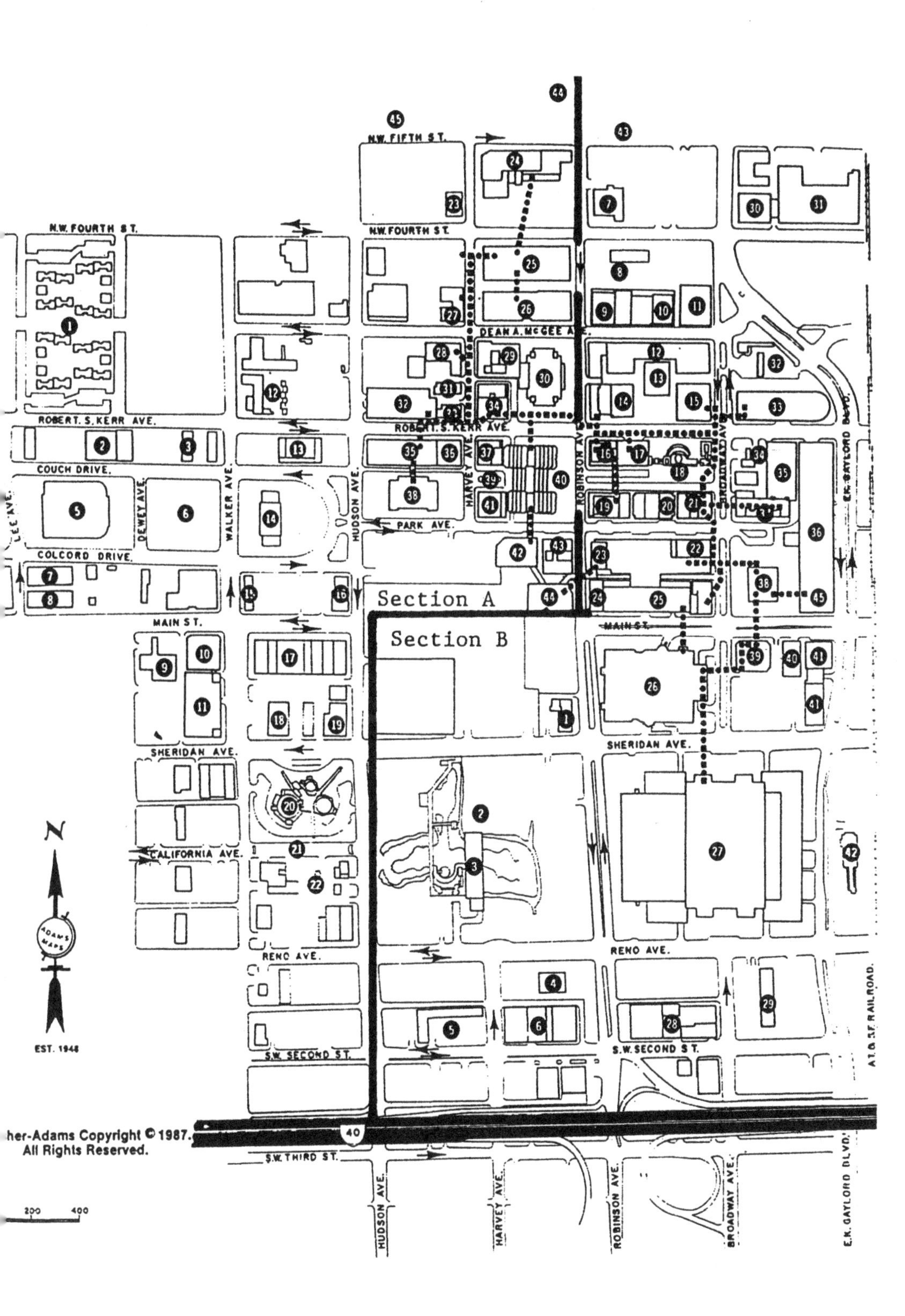
N.W. FIFTH ST.
N.W. FOURTH ST.
N.W. FOURTH ST.
DEAN A. McGEE AVE.
ROBERT S. KERR AVE.
ROBERT S. KERR AVE.
COUCH DRIVE.
COLCORD DRIVE.
LEE AVE.
DEWEY AVE.
WALKER AVE.
HUDSON AVE.
HARVEY AVE.
ROBINSON AVE.
BROADWAY AVE.
E.K. GAYLORD BLVD.
PARK AVE.
Section A
Section B
MAIN ST.
MAIN ST.
SHERIDAN AVE.
SHERIDAN AVE.
CALIFORNIA AVE.
RENO AVE.
RENO AVE.
S.W. SECOND ST.
S.W. SECOND ST.
S.W. THIRD ST.
A.T.&S.F. RAILROAD
40
N
ADAMS MAPS
EST. 1948
200
400
HUDSON AVE.
HARVEY AVE.
ROBINSON AVE.
BROADWAY AVE.
E.K. GAYLORD BLVD.

Printed in the USA
CPSIA information can be obtained
at www.ICGtesting.com
JSHW022206140824
68134JS00018B/890